PETER MARTYR

A REFORMER IN EXILE

(1542-1562)

BIBLIOTHECA

HUMANISTICA & REFORMATORICA

VOLUME X

PETER MARTYR
A REFORMER IN EXILE
(1542-1562)

A chronology of biblical writings in England & Europe

by

M ARVIN W ALTER ANDERSON

NIEUWKOOP

B. DE GRAAF

1975

By the same author

GOSPEL AND AUTHORITY, A. P.T. FORSYTH READER

FOR ANN MARIE

The Church of Christ even under the cross hath from the beginning
of the world been victorious....sometime it seemeth to be shadowed
with a cloud or driven with a stormy persecution....If for a time
it lie covered with ashes, yet it is quickly kindled again by the
wind of God's Spirit; though it seem drowned in the sea, or parched
and pined in the wilderness, yet God giveth ever good success....

TO QUEEN ELIZABETH. GENEVA, 10 April 1560.

PREFACE TO THE GENEVA BIBLE

HOMO ENIM SUM ATQUE CHRISTIANUS, UNDE NULLUM HUMANUM

CONSILIUM ATQUE CHRISTIANUM NON POSSUM NON BONI CONSULARE.

PETER MARTYR TO JAN UTENHOVE

9 MAY /1549?/

CONTENTS

Preface   11

Short Titles and _Sigla_   17

Introduction   23

Notes to Introduction   30

PART ONE: REFORMER IN EXILE (1542/62)

I. DIALOGUE TO DISSENT (1537/62)

Cortese and Contarini   35
Vermigli's Theology of Dissent   49
Flight from Persecution   49
Reformer in Exile   51
English Influence   55
Christology and Exegesis   57
Spiritual Church, Not Sacramental   61
Notes to Chapter I   65

II. LECTURER TO PROFESSOR (1542/49)

Naples and Lucca   71
Strasbourg Lecturer (1542/47)   76
Oxford Professor (1548/49)   85
Foreign Divines   89
Eucharistic Debate (1549)   101
Notes to Chapter II   115

III. CRANMER AND ENGLISH REFORM (1549/53)

Eucharistic Discipline   127
Ecclesiastical Laws   142
Notes to Chapter III   154

IV. MARIAN EXILE (1553/56)

Sustainers and Sojourners   161
Religious Controversy   168
English Exiles   175

Calvin and Unio Christi   186
Heresy all Around   195
Notes to Chapter IV   200

V. ZURICH THEOLOGIAN (1556/62)

Theology of Election   211
Elizabethan England   219
Colloquy of Poissy (1561)   234
Notes to Chapter V   251

PART TWO: THE LEARNED STRANGER (1542/53)

VI. STRASBOURG LECTURES (1542/47)

Sola Fide (1542/51)   270
Theses ad Disputandum Publice (1543/45)   278
Una Semplice Dichiaratione (1544)   287
Genesis and Lamentations (1545/47)   295
Notes to Chapter VI   301

VII. OXFORD LECTURES (1547/53)

Sermons   313
I Corinthians (1548/49)   318
Romans (1550/51)   328
The Scope of Theology   354
Notes to Chapter VII   355

PART THREE: THE CHRISTIAN SCHOLAR (1553/62)

VIII. MARTYR'S LIBRARY AND LECTURES (1553/62)

A Scholar's Tools   369
Second Exile: Strasbourg (1553/56)   378
Romans (13) and Secular Magistrates   382
Judges and Sacred History   383
Inferior Magistrates   391
A Treatise of the Cohabitacyon (1555)   394
Zurich Scholar (1556/62): Fortitude and Faith   403
I Kings: Schism and Papacy   408
Notes to Chapter VIII   418

IX. PERSON OF CHRIST

Oxford Sermons   437
Polish Church and Stancaro   439
Conclusion   455
Notes to Chapter IX   460

APPENDICES

I.   Register Epistolarum Vermiglii   467
II.   Latin Letter to Musculus   487
III. Lambeth Palace Letters   491

BIBLIOGRAPHY

Bibliographical Essay   534
I.   Manuscripts   540
II.   Martyr Imprints   545
III. Early Printed Sources   551
IV.   Secondary Works   562
V.   Periodical Literature   571
VI.   Unpublished Dissertations   583
VII. Private Correspondence   585
VIII. Unpublished Lectures   585

INDICES

I.   Scripture References   586
II.   Persons and Places   590
III. Special Subject Index   601

PREFACE

This study has been prepared because the author could find no survey of Peter Martyr as a biblical exegete. I am grateful to Dr. John Tedeschi, Curator of Rare Books at the Newberry Library, Chicago for suggesting the viability of such a topic. I can not thank Dr. Tedeschi enough for his precise bibliographic citations, contacts with Italian and European scholars and the incentive to decipher the multiple unprinted sources which undergird this work. Dr. Tedeschi, Professor Robert McNally, S.J., of Fordham University, New York, Professor James S. McEwen of Aberdeen University, Scotland, Dean Virgil Olson of Bethel College, St. Paul and Dr. Ralph Turnbull of Seattle supported research grants to pursue postdoctoral research in England, Italy and Europe from June 1969 to August 1971.

My study seeks to provide the reader for the first time an English language account of Martyr's writings (1542-1562) examined in the setting of manuscript letters and documents in England, Geneva, Strasbourg and Zurich. A reading of this material shows the value of Martyr's biblical writings for his contemporaries. Their esteem of Martyr as an exegete and his career as a 'scholar of Christ' lead one to the core of Martyr's extant writings. McLelland's account of Martyr's sacramental theology (1957) has been updated by Sergio Corda's Zurich thesis (1974). In all of this one appreciates all the more Philip McNair's fine biography of Martyr's Italian career. I would like to add to McNair this interim study of Martyr from 1542-1562. The term interim is important, for as McNair has written in his preface quoting the late Professor Claude Jenkins of Oxford.

several studies of this Italian reformer as a protestant need to be
written. In addition no one has detailed Bullinger's influence in
England, Bucer studies are experiencing a renaissance and there is
no adequate account of Cranmer's theology. I am hopeful that readers
will find this account based on manuscripts and built on printed
primary sources useful in understanding Peter Martyr as an Italian
protestant writer in Northern Europe. Other studies in progress will
add to this facet of Reformed theology. It was helpful to sketch
Martyr's protestant career first and then to turn to the _Sitz im Leben_
of his writings. This account restricts itself by and large to sources
which mention Martyr. Its only claim to clarity lies in a chronological format.

Many individuals and institutions have made this study possible.
The American Council of Learned Societies funded a visit to several
Italian Archives in 1969. I am grateful to the American Association
of Theological Schools who supported a delightful sabbatical leave in
Cambridge, England during 1970-71. The Institute For Advanced
Christian Studies provided research funds to visit continental
libraries in March and April of 1971. Professor Gordon Rupp read the
entire first and fourth drafts in typescript. His help is reflected
on each page. Our weekly discussions in Cambridge extricated me from
many a cul-de-sac of Sixteenth Century research. His fine gift of
Martyr's Latin Commentary on Romans (1558) bespeaks the finest traditions of Academia. Dr. Philip McNair provided some of his own
materials at an early stage in my research. His knowledge of Peter

Martyr is impressive and his collation of Martyr imprints in the
Oxford Collegiate Catalogue sped my research.

The Librarians of the Vatican Library, Rome, Marciana Library,
Venice, the Bodleian, Oxford and the British Museum provided many
rare printed books and manuscripts, as did the University Library
and Villa Archives, Strasbourg, the Bibliotheque Nationale, Paris,
the Zurich Zentralbibliothek and Staatsarchiv, the Musee Historique
de la Reformation and University Library in Geneva and the Biblioteka
Uniwersytecka, Warsaw. M. Alan Dufour expedited my studies in Geneva.
Italian Archivists were of great help in providing manuscripts,
especially in Brescia, Mantua, Modena, Padua, Parma, Perugia, Rome
and Venice. Professor Antonio Rotondo at Modena, Roberto Abbondanza,
archivist of the Archivia di Stato, Perugia and Don Costanzo Tabarelli,
O.S.B. at the church of St. Peter, Perugia deserve special thanks for
locating documents not listed in Kristeller's Iter Italicum. At
Zofingen I spent a delightful day reading the correspondence of
Wolfgang Musculus.

I am grateful to Mr. E.W. Bill, Librarian of the Lambeth Palace
Library and his Grace, the Archbishop of Canterbury, The Most Reverend
Arthur Michael Ramsey for permission to include the Lambeth Letters in
an appendix. Dr. Gordon Huelin has redone his transcription and
provided a fresh account of these letters for this volume. Huelin's
dissertation opened up fruitful questions for further research. On
several visits to Kings College, University of London we explored
together facets of Martyr's English experience. Msgr. John Sankovit:

of St. Paul Seminary finished the translation after Dr. Huelin's
illness prevented him from completing work on letters 82 to Richard
Cox and 86 to John Jewel.

Cambridge University and College libraries proved to be the
finest source of Martyr imprints of any city in the world. I am
especially indebted to Mr. E. J. Kenney, F. B. A., Perne librarian
of Peterhouse for allowing me to use the Andrew Perne copies of
Martyr's first editions in this ancient Cambridge college library.
The librarian of Corpus Christi College granted access to the Parker
manuscripts and the librarians of Clare, St. Catharine's, Gonville and
Caius, and Trinity Colleges, Cambridge gave permission to consult
rare printed volumes of the sixteenth century. The staff of the
Cambridge University Library and the Anderson Room were most efficient.
Mr. Pettit also placed at my disposal the twenty-four Peter Martyr
items in the Peterborough Cathedral Library on permanent loan to the
Cambridge University Library, though not then entered in the main
catalogue. Mrs. Hand's checklist of English Cathedral Library holdings located in the North Room of the British Museum facilitated
location of related works in the British Isles.

Mr. Richard Durling, cataloguer of the University Library Cambridge gave invaluable assistance with sixteenth century bibliographic
problems. His skill in sixteenth century bibliography has few equals.
Mr. Richard Kerr of the University Library Cambridge transcribed two
manuscript letters from Zofingen and helped with paeleography. My
study in the University Library gained much from the daily friendship

of these scholars. The Bush Foundation of St. Paul, Minnesota provided funds and space to prepare the fourth draft of the typescript
at St. John's University, Collegeville in the Spring of 1972. I would
like to thank the Benedictine monks and the Alcuin Library for cour-
tesies extended and microfilm copies provided during that sojourn and
since.

Mrs. Frank Voth, faculty secretary of Bethel Seminary, turned my
multiple manuscript revisions into a readable typescript. I am indebted to her and my wife, Ann, who prepared the final typed copy. The
editors of Concordia Theological Monthly, Church History, Journal of
Ecclesiastical History, Scottish Journal of Theology, Sixteenth Century
Journal and Theologische Zeitschrift have given permission to quote
extensively from previously published papers.

Dr. John Patrick Donnelly, S.J. of Marquette University shared his
dissertation on Martyr and details of the Peter Martyr bibliography in
progress. Further details have been unraveled in correspondence with
the Library of Congress and Union Theological Seminary, New York. Miss
Katharine Pantzer, The Houghton Library, Harvard University, graciously
provided copy about printers and publications from the forthcoming revision of Pollard and Redgrave, A Short Title Catalogue of Books
printed in England, Scotland and Ireland, and of English books printed
abroad, 1475-1640....

Dr. Peter N. Brooks, Fellow and Dean of Downing College, Cambridge
discussed research in progress during the first and second drafts and
read the third draft in its entirety. Professor Patrick Collinson,

University of Sidney, Australia and Professor Rupp each read the fourth draft and made valuable suggestions. These scholars have improved successive recensions by their gracious yet authoritative comments. My Old Testament colleague at Bethel Seminary, Professor Ronald Youngblood, served as resident 'Rabbi' on all _Quaestiones Hebraicae_. All of the several errors of fact and judgment which remain are _mea culpa_. Translations unless identified are mine. John Harms checked many references for me in Cambridge libraries and the British Museum. He photographed the illustrations in Cambridge.

I dedicate this study to the patience of my family -- especially to my sons Stuart and Chad who often asked, "Can we go to Jesus Green today?" There and in Professor Rupp's study overlooking the Fellows' Garden of Jesus College we often thought of Thomas Cranmer, Archbishop of Canterbury and fellow of Jesus College who invited Peter Martyr to England. In many ways this study has been inspired by that other Thomas in Canterbury, whose dreams of an _Ecclesia Anglicana Reformanda_ were shared by a host of foreign theologians like Bucer, Lask nd Martyr. His invitation to these learned strangers strengthened his hand against the like of Gardiner and Tunstal. Their labors laid the foundation of English Puritanism in the reign of the young Josiah. So for six short years did Peter Martyr at Oxford, Thomas Cranmer at Lambeth and King Edward VI dream of building Jerusalem in England's green and pleasant land.

St. Paul, Minnesota

1 May 1974

SHORT TITLES AND SIGLA

I. PETER MARTYR IMPRINTS (BY DATE)

Fede Christiana	Una Semplice Dichiaratione Sopra Gli XII Articoli Della Fede Christiana (1544)
Tractatio	Tractatio De Sacramento Eucharistiae (1549)
Vitandis	De Vitandis Superstitionibus (1549)
Discourse	A Discourse or Traictise ... Concernynge the Sacrament of the Lord's Supper ... (1550)
Somerset	An Epistle unto ... the Duke of Somerset (1550)
Corinthios	Priorem Ad Corinth /ios/ Epistolam (1551)
Cohabitacyon	A Treatise of the cohabitacyon of the faithful with the unfaithful ... (1555)
Polonicam	Ad Ecclesiam Polonicam (1556)
Romanos	In Epistolam ... Ad Romanos ... (1558)
Defensio	Defensio ... ad Riccardi Smythaei (1559)
Iudicum	In Librum Iudicum ... (1561)
Ethics	Libri Ethicorum Aristotelis ad Nicomachum (1563)
Judges	Most fruitful & learned Comentaries (1564)
Preces	Preces Sacrae Ex Psalmis Davidis Desumptae (1564)
Samuelis	In Duos Libros Samuelis ... Commentarii (1564)
Melachim	Melachim id est Regum Libri duo (1566)
Romanes	Epistle of St. Paul to the Romanes (1568)
Genesis	In Primum Librum Mosis ... Commentarii (1569)
Prayers	Most Godly Prayers (1569)
Loci Communes	Loci Communes (1576). Other editions by date of publication.
Opuscula (1581)	Locorum Communium ... opusculis Tomus Secundus (1581)

Opuscula (1582)   Locorum Communium ... opusculis Tomus
Tertius (1582)

Analysis   Analysis Libri De Eucharistia Contra Gardinerum
(1581)

Proposita   Proposita Disputata Publice In Schola Argent.
(1582)

Common Places   Marten translation of Loci Communes   (1583)

Panoplia   Panoplia Christiana (1588)

Collect.   Collectanea Variorum (1617)

Lament.   In Lamentationes Sanctissimi Ieremiae Prophetae
(1629)

II. ARCHIVES & REFERENCE WORKS

A.S.T.   Archives Municipales Du Ville De Strasbourg:
Archive St. Thomas

C.C.C.C.   Corpus Christi College Cambridge

C.R.   Corpus Reformatorum

C.S.P.Eliz.   Calendar of State Papers,Elizabeth

C.S.P.Span.   Calendar of State Papers, Spanish

C.S.P.Ven.   Calendar of State Papers, Venetian

C.T.B.   Correspondance De Theodore De Beze

D.N.B.   Dictionary of National Biography

L.C.   Letters of John Calvin ... Dr. Jules Bonnet

O.L.I.   Original Letters, Parker Society (1537-58).

O.L.II.   Original Letters, Parker Society (1537-58) 2.

Oratio   Simler, Oratio de vita et obitu ... D. Petri
Martyris Vermilii (1563). Elizabethan English
version from Common Places (1583).

O.T.Z.   Operum Theologicorum ... Zanchii (1613)

Scripta Anglicana   Martini Buceri Scripta Anglicana (1577)

S.T.C.   Pollard & Readgrave, Short Title Catalogue

T.B.   Thesaurus Baumianus, Strasbourg

Z.L.I.   Zurich Letters, Parker Society (1558-79)

Z.L.II.   Zurich Letters, Parker Society (1558-1602)
Second Series.

Z.S.A.   Zurich Staatsarchiv

Z.S.S.   Zurich Zentralbibliothek Simmlerische Sammlung

III. PERIODICALS AND SERIALS

A.   Archaeologia

A.B.R.   American Benedictine Review

A.E.R.   American Ecclesiastical Review

A.H.R.   American Historical Review

A.P.S.R.   American Political Science Review

A.R.G.   Archiv für Reformationsgeschichte

A.S.G.   Anzeiger für Schweizerische Geschichte

A.S.I.   Archivio Storico Italiano

A.T.R.   Anglican Theological Review

B.   Benedictina

B.G.A.S.T.   Bristol and Gloucestershire Archaeological
Society, Transactions

B.H.R.   Bibliotheque De Humanisme et Renaissance

B.H.S.   Bulletin of Hispanic Studies

B.I.H.R.   Bulletin of the Institute of Historical
Research

Bl.F.W.KG.   Blatter Für Württembergische Kirchengeschichte

B.S.B.S	Bolletino Storico-bibliografico subalpino.
B.S.H.P.F.	Bulletin Societe De L'Histoire du Protestantisme Francais
B.S.S.V.	Bolletino Della Societa Di Studi Valdesi
C.H.	Church History
C.H.R.	Church Historical Review
C.R.	Contemporary Review
C.S.	Critica Storica
C.Q.R.	Church Quarterly Review
C.T.J.	Calvin Theological Journal
C.T.M.	Concordia Theological Monthly
E.A.	Etudes Anglaises
E.H.R.	English Historical Review
F.V.	Foi et Vie
G.	Gesnerus
G.S.L.I.	Giornale storico della letteratura Italiana
H.	Historian
H.M.P.E.C.	Historical Magazine of the Protestant Episcopal Church
H.Q.	Hartford Quarterly
H.S.L.P.	Huguenot Society of London, Proceedings
H.T.R.	Harvard Theological Review
He.J.	Heidelberger Jahrbücher
Hi.J.	Historical Journal
I.E.R.	Irish Ecclesiastical Record
I.R.	Illif Review

I.S.	Italian Studies
J.B.S.	Journal of British Studies
J.E.H.	Journal of Ecclesiastical History
J.G.N.K.G.	Jahrbuch der Gesellshaft für niedersächsische Kirchengeschichte
J.R.H.	Journal of Religious History
J.S.A.	Journal of the Society of Archivists
J.T.S.	Journal of Theological Studies
L.J.	Luther-Jahrbuch
L.Q.	Lutheran Quarterly
L.T.B.S.	Library, Transactions of the Bibliographical Society
M.A.H.	Melanges D'Archeologie et D'Histoire
M.P.	Modern Philology
N.A.S.G.A.	Neues Archiv für Sachsische Geschichte und Altertumskunde
N.Q.	Notes and Queries
N.R.S.	Nuova Rivista Storica
P.	Protestantesimo
P.B.S.A.	Papers of the Bibliographical Society of America
P.P.	Past and Present
P.Q.	Philological Quarte:
P.T.R.	Princeton Theological Review
R.H.	Revue Historique
R.H.P.R.	Revue D'Histoire e De Philosophie Religieuse
R.Q.	Renaissance Quarterly
R.S.I.	Rivista Storica Italiana

R.S.L.R.	Rivista Di Storia e Letteratura Religiosa
R.T.P.	Revue Theologie et Philosophie
S.C.E.S.	Sixteenth Century Essays and Studies
S.C.H.	Studies In Church History
S.C.J.	Sixteenth Century Journal
S.H.P.B.	Societe d'histoire du protestantisme belge
S.J.T.	Scottish Journal of Theology
S.M.	Studia Monastica
S.M.G.B.O.	Studien und Mitteilungen Zur Geschichte Des Benediktiner-Ordens
S.P.	Studia Patristica
S.R.	Studies in the Renaissance
S.Z.G.	Schweizerische Zeitschrift für Geschichte
T.Z.	Theologische Zeitschrift
W.T.J.	Westminster Theological Journal
Z.	Zwingliana
Z.H.G.P.P.	Zeitschrift der Historische Gesellshaft für die Provinz & Posen
Z.H.T.	Zeitschrift für die Historische Theologie
Z.K.G.	Zeitschrift für Kirchengeschichte
Z.T.K.	Zeitschrift für Theologie und Kirche

INTRODUCTION

Reginald Pole, English Cardinal and cousin of Henry VIII, faced assassin's knives for rejecting the annulment of King Henry's marriage to Catherine of Aragon.[1] Two years later in 1541 Pole praised catholic and protestant agreement on the theological doctrine of justification by faith signed at Ratisbon on 2 May 1541. Martin Bucer and Philip Melanchthon agreed with John Eck and Cardinal Contarini that "without faith no human nature is able to keep either primary or secondary precepts ... The cross silences human pride, which rules in every desire of the heart."[2] Caught between the politics of Pope and King on the one hand and the scholastic formulae of Italian theologians on the other, Cardinal Pole rejoiced that some men placed their sin and God's saviour at the heart of ecclesiastical reform. He could not stem his secret joy to Contarini on 17 May 1542.

> Indeed, I felt myself flooded with such joy when I saw this accord of opinions. No melody, however sweet, would ever have been able to have soothed the spirit and the ears so greatly. I felt this way not only because I saw that a mighty foundation of peace and concord had been laid, but also because I recognized this foundation as the one that above all, as it seems to me, adds luster to Christ's glory. It is the very foundation of all Christian teaching. For even if matters seem to be treated under different heads, as concerning faith, concerning works, or concerning justification, nevertheless they all are referred back to the single head of justification. And I am most devoutly grateful at this, that the theologians of both parties have agreed concerning it, and I give thanks to God through Christ, who has chosen you to be this kind of servant of Him and equipped (*reforciendae*) you to construct so resplendent an agreement on so solid a basis. From this we have come to entertain the great hope that He who has so mercifully begun in establishing this basis will with the same goodness perfect the remaining things that pertain to this salutary work. I command you not to divulge all this, but I am keeping in my private possession the written documents that pertain to this agreement. I lament that the times demand this.[3]

Contarini defended the agreement in his *Epistola* of 25 May 1541
by turning to St. John Damascene's commentary on *Hebrews*, Book IV.
There where faith is translated as *confidentia*, Contarini asserted
that works follow faith.[4] In the debacle of Curial resistance to his
theological attempt at reform -- Pole wrote to Alvise Priuli to influence its acceptance in Rome -- Contarini turned to publishing commentaries on the Pauline and Catholic Epistles. At *Romans* (4:16) Contarini settled in his own mind the priority of faith over works. Where
the *Vulgate* read "Et propterea ex fide, et secundum gratiam sit firma
promissio," Contarini replaced "et" by "ut" to restore the Greek text.

> But therefore according to grace, to the end that the promise may
> be firm, for if the matter depended on justice, so that namely,
> we should be rewarded according to our works and not according
> to God's grace, the promise would have no certainty because of
> the lack of our works.[5]

Cardinal Pole defended these views at Trent.

In Italy during these decades of the 1530's and 1540's not only
Cardinals but laymen as well turned from the letters of Pope Paul III
to those of St. Paul. Venetian testaments express similar concerns
as Miss Logan has shown.[6] Two Paduan residents wrote works between
1538-1540 which support this Italian fascination with a Pauline religious experience. Sperone Speroni in his *Dialogue on the Active and
Contemplative Life* chose Contarini as the antagonist of civil virtue.
Even though Speroni leans toward a critique of Contarini, he repro-
duces his religious views accurately.[7]

Biblical commentaries of this period have been neglected. There
was an Italian Reformation concerned with these matters. Peter Martyr

Vermigli was in the circle of Valdes in Naples. He was a scholar with whom Cortese and Contarini conversed and in whom they confided. Central to their common concern was an experience of faith which would reform the church from within. Martyr found by 1542 that in spite of popular support for these religious concerns it was dangerous to comment on St. Paul in Petrine territory. His curial supporters could no longer protect his freedom to explore the source of faith in scripture. 1542 was the beginning of the end for the nascent Italian Reformation on its native soil. John Tedeschi prefaced his *Exhibition Catalogue* with the following comment:

> Although, with the Waldensian exception, Reformation movements were finally suppressed in Italy by the year 1600, it is still possible to speak of an Italian Reformation through the activities of the exiles who found refuge in the Protestant north. A handful, notably Peter Martyr Vermigli and Jerome Zanchi, made important original contributions to the development of orthodox Protestantism. But the key historical role of the Italians is best seen in the context of the vexed and still largely unresolved question of the relationship of the Renaissance to the Reformation. The connection between these two movements is most obvious on two levels, the religious and the literary, in the work of the Italian refugees.[8]

In that battle over words Martyr's Biblical writings continued the struggle for Italian reform in Northern Europe.

The bulk of Martyr's writing is in the form of comments on the Biblical text of the Old and New Testaments. The following commentaries and editions appeared in Martyr's lifetime: I *Corinthians* (Zurich, two printings, 1551), *Romans* (Basle, 1558; Zurich, 1559; Basle, 1560), *Judges* (Zurich, 1561). The commentaries on I & II *Samuel* (Zurich, 1564), I & II *Kings* (Zurich, 1566), *Genesis* (Zurich,

1569) and *Lamentations* (Zurich, 1629) were published posthumously as

were the *Prayers on the Psalms* (Zurich, 1564). In so devoting himself

to grammatical and theological exegesis Martyr shared with his contem-

poraries a fascination for the strange new world of the Bible.

No study in any language mirrors the attention which these Renais-

sance men gave to the Bible. Neal Gilbert has shown the common meth-

odology employed by several scholars across a broad range of academic

interests -- law, medicine, literature and theology. In an article on

Laurentius Valla I sought to recreate interest in the philological

basis of Biblical study during the Quattrocento.[9] The most detailed

study of commentaries is by Professor Basil Hall in the *Cambridge*

History of the Bible. From a careful reading of Hall, Rupp and

Bainton one can see that much remains to be done before one can speak

accurately about this genre of Sixteenth Century literature.[10]

A few observations may help the reader to understand why the com-

mentaries of Martyr met the needs of his contemporaries for answers

to political, moral, intellectual and theological questions. Professor

Rupp in reviewing Brian Walton, *Zwingli's Theocracy,* observed that

Zwingli himself did not think in terms of a state governed by the

clergy as God's representatives.

> Indeed, one's starting point would better have been Zwingli's
> own stress in his characteristic lectures on Isaiah (like himself
> a statesman-prophet) on a godly commonwealth where God speaks
> through his servants the prophets and is concerned with the
> whole life of the whole community.[11]

Who indeed has explored the many commentaries and sermons of John

Brenz to ferret out his political views on a non-polemical level?[12]

The first observation therefore is that because reformers like
Zwingli and Brenz turned to these ancient documents, one should
follow them there to observe their private thoughts made public in
print.

A second observation is that both Catholic and Protestant scholars were influenced by the new exegesis. The Prologue which Cardinal
Ximenes prepared for Pope Leo X explained the purpose of the *Com-
plutensian Polyglot.*

> It is unavoidable that after translation the Scripture yet
> remains pregnant and filled with both various and sublime
> insights which cannot become known from any other sources than
> from the very fountain of the original language.[13]

As an example one might refer to Faber's influence in France and on
Luther. Faber Stapulensis (1455-1536) was a contemporary of Erasmus.
Faber's commentaries on the *Psalms* (1509) and the *Four Gospels* (1522)
were used widely in restating traditional opinions of these books. A
single quotation must suffice since neither space nor information is
available to detail a history of hermeneutics in this period. Faber
while at Meaux greatly influenced Margurite of Navarre, sister of
Francis I. In 1525 Faber left Meaux under suspicion and in 1530 saw
published at Antwerp his complete French Bible, the first printed in
that language. Faber wrote in 1521:

> Act, therefore, bishops, act, kings, act, generous hearts!
> Awaken the nations everywhere to the light of the Gospel, to
> the true light of God! Restore to life and cast out whatever
> does not aid or whatever impedes this pure worship! Pay no
> attention to what the flesh says or does, but to what God says
> and commands! Diligently bear in mind that maxim of Paul: Do
> not touch, nor taste, nor handle things that must all perish
> in their very use, following the precepts and doctrines of men,

which, to be sure, have a show of wisdom in superstition and
self-abasement! The Word of God suffices. This alone is enough
to effect life everlasting. This rule alone is the guide to
eternal life. All else, on which the Word of God does not shine,
is as unnecessary as it is undoubtedly superfluous. Nor should
such be reckoned with the Gospel as far as the purity of pious
worship and the integrity of faith are concerned, for it is not
the creation of God.[14]

That new exegesis went beyond philology to Christology.

One could multiply examples of sacred history permeating the

thought patterns and educational structures of society. Our third

observation is that the new biblical study did so affect society. For

example, Sebastian Castellio's very popular *Sacred Dialogues* rewrote

biblical history in the form of school plays.

Acts (23): The Trial of Paul before Ananias.

> Paul: Men, brothers -- up till the present time, I
> have always served God with a good conscience.
> Ananias: Somebody, hit him in the mouth!
> Paul: God will hit you, you painted wall! How can
> you dare to judge me by the Law, and command that
> I be struck, contrary to the Law?
> Attendant: Do you dare to shout at the high priest
> of God?
> Paul: Brethren, I didn't know that this was the high
> priest. Yes, it's written in Scripture, 'Thou shalt
> not revile the ruler of thy people.' Now listen to
> the truth, brothers present in this assembly. I am
> a Pharisee, and the son of a Pharisee. The charge
> against me is that I hope in the resurrection of the
> dead.
> Sadducee: The clever rascal! He hopes to get out of
> it that way.
> Pharisee: He has spoken well; I see nothing wrong in
> him. Perhaps a spirit or an angel /genius/ has spoken
> to him. Let's not fight against God!
> Sadducee: You're defending yourselves now, because he
> claims to agree with you!
> Pharisee: We're defending him, because he deserves our
> defense. What's he really done wrong? Do you want
> to attack the innocent?
> Sadducee: It's really the other way around -- do you

want to protect the guilty?
Lysias: Something's got to be done, or this man'll
be pulled apart. You! Command the army to go down
there, and bring him up into the castle![15]

Peter Martyr delivered his lectures at Strasbourg, Oxford, and Zurich in oral form. After careful editing Martyr issued them in published form. Those who turn to the *Loci Communes* read Martyr's *loci* extracted from their context in these commentaries. The tendency is to view them twice removed from their original oral form. The procedure at Lausanne may shed light on how Martyr lectured. Its program followed the educational reforms of John Sturm at Strasbourg and in turn was adopted at Geneva, Nimes, Orange and elsewhere. These *Leges scholae Lausannensis* promulgated on 25 August 1547 describe among other things how a theology lecture ought to be given.

The professor of theology should first give the sense of the Hebrew and Greek text. Then he would underscore essential points and clearly explain the sense of the passage by citing "modestly and with reverence the diverse interpretations of the commentators." After summarizing the chief divisions of the subject which the students were to investigate and report on, a practical application completed the lecture. This final step related the passage to individual edification, ecclesiastical profit and ended with a review of the previous lesson.[16]

Martyr's commentaries then were given as oral lectures for the edification of his auditors. They were meant to repristinate contemporary society with ancient truth -- to interpret scripture as Christology and with care according to the finest available humanistic tools of text, grammars and lexica. It was a practice which his contem-

poraries relished. Therefore to understand Martyr's thoughts one

must follow him via the printed page into the lecture halls of Oxford,

Strasbourg and Zurich. There like John Calvin who would have wrenched

these pages from Martyr's own hands, the Marian exiles and future

Elizabethan bishops listened with rapt attention to Peter Martyr

Vermigli, the Theologian of the Italian Reformation. Martyr himself

described the task of biblical reading as an exposure to the inner

clarity of the Word and Spirit:

> For herein we hear not the wisdom of man, but have God himself
> speaking before us, to whom if we give ear we shall conceive
> singular joy, we shall chase away pensive cogitations, and be
> lightened with most sweet comfort: we shall be strengthened
> beyond the condition of man: nothing shall be thought hard
> and shameful for us.

But to see why Martyr could not remain in Italy to accomplish his

life's task, one must explore the reactions of his countrymen to the

Italian events of 1537-1542. That lead to a crisis in Modena which

paralleled in many ways the Lucca experience.

NOTES TO INTRODUCTION

1. Letter to Cardinal Farnese of 12 May, 1539. Unpublished
autograph in Parmese State Archives. Archivio di Stato Parma, Raccoldi
MSS., busta n. 135, Cardinali pergamene e lettere autografe, "Pole
(Card.) Reginaldo -- S.A.," n. 3.

2. Acta Diaectae Ratisbonensis, Codices Vaticani Latini 10755,21.

3. Reginald Pole, Epistolarum Reginaldi Poli. S.R.E. Cardinalis
et Aliorum ad ipsum, III, 25-26.

4. Epistola de Justificatione in Quirini, III, CC_CCII.

5. Gasparo Contarini, Scholia In Epistolas Divi Pauli, Romans,
pp. 437-38.

6. O.M.T. Logan, "Grace and Justification: Some Italian Views of the Sixteenth and Early Seventeenth Centuries," J.E.H. XX (1969), 67 et passim.

7. Rita Belladonna, "Sperone and Alessandro Piccolomini on Justification," R.Q. XXV (1972), pp. 164-165.

8. John A. Tedeschi, The Literature of the Italian Reformation, p. 6.

9. Marvin Anderson, "Laurentius Valla: Renaissance Critic and Biblical Theologian," C.T.M. XXXIX (1968), 10-27. Of several recent studies on Valla see Salvatore Camporeale, Lorenzo Valla Umanesimo E Teologia (Firenze: Nella Sede Dell' Istituto Palazzo Strozzi, 1972), section III. "Le Adnotationes . Prima E Seconda Stesura," pp. 277-468.

10. Roland Bainton, "The Bible In The Reformation," pp. 1-37 and Basil Hall, "Biblical Scholarship: Editions And Commentaries," pp. 38-93 in The Cambridge History of The Bible. The West From The Reformation To The Present Day. E.G. Rupp, "The Bible in the Age of the Reformation," pp. 73-87 in Church's Use Of The Bible Past And Present, edited D.E. Nineham.

11. J.T.S., new series, 21 (1970), 517.

12. See W. Köhler, Bibliographia Brentiana.

13. Hall, op. cit., p. 51.

14. John Olin, The Catholic Reformation, p. 112. See also Henry Heller, "The Evangelicalism of Lefevre d'Etaples: 1525," S.R. XIX (1972), 42-77.

15. Lowell Green, "The Bible in Sixteenth-Century Humanist Education," S.R. XIX (1972), 126-127.

16. Anne-Marie Salgat, Aspects Of The Life And Theology Of Pierre Viret, (unpublished thesis) p. 46 from Henri Meylan, La Haute Ecole de Lausanne, 1537-1937, pp. 19-20.

PETER MARTYR

PART ONE: REFORMER IN EXILE
(1542/62)

What is exile? . . . I know that it is the scourge of the Lord;
but with what mildness and fatherly affection he deals with me,
I can readily learn even from this, that he has afforded me for
my comforters Bullinger, Melanchthon, and Martyr, and other most
shining lights in the church.

John Ponet to Heinrich Bullinger

CHAPTER I

FROM DIALOGUE TO DISSENT (1537/62)

CORTESE AND CONTARINI: THE CLIMATE OF DIALOGUE (1537/42)

The pontificate of Pope Paul III (1534-1549) marked a turning point for Roman Catholic Reform. In preparation for the proposed Council of Mantua to meet in 1537, Pope Paul named a reform commission of nine clerics. In March of 1537 their report was given by Contarini to Pope Paul III. It read in part as follows:

> And your Holiness...had rightly acknowledged that the origin of these evils was due to the fact that some popes, your predecessors, in the words of the Apostle Paul, 'having itching ears heaped up to themselves teachers according to their own lusts'...[1]

The nine commission members had impressive credentials to prepare an indictment of the hierarchy. One such member was Gregorio Cortese, Benedictine Abbot of San Giorgio, Venice. Cortese's involvement in the attempts at mediation in Italy from 1537-1542 helps one to explain Peter Martyr's theology of dissent in exile. To follow the career in Italy of one of Martyr's prominent friends in the five years prior to his 1542 flight is to move theologically from a climate of mediation to one of dissent. The parallel career of a reformer who rejected protestant theology in Italy sets the scene for Martyr's writings which accepted protestantism first in Italy and then in Northern Europe. Like Martyr, Cortese was a monastic theologian and abbot. Both were educated at Padua. The troubles at Modena parallel those at Lucca in 1542 and give one a wide perspective on a volatile scene in Italian religious history.

The 1537 *Consilium*, though the most searching in its indictment
of the papacy, is one of several sixteenth century treatises on reform.
Gregorio Cortese in 1513 to Pope Leo X and again in 1522 to Pope Adrian
VI joined in the chorus for Roman Catholic Reform. As a Benedictine
Abbot, Cortese provides a distinct perspective on that *crie de coeur*
of the Reformers. On the death of Cardinal Fregoso, Cardinal Sadoleto
proposed to Pope Paul III that Cortese become a Cardinal. In his 1541
letter Sadoleto mentioned the erudition and piety of the Benedictine
Reformer, claiming that no one can have failed to learn about his
excellence in character, advice, eloquence and doctrine. What one
reads in the extant literature confirms the reasons for Sadoleto's
nomination and Pope Paul III's selection of Cortese as a cardinal.
Though his theological writings have not survived, in particular the
1538 New Testament translation and commentary, Cortese was an excellent
scholar and monastic reformer. To understand the background of the
De Emendanda Ecclesia of 1537 which Cortese helped to draft one must
examine the lives of the men who prepared such a remarkable document.
Cortese also from 1526-1542 was an abbot in the reorganized (1504)
Cassinese congregations of the Benedictine order and after 1542 was
a cardinal who served on the preparatory commission for the Council of
Trent. Investigation of his monastic study and career as an abbot
until 1542 will enable us to understand Pastor's evaluation:

> Cortese's whole character bore a striking resemblance to that of
> his fellow-countryman and friend, Sadoleto: gentle, tender, peace
> loving, and in his criticism of the Protestant reformers often
> lenient to a fault.

Thomas Badia, Jacob Sadoleto and Gregorio Cortese were all born
in Modena. Cortese had much in common with the lenient Badia (who
as Master of the Sacred Palace ruled on the orthodoxy of theological
works) and his humanist countryman Sadoleto. The leniency, however,
has its sources in sophisticated patristic and biblical scholarship.
What seems like leniency and/or heresy prior to the establishment of
the Inquisition in Italy on July 21, 1542, or even prior to the 1546
debates on justification at the Council of Trent cannot be naivete in
theology. Wolfgang Reinhard finds that the religious crisis of Sadoleto's associates is located in the medieval Aristotelian tradition
taught in Padua. Since Cortese studied in Padua, this seems plausible
as one source for the reforming ideas to which this author of the
Consilium subscribed. One should also remember that Vermigli was in
Padua from 1518-1526. Josiah Simler in his oration linked Vermigli
to this milieu. When Martyr interpreting I *Corinthians* at Naples
attacked the catholic doctrine of purgatory from chapter III, his
enemies saw to it that he could not longer read biblical lectures.
Then men like Cardinal Gonzaga of Mantua, Contarini, Pole, Bembo and
others saw that Martyr's liberty to teach was restored.

Philip McNair has described the environment of evangelism and
Dermot Fenlon the setting in Italy of Cardinal Pole's crisis over
faith and justification. It is not necessary to repeat here what each
has elsewhere so carefully written. Neither are specific about
Contarini's or Cortese's theological views. It has seemed best therefore to describe these in matters relevant to Martyr, i.e. Contarini

on scripture and Cortese on reform.   Cortese in 1540 possessed a copy

of the *Beneficio*. Its author resided in Cortese's circle in Venice.

Therefore, Cortese is crucial to this scene in the 1540's.

Cortese wrote Contarini about the nature of grace in 1537.   After

Cortese became Abbot of San Benedetto Polirone near Mantua in 1540, he

read John Calvin's *Institutes of the Christian Religion*.   Cortese

felt it was directed against a universal council.   In 1540 Cortese

meant to attend the Worms Colloquy but fell ill on the way and stayed

in Genoa.   On 1 May 1540 Cortese wrote to Duke Frederico Gonzaga of

Mantua that he had the Lutheran chapters which the Duke sent him to

examine.   Cortese kept well informed of theological matters in this

period, perhaps explaining why Pope Paul III would ask him to help stem

heresy in Modena.   Cortese was created a Cardinal on 2 June 1542, and

named administrator of the bishopric of Urbino on 6 November 1542.

Cardinal Bembo wrote from Rome of Cortese's learning, excellence in

religion, and incomparable prudence.   Pope Paul III appointed Cortese

a Cardinal for all of these reasons.   Cortese's involvement with his

countrymen in Modena led to his endorsement in 1542 of a confession of

faith prepared by Gasparo Contarini.   This affair in Modena demon-

strates the orthodoxy of Cortese as well as the intransigent positions

being urged in the Curia.   It will also introduce us to the climate of

suspicion which led Peter Martyr to abandon his Italian Cardinal

friends Cortese, Contarini and Pole for the more congenial climate

of Northern Europe.

1542 was a good year for heresy in Northern Italy.   Pope Paul III,

alarmed by religious unrest in Modena and Lucca, reconstituted the
Inquisition on 21 July 1542. *Licet ab initio* sought to stem the tide
of error which had inundated the very home of the papacy. Pastor could
not retell the full story for, as he put it:

> Any description or estimate of the work of the reorganized
> Inquisition as it proceeded under Paul III is impossible to an
> historian, as no records are at his disposal. The archives of
> the Holy Office in Rome must certainly have documentary evidence
> to some extent but inspection is absolutely refused. If the
> present congregation of the Holy Office still persists in main-
> taining a system of absolute secrecy, which has almost univer-
> sally been abandoned elsewhere, with regard to historical docu-
> ments now more than three centuries old, it inflicts an injury
> not merely on the work of the historian but still more upon it-
> self, since it thus perpetuates belief in all and in the worst
> of all the innumerable charges leveled at the Inquisition.

Equally difficult is the status of local records scattered throughout
Italy. The story at Lucca appears in Professor McNair's *Peter Martyr
in Italy: An Anatomy of An Apostasy*. Venice stalled Papal action until
the interdict of 1606-1607, yet even so 1542 was also critical for
religious activity in Venice.

At Modena the populace was in an uproar over itinerant preaching;
while the classical academy suspected papal intentions and Paul III
reacted before the curia. That story can be somewhat reconstructed by
retelling the reaction of the Academicians, the mediating Cardinals
and Giovanni Domenico Sigbaldo, Cardinal Morone's Vicar in Modena.
What resulted was a *Confessio Fidei* of 1542 which has not recently
been studied in its setting. Since Cortese is involved in its implementation in Modena, the *Confessio* is important in assessing his attitude toward reform in 1542. Pastor claims that "the focus of

religious rebellion was a society of learned men" known as the
Accademia and that Morone was amazed at the state of affairs in
Modena on his return in 1542. Unpublished correspondence between
Sigbaldo and Morone now shows that Pastor's statement about Morone is
unwarranted. For example, Sigbaldo wrote to the Duke of Ferrara on
4 July 1541 that Bartholomew of Mirandola had been able to abate
Lutheranism in Modena by his excellent and sound Catholic doctrine.[2]

As early as 1538 the Academy at Modena fell under suspicion when
Francesco Parto met opposition for interpreting the Greek New Testament
in preaching. In 1540 Camillo Renato fled to Modena where both the
Court and Academy welcomed him. That Renato was arrested under orders
of the Duke of Ferrara and the Dominican inquisitors at Bologna reflects the unrest in Modena at this time. The trial at Ferrara late
in 1540 uncovered much evidence of heresy in Modena. In 1541 the
Inquisitor of Modena examined Lancelloto for his theological views.
What complicates matters is the association of these academicians with
the reforming Cardinals Cortese, Morone, Badia and other influential
clerics. These Cardinals by 1542 approved of the ideas in the *Beneficio*
di Cristo. The point is not that Modena was orthodox but that the
Academy was defended at Rome. To explain these complex relationships
between heterodoxy and orthodoxy, further research needs to be done on
the associates of Cortese. Folengo, under suspicion for heresy, dedicated his 1546 commentary on I *John* to Cardinal Pole. Onorato-
Fascitelli (1502-1564), a Benedictine associate of Cortese, also
frequented Pole's Viterbo circle and participated in discussion of

these views.

Certain questions need to be asked about the Papal accusation of the Modenese Academy and Contarini's *Confession of Faith* rejected by the Academy in 1542. What action did the moderate Cardinals take in Rome when fully informed by correspondents in Modena? Are there two confessions in Modena in 1542, one prepared by Rome and one by Contarini? There are no clear answersbut some questions can be formulated as one explores the desire for biblical study shared by these Catholic reformers before and after the crises of 1542. The events of 1542 in Italy slowed the development of such study. The tension in Rome can be sensed in the letters written by Contarini during his 1542 legation in Bologna describing the political and military situation. Cardinal Sadoleto kept in close touch with Modena during 1542. His correspondence describes many concerns of the Academy. In his first letter to Castelvetro of 12 June 1542 Sadoleto found it difficult to believe that the Modenese Academy was not "veri christiani." Castelvetro replied that he wished Sadoleto to secure his innocence and to protect him "with faith and affection." The following day, 3 July, Alessandro Milano also wrote to Sadoleto seeking protection at Rome: "It is far from the truth to doubt and say that the new opinions of the Academy are not truly Christian, since they are founded on the divine scriptures and quiet study." The same day Giovanni Grillenzoni wrote from Modena that for two years the "grande frate Bernardino" had preached about Christ, causing a division of opinion. Francesco Greco on 7 July informed Sadoleto that the disturbances in Modena did not arise from any conflict with teachings firmly held by the Catholic Church.

Extant correspondence leaves no doubt that the members of the Academy were suspected of heresy. Castelvetro signed the confession even though he possessed protestant works, and later was suspected of translating Melanchthon into Italian and fled himself to Geneva. Suspicion of the Academy's activity is understandable, but what is interesting is an awareness of its activities by Sadoleto, Pole, Morone, Cortese and Contarini as well as the accusations and the accelerating reaction in Rome. On 15 July 1542 Sadoleto assured Castelvetro that not only he but others could certify the christian and catholic spirit of the Academy. Sigbaldo as Vicar for Morone had earlier supported the Academy in a letter to Morone of 6 April 1541. Cortese endorsed Giambattista Tassoni in a letter of 17 June 1542. Tassoni signed the *Confessio* on 1 September 1542. Morone had sent the articles to Cortese at Mantua who approved the proposal, "as Catholic, genuine and godly, drafted with much seriousness and skill, not letting be accepted any controversial aspects at that time (without examination)." The letter suggests that Cortese added several lucid expressions on the necessity of works, transubstantiation, indulgences and free will. Cortese wished for Morone to sign the preface to remove all pretext for the others. He also suggested that some sign who were not under suspicion. This would enable the others to appear more inclined to witness to the truth than to give evidence of their own faith.

A look at the *Confessio Fidei* shows the degree of suspicion in Rome. It also gives a definition of catholic orthodoxy supported by

the Pauline circle of Contarini in a period of doctrinal uncertainty.
On 1 September 1542 in the heat of controversy and suspicion about
Modena, a treatise was approved in Rome under the title *Articuli
Orthodoxae Professionis*. An impressive list of Cardinals and others
in Modena signed it including members of the Academy. The preamble
added by Sadoleto urged removal of all suspicion of impiety from this
Catholic state and from the names of the subscribers. The preface
claimed that the Pope sent the 41 articles of faith to Modena and that
Cortese, Sadoleto and Morone discussed them on August 30. However, in
a letter of 25 July 1542 Morone mentioned to Cervini that Cortese
promised to subscribe willingly to the articles composed by Contarini.
He adds that the city will be in great danger "non tanto di tumulto,
quanto di confirmar l'heresia nella mente di molti." Morone meant the
Katechesis, sive christiana instructio which Contarini prepared in
Bologna. Its text is identical to the document signed in Modena on 1
September 1542. Contarini wrote to Pole on 22 July 1542 to thank him
for the annotations of his little work which "Joannes familiaris" had
made. Cortese seems to have had a hand in the final revision.

Can one assume that the articles were composed by Contarini and
sent by Rome to Modena? Were they then revised on 30 August after the
initial rejection by the Academy? Some revision by Cortese seems
likely. Since the articles are not well known, two of its questions
and responses are given as follows:

> 35th Question: What must one think of the pattern of life and
> worship in the church? or, more specifically, is every Christian
> freed from ceremonies and rites and human laws as Paul seems to

say when he writes: hold fast to the freedom which Christ has
given us?
Reply: Christ freed all Christians from the cememonies and legal
precepts of the Mosaic Law, for once they were separated from the
people to whom alone these laws had been given, the laws no longer
applied to them. Likewise, the ceremonies which foreshadowed the
coming of Christ were abolished after His Resurrection. Freedom
in ceremonies, rites, and laws was also given to Christians because
nothing other than the Sacraments was prescribed for us by Christ.
On the other hand, we must not interpret the freedom given to the
Christian people by Christ as though we are to have no rites or
ceremonies in common. Homer tells us the Cyclops lived like that.
If everyone set up and followed his own concept of ceremonies or
life style arbitrarily, he would be living more like the people of
Babel than the church of Christ. That church is His Body whose
members are joined together in the unity of the Holy Spirit. The
freedom given us by Christ (other than freedom from slavery to
sin) should be understood in this way: Christ has not prescribed
anything by way of judicial precepts for our lives on earth as
citizens, nor for our lives as members of the Christian political
community. Rather, He regarded these as matters of lesser importance and subject to frequent alteration according to time and
place, and left them to the decision of Princes and Bishops. We
simply cannot live our lives without such leaders nor can unity
exist if not the object of effort in common. It is only the
rebel or the fool who wants to turn the Christian church into the
church of Babel or the Cyclops. So we should obey our Princes and
their laws, provided these do not go contrary to divine and natural
law. It is written: Obey Kings and Princes; obey Bishops too and
the laws and rites (?) pertaining to the Christian political community. For it has been written again and again: Obey your
superiors and be subject to them, for they look after your (lives)
as though one day they must give an accounting for them. Therefore, the Christian should observe rites, ceremonies and obser-
vances instituted by our superiors and honored in the church universal. For, as Augustine says to Januarius, certain things are
observed by the universal church whose origins go back beyond
memory. Indeed, they must be embraced as the doing of the Apostles.
And there are certain things which are proper to this or that
Bishop's jurisdiction; these, too, should be obeyed within his
territory. The man who does not obey them offends against justice,
for we owe obedience to our legitimate superiors. And he also
offends against charity because he injures the unity of the church
to some degree when as a citizen he offends against the pattern of
civil life by wanting to change what has been established and
accepted in that particular state. On the other hand, if he obeys
the law with humility in his heart as a Christian should, and
lives and acts in charity, then such a life will receive an abundant reward in heaven; yet we do not term these actions "worship"

as if we could earn the forgiveness of our sins through them.
That comes to us solely through Christ in Whom we have our Redemption and the forgiveness of sins, as the Apostle says and as is
clearly explained by St. Thomas.
36th Question: Does the universal Church have a head who directs
it in the Christian life?
Reply: Yes it has, and that head is Christ by Whom our sense and
movement and spiritual life are all infused into every Christian
who lives in Him, and Who guides and sanctifies the Christian from
within. Likewise, in another and lesser way the head of the
church is the Vicar of Christ, the successor of Peter, the Roman
Pontiff, who does not infuse interior life into the church but
rules and guides her externally. For it is impossible for large
numbers of men to achieve unity unless it be under one man's
guidance. It is especially necessary that the Christian church
possess unity: not so much the unity enjoyed by the secular state
as that of the one body spoken of in the Scriptures. Therefore,
it ought to have one head. There are specific references to this
in the Gospels, and it is the clear opinion of all (Teachers),
both ancient and modern, that the Bishops of the various cities
rank after the Roman Pontiff, and after the Bishops come the various priests of the (parishes) who lack any legitimate designation
allowing them to act separately or on their own authority.

It would be tempting at this point to settle the orthodoxy of the

1542 *Confessio* on the presence or absence of the slogan, *sola fide*.

One should resist that temptation and turn instead to other contempo-

rary expressions of faith in biblical commentaries. Professor Rupp well

describes the nature of the task when he says about patterns of salva-

tion in this period that it would be much harder to answer such ques-

tions by a history of hermeneutics in the 16th century, showing from

decade to decade how the Reformers expounded the Holy Scriptures. That

suggestion would be as valuable for catholic as for protestant exegesis.

In the absence of such a detailed study one turns to the Benedictine

setting in which Cortese lived and which produced the famous *Beneficio*

di Cristo. One reason for support of the Modena Academy by certain

Cardinals in Rome was their own interest and involvement in activities

similar to those of the Academy. The intense desire for and practice
of biblical study in Italy at this time is well known. Such a desire
explains in part the acceptance of works as the *Beneficio di Cristo*
first published in 1543. Tommaso Bozza claims that the activities of
Cortese, Isidore Clarius[3] and others cannot be ignored in describing
"evangelism." Cortese, while supporting men like Don Benedetto in
Venice, engaged in intense biblical study himself. Though his published
theological studies have disappeared, a thorough check of Cortese's
career in Italy indicates his agreement with the activities of many
like Isidore Clarius and the contents of the *Beneficio di Cristo*.
Cortese declared, "In the midst of the night I put on no other garment
than this beneficio di Cristo."

In September of 1541 Martyr had daily conversations with Cardinal
Contarini at Lucca. Elisabeth Gleason finds a Pauline dimension of
faith in the writings of Contarini. Martyr met with Contarini after
the debacle of Ratisbon where an agreement on faith between Lutheran
and Catholic was ridiculed in Wittenberg and rejected at Rome. The
dream of reform by dialogue was at an end. Men like Pole, Cortese and
Contarini were now faced with dissent from the catholic doctrines of
the Eucharist and Papal authority. In this maelstrom of catholic
religious and doctrinal confusion one ought to cite again an undated
opinion of Contarini on Luther. It was one option possible for several
Italian reformers until Pope Paul III moved against Modena, Lucca and
Venice with the Index and Inquisition. In spite of the articles of
faith prepared for Modena – the last such attempt by the devotees of

"evangelismo" in Sixteenth Century Italy - Pope Paul III established

the Inquisition as an offical response of the Papacy to its own

native Italian reformation. This statement by Contarini sums up his

views on religious faith.

> The basis of /Lutheranism/ takes into account the deformity of
> sin, and all the harm it brings ... from it nothing liberates but
> the merits of Christ ... through the merits of Christ we receive
> the Holy Spirit, by whom is dispersed the darkness of our soul ...
> Here we do not need our /good/ works ... Thus the basis of the
> Lutheran edifice is most true, and we must not contradict it by
> any means, but accept it as true and catholic, even as the basis
> of Christian religion.[4]

The dialogue which a native catholic religious experience in Italy had

supported was at an end. Small wonder that Martyr fled with Ochino in

that summer of their discontent.

Contarini emerges as the most impressive member of the Italians

who urged and practiced dialogue with the protestants in the 1540's.

When one reads recent literature on Contarini one is struck by the

credentials which Contarini commanded to reform catholicism in Italy

on the basis of Paulinism. Matheson claims that the dialogue between

protestantism and catholicism did not fail at Regensburg in 1541; it

never took place! J. B. Ross documents the materials for a modern

biography of Martyr's impressive friend while Felix Gilbert and

Elizabeth Gleason disagree over the primacy of political or religious

motives in Contarini's reform career. Professor Hall finds in a

survey of the Colloquies of 1539-41 that if theology alone was in

question, intransigence would not have been the only possible catholic

response.

Fenlon's theme of *Heresy and Obedience* touches Peter Martyr's response to the same crisis which faced Pole, Contarini and others. Because Pope Paul III forced obedience by violating basic human freedoms, Martyr chose freedom and charged the Papacy with heresy. That accounts for the tone of his writings on the Eucharist and the Papacy. Martyr's theology of dissent came after the Papacy in 1542 closed off the possibility of dialogue in Italy. Martyr realized that the theological dialogue at Ratisbon was a failure. Contarini and Cortese tried again at Modena: Pole and Seripando would make the last catholic attempt to defend *sola fide* at Trent. Their failure at Trent is one additional comment on Martyr's prior choice to flee persecution.

Pietro Martire Vermigli left the scene of papal oppression in 1542 for the interminable protestant colloquys of the North. For Martyr it was the religious side of the Renaissance struggle for human liberty.[5] Pope Paul III by his actions in 1542 greatly enriched the reformers of Strasbourg, England, Zurich and Geneva by sending them a man who in exile became the theologian of the Italian Reformation.

John Norton, pastor at Ipswich, wrote his *Orthodox Evangelist* to which John Cotton contributed a preface dated 20 September 1652. There, in far off New England, John Cotton at Boston could endorse Peter Martyr in the controversy over salvation. "'The most judicious and Orthodox of our best writers, Calvin, Martyr, Bucer and the rest,' have been 'slighted' in New England."[6] A century after contributing to Cranmer's lovely *Prayer Book* (1552) Peter Martyr once again became part and parcel of a theological controversy. This time it was over preparation of the heart for God's initiatory work of salvation.

There was no such preparation necessary for those whom God had chosen.

No antinomian of the seventeenth century or Pelagian of the sixteenth

could cite Martyr on his behalf. In McNair's phrase, though the re-

former who set out for Switzerland in 1542 was half racked by fever,

he was wholly justified by faith.[7]

VERMIGLI'S THEOLOGY OF DISSENT

ON FLIGHT FROM PERSECUTION

When Pope Paul III issued *Licet ab initio* which established the

Inquisition in Italy,[8] several crises of conscience surfaced for the

devotees of catholic evangelism such as Reginald Pole, Cardinal of Eng-

land,[9] and Gasparo Cardinal Contarini.[10] When the Emperor Charles V

met at Lucca with Pope Paul III during September of 1541, Contarini

renewed acquaintance with the Prior of S. Frediano--Pietro Martire

Vermigli.[11] This native of Florence had given lectures on I *Corinthians*

at Naples in 1540[12] and was one of several prominent Italians for whom

the Papal bull would be decisive. Contarini selected Martyr and Cor-

tese to be his advisors in 1540 at the Worms Colloquy. By that date

one can see that Martyr moved in the environment of Italian evangelism.

Both McNair and Donnelly document Martyr's stature as an Italian theo-

logian trained in scholastic, humanistic and evangelical circles.

Though precipitated by clandestine protestantism at Modena and

Lucca, the Inquisition reached into every corner of Italy. The

Inquisitors moved swiftly against the Anabaptists when suddenly on 4

October 1551 Peter Manelfi defected at Bologna.[13] Pietro Carnesecchi

for circulating the tract *On The Benefits of Jesus Christ Crucified*
confessed his heresy to the Inquisition on 21 August 1566 and was
burned at the stake for this and other revelations about his associ-
ations with the circle of Valdes.[14] It was dangerous to confess Pauline
theology in Petrine territory.

The choices were clear-cut. Either one became a Nicodemite[15]--
making a cloister of his heart--or he selected the narrow way of the
stake, or he could flee into exile. Martyr, like Ochino and later
Vergerio,[16] fled into Northern Europe in 1542. In the famous *De Fuga
in Persecutione*,[17] Martyr justified that flight. His title reminds
one of Tertullian's treatise of A.D. 207/208. In fact, Martyr took
great care to refute Tertullian's exegesis of *Matthew* 10:23:

> But when they persecute you in this city, flee into the next:
> For verily I say unto you, Ye shall not have gone through the
> cities of Israel, till the Son of man be come.

Tertullian observed that Christ urged flight from one Palestinian
city to another rather than exile from the entire country.[18] Since
Mark (6:7-11) and *Luke* (9:1-5), (12:1-12) mention the Gentile mission,
Martyr clearly saw the eschatological framework of Matthew's account.
When the end is near one ought to abandon all things. Montanism was
not one of Martyr's options when he wrote:

> Wherefore, since I am delivered from so great a danger, being not
> ignorant of these kinds of troubles, since I was certified from
> Rome, from the society, from the monastery, and from your city,
> of the persecution even at hand, since I did harm unto none, but
> by lectures and sermons did manifest the truth, all dignities,
> riches, and commodities set aside, being rid out of the bonds of
> superstitions, and delivered from so many hypocrasies: if I
> delivered my life from imminent oppression, there is no cause
> why any man should take occasion of offence. And doth not the
> Lord grant that we should avoid persecutions?[19]

Martyr also quoted from the *Psalms* the Greek verse, "He who flees shall also again do battle." His purpose was to serve God "more commodious-lie."[20]

Delio Cantimori in an essay on the problem of heresy in sixteenth century Italy observed that:

> The religious struggles of the age were carried on *religionis causa*--for the sake of religion, for the sake of salvation, for the sake of conscience. . . . Since we are dealing with struggles that were primarily religious, we cannot subordinate the religious, and hence the theological, elements to the non-religious elements within them.[21]

Ochino's flight ended in anti-trinitarian radicalism; Vergerio's in anti-catholic invective. By contrast the sober and profound patristic scholar Peter Martyr created an impressive series of Biblical commentaries which clarified the *furor theologicus*. He accused the Papacy of errors *in materia fidei*, of schism, heresy and idolatry. Who was this peripatetic Protestant theologian, confidant of Bucer and Bullinger, Calvin and Cranmer, Beza and the Marian exiles?

From 1499 to 1542 Martyr lived in Italy. Educated at Padua and having served at Spoleto, Naples and Lucca, Martyr not only came to the attention of the Inquisitors, but knew many of the leaders in Italian evangelism such as Juan de Valdes, Carinals Corcese, Pole and especially Contarini. It was the latter who requested Martyr's presence at the Worms Colloquy and himself represented the Pope at the illfated 1541 Ratisbon Colloquy where protestants and catholics agreed on justification.[22]

REFORMER IN EXILE

Martyr lived in Strasbourg from 1542-1547 where he lectured on the Old Testament.[23] At Cranmer's invitation Martyr joined the Archbishop of Canterbury at Lambeth in 1547 and became Regius Professor at Oxford in 1548. Martyr led the famous 1549 Oxford debate on the Eucharist, contributed an exhortation to the Prayer Book of 1552, a sermon to the Book of Homilies, was possibly the source for several of the Forty Two Articles and helped Cranmer draft the Edwardian *Reformatio Legum Ecclesiasticarum*. In all of the above one can see Martyr's imprint on English reform during Edward VI's reign. When the Catholic Mary Tudor ascended the English throne in 1553, Martyr fled to Strasbourg. In 1556 he left a host of Marian exiles and Lutheran opponents at Strasbourg to join Bullinger at Zurich. While at Zurich Martyr lectured on the Old Testament and attended the Colloquy of Poissy in 1561. His correspondence with Bullinger and Calvin marks Vermigli as an important reformed theologian.[24] His amanuensis John Jewel wrote the famous *Apology* for the Church of England in 1562 and Zacharias Ursinus who met Martyr in Zurich and followed his theology co-authored the Heidelberg Catechism of 1563. In 1562 Bullinger showed Martyr a draft of what became the second Helvetic Confession.

In his Theses of 1543 Martyr proposed that a Law/Gospel motif permeated the cannonical scriptures.[25] His use of scripture to sustain a godly life occurs in Martyr's proposition XII from *Exodus*.

> God's law requires of our perfect actions three things:
> first, that we be honest in outward affairs; next, that
> we avoid violence of our own accord; and finally, that
> we refer every good and spiritual impulse totally to
> God.[26]

The *Romans* commentary (1558) was given as lectures during 1550 at Oxford. In these pages one reads a clear Christological basis for a new quality of life. After noting that the sorrow of death no longer held Christ, Martyr went on to assert with St. Paul that sin's tyranny no longer binds the Christian man.

> Righteousness and purness of lyfe shall daily be renewed in us: which thing is brought to passe, when we depart from sinne: for as long as we live in sinne, we lead not a new life, but the olde life. There is no entraunce open unto the lyfe of the resurrection, but by death.[27]

The same theme occurs in his Oxford sermons, especially on *Philippians* (2). God has tempered a medicine out of the death and resurrection of Christ. Of this wholesome medicine we drink healthfully, argued Martyr, whenever by reading or preaching mention is made of Christ's death and resurrection, "and we with a lively faith embrace the same."[28] So must the biblical scholar orient his exegesis about the twin foci of scripture's scope and its clarity.

The scope of scripture includes theology, philosophy, and grammatical analysis. Those who recall Luther's dictum that at Wittenberg Aristotle was everywhere heading for a fall may be surprised to learn that in Martyr's view, scholastic method aids the scholar to set forth his views in a plain way.

While in Strasbourg Martyr lectured on the *Nichomachean Ethics*. In Zurich because the polymath Conrad Gesner lectured on the *Ethics* at the Carolinum, Martyr could prepare his commentary for publication. As stated in this commentary on the *Ethics* the scope of a biblical text first rested upon its explanation through theological loci. An example

would be in Martyr's *Romans* (1558) after chapter 11.[29] Together with
the theological definition of justification, Martyr added a catena of
patristic citations on *sola fide* and lamented that Albert Phigius taught
that love justified rather than faith. Martyr held that all a man's
deeds prior to justification are "occupied in evil works and wandreth
in the hatred of God."[30] Secondly in this commentary on method, Martyr
urged that grammatical and textual matters must be analyzed prior to a
final exposition of the text. Not only did Martyr set forth a scholastic method in theology, but also moral instruction, "ad uitam componendam."[31] Both were controlled by the biblical text as revealed knowledge. Such a moral dimension noted in his study of St. Paul marks
Vermigli as a biblical commentator unabashed to speak about the text
which taught him to amend his life intellectually and morally--to admit
both his ignorance and his sin. This triple method of loci, text and
exposition developed in lectures on Aristotle served as Martyr's exegetical model for scripture. Arabic commentators on Aristotle were
aware of such an approach to philosophical texts.[32]

Theodore Beza contrasted Martyr's clarity to Bucer's prolixity.
Bucer's attempt to explain the Eucharist only confused Beza. In a
letter of 23 June 1565 Beza urged Cassiodora De Reina to use "the
clearer and more certain writings of our Martyr."[33] In January of
1555 John Calvin sent Martyr a lengthy comment on the Eucharist.
Martyr cautioned Calvin against such ambiguous terminology. Calvin in
turn reminded Martyr that Bucer went far amiss in his attempt to resolve this issue. "For he, wishing to calm the violence of Luther

and his partisans, stooped so severely that he was entangled in continual complexity by single words."[34]

The clarity of Martyr's biblical writing was noted by his catholic opponents, especially Cornelius Schulting who in 1602 contrasted Martyr to Calvin. Schulting claimed that:

> In Martyr's *Common Places* there is great perspicuity of diction. In Calvin's Institutes as well as in his biblical commentaries, though industrious and studious, it seems that a tortuous serpent deceives and conceals from the reader the form which meanders so much that he sees only the tail which he can scarcely hold on to.[35]

The clarity of Martyr's exegesis would seem to derive from his personal orientation in which to the question of hermeneutical scope he gave a clear Christological answer. There can be no doubt that Martyr defended Chalcedonian terminology against Francesco Stancaro. This Anti-trinitarian professor of Hebrew challenged Martyr's exegesis of *Romans* (8). As Stancaro would have it, the true understanding of Christ was obscured by the theologians of Zurich and Geneva.[36] Though Martyr defended the non-biblical terms of Chalcedon, he also pressed on Calvin and Beza the biblical model in *Romans* (5) and I *Corinthians* (15). His positive analysis of the Two-Adam Christology is as significant as his defense of a two-nature Christology. Martyr's comments are refreshing on this subject.

ENGLISH INFLUENCE

Thomas Cartwright, the leading Puritan dissenter, answered Archbishop Whitgift by citing from important theologians of the time. The 1573 A *Replye to an Answere made of Dr. Whitgifte Agaynste the*

Admonition to the Parliament summarized several key issues at stake

in the Puritan controversy. On the Apostolic regiment of the Church

Cartwright cited John Calvin's *Institutes*, Peter Martyr on *Romans* (3)

and Martin Bucer's *De Regno Christi*.On elders it was Calvin, Beza,

Bucer and Martyr on *Romans* (11). On chancellors Cartwright appealed

to Martyr on *Romans* (13); on the sacraments, Martyr on I *Corinthians*

(11). Thomas Cartwright summarized the question of ceremonies and

apparel by quoting from Bucer, Bullinger, Gualter and Peter Martyr on

I *Kings*.

> P. Martyr upon the 10. C_+ of the 2 boke of the Kings/sayeth that
> the Lutheranes must take heede/least whilest they cutte of many
> popishe errors/they follow Jehu by retauuing also many popishe
> thynges. For they defende still the reall presence in the breade
> of the supper/and images/ and vestments, etc. and sayth that
> religion must be wholy reformed to the quicke.

This 1573 work reminds students of the Sixteenth Century that

Peter Martyr played a major role in shaping Reformed thought. Beza,

Bullinger, Bucer and Calvin considered him to be their equal.

When Henry VIII died in 1547 Archbishop Thomas Cranmer moved

quickly toward liturgical and theological reform. In 1547 Martyr and

Bernardino Ochino moved to England at Cranmer's invitation. In 1548

Cranmer publically repudiated transubstantiation. By 1549 under the

boy-king Edward VI Cranmer taught a spiritual eating and drinking of

the very flesh and blood of Christ. Peter Martyr as professor of the-

ology at Oxford publicly disputed these issues in 1549. Martyr assist-

ed Cranmer with the second Prayer Book of April, 1552. Peter Martyr

wrote a lovely prayer of invitation to the Lord's Supper for this

Edwardian Prayer Book.[37]

Peter Martyr had a greater influence on the English Reformation than one might conclude from a cursory glance at the 1576 Latin edition or Marten's translation of his *Common Places*. Martyr's correspondence is difficult to obtain. Three hundred and one extant letters from 1542-1562 may be divided as follows: (1) Fifty-eight have never been published, (2) Fifty-nine Latin letters are in the *Corpus Reformatorum*, (3) Sixty-nine Latin letters are found in the several editions of the Latin *Loci Communes* published between 1576 and 1656. The remaining Latin letters are widely scattered so that only thirty per cent of the three hundred and one letters are accessible. Solving these bibliographical problems enables one to appreciate Van der Delft's report of 16 May 1548 to the Emperor, Charles V.

> Very few of these returned refugees are Sacramentarians, but there are amongst them some who conform with the ideas of the Italians Friar Bernardin and Peter Martyr, who are the pet children of the Archbishop of Canterbury.[38]

Thomas Cranmer praised Martyr's learning and piety as did John Calvin, Theodore Beza and Heinrich Bullinger. A careful study of Martyr's protestant career from 1542-1562 will reveal why men like Cranmer and Calvin appreciated Peter Martyr's biblical writings. One result of such study is Donnelly's caution against viewing William of Occam as the father of protestant theology.[39]

CHRISTOLOGY AND EXEGESIS

When Zwingli wrote his 1522 treatise *On the Certainty and Clarity of The Word of God*, he wished that one would compare scripture with scripture and test the whole by what it said about Christ. Martyr who

read Zwingli's 1525 *De Vera et Falsa Religionis* used scholastic meth-

odology to analyze the scope of scripture. In so doing he found that

to know Christ made the scripture clear. Small wonder that in the

frontespiece of his Commentary on I *Corinthians* (1551) Martyr placed

the verse from *Galatians* (6:14). This made him a scholar of Christ

as well as a Christian scholar. As Sir Herbert Butterfield has well

said: "Hold fast to Christ, and for the rest be totally uncommitted."[40]

Peter Martyr in fleeing the Inquisitors of Italy fled to fight

again, not against flesh and blood, but against idolatry in the Eucha-

rist and hypocrisy in theology.[41] In the only extant letter from

Martyr's Italian days is a postscript to the Canons at Lucca. "I am

free from Hypocrisy through the grace of Christ."[42] While the Defend-

ers of the Faith lanced Italy with the stake and *Index* over their view

of biblical interpretation, Peter Martyr laboured over his books and

parchments in Northern Europe. In the end they could not keep Martyr

from his first love which was a study of scripture.

Professor Gordon Rupp sums up Martyr's concern when he wrote of

early English protestants:

> The case for the open Bible rests in the end not on an estimate
> of the intellectual capacities of common men.... But it rests in
> the main on the fact that the God who made all men and spent him-
> self in their redemption wills by his Spirit to lead men home in
> a plain way to himself, and that in the end we are not as child-
> ren to be protected from the adventure of truth, nor slaves who
> need not be told more than is good for them, but sons of God.[43]

Peter Martyr among many others opened the Bible to show his confreres

in exile the truth of God's redemption--that the scope of scripture and its clarity is found in the "Benefits of Jesus Christ Crucified." Or

again the words of the fourth Gospel, *John* (5:39):

> You study the scriptures diligently, supposing that in having
> them you have eternal life; yet, although their testimony points
> to me, you refuse to come to me for that life.

Bishop Edmund Scambler issued orders for Norwich Diocese on 16

April 1589. Among his first order for reading the Holy Scripture and

second to gather notes every quarter from one book of the Old or New

Testament, every deacon and minister who did not understand Latin had

a special order.

> 4. Item, such deacons and ministers as do not understand the
> Latin tongue shall provide Calvin's *Institutions*, Peter Martyr's
> *Common Places*, and Musculus his *Common Places* in English to read
> and profit in the same.[44]

Forty-two years earlier Peter Martyr had come to England.

Peter Martyr described exactly what he meant when in the *Defense*

of the Eucharist Against Stephen Gardiner he accused the Bishop of

Winchester of obscuring the Gospel. Prefaced to the 1582 edition of

Martyr's *Defense* is his own *Analysis* first published with Simler's

Oratio of 1563 in Geneva. Its thirteenth proposition clearly asserts

the Christological nature of Holy Scripture.

> The word of the divine letters, whether heard or read, when it
> is received by our faith is the body of Christ and bread which
> nourishes our souls.[45]

Since Martyr himself wrote that the scriptural doctrines of

Christ's death, Holy Spirit, Calling, Faith and Justification were the

substance of salvation, one will find in his exposition of those scrip-

tures the body of Christ offered to those who have received the gift of faith. This paper has been written with Martyr's thesis in mind that though the sacraments are visible signs, the scriptures alone incarnated Christ, "substantialiter et realiter." This conviction has been confirmed by an analysis of Martyr's biblical writings. The sacraments are the visible expressions of Martyr's concern for the propagation of the gospel by preaching, teaching, hearing and obeying the Word of God in scripture. Martyr's view of scripture then at all points precedes his discussion of the Dominical sacraments. His primary concern is our major premise in this study of a *Reformer in Exile*: 1542-1562.

Robert Masson in 1576 printed topics from Martyr's biblical commentaries into a Latin *Loci Communes*. Expanded editions of this work by their format distort Martyr's own method of commenting on scripture. John Donnelly cautions that though Martyr employed scholastic method, he was also a humanist. Martyr's exegesis led him into Eucharistic controversy. Rather than duplicate what McLelland and now Corda have done on that aspect of Martyr's thought, this study is set forth as an introduction to Martyr's views on the death of Christ, Faith, Justification and Calling or Vocation. If a study of Luther's exegesis has led to a fresh understanding of the early Reformation, would not a probe into Martyr's exegesis help to sort out the chief concerns of international Calvinism in the mid-sixteenth century? In its own way this would seem important. Professor Rupp argues that Calvin himself is best understood by flanking him with Martyr and Musculus.

> 'If we would gloss Calvin at this point,' i.e., union of sanctification and justification, 'perhaps it should not be by flanking him with Karl Barth and T. Torrance, but with the vast Common

places of Wolfgang Musculus and Peter Martyr—compared with
which the Institutes is the third dinosaur, which survived.'[46]

This pursuit after the adventure of truth motivated Martyr's career in

exile, a journey undertaken so that he might become a child of God in

the midst of a crooked and perverse generation. Peter Martyr set forth

as clearly as any protestant theologian of the sixteenth century these

concerns for the salvation of God's elect. For anyone who wonders as

I have what that *furor theologicus* was all about, a reading of Peter

Martyr will be helpful.

SPIRITUAL CHURCH, NOT SACRAMENTAL

Soon after his arrival in England in November 1547, Peter Martyr

lectured on I *Corinthians* at Oxford. His dedication to King Edward VI

of this 1551 commentary explained that if soundly interpreted such

lectures would heal all the faults of the Church. During 1548 a crisis

arose when Martyr reached I *Corinthians* (10:16-17) and began to dispute

the Roman view of the Lord's Supper. It was before the Oxford Disputa-

tion of May 1549 that Martyr wrote to Jan Utenhove on 15 January 1549

as follows:

> There is nothing more difficult in the world than to found a
> Church. The stones are generally rough and very unpolished;
> hence, unless they are rendered plane and smooth by the Spirit,
> the Word, and examples of holy life, they cannot easily be made
> to fit each other.[47]

One who seeks to understand the career of Peter Martyr in exile (1542-

1562) ought not concentrate on Martyr's sacramental disputations and

miss his theology of communion with Christ. The context of Martyr's

biblical writings if taken as a whole explains what he wrote to

Utenhove. One such example of Martyr's concern for a pure church is

the following comment to Martin Bucer made the end of August in 1549:

> For the Papists do not care what, or how much we conceed to them
> in these Adiaphora: this is not their point: their chief object
> is this - that the whole of that religion, which we have received
> as delivered to us by Christ through the enlightening of the Holy
> Spirit, may be entirely obscured and radically extirpated.[48]

If his opponents in England would obscure Martyr's attempts at

reform by challenging his biblical theology, one must examine Martyr's

biblical writings to understand his importance as a sixteenth-century

reformer. The most recent account of his career in English[49] needs to

be expanded since there are several aspects of theology which Martyr

held to be crucial to a celebration of these external signs of the

sacraments.

The widely scattered nature of the Vermigli correspondence togeth-

er with the multiple editions of his printed works and the primary

sources reprinted only in part in the *Corpus Reformatorum* suggest the

need for a fresh chronology.[50] Use of these manuscript sources pro-

vided this author with a deep appreciation for Martyr's thought. Since

1957 new information in the form of unpublished letters has been re-

covered which fleshes out this historical setting. There is need for

an English language account of Martyr's protestant life which notes the

published and unpublished correspondence available.[51] The paucity of

letters in the various editions of the *Loci Communes* is disappointing.

The vital issue in this study will be Martyr's view of the

Church[52] as created by the Holy Spirit, nourished by the Holy Scriptures

and expressed by believers growing in conformity to Christ.[53] If for

Martyr the sacraments were indeed visible words of God, how one ought
to celebrate them and receive them needs careful study. Martyr himself raised this issue when he wrote to John Calvin in 1555:

> ...t o the elect, faith hath access at the time appointed, where-
> by they believe in Christ, and so they are not only forgiven their
> sins and are reconciled unto God, where in consisteth the true and
> sound respect of justification, but also there is added a renew-
> ing power of the spirit, whereby our bodies also, flesh, blood and
> nature, are made capable of immortality, and become daily more and
> more as I may say fashioned unto Christ....[54]

Because of that crisis reached during Martyr's lectures at Oxford,
a 1549 disputation was held on I *Corinthians* (11). The printed account
circulated in England and on the Continent. The tractate preceeds the
account of the disputation in the 1549 edition. Martyr concluded his
treatise by taking up the crucial issue of faith among participants at
the Eucharist. Martyr's response here gives in capsule form the
essence of his biblical writings. After citing Origen on *Matthew* (15)
that the quality of faith is profitable, Martyr then defined union with
Christ. This definition which concludes Martyr's 1549 tractate serves
as an introduction to a narrative of his life, analysis of his biblical
writings and description of his work as a scholar.

> There is yet another thyng that I would have them to beate into ƥ
> mindes of ȳ people: which is ȳ through the cõmunio we are incor-
> porated, (as ye would saye) embodied unto Christe whiche worde of
> enbodyeng, is no straunge nor no newe deuised worde in scripture.
> For in Paule to the Ephesians it is sayd, that the Gentiles ARE
> MADE FELOWE HEYRES AND CONCORPORALL WYTH Christe: and the greke
> woorde therof is σύσσωμα For although we putte that the under-
> standing and takyng of Christes bodye is dooen by feyth: yet not-
> wythstanding at thys conceiuing and takyng, there foloweth effec-
> tually a true coniunction (I saye) betwene us and Christe, (and
> not a feigned or ymaginatiue coniunction) whiche first perteyneth
> to the solle and then redoundeth unto the bodye.[55]

Martyr's intense feelings about this matter can be seen from *inculco* (to kick down-force) from *calx* (a heel), which has been vigorously translated by Nicholas Udall. Udall's translation contains many fresh turns of phrase.[56] When using Paul's image of the head and body in scripture Martyr reminded his audience that Cyril explained the image of wedlock by the example of molten wax joined to wax. When Paul said that Christians were of Christ's flesh and bones (*Ephesians*), he meant flesh cleansed from sin and prepared to receive resurrection and immortality. The faithful have this from Christ through the sacraments and faith.[57] Martyr then concluded with Paul's affirmation to the Galatians:

> Thus than there happeneth a certain slidynge and issuyng of Christe into us, and a certain spirytuall touchynge whyche Paule considered wel weighed, whan he sayd to the Galathians: I lyue, yet not I, but Chyste (sic) lyueth in me.[58]

It is clear that every Eucharistic debate of the sixteenth century involved exegetical decisions. Whether Zwingli at Marburg who noted the article before $\sigma\alpha\rho\xi$ in *John* 6, or Martyr who paused in the midst of biblical lectures to draw out the implications of his text, the plain method was novel. To follow the discussion in these commentaries is to see why exegesis provoked a fresh look at the Eucharist. To reverse Martyr's order which is what one does who views him only as a sacramental theologian is to miss his point made to Stephen Gardiner. Martyr's prior world view of faith in Christ would seem then to steer him away from running the ark of Salvation aground in the mud of scholastic Eucharistic theology.[59]

NOTES TO CHAPTER I

1. Complete documentation on Cortese is published in Sixteenth Century Essays and Studies I (1970), 75-106.

2. I am grateful to Roberto Abbondanza, Director of the Archivio di Stato, Perugia for access to a private ms. collection. See Ansidei Miscellanea, no. 25 for letter to Morone. Sigbaldo also wrote to the Duke of Ferrara. This is in the Archivio di Stato, Modena.

3. H.O. Evennett, "Three Benedictine Abbots at the Council of Trent, 1545-1547", S.M. I (1959), 343-377.

4. Elizabeth Gleason, Cardinal Gasparo Contarini (1483-1542) and the Beginning of Catholic Reform, p. 165.

5. John Tedeschi, "Florentine Documents for a History of the 'Index of Prohibited Books'", pp. 579-81 in Anthony Molho and John Tedeschi, Renaissance Studies In Honor of Hans Baron.

6. Cited in Norman Pettit, The Heart Prepared, p. 178.

7. Philip McNair, Peter Martyr In Italy, p. 179.

8. Text in B. J. Kidd, Documents Illustrative of the Continental Reformation, pp. 347-350.

9. W. Schenk, Reginald Pole Cardinal of England. Pole changed his mind, rejecting sola fide between September 1546 at Trent and his response to the Cardinal of Augsburg in 1554. D.B. Fenlon, Reginald Pole and the Evangelical Religion: Some problems of Italian Christian Humanism in the Early Counter-Reformation, (Unpublished thesis), p.271. See also Marvin Anderson, "Trent and Justification (1546): A Protestant Reflection," S.J.T. 21(1968), 401-402.

10. See Elizabeth Gleason, Cardinal Gasparo Contarini (1483-1542) and the Beginning of Catholic Reform, (unpublished thesis). See also James Bruce Ross, "The Emergence of Gasparo Contarini: A Bibliographical Essay," C.H. 41(1972), 22-45.

11. Philip McNair, Peter Martyr In Italy. An Anatomy of Apostasy, pp. 231-235.

12. Ibid., pp. 150-179.

13. George H. Williams, "The Two Social Strands In Italian Anabaptism, CA. 1526-CA. 1565," p. 183 in The Social History of the Reformation, edited by Lawrence P. Buck and Jonathan W. Zophy.

14. See Oddone Ortolani, Pietro Carnesecchi: Con estratti dagli Atti del Processo del Santo Officio.

15. Carlo Ginsburg, Il Nicodemismo: Simulazione e dissimulazione religiosa nell' Europa del '500 shows that Calvin's famous treatise of 1544 was directed against Otto Brunfels of Strasbourg. Martyr's comments of 1545 were published with those of Melanchthon, Bucer and Calvin in the 1549 De Vitandis Superstitionibus. An Italian version of 1553 exists in the Gucciardini collection, Firenze. For Italy one must now consult Antonio Rotondo, "Atteggiamenti Della Vita Morale Italiano Del Cinquecento La Pratica Nicodemitica," R.S.I. 79(1967), 991-1030. See C. R. XXXIV, cols. 627-628 for Martyr's treatise of 1545.

16. Ann Cole Jacobson Schutte, Pier Paolo Vergerio: The Making of An Italian Reformer, (unpublished thesis). See Roland Bainton, Bernardino Ochino, Esule E Riformatori Senese Cinquecento1487-1573.

17. Latin text by Taddeo Duno in all versions of the Loci Communes (London, 1576 - Frankfurt, 1656). There were several medical treatises of the period which discussed flight from pestilence, i.e. Gabriel Biel, De Pestis (1500). See also Luigi Santini, "La Tesi della fuga nella persecuzione nella teologia di P. M. Vermigli, B.S.S.V. 108(1960), 37-49.

18. Quintus Septimius Florens Tertullian, "De Fuga In Persecutione," Corpus Scriptorum Latinorum Paravianum (edited Iosephus Marra, 1957), pp. 69-72. Timothy David Barnes, Tertullian/A Historical and Literary Study, pp. 178-183.

19. George Cornelius Gorham, Gleanings of a Few Scattered Ears, During the Period of the Reformation in England and of the times immediately succeeding, A. D. 1533 to A. D. 1588, p. 26. In the Genesis Commentary (1569) Martyr saw the continuing command of God at Matthew (10:9, 16 and 28) and Luke 10:16). Flight therefore was God's will.

20. Genesis, (1569) fol. 130^v.

21. Delio Cantimori, "The Problem of Heresy: The History of the Reformation and of the Italian Heresies and the History of Religious Life in the First Half of the Sixteenth Century--the Relation Between Two Kinds of Research," The Late Italian Renaissance 1525-1630, edited by Eric Cochrane, p. 225.

22. McNair, op. cit., p. 197.

23. Klaus Sturm, Die Theologie Peter Martyr Vermiglis wahrend seines ersten Aufenthalts in Strassburg 1542-1547.

24. Marvin Anderson, "Peter Martyr, Reformed Theologian (1542-1562): His letters to Bullinger and Calvin," S. C. J. IV(1973), 41-64.

25. Thesis IV on Genesis, Proposita, p. 431.

26. Ibid., p. 471.

27. Romanes, (1568), p. 149^r.

28. Common Places (1583), Part three, p. 355.

29. See Marvin Anderson, "Peter Martyr on Romans," S. J. T. 26 (1973), 401-420.

30. Romanes (1568), p. 397^r.

31. Ethics (1563), pp. 7-8.

32. Richard Walzer, "Zur Traditionsgeschichte der Aristotelischen Poetik," Greek Into Arabic, p. 134.

33. C. T. B. VI(1565), p. 115.

34. L. C. III, p. 121. C. R. XLIII, 2089. 18 January 1555.

35. Cornelius Schulting, Bibliothecae Catholicae Et Orthodoxae, Contra Summam Totius Theologiae Calvinianae in Institutionibus Ioannis Calvini, Et Locis Communibus Petri Martyris, breuiter comprehensae (1602), vols. in two, I, sig A^1.

36. Franciscvs Stancarvs Mantvanvs De Trinitate & Mediatore Domino Nostro Iesu Christo, Aduersus Henricum Bullingerum, Petrum Martyre & Ioannem Caluninu, & Reliquos Tigurinae ac Genuensis Ecclesiae Ministros, Ecclesiae Dei Perturbatores (1562), sig. D.VI^r.

37. Alan Beesley, "An unpublished source of the Book of Common Prayer: Peter Martyr Vermigli's Adhortatio ad Coenam Domini Mysticam," J. E. H. XIX (1968), 83-88. The Adhortatio first appeared in the 1581 Basle edition of Martyr's works, not the 1583 London edition, contra Beesley, p. 188.

38. C. S. P. Span./1547-49, IX, p. 266.

39. John Patrick Donnelly, S. J., Peter Martyr on Fallen Man: A Protestant Scholastic View (unpublished thesis), p. 347.

40. Herbert Butterfield, Christianity and History, p. 146.

41. Luigi Santini, "'Scisma' e 'eresia' nel pensiero di P. M.

Vermigli," B. S. S. V. XC, 27-43.

42. McNair, op. cit., p. 288.

43. Gordon Rupp, Six Makers of English Religion 1500-1700, pp. 30-31.

44. W. P. M. Kennedy, Elizabethan Episcopal Administration III. Visitation Articles and Injunctions. 1583-1603, pp. 255-256. See Robert B. Ives, The Theology of Wolfgang Musculus (1497-1563). Unpublished thesis.

45. Analysis (1581), p. 151. Also in 1563 Latin life by Simler (Zurich) fols. 30^V-35.

46. Gordon Rupp, "Patterns of Salvation in the First Age of the Reformation," A. R. G. 57(1966), 63. See especially Paul Joachimsen, "Loci Communes/Eine Untersuchung zur Geistesgeschichte des Humanismus und der Reformation," L. J. VIII (1926), 27-97. Philip Melanchthon while at Tübingen received a copy of Agricola's Dialectics from Oecolampadius. This was formative for protestant theological method. See Robert Stupperich, Melanchthon (translated by Robert H. Fischer), p. 29.

47. Gorham, op. cit., p. 74.

48. Ibid., p. 98.

49. "Portrait of an Ecumenical Reformer" in Joseph C. McLelland, The Visible Words of God: An Exposition of the Sacramental Theology of Peter Martyr Vermigli A. D. 1500-1562, pp. 1-68.

50. See the partial account not used by McLelland in Benjamin F. Paist, Jr., "Peter Martyr and the Colloquy of Poissy," P. T. R. XX (1922), 212-31, 418-47, 616-46.

51. See C. Schmidt, Peter Martyr Vermigli, Leben und Ausgewahlte Schriften. Schmidt gives reference to the letters only by date and the rubric, MS. G. Huelin, Peter Martyr and the English Reformation (unpublished thesis), pp. 1-20 has an excellent short account. Since Schmidt does not give the Latin text, I have preferred to make a fresh account by examining the Latin text where relevant.

52. See Luigi Santini, "Appunti sulla ecclesiologia di P. M. Vermigli e la edificazione della Chiesa," B. S. S. V. CIV (1958), 69-75.

53. Marvin W. Anderson, "Word and Spirit in Exile (1542-61): The Biblical Writings of Peter Martyr Vermigli," J. E. H. XXI (1970), 193-201.

54.   8 March 1555 from Strasbourg.   Peter Martyr Vermigli, The Commonplaces (1583), Part five, pp. 96–97.   Text in C. R. XLIII, 2142.

55.   Tractatio (1549), fol. CVIII^r-v and Discourse (1550), p.66^v.

56.   G. A. Starr, "Antedatings from Nicolas Udall's translation of Peter Martyr's Discourse," new series N. Q., new series XIII (1966), 9–12.

57.   Discourse (1550), fol. CVIII^v-CIX^r. Tractatio (1549),

58.   Ibid., fol. CIX^r. Tractatio (1549), p. 67^r. "Fit itaque illapsus quidam Christi in nos, et contactus spiritualis, quem Paulus expendebat cum diceret ad Galatas, Viuo ego iā non ego, sed uiuit in me Christus."

59.   See unpublished letter of 26 August 1558 where Martyr answers Bullinger's letter of 8 August that peace is desired by all christians in the confession of faith and in doctrine.   Sacramental doctrine is crucial where questions about the transfer of flesh in Christ are not discussed in scripture (fol. 389^r).   Martyr then rehearsed his views on spiritual, total and real presence though he did not like at all the term substantialiter (fol. 389^r).   Z. S. A. E II 346a, fols.389^{r&v}+390^r.

CHAPTER II

LECTURER TO PROFESSOR (1542/49)

NAPLES AND LUCCA

Peter Martyr when in Naples was governor of the College of St. Peter.[1] Josiah Simler recalls that Martyr read Martin Bucer's commentaries on the Evangelists, his annotations on the *Psalms*, Zwingli's *On True and False Religion* and *On the Providence of God* as well as "some books of Erasmus."[2] Juan De Valdes settled in Naples during 1535. This most fruitful period of Valdes' literary and religious activity lasted six years from mid-1535 to July of 1541.[3] Pietro Carnesecchi and Pietro Martire Vermigli are the better known of those in contact with this Spanish reformer. To what extend Valdes influenced Vermigli in his Neapolitan study circle is a moot question so long as no writings of Vermigli survive from this period. Nieto argues that Carnesecchi did not read the works of Luther, Bucer and Calvin in Naples, but in Viterbo after Valdes' death. From this he seeks to prove that the works of the reformers were not read in the Valdesian group. This may be true of Carnesecchi who did not meet Valdes in Naples until 1540.[4] To use this to claim that Martyr was more influenced by Valdes than by Bucer, Zwingli or Melanchthon claims too much for Valdes.[5] Simler put it well when he said,

> And albeit that the first praise of this church is due unto Valdesius, yet notwithstanding is Martyr's virtue also to be remembered: who, after that he had given him by the Lord a greater light of God's truth, and had joined himself to the congregation of the godly, that doctrine which he knew to be true, he would straightway preach it also unto others.

CONRAD GESSNER,
Né à Zurich en 1516. Médecin et Naturaliste,
dit le Pline de l'Allemagne. Mort à
Zurich le 13. Dec. 1565.

Huelin points to the most striking difference in their lectures.
Martyr made much of his Patristic study, while Valdes scarcely touched
on these sources. From this Huelin argues that the influence of Valdes
on Vermigli has been greatly exaggerated.[6] It seems however that the
moral tone of Valdes' theology was absorbed by Martyr and communicated
during his career in exile. One example must suffice from Valdes'
Commentary On The Gospel of St. Matthew. On the warning in *Matthew*
(3:7-10) to the religious leaders of Israel that their coming to John's
baptism of repentance was from fear, Valdes commented:

> We who have repented bear testimony to our Christian faith by
> living mortified as to the flesh and Quickened as to the Spirit
> . . . . confidence in Christian regeneration is efficient in
> man to make him live in holiness and righteousness all the days
> of his life . . . .[7]

A recent study of Valdes argues that Nieto exaggerates his denial
of Erasmian influence on Valdes in order to emphasize the teachings of
Alcaraz.[8] Haggard concludes that neither Bataillon's emphasis on the
Doctrina nor Nieto's appeal to the later works of Valdes can preserve
the balance provided when one commences a study of Valdes via his
Alfabeto christiano.[9] Nieto does make a telling point when he isolates
Law and Gospel as twin approaches in Valdesian theology to the questions
of knowledge and experience. Valdes seems to have developed this as
early as 1529.[10]

One ought then to pose a question about Martyr's use of Law/Gospel
in the lectures of 1543/45 at Strasbourg. Martyr would have known
these terms as early as Valdes' discussion in Naples. Did Martyr use
them with the same content which Haggard describes as the analytic

foundation of the Erasmian Neoplatonic dualism of flesh and spirit?[11]
Martyr's epistemological pattern seems different in the following ways.
First of all Martyr has examined Patristic literature and been impressed by Orthodox spirituality. More to the point however, while at
Strasbourg Martyr used the Law/Gospel motif to explicate the relationship of the Old to the New Testament, not to relate knowledge to experience.[12] In the *Romans* commentary Martyr defined Law/Gospel also in
the Melancthonian scheme of trust in the Divine promises. One will see
too the possible influence of Brenz as well as the companionship of
Bucer during the first Strasbourg sojurn. Thus Martyr has gone beyond
the Erasmian Neoplatonic Christ mysticism of Valdes perhaps as early
as his stay in Naples. I think his reading of Bucer and Zwingli sets
him apart from Valdes in many ways. Perhaps Simler meant that Martyr
was distinct from Valdes when he said that Martyr "had given him by the
Lord a greater light of God's truth" - greater, that is, than Valdes,
Bucer or Zwingli.

In Naples Vermigli lectured on I *Corinthians* to an influential
following. In the third chapter Martyr did not find (verse fifteen)
that the fire which burns any man's work was thought to be purgatory
by the Patristic Fathers. When for these kinds of thoughts Vermigli
was forbidden to continue reading his lectures, he appealed to friends
in Rome.

> Howbeit Martyr would not obey this prohibition, as being unequall
> and unjust: and having affiaunce in the goodness of his cause
> appealed at Rome unto the Pope. At that time he had in the city
> mighty and favorable friends: namely Hercules Gonzaga Cardinal
> of Mantua, Gaspar Contarenus, Reginald Pole, Peter Bembo and

Frederick Fregoso, all learned men and in favour with the Pope, and who then seemed to be desirous of some reformation of the church.

The prohibition was lifted and the lectures continued.

When Vermigli after ill health in Naples took up the post as prior of S. Frediano at Lucca in 1541, the climate in Rome had changed.[13] Camillo Renato visited Modena in 1540 where he was welcomed by the Academy. The Modenese chronicler described his arrest on 17 October 1540. The trial of Renato at Ferrara from late 1540 to 1542 indicated the nature of radical reform being preached in various circles.[14] In Lucca the Senate was concerned over the impending inquisitorial storm. In their letter of 21 April 1542 to the Lateran Congregation the Senators expressed fear that Martyr might be removed.[15] All the more critical then were the summer months of June, July and August of 1542.[16] Martyr fled in good conscience as he described in an undated letter, "On the Flying Away in Time of Persecution."[17] The previous year he met Contarini in Lucca.

Peter Martyr addressed a letter to the Church at Lucca explaining his reasons for flight into exile as an attempt to do God's will.[18]

> Wherefore, since I am delivered from so great a danger, being not ignorant of these kinds of troubles, since I was certified from Rome, from the society, from the monastery, and from your city, of the persecution even at hand, since I did harm unto none, but by lectures and sermons did manifest the truth, all dignities, riches, and commodities set aside, being rid out of the bonds of superstitions, and delivered from so many hypocrasies: if I delivered my life from imminent oppression, there is no cause why any man should take occasion of offence. And doth not the Lord grant that we should avoid persecutions?[19]

Martyr traveled to Pisa where he wrote a "letter of departure" to

Cardinal Pole which has not survived. It seems that Ochino who also
fled in 1542 had been informed by Contarini that Carafa intended to
persecute him for his heretical preaching. A recent study of unedited
documents support Ochino's reasons for departure and sheds light on
Martyr's path to exile.[20] McNair places the time when Martyr left
Florence as 25 August 1542.[21] A letter of the Lateran canon Gregorio
da Milano to Cardinal Farnese from Reggio on 24 August describes
Martyr and Paolo Lacizi da Verona, his Vicar at Lucca, as "Lutherani".[22]

This letter recently uncovered is important to understand why
Martyr left Lucca on 12 August and Florence on 25 August. That Martyr
stayed in the Lateran Congregation at Reggio suggests some collabora-
tion in his flight from Italy. The use of the term "Lutherani" in the
letter to Cardinal Farnese is interesting since Fragnito's thesis that
Ochino had help in his flight adds to the reasons for Martyr's journey
to Florence in August 1542.

Martyr not only was considered a heretic but it also seems that
his order collaborated in his flight from Italy and one member at Reggio
communicated that information to Cardinal Farnese. After preaching in
Ferrara and visiting Verona Martyr came to Zurich.[23] Since there was
no place for him in the Church or School at Zurich, Martyr continued on
to Basle for a month's stay. There Martin Bucer called him to Strasbourg.

STRASBOURG LECTURER(1542/47)

Martyr contacted Bullinger on 5 October 1542 while he was still at
Basle. Martyr could find no secure position in Basle, felt the

ambiguity of his presence among the Baselers and requested prayer from Bullinger that Bucer at Strasbourg would provide for his needs.[24] By 19 December 1542 Martyr could inform Bullinger about the liberality of the Strasbourgeoise. Bonifacius Amerbach in particular gave Martyr books and money.[25] Amerbach (1495-1562) was named Erasmus' principal heir in 1536. His evangelical confession of faith seems to have been submitted in 1534 to the Basle council. Amberbach's encyclopedic knowledge was well known. His patronage of Martyr during Martyr's initial contact with the scholarly reformation in Northern Europe is a harbinger of Martyr's future as a protestant theologian of stature and esteem in Strasbourg, England, Zurich and Geneva.[26]

Bullinger wrote about Martyr to Vadian on the same day. On 14 January 1543 Martyr informed Bullinger of Amerbach's aid,[27] while both Philip Melanchthon and John Calvin learned about the remarkable Florentine who had joined Martin Bucer at Strasbourg. Bucer wrote to Calvin on 28 October 1542 that an Italian learned in Greek, Hebrew and Latin had come from Italy, "et in scripturis feliciter versatus, annos natus quadraginta quatuor, gravis moribus et iudicio acri, Petro Martyri nomen est."[28] Melanchthon answered Martyr on 14 July 1543. He had read a letter from Martyr to Bucer. Melanchthon was impressed by what he read: Martyr had a lucid manner of expression, a critical mind and singular erudition. This was no small praise from the "Teacher of Germany."[29]

Martyr's comments on Nicodemism while in Strasbourg were included with those of John Calvin, Philip Melanchthon and Martin Bucer in a

treatise published in 1549 under the title *De Vitandis Superstitionibus*[30]
Calvin's two replies to the French Nicodemites were written in 1543 and
1544. Martyr's opinion might also have been added in 1549 because of
the case of Francesco Spiera, an Italian Lutheran whose abjuration and
recantation in 1548 troubled the Italian Reformers.[31]

Martyr's counsel on Nicodemism is undated. Since it cites Melanchthon and Bucer dated May 1545, surely it is a reply to their 1545 responses of April and May. Martyr may even have talked to Bucer about
the synod which forced Brunfels' retirement from Strasbourg in 1533.[32]
One remembers that Martyr wrote in 1543 to the Lucca congregation about
flight in time of persecution. Now two years later he did not hesitate
to condemn those secret believers who hung on to the external signs of
baptism and Eucharist but did not make public their own confessions of
faith. Calvin broached the issue as early as 1537 in his letter on
flight. Martyr might have seen a copy on arrival in Strasbourg. The
relation between his own public identity with protestantism and Calvin's
condemnation of those who kept silent would not have escaped Martyr's
attention.

Since Martyr was in process of flight from his native land, his
conclusion in this treatise may well mean that the holy covenant of a
life in exile (Babylonian Captivity) must be nourished by the preached
word of God rather than the practice of religious ceremonies. One
notices Martyr's use of the present tense to describe captivity.

> Finally, so long as our brothers are scattered in the Babylonian
> Captivity they see that they may have among them, if they are able,
> a holy covenant. On the other hand the Apostles in Jerusalem

after Christ was slain were different. They practiced Jewish
ceremonies in the temple, yet though they had the Lord's Body
among one another, they were without sermons or indeed the word
of God at the same time.[33]

Martyr while writing this judgment of dependence on external forms was

himself giving lectures on the Old Testament. One can conclude that

Martyr had begun his attack on ceremonial rites in biblical lectures

by 1545. On the other hand in 1549 Laelius Socinus noted in letters

to Calvin a note of caution in Martyr's response that one ought not to

eschew papal baptism.

During those five years at Strasbourg Martyr lectured on the Old

Testament books of *Jeremiah*, the *Twelve Minor Prophets*, *Genesis*, *Exodus*

and much of *Leviticus*. Martyr now could escape poverty since Bucer

obtained a stipend for him from the Senate.[34] Martyr arrived in Stras-

bourg on 16 November 1542 where he lived in Bucer's house for seventeen

days. He later described the reformer's household as a place where one

might experience a growing conformity to Christ. Martyr noted that be-

fore and after meat something was read out of the Holy Scriptures,

"which might minister matter for godly and holy communications."[35]

Martyr went on to comment on the office of a bishop as he observed it

in the life of Martin Bucer.

Behold, well-beloved brethren, in our age bishops upon earth, or
rather, in the Church of Christ, which be truly holy. This is
the office of a pastor, - this is that bishop - like dignity
described by Paul in the Epistles unto Timothy and Titus. It
delighteth me much to read this kind of description in those
Epistles, but it pleaseth me a great deal more to see with the
eyes the patterns themselves. Perhaps those of yours which only
have the bare name of bishops will object that the dignity and
bishop - like majesty cannot by this means be preserved. If a
bishop should preach and teach everyday; if he must every day

teach and visit the schools; if care should be taken of the
needy strangers and wayfarers; if poverty should be suffered
with an indifferent mind, without the greatness of revenues –
where shall be the dignity, where shall be the glory, where shall
be the majesty of a bishop? We answer, that honour, riches, and
glory are in no estimation among the pastors of souls and
apostolical bishops: – contrariwise we grant that, unto bishops
which be not of the Church but of the world; unto parents not of
souls but of children; unto pastors not of men but of dogs,
horses, and hawks; these (temporal) things are most of all regarded, these are among the delights, unto these must be bended
all their strength.[36]

Martyr taught differently than did Bucer. Simler wrote that by
all men's judgments Martyr excelled Bucer in the use of an exact method
or a pure and plain style.[37] "And moreover even in the Lectures themselves he with a singular gravity sometime exhorted to godly life."[38]
Bucer urged Martyr in speaking of the Lord's Supper to use a "certain
obscure and doubtful kind of speaking," which Martyr would reject as no
means to foster peace in the Church. To speak the truth in love and
with clarity was his goal in lecturing and preaching.[39] A short note
from Frectus to Ambrosius Blauer describes Martyr's lectures in Strasbourg as very profitable. Calvin seems to have expected Martyr's
lectures on the *Minor Prophets* to supplement his commentaries on St.
Paul's letters. These works on the *Minor Prophets* were never published.[40] On 7 July 1545 Martyr sensed in his letter to Bullinger that
future conflict over religion at Strasbourg could not be avoided. He
deplored such controversies.[41]

Bucer was not alone in his impact on Martyr. John Sturm had reorganized education in Strasbourg by his famous memorandum to the magistrates of 24 February 1538. This plan would regroup the advanced

Latin schools in a single college with a progressive course of nine
classes. As rector from June of 1538 Sturm received considerable help
from the arrival in 1542 of Sleidan and Peter Martyr. In 1545 the
enrollment was 644. Pedagogy was at the center of Sturm's direction.
In spite of the political pressures which forced Strasbourg to adopt
a theological compromise – keep the *Confessio Tetrapolitana* and subscribe to the *Augustana* – it was not until Marbach from 1553 put pressure on Sturm as a 'crypto-calvinist' that the gymnasium was negatively
affected. In 1563 Sturm signed a new formula and in 1581 Marbach
finally forced Sturm to leave.[42]

Strasbourg pedagogy as perfected by Sturm sheds some light on
Martyr's happy letters to John Sturm and Conrad Hubert. Sturm sought
for impregnation, continuity and progression. Memorize, repeat, analyze, recompose and imitate meant that over three years or so an incredible amount of information could be communicated.[43] That Roger
Ascham visited Strasbourg is of real interest since *The Scholemaster*
of 1570 was written after Ascham visited Strasbourg,[44] corresponded
with Sturm whom he never met and offered to aid Sturm in writing a life
of Bucer.[45] At Strasbourg Martyr not only found theological friends
but educational views compatible with his own humanistic concerns.

Though the lectures on the Minor Prophets (*Amos, Joel,* etc.) have
not survived, one could reconstruct how Martyr lectured in Strasbourg
during 1545. In the St. Thomas collegiate church in the Dominican
convent Martyr as Simler put it "sometime exhorted to godly life, sometime by a sharp rebuking he stirred up to repentance." The letter to

Neuchatel of 1544 which Martyr helped to draft indicates such direct

concern for repentance. Sturm's letter to Marbach in which he defined

the limits of a reformed zeal in teaching would perhaps explain Simler's

comment that in method Martyr was clearer than Bucer.

> Maintain in our schools of Theology Moses, the prophets, the
> evangelists, the apostles, and, in order to explain them, the
> authority of the fathers, before whom all those who are hostile
> to our doctrine must of necessity bow. But it is neither nec-
> essary nor useful to read the fathers in class as long as there
> remains some text to read of the four types which I have mention-
> ed, and there will always be some. Experience itself has taught
> our era what evils insinuated themselves into the academies and
> churches during past centuries, after collectors of sentences
> and writers of epitomes had chased better writers from their
> places. These were the inventions of an ignorant laziness, an
> ingenious advocate of its own cowardliness. Our era has better
> commentaries and better methods of teaching which need neither
> intermediary nor glossator, and the church finds in them a sure
> protection against corruption of doctrine and against idolatry.
> Therefore let us fight for religion and for letters and wish
> that only the authors cited above may have their place in the
> school.[46]

Sturm's letter explains why Martyr in 1543 lectured on Moses and the

prophets, for Bucer lectured on the evangelists and the apostles.

Mesnard then describes the unique method which Sturm introduced

in the College of St. Thomas. Lecturers were to explicate the holy

books in a good Latin edition. Then

> they assign to groups composed of two or three students each the
> study of a prophet, of a psalm, or of a gospel; for the more ad-
> vanced students, that they distribute to them in the same way a
> chapter of doctrine, a controversy, the commentary of a father
> or of a Protestant theologian. These preparations will be natu-
> rally followed by analyses and discussions.[47]

Martyr was impressed by the piety of Bucer, but in the lectures at

Strasbourg he followed the pedagogy of John Sturm.

By 1545 the civic authorities at Lucca proscribed Martyr's
opinions and those of others who held to "the new religious opinions."[48]
This document may help to date a tractate which is prohibited under the
rubric, "et libri dicti Petri Martiris et Bernardi Ochini de Sensis,
post eorum lapsum ab unitate Sancte Matris Ecclesie."[49] The document
does not specify the 1544 *Una Semplice Dichiaratione* on the Apostle's
Creed. Since Martyr's letter to Lucca of 8 January 1543 does not
charge the Roman Church with heresy, it is possible that the Lucca
civic law means the 1544 book, the only one of Martyr's works in print
at that date. A less likely possibility would be an early edition of
the treatise published in the Latin Commentary on the Book of *Kings* in
1566 attacking a corrupt ecclesiastical hierarchy under papal authority.[50]
That Martyr was aware of affairs in Lucca and wrote other tracts on his
flight from Catholicism can be seen from his treatise on the study of
divinity written in 1553 and included in the various editions of the
Loci Communes.[51]

Martyr described his first stay in Strasbourg in a letter of 6
September 1550 to Bucer. None in the College of St. Thomas cared much
about Martyr except Bucer. Martyr spent a good bit from his income to
repair and improve his quarters. Even that was misunderstood. Martyr
trusted that, "as they have dealt with me, so will God deal with them."[52]
One detects in this 1550 Oxford letter about matters in Strasbourg that
Martyr faced opposition within the College of St. Thomas. On 8 December
1549 Martyr lamented Paul Fagius' death in Cambridge.[53] This fine
Hebrew scholar came with Bucer from Strasbourg earlier that year.

Martyr seemed discouraged at his opponents but endorsed Bucer's friendship with enthusiasm in his Oxford letter.

> . . . you have a firmer mind. You have a familiar acquaintance
> with the Divine Scriptures; a consciousness of having well ad-
> ministered the affairs of the Kingdom /Respublica/ of Christ; and,
> above all, the invincible shield of faith, by which you possess a
> full confidence (πλφροφορία) and entire persuasion, that none of
> the calamities of this world can tear us away from that immense
> love of God, which He has freely and most abundantly bestowed on
> us through Jesus Christ our Lord.[54]

Martyr married Catherine Dampmartin in 1545. She died childless
in England after eight years of marriage, loved by the people of Oxford.
Cardinal Pole had her body exhumed and cast on a dung heap because of
its proximity to the bones of St. Frideswyde in Oxford. Later after
1558 an ecclesiastical commission had Catherine reinterred in a grave
with the relics of St. Frideswyde. Simler calls her one who "feared
GOD; loved her husband, wise and industrious in governing of her domes-
ticall affairs, bountiful towardes the poor, who not only aided them
with her substance, but also with all the counsel and help she could".[55]

In 1546 the Zurich and Strasbourg churches disagreed so severely
that in 1547 Zurich refused communion with Strasbourg. Martyr joined
Bucer and Hedio in drafting a letter to the Zurich pastors sent on 6
December 1546. The crucial issue was the Eucharist. Characteristic of
Martyr's teaching was the statement to the Zurich pastors that the Word
of God was to be simply communicated with faith in order to avoid con-
troveresy or scrupulous inquiry into how Christ was communicated under
bread and wine.[56]

Martyr joined in a letter to the Church at Neuchatel about the

discipline of ministers in its city. The Strasbourg ministers recalled
that Paul sent Timothy and Titus to Corinth to correct corrupt church
leaders.[57] By this time Martyr shared in such corporate decisions with
Hedio, Bucer, Niger, Fagius, Poullain and others. Martyr also faced
disciplinary problems in the city and school of Strasbourg. Francis
Dryander reported that in 1547 a certain Belgian had the city in an
uproar. Again Martyr is mentioned together with Bucer as prominent in
Strasbourg civic affairs.

> There is in this town a certain Belgian gentleman named Valerando
> (Polano), a turbulent and fraudulent man who for his own iniquitous
> and unworthy sake upset the entire state. This is well known to
> all the most eminent citizens of his own town and of Strasbourg,
> Bucer, Peter Martyr, Myconius and our magistrate.[58]

After Henry VIII died on 31 January 1547 events transpired to bring
Martyr to England. In that year the Senate of Strasbourg gave Martyr
leave to accept Archbishop Thomas Cranmer's invitation to come to England. Later the Augsburg Interim put pressure on Strasbourg so that it
was expedient for Bucer to accept a similar invitation in 1549.[59]
Martyr sought to accomplish at Strasbourg that which Philip Melanchthon
addressed to him in a letter of 14 July 1543. Martyr was to pray for
the German church and that universal church which exists by the will
and work of God.[60]

Now in England under Edward VI and Cranmer Peter Martyr could
begin to reform the legal and liturgical expressions of the Church
while avoiding political rebellion.[61]

OXFORD PROFESSOR (1548/49)

In his final speech to Parliament on 24 December 1545 Henry VIII gave his last will on political matters.[62] That the monarch was deeply

concerned about religion in the realm appears in his own words.

> I see and hear daily that you of the clergy preach one against
> another, teach one contrary to another, inveigh one against
> another without charity or discretion. Some be too stiff in their
> old Mumpsimus, other be too busy and curious in their new Sump-
> simus. Thus all men almost be in variety and discord, and few or
> none preach truly and sincerely the word of God according as they
> ought to do. Alas how can the poor souls live in concord when you
> preachers sow amongst them in your sermons, debate and discord: of
> you they look for light, and you bring them darkness.[63]

One means Henry chose to ensure concord was the education of his young

heir, the future Edward VI. In the *Chronicle* and political papers of

the boy King, "almost nothing of personal warmth, of boyish affection,

of youthful preoccupation"[64] appears. The lad's tutors had done their

work well, though W. K. Jordan's memorable phrase about them is a bit

harsh: "The tutors selected with such a shrewd care by Henry VIII had

made a king: they had also destroyed a boy."[65] King Edward VI was

firmly protestant, deeply religious and alert to the duties expected of

him in Church and State. Though the *Chronicle* shows little religious

warmth, Edward VI cherished the *Beneficio di Cristo* and similar theo-

logical documents.[66] It is small wonder that under Archbishop Cranmer

and King Edward VI foreign refugees spread continental protestantism in

their desire to fulfil the mission implied in Cranmer's invitation to

the island realm. As we have seen from Martyr's letter to Jan Utenhove

of 1549, there were foreign churches in London.[67] Martin Micronius re-

ported to Bullinger that after some delay, on 5 October 1550 four elders

were appointed in the Stranger's Church and on 12 October four deacons.

The multitude of believers (praised be God!) is increasing every

day. Should we be permitted, by God's blessing to go on in this
way for some years, we shall attack our Flanders with fiery darts
and, I hope, take it by storm, that antichrist being put to
flight, or at least weakened our Saviour may reign there.[68]

In 1550 King Edward VI granted formal letters patent to establish

Jan Laski, noted Polish reformer, as superintendent of the London

Stranger's Church. On 24 July a unique document set apart in London a

church to be called the "Temple of the Lord Jesus." The formal reason

was compassion for exiles. King Edward VI in his diary singled out

another motive - to guard against heresy. The entry for 29 June reads

that the Germans were given the Church of Austin Friars, "for avoiding

all sects of Anabaptists and the like."[69] Firpo has described the

Italian congregation under Michael Angelo Florio. Martyr would have

had some contact with his countrymen in London, for Florio like Martyr

was a native Florentine.[70]

Martyr preached at Oxford in Italian and may have done so in Lon-

don. At any event the liturgical form used by the Italian congregation

was published by Vergerio about 1550. Since Firpo omits this document

it will be of interest to cite from it. Also, this document in the

Westdeutsche Bibliothek, Marburg has been assigned to Peter Martyr.

John Tedeschi concurs that it is edited by Vergerio. *La forma delle*

publice orationi . . . . la qual si usa nella chiesa de forestieri . .

. . instituta in Londra is prefaced by an undated letter from Vergerio

to the Italian church in the Grison. It contains "the sum of the best

Christian doctrine which was preached in that felicitous reign..."[71]

The opening petition asks that the perfect Heavenly Father might

convert the mind, restore wisdom and illumine the eyes through the
prayer of supplication.[72] Vergerio in 1550 also composed a work on
Pope Paul III for Edward VI under the title, *Al Serenissimo re d'
Inghilterra Edoardo Sesto, de portamenti di Papa giulio III.*

Though there is no way to assign the document or parts of it to
Peter Martyr as the modern Marburg librarians have done, the Italian
phrases are similar in tone and content to Martyr's *Preces* on the
Psalms. One illustration from this liturgy would be the lovely prayer
after the Creed entitled *Oratione per tutte le neccessita della chiesa.*
Vergerio may even be following Laski's *Forma ac Ratio* not printed until
1555.

> Allpowerful, heavenly and merciful Father, according to your
> infinite goodness by which Thou hast freed us from the darkness of
> ignorance and Roman idolatry . . . may Thou also fortify us by the
> grace of Thy Spirit and restore this constant Christian faith . . .
> with piety and innocence of the life which Thou hast made according
> to Thy glory.[73]

These religious sentiments were tolerated by Royal patent on 24 July
1550. They form part of the setting for Martyr's sojurn in England.
The term *chiesa de forestieri* is of interest since *forestieri* would be
a literal translation of St. Paul's phrase in *Ephesians* (2:19). In
Edwardine England Martyr and his countrymen felt themselves "no more
strangers and sojurners, but . . . fellow-citizens with the saints and
the household of God." Diodoti in seventeenth century Geneva translated
this as "Voi dunque non siete piu forestieri, ne auueniticci: ma con-
cittadini de' santi, e domestici di Dio."

Archbishop Cranmer by 1547 had begun to promote liturgical reform in the Church of England. In 1544 Cranmer addressed a processional in English to Henry VIII. This Litany of 1544 did not lead to an immediate revision of worship, but indicated Cranmer's purpose, that "I trust it will much excitate and stir the hearts of all men unto devotion and godliness: . . ."[74] The 1549 *Prayer Book* reflects the influence of Lutheran liturgies.[75] Cranmer's Eucharistic Canon in English is a substitute for the Roman Canon of the Mass with its emphasis upon an oblation or material sacrifice.[76] By 1552 Peter Martyr's influence appeared in the second Exhortation to the revised *Prayer Book.*[77] So did Martyr's work become a permanent part of Cranmer's reform. For these views on the sacrament Martyr found his stay at Oxford difficult.

FOREIGN DIVINES

Hugh Latimer in a sermon before Edward VI said, "I wish that we could collect together such valuable persons in this kingdom; it would be the means of ensuring its prosperity."[78] In two letters to Dryander, Martyr indicated something of his scholarly activity and anticipated residence in England. On 22 August 1547 Martyr endorsed the letters of Theodosius, indicating that while still in Italy he had copied them from a manuscript in Siena.[79] Martyr was upset by the state of affairs in Italy, but would find consolation "ex sacris litteris desumpti."[80] In October 1547 Martyr reported to Dryander that the negotiations for a royal invitation to England were progressing marvelously. He hoped to go in November with Dryander's prayers accompanying him.[81]

Peter Martyr traveled to England in November of 1547 where he was welcomed at Lambeth Palace by Cranmer. Martyr stayed on at Lambeth

through the winter of 1547 until he took up residence at Christ Church,
Oxford with a stipend of forty marks.[82] Strype comments that Martyr
was "a Papist, or a Lutheran, as to the belief of the presence" until
talking at length with Cranmer and listening to the patristic sources
he had collected.[83] McLelland, however, points to the extensive patristic study undertaken by Bucer and Martyr in Strasbourg before 1547.
Cranmer borrowed from Theodoret in the "Defence" of 1550 and learned
much from Martyr's patristic study by using a transcript from a Chrysostom manuscript copied by Martyr in Florence. Then too, Martyr's 1544
Commentary on theApostles' Creed shows Strype's comment on his Papist
or Lutheran views to be inaccurate.[84]

This *Epistola ad Caesarium Monachum* Martyr discovered among the
manuscripts in the Dominican monastery of San Marco in Florence. Cranmer made use of it in his own *Defence of the True and Catholike Doctrine
of the Sacrament.*

> And yet more plainly St. Chysostom declareth this matter in another
> place, saying: 'The bread before it be sanctified is called bread,
> but when it is sanctified by the means of the priest, it is deliv-
> ered from the name of bread, and is exhalted to the name of the
> Lord's body, although the nature of bread doth still remain.'

Gardiner responded, "The second saying of Chrysostom, which I never
read but in Peter Martyr's book, who saith it is not printed, toucheth
this author's doctrine much..."[84a]

The Theodoret used by Martyr in the 1549 Oxford Debate and questioned by Tresham can now be identified. McLelland observes that Martyr
cited the *Eranistes Seu Polymorphus*. Martyr's copy of this 1548 work
was printed in Venice by J. Farreus and is in the Genevan University

Library. Cranmer used it in his *Defence* of 1550. McNair thinks Martyr

brought this with him from Italy. In fact Martyr's copy used in the

Oxford Disputation was published in 1548 at Venice.

Ochino and Martyr arrived in 1547, Laski in 1548 and Bucer in

1549. Among others, these "learned strangers" as Dixon calls them were

part of Cranmer's strategy for a religious renewal of England. W. K.

Jordan has well described Cranmer's triple purpose in inviting at one

time or another almost all the leaders of Continental Protestantism.

> In part, as we shall see, Cranmer's purpose was irenic, for he
> bore steadily in mind the spiritual goal of associated Protestant
> churches, of which the English would be but one, united in the
> profession of a common faith and worship. He was likewise moved
> in his extraordinary policy of seeking the fellowship and help of
> Protestant leaders from the Continent, men of diverse persuasions,
> by the fact that England lacked a preaching clergy; that much had
> to be done, and that quickly, to raise the intellectual level of
> those who professed Protestantism; and that these eminent divines
> to whom he was steadily addressing attractive invitations would
> greatly assist him in this intention. And, finally Cranmer re-
> acted quickly and generously to political developments on the Con-
> tinent which were for a season gravely to threaten Protestantism
> in Germany and the imperial dominions generally.[85]

Martyr's reputation as a preacher was as well known as his irenic char-

acter. Those traits would be tested to the breaking point during Mar-

tyr's six years in England when Cranmer's attempt to implement his goal

of a learned preaching clergy in England met stiff resistance from

Bishops such as Stephen Gardiner and Edmund Bonner.

Despite the hyperbole, Hugh Latimer's sermons to Edward VI in

1549 indicate his feelings and undoubtedly those of Cranmer that the

task of reform would be arduous.[86] Certainly Martyr's reception at

Oxford lends credence to Latimer's sermonic warnings. At times Martyr was in good spirits while at Oxford.[87] Martyr's predecessor as Regius

Professor of Divinity at Oxford was Dr. Richard Smith. On 15 May 1547

Smith repudiated publicly at St. Paul's Cross the authority of the

Roman Bishop. Smith was the first holder of this post at Oxford and in

1537 was made Master of Whittington College. McConica describes the

other Regius Professors who were John Harpsfield and George Etherege.

John Harpsfield was the brother of Nicholas Harpsfield, biographer of

Thomas More. Etherege succeeded Harpsfield when the Kings College was

refounded in 1546 as Christ Church. He would then have been Martyr's

collegue until 1550.

Humanism was present at Corpus Christi College in John Morwen,

Reader in Greek. One of Morwen's pupils was John Jewel, later Martyr's

secretary, protege and author of the *Apology* as Bishop of Salisbury

under Queen Elizabeth. Etherege at Christ Church and Morwen at Corpus

Christi were eminent Greek scholars. Martyr joined a coterie of

learned if somewhat conservative catholic apologists when Cranmer ap-

pointed him early in 1548 as Regius Professor of Divinity with residence

at Christ Church College.[88]

In a letter to Bucer of 6 September 1550 Martyr commented on his

crafty colleagues. At the Convocation Martyr was to present several

candidates for promotion to the B.D. degree and to preside at the the-

ological disputation. The question was kept a secret from Martyr so

that he must speak extempore before a great crowd. Perhaps they might

outflank his views. In spite of such "incredible craftiness," Martyr

concluded, "I rely upon God who has neverfailed to give a mouth, a tongue, and wisdom to His people. . . ."[89]

Jewel entered Merton College, Oxford in 1535. In 1539 Jewel accepted a scholarship to Corpus Christi where he proceeded to B.A. in 1540. In 1548 Jewel was elected to the post of Reader in Humanity and Rhetoric attached to Corpus but open to all university students. Of the only two addresses to survive, the *Oratio Contra Rhetoricam* depicts Jewel as an Erasmian humanist. Martyr's coming to Oxford in 1548 made a difference for Jewel, who served as Martyr's assistant and notary at the 1549 Oxford Disputation on the Eucharist. In December 1551 Jewel obtained a license to preach at the rectory of Sunningwell just south of Oxford. In December of 1552 Jewel delivered the commemorative address on Richard Foxe, founder of Corpus Christi College. Martyr and Jewel many times accompanied the shadowy figure Richard Chambers, a layman who seems to have financed the Marian exiles for the Earls of Bedford. On Chamber's rounds to seek out worthy scholars, he often had a cleric like Martyr rule on the worth of candidates. The *Articuli verae Religionis* used in these activities asked young men to deny papal power, reject transubstantiation and affirm justification by faith. One wonders whether Martyr's hand was in the composing of these articles used in 1559 by Jewel against Harding after Jewel had been with Martyr at Strasbourg and Zurich.[90]

In his *Reioindre* (1566) to Jewel, Harding described what life was like in Martyr's house at Oxford. One detects a jealous note in the account which follows:

. . .what wayes and meanes did not Peter Martyr practise with me

after my returne from biyonde the sea, to preswade me thorowly?
To how many private Sermons was I called, which in his house he
made in the Italian tongue to Madame Catherine the Nonne of Letz
in Lorvaine his pretended wife, to Sylvester the Italian, to
Frauncis the Spaniard, to Iulio his man and to me? For al this
I remained as before: and you know M. Jewel no man better, how
far I was from his inward familiaritie whereunto you were admitted, and what strangenesse there continued alwaies betwen him and
me. . . [91]

In his letter to Bucer of 26 December 1548 Martyr mentioned the

growing storm over Eucharistic reform.

The other matter which distresses me not a little is this, that
there is so much contention among our people about the eucharist,
that every corner is full of it. And even in the supreme council
of the state, in which matters relating to religion are daily
brought forward, there is so much disputing of the bishops among
themselves and with others, as I think was never heard before.
Whence those who are in the lower house, as it is called, that is,
men of inferior rank, go up every day into the higher court of
parliament, not indeed for the purpose of voting, (for that they
do in the lower house,) but only that they may be able to hear
these sharp and fervent disputations. Hitherto the popish party
has been defeated, and the palm rests with our friends, but especially with the archbishop of Canterbury, whom they till now were
wont to traduce as a man ignorant of theology, and as being only
conversant with matters of government; but now, believe me, he
has shown himself so mighty a theologian against them as they
would rather not have proof of, and they are compelled, against
their inclination, to acknowledge his learning, and power and
dexterity in debate. Transubstantiation, I think, is now exploded,
and the difficulty respecting the presence is at this time the
most prominent point of dispute: but the parties engage with so
much vehemence and energy as to occasion very great doubt as to
the result; for the victory has hitherto been fluctuating between
them. May the Holy Spirit grant that nothing may be determined
upon but what may be for the advantage and welfare of the church!
With respect to a change of religion, they can no longer retrace
their steps; for such great innovations have every where taken
place, and all things are so changed and removed from their former
state, that if they were long suffered to remain so, wonderful
disorder would ensue. Wherefore I have no doubt but that something must be decided upon; and I hope it may be under good auspices, and with the favour of Christ: and when this shall be the
case, we must also entreat the Lord that the powers of hell, which
are everwhere in arms, may not prevail against the truth of his
word.[91a]

Martyr's view of Cranmer as a mighty theologian who aided in exploding
transubstantiation brings one to consider Martyr's own role at Oxford.
He first expounded I *Corinthians* in 1548. In the dedicatory letter to
Edward VI in the printed edition of 1551 Martyr explained his choice
of this Epistle, for nowhere else in scripture could one find such a
variety of topics pertinent to the controversies of the time. The
doctrine of this Epistle if skillfully used would heal all the faults
which corrupt the Church.[92]

The Order of Communion published on 8 March 1548 certainly denied
both transubstantiation and real presence in the Eucharist. It reads
in part as follows. (The priest is to say:)

> Dearly beloved in the Lord, ye coming to this holy communion, must
> consider what Saint Paul writeth to the Corinthians, how he exhort-
> ed all persons diligently to try and examine themselves or ever
> they presume to eat of this bread or drink of the Cup, for as the
> benefit is great, if with a true penitent heart, and lively faith
> we receive this holy Sacrament (for then we spiritually eat the
> flesh of Christ and drink his blood: then we dwell in Christ and
> Christ in us, we be made one with Christ and Christ with us) so is
> the danger great, if we receive the same, unworthily. . . .[93]

Martyr's *Sermon of Thanksgiving* dedicated to Somerset in 1548 developes
this theme. One wonders whether the above phrases in the *Order of
Communion* are not being explained by Martyr to Somerset. The wording
is as follows:

Martyr	Order of Communion
They that do believe when they do commune, they uerely receive the body and blood of Christ, but they that be without faith and very ungodly, they receive nothing else but the tokens of bread and wine.	If with a true penitent heart and lively faith we receive this holy Sacrament (for then we spiritually eat the flesh of Christ and drink his blood:...) so is the danger great, if we receive the same, unworthily....

At this point in the narrative a summary of the debates on the Eucharist is necessary as a backdrop to Martyr's influence on Cranmer. Martyr's *Sermon of Thanksgiving* was used by Somerset in the informal debate on the *Prayer Book* in the House of Lords between 14 December and 21 December 1548. Somerset proposed in opening the debate that the issue centered on remnance, i. e., did bread remain bread after consecration in the Eucharist? Tunstal objected that the language of the new *Prayer Book* was evasive. Tunstal would support nothing but a clear definition of transubstantiation.

Cranmer explained his interpretation of the position which altered the Catholic Canon of the Mass. The framework as Ratcliff has shown is the traditional Latin Mass with Lutheran exhortations, extended communion devotions and postcommunion prayer in place of the usual collect of the Mass. Offertory prayers are omitted in Lutheran fashion. Cranmer excised the Latin Canon of oblation of bread and wine, the blessing of oblation and its offering to God. What Cranmer substituted was defended in these discussions. Cranmer's English Canon gave a brief thanksgiving for the saints after intercession for the living and the dead. The second section seems to follow the 1540 Church Order of Electoral Brandenburg with its affirmation of Christ's unique and perfect sacrifice on the cross rather than the altar. The third English section memorialized Christ's passion, the sacrifice of praise and thanksgiving, and seeks the benefits of a worthy reception.

In his explanation of December 1548 Cranmer gave his theological views. The sacrament was the remembrance of Christ's sacrifice and the

memorial of his gift of salvation. The unworthy eat to their own
damnation, but the righteous partake of Christ's sacrifice because "He
is in heaven." Somerset on 17 December 1548 attacked Thirlby's reminder that this matter was not yet agreed upon but still a matter of
dispute. Ridley then argued in support of the English *Prayer Book* that
"bread made by the Holy Ghost /is/ holy and remaineth bread still."[94]
What is well known is Ridley's agreement and defence of Cranmer; what
is less well known is Martyr's support of Somerset, Cranmer and Ridley
on these matters.

Peter Martyr in his 1549 Oxford lectures on I *Corinthians* (10: 16-
17) provoked a debate on the Eucharist which is well known from John
Foxe's account in his *Acts and Monuments*. Printed versions of this
1549 Debate appeared in Latin; (1549,1552,1557,1562,1581), English (1550),
Italian (1557) and French (1557,1562). Thus in 1548 for Somerset and
in 1549 for Cranmer, Martyr defended the view which Bullinger and Calvin
agreed upon in the *Consensus Tigurinus* of 1549. In 1550 and 1551 Martyr
examined the revised Prayerbook and contributed to it a prayer of exhortation. In 1550 Gardiner thought Cranmer's *A Defence of the True and
Catholic Doctrine of the Sacrament* was written by an author who "doth
but as it were translate Peter Martyr."

However one views Martyr's Eucharistic theology – and it is at one
with Bullinger of Zurich whose treatise converted Beza to protestantism–
Martyr's views are supported by Somerset and endorsed by Cranmer in the
Prayer Book of 1552. According to the account of the troubles at Frankfurt, Cranmer wrote a clearer statement of Reformed views by 1554 "an

hundreth tymes more perfect then this that we nowe have." The auster-
ity of the 1552 *Prayer Book* was to remove the confusion of 1549. Whatever Lutheran form Cranmer used for the 1549 *Prayer Book*, Peter Martyr
helped him to make explicit the Reformed content in that of 1552. At
least one can conclude that Cranmer's contemporaries like Gardiner saw
matters that way even if Queen Elizabeth failed in making the 1549 Book
more protestant and settled for making the 1552 Book more catholic.[95]

On 3 January 1549 Martyr again wrote to Dryander. Referring either
to his lectures on I *Corinthians* and/or disputes over the Eucharist,
Martyr reported that conditions in Oxford were optimum for a circumspect
tract. One gains the impression that Martyr had already begun to prepare the *Tractatio* published later in 1549. Martyr protested that in
the English realm the Gospel was firmly opposed and that he in turn
fought for the Gospel.[96] On 15 January 1549 Martyr told Utenhove, "May
the Lord grant, that, among us, there may be rightly planted a vine
which in due time may produce fruit delicious both to men and to God."[97]
Again on 1 February 1549 Martyr wrote to Dryander that though the
enemies of the gospel were remarkably active, Cranmer leant his support.[98]

One ought here to sketch in the transition of political power during the years 1547-1553 so that a narrow focus on Martyr's career will
not distort the wider view of events in England under Edward VI. It
was after all an age of rather drab religious prose. All that men
thought and did in Church and State has not survived, though such documents which have survived limit the options which men dared to express

publicly as a sign of how they felt in private. For several there was the Tower of London in which Sir Thomas More discovered that the thoughts of men could lead to death. From William Tyndale's *Obedience of The Christian Man* and Sir Thomas Elyot's *Book of the Governor* to Reginald Pole's *Defense of the Unity of the Church* and Stephen Gardiner's *Oration on True Obedience* one can see that Englishmen of the sixteenth century cared about legitimate authority. In fact Gardiner, Martyr and Cranmer become the central religious players on the English stage during Edward's reign. Circumstances made cowards of the many and martyrs of a few.

Liturgical change preceeded what T. M. Parker has called "The Protestant Revolution." Edward VI was a lad of nine when his uncle the Earl of Hertford took the title Lord Protector in 1547. Under Somerset chantries were dissolved and episcopal lands secularized. Somerset House in London is a memorial today to the process. During the summer of 1547 new injunctions appeared which ordered each parish church to have a copy in English of Erasmus' *Paraphrases* and Cranmer's *Book of Homilies*. Gardiner opposed these as well as the injunction for an English Bible in each parish. Even so, a new Act charged bishops to preach four times a year in their dioceses. Under Somerset foreign theologians came to England such as Martyr, Bucer, Fagius, Poullain, Laski, Ochino and Dryander. Prayer book reform appeared in 1549 and foreign congregations were authorized to meet in London in 1550. Then John Dudley, Earl of Warwick whose army suppresed the 1549 rebellion seized power.

On 14 October 1549 Somerset entered the Tower of London. When in 1550 the Earl of Warwick became Lord President of the Council he released Somerset. In 1552 Warwick became Duke of Northumberland. By January 1552 Somerset gained enough support to expect that Parliament would restore him to his previous high post. Northumberland had Somerset tried for treason. He was executed for felony on the day before Parliament gathered in 1552.

Under Northumberland events rapidly moved to establish Protestantism. In spite of John Knox who questioned the Duke's sincerity steps were taken to solidify Cranmer's plans. Bonner was deprived as Bishop of London to be replaced by Nicholas Ridley from Rochester. As Bonner languished in the Tower, Gardiner was prosecuted and his see of Winchester given to John Ponet. Miles Coverdale succeeded to Exeter as Bishop. A symbol of the new prelatry was John Hooper whose 1550 scruples over vestments and administration of Gloucester mark a new care for the Word of God.

The 1552 *Prayer Book* appeared under Northumberland as did the *Forty-Two Articles* of 1553, while Ponet's *Short Catechism* and a new *Prymer* also emerged in print in 1553. However Knox and others may have questioned Northumberland's religious sincerity, a great number of events transpired to make Northumberland's presidency a protestant revolution. In the final analysis all hung on the health of the young Edward VI. When Edward died his sister Mary as Queen had John Dudley, Duke of Northumberland executed as he recanted his protestant "heresy." It was an epoch of huge proportions for English political and religious history which

Martyr helped to shape from 1547-1553. In the end his beloved Cranmer went from Lambeth to the Tower of London to martyrdom at Oxford. Hoak's dissertation on the King's council in Edward's reign does not mention Martyr. That only shows when taken with Professor Jordan's magisterial political biography of Edward VI how much can be added about Martyr's influence during these six years.

EUCHARISTIC DEBATE (1549)

When Martyr reached I *Corinthians* (10:16-17) in his Oxford lectures a clamor arose headed by Richard Smith.[99] Notices were posted in Oxford churches announcing a public debate the next day,

> against the presence of Christ's body in the holy supper. Wherefore the day following they occupy the auditorie, they dispose of their travels in places convenient, and command them to be ready as need should require to make clamors and tumult, yea and to fight too.[100]

Martyr's friends persuaded him not to participate since he was at study to prepare himself for the appointed lecture, oblivious of the dangers to come. Martyr refused to retire, saying that he was not himself the author of tumult; moreover he could not disappoint some in his audience who were waiting for the accustomed reading. Martyr lectured the next day with no sign of distress in his speaking or physical appearance. After the lecture friends arranged a dispute between Smith and Martyr. When the Royal Visitors of the university arrived at the beginning of May, Smith lost his nerve and fled to Scotland.[101] Later from the safety of Louvain Smith attacked Martyr in a diatribe which Martyr answered in published form in 1559.[102] Martyr described Smith in a letter to Bucer of 10 June 1550.

I have nothing new to tell you. A certain adversary of mine, Dr.
Smith, who preceded me as Professor of Divinity at Oxford, and
fled hence last year to Louvain, (-having conducted himself very
turbulently here, by challenging me, with excessive petulance, to
a public disputation with himself, -) has published two books: -
one, *On The Celibacy of Clerks*, pretendedly against Luther, whose
character he impudently assails with abuse, in reality however
against myself, often naming me reproachfully, as having inculcated
the same doctrines: - the other, *On Monastic Vows*, professedly
written against me, stuffed so full with maledictions, accusations,
and the bitterest contempt, that I think I never have heard before
of any tongue so unbridled in abuse. He does not even spare my
wife, whom he most filthily traduces as my harlot. Now and then he
makes mention of your Calvin, representing us all as having con-
spired together in (support of) the same opinions. He heaps together the opinions of the Fathers with all possible zeal; but he
heaps together very many, by which he strives to prove that vows
of Celibacy are both lawful and laudable, and having once been
taken, are rigidly to be fulfilled. By the same authority of the
Fathers he endeavours to prove that every one of us have the power
of making such vows, provided we be willing, and prayers be offered
up: in which particular he imitates (the Bishop of) Winchester;
although he does not equal him either in style or in acuteness of
argument, for he adopts a very impure phraseology, and weaves sill
sophisms; but he is more copious than Winchester in collecting the
opinions of the Fathers. I think he was induced to select this
particular subject, above all others, in writing against me (- for
he had often heard me deliver opinions in the Schools directly
opposed to his Papistical dogmas -) for the following reason - that
he sees that, on this point, he has a sufficiently rich and copious
testimony in the Fathers. Perhaps he has fully persuaded himself
that he will gain this advantage - namely - that, in this question,
I shall be compelled, however unwilling, openly to dissent from the
Fathers; from whose field, should I leave him master of it, he will
immediately sing his *Epinicia* among his comrades, and splendidly
proclaim his triumph as having gloriously won the battle. You have
been frequently and happily conversant with this topic, both with
Latomus, and with Winchester. Wherefore, now I hold the wolf by
the ears. If I answer, I shall seem to do what has already been
done: for it would be impossible for me to bring forward more than
has been written either by you or by others on this controversy; or
to add much to what I have taught in the Schools, that fellow Smith
himself being a hearer and a diligent annotator of all that was
said. But if I take no notice, I shall be reminded of my duty by
those who are on our side; and other nations, in which his book
will be generally read, will easily be imposed on. For, although
his books are not dispersed in England, (having been prohibited) by
the order of the Magistrates, and chiefly, as I think, of the Most
Reverend (the Archbishop) of Canterbury, yet since they have been

printed at Louvain, they will be universally circulated. The
writer has never appeared here, and no one knows where he is.
What a pure and innocent life he leads, you may conjecture from
this. He had a man-servant who took to himself a wife: he
lodged with them; and, as it is generally reported, they had all
things in common. Such are the advocates of *The Celibacy of
Clerks and Monks*.[103]

When Cox proceeded to reform the Oxford colleges, Magdalen College

became pivotal. Its head was Owen Oglethorpe, an outspoken catholic,

and its students had been warned by Somerset in January of 1548 to

stop defacing property. The fellows demanded a visitation which led

to religious changes such as the end of daily masses and whitewash of

the chapel. When Cox saw that nineteen protestants and some Irish were

named fellows of St. Mary Magdalen College, all the factors were present

to make Martyr's dispute a major event in Oxford life. Not only Richard

Smith of Merton but the students of Magdalen awaited the debates of 1549.

The presence of Cox represented governmental supervision of the entire

affair.[103a]

The disputation took place on 28 May - 1 June 1549 after Martyr

finished commenting on I *Corinthians* (XI).[104] Martyr in his notice post-

ed on the door of St. Mary's Church stated that even though Smith was

said to have departed,

> I offer publicly, for the edification of godly minds, to dispute
> the same points which we desired to treat, with him or any other
> who will appear in his place, and I take it upon me with God's
> help, to defend and to prove my propositions.[105]

Martyr in his propositions drawn up for debate demanded that the grounds

of the disputation analyze the signs under which the body of Christ is

corporeally and carnally present.[106]

The 1577 *Scripta Anglicana* printed Bucer's response to Martyr's three propositions. First, Martyr claimed that "in the sacrament of the Eucharist bread and wine are not transubstantiated into the body and blood of Christ." Bucer concurred. Secondly, Martyr contended that "the body and blood of Christ are not corporeally or carnally in the bread and wine. . . ." Bucer added that they were not contained "locally in bread and wine." Finally, Martyr taught that "the body and blood of Christ are united sacramentally in bread and wine." Bucer demurred that this must be understood by faith and not the senses.[107] Martyr's preface to the *Tractatio* of 1549 stated:

> For I know well that Scripture, to demonstrate its great compactness, is accustomed to declare that not only are we endowed with the Spirit, merit and intercession of Jesus, and act and live by His inspiration and Spirit, but also He Himself is with us, and dwells in us and we in Him, we are born again in Him, His flesh is both given and received to be eaten and drunk. But I understand statements of this kind to be metaphorical, since proper speech cannot easily be had for these things - for words signify this or that as they are appointed to serve human ends. Wherefore when it comes to heavenly and divine things, natural man who understands not such great secrets, cannot as much as name them.[108]

Martyr discussed his academic life in two letters of 1549 to Utenhove and Bucer written prior to the May dispute at Oxford. Martyr told Utenhove that when he had information he would comment "on the present state of matters connected with religion; I will do so with pleasure, as soon as I have any accurate information."[109] Martyr's mention of Cranmer's strenuous fight might refer to revision of the *Prayer Book*.[110] He wrote on 22 January 1549 to console Bucer on the sorry state of the church in Strasbourg. "I am at present, as you know, at Oxford, and cannot communicate with (the archbishop of Canterbury) except by letter, which I do not consider adviseable."[111] At that time Martyr was en-

couraged at the "progress of religion,"[112] though by June 1549 his

attitude was less than optimistic in comments to Bucer on theology and

its prospects at Oxford. If the dispute continued beyond four days,

"undoubtedly more light would have come to the cause."[113] Martyr then

summarized the points he was attempting to establish.

> I admit that we verily partake of the Thing of the Sacrament, that
> is, the Body and Blood of Christ; but so that I hold, that this is
> done by the mind and by faith; and in the meantime I grant that the
> Holy Spirit is efficacious in the Sacraments by force of the Spirit
> and institute of the Lord. This, however, I endeavour to maintain,
> in opposition to superstitious notions; chiefly with the view that
> people should not confuse either the Body or Blood of Christ, car-
> nally and through a corporeal Presence, with the Bread and the Wine.
> But that we ourselves are verily conjoined to Him (is a point on
> which) I have no hesitation; nor do I desire that the Sacraments
> should be (considered as) Symbols without honour and dignity.[114]

Martyr attributed to the sacraments as much honor and dignity as

the Word of God would allow him.[115] William Tresham engaged Martyr in

debate on 28 May, William Chadsey on 29 May, Tresham and Morgan on 31

May and Chadsey on 1 June.[116] Though Martyr's account of the debate was

endorsed by the Royal Commissioners and translated by Udall, it was not

his most important theological labour while in Oxford.[117] Tresham com-

mented on the debate that "Peter Martyr Vermigli is a certain delerious

old man, subversive, shameless, and a distinguished teacher of error."[118]

Richard Cox the chancellor of Oxford had defended protestant Eucharistic

views as early as 1540 when Cranmer circulated seventeen questions on

the subject. Cox could not agree that the sacraments had scriptural

support. In becoming chancellor by an election in London and by virtue

of his marriage, Cox also antagonized conservative Oxford and Richard

Smith in particular. That Cox as a 'Zwinglian' and a married cleric
was dean of Christ Church may explain why Cranmer attached Martyr to
that college. Cox defended Martyr in the June Oxford debate. As a
tutor to Edward VI and Somerset's agent of change for Oxford, one could
expect Cox to support Martyr. Cox was blunt in his summary of the
debate:

> He so singularly well answered the expectation of the great
> magistrates, and indeed of the King himself, while he not only
> has delivered unto the University the doctrine of Christ, out of
> the living fountains of the Word of God, but, so far as lies in
> him, has not suffered any man to disturb or stop the fountains.[118a]

After he heard from Julius Terrentianus in person about the debate,
Bucer responded to Martyr on 20 June 1549. Did Bucer's comments alter
Martyr's views somewhat between the debate and its published record?[119]
Bucer suggested that Martyr's opponents be given a copy and react to
it before final publication of the Acts of Disputation.[120]

Stephen Gardiner for example had complained of Martyr's cunning in
a letter of 1549/50 later attached to his tract attacking the 1549 debate.

> You discuss the Eucharist in a wicked and shameful way; with
> subtlety and shrewdness you cunningly twist certain considerations
> to your purpose, and openly and forcibly distort certain others;
> you treat nothing with honesty and integrity. These are the things,
> Peter, of which, in the name of the Eucharist, I complain; whether
> rightly or wrongly, the facts of the case shall be judge. But
> without further preface and with the utmost dispassionatness (as
> far as this is possible), I shall address myself to the subject.
> I shall subjoin my own arguments after first setting forth yours,
> that everything may be perfectly clear to the reader.[121]

McLelland has no reference to Gardiner's manuscript response to Martyr.
It is in 264 folio pages with the title *In Petru Martyrem florentinum*

malae tractaconis querela Sanctissimae Echaristiae noñe edita, authore

Stephano Winton. Gardiner mentions this in his manuscript answer to

Hooper of 1550, folio 22. The chronology of responses becween Martyr

and Gardiner involve Cranmer. Arundel MS. 100 answers Martyr's

Tractatio of 1549. Gardiner answered Cranmer in his 1550 *explicatio*

which responded to Cranmer's A *Defence of the true & catholike Doctrine*

(1550). Cranmer replied again in the An *Answer . . . Unto a craftie*

and Sophisticall cavillation (1551). Gardiner retorted with the

Confutatio Cavillationum (1552 and 1554) which Martyr answered in his

massive *Defensio* of 1559. No thorough study of Martyr's Eucharistic

views can ignore these works of Cranmer and Gardiner.

Bucer worried whether or not Martyr had acknowledged sufficiently

the presence of Christ by faith, as St. Paul says:

> yet nearly the whole Disputation runs on in such a manner, that I
> fear too many who may read the Acts of this Disputation will come
> to the conclusion that you maintain that Christ is absent alto-
> gether from the Supper, and that whatsoever is done in it has no
> further results than that faith, excited concerning Christ truly
> absent, is increased through the Spirit of Christ, by His benefits
> brought to mind and by meditation; and that you do not acknowledge
> that the very Christ, (beginning (to do this) in Baptism, and con-
> tinuing (to do it) more and more in the Eucharist,) exhibits and
> communicates Himself present to His own by that communication, by
> which they verily are and remain in Him, and have Him being and
> remaining in themselves. To sum up: they will think you maintain
> the presence, not of Christ, but only of the Spirit of Christ and
> of His influence; although I know that you acknowledge that Christ
> exhibits Himself present to faith.[122]

Peter Martyr seems to have been left in peace at Oxford until an

insurrection broke out later in 1549.[123] Martyr fled to London when the

Oxford mob threatened him with violence as a leader of the reform. In

his sermon on this troubled moment Martyr refers to Job; "We must take

the Word of God for our comfort and instruction; we must confess that
tumult and sedition spring from sin."[124] Cranmer preached two sermons
against rebellion on 21 July and 10 August at St. Paul's in London
based on Latin originals composed by Martyr. Valdo Vinay has noted
that Corpus Christi College MS. 102 which contains the sermons is
divided. At page 480 the final two paragraphs as well as pages 481-
482 are cancelled out, perhaps by Cranmer himself, since a note in his
own hand is in the margin.[125] Manuscript 102 also contains on pages
529-534 Cranmer's note on biblical passages attacking spiritual sedition.
Since Martyr composed a treatise with the title *Cogitationes contra
Seditione* which uses similar themes, it is clear that on this question
Martyr provided a political – theological program for Cranmer and
Somerset.[126]

W. Lynne in 1549 translated a sermon of Henrich Bullinger on magistrates and civic obedience. This work printed by Gwalter Lynne in
London, 1549 is an early translation of the Ninth Sermon in Bullinger's
Second Decade. Lynne's prefatory letter indicates Bullinger's influence
at this crucial moment for liturgical reform in England. Lynne could
not find a more pertinent sermon to translate than this one by Bullinger
under the title, *A treatise or Sermon of Henry Bullynger, much fruitfull
and necessarye for this tyme, concernynge magistrates and obedience of
subiects. Also concernyng the affayres of warre, and what scryptures
make mension thereof.* etc. Calvin's letter to Somerset and Cranmer at
this time are also pertinent. First Bucer and then Farel received com-
plaints from Calvin about popery and clerical weakness in England. On

1 April 1552 Calvin urged a speedy reform so that "the cold of an eternal winter" might not prevail. In June of 1552 Calvin would urge Cranmer to set himself to reform of the Prayer Book with Peter Martyr's aid.[127]

Cranmer and Somerset received much encouragement at this time from the continental party and refugee theologians. When Somerset languished in prison in 1550 Calvin addressed a letter similar to that sent by Peter Martyr. Here one sees the assessment of English reform made by these two protestants. That Somerset himself translated Calvin's epistle is of more than passing interest, for it confirms the theological convictions held by Somerset which Peter Martyr alluded to in his letter. Calvin wrote that, "Truely the brute that I have heard a far of, both caused me to have a great griefe in my heart, unto such time that I did know ỹ God had begon to put some rememdy."[128]

Calvin went on to remind Somerset of the good King Hezekiah. Civil rebellion would harm the reform envisaged by Cranmer and supported by the foreign theologians who encouraged him and Somerset.

The Duke of Northumberland disliked the 1549 Prayer Book. On 6 October 1549 the storm broke as Somerset hurried from Hampton Court to Windsor Castle. The Council in London failed to accept Cranmer and Paget's attempt at mediation. The Council broke its promise not to have Somerset suffer in lands, goods or in honour. The Protector submitted, was sent to the Tower and Northumberland captured the Government. Northumberland even sought to appoint John Knox as Bishop of Rochester to check Cranmer. When the Duke offered Hooper the bishopric of Gloucester in 1550, Hooper refused to take the oath swearing by the Saints and to use the vestments required in the Ordinal. Cranmer appealed to Bucer and Martyr when Ridley could not remove Hooper's scruples. Small wonder that Cranmer moved slowly when the formidable Northumberland sought to check his moves. Cranmer depended on his "learned strangers" to counter the political realities of 1550. He needed them every bit as much as his own patristic scholarship to reform English worship on continental models. The letter to Bullinger of 1 June 1550 and the lectures on *Romans* at Oxford in 1550 continue Martyr's opposition to rebellion, especially at *Romans* (13). This letter indicates amity between these theologians.

Martyr outlined his daily expositions of St. Paul and deplored the new royal decree that weekly public disputations be held in the Universities. His opponents were obstinate, the "business of religion" made more progress in England than his sins deserved and reform needed the restoration of the pure sources. Martyr praised Bullinger's *Decades*, apparently using the scriptural references. He sent his greetings to Bibliander and "Doctor Gesner."[129] It is possible that Nicholas Udall's answer to the rebels used these works of Martyr, especially as noted in the Fifth Article. "Item, we will have the sacrament of the Altar but at Estur delivered to the lai people, and then but in one kind."[130] The Corpus Christi MS. 340 also contains Ochino's *Dialogus Regis et Populi* in his own hand.[131] Vinay points to similar themes shared by Martyr and John Cheke's *The Hurt of Sedition, howe greueous it is to a Commune Welth* (London: John Day, 1549). Cheke has an illustration of Absalom

on the frontespiece with the words, "The reward of Absalon the Rebell."
This theme occurs frequently in Martyr's writings.[132] The very least
one can conclude is that Martyr assisted Cranmer during this thorough
revision of the discipline and theology of the English Church. Edward
VI would guarantee its implementation if he lived.

It seems from a reading of the *Cogitationes* that Vinay claims too
much of a role for Martyr on the basis of this document alone. It is
important, however, to note Martyr's conclusion about the rebellion.
"Three extraordinary causes can be assigned for this sedition. One is
the change of religion, another the excessive oppression of the poor,
the third is the leisure of otherwise robust men."[133]

Arthur B. Ferguson describes the concern for poverty on pages 253-
261 of his *The Articulate Citizen And The English Renaissance,* citing
from *The Three Fruitful Sermons* by Thomas Lever of 1550 and Henry Brin-
helow's *The Complaynt of Roderyck Mors.* Martyr's comments on poverty
bespeak sympathy for the plight of peasants as well as a rejection of
their theological appeal.

Martyr had resumed his lectures on returning to Oxford as a canon
of Christ Church. At the end of August 1549 Martyr wrote to Bucer answering a letter of 7 August no longer extant. Flacius Illyricus bothered
Melanchthon when he conceded the *Adiaphora* at Leipzig. Martyr thought
that the Papists' chief object was not to grant such concessions, but
rather "that the whole of that religion, which we have received as
delivered to us by Christ through the enlightening of the Holy Spirit,
may be entirely obscured and radically extirpated."[134] Martyr would

labor long in England in several attempts to preserve the "whole of

that religion."

Martyr expressed the extent of that task to Henry Bullinger.[135]

> . . . many things yet remain to be done, which we have in expecta-
> tion rather than in reality. The perverseness of the bishops is
> incredible; they oppose us with all their might: yet some of that
> order, though very few, are favourable to the undertaking . . . .
> we are in hopes that at the end of the parliament, which is now
> sitting, some enactments will come out, which will in no small
> degree promote the reformation of the church. May the Lord give
> us quiet times; for whatever tumult, or disturbance, or sedition
> breaks forth in this country is altogether, both by the enemy and
> the people at large, imputed to the reviving gospel.

The initial impression one gains is that Martyr played a signifi-

cant role in the development of Reformed Theology in England. Martyr

addressed the Duke of Somerset in March of 1550 after Northumberland re-

leased him from the Tower of London.[136] On 20 December 1549 Somerset

had been stripped of his office as Protector. In a reflective mood

Martyr admonished the Duke that though "Christ shall care for us," the

frailty of human flesh should remind one to give "hearty thanks to the

mercy of God."

> But leaste the power of the fleshe make us lese so greate fruit, we
> muste consider ỹ plentyous and full light of Christian doctrine,
> least while we be to earnestlie moued with those things which the
> flesh putteth in our head, we take ỹ lesse hede to those things
> which we ought to loue. What can happen more happie to a Christian
> man, than bothe to be & be accopted, the scholer of Christe? What
> more luckie ching can he desyre, than to reigne for euer in hys
> maister? What more to bee wished for, than to obteine euerlasting
> life with great glory. But these things are not attayned but by
> the crosse.[137]

The above letter appears to be an autobiographical account of

Martyr's Oxford troubles. He was quite happy to be a scholar of Christ

in a two-fold sense; to learn dependence on the mercies of God in Christ
crucified, and to work so that the Church might share that humility in
the English realm. Martyr outlined that task at Christ Church, Oxford
in another letter to Bullinger, telling how he gave daily expositions
of St. Paul, held weekly theological debates in the College and fort-
nightly participated in a university disputation. Martyr served as
moderator of these disputations in which he met much opposition.[138]
Martyr's greatest comfort was the support of Edward VI.

> But, on the other hand, we derive no little comfort from having a
> king who is truly holy, and who is inflamed with so much zeal for
> godliness. He is endued with so much erudition for his age, and
> already expresses himself with so much prudence and gravity, as
> to fill all his hearers with admiration and astonishment: where-
> fore we must entreat God with most fervent prayers very long to
> preserve him to the kingdom and to the church. There are also very
> many of the nobility and men of rank who entertain right views; and
> we have some bishops who are not illinclined, among whom the arch-
> bishop of Canterbury is as a standard-bearer. And then, Hooper is
> enrolled among them, to the exceeding joy of all good men, and, as
> I hear, a people not ill-disposed has fallen to his lot. I hope to
> see him when he visits his diocese; for if he goes to Gloucester,
> where his cathedral is, he will pass this way. By what means he
> was induced to accept a bishoprick, I would relate at large, were
> I not wholly assured that from his respect towards you he would
> write you a most full account of the entire proceedings. There is
> likewise another excellent man, Michael Coverdale, who some few
> years since had charge of a parish in Germany. He is actively en-
> gaged in Devonshire, both in preaching and interpreting scripture.
> You are, I think, well acquainted with him. He is to be made
> bishop of Exeter; and nothing can be more convenient and conducive
> to the reformation of religion, than the advancement of such men to
> the government of the Church. Master A Lasco too has come over
> hither on account of his country Friesland having received the
> imperial Interim; and I expect he will preside over the German church
> in London, which event will gratify me exceedingly. He is now re-
> siding with the archbishop of Canterbury.
>
> You have now heard the state of our affairs in England, which this
> peace made with the French king, and which seems daily to be con-
> solidated, will in some measure tend to improve. Only some persons
> are afraid lest, as they are beginning to boast, a council should be

held by the pope for the destruction of the godly: but if we are
wise, we shall cast all this kind of care upon God. The sermons
you have published have been useful monitors at this period, which
as they are strengthened by quotations from the holy scriptures,
were both agreeable, and will I hope be read with advantage.[139]

Hooper had initiated a stand against vestments in 1550 on the

grounds that they were Aaronic, hence unchristian.[140] Martyr true to

his earlier views on *adiaphora* held that "their use, if other things

prescribed to us by the Word of God remain sound, are neither wicked

nor pernicious in themselves or by their own nature."[141] This well

known affair may be followed in Patrick Collinson's second chapter,

"That Comical Dress" and Bucer's attitude in Constantine Hopf IV. The

Ordinal of 1550 required that Hooper wear episcopal garb. Martyr's

letter of 4 November 1550 was included in two English treatises of

1566. One was A *briefe examination of the time* . . . . which also gave

Bucer's judgment. The other treatise of 1566 was *VVhether it be*

mortall sinne to transgresse ciuil lawes . . . . In this later work

Grindal published a long letter from Bullinger and Gualter at Zurich to

Humphrey and Sampson in 1566. This letter exists in Latin and English

(S.T.C., 4063,4,75) and in *VVhether it be mortall sinne* . . . .[142]

Martyr's opinion was therefore part and parcel of the Puritan contro-

versy under Grindal in 1566. Another thought comes to mind at this

point. Hooper's stand was against the 1550 *Ordinal* which was the law

of the realm. Could not Martyr's letter in addition to its making a

distinction between essentials and non-essentials, be read as a defense

of the legal *status quo*? Martyr's letter then is consistent with his

political views expressed in the *Sermon on Rebellion*. More recently

Paul Bradshaw shows that the 1550 *Ordinal* was changed by 1552 even

though Hooper submitted. The Oath of Supremacy to the King changed

from "so help me God, all Saints and the holy Evangelist" to "so

helpe me God through Jesus Christ."[143]

NOTES TO CHAPTER II

1. On Martyr's life prior to 1542 see Philip McNair, Peter Martyr
in Italy: The Anatomy of an Apostasy.

2. Josiah Simler, "An Oration of the life and death of that wor-
thie man and excellent Divine D. Peter Martyr Vermillius, professor of
Divinitie in the Schools of Zuriche," in Peter Martyr Vermigli, The
Commonplaces (1583), no pagination. Checked at all points against the
1563 Oratio.

3. Jose C. Nieto, Juan De Valdes and the Origins of the Spanish
and Italian Reformation, pp. 146-147. McLelland, op. cit., p. 6
wrongly gives Valdes' death as 1536 and Martyr's lectures in Naples as
1535-36.

4. Ibid., p. 148. See on the background in Naples, Mario Rosa,
"Vita religiosa e pieta eucharistica nella Napoli del Cinquecento,"
R.S.L.R. IV (1968), pp. 37-54.

5. Ibid., p. 16. The term disciple here is misleading when one
reads p. 148, n. 48 of Nieto. See McNair, op. cit., pp. 150-151. To
argue from cause to effect could mean attributing Seripando as a common
source for both Valdes and Vermigli. It might as well be argued that
St. Paul is the logical source for all three. The absence of manuscript or printed sources for Vermigli prior to 1542 makes the term
'disciple' problematic in extremis, especially since Vermigli uses
Patristic sources in his exegetical study while Valdes virtually
ignores the Fathers. See Tedeschi's review of Nieto in Church History
41 (1972), pp. 120-121.

6. Huelin, op. cit., pp. 27-28.

7. Commentary on the Gospel of St. Matthew, pp. 34-35. But see
the caution expressed by Margherita Morreale, "Juan De Valdes as
Translator and Interpreter of St. Paul: The Concept of GNOSIS,"
B.H.S., XXXIV (1957), 89-94. An Italian ms. version /Curione's?/ was
known to Simler in 1555 and has been found in Turin.
8. Theodore M. Haggard, The Church And Sacraments In The Theological Writings Of Juan De Valdes (unpublished thesis), p. 52.

9. Ibid., p. 132.

10. Nieto, op. cit., p. 198n.7 and p. 200 n.11.

11. Haggard, op. cit., p. 263.

12. Proposita, p. 431.

13. See the entire issue of A. S. I. X (1847) devoted to Lucca. Also see A. Pascal, "Da Lucca a Ginevra," R. S. I. (1933). On Modena see the following footnote reference.

14. George Hunston Williams, "Camillo Renato (c. 1500? 1575)," Italian Reformation Studies In Honor of Laelius Socinus (ed. John A. Tedeschi), p. 130. See pp. 131-135 for Renato's beliefs.

15. McNair, op. cit., pp. 236-237.

16. Ibid., pp. 239-268.

17. The original Italian text has not survived--a Latin translation by Taddeo Duno is in all editions of the Loci Communes.

18. McNair, op. cit., p. 292, n.4.

19. Gorham, op. cit., p. 26. The setting of Martyr's letter is Matthew (10:1-16). Matthew restricts the saying to Galilee and the Jews, whereas Mark (6:7-11) and Luke (9:1-5) and Luke (12:1-12) mention the Gentile mission. The restriction in Matthew to Israel and the geography of Palestine must be seen in the eschatological framework that the end time is so near that one ought always be prepared to abandon all things for sake of the Kingdom. Vermigli realized this in a way that Tertullian refused to accept.

20. Gigliola Fragnito, "Gli₁₁ spirituali" e la fuga di Bernardino Ochino," R. S. I. 84 (1972), 717-813.

21. Mc Nair, op. cit., p. 290.

22. Fragnito, op. cit., p. 779, n. 8. Archivio di Stato, Parma, Sez. VI. b. 58, Eretici d' Italia, f. 33[r-v].

23. Simler, Oration.

24. Z. S. A. EII (340), fol. 112. III Nones Oct. 1542. Autograph letter from Basle. Copy in Zurich Zentralbibliothek, Simmlerische Sammlung MSC.S.52.

25. Z. S. S., MSC.S.52 (86). "Domini Bonifacii Amerbachii

liberalitas in nos mihi semper erit memorabili."

26. Myron P. Gilmore, "Boniface Amerbach," Humanists And Jurists: Six Studies In The Renaissance (Cambridge: Belknap Press of Harvard University Press, 1963), pp. 146-177.

27. Z. S. A. EII (340), fol. III. XIIIIKL. Januarias M.D. XLII.

28. C. R. XXXIX, 430, cols. 456-457.

29. C. R. V, 2726, col. 143. There are three other extant letters between Melanchthon and Martyr.

30. C. R. XXXIV, Cols. 617-644. See Antonio Rotondo, "Atteggiamenti Della Vita Morale Italiana Del Cinquecento La Pratica Nicodemitica," R. S. I. 79 (1967), 991-1030. N.B. p. 993, n. 7. Ginzburg, Il Nicodemismo traces the object of Calvin's wrath to Strasbourg in the person of the learned physician Otto Brunfels. His 1527 Pandectorum veteris et novi testamenti is now seen as the principle source for the view that confessional adherence to a visible church is incompatible with true faith in the God who alone discerns the thoughts of men.

31. Delio Cantimori, "Nicodemism and the Expectations of a Conciliar Solution to the Religious Question," The Late Italian Renaissance 1525-1630 (edited by Eric Cochrane), pp. 246-47.

32. Miriam Chrisman, Strasbourg and the Reform, p. 82.

33. De Vitandis (1549).

34. "To the Faithful of the Church at Lucca," Common Places (1583) Part Five, p. 63. See Marino Berengo, Nobili e mercanti nella Lucca del Cinquecento, pp. 438-39.

35. Gorham, op. cit., p. 21.

36. Ibid., p. 22.

37. Oratio.

38. Loc. cit.

39. "I will teach and speak that which I judge true concerning that matter wherein I know they disagree from me, and that with such moderation and temperance, as I will not grieve or bitterly taunt any man that is of another judgement." 26 June 1554 in letter to a certain friend, from Strasbourg. Common Places (1583), Part five, p. 95. The friend is Melanchthon. See Melanchthon's letter of 29 May 1554 to which this letter is probably a response. Henricus E. Bindseil,

Philippi Melanchthonis Epistolae, pp. 359-60. Calvin wrote Melanchthon at the same time to be more decisive about Marbach.

40. C. R. XXXIX, 503, col. 618. 23 September 1543. Ulm.

41. Z.S. A., EII (340), fol. 157^{r-v}.

42. Pierre Mesnard, "The Pedagogy of Johann Sturm (1507-1589) and its Evangelical Inspiration," S.R. XIII (1966), 204-208.

43. Ibid., pp. 210-213.

44. D. N. B. I, 626-627. See Jean Rott and Robert Faerber, "Un Anglais a Strassbourg au milieu du XVIe Siecle: John Hales, Roger Ascham et Jean Sturm," E. A. 21 (1968), 381-394.

45. Ibid., p. 627.

46. Mesnard, op. cit., p. 214 n.8.

47. Ibid., p. 215.

48. "1545. Legge riguardante le nuove opinioni religiose, e divieto di libri ereticale," A. S. I. X (1847), Documenti, pp.165-168.

49. Ibid., p. 168. See p. 167, "Et inoltre, perche patria essere che alcuno temerario publicamente tenuto dalla Santa Romana Chiesa infedele et heretico, et spetialmene fra Bernadino Ochino et Pietro Martire."

50. Karl Benrath calls it, Se gli Evangelici siano scismatici per essersi separati dai Papisti. "Vermigli, Pietro Martire," Realencyclopedie für protestantische Theologie und Kirche, pp. 550-552. This is the 1572 Italian translation of De Schismate from Melachím (1566) which exists in the Gucciardini collection in Florence.

51. Oratio de Utilitate...Ministerii. See D. N. B. LVIII, col. 256 where it is wrongly dated to 1543.

52. Gorham, op. cit., p. 179.

53. Fagius died on 13 November.

54. Ibid., pp. 124-25. C. C. C. C., Parker MSS. 102, 107-109.

55. Oratio. Account published by Conrad Hubert & Sir John Cheke, Historia uera: de vita M. Buceri & P. Fagii. Item historia Catharinae Vermiliae. (J. Calfhill, London: John Day, 1561).

56. C. R. XL, 860, col. 438.

57. C. R. XXXIX, 597, col. 816. 29 December 1544.

58. Z. S. A. VI, 156, fol. 34. 8 May 1547 to Bullinger. Printed in Eduard Boehmer, "Francesci Dryandri, Hispani, epistolae quinquaginta", Z. H. T. XL (1870), 387–442. Quotation is taken from p. 415.

59. Bucer to Calvin of 7 February 1549: "Jam episcopo promissuru sic est hic non permittendum praedicari contra Interim. Vel hodie itaque, vel intra perpaucos dies, obsignabitur meum et praecipuorum collegarum ministerium."

60. C. R. V, 143–144. Schmidt, op. cit., p. 48 in MS. mentions a letter of 17 October 1542 from Martyr to Bullinger. The letter to Bucer on 13 April 1544 in Schmidt, p. 62 MS., is in the Thesaurus Baumianus of the University Library, Strasbourg. MS. 674: Reg. XV, fol. 32–33. Martyr here expressed gratitude for his reception as lecturer in the College of St. Thomas. See also MS 675, Reg. XVI: fol. 158 for Bucer's letter to Fellio, Martyr and Fagius of 23 December 1545 from Ratisbon. Bucer worried about discipline in the College of St. Thomas.

61. See the letter to Elizabeth of 1558 for Martyr's ability to find Biblical concepts personified in sixteenth century events.

62. Lacey B. Smith, "The last will and testament of Henry VIII: a question of perspective," J. B. S. 2 (1962), 14–27. Mortimer Levine, "The last will and testament of Henry VIII: a reappraisal appraised," H. 26 (1964), 471–85.

63. The Letters of King Henry VIII (edited by M. St. Clare Byrne), pp. 420–421.

64. The Chronicle and Political Papers of King Edward VI (edited by W. K. Jordan), p. xxiii.

65. Ibid., pp. xxiii–xxiv. That Henry VIII had no intention of creating a Protestant England by his selection of Edward's tutors is clearly argued by Lacey Baldwin Smith, "Henry VIII and the Protestant Triumph," A. H. R. LXXI (1966), pp. 1237–1264. See especially p. 1240.

66. Carol Maddison, Marcantonio Flaminio, Poet, Humanist & Reformer, p. 142.

67. Luigi Firpo, "La Chiesa Italiana Di Londra nel Cinquecento e i suoi rapporti con Ginevra," Ginevra e l' Italia (edited by Delio Cantimori et al.), pp. 309–412. On the Spanish Church see Paul J.

lauben, "A Spanish Calvinist Church in Elizabethan London, 1559-65," C. H. XXXIV (1965), 53 where the Dutch, French, Italian and Spanish Churches in London kept in close contact. On the Dutch Church and Laski see Frederick A. Norwood, "The Strangers' 'Model Churches' in Sixteenth-Century England," Reformation Studies In Honor of Roland H. Bainton (edited by Franklin H. Littell), pp. 180-196. On the work of Utenhove see J. Lindeboom, Austin Friars History of the Dutch Reformed Church in London 1550-1950, pp. 1-28. On the wider influence of these churches see Fernand de Schickler, Les Eglises du Refuge en Angleterre.

68. O. L. II, pp. 570-71. London, 13 October 1550.

69. Norwood, op. cit., p. 184.

70. In a letter of 4 June 1558 Ochino told Fredrich von Salis that Martyr and Florio wrote each other about Laelius Socinus. Martyr asserted the satisfaction of Christ's merits for human sin. See Karl Benrath, Bernardino Ochino von Siena, pp. 306-307.

71. Pier Paolo Vergerio, La forma . . . nella chiesa . . . in Londra, sig. A2^r.

72. Ibid., sig. A3^r.

73. Ibid., sig. A7^r. In 1553 Florio translated Ponet's Catechism into Italian. It was dedicated to the Duke of Northumberland and suggested that it would "give a new knowledge of Christ and entrance to his doctrine." Cathechismo (1553?), sig. A4. Florio therefore introduced the Italian congregation to the fresh statements of English reform, albeit in a Calvinist cloak.

74. E. C. Ratcliff, "The Liturgical Work of Archbishop Cranmer," J. E. H. VII (1956), p. 190. William P. Haugaard, "The English Litany from Henry to Elizabeth," A. T. R. LI (1969), 177-203. On the 1559 Elizabethan changes see pp. 199-200 and notes 39-41.

75. Peter Brooks, Thomas Cranmer's Doctrine of the Eucharist.

76. Ratcliff, op. cit., p. 197.

77. Beesley, op. cit., pp. 83-88.

78. Lindeboom, op. cit., p. 3. I cannot locate this phrase in the Parker Society Edition of Latimer's sermons. See John K. Yost, "Hugh Latimer and the Reformation Crisis in the Education of Preachers," L. Q. XXIV (1972), 179-189.

79. A. S. T. 40, fol. 837^r. 22 August 1547. Autograph.

"Theodosii litteras quas mihi curasti perferandas et una hias ipsius libenter . . . cum voluptate perlegi." If one retains the reading 'Theodosii,' then Martyr may have meant the Theodosian Canons of the early ecumenical councils now in Verona MS. LX (58). See W. Telfer, "The Codex Verona LX (58)," H. T. R. XXXVI (1943), 169-246. Since Martyr used Theodoret as well as the Theodosian Code, the reference could be to a MS. version of the Codex on heresy or certain letters of Theodosius, Monophysite Patriarch of Constantinople.

80. Loc. cit.

81. A. S. T. 40, fol. 839^r.

82. Public Record Office, Calendar of the Patent Rolls, Edward VI, Vol. I, A. D. 1547-1548, p. 266. A stipend of forty marks each for Ochino and Vermigli was granted on 9 May 1548. On 24 October 1550 Martyr was granted the canonry or prebend in the cathedral church of Oxford, of Henry VIII's foundation. Vol. III, A. D. 1549-1551, p.174.

83. John Strype, Memorials of the Most Reverend Father In God Thomas Cranmer I, p. 370. Hereafter cited as Cranmer (1812).

83a. See Writings And Disputations of Thomas Cranmer (Parker Society, 1844), pp. 274-275 and McNair, op. cit., pp. 289-90.

84. McLelland, op. cit., pp. 270-271.

85. W. K. Jordan, Edward VI: The Young King. The Protectorship of the Duke of Somerset, pp. 189-190.

86. Sermons by Hugh Latimer, Sometime Bishop of Worcester, Martyr, 1555, p. 141. "There is yet among us two great learned men, Petrus Martyr and Barnard Ochin, which have a hundred marks apeice: I would the king would bestow a thousand pound on that sort."

87. Gorham, op. cit., pp. 53-54. Martyr to Utenhove. Oxford, 21 September 1548.

88. James K. McConica, English Humanists And Reformation Politics Under Henry VIII and Edward VI, pp. 266-67.

89. Gorham, op. cit., p. 178.

90. W. M. Southgate, John Jewel, pp. 4-11.

91. John Booty, John Jewel as Apologist, p. 74.

91a. O. L. II (1537-1558), pp. 469-70. "At modo cum templum Dei uium reparari oporteat, quaeritur sana doctrina cum experientia coniuncta, quae ut diuinitus datur, ita etiā rara, & in quam paucissimis occurit." Corinthios (1551), sig. A3.

92. See Anderson, "Word and Spirit in Exile," pp. 200-201.

93. English Historical Doctuments, V. p. 846.

94. W. K. Jordan, Edward VI: The Young King, pp. 315-316. Ratcliff, op. cit., pp. 197-200. Neither Jordan nor Ratcliff cite Martyr's Sermon of Thanksgiving whose Latin original has not survived.

95. William Haugaard, Elizabeth and the English Reformation, p. 110. Richard Hills in March of 1559 anticipated a liturgical reform which would follow the Lutheran Prayerbook of 1549 (form) or the Reformed Prayerbook of 1552 (content). Ibid., p. 108.

96. A. S. T. 40, fol. 881^r. 3 January 1549 from Oxford.

97. Gorham, op. cit., p. 74.

98. A. S. T. 40, fol. 883^r.

99. McLelland, op. cit., p. 18, n. 39 who improves on Simler and Young by examining the published commentary of 1572. Huelin goes a step further in translating the unpublished letter of Martyr to Cox of 22 August 1559 in Lambeth Palace Library MS. 2010, f. 133: "And when I had arrived at chapter 7, where the Apostle writes a good deal concerning virginity and marriage, according as my opinions were regarding vows, I disputed at length." Smith also noted down Martyr's reference to the Eucharist when Martyr lectured on chapter seven. Translation from Heulin, op. cit., p. 49. See appendixIII for text of entire letter.

100. Oratio.

101. Charles H. Smyth, Cranmer and the Reformation under Edward VI, p. 118.

102. Smith's Diatriba was published in 1550.

103. Gorham, op. cit., pp. 152-155.

103a. Vander Molen, Richard Cox, pp. 124-27.

104. Smyth, op. cit., pp. 118-119. See title page of Discourse (1550) translated by Udall.

105. McLelland, op. cit., p. 21.

106. Ibid., p. 19.

107. "Censvra Martini Bvceri De Tribvs Propositionibus a P. Martyre Oxonii ad disputandum propositis, clarissime hic comprehensa," Scripta Anglicana pp. 550-551.

108. McLelland, op. cit., Appendix D, pp. 283-284. The importance of the Disputatio and Tractatio of 1549 can be seen from noting the license given to Nicholas Udall in 1550 to print, reprint and sell these two works granting a "Prohibition of all others from printing the said works of Peter Martyr in English or any portion of them. . ." for a period of seven years from the printing or reprinting by Udall. Calendar of the Patent Rolls, Edward VI, Vol. III. A.D. 1549-1551, p. 315. That Udall sought such protection argues for the popularity or notoriety of these published accounts of the Oxford Debate in May of 1549. The Catholic account in the Bodleian Library, Oxford was never published. MS. 29279. Gardiner's 1550 response is British Museum, Arundel MS. 100.

109. Gorham, op. cit., p. 74. 15 January 1549.

110. Loc. cit.

111. O. L. II, p. 476.

112. Ibid., p. 477.

113. Gorham, op. cit., p. 81. 15 June 1549.

114. Loc. cit. In the dedicatory letter to the published Tractatio (1549) Martyr discussed these issues with Cranmer. The book is dedicated to Cranmer as an authentic defense of the truth of the Gospel and the Eucharistic sacrament. See Epistola Nuncupatoria in the Tractatio (1549).

115. Gorham, op. cit., p. 82.

116. See Strype, Cranmer (1812), I, pp. 283-289. Tresham's letter is in Strype, Cranmer (1694), appendix LXV, p. 122.

117. Smyth, op. cit., p. 120.

118. Strype, Cranmer (1694), p. 122.

118a. McLelland, op. cit., p. 22. Strype, Cranmer (1694), II, 119-120. Cox went on to speak of the sacraments as mysteries of Christ, "sacrosancta & tremenda."

119. Gorham, op. cit., pp. 83-84.

120. _Ibid._, pp. 88-89. Martin Micronius wrote to Bullinger on 20 May 1550: "The English translation of Peter Martyr's book on the Lord's supper could not be printed, owing to the bishops, and those too gospellers." _O.L._ II, p. 561.

121. British Museum, Arundel MS. 100, 1. Printed and translated in James Arthur Muller, _The Letters of Stephen Gardiner_, pp. 445-446.

122. Gorham, _op. cit._, p. 88. See also Hugh Pope, O.P., "The Oxford and Cambridge Disputations on the Holy Eucharist 1549," _I. E. R._ 59 (1942), 403-424. Pope challenges Martyr's Patristic citations. Bucer wrote to Niger about the disputation and said that "Christi praesentiam et exhibitionem." See _Scripta Anglicana_.

123. "The Oxonians go on toloribly quiet, at present; God grant they may continue to restrain themselves within the same bounds." 18 December 1549 to Bucer. _Ibid._, p. 126.

124. _C.C.C.C._, MS 102. No. 29. "A Sermon concernynge the tyme of rebellion." The original is MS. 340. 4, _Sermo Petri Martyri manu propria scriptus in seditionem Devonensium_.

125. Valdo Vinay, "Riformatori e lotte contadine. Scritte e Polemiche relative alla ribellione dei contadina nella Cornouaglia e nel Devonshire sotto Edoardo Vi," _R. S. L. R._ III (1967), p. 207, n.12. An older account is silent about the Corpus Christi material. See Frances Rose - Troup, _The Western Rebellion of 1549_, p. 324.

126. _Ibid._, p. 239. Vinay discusses this treatise on pp. 224-239. See _Miscellaneous Writings and Letters of Thomas Cranmer, Archbishop of Canterbury and Martyr 1556_, pp. 190-202 where Cranmer's notes based on Martyr and Ochino are reproduced.

127. W. K. Jordan, _Edward VI. The Threshold of Power_, pp. 324-325.

128. _An epistle/both of Godly Consolation and/also of aduertissemente, written by John/Caluine the pastour and preacher/of Geneua, to the righte noble prince/Edwarde Duke of So=/merset, before the time/ of knowledge had/of his trouble, but de=/lyuered to the sayde/Duke, in the time of hys/trouble,/and so translated out of/frenche by the same/ Duke hymselfe, in/the tyme of his/imprieson=/mente_ (London: E. Whitchurche, 1550), sig. Aviii^v.

129. _O. L._ II, pp. 480-481. _Epistolae Tigurinae_, pp. 316-319.

130. _Udall's Answer to the Commoners of Devonshire and Cornwall_ (Royal MS. 18B. xi fol. 1. British Museum) printed in Nicholas Pocock,

Troubles Connected with the Prayer Book of 1549, p. 157. The response
to the Fifth Article here on pages 157-173 contains a more detailed
discussion of the Church Fathers than in Cranmer's response. See p.
XX where Pocock says that though written during the time of the rebel-
lions, only internal evidence can help describe it. Pocock has not
solved the authorship of this treatise. Udall's interest in Martyr
raises a query whether this tract is another translation of Martyr.

131. Text in Italian. See Philip McNair, "Ochino on Sedition.
An Italian Dialogue of the Sixteenth Century," I. S. XV (1960), 36-49.
Text reproduced on pp. 46-49.

132. Vinay, op. cit., p. 211. Vinay concludes on p. 239 that
Martyr's influence on the official response to this rebellion of 1549
was considerable. See also A. R. Mason, "Rebellion in Norfolk, 1549,"
C. R. (March, 1959), 164-167,

133. C.C.C.C. MS. 102:31, fol. 512.

134. Gorham, op. cit., p. 98.

135. O. L. II, pp. 479-480. 27 January 1550. See also "Of the
Sacrament of Thanksgiving: a short treatise of Peter Martyr's making"
of 1 December 1548: British Museum Royal MS. 17 C.V. Strype, Ecclesiastical Memorials, 1, XXV, pp. 336-337 translates an Ash-Wednesday
sermon of Martyr on Fasting. It was well received. Martyr's treatise
on fasting in the Common Places draws on Zwingli's 1522 Von erkissen
und freyheit der Speisen. Martyr possessed a copy of this tract,
drawing on it for this 1549 sermon. See F. Gardy, "Les livres de
Pierre Martyr Vermigli conserves a la Bibliotheque de Geneve," A. S. G.
I (1919). Huelin refers to this copy in Geneva but does not identify
the sermon other than preached at Oxford in 1549. Huelin, op. cit.,
p. 33.

136. Thomas Norton translated this letter. Somerset, (1550).

137. Ibid., "The Epistle Dedicatory."

138. O. L. II, p. 481. 1 June 1550.

139. Ibid., pp. 482-483.

140. Martyr gave his opinion in a letter to Hooper of 4 November
1550. See Constantin Hopf, Martin Bucer and the English Reformation,
p. 132. where Hooper accedes to Bucer and Martyr. Cranmer appealed to
Martyr and Bucer. See Popcock Troubles, p. 130 for letter to Bucer of
2 December 1550. Also in Hopf, Martin Bucer, pp. 169-170.

141. <u>Common Places</u> (1583), Part five, p. 120. The argument depended on Patristic writings as well. cf. p. 119 and John H. Primus, <u>The Vestments Controversy</u> now updated in John Opie, "The Anglicizing of John Hooper," <u>A. R. G.</u> 59 (1968), 150-177.

142. L. J. Trinterud, <u>Elizabethan Puritanism</u>, p. 80.

143. Paul F. Bradshaw, <u>The Anglican Ordinal</u>, p. 38. C. W. Dugmore, "The First Ten Years, 1549-59," Arthur M. Ramsey, <u>English Prayer Book</u>, 1549-1662, pp. 6-30 who claims that Cranmer had little to do with <u>1552 Prayer Book</u>.

CHAPTER III

CRANMER AND ENGLISH REFORM (1549/53)

EUCHARISTIC DISCIPLINE: THE PRAYER BOOKS OF 1549/52.

Recent study of Thomas Cranmer's *Commonplace Books* in the British
Museum shows that his theological sympathies inclined toward Wittenberg,[1] thereby countering the views of Zwingli and Oecolampadius with
the Lutheran doctrine. In the years before 1546 Cranmer had been considerably indebted to Wittenberg, especially to Luther's 1527, *Das
diese wort Christi noch fest stehen widder die Schwermgeister*.[2] Cranmer was not Zwinglian in 1550.[3] Cranmer published in 1550 A *Defence
of the True and Catholic Doctrine of the Sacrament*, a work for whose
authorship Stephen Gardiner feigned surprise. "I will not reckon Peter
Martyr, because such as know him say he is not learned; nor this author,
because he doth but as it were translate Peter Martyr . . ."[4] In his
epistle to the 1549 *Tractatio* Martyr refers to Cranmer's impressive
patristic scholarship. Alan Beesley has recently shown that Martyr was
the source for Cranmer's second exhortation to the revised *Prayer Book*.
In my view Martyr's work on the *Ecclesiastical Laws* in the period from
11 November 1551 to 12 February 1552 helps one to understand his impact
on Cranmer as early as 1550.[5] Martyr served on both the sub-committee
and the full committee of Commissioners.[6]

Professor Dugmore describes Martyr's 1549 discourse as "an exceedingly able discourse," though not quite what Bucer maintained at Cambridge. It is difficult however to accept an endorsement of Smyth on
page 148 of Dugmore's *The Mass And The English Reformers*, "that Peter

Martyr embraced Zwinglianism (of the Tigurine type) between 1 June 1549 and 25 April 1551." To follow Dixon and Smyth is to ignore the commentary on I *Corinthians* in which during 1548 Martyr developed his views of a true presence. No one has explained Cranmer's conversion from the Lutheran real presence to a sacramental view akin to Martyr in 1550. Peter Brooks cautions that the truth lies somewhere between Cranmer's scholarly independence with respect to the Fathers and Scripture on the one hand and his debt to Act II of a Continental drama in which Oecolampadius and Peter Martyr played the leading role. Brooks urges research on Oecolampadius which he himself has done in 1974. I support Martyr's influence on Cranmer as will be seen in the following pages and reject any view of Martyr's conversion to "Tigurine Zwinglianism" between 1 June 1549 and 25 April 1551 on grounds that such a view ignores both Martyr's previous writings, i.e., the unpublished sermon of 1 December 1548 drawn up for Somerset, and Cranmer's testimony. Long before Martyr's first visit to Oxford he discussed views in 1547 identical to those held in 1553 and endorsed by Cranmer.

On 21 January 1550 a first reading was given in the House of Commons to a bill reviving statutes from Henry VIII's reign which called for a committee to revise and reform the ecclesiastical laws. This suggestion arose as early as the *Submission of the Clergy* presented to Henry VIII on 16 May 1532 and drawn up by 1535. Cranmer and other bishops opposed this earlier Commons bill, perhaps fearing it was a stalling action to shelve the entire project for several additional years.[7] By March of 1552 Martyr could report on the sub-committee's work to Bullinger. Prior to this letter to Bullinger, Martyr described

his Annotations for the *Prayer Book* in a letter to Bucer of 10 January

1551. In fact, a reading of Martyr's correspondence from January of

1550 to March of 1552 is crucial for an understanding of his relation

to Cranmer. In December of 1549 Martyr asked Bucer whether the hand

of the Lord always rested so heavily upon His people. Paul Fagius had

died on 13 November 1549 at Cambridge, a death which meant not only a

personal loss for Martyr but also a deep loss for Hebrew Literature.[8]

> As to my private matters, I will just say one or two words. The
> Oxonians go on tolerably quietly, at present; God grant they may
> continue to restrain themselves within the same bounds. Theolo-
> gical Disputations have not yet been resumed, agreeably to the
> recent Royal proclamations; indeed, I much fear, should they take
> place, that they will be promotive of tumult rather than of edi-
> fication – which is the necessary result, when men are searching
> for a handle of contention, not for the truth.[9]

On 10 January 1550 Martyr thanked Bucer for sending him the *Librum*

Sacrorum, a reference to the *Censura* on the revised Prayer Book.[10] That

the *Censura* are meant is clear from Martyr's reference to the transla-

tion of the proposed prayer book revision made for Martyr by Sir John

Cheke.[11] Martyr contacted Bullinger to endorse the *Consensus Tiguri-*

nus[12] whose agreement Martyr would have liked to have seen made per-

petual.

After a series of letters from 1544 Calvin and Bullinger signed a

statement on the Eucharist in 1549. In Article X Bullinger insisted

that the sacrament was efficacious only as far as faith in the promise

prevails. Since this *Consensus Tigurinus* was not published until 1551,

it is important to note Martyr's comments on the agreement in 1550.

Calvin and Bullinger had drawn up the original agreement in November

1548 and discussed it in May of 1549 with Farel.[13] In March 1550

Martyr encouraged the Duke of Somerset in prison and Martin Bucer who

suffered from fevers. That Martyr and Bucer agreed on the nature of

the sacrament can be seen from Bucer's letter to Theobald Niger of 15

April 1550.[14] Those who had listened to Bucer's explanation approved

of Martyr's observations on the Eucharist. Bucer urged Niger to sup-

port Martyr.

> You know the piety and erudition of that excellent man; therefore,
> as far as you have any influence over those who take offence at
> his Disputations, reconcile them by the Preface to those Disputa-
> tions. When we cannot obtain all that we wish, it is our duty,
> as far as lies in our power, to bend to the glory of God those
> things which are given us, especially when they come from men so
> pious and learned.

On the other hand one wonders from Bucer's letter to Brenz whether

Bucer did agree with Martyr. How far could Bucer bend Martyr's plain

speech without distortion?

On 1 June 1550 Martyr wrote to Bullinger from Oxford that the

worldly prudence of some would make as few alterations as possible in

the legal discipline of the church, "for feeling as they do, and

thinking as civilians, they consider that any great changes would be

dangerous to the state." Martyr went on to say that when corruptions

and superstitions have grown everywhere, a proper reform cannot be

effected, "unless those things which have been perverted to abuse, be

restored to their true origin, their most pure sources, and unadulter-

ated beginnings."[15]

On the same day Martyr also wrote to Rudolf Gualter in Zurich

about the great pertinacity of his opponents in Oxford. Preachers
were plenteous in London, though rare in the rest of the kingdom. The
sheep were defrauded of their proper nourishment of the divine word.
Change of religion would be of small avail unless the people continued
to be taught. Then Martyr wrote a dramatic passage of hope for renewal
in England.

> We have, thank God, a king of such a disposition, that nothing can
> increase his inclination and love for religion: and very many too
> of the nobles of the kingdom are very favourably disposed. The
> people in most places are still opposing us, owing to their want
> of instruction, and they are secretly confirmed in their errors
> by the subtle artifices of the papists. The tender age, too, of
> our Josiah is no slight hinderance to the business; but we have
> placed our hope in God, and are daily looking for no less progress
> than was made at first: but when we compare the church of Christ
> at its earliest infancy with that which is now reformed, we can-
> not but sigh most deeply, and weep with the Jews on their return
> from captivity, that the appearance of this second temple is not
> to be compared with the glory of the first, unless perhaps Christ
> may glorify it sooner than we expect with the presence of his
> second coming. Do you, I pray you, aid the work of the Lord by
> your prayers, and continue to love me. Farewell in the Lord.[16]

A month later Martyr expanded on the need for pastoral preaching
to the people. He wrote to a friend that a penury of the Word of God
ought not keep him from strengthening himself by the words of God — to
rule his family in the spirit as well as in the flesh.[17] Nicholas
Pocock concludes from the phraseology in this letter that Martyr explains here exactly articles nine and twenty-seven of the Forty-Two
Articles.[18] On the vestment controversy Martyr would have ecclesiastical attire taken away when possible so that the affairs of the Church
might be conducted "with the utmost simplicity." Ecclesiastics if
divorced from their robes and cap would have little left to commend

themselves as ministers of the Church.[19]   In this context Martyr cited

Augustine's *On The Spirit and The Letter* to show that good works fol-

low justification but cannot precede it.   After a lengthy discussion

of Augustine's other writings, Martyr concluded: "If, however, they

shall say that Augustin opposes himself; let him be left for reconcil-

iation to those who prop themselves up by the Fathers, leaving the

Scriptures."[20]

A week later on 6 September 1550 Martyr again commented on public

disputations, expressing in this letter to Bucer his concern that

judges should be appointed to settle the outcome of such debate. Fresh

contentions might in this way be foiled and scurrilous accounts in

print would be avoided.[21]   In a subsequent reply of 10 September Martyr

rejoiced that at Cambridge the disputations were successful even with-

out the presence of judges.   To Martyr's surprise and joy the Vice-

Chancellor of Oxford forbade theological disputations at convocation.[22]

Two additional letters from Martyr to Bucer in 1550 provide opin-

ions on theological questions.[23] In a letter of 11 November Martyr men-

tioned Laski's desire to draw up a confession on the sacramentarian

question in such a way that Ochino, Laski, Martyr and Bucer might agree

to it.   Martyr went on to say: "I answered, that I did not disapprove

his design; and I advised him to talk the matter over with you.   I took

this course, because I feel assured that, if both of you should sub-

scribe to the same opinion, it would be easy for me also to accede to

it."[24]   A treatise recently recovered by the Lambeth Palace Library and

ascribed to Laski may be the final result of this conversation.[25]   If so, it demonstrates the desire of these learned strangers to achieve

unanimity on a crucial issue for church life which would also have its

impact on Cranmer's liturgical reforms. One problem with Laski's

authorship of this document dated 14 May 1557 is that on 14 May 1557

Beza and Farel signed the Göppingen confession. Perhaps their confess-

ion of 1557 follows or endorses a draft by Laski.

An additional example of Martyr's influence is in a letter of 10

January 1551 on the *Censura* prepared by Bucer for Cranmer's revision

of the *Book of Common Prayer*. Since Martyr's own annotations have not

survived, this letter to Bucer is invaluable.

> At this time nothing could happen more desirable or agreeable to
> me than that I should see your "*Censura*" on the Book of Sacred
> (Offices). I therefore return you infinite thanks for your con-
> descension in sending it to me. A request had already been made
> to me, that I also would myself state my opinion respecting it.
> And when, by reason of my want of knowledge of the (English)
> language, the version of Mr. Cheke was given me for perusal, I
> noted those things which appeared to me worthy of correction, as
> far as I was able to collect them from that (translation).
>
> But because, in the version put into my hands, several things were
> wanting, on that account I passed over many things, concerning
> which I have said nothing in my Annotations. Afterwards, when I
> discovered, from your Writing that these things were contained in
> that Book, I regretted that, two or three days before, I had al-
> ready carried my *Censura* to the Most Reverend (the Archbishop),
> who had pressed me for it.
>
> However, I at length applied this remedy: I collected the heads
> of those matters which, from your Writing I perceived to be defi-
> cient in my (copy of the) book: and, since the same thing which
> you disapproved appeared also to myself not to be borne, I reduced
> them into short articles; and I stated to the Most Reverend (who
> already knew that you had written on these matters to the Lord
> Bishop of Ely) that I agreed with you that a change should be made
> in all those particulars which I laid before him as noted in those
> articles.
>
> However, in my former Annotations, almost all those things which

had offended you had been annotated by me. I would now send you
a copy, but I have it not so written out that you would be able
to read it. I have only wondered how you could have omitted to
disapprovethe order which is given in the Communion of the Sick,
if it shall happen to be on the Sunday on which the Lord's Supper
is celebrated, that the Minister should in that case, take with
him a portion of the elements, and so should administer the Communion in the house of the sick person. In which matter, it
offends me that they do not there repeat those things which particularly belong to the Lord's Supper; since I agree with you in
thinking that the words of the Supper belong more to men than to
bread or to wine. I stated, that it clearly seems to me, that
all things that are necessarily required for the Lord's Supper,
should be both said and done in the presence of the sick person,
of those who communicate with him. And it is, indeed, wonderful
that they should scruple to say those words in the presence of a
sick person, which might be very profitable to him, - though they
choose to repeat them, uselessly, whenever it happens during
communion in the Church that wine is wanting in the cup, although
the per(sons) who take the Sacraments, have already heard them.

These are the points which I have considered as of some m(oment);
and I do not fully understand why you have omitted them. But in
all those matters which you have judged to need amendment, I(am
of) your opinion. And I thank God who has given us an opportunity
of laying before the Bishops our suggestions on all these things.
It has now been decided in their conference, as the Most Reverend
informs me, that many things shall be changed: but what corrections
they have decided upon, he did not explain to me, nor was I so bold
as to ask him. But I have been not a little gratified by what Mr.
Cheke has told me; he says, that if they will not make the changes
which have been considered necessary, the King himself will do this;
and that, when Parliament meets, he will interpose his Royal authority.[26]

This comment, as McLelland notes, refers to the words of consecration.[27]

The efficacy of the Lord's Supper is another question which Martyr took

up in a letter to Bullinger of 14 June 1552. Meanwhile Hooper once

again came to his attention,[28] for by February of 1551 Martyr grieved

over Hooper more than words could express.[29] Martyr also had been to

Lambeth with Cranmer to consult on the Prayer Book revision. Martyr's

lack of English did not permit him to comment on the changes, other

than that the Bishops had not yet entirely adopted their suggestions.
Cheke was the only person who favoured simplicity!30

On 25 November 1551 in the private residence of Secretary William
Cecil members of a conference on the Eucharist debated the term bodily
presence. Sir John Cheke and Edmund Grindal were present on the protestant side when Cheke questioned whether the words of the Supper were
to be understood in a grammatical or literal sense. Sir Anthony Cooke
also listened to this first session. A second conference met on 3
December 1551 in Sir Richard Morison's quarters with the same question
advanced by Cheke.31 That prominent persons met privately to debate
this issue between the two editions of the *Prayer Book* demonstrates
the protestant dissatisfaction with catholics that the 1549 version
taught real presence. This explains in any event Martyr's comment on
Cheke.

Recent studies of liturgical transition from 1549 to 1552 overlook
several documents which appeared while Cranmer contemplated a clear
denial of real presence in the second *Prayer Book* of 1552. Thomas
Lancaster's *The ryght and trew Understandynge of the Supper of The Lord
and the Use thereof* said that the minister of the Supper must be
"called of a Christian congregation compelled through the Holy Ghost to
come into the Lord's vineyard . . . without fault . . . both in his
life and learning." The treatise is completely Reformed and written in
1549!32

There seems to be no reason to adopt C. W. Dugmore's suggestion
that Martyr altered his views between the 1549 Oxford dispute and the

year 1551.[33] Dugmore goes on to state that Bucer's subsequent defection to Martyr's 'Tigurine' view weakened Cranmer's hand. That it intensified Cranmer's struggle with Gardiner is true but one has difficulty with this thesis advanced by Smyth that Laski is responsible for
a continental protestant replacement of a patristic realism in the
Supper held by Cranmer prior to 1549.[34] Pocock goes on to discuss
Ochino's 1549 A *Tragoedie or Dialoge of the unjuste usurped Primacie
of the Bishop of Rome.* The British Museum copy has a dedication to
the Protector Somerset. The ninth dialogue between the young King
Edward and his uncle declares the method of extirpating Anti-Christ
from England, that "the worde of God ought to be sufficient. . ."[35]
Parliament enacted a provision to destroy all old service books and
passed an act for a new *Ordinal* to take effect on 1 April 1550.

Historians have overlooked, concludes Pocock, the appearance of
five different editions of Tyndale's *New Testament* with Calvinistic
notes in 1550 and its new revision called Jugges just before release
of the 1552 *Prayer Book.*[36] The notes were influenced by the *Consensus
Tigurinus* (1549) and the *Genevan Consensus* of 1552. The note on
Matthew VIII reads: "The corporal presence of Christ is nothing necessary and needful unto us. For it is His word only received through
faith, that healeth us."[37]

It is necessary to look at Martyr's works, Cranmer's support of
Martyr and the deliberate progress from denial of transubstantiation in
the 1549 *Prayer Book* to the affirmation of spiritual reception in that
of 1552. Cranmer invited these foreign theologians because he needed

their help to strengthen his hand in Eucharistic reform, not weaken it.
Peter Brook's brief work then is of enormous significance for document-
ing Cranmer's protestant views expressed in the two Prayer Books. Cranmer and Martyr denied real presence following Ratramn and asserted the
necessity of faith. That was another excuse for Gardiner to banish
the stranger and burn Cranmer for holding to the opinions of foreign
divines like Martyr.

Van den Brink's comments on Ratramn's Eucharistic influence in
England call for a brief evaluation. Van den Brink misquotes Foxe that
a rare treatise by Thomas Lovell is "a compilation of the works of
Peter Martyr made by Ridley."[38] John Foxe cites from A *Dialogue Be-*
tween Custom and veritie /S.T.C. 16860 only in Huntington Library,
California/ in his *Actes and Monuments* (1583) that it seems to be a
compilation of Martyr's tracts and other authors. That Foxe included
Martyr here as well as a description of his 1549 Oxford Eucharistic
debate is important. It means that generations of Englishmen read an
account of Martyr's agreement with Ridley and Cranmer. Foxe introduced
the *Dialogue* to demonstrate that the English Church under Edward VI and
Cranmer intended to replace in stages the catholic view of transubstantiation with a transitional position on real presence and a firm statement on spiritual feeding or true presence. It all bore the stamp of
Cranmer's liturgical genius upon it. It seems best to cite Foxe:

> In the meane season because great controversie hath bene and is
> yet amongst the learned, and much effusion of Christen bloud about
> the wordes and meanyng of the Sacrament: to the intent that the
> ueritie thereof more openly may be explained, and all doubtfull
> scruples discussed, it shall not be out of place to adioyne to the

former discources of Peter Martyr, and of Doctour Ridley aboue
mentioned, an other certayne learned treatise in fourme of a
Dialogue, as appertaynyng to the same argument, compiled (as it
seemeth) out of the tractations of Peter Martyr and other
Authours, by a certayne learned and reuerend person of this
Realme who under the persones of *Custome* and *Veritie*, manifestly
layeth before our eyes, and teacheth all men not to measure
Religion by Custome, but to try Custome by truth and the word
of God, for els custome may soone deceyue, but the worde of God
abydeth for euer.[39]

The most recent account of the sources used for the 1549 *Prayer
Book* and its revision in 1552 denies the probability that Cranmer

plotted either a theological or liturgical revolution. Nor does Horton

Davies find that evidence convincing which suggests that Cranmer delib-

erately used equivocal language. Davies suggests a fourth possibility

open to Cranmer apart from Catholic, Lutheran and Zwinglian alterna-

tives. Virtualism is a term which Davies prefers but does not define.

"This was the view of the Eucharist affirmed by Martin Bucer, Henry

Bullinger, Peter Martyr, and John Calvin."[40] In distinguishing Cran-

mer's views from those of Calvin, Davies finds that the 'black rubric'

adopted in the 1552 *Prayer Book* at the last minute under John Knox's

insistence and royal request cannot therefore be used as an example of

Zwinglianism.[41] Davies does not describe Martyr's role in this matter

nor his contributions to the 1552 *Prayer Book*.[42] Alan Beesley's note

on the *Adhortatio ad Coenam Domini Mysticam* shows that Martyr prepared

this exhortation while staying with Cranmer at Lambeth from November

1551 to April 1552. Beesley finds that the *Adhortatio* first appeared

in the 1583 London *Loci Communes* when in fact it was published in 1581

at Basle.[43]

Lorimer published a letter of Cranmer dated 7 October 1552 in which Cranmer addressed the Privy Council on the offense which kneeling to receive the sacrament caused some communicants.

> And whereas I understand farther, by your Lordships' letters, that some be offended with kneeling at the time of receiving of the Sacrament, and would that I, calling to me the Bishop of London, and some other learned men, as Mr. Peter Martyr or such like, should with them expend and weight the said prescription of kneeling, or to be left out of the Book, I shall accomplish the King's Majesty his commandment, albeit I trust that we with just balance weighed this at the making of the Book . . . .[44]

It is clear that Ridley and Martyr were called in for consultation between 11 October and the 20th to consider Knox's proposal. Between 20 October and the 27th objections were also made to article thirty-eight of the Thirty-Nine Articles. The document published by Lorimer as the Memorial to the Privy Council quite possibly represented Martyr's sentiments and may mean that Martyr and Ridley were co-authors with Cranmer of the 1552 *Prayer Book*.[45]

At this stage in his Oxford career Martyr had not ceased to hope for parliamentary reform aided by Edward VI and Archbishop Cranmer. His numerous contacts both in London and on the Continent, his conversations with Cranmer at Lambeth Palace and contact with his colleague Bucer at Cambridge fortified that hope. Many of his statements demonstrate the tenacity with which Martyr prayed, hoped and labored for reform. Though the minority of the monarch and the obstinacy of some bishops worried him, the patience of Job and the example of Christ sustained him.[46]

A letter to Bullinger in January 1551 again took up the nature of

Martyr's work at Oxford.[47] His commentary on I *Corinthians* had been

given to Byrchman the bookseller who wished to publish it in Zurich.

Martyr would like Bullinger to see to its correction before printing.

Even though Martyr did not think that he had written anything valuable,

an (importunate) clamour for his commentary in the kingdom might pro-

duce some fruit.[48] Then Bucer's death on the last day of February

depressed him. Martyr sent a letter for the College of St. Thomas at

Strasbourg in which he expressed a vast loneliness.

> O wretched me! as long as Bucer was in England, or while we
> lived together in Germany, I never felt myself to be in exile.
> But now I plainly seem to myself be alone and desolate.[49]

The learned stranger and scholar of Christ was now a reformer in

exile. During the eleven days Bucer was at Oxford in the summer of

1550 their thoughts were of the silver church (Strasbourg-Argentia);

now Bucer has outstripped Martyr and betaken himself to the golden

church of heaven.[50] In his letter to the College of St. Thomas at

Strasbourg, Martyr eulogized his lost companion. "We are to be account-

ed miserable, or rather unhappy, who are yet tossed in the storms of

calamities."[51] John Warner the Regius Professor of Medicine at Oxford

answered Martyr's inquiry about Bucer's terminal illness. His detailed

response indicates Martyr's interest in medical science. Warner de-

scribed various types of fevers and their remedies, warning Martyr in

a postscript that wine should not be diluted without first boiling the

'crass' water available in Oxford.[52]

In April of 1551 Martyr solicited Bullinger's prayers in the face

of extreme opposition at Oxford.[53] By 6 August he could rejoice over

good health, even encouraged by Hooper's episcopal labors. "God
grant that we may at length have many other bishops who shall bestow
the like diligence and labour on the church!"[54] An interesting reference is to the circle of Zurich youth studying in Oxford.[55] Huelin has
an excellent account of these students among whom were John ab Ulmis
and John Rodolph Stumphius. In view of his caution about an uncritical
use of ab Ulmis' letters,[56] Smyth's use of correspondence between ab
Ulmis and Julius Terrentianus to show the Zwinglian or 'Suvermerian'
nature of Martyr's Eucharistic lectures is incredible.[57] The "shadow
of Zwinglianism" is not adequate to describe Martyr's lectures at
Oxford.[58] In Martyr's *Book of Prayers* used in lecturing at Strasbourg
after 1553 one finds a prayer written not on the *Psalms*, but rather
against superstitious worshippers of bread in the Eucharist. Certainly
this prayer summarized his feelings already expressed in the letters of
1549-1551. McLelland omitted the pejorative references in his version
printed in *The Visible Words of God*.

> And as nowe at length I humbly beseech thee (O heavenly father)
> by liganing the mindes and heartes of thy Christian people wyth
> the spirit of thy sonne Christ Jesus: who (laying Idolles and
> superstitions apart) may returne to the pure and uncorrupt wor-
> shipping, honouring, and calling upon thee onely: nyther suffer
> the honor due to thee alone to be wickedly and devilithly attri-
> buted unto bread, wine, pictures, Images, and bones of dead
> persons: thy holye name hath alreadie beene to long slaundered,
> to long hath the puritie of thy blessed Gospell beene polluted:
> men have ynough & to much abused the institution of thy sonnes
> supper, by converting the same to most fithie Idolatry. Mittigate
> at length these outrages of mad brayned men, that miserably over-
> throwe themselves hedlong, as they may no more go a whoring lewdly
> and voyde of shame, upon every hill, under every tree, in all by
> wayes, streetes, Churches, and Chappels, with bread and wine under
> the name of thy deere sonnes Sacrament, and let them not defile
> the true honoring of thee after this wicked and blasphemaus maner.

Unlesse thou (O most good and mercifull God) doest with thy
puyssant hand, take away & utterly subvert this worshipping of
bread, the saluation of mankind and reedifying of thy sacred
Church can never be looked for.   Helpe (O God) succour thy
faythfull people whome thou hast redeemed with the blood of thy
deere sonne.   And thou, O Christ Jesu (who art a true and everlasting God) establishe this worke which is begunne by thee,
and bring it to the desired ende: or if the fore bee without
hope of recouery, and that thy truth maye not any more take place
commonly and openly in thy sacred Church, then come and exercise
judgment with all speede, and drive awaye (for the glorie of thy
name) so shamefull a reproche from thy holy supper, which thou
of thy incredible mercee and singuler goodnesse hast instituted,
who lyuest and reignest with the father, and the holy ghost ever-
more world without ende.   Amen.[59]

ECCLESIASTICAL LAWS

Peter Martyr's work on the *Ecclesiastical Laws* should be seen in

the context of the above prayer.   His purpose in debating the Eucharist

was not to establish a Zwinglian shadow over the Lord's Supper, but to

simplify the church's understanding of the Eucharist.   Martyr meant by

this to eliminate the Roman and Lutheran "worshipping of bread."   Unless

this could be done, "the salvation of mankind and reedifying of thy

sacred Church can never be looked for."   The Oxford lectures, disputes

and tractates were necessary therefore as important prolegomena to the

creation of a church purified by Word and Spirit.   Martyr's work during

the remainder of 1551 until the death of Edward VI and his own return

to Strasbourg in 1553 must be viewed as the beginning of reform in

England but certainly not its completion.   The extraordinary attention

paid to the Eucharist in this or any period of Martyr's career-in-exile

elucidates his primary pastoral concern for a faith made pure through

preaching and teaching of the Word of God.

During 1551 Martyr wrote to a variety of persons on the continent

of Europe. In February to Bucer he had expected little fruit from
the reform of order in the parishes. Only Cheke favoured simplicity,
though if Cranmer were to accomplish the task himself purity of cere-
mony would easily be achieved.[60] Three letters of 8 March 1551 were
written to Rosenblatt, Hubert and the Governors of the College of St.
Thomas in Strasbourg.[61] Martyr told the Governors about the great loss
that Bucer was to the Church, the school and their college.[62] On 25
April Martyr wrote to Bullinger and Gualter in Zurich. Martyr felt
indebted to Gualter for seeing his Commentary in I *Corinthians* through
the press. Martyr was astonished at the care with which his manuscript
copy was being edited.[63]

Martyr wrote to help a student gain a stipend in March of 1552.
This letter comments on the alacrity with which the young outstrip
their elders in doctrine. Then came a comment on his wife Catherine.
Martyr did not care to write much about his affairs since his most holy
wife of remarkable piety in Christ was deadly ill. Thoughts about the
death of his dear wife though she would sleep in the Lord left Martyr
deeply oppressed. Not even that earthly loss could shake his trust in
Christ.[64]

In four letters to Bullinger prior to October 1552 Martyr outlined
his concern for simplicity and purity of faith and worship. On 14 June
1552 Martyr told Bullinger that since the sacrament was in dispute, the
Forty-Two Articles could not be passed. Such efficacy of faith was
central to Martyr's concern for a valid partaking of the Eucharist.

> For unless faith is present, they are always received unworthily:
> but if they who came to the Sacraments are endued with faith,
> they have already received through faith the grace which is

proclaimed to us in the Sacraments, and then the reception and use of the Sacraments is the seal and obsignation of the promise already apprehended. And as the external words of God avail to the quickening and exciting our faith which is often torpid, and in a manner laid asleep in us, this same thing also the Sacraments can effect by the power of the Holy Spirit, and their use is of no little benefit to confirm our minds, otherwise weak, concerning the promises and the grace of God. But in the case of children, when they are baptized, since on account of their age they cannot have that assent to the divine promises which is faith, in them the Sacrament effects this, that pardon of original sin, reconciliation with God, and the grace of the Holy Spirit, bestowed on them through Christ, is sealed in them, and that those belonging already to the Church are also visibly implanted in it. Although of those that are baptized, whether children or adults, it is not to be denied that much advantage and profit comes to them from the invocation of the Father, the Son, and the Holy Spirit, which takes place over them. For God always hears the faithful prayers of His Church. We were anxious that these things should be determined and established by authority concerning the Sacraments, that their use might at length be restored to a state of purity and simplicity. But it was opposed; and many are of opinion, and those otherwise not unlearned, nor evil, that grace is conferred, as they say, by virtue of the Sacraments. Nor are they willing to grant that little children are justified or regenerated previous to baptism. But when we come to their reasons, there are none which do not most readily admit of solution. Nevertheless no little displeasure is excited against us on this account, namely, that we altogether dissent from Augustine. And if our doctrine was approved by public authority, then, say they, Augustine would manifestly be condemned. Why need I add more? Men cannot be torn away from the merit of works; and, what is more to be lamented, they are unwilling to confess it; and there are always innumerable impediments, and they mutually succeed one another, so as to retard day after day the restoration of the worship of God. A work of so great labor is it to bring back into the Church pure truth. But we must not, on that account, despair; nay, we are not a little confident, that that may be accomplished at some other time which has now failed of success.[65]

Parliament had been postponed even though Martyr hoped that many things would be established by the autumn session.[66] By March of 1552 Martyr stayed with Cranmer at Lambeth during the sessions of Parliament, anxious to complete his commentary on *Romans*.[67] This letter of 8 March 1552 shows the importance Martyr gave to his work on the ecclesiastical laws.

> I came to London some time since, on account of the holding of the assembly commonly called a parliament. For the king's majesty has ordained, that, as the gospel is received in his kingdom, and the bishop of Rome is driven out, the church of England shall be no longer ruled by pontifical decrees, and decretals, Sixtine, Clementine, and other popish ordinances of the same kind: for the administration of these laws has for the most part prevailed up to this time in the ecclesiastical court, under the tacit authority of the pope; though many other laws were enacted by which the external polity of the church might be regulated. To the intent therefore, that so powerful a kingdom should not be deprived of this, as it appears, necessary advantage, the king has appointed two and thirty persons to frame ecclesiastical laws for this realm, namely, eight bishops, eight divines, eight civil lawyers, and eight common lawyers; the majority of whom are equally distinguished by profound erudition and solid piety; and we also, I mean Hooper, a Lasco, and myself, are enrolled among them. May God therefore grant that such laws may be enacted by us, as by their godliness and holy justice may banish the Tridentine canons from the churches of Christ! But as I am conscious we have need of the prayers of yourself and your colleagues in furtherance of so great an undertaking, I implore them with all the sincerity and earnestness in my power. For it is not only necessary to entreat God that pious and holy laws may be framed, but that they may obtain the sanction of parliament, or else they will not possess any force or authority whatsoever.[68]

Several articles of religion appeared in 1552 known as the *Forty Five Articles*. Article XI on justification refers to the homily on justification, an apparent link with Cranmer as the author. Charles Hardwick thinks on the basis of test articles presented to Hooper in 1548 that the *Forty-Two Articles* of 1553 originate in that year with Cranmer. Hooper's letter of 27 February 1549 to Bullinger is decisive for such an early dating. The Bishops seem to have had these articles from the summer of 1551 until the spring of 1552. Sir John Cheke and Sir William Cecil both examined the Articles as is clear from Cranmer's letter to Cecil of 19 September 1552. Six royal chaplains among whom were Grindal and Knox subscribed to forty-five articles in Latin.

From 20 November to the 24th a weary Cranmer made final corrections

for the council. Richard Grafton published the *Forty-Two Articles* in

May of 1553.

Article XVII on Predestination and Election is similar in the

Forty-Five Articles, Grafton's English version, the *Forty-Two Articles*

of 1553 and its 1571 English version. Martyr lectured on predestina-

tion while teaching *Romans* at Oxford. It may well be that during 1552

at Lambeth Martyr and Cranmer discussed article XVII. The wording is

given below so that the reader can compare some similarities. The

phrase *in Christo* is added to the *Forty-Five Articles* approved by

Grindal and Knox. That this phrase is in Martyr almost convinces one

that Cranmer followed Martyr in composing this article. Calvin does

not use similar language in his *Institutes* and in III.21.5 includes

reprobation on which the English articles and Martyr's definition are

silent.

XVII (1553)

Praedestinatio ad uitam, est
aeternum Dei propositum, quo
ante iacta mundi fundamenta,
suo consilio, nobis quidem
occulto, constanter decreuit,
eos quos in Christoelegit ex
hominum genere, a maledicto et
exitio liberare, atque ut uasa
in honorem efficta, per Christum ad aeternam salutem addu-
cere: Vnde qui tam praeclaro
Dei beneficio sunt donati, illi
spiritu eius opportuno tempore operante, secundum propositum eius uocantur:

Martyr, *Romans* (1558)

Dico igiter, praedestinationem
esse sapientissimum propositum
Dei, quo ante omnem aeternitatem
decreuit constanter, eos, quos
dilexit in Christo, uocare ad
adoptionem filiorum, ad iustificationem ex fide, & tandem ad
gloriam per opera bona, quo
conformos fiant imagini filii
Dei, utque in illis declaretur
gloria, & misericordia
Creatoris.

XVII (1553)

Predestination to lyfe, is the euerlasting purpose of God, whereby (before the foundations of the world were layd) he hath constantly decreed by his councell secrete to vs, to deliuer from curse and damnation, those whom he hath chosen in Christe out of mankynde, and to bryng them by Christe to euerlastyng saluation, as vessels made to honour. Wherefore they which be indued with so excellent a benefite of God, be called accordyng to Gods purpose by his spirite workyng in due season: they through grace obey the callyng: they be frely, thei be made sonnes by adoptione, thei bee made like the image of Goddes onely begotten sonne Jesu Christe, thei walke religiouslie in goode woorkes, and at length by Goddes mercie, thei atteine to euerlasting felicitie.

Martyr's wording looks like one of the sources for Cranmer's final product. The entire section *De Praedestinatione* is on pages 404-441 of Martyr's Latin *editio princeps* at the end of *Romans* IX. The Elizabethan *Thirty-Nine Articles* retain Cranmer's wording. It is difficult to call article XVII "as Calvinistic in meaning and intent." One should instead view this as another example of Martyr's influence on Cranmer.[69] If Pocock is correct, Martyr also influenced articles nine and twenty seven.

By June after the 1552 *Prayer Book* had been passed in which Martyr aided Cranmer, Martyr turned to the question of sacramental efficacy.[70]

That matter which was desired by all good men, and which the King's Majesty had not a little at heart, could not be accomplished; wherefore as yet things remain to a great extent as they were before, except that The Book of Order of Ecclesiastical Rites and the Administration of the Sacraments is reformed, for all things are removed from it which could nourish superstition. But the chief reason why other things which were purposed were not effected, was that the subject of the sacraments stood in the way; not truly as regards transubstantiation, or the real presence (so to speak) either in the bread or in the wine, since, thanks be to God, concerning these things there seems to be now no controversy as it regards those who profess the Gospel; but whether grace is conferred by virtue of the sacraments is a doubtful point to many.[71]

In October Martyr notified Bullinger of his work on the *Ecclesiastical Laws* which he and Cranmer hoped to see approved.[72] Martyr's work on the *Ecclesiastical Laws, The Book of Common Prayer* and the *Forty-Two Articles* has been somewhat neglected. For one thing, since he did not know English, the final wording of the 1552 *Prayer Book* and *Forty-Two Articles* can not be Martyr's. Cranmer deservedly claims praise for these liturgical disciplinary and doctrinal reforms. When the *Ecclesiastical Laws* are more carefully examined, Martyr's direct influence is apparent.[73]

Professor Spaulding furnished a translation of the section *De Prescriptionibus* from folio pages 209-211 of the manuscript. It reads in part with Martyr's marginal notation in brackets:

> A prescription is said to cease when the prescription does not have place because of some privilege of a person involved or because of a condition of the involvement itself. An impediment can seem similar to this cessation when a prescription as it were intervenes as when one is not permitted to exercise judgements because of some public movement and one is not permitted to seek one's own right, as in time of war /or when justice is not rendered in a situation because of defect of the judge or of the defendent (case?) and in time of pestilence/.[74]

Spaulding has provided a plausible translation of Martyr's addition on folio 210 of Harleian MS. 426.65.C. Martyr wished to safeguard the interference in a bishop's diocese when it ran contrary to common law or when one prescribed acts in bad faith (chapter seven). Those subject to higher visitation by bishops seeking carnal things (chapter five) must have the claim proved (chapter six) and not be harrassed by clerics of bad faith (chapter seven). These were moral safeguards

against legal claims by heretical bishops. Martyr's concern about

common law and his wish to add a moral basis to the *Ecclesia Anglicana*

stands out in this comment.

Though never passed into law and thus fulfilling Martyr's fears,

the *Ecclesiastical Laws* do aid one to see the impact Martyr was having

on England at this time.

> Leaders of the Church of England itself had been preparing a
> discipline as the basis for Jerusalem in England before those
> exiles ever saw Geneva. The failure of their discipline to be
> accomplished within the context of episcopal government in
> England created tinder in which later Puritan fire could be
> ignited.[75]

When Edward VI died on 16 July 1553 it seemed as though all

Martyr's work had been in vain. His wife had recently died and he

was racked with pain from a fever. Julius Terentianus described the

scene to ab Ulmis where Martyr was forbidden to leave his house, per-

haps under guard for six weeks for his own protection. Julius peti-

tioned the Queen in London to permit Martyr to leave England. On 5

September Cranmer announced a public dispute in which together with

Peter Martyr and others of his choosing he would prove that the doc-

trine and religious order established by Edward VI was agreeable to

the Word of God, sound and the same with that of the primitive church

"approved by the authority of the ancient fathers."[76]

That Cranmer was serious about the changes in the 1552 *Prayer*

Book can be seen from the experience of the aged Cuthbert Tunstal,

Bishop of Durham. On 20 May 1551 Northumberland had Tunstal placed

under house arrest and on 20 December 1551 committed to the tower.
Even though the rich see of Durham was the prize rather than his
person, Tunstal chose to finish his great treatise on the Eucharist.
That Tunstal in this published work of 1554 thought it hopeless to
maintain belief in the real presence indicates the intended permanence
of Cranmer's 1552 words "Take and eat this in remembrance . . . ."[77]
It seems clear that with Martyr's help, Cranmer discarded the real
presence doctrine, which his earlier Lutheran contacts had urged him
to maintain, in favour of the Reformed doctrine of necessary prior
faith for a valid communion at the Eucharist. Only Edward's death
kept that reform from its intended permanence.

While Martyr and Cranmer prepared for the 1553 disputations, Cranmer was cited for treason on 13 September. Cranmer advised Martyr to
leave the country illegally if he did not quickly obtain leave from
the Council, for Cranmer was certain that Martyr would be in great
danger in England. Cranmer prepared a *Declaration Concerning the Mass*
to refute rumours that he was responsible for mass being said in
Canterbury Cathedral. Martyr may have assisted Cranmer with the
Declaration though he was not in London at the time. Copies of this
treatise were scattered through the city, an action which led to
charges of sedition against Cranmer.[78] As the two friends dine together for the last time Cranmer told Martyr that he should never again
see him.

Martyr left England in secrecy, arriving back in Strasbourg on 30
October 1553. He told John Calvin that it was like being plucked out

of the Lion's mouth.[79] This expression is supported by Terentianus'

report to John ab Ulmis on 20 November 1553. Martyr was placed under

house arrest in Oxford for six weeks soon after Bradford was thrown

in the tower on 14 August 1553. Terentianus and William Whitingham

went to London to petition the Queen and council for Martyr's leave

from England. Peter Martyr was at last allowed to come to London

where Cranmer told him that he had offered to give all his property

as a security for master Peter.

> About five days after the archbishop of Canterbury had been
> committed to the Tower, a safe conduct, and a most honorable one,
> was given by the queen to master Peter; who, therefore, on the
> public guarantee, at the persuasion of his other friends, and
> also bearing in mind the words of the Archbishop, commits himself
> to sea, spreading a report that he was going to Hamburg, when in
> reality he was proceeding to Antwerp. This he did, to escape the
> snares of the papists in the dominions of the emperor. . . .[80]

Referring to Bishops in prison Martyr described his sojourn in

England as a time when,

> In that nation were laid the foundations of the Gospel and of
> a noble Church, and with a few years labor the holy building was
> in good forewardness, and better and better was every day hoped
> for. But now finally unless God put to his helping hand, it is
> like to come to pass, that not so much as a step of godleness in
> outward profession will be left.[81]

In four years' time Martyr would write a remarkable letter to Elizabeth.

Then too, though no longer in England in person, by his writings Pietro

Martire Vermigli would help ignite the Puritan fire in the tinder of

episcopal England and the wilderness of New England.[82] Peter Martyr

must be included together with the Geneva Bible, the Marian Exiles and

the Cambridge Puitans in assessing steps towards "godliness in outward

profession" in sixteenth century England.

When Cranmer replied to Smith's work on the Eucharist he indicated

the importance of Peter Martyr for his own development.

> After this he falleth to railing, lying, and slandering of M.
> Peter Martyr, a man of that excellent learning and godly living,
> that he passeth D. Smith as far as the sun in his clear light
> passeth the moon being in the eclipse.
> "Peter Martyr," saith he, "at his first coming to Oxford, when
> he was but a Lutherian in this matter, taught as D. Smith now
> doth. But when he came once to the court, and saw that doctrine
> misliked them that might do him hurt in his living, he anon after
> turned his tippet, and sang another song."
> "Of M. Peter Martyr's opinion and judgment in this matter, no
> man can better testify than I; forasmuch as he lodged within my
> house long before he came to Oxford, and I had with him many
> conferences in that matter, and know that he was then of the same
> mind that he is now, and as he defended after openly in Oxford,
> and hath written in his book. And if D. Smith understood him
> otherwise in his lectures at the beginning, it was for lack of
> knowledge, for that then D. Smith understood not the matter, nor
> yet doth not, as it appeareth by this foolish and unlearned book,
> which he hath now set out: no more than he understood my book
> of the catechism, and therefore reporteth untruly of me, that I
> in that book did set forth the real presence of Christ's body in
> the sacrament. Unto which false report I have answered in my
> fourth book, the eighth chapter.[83]

While at Oxford druing 1550 Martyr also lectured on *Romans*. The

lectures were given every day at 9:00 A.M.[84] Though Peter Martyr's

Romans was not published until 1558 he had made progress toward publica-

tion by 1552. Apparently from his letter of 8 March Martyr prepared

a copy for publication before taking up residence with Cranmer in the

autumn of 1552.[85] Consequently, the comments in the first Latin edi-

tion of 1558 have some bearing on Martyr's feelings about his experi-

ences in England.

Martyr wrote in the 1558 prefatory letter to Sir Anthony Cooke

about his experiences five years before when Edward VI died and protes-

tant hopes for a simplified church structure collapsed.

When I oftentimes consider . . . all those things which happened all that whole time that I dwelt in England, it driveth into me a great and manifolde griefe. And in especiall it is a grief unto me, that so great an hope of the gospell of Jesus Christe, and of pure doctrine in that Realme, geuen by the most mighty and most mercifull God, and confirmed by the great laboure, industry, and study of godly men, hath now in a maner utterly pearished.

The political views in the *Romans* commentary are important for what they suggest about Martyr's attitude toward rebellion under a catholic monarch. At *Romans* (13) Martyr stated that the Prince was appointed in God's place between God and men.[86] In *Judges* given as lectures during this second Strasbourg period Martyr taught that the magistrate was subject to the clerical preaching of the Word of God.[87] Passive resistance was necessary for the people but resistence could be sanctioned for the lesser magistrates.

For what, if the superior prince commaunde the inferior Magistrates, to receave the Masse in their Cityes? Undoubtedly they ought not obey. If a manne will saye: It is the superior power, therefore it must bee obeyed: I will aunswere: In thynges civile and humane let them obeye as muche as they ought, but nothyng againste God.[88]

Generations of Englishmen read in the *Prayer Book* an exhortation to communion which Cranmer prepared from a Latin text of Peter Martyr. The text of the Basle *Opuscula* is the earliest known Latin version of this lovely prayer. John Booty points to the two exhortations which accompany the Martyr prayer. These are from the *Order of Communion* (1548) and all three focus on the general call to repentance read before the call to General Confession and Absolution.[89]

Martyr's exhortation used the Parable of the Great Feast in *Luke* (14:6-24) to the effect that God's anger might come against those who refused His invitation to commune.

> Now, if you will in no wise thus do, consider with yourselves,
> how great injury you do unto God, and how sore punishment hangeth
> over your heads for the same . . . . I pray you what can this
> be else, but even to have the mysteries of Christ in derision?
> . . . These things, if ye earnestly consider, ye shall by God's
> grace return to a better mind: for the obtaining whereof we
> shall make our humble petitions, while we shall receive the
> holy Communion.[90]

In this exhortation as in his Oxford lectures and sermons Martyr

cared much for the truth of the Gospel.

NOTES TO CHAPTER III

1. Brooks, op. cit., p. 21. Dated by Brooks from mid-1530's
until early 1540's. See also J. McGee, "The Nominalism of Thomas
Cranmer," H.T.R. 57 (1964), 189-206, and J. N. Bakhuizen van den
Brink, "Ratramn's eucharistic doctrine and its influence in sixteenth-
century England," S.C.H. II 54-77.

2. Ibid., pp. 24-34.

3. See contra, Cyril Richardson, Zwingli and Cranmer on the
Eucharist - Cranmer dixit et contradixit, pp. 48 and 51f. where Laski's
stay at Lambeth in 1548 according to Richardson shifted Cranmer's
views toward Zwingli. See McLelland, op. cit., p. 271 for arguments
that Martyr influenced Cranmer. C. W. Dugmore, The Mass and the English
Reformers attempts to establish direct links with the Patristic writers.
See the review by T. H. L. Parker, J. T. S. New Series, XII (1961),
134-46. On a mediating attempt see J. R. Parris "Hooker's doctrine of
the Eucharist," S. J. T. 16 (1963), pp. 151-64.

4. James Arthur Muller, Stephen Gardiner and the Tudor Reaction,
p. 209.

5. On 11 November a sub-committee of eight was commissioned to
draw up a preliminary summary of the ecclesiastical laws then in use,
later to be submitted to the judgement of a thirty-two member committee.
Calendar of the Patent Rolls, Edward VI, Vol. IV, A.D. 1550-1553,p.114.
The Henrician Canons have recently been recovered after an absense of
four centuries. This is the collection Cranmer remembered when on 23
January 1546 he wrote to Henry VIII that the Bishop of Winchester would
"enquire out their names, and the book which they made, and to bring
the names and also the book unto your majesty." F. David Logan, "The
Henrician Canons," B. I. H. R. XLVII (1974), 101. Henry intended to
depapalize the English Church through this instrument as early as

October 1535 but never promulgated these canons.

6. *Calendar of the Patent Rolls*, Edward VI, III, p. 354 where Martyr's name appears among those of the thirty-two Commissioners.

7. James C. Spaulding, "The Reformatio Legum Ecclesiasticarum of 1552 and the Furthering of Discipline in England," C. H. XXXIX (1970), pp. 162-163. See also Jasper Ridley, *Thomas Cranmer*, p. 331. Martyr confessed his feelings in a letter to Otto Heinrich, Count Palatine on 23 November 1551. This unpublished letter is in the Zurich Zentralbibliothek, *Simmlerische Sammlung* MS. 76:93. Latin text transcribed in Huelin, op. cit., pp. 255-57. The reform of the Eucharist is to be postponed. "But on what grounds I do not know, it is to be deferred until next January when we all pray that God will deem it worthy to provide for it the desired beginning and happy success." Huelin, op. cit., p. 87. On 27 February 1559 it was reintroduced in the House of Commons where it passed but survived only a first reading in the Lords. It next appeared in the Lower House of Convocation in 1563, and was printed by John Foxe in 1571 as part of an attack on the Elizabethan Prayer Book. This 1559 episode "demands our thesis of an organized movement operating through the House of Commons, the object of which was to force upon Elizabeth and her government a complete Protestant programme, at least as radical as that achieved by the close of Edward VI's reign." J. E. Neale, *Elizabeth I and Her Parliaments 1559-1581*, p. 64.

8. Gorham, op. cit., p. 123. 18 December 1549 from Oxford.

9. *Ibid.*, p. 126.

10. Roger Ascham, *Epistolarum Libri Quatuor*, p. 437.

11. *Loc. cit.*, "& cum propter ignotam mihi linguam fuisset data versio Domini Cheeki legenda . . ."

12. *O. L.* II, p. 479.

13. See Otto Erich Strasser, "Der Consensus Tigurinus," Z. 9 (1949), 1-16 and especially pp. 7-9.

14. Gorham, op. cit., pp. 128-142 for letters to Somerset and Bucer. Quotation from Bucer to Niger is in Gorham, op. cit., p. 143.

15. *O. L.* II, p. 482.

16. *O. L.* II, p. 485.

17. Gorham, op. cit., p. 161. 1 July 1550. See his letter of 18 April 1553 to procure a license from court for one of his auditors

to preach. Strype, _Cranmer_ (1812) II, p. 1002.

18. Nicholas Pocock, "The condition of Moral and Religious Belief in the Reign of Edward VI," _E. H. R._ X (1895), pp. 417-44. See especially p. 444.

19. Gorham, _op. cit._, p. 162.

20. _Ibid._, p. 172. 31 August 1550.

21. _Ibid._, pp. 176-177. 6 September 1550. Details of an unsuccessful attempt to draw Martyr into a second disputation in 1550 are in an unpublished letter of 20 September 1550. British Museum Add. MS. 21, 524.

22. _Ibid._, pp. 180 and 182. 10 September 1550.

23. Hopf. _op. cit._, pp. 162-164. 25 October 1550. Gorham, _op. cit._, pp. 196-199. 11 November 1550.

24. Gorham, _op. cit._, p. 198.

25. John a Lasco, _De Sacrament_. 14 May 1557 signed by Farel and Beza. _Epistolae Virorum Doctorum de Rebus ecclesiastices tempore Elizabethae reginae_, Lambeth Palace Library MS. 2010, Fairhurst Paper (Selden Papers), no. 101. Several letters of Continental reformers are included here, not available to the editors of the Parker Society Letters. For the three-hundred year absence of this MS. from Lambeth Palace see E. G. W. Bill, _J. S. A._ III (1965-69), 24-26.

26. Gorham, _op. cit._, pp. 227-229.

27. McLelland, _op. cit._, p. 32.

28. Letter of 17 October 1550, Hooper to Bucer and Vermigli. _2 Hooper_ XIV (Parker Society).

29. Gorham, _op. cit._, pp. 232-233. Early February, 1551 to Bucer.

30. _Ibid._, p. 232.

31. Strype, _Cranmer_ (1964), p. 269.

32. Nicholas Pocock, "Preparations for The Second Prayer Book of Edward VI," _C. Q. R._ 37 (1893), 138.

33. Charles W. Dugmore, _The Mass and the English Reformers_, pp. 148-149.

34. _Ibid._, p. 149.

35. Pocock, _op_. _cit_., p. 144. Now see Philip McNair and John Tedeschi, "New Light on Ochino," B. H. R. XXXV (1973), 289-301.

36. _Ibid._, p. 148.

37. _Ibid._, p. 150.

38. Van den Brink, _op_. _cit_., p. 73.

39. John Foxe, _Actes and Monuments_ (1583), p. 1388.

40. Horton Davies, _Worship and Theology in England From Cranmer to Hooker 1534-1603_, p. 183.

41. _Ibid._, pp. 184-185.

42. Peter Lorimer, _John Knox and the Church of England_, p. 103.

43. Beesley, _op_. _cit_., p. 88.

44. Lorimer, _op_. _cit_., p. 103.

45. _Ibid._, pp. 267-274.

46. "A sermon concerning the tyme of rebellion."

47. O. L. II, pp. 488-89. 28 January 1551. See letter to Gualter of 25 April 1551 in _Common Places_ (1583), Part five where Martyr uses term "uncorrected copies," thus expressing some concern about the accuracy of the printed edition.

48. _Ibid._, p. 492. Printed in _Common Places_ (1583), Part five, p. 81.

49. _Ibid._, p. 491.

50. Martyr wrote a letter of consolation to Bucer's widow. Sir John Cheke described the funeral at Cambridge to Martyr on 10 March 1551. Gorham, _op_. _cit_., pp. 238-241.

51. _Common Places_ (1583), Part five, p. 81.

52. C.C.C.C. MS. 119: fols. 109-114.

53. O. L. II, p. 494. 25 April 1551. That such a request was not unusual can be seen from a perusal of Clyde A Manschrek, _The Prayers of the Reformers_.

54. O. L. II, p. 497. See F. Douglas Price, "Gloucester diocese under Bishop Hooper, 1551-3," B. G. A. S. T. 60 (1938), 51-151.

55. The letters addressed to Geneva which Martyr sent with this letter have not been recovered.

56. Smyth, op. cit., p. 136.

57. See Ibid., pp. 127-133. Letters of ab Ulmis & Stumphius are in O. L. II, pp. 377-468. See Hopf, Bucer in England for a chapter on the term 'Suvermerian'.

58. Smyth's references to separate lectures on Lutheranism and Zwinglianism by Martyr at Oxford are not documented. Huelin calls attention to Martyr's 1549 Oxford defence of Bullinger's teaching in O. L. II, p. 493. 25 April 1551.
"As far as my own opinion is concerned, I go along with you altogether, and scarcely deliver any other sentiments in this place, when any conversation or disputation takes place respecting the Lord's supper."

59. "A Prayer of Doctor Peter Martyr agaynst worshippers of bread and all maner of superstition," Prayers (1569) at end of volume. Simler's preface dates these prayers to the second Strasbourg period.

60. Gorham, op. cit., p. 232.

61. Letter to Rosenblatt is printed in Loci Communes (1580), p. 572 and Loci Communes (1613), pp. 1088-89.

62. Gorham, op. cit., p. 237.

63. Ibid., p. 261,

64. Clarissimo Viro Domino Guglielmo Sicello. (William Cecil) Oxford, March, 1552. Strype, Cranmer (1694), II, Num. XCV.

65. Latin text in Bradford, Letters, p. 400. Gorham, op. cit., pp. 281-282 and William Goode, An Unpublished Letter (1850), pp. 6-7.

66. O. L. II, p. 500. 26 October 1551.

67. Ibid., p. 504. On the Romans Commentary see J. C. McLelland, "The Reformed Doctrine of Predestination according to Peter Martyr," S. J. T. VIII (1955), pp. 257-65.

68. Ibid., pp. 503-504.

69. Charles Hardwick, A History of The Articles of Religion,

pp. 310-11. <u>Romanos</u> (1558), p. 411. W. K. Jordan, <u>Edward VI</u>: <u>The</u> <u>Threshold</u> <u>of</u> <u>Power</u>, p. 356.

70. See McLelland, <u>op</u>. <u>cit</u>., pp. 34-35 where McLelland discusses Martyr's influence on Articles 26 and 27 of the <u>Forty-Two</u> <u>Articles</u>. ab Ulmis informed Bullinger that Cranmer, Martyr, the Archbishop of York, Bishop of London, Thomas Goodrich the Chancellor and Skinner were to form a select committee "to consult about a proper moral discipline and the purity of doctrine." <u>O</u>. <u>L</u>. II, p. 444. 10 January 1552.

71. Gorham, <u>op</u>. <u>cit</u>., p. 281. 14 June 1552.

72. <u>Ibid</u>., pp. 287-288. 4 October 1552. Cranmer's invitation to Melanchthon, Bullinger and Calvin for a conference on the Eucharist was part of his attempt to reform English church life as a response to Trent. See letters of 20 March 1552 to Bullinger and Calvin, and 27 March 1552 to Melanchthon in <u>Miscellaneous</u> <u>Writings</u> <u>and</u> <u>Letters</u> <u>of</u> <u>Thomas</u> <u>Cranmer</u>, pp. 430-434.

73. British Museum, Harleian MS. No. 426. 65. C contains corrections and notations in the hands of Cranmer and Martyr. Gordon Huelin, <u>op</u>. <u>cit</u>., p. 258, n. 52 notes that all alterations in the section <u>De</u> <u>Prescriptionibus</u> (208-211) are in Martyr's hand. On page 211 of the manuscript there is a note almost a page long. In his prefatory letter to the 1571 edition John Foxe sets forth these ecclesiastical laws as a concrete means of reforming worship. "Nos vero perfectum omnis divini cultus magistrum solum Dei verbum agnoscimus, cum interim in hoc libro non esse nulla constat, quae per omnia minus quadrare ad amussim ecclesiasticae reformationis videantur, multoque; rectius fortasse mutarentur. Sed haec ab aliis rectius perspicientur, quam a me admoneri paterint." <u>Reformatio</u> <u>Legum</u> <u>Ecclesiasticarum</u>, (1571).

74. Private letter of Professor James Spaulding to author, 28 November 1973. Included by permission.

75. Spaulding, "The Reformatio Legum Ecclesiasticarum of 1552 . . .," p. 171.

76. <u>O</u>. <u>L</u>. I, p. 371. 20 November 1553. For Cranmer's manifesto of 5 September 1553 see Gilbert Burnet, <u>The</u> <u>History</u> <u>of</u> <u>the</u> <u>Reformation</u> <u>of</u> <u>The</u> <u>Church</u> <u>of</u> <u>England</u> (1681), II, appendix II, pp. 249-50.

77. Morley Thomas, "Tunstal-Trimmer or Martyr?", <u>J</u>. <u>E</u>. <u>H</u>. XXIV (1973), 345-346.

78. See Henry Jenkyns, <u>Remains</u> <u>of</u> <u>Thomas</u> <u>Cranmer</u> IV, 1-3 and John Foxe, <u>The</u> <u>Acts</u> <u>and</u> <u>Monuments</u> <u>of</u> <u>John</u> <u>Foxe</u> (1877), VI, p. 394.

But see Garrett, <u>Marian Exiles</u>, p. 328, who claims Martyr was chosen as "one of the earliest advocates of the cause of English protestants abroad." See also <u>Spanish Calendar</u> for 9 September 1553, p. 217.

79. <u>Common Places</u> (1583), Part five, p. 92. In a letter of November 1553 Wolfgang Musculus wrote to Bullinger, "I have not yet learnt where he is; I fear exceedingly for him from the English Papists. I ask if you should have any information concerning him and other good men, you will communicate it to me." Huelin, <u>op</u>. <u>cit</u>., p. 96. Z. S. S. MS. 79: 188.

80. <u>O</u>. <u>L</u>. I, p. 372.

81. <u>Common Places</u> (1583), Part five, p. 95.

82. Giorgio Spini, "Riforma italiana e mediazioni ginevrine nella nuova Inghilterra puritana," <u>Ginevra e I'ltalia</u>, pp. 451-89.

83. <u>Writings and Disputations of Thomas Cranmer, Archbishop of Canterbury, Martyr, 1556, Relative To The Sacrament Of The Lord's Supper</u> (1844), pp. 373-4.

84. <u>O</u>. <u>L</u>. II, p. 419. ab Ulmis to Gualter. 5 November 1550.

85. <u>O</u>. <u>L</u>. II, p. 504. 8 March 1552.

86. <u>Romanes</u> (1568), p. 430^{v}.

87. <u>Judges</u> (1564), p. 430^{v}.

88. <u>Ibid</u>., p. 265^{r}.

89. John E. Booty, "Preparation For the Lord's Supper in Elizabethan England," <u>A</u>. <u>T</u>. <u>R</u>. XLIX (1967), 137-139.

90. Beesley, <u>op</u>. <u>cit</u>., pp. 85-86.

CHAPTER IV

MARIAN EXILE (1553/56)

SUSTAINERS AND SOJOURNERS

Pope Julius II, counselled by Simon Renard, the Spanish ambassador
of Charles V to Queen Mary and the Spanish monarch, realized that haste
was Queen Mary's worst enemy.[1] Renard urged a 'step by step' approach.
The first would be the expulsion of foreign protestants from England,for
once the land was rid of these her majesty could concentrate on
restoring the Roman forms of worship.[2]

The protestant foreigners had indeed become influential in England
for in addition to Martyr at Oxford and Lambeth Martin Bucer was active
as a divinity professor at Cambridge,[3] Jan Laski directed the influential foreigners' church in London,[4] Valerand Poullain led a refugee
group to worship in Glastonbury while another group met in Canterbury
under the leadership of Utenhove.[5]

In keeping with Renard's advice Queen Mary proclaimed that all
protestant foreigners were to leave the country within twenty-four days
of her proclamation. Failure to do so would result in "most grievous
punishment by imprisonment, and forfeiture and confixcation of all their
goods and movables; and also to be delivered unto their natural princes
or rulers, against whose laws or persons they have offended."[6] Port
cities were ordered to grant passports and the majority of these aliens
became refugees once more.

Peter Martyr was quickly opposed at Oxford and chose to flee to
Lambeth. But Cranmer was in no position to aid him for he was summoned

to appear before the Council[7] and Martyr made his way to the continent. The congregations shepherded by Laski, Poullain and Utenhove left while the leaving was good. Two ships took Laski's congregation to a hostile reception in Denmark since they adhered to the Helvetic Confession. Lubeck, Weismar and Hamburg also refused them refuge and it was six months after leaving England in March of 1554 that they were permitted to settle in Friesland.[8]

Not all refugees were ready to leave England since members of the group had remained in London.[9] Because bloodshed was not part of Mary's original design[10] individual prodding was necessary to ferret them out. Gardiner boasted about his technique of dealing with them. He would begin "by summoning the undesired alien to come to the chancellor's house. If that did not dislodge him, the next step was to let him know, if he were a Frenchman, that the King of France, if a Netherlander, that the Emperor, was about to demand his extradition. This last never failed."[11]

Contending with the English protestants was, however, a different matter. Here the Queen began by permitting only licensed men to preach the gospel. For protestants licenses were non-existent. Because they interpreted this as an attempt at submission they concluded they were not in conscience bound to obey. Many continued preaching and most were arrested. Others left the country.[12] In all over eight-hundred Englishmen made their way to the continent.

Escape was relatively easy since few obstacles had been placed in their way. Thus Cox, Grindal, Coverdale, Knox, Sandys, Scory and men of their esteem were able to leave England.[13] Latimer could have "emigrated" but preferred to die for his faith. Prescott thinks that it was in fact the Queen's wish that such men leave the country. Opportunities for escape were too numerous to be accidental. It is hardly an oversight that the Tower was left open and unguarded on the day of her coronation.[14] Few of the exiles appear to have been commoners. Norwood lists four hundred seventy-two persons in which there were one hundred nineteen theological students, sixty-seven clergy, one hundred sixty-six gentry, forty merchants, thirty-two artisans, seven printers, three lawyers, three doctors, three yoemen, thirteen servants and nineteen with no listed profession.[15]

Not all Europe welcomed the Marian exiles. Because Germany in particular appears to have been quite hostile most groups sought refuge among the Zwinglian and Calvinistic centres of Switzerland and the Upper Rhine. Frankfurt, Emden, Wesel, Arrau, Geneva, Basle, Zurich and Strasbourg became their new homes.

In May of 1555 Grindal wrote to the imprisoned Ridley saying "Here /at Frankfurt/ is a church now well settled by the prudency of Master Cox /former Oxford reformer/ and others which met here for that purpose, who most earnestly and unceasingly do cry unto God for the delivery of His Church." At first this group followed the liturgy prescribed in Cranmer's prayer book. Later however they were urged to conform to the French form of worship common to the area. It was also during this time that they were joined by other refugees. John Knox was among these and he quickly sought to make "Genevans" out of them. Dissension followed.

Cox feared the Calvinistic influence could be disastrous for the future
Anglican church. In an effort to settle the issue Peter Martyr's
counsel was obtained.[16] The degree of his success appears uncertain
but the issue was partially resolved when the ever tactful Knox expressed himself regarding the emperor. Knox and many of his followers eventually turned to Geneva.

The port city of Emden on the North Sea became the home of another
group of refugees. Under the watchful eye of John Scory they seem to
have maintained a fair sense of unity and channeled their energies
toward polemics rather than internal rivalries. Wesel too opened her
doors to the "enemies" of Mary Tudor. Miles Coverdale joined them sometime after February 1555. Because of their political activities this
group was compelled to relocate and found a new Swiss home in Aarau.
This appears to be the only group of English refugees who were gainfully
employed. Many refugees also made their way to Basle because as Strype
says the city was especially kind to the English and because "those
that were of lesser fortune might have employment in the printing houses
there."[17] At first facilities for worship were quite restricted. Later
they were able to rent the so called Clarakloster for twenty-four pounds
per year. Here they ate, slept, and worshipped and referred to their
life as "in collegio."[18]

The Genevan records list nearly one hundred eighty English refugees. Strype makes reference to their activities when he says that "At
Geneva a club of them employed themselves in translating the Holy Bible
into English . . . having the opportunity of consulting with Calvin and

Beza."[19]

The activities of the Geneva club were not unique. Other groups became engrossed in parallel activities. The Emden group, according to Strype, committed themselves to the writing of "good books in English" and shipped them to England. Scory, former bishop of Chichester, wrote *A Very Comfortable Epistle Unto All That Were In Prison, Or In Any Other Trouble.*[20] While referring to the haven of the exiles Strype also says that "In these places some followed their studies, some taught schools, some wrote books, some assisted at the printing press . . ."[21]

Possibly few exiles would claim to have received such commands from the Almighty as John Ponet who argued in the 1556 *A Short Treatise of Politike Power* that if necessary a Christian should liquidate a tyrant. Nevertheless anticipation of a return in the not too distant future ran high. Norwood claims for several reasons that long range plans for a return existed. Few refugees sought citizenship but were in constant touch with their homeland, often receiving information and instruction from imprisoned or silenced leaders.[22] Robert Horn and Richard Chambers relayed detailed data in a letter addressed to Bullinger in 1556. They included information on some of the martyrs, the Suffolk rebellion and the Queen's suspicions of Elizabeth. Another letter also addressed to the Zurich reformer by these two exiles spoke of their hopes for a swift return to their homeland.[23]

If most Marian exiles considered the continent a temporary home, and if few obtained gainful employment, how did they maintain their livelihood? They were after all exiles not tourists. And exile for most lasted a minimum of three years. Strype is careful to note that

during the early years of Mary's persecution "very liberal contribu-

tions came from England . . . From London especially came often very

large allowances."[24] Gardiner, incensed at this outflow of capital,

vowed that the money would stop; "that for very hunger they should eat

their own nails, and then feed on their finger ends."[25] Though Gardiner

was in some measure successful, the reduced income from the homeland

was supplemented by generous gifts from continental sympathizers. On

one occasion the Duke of Würtemberg gave the Strasbourg exiles between

three and four hundred dollars and on another he aided the Frankfurt

group.[26] The Zurich city fathers at Bullinger's request opened the

city treasury to aid Englishmen who refused such largess. Norwood

claims that those in Zurich probably lived in the greatest ease of all

English refugees.[27]

Horn and Chambers in a letter to the Zurich council described

themselves as "wandering, dispised, and wretched members of the

church," yet at the same time they thanked the council for kindness

and support while praising the liberality of the townsmen.[28] John

Ponet corresponded with Bullinger concerning his state as a refugee:

> What is exile? . . . I know that it is the scourge of the Lord;
> but with what mildness and fatherly affection he deals with me,
> I can readily learn even from this, that he has afforded me for
> my comforters Bullinger, Melanchthon, and Martyr, and other most
> shining lights in the church.[29]

It is this 'mildness and fatherly affection' that have caused

some to question the whole concept of a Marian exile, hypothesizing

instead that the migration was not a flight but a pre-planned well-

organized and funded exodus. Conceived in the mind of Lord Cecil, and
aided by the likes of the Duke of Suffolk and William Parr, the 'Sustainers' became an organization dedicated to the restoration of Angli-
canism in England. Organized in December of 1553 they intended to
finance the education of theologians who would become the future leaders of Anglican England. Evidence in support of such a view is the
predominence of teachers and students among the refugees. Their arrival on the continent at least six months before the Marian persecutions began needs also to be considered. Furthermore their hesitation
to seek employment and citizenship may indicate more than appears on
the surface. Financial support from England could have been motivated
by more than humanitarianism.[30]

It does seem unlikely that the protestants would submit without
an energetic attempt at a restoration. That the 'Sustainers' existed is
a known fact. That English protestants funded and directed exiles is
also evidenced by extant correspondence. But that all who left England
did so with the consent and support of the "Sustainers" is unlikely.
Elements of flight did exist. The foreigners shepherded by Laski,
Poullain, and Utenhove indicated little desire to return to the continent, yet they were ordered out of the country. Prescott also claims
that protestant bishops used their pulpits to recommend a general
exodus.[31] Furthermore, the Queen's belief that protestantism was the
aberration of a few and would easily be overcome by proper teaching[32]
may well account for the pressure put on protestant scholars and teachers but not on artisans. Scholars were after all economic leeches

and artisans the backbone of a growing economy. Why force artisans out of the country when they could be converted?

Strangely enough the conclusion of the matter did not depend on an exodus or flight. In 1558 those on the continent still had their fingernails, while Gardiner who had vowed starvation for the exiles, and the Queen whom he served were enjoying purgatory. And the exiles were enjoying a hero's return for a season.

RELIGIOUS CONTROVERSY

Martyr's second exile and stay in Strasbourg involved him in further religious controversy - this time with the Lutherans. In his prayer on *Psalm* (56) Martyr clearly sensed the precarious reception of his theology in Strasbourg. Martyr prayed for a steadfast confession of the gospel, Lutheran adversaries notwithstanding.

> Wicked men (O moste good and mercifull God) go about to swallow us up: they doe assault and afflict us so much as in them lyeth. But seing that thy mightie power far excelleth the princes and kinges of the earth, and our whole affiaunce dependeth on thee onely, extende nowe thy favourable mercy unto us. . . . Thou shalt be present at thy owne case, and shalt see howe they ungodly doe all the day long rayle upon thy glorious Gospell, and true worshipping of thee, and how they continually imagine mischiefe agaynst thy deere and chosen people. Forsomuch as therefore they deale lewdely agaynst those whome thou hast redeemed, how shall they escape thy wrathful indignation.[33]

One such confession was Martyr's treatise or *Oration concerning the Study of Divinity*. As Paul in *Romans* (1:10) expressed his heartfelt desire to be with the faithful in Rome, so too Martyr had not been forgetful of the School of St. Thomas or the Church in Strasbourg. In fact Martyr several times requested tnat Edward VI return him to Strasbourg.[34]

From a series of unpublished letters between Conrad Hubert in
Strasbourg and Peter Martyr during 1551-1553, it is clear that Martyr
kept himself informed about the College of St. Thomas. For example,
Hubert praised Martyr's Commentary on I *Corinthians* whose prologue
especially impressed him, "& pro amore & studio quis in re sum."[35]
Equally important for Martyr was the report that under the rector the
school made excellent progress.[36] Though the church in Strasbourg was
mediocre, the Senate in Hubert's report continued to seek the glory of
Christ.[37] An important letter of 23 February 1552 informed Martyr of
Trent, of Osiander's controversy on justification and inquired about
Martyr's lectures on the *Minor Prophets*.[38] An interesting bit of information is Hubert's report on recent publications such as Bibliander
on *James* & *Mark* (?) and especially a new edition of Chrysostom. Hubert
mentioned that Amerbach's *vita Chrysostomi* appeared with it.[39] The
Cronologia Mundi in formam tabulae seems to have impressed Hubert.
Among the other letters is a reference to two manuscript works of Bucer
in the Royal Library (Oxford?).[40] Clearly Martyr knew about the sympathetic reception which he would have from Sturm and Hubert were he ever
to return to Strasbourg. Martyr's letter to Hubert of 23 April 1553
not only lamented the death of his wife, but also requested news about
the church and schools of Strasbourg.[41]

Martyr's comments on Edward VI also illustrate during his second
residence in Strasbourg a continuous concern for the English Protestant
Church in martyrdom and in exile.

Howbeit contrarie to the expectation of all men, was King Edward

of Englande the bright light of Christian kingdomes, the verie
nurse of godlynesse and a stoute defender of the Gospell of
Christ by cruell and lamentable death taken away. The light was
turned into darknesse, impietie succeeded pitie, and most cruel
Woolves invaded the newe and late (restored) Churche, good men
are wickedly oppressed, from whose perils and misfortunes howe
I by the providence of God have bin delivered, I cannot sufficiently imagine, much lesse declare.[42]

On 3 November 1553 Martyr wrote John Calvin that though his intention after leaving England was to go to Geneva, the winter terrified
him. John Sturm also labored to keep Martyr at Strasbourg.[43] On the
same day Martyr intimated to Bullinger that his stay would be temporary
but he was not anxious about it.[44] Controversy came by 15 December
even though Sturm worked strenuously with the clergy for his stay. Two
or three of the ministers raised such a formidable challenge to Martyr's
sacramental views that he urged Bullinger to look elsewhere for a position in which he might "exercise my calling with honour and advantage".[45]
John Marbach objected with the other Lutherans and insisted that since
Martyr had departed from the Augsburg Confession, only his signature on
the 1536 Wittenberg concordat between Bucer and Luther would avoid
trouble.[46] Martyr replied in a formal statement to the college on 27
December 1553 that the Augsburg Confession was profitable if properly
understood. Since Martyr had already published his views he could not
assent to the concord between Bucer and Luther. Bucer taught otherwise
in his public expositions of Acts while at Strasbourg. This opinion
that "those who are destitute of faith eat the body of Christ in receiving the sacrament" might seem if endorsed by Martyr to "condemn the
Church of Zurich, Basle, Berne, Geneva and England, and all the brethren

scattered throughout Italy and France."[47]

In a series of letters Martyr described this controversy and that
on Predestination to Bullinger and Lavater. On 30 December Bullinger
wrote Martyr:

> I have read your writing on Predestination with great delight.
> Since I know you, I am not concerned that you will cause dissension
> over this doctrine. I know that your reputation would set aside
> such controversy regardless of whomever might raise the issue.[48]

On the same date Martyr informed Lavater that he had not yet determined
what he would do. The authorities had not restored him to his former
position, though a postcript to the letter reports his restoration to
the position held before leaving Strasbourg in 1547.[49]

Soon after his arrival in Strasbourg on 30 October 1553, Martyr
found himself embroiled with John Marbach, a Lutheran enthusiast who
challenged Martyr's views on the sacraments and his interpretation of
the Augsburg Confession which Martyr had signed on his return from
England. When in 1530 the Imperial Diet convened at Augsburg, Melanchthon drew up a confession signed by the protestants known by its Latin
title as the Augustana. Strasbourg had been unable to sign this Lutheran document and instead submitted with the three Swiss cities of Lindau,
Constance and Memmingen an alternative statement known as the Tetrapolitan. When Martyr first arrived in Strasbourg (1542), political
events had forced the city to accept the Augustana. Jacob Sturm agreed
in negotiations to do so if the Tetrapolitan also remained in effect.

The background to Martyr's dispute with Marbach is crucial for in
1552 John Sturm hired Marbach when Caspar Hedio died of the plague.

Marbach was from Lindau, one of the original signers of the *Tetrapolitan*. Marbach who lived in Luther's house at Wittenberg completed a

brilliant course of study in 1543. The letter cited above from Sturm

to Marbach reflects something of the difficulty over this new Super-

intendent. [50]

When Martyr signed the *Augustana* he would have interpreted it in

the light of the *Tetrapolitan*. A brief selection from this confession

will show what theological options were officially open to Martyr at

Strasbourg. Its statement on the sacraments forbade "all superfluous

and curious inquiry into that which is alone profitable . . . namely,

that, fed upon him, we may live in and through him a life pleasing to

God, holy, and therefore eternal and blessed, and that we who partake

of one bread in the Holy Supper may be among ourselves one bread and

one body."[51] Martyr then knew chapter three of the *Tetrapolitan* with

its poignant definition of salvation which ran counter to Marbach's

Lutheran sacramental views. As a legal document for Strasbourg and one

also compatible to his views gained long before in Italy the *Tetrapolitan* explains Martyr's reluctance to agree with Marbach. The sacraments

did nothing more than to seal the prior work of the Holy Spirit.

> But the beginning of all our righteousness and salvation must
> proceed from the mercy of the Lord, who from his own favor and
> the contemplation of the death of his Son first offers the
> doctrine of truth and his Gospel, those being sent forth who
> are to preach it; and, secondly, since "the natural man receiveth
> not the things of the Spirit of God," as St. Paul says (I Cor.
> 2:14), he causes a beam of his light to arise at the same time
> in the darkness of our heart, so that now we may believe his
> Gospel preached, being persuaded of the truth thereof by his
> Spirit from above, and then, relying upon the testimony of this
> Spirit, may call upon him with filial confidence and say,

"Abba, Father," obtaining thereby sure salvation, according
to the saying: "Whosoever shall call upon the name of the Lord
shall be saved."[52]

In a formal document of 22 January 1554 Martyr reaffirmed his

position.[53] Philip Melanchthon heard about the disturbances and wrote

to Martyr and Marbach on 24 May 1554. He warned Marbach not to disturb

the tranquillity of the church, since the Son of God governs both church

and state at Wittenberg and at Strasbourg.

> I desire tranquillity for your churches and ours, and I pray to
> God's Son that He may rule over us both. I also pray that you
> may esteem with love the English exiles and Peter Martyr. I have
> written to him as well to exhort him to care for the harmony of
> your churches.[54]

Melanchthon was polite but firm in his letter to Martyr on peace

in the Strasbourg Church. He consoled Martyr on the loss of Edward VI,

whose wisdom and doctrinal acuity would have graced the Universal

Church. "Sed haec fota aspera huius extremae mundi . . ." Then Melan-

chthon cautioned Martyr not to add to the church's sorrow by disturbing

the tranquil and aristocratic city of Strasbourg.[55]

Martyr responded to Melanchthon on 26 January 1555 that concord

was a desirable goal, but compromise of the truth was unthinkable.

> I will teach and speak that which I judge true concerning that
> matter wherein I know they disagree from me, and that with such
> moderation and temperance, as I will not grieve or bitterly
> taunt any man that is of another judgement.[56]

John Calvin wrote Melanchthon on 27 August 1554. In his letter

Calvin berated the silence of Melanchthon, which "as I esteem it to be

detrimental to the Church of God, cannot for that reason but be painful

and annoying to me."[57] Calvin selected this disturbance in Strasbourg

to charge Melanchthon with timidity. Numbers of believers were left
floating in doubt from his ambiguous teaching.

> But if you are not at liberty to declare, candidly and fully,
> what it would be advantageous to have made known, at least you
> should make an effort to bridle the fury of those who brawl
> unseasonably about nothing.[58]

Martyr had written Calvin on 24 September 1554 about the sacraments. This letter indicates that Calvin knew full well the disturbances created at Strasbourg by Marbach. On 29 August 1559 Martyr
endorsed Melanchthon's 1559 commentary on *Colossians*. Melanchthon
argued that Christ's human nature was in heaven and that no human
allegory was necessary to understand its confinement to a place in
heaven. If Melanchthon would publish these remarks, meaning Martyr
had seen a manuscript version, the Church of Christ would greatly
profit. One recalls here a basic theological definition raised at
Marburg by Luther in 1529 and defended by Brenz against Martyr and
Bullinger in 1562 - ubiquity. In this view the body of Christ can not
be confined to space and therefore is everywhere. In Martyr's mind
Brenz taught that it was nowhere, or at least he lost it in the exchange of the human and divine natures known as the *communicatio idiomatum*. The Zurich - Genevan theologians kept their eyes on Melanchthon
so carefully that in these comments they seem to have caught a glimpse
of hope in a time of theological rigidity and despair.[59]

In summary then, the Strasbourg dispute broke out when Martyr
returned in 1553. The pastors demanded that before Martyr could offer
a course on philosophy he must sign the 1536 Wittenberg concord. In

that year Luther, Bucer, Capito and others signed a formula drawn up by
Melanchthon which gave some latitude to the Swiss. For this reason
Martyr felt he could sign the Augsburg confession on 28 December 1553
with the same latitude of understanding. It is important that Martyr
did not sign the 1536 Concord which used the phrase, "with the bread
and wine the body and blood of Christ are truly and substantially
present, offered and received." Martyr was not like Bucer on this
question.

ENGLISH EXILES

Martyr lectured on *Judges* and Aristotle's *Nichomachean Ethics*
when he resumed his former post in the College of St. Thomas. Zanchi
expounded the *De Natura*. During this period several exiles from England
joined Martyr at Strasbourg, especially John Jewel who was later Bishop
of Salisbury. It is to Jewel's contemporary biographer Lancelot
Humphry that we owe a description of this study circle which met in
Martyr's home.[60]

An example of their attitudes may be read in Thomas Sampson's,
*A Letter to the trew professors of Christes Gospell inhabitinge in the
Parishe off Allhallowis in Bredstrete in London* (Strasburgh: Hugh
Singleton - types, Auguste 1554). "Oh! London, London, is this the
gospelling fruit, to be the first that without a law shouldst banish
true preaching out of thee . . . to be the first that shal give the
example of stumbling to al England?" After citing the abominations of
transubstantiation, worshipping the host etc, Sampson spoke out in
defense of justification. His statements are valuable since Sampson

at this time was Martyr's student at Strasbourg.

> In the doctrin of justification they wander, enwrapt in labrinths
> inextricable. They erre in extenuating sin, both original and
> actual, in not understanding the law, the force of it I mean, nor
> the end of it: in making a justification partly of Christ's grace,
> partly of man's freewil, good motions, and good works. And herein
> they so enwrap themselves with their terms of the first grace, the
> second grace, grace precedent, grace concomitant, grace following,
> with merit of congruence, and merit of condignity; that they
> neither understand the true justification, neither can other men
> understand what they do mean by their justification. But their
> doctrin is to bring men into a continual doubting of salvation;
> and leadeth them clean from that free justification which we have
> in Jesus Christ.
> But you, my brethren, have out of the scripture received, and I
> trust by the practices of your own consciences have tasted, that
> by nature ye are the children of wrath of your selves; and of
> your selves that yee are but such a lump of sin, that in you
> dwelleth no good thing. For which the law justly condemneth you,
> as guilty of God's curse and wrath: and so driveth you to Christ,
> by whose grace ye be freely justified: by whose bloud-shedding
> only and alone the attonement is now made betwene God and you.
> Which you believing, are made the heirs of blessing, and of which
> your consciences by faith being assured by the work of Gods Spirit,
> ye be at peace with God. Because yee do seal even in your hearts
> by lively persuasion of faith, that God hath loved you, and given
> himself for you. For whose only sake ye are justified and saved.
> Which you thus feeling, are led by the same Spirit that worketh
> this in you, to render unto God the sacrifice of your body, in
> living and doing those works which in his sight are acceptable;
> and that in a freedome and liberty of the Spirit. I mean no
> fleshly liberty, but that liberty of the Spirit by which we draw
> nigh unto the sight of God's grace, calling him *Abba, Father;*
> that liberty that subdueth the liberty of the flesh, and maketh it
> captive, and bound to serve the Spirit. In which you also walking,
> when you have don al that you can do, if ye could do al that is
> commanded you to do, yet seing al mans righteousnes is but as a
> defiled cloth, ye seek not thereby the perimplishment of your
> justification, which is already fully given you in Christ Jesus;[61]

This is very similar to statements in Martyr's unpublished *Romans*

lectures.

Miss Garrett has shown that Martyr's letter to a "Friend" in the

Common Places (1583) was sent to Thomas Sampson, expressing Martyr's

displeasure at the 1554 *Confession* co-authored by Sampson and Ponet.
This *Confession of the Banished Ministers* seems to have been submitted
to Martyr for approval in 1554. Martyr's testy tone disbelieved that
such matters were "circulated in our name."[62] From this one garners
that Martyr was unhappy with John Ponet as well as Thomas Sampson over
their political views but not their theological ones.

Jewel transcribed the lectures on *Judges*. To Bullinger in January
Martyr wrote, "May the Lord grant that I may some time reap the desired
fruit of my labour."[63] The "collegium" encouraged Martyr to work on a
major refutation of Stephen Gardiner's sacramental views which appeared
in 1559. Meanwhile Martyr shared his work with the English exiles at
Strasbourg and elsewhere on the continent. Not only did Martyr lecture
publicly on Aristotle and *Judges*, but in private read much from Augustine and other patristic writers with the "Angloargentinenses."[64] On
6 May 1555 Grindal reported from Frankfurt to Ridley who was by then a
prisoner at Oxford. The exiles were dispersed in several places, especially well treated by Bullinger at Zurich and Martyr at Strasbourg.

> Another number of us remain at Argentine, and take the commodity
> of Master Martyr's lessons, who is a very notable father . . .
> The greatest number is at Frankfort, where I was at this present
> by occasion; a very fair city, the magistrates favourable to our
> people, with so many other commodities as exiles can well look
> for. Here is also a church, and now (God be thanked!) well
> quieted by the prudence of Master Coxe, and other which met here
> for that purpose. So that now we trust God hath provided for
> such as will flee forth of Babylon a resting-place, where they
> may truly serve him, and hear the voice of their true pastor.
> I suppose, in one place and other dispersed, there be well nigh
> an hundred students and ministers on this side the seas. Such
> a Lord is God to work diversely in his, according to his unsearch-
> able wisdom, who knoweth best what is in man.[65]

A partial list of English exiles in Strasbourg would include John
Aylmer, Thomas Becon, Thomas Cole, Thomas Gibson, James Haddon, Robert
Horne, Thomas Lever, John Pedder, John Ponet, Michael Reniger, William
Turner and Robert Wisdom. At Christopher Froschouer's house in Zurich
about twenty Englishmen also met for study. Together with Pellican,
Lavater and Bullinger there was a brilliant school at Zurich to attract
these Marian exiles.[66] In a letter from Calvin to these friends at
Strasbourg one reads an exhortation to patience that their work would
be fruitful in spite of exile.

> I do not doubt the counsel of God who miraculously assists your
> pious doctrinal studies. He wishes that you discipline your-
> selves under the cloud that after a long time He may bring your
> endeavors to light, and use them for a more serious purpose (in
> seriam militiam).[67]

Henry Cowell reports that no original records can be traced at
Strasbourg of that group of English exiles in the city from 1553-1558.[68]
Cowell proceeds with a series of biographical accounts of the English
refugees in Strasbourg based on other records. One report is that of
John Ayre who mentioned Jewel's close ties with Martyr.

> For he speedily received pressing invitations from Peter Martyr
> to join him at Strasbourg, in whose house there he was received
> and treated as a beloved son. Many of the exiles were collected
> in this city: among them Grindal, Sandys, Ponet, Nowell, Cheke,
> Cook, Worth, and a host of other scarcely less distinguished
> persons. Here they formed a kind of college, converting their
> place of exile into a seminary of learning and a school of piety.
> Peter Martyr lectured on the Ethics of Aristotle and the Book of
> Judges, and here, as at Oxford, Jewel was one of his most diligent
> auditors. In the following year Conrad Pellican, Professor of
> Hebrew at Zurich died, and Martyr was invited to succeed him. He
> complied with the invitation and removed to Zurich in July 1556.
> Hither Jewel accompanied him and as before was lodged in his house.
> For almost all the remainder of his exile Jewel continued at Zurich,
> but it seems probable that he visited Padua from there. His course

of life at Zurich was similar to what it had been at Strasbourg.
He diligently pursued his private studies and was always ready
for Martyr's public lectures.[69]

The group of English exiles at Frankfurt consulted Martyr. An
important document appeared in Heidelberg in 1574 and 1575 printed
anonymously under the short title, *A Brieff Discours off the Troubles
Begonne at Franckford*. In 1554 trouble arose among the English exiles
in Frankfurt over liturgical worship, especially the use of the 1552
Book of Common Prayer. On their arrival in June of 1554 the exiles were
offered the same church used by the French exiles with the condition
that they not "dissent from the Frenchmen in doctrine or ceremonies."
They thus abandoned the litany and congregational responses to the minister. The author who used documents from 1554 is now thought to be an
original member of the group named Thomas Wood.[70] On 6 February 1555
the group agreed to appeal to Calvin, Wolfgang Musculus, Bullinger,
Martyr and Viret if their agreement to use the English Prayer Book did
not last. On 22 March 1555 they appealed to these men after the arrival
of Cox and an additional group of English exiles disturbed the February
concord.[71] As part of the involved controversy between John Knox and
Cox a letter from John Calvin of 25 January 1555 circulated widely.
Calvin had described the 1552 *Prayer Book* used in Frankfurt as "popish
dregs."[72] It is important for this account to note that the Frankfurt
group appealed to Martyr for a decision. Martyr earlier had sent them
a letter on 30 September 1554.[73] Foxe sent a letter in October to Martyr
urging a response. In it he styles Martyr, "the apostle of the English
nation."[74]

The February concord involved the soliciting of opinions by the Frankfurt groups of exiles from "Strasbourg/Zurich/Dens brugh/ and Emden in the 2. off Auguste."[75] This was soon after their arrival in Frankfurt on 27 June 1554. To this end a general letter was sent to each of the above mentioned churches. The Strasbourg answer was that one or two men ought to take charge of the congregation, either Ponet, Scory, Bale or Cox. Grindal wrote to Scory at Emden while the congregation invited Knox at Geneva, Haddon at Strasbourg and Lennox at Zurich.[76] After letters had arrived from Zurich and Haddon, the group at Frankfurt reached an impasse with Cox's arrival in 1555. One problem was that the lay exile Richard Chambers aided the Frankfurt congregation to reject the help of other exilic groups. The Strasbourg response was that sixteen scholars would come in February of 1555 to enforce the 1552 *Prayer Book*. Frankfurt thus adopted the Genevan service with Knox as minister. Thomas Lever would not accept this and made a temporary service.

The February concord agreed on 6 February 1555 to use the Liturgy reported on pages XXVIII-XXXIIII of the 1575 edition. Of the English Service as described by Knox Calvin said in his letter of 20 January 1555: "I cannot tell what they meane whiche so greatly delite in the leauinges off Popishe dregges."[77] If any contention were to arise between 6 February and the end of April 1555, then Calvin, Musculus, Martyr, Bullinger and Viret would decide the matter. On Sunday, 13 March 1555, Cox and other who had recently arrived in Frankfurt broke with the agreed litany by responding to the minister during the service.

On the following Sunday afternoon John Knox in a sermon attacked the breaking of the February agreement.

John Knox resorted to prophesying which was an application of biblical texts to contemporary situations. Knox used the *Genesis* account of Noah where after leaving the ark he became drunk. As Noah's sons covered their father's nudity and shame, so must some things be kept secret and others open. The *Prayer Book* difficulties belonged in the latter category. In addition Knox attacked the sins of the English church: its want of discipline, persecution of Bishop Hooper for his failure to wear vestments, superstitions in the *Prayer Book* and even the wealth of the English clergy.[77a] When Cox rebuked Knox on the following Tuesday, the congregation withstood Cox. Knox declared that though not all things in the English Book were necessary, a breach of order could not be justified.[78] This well known affair of 1555 seems to have led scholars to view the troubles at Frankfurt as liturgical ones.

Martyr's letter of 30 September 1554 was important enough for Bullinger to obtain a copy. The Zurich document has Bullinger's autograph title at the top of the manuscript.[79] Martyr above all desired unity in the exiled Church.

> Therefore since wee be most desirous of the unitie of $\bar{y}$ church, we would maruelouslie wishe, that the controuersie which is sponge uppe amongest you should be pacified, which we suppose might bee doone, if yee will deliuer your children to be baptised unto those churches, with whome ye agree in faith and doctrine.[80]

It is important to observe that Martyr advised the Frankfurt congregation on *two* significant issues, one in 1554 and the other in 1555. Such events reflect how important Martyr had been to the reforming party while in England and still was now that they were scattered in Europe.

The letter printed in *Common Places* (1583) as *An Epistle to the English Church* is addressed to the Frankfurt congregation. Bullinger's autograph title on his copy helps in its identification. This letter indicates that in the Frankfurt refugee congregation the doctrine of baptism was an issue as well as liturgy. The controversy of 1554 was over Lutheran views of baptism. It introduces one to Martyr's scholastic method.

> The matter which ye propounde we reade not to be defined by the worde of God extant and pronounced in plaine and expresse wordes: Wherefore wee must dispute thereof according to that which we may cōiecture by that which we gather out of the holie scriptures.

This can be a difficult anddangerous process, argued Martyr, since Christianity must be kept inviolate. The question which the English congregation at Frankfurt asked Martyr was whether or no "it be lawfull for men that professe the gospell, to receive baptisme of the Lutherans." Martyr answers that "this can not be doone of them without fault."

Martyr did not deny the ecclesiastical validity of Lutheranism as a church nor the significance of Lutheran baptism in spite of the cruelty which their ministers exercised against him. That reference to cruelty must be to John Marbach. One thinks of Melanchthon's twin letters of 24 May 1554 to the two theologians Martyr and Marbach in Strasbourg. Martyr's answer to the Frankfurt Church outlined the difference between "our faith and the faith of the Lutherans." Since baptism is a sealing of the faith of the one baptized and since the

faith of a Lutheran in Martyr's mind was not that of the English exiles,
"we cannot deliver our faith to be sealed of them." To do so would
seem to consent to the Lutheran faith.

Martyr argued that baptism succeeded circumcision in which the
Jews would not circumcise a stranger unless he became a proselite instructed for forty days. One cannot have children baptized into a
faith where the view of the Eucharist is wrong. Lutheran ministers did
not agree with the English exiles at Frankfurt on the meaning of the
sacraments.

> They attribute unto the sacramentes a great deal more than is
> requisite, and tie the grace of God unto baptisme interpreting
> amisse that saying which is in John: Except a man be borne
> againe of water and of the spirite he shall not enter into the
> kingdome of heaven:.

Not only did the Lutherans refuse to give Martyr the Eucharist - a
possible explanation for Martyr's controversy with Marbach at Strasbourg - but they also denied that children could be saved without
baptism. This view Martyr could not accept, for

> undoubtedlie your infants are not in ioperdie of salvation, if
> they die without baptisme for somuch as neither the grace of
> Christ, nor the effects of predestination must bee tied to out-
> warde things and sacraments.

One notes too Martyr's theological method in the conclusion of this
very important letter which Bullinger had copied and Humphrey included
in his account. Baptism, said Martyr, is either forbidden, necessary
to salvation or it is a thing indifferent. It is not necessary to
salvation "seeing the Grace of God is not tyed unto the sacraments."
It is forbidden of God for the English to practice Lutheran baptism.

Since they must abstain from Lutheran baptism is baptism a matter of
indifference? No, answered Martyr, for the weaker brethren /at Frank-
fur_t/ will be scandalized. St. Paul provided in *Romans* (14) for the
weak conscience and in I *Corinthians* (6:12) that not all lawful things
are expedient.

> Consider (I beseech you) with your selves, although that the
> baptisme of the Lutherans shoulde be lawfull, yet shoulde it
> not be expedient at this time and for your brethren.

Martyr loved some of his Lutheran friends whose *Augsburg Confes-*
sion he signed at Strasbourg. They would not have him, it seems, because they tied the grace of God to the sacraments. This letter of 1554
demonstrates Martyr's value to the English exiles in Frankfurt as well
as the origin of his controversy at Strasbourg with the Lutheran theologian Marbach. Melanchthon's advice could not resolve such a fundamental division about the nature of the Gospel as understood by Martyr
and Marbach. One does disservice to suggest that neither was serious
about his own understanding of grace, that on the one hand the sacraments conveyed grace and in Martyr's view on the other hand that such
talk obscured the central message of scripture. Finally, this letter
suggests that the liturgical dispute of 1555 at Frankfurt was the
second time men at Frankfurt sought Martyr's mind on sacramental issues.
The sacraments did not convey grace in Martyr's manner of thinking;
therefore he often was called upon to settle sacramental disputes over
baptism and Eucharist.

If the Marian exiles are crucial to an understanding of English
puritanism, then this letter co an important center of their refugee

activity takes on remarkable significance. That Laurence Humphrey included it in his life of Jewel and that Bullinger kept a copy at hand means much. Many in the formative movement behind Elizabethan puritanism were sharing Martyr's views expressed in this letter. Baptism was of equal concern to liturgical dispute and arguments over vestments. One suspects Cranmer's views are represented here as well.

Martyr continued to report to Bullinger on affairs in England such as Thomas Wyatt's rebellion. Martyr neither approved nor disapproved of this revolt against Mary's marriage to Philip of Spain, though he did call Wyatt "a vigorous leader . . . well skilled in military affairs."[81] By April Martyr reported that affairs were worse then ever. He was distraught at the course of events leading his beloved Archbishop to martyrdom.[82] In his June letter Martyr asked Melanchthon to request God's pity on an afflicted England.[83] Within a few hectic months Martyr had been reinstated at the College of St. Thomas, began to lecture on Aristotle and the Old Testament, became involved with baptismal and liturgical disputes in Frankfurt, sacramental doctrine in Strasbourg and read patristic literature with John Jewel and other friends in his home. From his correspondence with Bullinger, Calvin and Melanchthon one can see that Peter Martyr was held in great esteem. Martyr kept in the center of theological activity during a critical phase of the expanding Protestant Reformation. Though feeling himself an exile since the death of Bucer in England, other exiles were to find great consolation in this Florentine reformer.

CALVIN AND UNIO CHRISTI

On 25 September 1555 Martyr wrote a lengthy treatise to Albert
Hardenburg of Bremen, defending his own opinions and those of Calvin.
It reads in part as follows:

> . . . While others rage with great anger against the sons of God
> and proceed to pursue and destroy more bitterly those afflicted
> by exile and the scattering of the English Church, you have
> treated them with uncomon kindness and received them with hospi-
> tality and have not refused to have intercourse with the Phrysican
> Church . . . I allow each one freely, provided the firm truth
> of the scripture remains inviolated, to use his own judgment in
> explaining and settling controversial questions. I see our people
> do this for the most part. The people of Zurich all thank me most
> heartily for my studies. The Genevans approve, they love me as a
> brother and more than I deserve, they beseech me to go to them.
> The people of Berne do not contradict, the churches of Rhetica
> refer to those writings more than I wish. And so we have settled
> all these things amongst ourselves so that when we have come to
> an agreement concerning the chief point of a matter, each one is
> ready to hear the other unfold the disputed questions more fully.
> But the Saxons are so inflexible, I will not say anything more
> severe, that they endure hearing no one except one who speaks most
> stupidly, and they want men to swear, not so much by their own
> opinions, as by phrases and words. Now, as you rightly say, all
> these things incline towards papistry. What are they seeking to
> obtain? Why are they collecting votes? Is it that they may ex-
> communicate us in Saxony by general consent? Let them cleave the
> Church in sunder and tear it to pieces as they will, there will
> remain, whether they like it or not, those who are of God. What
> have they against us? Have they not, they say, accepted the word
> of God simply? This is my body. But do they receive that sen-
> tence simply without any interpretation? I do not think so. They
> certainly reject transubstantiation whence some of them, when they
> exhibit the bread they have in their hands interpret this, be-
> neath this, with this, or in this, is my body. But where do they
> read the words, with this, beneath this, in this? Certainly not
> in the gospels, nor in Paul, nor any sacred book . . . I have
> explained enough, as I consider, in the discussion, disputation,
> and letter prefixed to the Canterbury book. Besides, Calvin in
> the consenses of our churches which he published this year,
> stooped so far, laid bare the matter so aptly, that I have no mind
> at present to add anything further.[84]

Geneva continued to attract Martyr with friends like Martinego

and Carraccioli in the Italian refugee church there. When anti-trinitarianism became a problem, Calvin appealed to Martyr to come and
serve the Italian congregation in Geneva.[85] When Martenigo died in
1557 Calvin wrote another letter to the Zurich Senate suggesting that
Martyr would be of great value to Genevan reform.[86] Meanwhile from 1554
Martyr and Calvin kept in close contact on theological issues such as
predestination.[87] Their primary concern was to teach a pure gospel
which would avoid idolatry.[88] On 27 November 1554 Calvin sent a treatise to Martyr who responded that to write theology with such ambiguous
words was to court disaster.[89] In January of 1555 Calvin sent a lengthy
statement on the Eucharist to Peter Martyr. Calvin accepted Martyr's
advice to avoid ambiguity, pausing to note that Bucer in wishing to
calm the violence of Luther had entangled himself by single words.[90]
Calvin went on to add that if the *Zurich Consensus* had not been published, he would have added Martyr's phrase on the efficacy of the Spirit.

At the end of a series of letters in which Martyr commented on
exegesis and theology, he raised a crucial matter with Calvin that takes
one to the core of Martyr's theological thought.[91] The activity of the
spirit of Christ constitutes true communion with Christ. The sacraments and the Word of God are "tokens and signs of the true communion
with Christ."[92] Martyr's biblical reference is to *Hebrews* (2:15) that
Christ by his death "set free all those who had been held in slavery
all their lives by the fear of death."[93] His letter to Calvin of 8
March 1555 touched on the renewing power of the Holy Spirit in one's
daily life. A careful analysis of this theme in Bucer, Calvin and

Martyr will show their agreement on this issue.

> It is a thing of great importance that he which is of Christ,
> should understand by what means he is joined unto him. First, I
> see, that he by the benefit of his incarnation, (as it is said
> unto the Hebrews) would communicate with us in flesh and blood.
> For since that the children were partakers together of flesh and
> blood, he himself would also be a partaker thereof. But unless
> that another kind of communion had happened therewithall, this
> would be very common and weak. For so many as are comprehended
> unto mankind do now after this manner communicate with Christ:
> for they be men as he was. So as besides that communion this
> happeneth, to wit, that unto the elect, faith hath access at the
> time appointed, whereby they believe in Christ, and so they are
> not only forgiven their sins and are reconciled unto God, wherein
> consisteth and true and sound respect of justification, but also
> there is added a renewing power of the spirit, whereby our bodies
> also, flesh, blood and nature, are made capable of immortality,
> and become daily more and more as I may say fashioned unto Christ:
> not, that they cast away the substance of their own nature, and
> pass in very deed into the body and flesh of Christ, but that
> they no less draw near unto him in spiritual gifts and properties,
> than they did naturally even at very birth communicate with him
> in body, flesh and blood. Now therefore we have here two con-
> junctions with Christ: The one natural which by birth we draw
> even from our parents, but the other commeth unto us by the Spirit
> of Christ, by whom at the very time of regeneration we are made
> new according to the image of his glory.[94]

By August of 1555 Calvin responded that the subject was one of
vast importance.[95] Calvin's purpose in answering so briefly was to
demonstrate his entire agreement.[96] There are, said Calvin, two com-
munions to be understood: the one in which fellowship with Christ is
created by His death, and the other in which there is "a second influence of His Spirit, enriching us by His gifts."[97] Calvin felt that
St. Paul's expression in I *Corinthians* (1:9) that the faithful are
called in the κοιvωvία of His (Son) was a better term than either
Consortium or *Societas* to describe the first communion. The second
communion stems from the indwelling Christ and is received in the

Sacred Supper.

> Hence, - that we are strong in hope and patience, - that we
> soberly and temperately keep ourselves from worldly snares, -
> that we strenuously bestir ourselves to the subjugation of carnal
> affections, - that the love of righteousness and piety flourishes
> in us, - that we are earnest in prayer, - that meditation on the
> life to come (snatches us above (Sursum rapit) - this, I maintain,
> flows from that second Communion . . .[98]

Martyr also discussed this subject in a letter to Theodore Beza

of 1555.

> Now it remaineth that I should aunswere unto those thinges which
> you demaund as touching our communion with Christ . . . Wherefore
> it behooueth that there come an other likenesse whereby the nature
> of euerie Christian, as touching soule, bodie, and bloud, be
> ioyned unto Christ: and that is when by the helpe and indowment
> of Christes benefites we are renued unto all things, and being
> adorned with diuine properites, are made holie and iust,and through
> the giftes of God, doe claime unto our selues the gift of immor-
> talitie and of eternall glorie.[99]

Martyr went on to describe those benefits of Christ as gifts which re-

store the believer to Christ. Then Martyr concluded:

> Then doe wee beginne after some sort to be like unto him when we
> be borne men, and finallie when by the faith of Christ we are
> restored unto his merites, giftes, benefites, and properties.[100]

On this question of union with Christ, Kilian McDonnell has given

an excellent account of Calvin's eucharistic and ecclesiastical con-

cerns in which Calvin is "in large part indebted to Martin Bucer."[101]

This "ecclesiology of inwardness" had union with Christ as its norm.

From Martyr's letter cited above and Calvin's response, one wonders if

Martyr did not equally influence Calvin on this normative "ecclesial

moment." Since Martyr discussed the same question in his I *Corinthian*

Commentary of 1551, there is a possibility that Martin Bucer's *Pra-*

electiones In Epistolam ad Ephesios given in Cambridge during 1550/51

reflect what Martyr may have gained from Bucer then and even earlier.[102]
Martyr had read Bucer on the *Psalms* and *Gospels* while in Naples. Even
so on this question of union with Christ, Bucer's influence on Martyr
is negligible.

Bucer's *Praelectiones* were edited by Tremellius, who points out in
his preface that death prevented Bucer from proceeding beyond the Fifth
Chapter. In Chapter Four one finds a treatise called, *Quid Sit
Ecclesia.*[103] There Bucer wrote similar thoughts to those of Martyr
expressed in the 1549 *Tractatio.*

> Moreover, every Christian because he is a new creature must also
> live that life by new customs and duties. These he must do so
> that everything might naturally serve God's glory in accomplishing
> human salvation. This true and efficacious power is life itself
> whose customs and actions minister Christ Himself, to one another,
> who is one living body directing all things. I live, yet not I,
> but Christ lives in me.[104]

It is important to note that the section of Calvin's *Institutes*
on the life of Christian men which ended all editions of the *Institutes*
since its first inclusion in the 1539 edition shifted to Book III in
1559. In the 1559 edition it is found in Book III, chapter VI. There
Calvin added an expression which he deduced from the Scriptural premise
that the Christian is conformed to the image of Christ. The new emphasis is this chapter's manifestation of the work of the Spirit. On the
subject of total conversion by the Spirit, Calvin said that what Paul
called renewal of the mind is the means whereby Christ lives and reigns
in us. This kind of Christian philosophy is foreign to all the philosophers.[105] Certainly Calvin's 1548 Commentary on *Ephesians* was available to Martyr by 1549. Even so, it seems likely that Martyr's letter

of 8 March 1555 was partially responsible for these alterations in the

1559 *Institutes*. Niesel has shown that Calvin's polemic against

Osiander led him to define these issues in 1550 or 1551.[106] In the

Commentary on John (17:21) Calvin said in 1553:

> So that the unity of the Son with the Father be not vain and use-
> less, it is necessary that the virtue of the same should spread
> throughout the body of the faithful. Whence we also gather that
> we are one with the Son of God, not to say that he transmutes his
> substance into us, but because by virtue of his Spirit, he com-
> municates to us his life, and all the benefits he has received
> from the Father.[107]

Again in a sermon on *Ephesians* (3:9-12) in 1558 Calvin insisted that

union with Christ makes even the angels "wonder at the riches that God

has displayed in uniting us with the body of his Son.[108] Long before

this Calvin had used the phrase "bone of his bones and flesh of his

flesh" in his *Sermon to flie Idolatrie* (1537, translated 1551, fol.

E V[r]).

It would seem that Calvin and Martyr shared a common concern to

avoid Osiander's essential righteousness while at the same time they

took care to assert the union with Christ which St. Paul clearly enun-

ciated in his *Epistles*. Prior to Martyr's 1555 letter to Calvin there

is a hint in the I *Corinthian* Commentary (1551) that Martyr arrived at

his understanding of union with Christ by a reading of Patristic sources.

In discussing union at chapter 10, Martyr cited from Cyril on *John* (15),

Hilary's *Eighth Book on the Trinity* and Irenaeus' *Book Four Against

Valentinian*, all of whom refuted heretical views which deny that human

nature of Christ through faith or any other way when partaking of the

Eucharist.[109] This section from Hilary was well known and central to

Melanchthon's Eucharistic thought. See the valuable discussion by
Pierre Fraenkel, "Ten Questions Concerning Melanchthon, The Fathers
And The Eucharist," in V. Vajta, *Luther and Melanchthon*, pp. 148, 150,
163 - 164. That Martyr cites Hilary raises the question of his use of
Melanchthon's *Sententiae Veterum*. Bucer certainly knew about this work
whose quotations were used in the *Wittenberg Concord* of 1536. Hilary's
comments were used to circumvent the question of ubiquity so crucial
at Marburg in 1529 and thereafter for the Genesio-Lutherans.

The common source for this reformed doctrine of sanctification
would seem to be two Pauline passages in *Romans* (5) and I *Corinthians*
(15). B. C. Milner argues that neither Krusche, *Das Wirken des
Heiligen Geistes nach Calvin* nor T. F. Torrance, *Kingdom and Church*
relate the simultaneity of justification and sanctification in Calvin's
thought. Torrance would seem to dissolve sanctification in justification, while Krusche makes justification logically prior. Niesel, *The
Theology of Calvin*, is aware that real progress in righteousness is
spoken of in the *Institutes* but never perfection (*Institutes* III.3.14).
Milner does well to point out that, "Simultaneity means, then, that
sanctification and justification begin together in faith and end together in salvation."[110] Calvin and Martyr agreed with St. Paul's
view of the two Adams expressed in *Romans* (5). Salvation is accomplished by the work of Christ, experienced in the believer by faith and
nourished by the Eucharist.

St. Paul used the parallel between Adam and Christ at *Romans* (5:
12-21) and I *Corinthians* (15:22, 34-39). The typology in *Romans* (5)

clarified redemption and in I *Corinthians* (15), resurrection. Calvin's comparison of Christ and Adam followed St. Paul and "contains *in nuce* Calvin's anthropology, Christology and soteriology."[111] In spite of a recent article by Gordon Bates that Calvin followed St. Paul, Calvin himself qualified the Second Adam Christology in his I *Corinthian* commentary of 1546. There at 15:47 on St. Paul's reminder that "the first Adam was from the earth," Calvin commented:

> Let us observe in the first place that this is not an exhortation, but pure doctrine, and that he is not treating here of newness of life, but pursues, without any interruption, the thread of his discourse respecting the resurrection of the flesh.[112]

In the *Institutes* Calvin saw that relationship as one in which "Adam, implicating us in his ruin, destroyed us with himself; but Christ restores us to salvation by His grace" (*Institutes* II.1.6.). Martyr at *Romans* (5:12) commented on this antithesis. There, too, Martyr viewed the relationship of Adam to Christ as "an obscure and very difficult thing" (*Romans* 1558, p. 152). He went on to assert the identity of Christ with Abraham and therefore as a true son of Adam the only one who could restore men to righteousness through the long-suffering of God. Martyr helped Calvin to see from Patristic witness that the Son of Man of the Gospels was the Second Adam of Paul. The One who suffered to give His life a ransom for many undid by His saving act the ruinous act of the first Adam. His triumph was the surety of their faith.

In the 1546 I *Corinthians* commentary Calvin preferred not to grant any progress in righteousness, while in *John* (1553) he spoke of the Spirit who communicated the benefits of the Father – God. After

Martyr's I *Corinthians* (1551), letters to Calvin and Beza of 1555 and

Romans of 1558, Calvin spoke about union with Christ. Martyr left his

mark on Calvin's theology. It was stated most clearly in the conclu-

sion of Martyr's 1549 *Discourse* at Oxford. There in commenting on

Ephesians (3:6) that the Gentiles were made fellow heirs and "concor-

porall wyth Christe," Martyr made an observation on St. Paul's term

σύσσωμα. Though one might feel this is by faith, "there foloweth

effectually a true coniunction (I saye) betwene us and Christ, (and

not a feigned or ymaginatiue coniunction) whiche first perteyneth to

the solle and then redoundeth unto the bodye."[113] Where St. Paul said

"we are of his fleshe, and of his bones," Martyr concluded that the

flesh was uncommonly cleansed from sin.

> fleashe apte to receiue the resurrectiō and immortalitee. Whyche
> kinde of fleashe the feithfull, for asmuche as they have it not
> of theymselfes, nor yet by the procreation of Adam they doe
> chalenge & take it of Christ whō thei are incorporated into him
> by the sacramentes and by feith.[114]

During the remainder of 1555 Martyr continued to lecture and to

work on his response to Stephen Gardiner.[115] The Church in Strasbourg

made "marvelous strides in spiritual prosperity." Such a phrase sug-

gests that Martyr preached or lectured on the positive theme of Com-

munion with Christ in addition to the many hours spent answering his

critics in Strasbourg and elsewhere.[116] His term "ecclesiola" may

refer to the English exiles and have been patterned after the study

circle of Valdes in Naples to which Martyr added his own accents in

divinity. "nostra vero ecclesiola, quam tamen et frequentiorem et

numerosiorem solito habemus, uti divinas, potius est sedata quam
tranquilla."[117]

HERESY ALL AROUND

Martyr's status as a reformer at this time may be observed from
two lengthy letters. On 14 Feburary 1556 he wrote "To the Lords of
Poland, professors of the Gospel, and to the Ministers of the Churches
there."[118] The Polish Church was troubled by heresy. Osiander and
Stancaro opposed one another in Christology. Martyr's plea was for
plain teaching and discipline.

> But when I speak of faith, I mean not that which men of their
> subtilty have framed by the judgement of human wisdom, but I
> speak of that, which as Paul teacheth, is by hearing, yet not
> every hearing, but that which is only of the word of God, as we
> have it now by the grace of God comprehended in the holy
> scriptures.[119]

The opinions of Arius or Servetus are to be avoided where either the
two natures are confounded in Christ or his humanity is denied.[120] A
discipline based on plain rites for the sacraments would be an answer
to such vacuities.[121] Martyr then responded to four questions proposed by Lismanini. Christ as touches his divine nature did not suffer;
Christ is mediator with respect to both his divine and human nature;
Christ by nature is the son of God and the son of man; Osiander's
"essential justice" is especially contrary to Paul's teaching in
Romans (4).[122]

By the time Martyr wrote about Christological heresy to the Polish
Church his former friends in Lucca had also fallen on unhappy times. As
early as 1545 the Luccan Senate prohibited Martyr's and Ochino's

writings. Now persecution made its inroads among Martyr's countrymen.
Martyr urged them to constancy and prayer.[123] He advised in his letter
that a road would be made for the Gospel in Italy by martyrdom and
death. Martyr warned that it was time for tears not words[124] since
they long since should have fled to another city.[125] Because love of
riches kept the Lucchese from thinking that so great a calamity would
come it was difficult for them to endure persecution.[126] Martyr consoled his brethren in Lucca to forget prestige and endure what had
suddenly overtaken them. Martyr worried about two possible reactions:
either the believers would apostasize or they would become desperate
and suffer "the eternal death of desperation." Martyr's letter to
Lucca defends his own flight of 1542 as an exile through his detailed
analysis of scripture and patristic writings. Martyr's attitude amidst
continuous controversy in Strasbourg reflects a mature understanding
that God directs human affairs. Perhaps it was then that Martyr composed a prayer for the comfort and consolation of Christ's Church.
"Have an eye therefore unto the troublesome estate of thy blessed
Church, and diligently regarde the mostee greeuous oppression of thy
faythful people."[127]

During these busy months predestination should have been a great
consolation to Martyr. Instead it became the subject of pernicious
contention.[128] Martyr urged the brethren at Lucca to endure their
calamities as a sign of predestination which pertains only to the elect.
One result of such contention at Strasbourg was a further delay of
Martyr's *Romans*. Martyr deplored to Calvin the foul and false reports

spread by the Lutherans at Strasbourg concerning the eternal election

of God. Martyr and Zanchi defended Calvin as far as they could.[129]

While at Strasbourg Martyr became deeply involved with John Calvin.

After 13 July 1556 when Martyr left Strasbourg to succeed to Conrad

Pellican's position in Zurich the contact between these two widened on

several levels. They agreed that Gardiner's work was prolix and use-

less.[130] In June of 1556 Martyr briefed Calvin on his Eucharistic

views under four headings.[131] This clear statement of sacramental teach-

ing met with Calvin's approval. Martyr summarized his convictions as

follows:

> First, I do not deny that the Body of Christ is substantially
> present in the bread; secondly, the impious because they are
> devoid of faith eat only symbolically and do not lay hold of the
> true body and blood of Christ; thirdly, these words, 'this is
> my body' are spoken tropologically; in the fourth place, the
> Body of Christ can not at one and the same time be everywhere
> and in many places.[132]

Such were the themes which Martyr defended at Strasbourg when challen-

ged by the Lutheran party. The growing agreement between Calvin and

Martyr is one positive result of that struggle. Clarity of expression

and simplicity in thought mark Martyr as a mature theologian with

imaginative gifts as a writer, teacher and mediator in theological

disputes. It was exactly that clarity and refusal to use ambiguous

language in these vital issues which intensified the controversy with

the Romanists and Lutherans. Martyr would not compromise the truth

of the Gospel as he understood it.[133]

On 16 February 1556 Martyr thanked Calvin for his treatise against

Westphal. He devoured it in a single night. This would be the *Secunda defensio piae et orthodoxae de sacramentis fidei, contra Ioachimi Westphali Calumnias* (Geneva: Jean Crespin, 1556). Calvin accused Westphal of separating the promise of the Spirit from the sacraments. Martyr's enthusiastic response supported Calvin who held that the Spirit fused the sign and promise. The Spirit fructifies the sacraments for those whom He has adopted (*Secunda defensio*, pp. 170-171).

Other letters from June of 1555 show Martyr's increased concern for theological harmony. To Peter Alexander he lamented Marbach's hyper-Lutheran activity.[134] Martyr in July discussed the French congregational pastor Garnerius' suspension based on Marbach's suspicions. Martyr sought Bullinger's consolation for his own precarious position in Strasbourg.[135] To Calvin in September he wrote, "Verily they which disquieted Garnerius, do still remain; they be, as they have ever been, of a troublesome nature."[136] Martyr delighted at the harmony existing in Zurich when he wrote with relief to John Wolf that a Zurich report of suspicion about his own work in Strasbourg was false. He congratulated himself on belonging to the Zurich Church!

We have already noted Martyr's sympathies for Zurich in the letter to Bullinger on 1 May 1556.[138] Now to Lavater in April and June some of his reasons for sympathy with Zurich are stated. "Whereas contention is renewed about the sacrament, it is to be lamented: but since that the strife is grown up by the obstinacy of others, it is not meet for our men to leave the truth undefended."[139] In a letter to Bullinger during May of 1556 Martyr mentioned how difficult it was to leave Strasbourg.[140] By June permission came, as Martyr wrote to Lavater.

. . . upon St. John's day leave was given me to depart. In which matter I so greatly laboured, as I never in all my life obtained anything with greater difficulty.[141]

On 8 June 1556 Martyr thanked the Zurich magistracy for their aid when he first fled Italy. Now Strasbourg had changed even though Martyr labored with difficulty after returning from England. The situation which Conrad Hubert could describe in detail had deteriorated. Martyr was ignorant of the conditions under which he would be of use to the Zurich civic authorities.[142] The Strasbourg magistrate permitted Martyr to depart even against the civic wish.

> Herr Peter Sturm and the other Schulherren report that, with regard to the request from Zurich, they have discussed the matter with Doctor Peter Martyr, and have made every effort to retain his services themselves. But he has pointed out that when he accepted the position here, he signed the Augsburg Confession – conveniently interpreted to accord with his Calvinism – but that since then he has been subjected to all manner of unpleasantness from the preachers, and has suffered from considerable interference with his lectures. He makes freedom from such interference his condition for remaining. Decided: that the Council does not wish to oblige him to do anything against his will, and in either case will try to meet his desires. If he wishes to go it will be readily allowed and a letter of recommendation sent to Zurich.[143]

Martyr was elected to the position vacated by the death of Conrad Pellican and left for Zurich on 13 July 1556.[144]

The academic protocol involved in becoming Pellican's successor is of some interest.[145] Martyr left Strasbourg because he could no longer discuss the Eucharist in disputations.[146] At the end of July Zanchi wrote Calvin about Martyr's reception in Zurich. "Quum igitur hoc optime praestaret Martyr noster, et eius autoritas plurimum valeret ad veram doctrinam studiosis persuadendam . . ."[147] Martyr labored and longed to leave the city which no longer attracted him. Martyr's most complete description of these problems may be found in Martyr's letter to Wolfgang Musculus printed in Appendix II. As he earlier wrote to Melanchthon, Martyr would neither compromise the truth of the Gospel as he read it in sacred scripture, nor could he provoke a bitter theological opponent like Marbach with invective and irony. This period in Strasbourg equipped Martyr for a major role in Zurich.

NOTES TO CHAPTER IV

1. D. M. Loades, "The Enforcement of Reaction", J. E. H. XVI, (1965), p. 55.

2. Loc. cit.

3. Edward L. Cutts, Turning Points of English Church History, p. 10.

4. Actually there were two churches sponsored by Laski. One was the famed Church of Austin Friars. The other was a French congregation which met in a building on Threadneedle Street.

5. Frederick A. Norwood, The Reformation Refugees as an Economic Force, pp. 809.

6. John Foxe, The Acts and Monuments of John Foxe, (1838), p.430.

7. Gilbert Burnet, The History of the Reformation of the Church of England, (1843), p. 384.

8. Ibid., pp. 387-388.

9. Loc. cit.

10. A. F. Pollard, The History of England, p. 100.

11. H. F. M. Prescott, Mary Tudor, p. 201.

12. Burnet, op. cit., p. 383.

13. Ibid., p. 388.

14. Prescott, op. cit., p. 200.

15. Frederick A. Norwood, "The Marian Exiles - Denizens or Sojourners?"C. H. XIII (1944), p. 102.

16. John Strype, Memorials of Thomas Cranmer, (1694), p. 355.

17. Strype, op. cit., p. 356.

18. Norwood, op. cit., p. 106.

19. Strype, op. cit., p. 355.

20. Ibid., p. 356.

21. Ibid., p. 354.

22. Norwood, op. cit., p. 106.

23. Letters by Horn and Chambers (Sept. 19, 1556 and February 3, 1556), O. L. II, 132, 130.

24. Strype, op. cit., p. 361.

25. Norwood, op. cit., p. 105.

26. Strype, op. cit., p. 361.

27. Norwood, op. cit., p. 104.

28. O. L. II, p. 127.

29. Ibid., p. 116.

30. Norwood, op. cit., p. 103.

31. Prescott, op. cit., p. 200.

32. Ibid., p. 195.

33. Prayers (1569), "A Prayer out of the LVI. Psalme," i-ii.

34. Common Places (1583), Part five, "An Oration concerning the studie of divinitie, made to the Vniuersitie of Strasbourg after his returne out of England," p. 44.

35. A. S. T. 41, fol. 97. 7 September 1551. Strasbourg.

36. Loc. cit.

37. Ibid., fol. 99.

38. A. S. T. 41, fol. 105.

39. Ibid., fol. 107. "Noremborgae impressa."

40. A. S. T. 41, fol. 123.

41. "Quam uero de nostra Republica, Ecclesia & Schola Argentin-ensi, denique omnibus germanis Euangelicis, audiendi sim cupidus, modo non dicam: quoniam & tu fortasse uix crederes, & ego prorsus non possem exponere." 23 April 1553. Oxford. Conrad Hubert, Historia vera, p. 194^V.

42. Common Places (1583), Part five, p. 44.

43. Ibid., p. 92. John Sturm was rector of Strasbourg. See "la Pietas litterata de Jean Sturm et le developpement a Strasbourg d'une pedagogie oecumenique (1538-1581)," B. S. H. P. F. CXI (1967), 281-302.

44. O. L. II, p. 505. 3 November 1553.

45. O. L. II, p. 509. 15 December 1553 to Bullinger.

46. Oratio. He was born on 24 April 1521 and returned to Stras-bourg in 1545 after study in Wittenberg.

47. McLelland, op. cit., p. 286.

48. Translated from Alexander Schweizer, Die Protestantischen Centraldogmen in Ihrer Entwicklung Innerhalf Der Reformirten Kirche I, p. 275. Schwiezer gives neither the Latin text nor its location.

49. Common Places (1583), Part five, pp. 110-111. Calendes of January 1554.

50. Henri Strohl, Le Protestantisme en Alsace, pp. 77-79.

51. Arthur Cochrane, Reformed Confessions of the 16th Century, p. 75.

52. Ibid., p. 58.

53. A. S. T. 346, fol. 114.

54. C. R. VIII, 5613, col. 298.

55. Bindseil, Philippi Melanchthonis Epistolae, pp. 359-360.

56. Common Places (1583), Part five, p. 95.

57. L. C. III, p. 61.

58. Ibid., p. 63.

59. C. R.,XLIV, no. 2690, cols. 586-87. Reference to Melanchthon is to C. R. XV, cols. 1271-72. See the helpful survey in Charles Schmidt, La Vie Et Les Travaux De Jean Sturm, pp. 111-129: "Discussions avec les lutheriens de Strasbourg 1553-1563."

60. Laurentius Humfredus, Ioannis Iuelli Angli, Episcopi Sarisburiensis vita et mors . . ., pp. 87-91.

61. Reprinted in Strype, Memorials of the Reformation VII, 61 and 66-67.

62. Text of letter in Gorham, op. cit., pp. 333-335. See Christina M. Garrett, "John Ponet and the confession of the banished ministers," C. Q. R. 137 (Oct.-Dec. 1943), 47-74; 137 (Jan.-Mar. 1944), 181-204, especially pp. 187-191. The document under scrutiny is S. T. C. 5630: Nicolas Dorcastor. THE HVMBLE and vnfained confessio of the belefe of certain poore banished men.

63. O. L. II, p. 511. 22 January 1554.

64. Humphrey,op. cit., p. 89.

65. Remains of Edmund Grindal, p. 239.

66. Humphrey, op. cit., p. 89. See Henry J. Cowell, "English Protestant Refugeesin Strasbourg, 1553-1558," H. S. L. XV (1933-37), 69-120. On the temporary plans of the exiles see Frederick A. Norwood, "The Marian Exiles=Denizens or Sojourners?," C. H. XIII (1944), 100-110.

67. Ibid., p. 92. Geneuae idibus Junii, 1555.

68. Cowell, op. cit., pp. 77-78. My own search in 1971 found no surviving records in Strasbourg.

69. Ibid., p. 117. Jewel took down Martyr's lectures and sermons in shorthand.

70. Patrick Collinson, "The Authorship of a Brieff Discours off the Troubles Begonne at Frankford," J. E. H. IX (1958), 201-208.

71. There is a summary in Jaspar Ridley, John Knox, pp. 201-208. On this and other centers see Henry J. Cowell, "The sixteenth-century

English speaking refugee churches at Strasbourg, Basle, Zurich, Aarau, Wesel and Emden," H. S. L. P. XV (1937), 612-65, and "The sixteenth-century English speaking refugee churches at Geneva and Frankfort," H. S. L. P. XVI (1939), 209-30. Also Michael Walzer "Revolutionary ideology: The case of the Marian exiles," A. P. S. R. 57 (1963), 643-54. Walzer attacks John Knox here and in his volume, The Revolution of the Saints, pp. 66-67 and 100-109.

72. Latin text in The Works of John Knox IV, pp. 51-3.

73. Found in Humphrey, op. cit., pp. 93-95 and Loci Communes (1623), p. 767. Cox quotes from it to Gualter on 12 February 1571: "I find nothing in (Second Prayer Book of 1551 /sic/) that book contrary to godliness. We know that some contentious men have caviled at and culminated it. Such persons ought to have remembered that our Lord is not a God of contention, but of peace." Z. L. I., p. 235. Ronald J. Vander Molen, "Anglican Against Puritan: Ideological Origins during the Marian Exile," C. H. (1973), 45-57 omits reference to this correspondence.

74. John Strype, Ecclesiastical Memorials, (1816), VII, pp. 151-154, contains two letters of Foxe to Martyr. The second of 12 October 1554 urges Martyr to join the group to read divinity to them, going on to say: "Jam etsi nullus locus te vendicare poterit, attamen si indigentiam spectet excellentia tua, nulla certe Germaniae pars impensius eget operatura: si voluntatem ac vota hominum, nulla impotentius desiderat, quam Anglia nostra Francfordiana."

75. A Brieff discours off the troubles begonne at Franckford in Germany Anno Domini 1554. Abowte the Booke off common prayer and Ceremonies/and continued by the Englishe men theyre/to thende off O. Maries Raigne/in the which discours/the gentle reader shall see the uery originall and beginninge off all the contention that hathe byn/ and what was the cause off the same (Zurich: Christopher Froschouer?, M.C. LXXV), pp. VIII-XIII.

76. Ibid., p. XIII.

76a. Ibid., pp. XXII-XXIV.

77. Ibid., p. XXXVI.

77a. Ibid., pp. XXXVIII-XXXIX. Vander Molen, Richard Cox, pp. 186-187.

78. Ibid., pp. XXVII-XXXIX. Knox's account is also given in Works of John Knox (Laing) IV, pp. 41-49.

79. Common Places (1583), Part five, pp. 136-139. Bullinger's

copy in the Zurich Zentralbibliothek, Car. XV.20.S.89-97 has the following title in Bullinger's hand: <u>Ad peregrinae ecclesiae apud Francfordi-
enses fratres, de baptismo a Lutheranis administratio</u>. The <u>Loci
Communes</u> (1627) dates the letter to 30 September. The Latin text is
reprinted in <u>C. R.</u> XLVIII, 2014 and may be found in Humphrey, <u>op</u>. <u>cit</u>.,
pp. 93-95. Professor Rupp in conversation thinks the letter may be
about Strasbourg and not Frankfurt. Professor Stanford Reid reminded
me that if that was Martyr's advice to Frankfurt, apparently it was
not followed consistently. I follow Bullinger's title that the letter
was sent to Frankfurt but I also think it would be consistent with
advice given by Martyr to the Strasbourg refugees and thus additional
fuel for the Marbach conflict.

80. <u>Common Places</u> (1583), Part five, p. 137. The quotations
which follow are from pp. 137-139. McLelland, <u>op</u>. <u>cit</u>., p. 156 n.42
does not notice the Frankfurt setting of this letter. See McLelland,
pp. 154-159 for Martyr's comments on baptism from I <u>Corinthians</u> (7:14).

81. <u>O</u>. <u>L</u>. II, p. 513. 24 February 1554. This is an interesting
comment on Martyr's views on rebellion. Is it legal in his view to
oppose a catholic monarch and not a protestant one? The doctrine of
lesser magistrates permits them to intervene when the higher authority
abandons the Gospel.

82. <u>O</u>. <u>L</u>. II, pp. 515-16.

83. Gorham, <u>op</u>. <u>cit</u>., p. 319. Letter seems to be a response to
Melanchthon's letter of 29 May 1554. See letter to Calvin of 23
September 1555. "The Saxons do not rest. They have issued a most vain
Farrago (for so they call it). They gather certain sentences out of
the Fathers, and also out of Luther, Philip, Brentius, Pomeranus and
such like. They add to this Bucer, Illyricus and Joachim Westphal,
that they may be shown to agree among themselves."

84. Biblioteca Nazionale Centrale Vittorio Emanuele II, Roma,
Fondo Autografi, Busta 153, n. 23. Pietro Martire Vermigli, dissertaz-
ione (signed in Latin autograph letter). Calvin's <u>Defensio sanae
et orthodoxae doctrinae de sacramentis</u> was published in 1555 by
Stephanus at Geneva and Froschouer at Zurich.

85. See Antonio Rotondo, <u>Calvin and the Italian Anti-Trinitar-
ians</u>. <u>Common Places</u> (1583), Part five, pp. 96-98. Also William E.
Monter, "The Italians in Geneva, 1550-1600: A New Look," in <u>Geneve
et l'Italie</u>.

86. 31 August 1557 in M. Young. <u>The Life and Times of Aonio
Paleario</u> I, p. 582. "If it was desired to seek a professor for our
school, which does not equal yours in either numbers or in talent, it
would be unwise to attempt to draw away so superior a man from you."

87. <u>C</u>. <u>R</u>. XLIII, 2053 and 2089.

88. <u>C</u>. <u>R</u>. XLIII, 2014, Col. 236. 24 September 1554. "Ideoque consultum esse ut pios ministros sibi procurent, qui popolo evangelium pure doceant in aliis templis, ab illis abstineant, nec ibi quidquam coneantur reformare: quum tamen suos cives queant iure prohibere, ne ses idolatria contaminent."

89. <u>C</u>. <u>R</u>. XLIII, 2053. Calvin's answer to Martyr may be found in 2089 of 18 January 1555. See especially the interesting comment in col. 386: "Prudenter quidem admones quantum in ambiguis loquutionibus sit periculi, nec intempestive optimi Buceri exemplum profers. Siquidem nostra similis esset ratio."

90. <u>C</u>. <u>R</u>. XLIII, 2089. 18 January 1555.

91. See the comment on an expected <u>Genesis</u> commentary in a letter of 6 September 1554 in <u>C</u>. <u>R</u>. XLIII, 2003, col. 220.

92. <u>Common Places</u> (1583), Part five, p. 98.

93. <u>Hebrews</u> (2:15).

94. <u>Common Places</u> (1583), Part five, pp. 96-97. The same concern appears in a letter to Beza. <u>Ibid</u>., p. 105.

95. Gorham, <u>op</u>. <u>cit</u>., p. 349. 8 August 1555.

96. <u>Ibid</u>., p. 352.

97. <u>Ibid</u>., pp. 350-351.

98. <u>Ibid</u>., p. 351.

99. <u>Common Places</u> (1583), Part five, p. 105.

100. <u>Ibid</u>., p. 106.

101. Kilian McDonnell, <u>John Calvin, the Church, and the Eucharist</u>, p. 177. McDonnell nowhere documents this debt to Bucer.

102. <u>Praelectiones Doctiss</u>. <u>In Epistolam D. P. ad Ephesios</u>, <u>eximij doctoris D. Martini Buceri, habitae Cantabrigae in Anglia, Anno MD.L. & LI</u> (Basle: Petrus Perna, M.D.LXII). Neither Hopf, <u>op</u>. <u>cit</u>., nor Herbert Vogt mention Martyr with respect to this work. See Herbert Vogt, <u>Martin Bucer und die Kirche von England</u>.

103. <u>Praelectiones</u>, fol. 111-129.

104. _Ibid._, fol. 114F. Even so Peter Stephens endorses the much argued weakness in Bucer's understanding of the person of Christ. "Bucer does not sufficiently do justice to that element in the New Testament which stresses the newness of the situation created by the life, death, and resurrection of Christ, and the gift of the Holy Spirit." W. P. Stephens, _The Holy Spirit in the Theology of Martin Bucer_, p. 264.

105. John Calvin, _Institutio Christianae religionis_ fol. 245 and fol. 246.

106. W. Niesel, "Calvin wider Osianders Rechtfertigungslehre," _Z. K. G._ 46 (1928), 410-430.

107. Francois Wendel, _Calvin. The Origins and Development of His Religious Thought_, p. 238.

108. _Loc. cit. C. R._ LXXIX, col. 470. This series of sermons was begun in May of 1558.

109. _Corinthios_ (1551), p. 259[r], "Et recte patres aduersus haereticos, qui uel naturam humanum, uel naturam diuinam, uel utriusque coniunctionem in una persona, quod Christum, negabant, argumenta sua ex eucharistia deduxerunt."

110. Benjamin Charles Milner, Jr., _Calvin's Doctrine of the Church_, p. 168.

111. Gordon Bates, "The Typology of Adam and Christ in John Calvin," _H. Q._ 5 (1964), p. 47.

112. John Calvin, _Commentary on the Epistles of Paul the Apostle to the Corinthians_ II, 55-56.

113. _Discourse_, (1550), fol. cviii[v].

114. _Ibid._, fol. cix[r].

115. _C. R._ XLIII, 2357. Martyr to Calvin, 8 December 1555. The Basle edition printed in 1581 by Peter Perne has a separate analysis not found in the 1559 edition. This first appeared with the 1563 _Oratio_.

116. _Ibid._, col. 883. "De nostratium ecclesiae augmento et spirituali prosperitate mirifice gaudeo."

117. _Loc. cit._

118. _Common Places_ (1583), Part five, pp. 85-92.

119. Ibid., p. 86.

120. Loc. cit.

121. Ibid., p. 88. See letter to Calvin of 16 February 1556 in Common Places (1583), Part five, pp. 100-101.

122. Ibid., pp. 90-91. See K. E. Jordt Jørgensen,"Fejden mellem Lipomano og Radziwill i Wilno 1556," Festskrift til Jens Nørregaard, pp. 96-111.

123. Ibid., p. 139. "An Epistle to the Brethren of the City of Lucca."

124. Ibid., p. 140.

125. Ibid., p. 142.

126. Ibid., p. 141. "We promised to ourselves a quiet fruition of our goods with a holy Evangelical peace, sometimes going out of the City into the Country, and sometimes returning out of the Country into the City."

127. Psalms, (1569), "A prayer out of the cxiii Psalme."

128. O. L., p. 506. To Henry Bullinger on 3 November 1553.

129. C. R. 43, 1953. 9 May 1555 from Strasbourg. Dantine notes that in the Bolsec affair of 1555, Beza followed Martyr's counsel in preparing an explanation of the faith. This was published in the Tria Volumina Tractationem Theologicarum of 1570 in Geneva. This Summa totius Christianismi was translated in English in 1556. There is no evidence that Martyr compiled this treatise, except that his position would have been well known to Beza. Beza added Biblical references on Martyr's advice. Johannes Dantine, "Les Tabelles sur la Doctrine de la Predestination par Theodore De Beze," R. T. P, troisieme serie, Tome XVI (1966), p. 367. See C. T. B. I, 153 where letter to Beza commenting on same affair is dated to March 1555. Therefore the above letter to Calvin must be 9 May 1555. See the reference to Morrison, Cheke and Cox whom Martyr soon expected.

130. C. R. 44, 2377. 13 January 1556.

131. C. R. 44 2479, cols. 193-197. 4 June 1556.

132. Ibid., col. 195.

133. See above chapter two, note 39 on letter to Melanchthon.

134. C. R. XLIII, 2233, col. 663. 18 June 1555.

135. C. R. XLIII, 2237, cols. 667-668. 3 July 1555. See Peter Walser, "Glaube und leben bei Heinrich Bullinger," Z II (1959-63), pp. 613-14 for a sensitive discussion of Bullinger's views on the Christian life.

136. Common Places (1583), Part five, p. 99.

137. O. L. II, p. 519. 18 February 1556.

138. Z. S. A. EII (342), fol. 323.

139. Common Places (1583), Part five, p. 111. 4 April 1556.

140. Ibid., p. 110. Bullinger 7 May 1556. See also 22 May 1556 on p. 109: "Of my coming, stand you in no doubt; I do all things and I set all things awork that I may be dismissed."

141. Ibid., p. 112. 3 June 1556.

142. A. S. T. 43, fols. 313-314. 8 June 1556.

143. Archives of Strasbourg, "A Calendar of the 'Protocols of the Council and 21' of Strasbourg, 1554-8," Vol. 34, 1556, ff. 287-r-v. Monday, 29 June 1556. Cited in C. H. Garrett, The Marian Exiles 1553-1559, p. 368.

144. See Ibid., p. 367 for request from Zurich for Martyr to fill Pellican's position.

145. See Hottinger's discussion of the problem in a letter to Bullinger. C. R. XLIV, 2448, Col. 143.

146. "Non vult magistratus ut quaestio haec in schola disputetur . . . ." C. R. XLIV, 2494, cols. 221-222. To Calvin on 7 July 1556,

147. C. R. XLIV, 2507, col. 246. End of July, 1 August 1556.

CHAPTER V

ZURICH THEOLOGIAN (1556/62)

THEOLOGY OF ELECTION

The protocol description of Martyr's invitation to Zurich faces
one with the question of his honesty. Could he in good conscience sign
the Augsburg Confession and yet refuse to lecture on its basis? One
must recall Martyr's own formal statement given to the College of St.
Thomas on 27 December 1553.[1] "First, I readily embrace and acknowledge
the Augustan Confession, and whatever others do not differ from it, if
rightly and profitably understood." When one realizes that the Council
in 1556 had seen the outcome of Martyr's attempt to "rightly and profitably" understand this confession and others in the light of Holy
Scripture, their comment on his Calvinism ought not to be read as a
negative judgment on his motives. One of those other confessions would
have been the Tetrapolitan. Simler gives additional information on
Martyr's discussion with the Strasbourg Senate in 1556.

> Therefore when he was demanded by the magnificall and noble Senate
> what his mind was, he nothing dissembled, but showed that leave to
> depart would be very welcome to him: and he testified at large of
> his good will towards the common weale . . . . And to be desirous
> of this leave, first he said he was urged by his vocation, and then
> moved by threates and comminations. Besides that he feared the
> judgements of the gravest men who had read his writings and had
> heard him teach, if by his silence he should seem not only to for-
> sake, but also as it were to betray the truth, at other times de-
> fended with the peril of his life, and now many and sundrey ways
> privily and openly oppugned. For of these men of whom some of
> them either for the very same cause would be burned with fire, or
> else remaining yet alive did to great purpose bear rule in the
> Churches of Christ, he said he might not choose but be greviously
> reproved, as that he either departed from his upright judgement
> (which crime of inconstancy is not to be suffered in a Christian
> man) or else who would in silence let slip those things, which he
> knew to be profitable and necessary unto salvation.[2]

The point is that the Strasbourg Senate could not continue Martyr's license to teach because they knew what would be the outcome. They and Martyr then agreed that he should go to Zurich where his vocation would permit him to defend the truth openly in lectures and sermons. So Martyr left Strasbourg on 13 July 1556 with John Jewel to be lodged in Bullinger's house at Zurich where he was warmly received by the Senate of the School and the ministers. Simler's statement, "and of all godly" should not be dismissed as hagiography, but rather taken that not all in Zurich were pleased at their new lecturer in Old Testament studies. Martyr lectured on the *Psalms, Minor Prophets, Samuel* and *Kings*. Unmarried when he arrived in Zurich Martyr soon married one Catharine Merenda from Brescia, a member of the Italian Church in Geneva.[3] In his inaugural address at Zurich Martyr set forth that quality of life which ever since his Italian days had been sustained by the knowledge of the truth and the Holy Spirit.[4]

During this residence in Zurich Martyr involved himself in a quarrel over predestination, declined Calvin's call in 1557 to join the Italian congregation in Geneva as pastor and participated in the 1561 Colloquy of Poissy. Through Jewel and the several English residents of Zurich who became Bishops under Queen Elizabeth, Martyr contributed to the restoration of protestantism in England. James Pilkington described the import of Martyr's move for the Marian exiles in a letter to Bullinger of 27 June 1556.

> Continue, moreover, as you have begun, and do honour to yourself
> and all your friends by your kindness to the exiles: for the Lord
> is pleased by such offerings, he has them in everlasting

remembrance, and can never forget your beneficence towards his proscribed people. But though your numerous noble actions are quoted by many with much grateful acknowledgment, there is not any thing in which they really rejoice more, than in that you are endeavouring to draw over to you Peter Martyr. Many persons remark how unbefitting it is, and especially in these times, that the mouth of such a man should be stopped; and many persons are promising themselves great things concerning him, when they perceive how great an accession he will be to the cause of truth in your most free city.[5]

Martyr's Zurich stay will be described in chronological order so that one can follow Martyr's thought as it developed in response to the realities of his time. It was Robert Masson who collected Martyr's writings posthumously in the *Loci Communes* of 1576. To provide a chronology of those writings and to sketch Martyr's career from his larger literary deposit is to understand the setting of these commonplaces which Masson compiled from Martyr's writings.

Again Martyr wrote to Calvin about predestination which he had taken up when lecturing on *Romans* at Oxford. Martyr notified Bullinger in 1553 that he would publish the *Romans Commentary* in that year. There Bullinger could perceive the nature of Martyr's teaching.[6]

I must however candidly confess that I cannot but lament that our churches are agitated from time to time by new controversies: we have had, I think, quite disputing enough. May God of his goodness grant us all so to feel respecting predestination, that what ought to be the greatest consolation to believers, may not become the painful subject of pernicious contention.[7]

Bullinger who later dissented from Calvin's response to Bolsec, had refused to sign the *Consensus* of 1551 on predestination. In June of 1557 Theodore Bibliander openly opposed this doctrine in his College at Zurich. Martyr who was in the midst of lectures on the passage in I *Samuel* where Saul was rejected as King, discussed the doctrine at length with Calvin:

> I have read your book (the two works against Castellio) with the
> greatest delight; God redounded your defence unto honour and to
> the defence of the orthodox faith − so hold I for my own part,
> I concur with you in all points. I have begun to treat of pre-
> destination, and shall continue with it the whole week. Not only
> does the inducement of the passage move me to declare it, but
> also because my College, as you know, is widely separate from me
> in regard to this, and has spoken against the doctrine in lectures
> the past week.[8]

In 1554 Martyr told Calvin that he and Zanchi defended Calvin on
the eternal election of God.[9] This continued at Zurich when Martyr in
January of 1560 answered Bibliander's challenge to a debate issued in
December of 1559. Staedke has unraveled the threads of this issue.
Bibliander's initial joy over Martyr's Zurich residence was short lived
indeed. Bullinger wrote Martyr on 1 May 1556 that "Theodore himself .
. . greets you singularly."[10] In fact, Martyr viewed Bibliander as his
Barnabas. Like St. Paul's disciple, Bibliander was "an honest man."
Details of the controversy in 1557 can be seen in Martyr's letter to
Calvin of 1 July 1557.

On 10 December 1559 Jacob Rüger at Schaffhausen received a letter
from Bullinger rumoring a debate between Martyr and Bibliander (de
prouidentia pugna). In January 1560 Martyr defended his views before
the College. There seems to be some question about Martyr's response
printed in the *Loci Communes* of 1576 and subsequent editions. Staedke
evaluates the inclusion of three tracts on this subject in the *Loci
Communes*. The three are *Propositiones De Libero Arbitrio*, *Propositiones
De Providentia et Praedestinatione* and *Propositiones An Deus sit Causa
et Author peccati.*[11] These three treatises are in manuscript in

Zurich.[12] Staedke finds Brassel's discussion assigning them to Bullinger so full of mistakes that a new study is necessary. It seems that
since Bullinger's *Diary* is wrong and the handwriting is not Martyr's,
one can still question their authorship. Staedke thinks the tracts are
not from Martyr's hand nor by Bullinger, though the hand may be that
of their Zurich contemporary Rudolf Gualter.[13] The author of these
tracts can not be determined by paeleography alone.

A longer treatise seems to be by Martyr since its comments on free
will parallel those in the *Romans* commentary. The interesting reference
in this treatise is to Oecolampadius on *Isaiah,* perhaps to the 1525
edition at Cologne. One reads that Oecolampadius is "Ecclesiae nostrae
Tigurinae bene coniunctus . . ."[14] Martyr went on to say with St. Paul
in II *Corinthians* "What are we to think? If the Spirit of God shall
relate to us either the law or promises, or the words of sacred scripture, neither is a change decreed nor shall we be moved so that we are
worthy and suitably disposed toward them."[15] This would seem to confirm Martyr's language in *Romans* (9) that God does not coerce a man to
change his mind but rather compels the predestinate to be conformed
by the Spirit. It is not surprising to find direct references to
Zwingli on *Romans, On True and False Religion* and several patristic
writers in *De Libero Arbitrio.*[16]

One notes the terminology used in the longer tract *De Libero
Arbitrio.* In *Romans* (9) and its commonplace on predestination and
election the opposite terms are "predestinate" and "reprobate." In
the theological treatise which should be assigned to 1560 one reads

about "regenerate" and "impious."[17] The language has taken on a moral

tone which may mean one of several things. Since Martyr according to

McLelland wrote the *An Deus sit causa et Author peccati,*[18] his theme

of *unio Christi* has led Martyr between 1550 and 1560 to alter his

vocabulary from "predestinate" to "regenerate." There is no question

that a debate took place in Zurich at this time over predestination.

Schmidt discusses Martyr's 1561 defense of Zanchi on predestina-

tion. Zanchi remained in Strasbourg until 1564 while Martyr took up

residence in Zurich. In a letter to Peter Sturm Martyr supported the

fourteen theses of Zanchi drawn up after an eight day visit to Zurich[19]

There Martyr reminded Sturm that wisdom and leniency no longer would

do. Extreme and harsh remedies were needed.[20] Martyr could not accept

the views current at Strasbourg since Zanchi who opposed them taught

nothing contrary to the divine letters, Augustine, Luther or Bucer.[21]

On 29 December 1561 Martyr composed a Zurich view on predestina-

tion.[22] Since it not only supports Zanchi but also represents Zurich,

an analysis of its language is valuable. Point ten is decisive where

Martyr supported Zanchi's view that the *regenerate* man struggled over

sin which was the victory of the outward man. Martyr's agreement added

that a *regenerate* man sinned reluctantly as in *Romans* (7:15).[23] The

entire experience led Martyr to reaffirm predestination *in Christo* as

he had in lectures at Oxford and with Cranmer at Lambeth . Thus

Bullinger who refused in 1551 to sign any synthesis let Martyr speak

for the Zurich theologians a decade later.[24]

Calvin in February of 1557 urged Martyr to come to Geneva as

pastor of the Italian Church. Calvin would share the Biblical
lectures, or even "resign the whole task to you, so far as your con-
venience will permit."[25] In September Calvin in a letter to the Zurich
Senate again invited Martyr to be pastor of the Italian Genevan Church.
There Calvin called Martyr a man whose mission in Geneva would be "to
the incredible profit of both the men of his own nation and ourselves."[26] In April Calvin received a reply from Martyr on the forthcoming August dispute in Worms. Martyr commented on Melanchthon, Brenz
and Marbach who would defend them against the Papal Party.[27] "What
will you say, is Saul among the Prophets? The matter is come to these
men." By August Martyr could endorse the Göppingen confession drawn up
by Farel and Beza with the Lutheran Jacob Andreae.

> What you did write unto me a few days since of the confession of
> Farellus and Beza, seemeth to be even as you say: to wit, that
> all things were done simply and sincerely of them. Wherefore for
> my part I think well of it, neither have I perceived any offence
> in any other thing whereby the content and ecclesiastical unity
> should be one iota diminished in any respect.[28]

Valerand Poullain wrote Martyr from Heidelberg about the confession.
His letter of 5 June 1557 has recently been published for the first
time. Among other questions Poullain worried about the ambiguity of
terms such as *sola fide* in Article 2.[29] Poullain had been in England
with Martyr where he arranged a mass exodus of French-Walloons to England at Glastonbury during 1550-1553.[30] Beza's comment to Bullinger
and Martyr is apropos of such simplicity. Beza amplified his and
Farel's confession by adding the New Testament references desired by
Martyr.[31]

This confession is that drawn up at Göppingen on 14 May 1557 after

Beza had a lengthy interview with Jacob Andreae. The confession was an

attempt to unify the German and Swiss churches which pleased the

Germans but not Bullinger, who was unhappy that Martyr received a copy.[32]

Calvin saw nothing dangerous in this confession.[33] What is interesting

about the confession is Martyr's endorsement though Bullinger rejected

it. Since the Lambeth Palace document has not been used in this discus-

sion some questions remain to be solved. The Lambeth document dated 14

May 1557, is signed by Farel and Beza but ascribed to Jan Laski![34]

Jacob Andreae (1528-1590) received his doctorate in 1553 and that

year became pastor as well as general - superintendent at Göppingen.

Beza would meet Andreae again at Poissy (1561) and in the famous Collo-

quy of Montbeliard in 1586.[35] Martyr's conciliatory attitude in this

affair of 1557 is important for assessing his relation to Bullinger.

Bullinger was out of sorts with Beza, Martyr, Farel, Calvin and several

others on this issue.

Martyr's influence on Bullinger, Beza and Calvin can best be seen

where he urged each to explain that communication with Christ which he

noted in letters to Calvin and Beza during March 1555. That each

responds positively to Martyr is evidence of their theological agree-

ment. The debates at Oxford, Strasbourg and Zurich are now developed

as part of a positive concern for experiencing the benefits of Christ.

On sacramental theology and predestination there is a growing consensus

between Calvin, Beza, Bullinger, Martyr and Farel. Martyr defended

predestination because for him it was a great consolation.[36]

One should note two facets of this ancient theological issue.
Martyr seems to follow St. Paul at *Romans* (9-11) in using the plural.
Corporate predestination is the biblical manner of speaking, a nuance
in all these reformers from Wyclif's *De Ecclesia* to Calvin which their
opponents like Erasmus and Castellio seem to overlook. If election
seemed difficult to explain, the fact that Jesus spoke in parables was
likewise hard to understand. *Mark* (4:11-12) states that Jesus did this
on purpose so that, "while seeing they may see and not understand, and
while hearing they may hear and not comprehend, lest they might turn
and it be forgiven them." This Markan citation of *Isaiah* (6:9-10) is
paralleled in *John* (12:40) and *Acts* (28:26-27) in a shift to result.

ELIZABETHAN ENGLAND

While absent from England Martyr maintained his interest in the
English Church by advising the Marian Exiles in Frankfurt, opening his
quarters to exiles in Strasbourg and assisting the English colony in
Zurich. After Martyr left Strasbourg in 1556 Edmund Grindal wrote from
Strasbourg to John Foxe about Cranmer. On 28 December 1557 Grindal
discussed Cranmer's views on the Eucharist published in 1556.

> I have heard it sometimes muttered in England, that occasionally
> the archbishop of Canterbury falsely attributes to the papists
> what they do not hold. And, if I rightly remember, he has certain
> contrasts between the popish doctrine and ours, expressed in this
> form: 'They say' – 'We say.' He states, I believe, in the same
> place, that the papists affirm the body of Christ to be every
> where: which they nowhere teach; but earnestly maintain, that it
> is upon every altar. If in course of translating you should find
> things of this kind, (for I bring forward this merely for example,)
> or if any where he does not fully satisfy your own judgment, you
> would, in my opinion, do well, if you were to send to Peter Martyr
> a list of such places, and ask his advice on the work of his most
> loving patron. He would communicate it, I well know, most

willingly; and perhaps, if he has himself marked any similar passages besides, would point them out to you.[37]

When John Jewel went with Martyr to Zurich in 1556 he found a group of English students with Thomas Lever, Master of St. John's College Cambridge. Twelve students came with Lever when he fled two months after Queen Mary's accession. Lever traveled from Zurich to Geneva via Berne and Lausanne, where on 13 October 1554 he began regular attendance at Calvin's lectures. After vain efforts to reconcile the parties at Frankfort, Lever in September of 1556 became minister of the English congregation at Aarau.[38] The number of prominent English students can be seen by consulting Boesch's list. Among those in Zurich were Robert Horn, in 1560 Bishop of Winchester; James Pilkington, in 1560 Bishop of Durham; Thomas Bentham, in 1560 Bishop of Coventry and Lichfield; Laurence Humphrey, President of Magdalen College, Oxford; William Cole, President of Corpus Christi College, Oxford; Robert Beaumont, Master of Trinity College, Cambridge; John Parkhurst, in 1560 Bishop of Norwich; Edwin Sandys, in 1559 Bishop of Worcester and in 1570 of London; and Jewel, who became Bishop of Salisbury in 1559.[39] Many of these Martyr influenced, so much so that he received invitations during Elizabeth's reign to return to England.[40] England was still Martyr's "altera patria."

Martyr's zeal for English affairs quickened by January of 1558. Sir Anthony Cooke wrote from Strasbourgurging compassion for an England which was afflicted in so many ways.[41] By April Sampson could write from Frankfurt: "We have no news from England, except that the Queen

is wholly occupied in raising money and troops, it may be, possibly,
to make war against herself."[42]

Three weeks later Martyr mentioned to Calvin the marvel of the
Imperial coronation. Ferdinand of Austria was crowned without a mass.[43]
The authority of the Roman Antichrist had been breached; now perhaps
with Maximilian of Bohemia and Philip of Saxony an evangelical religion
could be established in which the mass would be abolished and the Eucharist might no longer be a matter of discord![44] On 22 May 1558 Calvin
was pleased that Martyr agreed with him on predestination in the soon
to be published *Romans*. He also inquired into the state of Martyr's
commentaries on *Genesis* and the *Prophets*. "Why are you not here",
wrote Calvin, "that I might wrench from your hands what you long keep
back." Martinego was very ill. The Italian church at Geneva was in
turmoil over the teaching of Gribaldus that "there is one God who is
the father of Christ . . . who is in truth secondary and first born
among many gods."[45]

Gribaldi in 1554 prepared a heterodox confession of faith which
established his reputation as an Anti-trinitarian.[46] Beza described the
confession in his letter to Bullinger of 1 January /1556/.[47] Martyr
also received a copy of Gribaldi's confession from Beza. Zanchi mentioned the situation in a letter to Beza of 6 July 1556.

> While in Zurich I have seen Bullinger's confession in his own hand
> against Gribaldi in which nothing seems to be lacking. Before
> that I have also seen Gribaldi's own written account which fights
> against this confession itself. Doubtless it is that account
> whose copy some time ago you sent to Martyr.[48]

Gribaldi's confession was addressed to his brothers in Christ because of public dispute over the unity of God. His primary exegetical support came from *John* (10:30), "I and the Father are One."[49] To use the abstract language of hypostasis will not do, for Gribaldi said that where St. Paul and Apollus are said to be one in the scriptures, that one analogy is one of two apostles and one apostolate. In this way one can easily understand the unity among many hypostaseis.[50] The sequel in Geneva to this 1554 confession is recorded by the *Register of the Company of Pastors*. On 29 June 1555 Gribaldi appeared before this body.

> The following Saturday, because Matteo Gribaldi, Sire de Farges, had maintained and written a number of heretical opinions and had criticized the doctrine preached in this church, the Syndic of the Consistory, Pierre-Jean Jesse, and M. Jean de la Maisonneuve and the ministers assembled, and Gribaldi was summoned. He arrived accompanied by several Italians and in particular by the physician Maitre Francois. On entering he asked: "Where is Master Calvin?" and offered his hand to him. M. Jean Calvin, however, refused to take it, saying: "I will not shake hands until we are in agreement over doctrine, for we should not open these proceedings with formalities." Thereupon Gribaldi said: "Adieu, messieurs," and went off. Soon afterwards he was summoned to the city hall and reproved for his errors by M. Calvin, in the presence of the Syndic and other members of the Council.[51]

Martyr saw that Calvin's description was accurate when he talked to the physician George Blandrata.

> By these men is appointed in the divine nature a monark of the father only, and they affirm not that there is one essence of the father and of the son. And since they will have a distinction or diversity in the divine essence, they cannot avoid but that they confess a multitude of Gods, which Gribald in plain terms (as I hear) did affirm.[52]

Martyr seems also to have advised the Italian congregation in Zurich. Ochino in his 1558 letter about Martyr and Florio discussed the same issue in that congregation. It came down to whether or not

Christ made an infinite sacrifice for human sin by his obedience to the Father's will and death on the cross. Ochino has preached that fundamental matter in Zurich. "Especially did Peter Martyr approve of my sermon on the true faith and has written a letter to Michael Angelo . . . ."[53]

One catches here that Martyr was called upon to defend his dear friend Ochino at a time when so many doctrinal aberrations split the Italian refugee congregations. This whole affair saddened Martyr and he could no longer restrain himself when he wrote Utenhove on 29 November 1559. During that year and a half one reads between Martyr's lines a bitterness that must refer to his countrymen in Zurich and Geneva even though the letter is addressed to Poland. By then an incredible situation had arisen for the number of alien sects brought on the Church by God was "because of our sins." That seems to be the point alluded to in Ochino's letter of 4 June 1558.[54] Ochino's sympathy and toleration for Anabaptists was the cruelest blow of all to the orthodox Martyr. Does not his letter to Utenhove suggest Martyr's chagrin about Ochino? When in 1563 Castellio latinized the *Thirty Dialogues*, including one in defense of polygamy, Ochino was compromised.

When Sampson wrote Martyr again on 10 July 1558 he mentioned the preparation for war between England and Spain. Sampson found on his return from Strasbourg that the English at Frankfurt "are in a perpetual motion, more perverse than useful."[55] From Geneva Martyr heard about the apostasy of Sylvester who had fallen prey to the anti-trinitarianism disturbing the Italian congregation. Christopher Goodman

remarked, "I pray God speedily to purge his church from such a pestilence . . ."[56] Goodman would have enjoyed the peace in Frankfurt

which he and John Knox had as English pastors in Geneva if it had not

been for the "dregs of popery" which contaminated the purity of reli-

gion in Frankfurt. In September Martyr warned Calvin about France:

"Others perhaps do marvel at the Queen. But I marvel not: for I never

perceived hithertoo any token of her godliness towards sincere reli-

gion."[57]

Martyr found himself involved in the extension of protestantism

in Poland, Bohemia, France and the cities of the Marian Exiles. Martyr

prayed for restoration of the "pure gospel" in England. When Elizabeth

gained the throne Martyr sent her a lengthy treatise which not only

rejoiced at her coronation but also provided a detailed explanation of

those biblical passages which discuss a godly ruler. Elizabeth burst

into tears when she read his letter.[58] Martyr compared England's re-

cent experience to the death and resurrection of Christ, or again to

the wilderness wandering of the Israelites after fleeing from Egypt.

Martyr touched on this theme of restitution when he wrote:

> Wherefore by the mercy and goodness of the son of God, in whome
> only you did put your trust, you are revived and by good help
> of God do enjoy the kingdom of your father and grandfather, and
> that to the safty of the Church of Christ, and to the restitution
> of the commonweal of England falling into decay.[59]

The decay in the English Church could be ended if Elizabeth would follow

the biblical example of David. As David restored the holy Ark to Zion

with great joy among the people, so too Elizabeth has been given a

similar task "to restore again into his place the holy Gospel of

Christ."[60] Martyr was persuaded that Elizabeth "is both of a ready mind and will to restore the Evangelical Religion,"[61] going on to remind her that a ruler must serve God in two ways; as a man, by faithful believing and living, as a king by establishing laws which command just and holy things and forbid the contrary.[62] On 22 August 1559 Martyr wrote to Richard Cox about Elizabeth, "For she recalls religion to evangelical purity."[63]

Jan Utenhove had written the good news of Poland's possible conversion to the Reformed faith. Martyr surveyed the European scene in his reply by touching on England, Poland, Scotland, Spain, Flanders and France. He resolved to dedicate his confutation of Gardiner to the Queen of England.[64] From January of 1559 the bulk of Martyr's extant correspondence is with Elizabethan reformers such as John Jewel. Martyr's influence on the subsequent development of English protestantism has not been thoroughly investigated.[65] It is not possible to trace the process by which these Marian exiles were selected as bishops, though they scarcely "elected themselves."[66] Collinson does not mention Martyr's letter to Elizabeth nor indeed Cooke's report of her responses, perhaps because it may be historiographically fashionable to focus on the controversy over Vestments. One can hardly fail to see the ideological connection between Martyr and the Elizabethan Bishops. More recently Collinson has described the influence of Martin Bucer on Archbishop Edmund Grindal.[67] Thomas Sampson for example had scruples about episcopal service. His *nolo episcopari* occurs in a letter to Martyr from Strasbourg. "In case the queen should invite me to any ecclesiastical office, such, I mean, as the government of a church,

can I accept such appointment with a safe conscience . . .?"[68]

Collinson's "conundrum" as he calls it remains after one reads

Martyr's letter and senses the Queen's response. There is an interest-

ing report from Vergerio to Sir Henry Killigrew on 1 February 1559.

Duke Christopher of Württemberg reported to Vergerio,

> that he had heard by letter that the Queen had summoned Peter
> Martyr. When the writer expressed his disbelief, the Duke replied
> that such was the impression current among the Princes, and that
> this opinion would endamage her popularity, since it gave rise to
> the impression chat at the very outset of her reign she wished to
> introduce into her kingdom a doctrine contrary to that of those
> Princes."[69]

MacCaffrey points to the laymen of the period whose convictions he

feels were scarcely religious. The two ambassadors in Paris and Edin-

burgh, Nicolas Throckmorton and Thomas Randolf often used the rhetoric

of the new faith for their dispatches.

> For them independence from foreign ecclesiastical authority, the
> expulsion of the clergy from the political stage, and the shaping
> of the ecclesiastical structure to that of the state were at least
> as important, if not more so, than the renewed spiritual vigour
> and the rigorous enforcement of the godly discipline which the new
> faith offered . . . This curious blend of the hot Gospel and
> Machiavelli led to a basic confusion whenever the interests of a
> supra-national faith clashed with those of the English (or Scot-
> tish, or French) states and produced a wavering and uncertain
> note.[70]

If however a confusion arose in their conduct of foreign policy, it

would seem to argue for sincere religious views which interfered with

political doctrine.

Since only Christ according to scripture is the head of the church,

Sampson had demurred on three points. First of all, a bishop cannot discharge properly his office when there is no church discipline. Then, too, little revenue is left after civil burdens have been met to support learned men or give relief to the poor. Finally Sampson deplored episcopal election without consent of clergy or people. These scruples are substantial matters to be kept in mind if one interprets Collinson's remark to mean that some of the exiles elected themselves as bishops under Elizabeth. In private correspondence Professor Collinson has clarified that phrase. ". . . while the processes which made these men bishops are largely obscured from us, such processes there must have been, since they cannot be held to have elected /or selected/ themselves."[71]

John Jewel reported that fourteen English episcopal sees were vacant.[72] Though he had traveled only to Strasbourg on his journey to England, Jewel told Martyr on 28 December 1558 about the uncertainty over the Queen's prohibition of preaching.[73] From London on 20 March 1559 Jewel reported on the state of religion. Things were beginning to shake and almost fall as Elizabeth moved cautiously though openly favouring their cause.[74] Whatever accuracy this report may or may not contain, it is important that Jewel felt this way and communicated it to Martyr. A disputation was to commence on 31 March against the Bishops who were acting as sole monarch. "The Queen regards you most highly: she made so much of your letter, that she read it over with the greatest eagerness a second and third time."[75]

In April 1559 Jewel described the March disputation to Martyr. The assembly gathered at Westminster on 31 March where Dr. Cole harangued to the effect that public prayers must be retained.[76] He

first queried the use of Latin, secondly the power of a provincial

church to establish or abrogate ecclesiastical rites for edification

and finally challenged any thought of a propitiatory sacrifice in the

mass "which cannot be proved by the holy scriptures."[77] A subsequent

disputation did not occur though there was a meeting on 3 April 1559

which weakened the people's opinion of the Bishops.[78] On 14 April

Jewel reported about his party's circumspection. People joked that

under Mary "Christ was cast out by his enemies, so he is now kept out

by his friends."[79] Many persons inquired whether Martyr's recall would

make him feel disposed to return to England.[80] Martyr responded to all

of this in an unpublished letter to Cox of 22 August 1559. "For she

recalls religion to evangelical purity."[81]

During the remainder of 1559 Martyr by his recently published book

against Stephen Gardiner and his *Romans* Commentary aided the continental

party in England.[82] Jewel hoped that the prior state of religion under

Edward VI could be restored, presumably through episcopal appointments

among the continental party. There was small hope of Martyr's return

to England.[83] Martyr's 1559 letters to Sampson answered his scruples

about accepting episcopal appointment.[84] He appreciated Sampson's

dilemma, that to act in variance with one's teaching would destroy

rather than build up the church. His advice to Sampson was radical.

> Truly, if we hated superstitions from the heart, we should endeav-
> or by all means that their very vestiges should be rooted out. I
> would that we had been somewhat better instructed by the obstinate
> zeal of our adversaries . . . Why do not we take care in like
> manner to depart as far as possible from their pernicious

institutions, and aim at apostolic simplicity, not only in doctrine, but also in the administration of the sacraments?[85]

Martyr urged Sampson to continue preaching but abstain from administering the sacraments. This was Bullinger's advice as well![86]

By August 1559 Jewel reported his work on a commission to establist religion which took in a journey of some seven hundred miles. The appointment of several friends to bishoprics must have been good news for Martyr.[87] In May Jewel wrote to Bullinger about the universities in which Martyr's work had been ruined.

> Our universities are so depressed and ruined, that at Oxford there are scarcely two individuals who think with us . . . That despicable friar Soto and another Spanish monk, I know not who, have so torn up by the roots all that Peter Martyr had so prosperously planted, that they have reduced the vineyard of the Lord into a wilderness.[88]

The reference is to the Dominican Thomist theologian Dominic Soto whom Charles V named Imperial Theologian at the Council of Trent. Soto succeeded to the Jesuit Melchior Cano's chair in theology at Salamanca in 1552. Jewel in this letter told Bullinger that even a dog from Zurich would be welcome in wicked and barbarous England. Patrick McGrath's comment is appropriate. "Whatever Jewel might think, the government was no more enthusiastic about welcoming dogs from Zurich than it was about welcoming unmuzzled wolves from Geneva."[89] In November and December more favorable reports passed from England to Zurich. In fact Martyr's books were eagerly awaited in England. Martyr's friends devoured the tract on monastic vows written against Richard Smith.[90]

Popular excitement in London led to the destruction of much church property, including the crucifix and candles from the royal chapel. In October the Spanish ambassador wrote, "the crucifixes and vestments that were burned a month ago publicly are now set up again in the royal chapel."[91] Jewel on 16 November 1559 wrote Martyr that there was too much foolery: "That little silver cross, of ill-omened origin, still maintains its place in the queen's chapel. Wretched me, this thing will soon be drawn into a precedent."[92] In spite of the circulation in England of Martyr's writings and the possibility of the Queen's invitation for Martyr to return, other slow-paced horses retarded the chariot.[93] Martyr was cautious after first opposing the crucifix/cross.[94]

By January 1560 the controversy upset the volatile Sampson who could no longer hope for any good while such idolatry continued or the Lord's Supper was celebrated apart from any sermon.[95] Martyr tried to salve Sampson's conscience by suggesting that in England there may be a political reason for using the square cap and external episcopal habit. Martyr suggested that even if one's conscience were bothered, doctrinal accord could still be reached if one could bear with such practices.[96] Jewel also mentioned the disputation to take place on 5 February 1560 about the crucifix.[97] "For matters are come to pass, that either the crosses of silver and tin, which we have everywhere broken in pieces, must be restored, or our bishopricks relinquished."[98] In March Jewel informed Martyr that his Divinity lectureship was still open at Oxford and that Cecil and the Queen though busy with affairs of religion and state kept Martyr in mind.[99] In April Bishop Sandys in mentioning the image controversy went on to say how much Martyr was

needed in England.

> How much injury England is now receiving by your absence, as to
> the affairs of the church and religion, I am accustomed very
> frequently and earnestly to impress upon those to whom is
> committed the management of the state. But their minds are so
> much occupied with other matters of the greatest importance,
> that nothing, I see, has been hitherto determined with respect
> to inviting you back. The queen I know was at one time very
> desirous of recalling you: you will easily comprehend, I suppose,
> what prevented it. The cause of Christ has always many adver-
> saries, and the best persons are always the worst spoken of. This
> pretence of unity is daily giving rise to many divisions.[100]

Martyr had many such episcopal supporters even though he was not in

England at this time. What use was made of his writings in the later

Puritan debacle is another subject for another day. Thomas Cartwright

in the 1570's made good use of Martyr's biblical writings.

During 1560 controversy continued.[101] Jewel's letters reflect his

own dismay that external display carried such weight among the defenders

of the faith. For example, when Jewel wrote from Salisbury that the

Church was finally at peace his reference must have been to these ques-

tions. Elsewhere there was quiet, as he understood it. Doctrinally

there was in his view no longer any danger from Arianism, Anabaptists

and other such pests.[102] Meanwhile in London reports came of trouble

in the Stranger's Churches. Martyr sent a long letter to the church in

London on 15 February 1561, in July declined an inquiry to reside once

more in England, and in August Parkhurst of Norwich heard from Martyr.

In all of these letters one can see Peter Martyr's theological acumen.

The Stranger's Church requested Martyr's opinion on the person of

Christ. Martyr refuted the Anabaptist position by showing that such heresies removed their holders from the Church. The teaching in question was whether or not Christ came in the flesh from heaven apart from a virgin birth. That Christ has only heavenly flesh was an attempt on the part of some to escape attributing human error to the Christ by virtue of his natural birth.[103] It is important that such an issue should elicit a vigorous response from Martyr, when over a crucifix or vestments he could urge moderation. It shows that Martyr established a hierarchy of values with respect to external and internal ecclesiastical questions, as in the 1550 letter to Cooche on Christ's divinity.

This controversy arose in the Dutch Strangers Church as Adriaan von Haemstede appealed to Martyr when cited before the authorities. Grindal's letter of 4 September 1560 to Peter De Loene and Jan Utenhove describes the issue (*Remains of Grindal*, 243). These Anabaptists held that Christ did not derive his human nature/flesh from the Virgin Mary. A recent study by A. J. Jelsma, *Adriaan-von Haemstede en zijn Martelaarsboek* (The Hague: 'S - G. Gravenhage, 1970) documents the affair. Martyr began his letter with the words, "Hadrianus incommode fecisse videtur, qui Ecclessiam turbauerit . . . ." Horst mentions Haemstede with no reference to Martyr or his letter.

The *Dialogus de utraque in Christo natura* is one of Martyr's clearest theological works. Latin editions appeared in Zurich in August and again in November of 1561. A second edition of 1563 and a third one of 1575 also were printed at Zurich. A Basle edition of 1581 completes the Latin versions, though a German edition of 1563 is suspect and a French *Dialogue des deux natures de Christ* is known to have been translated by Claude de Kerquefinen in Lyons, 1565.[104] Though written

against Brenz and the doctrine of ubiquity, readers in England would

have this recent "left-wing" controversy in mind. With his letter to

Parkhurst Martyr sent this dialogue he had written against the Lutheran

Brenz who taught the doctrine of the ubiquity of Christ's body.

The coming Colloquy at Poissy in France called Martyr to examine

yet another theological issue. The Royal invitation was so insistent

that Martyr could not defer it.[105] It is to that Colloquy of Poissy

that one must turn to see Martyr's greatest public contribution to the

Reformed Faith. When the Earl of Bedford finally invited Martyr to

England in 1561 Martyr declined, saying:

> Truly if I might have my own will I would no less serve the Church
> of England than before time I have done: howbeit neither mine age
> nor the strength of my body will any longer endure the same, being
> not able to endure a voyage so long, so diverse and not altogether
> easy.[106]

That this reply is to one of the Puritan extremists rather than to

Jewel leads Southgate to question at face value McLelland's interpreta-

tion of this letter as a refusal of a *bone fide* invitation.[107] It was

too late to expect Martyr to come again to England.

Martyr's last letter to England was sent to Cox on 4 October 1562.

He explained the urgency to finish the biblical commentaries which

Calvin had asked about and the English theologians expected. This was

potentially his most significant contribution to the cause of the

gospel in England.

> Then I proceed with the task of the interpretation of the
> Scriptures, that I may give it as much diligence as I can. For
> I am wholly devoting myself to my commentaries both on Samuel

and on Kings, now co the reviewing, now again to the copying, in order that they may be produced as quickly as possible.[108]

Martyr did accept a royal invitation to France rather than England, where he journeyed to debate the nature of the faith at the Colloquy of Poissy.[109]

COLLOQUY OF POISSY (1561)

In the same way the controversy over predestination drew Martyr into close contact with Beza and Calvin, it also marked him as an important theologian for the Reformed Churches in France. One glimpses in Martyr's correspondence a deep concern for the French congregations. This concern appears in a letter from Folkertzheimer to Martyr of 9 May 1560 in which he asked Martyr's judgment on civic strife in France. Beza had reported a variety of opinions in Zurich. Folkertzheimer worried whether or not there was sedition in France. Martyr's response has not survived but clearly he was considered an important source of information on such questions in 1560.[110] In January Hotman wrote to report the misery created by the law of Francis. He urged Martyr to plead with Navarre.[111] On the same day Beza sent a similar letter to Bullinger at Zurich.[112] These two letters of 22 January 1561 would prepare Martyr for Beza's visit from Geneva to Zurich, urging him to attend Poissy. It was at the urgent call of Catherine de' Medici, Quuen-Regent of France, that Peter Martyr pled the Huguenot cause in person at the Colloquy of Poissy.[113]

King Charles IX of France formally called the Colloquy on 25 July 1561. Among the catholics present were six cardinals, including

De Lorraine[114] and Odet de Chatillon, Admiral de Coligny's elder
brother who died as a protestant.[115] Martyr joined Beza in this
dramatic Colloquy amongst other such debates in the Sixteenth Century,
dramatic since national unity was its purpose. John Calvin kept fully
informed of the proceedings as is clear from Beza's letter sent two
days after arriving at Poissy: "Mr. Martyr is awaited with great longing, as I have heard from the words of the Queen herself."[116] Five
days later Beza wrote to Calvin:

> If our Martyr come in time, i. e., if he greatly hasten, his
> arrival will greatly refresh us. For we are to deal with Veteran
> sophists, and although we are confident that the simple truth of
> the Word will prevail, yet it is not in the power of everyone
> instantly to resolve their artifices and allege the sayings of
> the Fathers.[117]

In letters to Calvin and Bullinger early in 1561 Martyr showed his
willingness to obey the French Churches, for he could not refuse to
labor or escape the perils of so notable a cause.[118] On 13 August 1561
Martyr reported a safe-conduct from the King.[119] His intense preparation for the Colloquy can be seen in Martyr's remark to Calvin that he
was too busy to read his books.[120] Two letters written in the next
week touch on those preparations. Martyr responded "non muto animam"
about his coming task at Poissy.[121] Calvin answered two days later
that the Genevan Senate had received letters from the King of Navarre.[122]
Apparently Martyr had been reviewing patristic writings on the sacrament, though this impression is gained *post eventu* from his reports to
the Zurich Senate. The die was cast for Martyr's public defense of his
French confreres.

Simler described Martyr's journey to Paris and conference with
the Queen. In addition to Simler's account there are letters from
Martyr to Bullinger and to the Zurich Senate which help to reconstruct
his role from 10 September to 19 October. Martyr took thirteen days
to travel from Zurich on 29 August via Bern, Neuchatel and Lyons to
Paris.[123] Julius Terrentianus and Johann Stuckius went with Martyr,
the latter as secretary. Martyr's letter to the Zurich Senate from
Neuchatel describes the journey via Berne where Martyr was publically
honored.[124] There the scholars, ministers and Senate feted him.[125]
Near Paris the Royal Treasurer Bautrad, a noted evangelical, entertained Martyr in his own house. Catharine sent salutations from the court
with her private physician, while on the next day the Prince Conde
sent his private secretary. On 10 September Martyr took up residence
with Cardinal Odet de Chatillon.[126]

Martyr was to act as a theological advisor at Poissy since the
discussions were to be in French. Antonio Caraccioli, Bishop of Troyes,
was Martyr's translator.[127] In his report to the Zurich Senate Martyr
described his cordial reception by the Queen on 12 September 1561. He
informed the Queen that his purpose in coming was to speed the reform
of the churches.[128] When Navarre intruded together with his chancellor
that the Augsburg Confession would be such a base for ecclesiastical
harmony, Martyr rejected their suggestion outright. For him sacred
scripture was sufficient. The Augsburg Confession would hardly be
acceptable since the papists had outlawed it.[129] His secretary described the interview to Hubert in Strasbourg.

The day following this one the Queen of France summoned Dr. P.
Martyr to her, and, when she had taken him aside, spectators being
removed, she held for several hours a very courteous conference
with him; and she earnestly besought of him to exercise care and
thoughtfulness, that, if it could be done, this matter might be
peacefully settled, and with the goodwill of the ecclesiastics.
To which Dr. Martyr replied that, so far as truth allowed, he
would indeed consult peace and tranquility, but that as a matter
of fact he altogether despaired of the good will of the churchmen;
by which response she was exceedingly moved.[130]

In his letter to Bullinger Martyr mentioned the four points to be
discussed. They were 1) the authority of the church; 2) the strength
and power of Councils; 3) the authority of Scripture; and 4) "the real
and substantial presence of the body and blood of Christ in the Eucharist."[131] When Martyr "defended, praised and confirmed what Beza had
done" to the Queen, this was quite important.[132] On 9 September Beza
had defined the Eucharist in the following terms: "We say that his
body is as far removed from the bread and wine as the Heaven is from
Earth."[133] This speech at the very start almost ended the Colloquy and
postponed discussion a week until 16 September.[134] While the Cardinal
of Lorraine prepared his response to Beza the radical party wanted the
Reformed group to submit to a confession of faith. The Reformed peti-
tioned the King who permitted the Colloquy to continue.[135] On the 15th
of September the Jesuits were introduced into France. Under these
conditions Martyr entered the Colloquy on 16 September, though not without opposition from many at Poissy. Martyr's letter to Bullinger of
19 September describes his initial participation.

The cardinals and bishops did not want Martyr present though the
Queen commanded him to attend and the Prince Conde even provided his

own mule. The Duke of Guise denied Martyr entrance to the hall. When
the Duke learned who he was he led Martyr in by the arm. Martyr waited
at one side until the brethren should appear.

> Cardinal Chatillon, together with two bishops in their cardinal's
> and bishop's apparel, came up to me and first asked if I were
> Peter Martyr. When I said that I was, he saluted me very kindly,
> proffered all courtesies, and testified that my coming was most
> acceptable both to himself and to all other good men. Likewise
> the two bishops who were with him earnestly besought me to labor
> for the restoration of peace and concord, and that the risen
> troubles might be calmed down. I thanked the Cardinal, and re-
> plied to the bishops that I would not fail the cause of peace and
> concord so far as the Word of God and evangelical truth would
> allow. This cardinal is a brother to the admiral and (as almost
> all men say) has very good views on religion.[136]

Martyr went on to report Lorraine's response to Beza, though saying nothing of the uproar over previous Eucharistic statements.[137] In
this second meeting the Cardinal of Lorraine distinguished between
ἀγραφον and ἐγγραφον, with the Church having the right to judge both.
The general councils cannot err, said the cardinal in his one and a
half hour speech, and at the close he knelt before the Queen mother to
urge her and her son to remain faithful to their baptismal faith. The
Reformed leaders wished to respond at once though Catherine deferred
their request to another day. Martyr's response came in a private
conference with the Queen on the evening of 17 September.[138] Martyr
agreed with Lorraine's moderation, but could not grant the authority of
the church above scripture. He conceded that the cardinal might relent
on the Eucharist though not really believing it. "I said this, however, not because I had any such hope, but that the design and hope of
the Colloquy might not be prematurely cut off."[139] Though Martyr did

not follow at all points the French speech of Lorraine, he did tell the
Queen that charity rather than charges of heresy ought to follow the
Colloquy. When some of the bishops urged an agreement based on Luther
and Brenz, for Lorraine had proposed use of the *Augustana,* Martyr rejected such a middle way when he replied, "We deny that this can be
done, but we constantly persist in this: the body of Christ is in
heaven and nowhere else."[140]

On 19 September Ippolito d'Este, Cardinal of Ferrara and Papal
legate-a-latere arrived at Poissy with a magnificent retinue of horses
and Jesuits. Laynez who was successor to Loyola as general of the
Jesuit Order only confirmed by his presence Martyr's pessimism about an
ecclesiastical solution. To Bullinger Martyr spoke about these learned
men as "determined to swallow us as a morsel of bread." At the third
meeting of the Colloquy, now reduced to private sessions by the Queen,
Beza responded on the 24 of September to Lorraine's speech of the 16th.
Suddenly drawing the *Württemberg Confession* of 1559 from his pocket, the
cardinal demanded that the reformers sign it. The text was that defined
by Brenz. Martyr identified the lines which Lorraine pressed on the
Reformed as "in sacramento adesse corpus Christi realiter uere ac
substantialiter atque et exhiberi et sumi." Nugent reports on the
problem that this passage poses since it is not in the *Confession of
Württemberg* even though Lorraine did have a copy of it in his possession.
Nugent clarifiesthe problem by proving that several confessions were
introduced into the colloquy. Lorraine introduced his own confession
as well as the one pressed on the Reformed on 24 September. The passage

did not speak of ubiquity. Therefore the lines referred to by Martyr
and the Jesuit Jean Polanco are in the 1530 *Inuariata* rather than the
softened 1540 *Variata*. The text of the Naumberg Convention of 1561
was identical to that of the 1530 *Inuariata*. This would be an olive
branch to the Lutherans via Württemberg and a sword to the Reformed in
case of war. Lorraine had political considerations in mind rather than
perfidy.[141]

Martyr had not yet spoken publicly because the sessions were in
French. Finally on the Queen's approvalMartyr addressed the session
in Italian on 26 September.[142] On 26 September 1561 Beza read a protest before the meeting that the reformers should neither be deprived
of their legitimate ministry because of Lorraine's words, nor should
the Augsburg Confession be forced upon them. His letter to Calvin of
27 September 1561 claims two results of the ensuing discussion. They
had finally answered their opponent, and by so doing had silenced their
own fears.[143] Martyr answered the cardinal's initial sally that the
reformers were guilty of sedition. "For truly we have not come here to
disturb royal rule, much less to overthrow it."[144] The ministry of
the evangelicals on the contrary was valid apart from episcopal ordina-
tion by bishops who held office by virtue of their royal appointment.[145]
After Martyr turned to the subject of the Eucharist and described the
figurative language used by the scriptures and the Fathers, Diego Laynez
replied in Italian. Laynez rebuked the Queen for judging matters belonging to the pope alone and his higher clergy. It was unthinkable to
hold a private conference during the public sessions of the Council of

Trent. Laynez called Martyr an apostate monk and "brother" to ill
effect. As Martyr reported to Bullinger, "This speech of the arrogant
man greatly offended the Queen, and had it not been for the Cardinal
of Ferrara, she would have taught the Jesuit modesty."[146]

Lorraine objected to Martyr's speaking in Italian, who responded
in turn that it was the Queen's pleasure that he do so though he would
be ready to debate in Latin. The Queen permitted Martyr to continue
in Latin. On transubstantiation Martyr claimed against Lorraine that
the Greek text of *Matthew*(26:26) places bread in the accusative.
Lorraine was then in error that scripture did not teach the giving of
bread in the Eucharist.

Martyr's oration came in two parts according to the *Diario dell'
assemblea de'Vescovi a Poissy*.[147] Before the Cardinal of Lorraine
Martyr discussed the history of the question of "the true presence of
the body of Christ in the sacrument."[148] In the final section of his
speech the *Diary* reports that Martyr used the authority of scripture to
settle the meaning of sacrument or testament. Here Martyr cited against
the text from Genesis (s *Genesis* 46:27), "All souls who went out from
Jacob's loins and went into Egypt were seventy in number," that these
were figurative. What else was the term used of God during the flood
than a trope when scripture called Him "angry?"[148a] Martyr's meaning of
sacrament was a seal or testament forwhich he alleged the authority of
Exodus: " Quod magnum est Phase) idest transitu (sic) Dominj ."[149]
Laynez then intervened after Lorraine countered Martyr's arguments. He
asserted that only the catholic church and apostolic see possessed the

correct understanding of scripture.[150]

The discussion continued as Martyr interjected two patristic arguments. First, he used Tertullian's Fourth Book against Marcion to argue that Christ did not mean his own body when he consecrated the bread. "Wherefore when he desired to celebrate the passover, he accepted bread and distributed to the disciples . . . saying, 'This is my body,' that is a figure of my body, etc."[151] Then on the passage in I *Corinthians*, "The bread which we eat, is it not . . ." and in *Acts*, "They communed in pieces of bread," Martyr used the authority of St. Augustine in his book *Contra Adimantum* who said: "I do not doubt that when the Lord said here, 'This is my body,' he signified his own body." Martyr cited from Augustine, *De Doctrina Christiana* that John (6) was a Eucharistic passage. He then called Laynez a *rabula Hispanus*.[152] The Queen dissolved the assembly when (according to Martyr) the debate approached violence.

The Queen further reduced the sesssions to ten participants. By the time of Martyr's letter to Bullinger of 2 October three of these meetings had taken place which discussed bodily presence in the Eucharist. At the first session Martyr placed truth above ecclesiastical union when he rejected a formula of concord. Martyr's report to the Zurich Senate shows his fear of an interim that would be neither protestant nor catholic.[153] His letter to Calvin of 4 October expressed a similar fear that a Lutheran and/or Papistical religion would be forced on France.[154] Martyr read a confession to the Committee of Ten on 30 September 1561 which marks the climax of his participation in the

Colloquy of Poissy. Above all else his distaste for ambiguity is clear.

Together with the letter to John Sturm one can see his views on the

Eucharist in 1561. The confession reads in part:

> And so I assert that there is no need of proving the body of
> Christ to be truly, substantially, and corporally present, either
> to us or in the symbols, by an illogical presence.[155]

Martyr relented so that no one could accuse him of forestalling an

agreement, for on 1 October he signed a joint statement. A note to the

2 October letter has been left out of all the editions of the *Loci*

Communes.[156] It reads as follows to Bullinger with the crucial passage

in capital letters:

> My colleagues appear to me to yield too much, (aliquid remittere)
> but nevertheless they maintain that the bread and wine are not in
> reality (reipsa) the body and blood of Christ, and that the par-
> taking (perceptionem) of the things signified is spiritual and
> occurs through faith. But they are compelled to make use of the
> word 'substance' (vocabulum substantiae) because they use it in
> their Catechism and in the Confession which they presented to the
> King before my arrival. We are still in this same deliberation,
> and nothing conclusive had yet been decided. I APPEAR SEVERE
> (durus), SO THAT SOME OF THE COMMISSIONERS SAY THAT IT IS ON
> ACCOUNT OF ME THAT THEY DO NOT COME TO AN AGREEMENT. And I doubt
> not but this is also the reason why I am less acceptable (minus
> gratum) to the Queen Mother and the other nobles, as these desire
> to effect an agreement between us by all methods as quickly as
> possible. For the more the settlement of the religious question
> is deferred the more they fear uprisings among the people.[157]

Martyr's refusal to concede on the Eucharist lost him his prestige with

the Queen. By 19 October the Colloquy ended with the departure of

Cardinal Chatillon. In his letters Martyr traces the problems of the

Colloquy. Too late did five German theologians arrive at Poissy on

19 October.[158] Geisendorf says simply of the accord reached on 1

October, "Catherine triumphed."[159]

Simler described the final interview between the Italian theologian

Martyr and Catherine de' Medici. After giving his reason for returning

to Zurich as the will of the Senate, Martyr took leave of his fellow-

country woman. He had come to further religion rather than to foster

sedition, and now sought nothing but "peace and concord, so far as it

might be agreeable with the word of God."[160] Martyr departed from St.

Germain with an escort of two nobles provided by Conde and Coligny who

conducted him in safety to Zurich.[161] Paist's encomium praises Martyr's

tolerance, a view which one must suspend in the light of Martyr's in-

tolerance toward the "blasphemy" of Servetus.

> The position taken by Martyr at Poissy is part of his contribution
> to evangelical Protestantism. It is the contribution of the right
> of religious freedom guided by the authority of the inspired Word
> of God. And it was upon this distinguishing essential of the
> Reformed Theology in its pristine purity that Martyr knew the
> Huguenots of France would have to stand or fall. They fought and
> bled and died for it. He taught and wrote, debated and traveled,
> in defence of it. The unwavering confession of it was upon his
> lips when he died, and its unfailing consolation supported and
> sweetened the closing hours of his gently (sic) and beautiful
> life.[162]

On 17 October Martyr wrote to Bullinger that the Cardinal of

Ferrara labored to interrrupt the Colloquy. The bishops and cardinals

so disagreed among themselves on 10 October that they almost came to

blows. Martyr attended a sermon preached to a crowd of Reformed wor-

shippers (eight thousand) who when shut out of the city of Páris by the

cardinals and bishops began a pitched battle in which some on both sides

were slain. Martyr noted that such activities in Paris and elsewhere

in the kingdom would force the Queen and ecclesiastics to grant rights

of assembly for the Reformed Church.[163] Again Bullinger need not worry about acceptance of the Augsburg Confession.[164] On 19 October Martyr

reported to Lavater that the reformed party had reason to hope for

rights of public assembly from the King. The conference broke off when

the cardinals and other prelates left St. Germain.[165]

Beza wrote on 22 February 1564 to Jean De Ferriere approving the

idea of a colloquy with the Lutherans somewhere in Würtemberg.   One

will recall the Göppingen confession issued by Farel and Beza in 1557.

Beza pointed out that there was no need to accept the doctrine of ubiq-

uity. The Lutheran princes did not understand the concerns of Beza and

Martyr, who believed that one must communicate with Christ personally

in the Lord's Supper.

> Consequently, we are not saying that the Lord's Supper be only a
> commemoration of the death of our Lord or the meaning of his body
> and his blood. So, we say that it is instituted mainly so that
> by faith we commune truly with his body and his blood even with
> him altogether in Eternal Life. The disagreement therefore does
> not lie either in the substance or in the practice of the Lord's
> Supper but its result.[165a]

By 1586 at the Colloquy of Montbeliard, Jacob Andreae and Luke Osiander

forced Beza into writing the pacific yet scholastic account of 1593

known as the *De controversiis in Coena Domini*. The views of Martyr ex-

pressed in 1561 at Poissy are an integral part of these concerns that

the faithful share in all the riches of Christ, experience freedom from

error and seek harmony and peace within the Church.[165b]

The return journey by way of Troyeson 5 November was a delight.

The bishop who entertained him had been confirmed by the Reformed elders

in a service rarely seen in the sixteenth century. Martyr said that his

consequent authority and godliness "greatly profited the Church of

Christic."[166] On 21 November Martyr arrived safely home where he was

honored together with the two captains by the Zurich Consuls and

Senate.[167] On 25 November 1561 Martyr told John Calvin,

> I was desirous in my return to see you . . . . Herewithall I
> considered, that it should make but small if we were asunder
> in body sith we have our minds and judgements most nearly joined
> together.[168]

During 1562 Martyr continued work on his biblical commentaries.

There would appear something in his experiences at Poissy. The treatise

on the Catholic Church included in the Commentary on I *Kings* published

in 1566 will deserve a careful reading to assess Martyr's views during

1561-62.[169] There is no indication when this "common place" was com-

posed, though it has the form of an oration which could date from

1542.[170] That Martyr continued to labor for the Reformed cause in

France can be read from some works in Geneva and Paris.[171] Then there

was correspondence with Bernard Mommeja who had been at Geneva from

1559 until in 1561 he was made minister of Chauny in Picardy.[172] One

little-known letter to Martyr is from Beza on 14 December 1561. Beza

summarized the difficulties in preparing for the future religious

parliament at St. Germain in December.[173]

Zacharius Ursinus, future author of the *Heidelberg Catechism* (1563)

was in Zurich for a while from December of 1561. While there he was

affected by Martyr's commentaries on I *Corinthians* and *Romans*. Ursinus

wrote to Crato about Martyr. One can surmise that Martyr left his mark

via his disciple Ursinus on yet another important document of the

sixteenth century known as the *Heidelberg Catechism*.[174] Bullinger wrote the Second Helvetic Confession in 1561 and showed it to Martyr who had his say there as well.

Martyr's letter to Bullinger of January 1562 illustrates his concern for ecclesiastical harmony. At Basle there was neither disputation nor turbulence and dogma was profitable.[175] To prepare a clear confession perspicacious to all would be difficult. Even at Basle they neglect the notes on *Romans* (9) in which Martyr had set forth his views on predestination. Such views which also reject the teaching of I *Corinthians* (10) are heretical.[176] By August 1562 Martyr repeated the closing phrase of the January letter in which he accused Castellio of teaching outright heresy.[177] Could Curione have reported this in person to Martyr on one of his many visits to Zurich? Only one letter is extant between Martyr and Curione,[178] though it is interesting to see Curione's name in Gesner's *Liber Amicorum*.[179] On 18 August 1562 Stanislaus Paclesius wrote to Martyr from Poland. Stancaro was a problem.[180] By September Martyr again abhored the views of Stancaro on the Trinity which he had earlier condemned in the letter to the Polish Church. Gregory Paulus wrote a letter on 24 September 1562 from Cracow to Martyr and Bullinger in which he discussed the patristic evidence for the Trinity in some detail.[181] Zanchi had written his response on 21 August 1562. Paulus would also like a response from Martyr and Bullinger.[182]

Earlier on 24 May Martyr wrote a second letter to John Sturm about the situation in Strasbourg.[183] Once again Eucharistic controversy came to the fore.[184] During these final months of his life Peter

Martyr emerged as a leader of the Reformed Churches in Europe to whom
all turned for advice from areas where the fight to establish the evangelical faith was raging. In 1560 the *Unitas Fratrum* established official contact with the Swiss reformers. Peter Herbert held discussions
in Zurich with Peter Martyr and Bullinger to clarify conflicting reports from Poland on the doctrinal position of the Unity.[185] Nicolas
Gallasius had written to Martyr on 25 November 1561 rejoicing with the
entire kingdom of Scotland that the mass had been withdrawn from that
kingdom in which before it had been totally extended /exulabat/.[186]
That many turned to Martyr is not surprising from the brief account we
have sketched of his life in exile.

Martyr ended his life in controversy with John Benz, Lutheran reformer of some reputation. Brenz had been at the famous 1529 Marburg
Colloquy on the Eucharist where Luther and Melanchthon on the one side
debated Zwingli and Oecolampadius on the other. On 3 October 1529 when
the question of Christ's body in *Philippians* 2:6ff was defined by Zwingli as a local presence, Brenz answered that the body was independent
of place. Brenz was Swabian and one of Luther's chief disciples at
Schwäbisch - Hall (1522-1548) and in the Duchy of Würtemberg (1550-1570).
In 1561 Brenz updated the controversy between Calvin and Westphal with
the appearance of his *De Personali Unione Duarum Naturarum in Christo,
Et Ascensu Christi in Caelum, Ac Sessione eius ad dextram Dei Patris.
Qua Vera Corporis et Sanguinis Christi Praesentia in Coena explicatio
est, & confirmata* (Tubingen: Ulrich Norhardi, 1561), two editions.[187]
Martyr responded with his *Dialogus de Utraque in Christo natura* (1561)

about which he wrote to Parkhurst: "I was here required by the brethren that I should answer him: which I have done as well as I could".[188]
Simler reports that "because hee knewe that Brentius did in other
writings not altogether deserue ill of the Church, he woulde not put
there unto his name, and expressely defame and speak ill of him, especially since this nothing furthered the cause . . . ."[189] Brenz retorted with a vicious attack on Martyr and Bullinger of 1562.[190] Martyr's
tract is one of his clearest writings, having gone through several Latin
editions as well as German and French translations by 1574.[191]

Martin Bucer in 1550 wrote to Brenz about the publication of Martyr's 1549 Oxford Tractate: "I am as sorry for master Martyr's book
as any one can be; but that disputation took place, and the propositions
were agreed upon, before I arrived in England."[192] Now Martyr as he
lay ill for the final time only regretted he could not respond in full
to Brenz. When Bullinger quoted the verse that one has a house not
made with hands and eternal in the heavens, Martyr retorted, "I knowe
it is, but not in Brentius heaven, which is no where."[193] Ten days
after Martyr's death, Bullinger wrote to Calvin comparing Brenz's
torture of scripture to that of Servetus. Bullinger's reference would
be to the 1561 treatise against himself and Martyr.[194]

A summary of Martyr's views may be found in his letter to Peter
Sturm of 24 May 1562. There Martyr defined his Eucharistic theology
as follows: "The body and blood of the Lord are not just present to
our minds spiritually and by faith so that our faculties are healthy
and strong from day to day . . . but we are justified and regenerated

by what is believed and the body and blood of Christ are valuable for
our salvation. Not only in the act of justification itself are we
sustained and confirmed by regeneration but justification and regeneration are the first principles of our joys of immortality."[195] It
seems odd therefore to view Martyr as a Bucerian believing in real
presence. True presence would be a better description in which the
regenerate alone share in the spiritual benefits of Christ. What
Christ's confessors get is moral mercy, not spiritual medicine, forgiveness rather than food.

The Florentine reformer took ill again in November for the last
time. Simler described the scene in the room around his bed with several close friends including the Pastors and Elders of the Italian
Church. It was 12 November 1562.

> When he thus sitting in his clothes as he was wont to go,
> commending his soul stoutly unto God, he begain to be at the
> point of death: there remained yet with him Conradus Gesnerus,
> and also his wife and two young men besides of his familiars.[196]

Bullinger wrote to John Calvin commemorating his colleague. His words
well summarize Martyr's six years in exile at Zurich.

> This man was incomparable and most dear to me of mortals.
> The loss felt in his death is not ours alone, but more
> surely an irreparable one for the universal church.[197]

When his beloved Bucer died at Cambridge in February of 1551,
Martyr wrote to John Warner who was Regius Professor of Medicine at
Oxford about the illness which felled Bucer. Martyr suffered even then
from fevers which sapped his physical strength. Now with Conrad Gesner
at his side there was no cool wine which could slake his feverish thirst

and restore his strength. There was no medicine of immortality in the
Eucharist on which Martyr would rely. One recalls the life of hope
Martyr had oft expressed in his biblical commentaries. That ancient
hope in the Living God was to be his final consolation. Thomas Cranmer,
put it well when he praised Martyr to Richard Smith.

> But as for Dr. Peter Martyr, hath he sought to please men for
> advantage? . . . /He/ for the truth and Glory of God came into
> strange countries, where . . . God of his goodness, who never
> forsaketh them that put their trust in him, provided for him.

Martyr described that trust in a sermon at Oxford on *Philippians* II:
"So God hath tempered for us a medicine out of the death and resurrection of Christ, whereby we be delivered, and death perisheth . . . ."

NOTES TO CHAPTER V

1. McLelland, op. cit., p. 286. In October of 1557 Martyr informed Melanchthon that through Bullinger he had heard about the Assembly at Worms. The endorsement of Melanchthon's work was important for
Martyr's theology. Not only did he sign the Augsburg Confession, but
he continued at Zurich to support its author. 20 October 1557 in
Common Places (1583), Part five.

2. Oratio.

3. Oratio.

4. Cesare Cantu, Gli Eretici D'Italia, Volume Secondo, p.75.

5. O. L. I., p. 137.

6. Martyr admired Bullinger's Decades, especially Book V. On
this aspect of Bullinger as an historian and educator see especially
Jacob Berchtold, "Die Grundquelle von Stumpfs und Bullingers Reformationschronik," S. Z. G. VII (1927), pp. 314-330. Also the review by
Walter Schmid, "Johannes Stumpfs Schweizer und Reformationschronik,"
Z. 10 (1954-58), 502-506. See Martyr's judgement on Castellio in a
letter of August 1562 to Bullinger. Commenting on I Corinthians (10)
Martyr says, "De iustificatione per fidem solam dicitur non recte
sentire. Praedicatur etiam docere, eam perfectionem in hac vita
obtineri ut operibus legi Dei satisfaciamus." C.R. XLVII, 3840,
col. 505.

7. <u>O</u>. <u>L</u>. II, p. 506. On the authorship of <u>De</u> <u>Libero</u> <u>Arbitrio</u>, <u>De</u> <u>Providentia</u> <u>et</u> <u>Praedestinatione</u> and <u>An</u> <u>Deus</u> <u>sit</u> <u>Cause</u> <u>et</u> <u>Author</u> <u>Peccati</u> which Masson included in the <u>Loci</u> <u>Communes</u> (1576) see Thomas Brassel, "Drei umstrittene Traktate Peter Martyr Vermiglis," <u>Z</u>. Xl (1959-63), p. 476 and pp. 553-4. Brassel denies Martyr their authorship.

8. Translated from Schmidt, <u>op</u>. <u>cit</u>., p. 216 in J. C. McLelland, "The Reformed Doctrine of Predestination," p. 266. See letters of 20 July 1557 in C. R. XLIV, 2665 and 2667, cols. 544-546. See also C. R. XLV, 2855, cols. 143-145 of 21 April 1558 where Martyr mentions his own section on predestination in his <u>Romans</u> (1558). He agrees fundamentally with Calvin. The undated letter to Beza in <u>Common</u> <u>Places</u> (1583), Part five, pp. 105-106 would be part of this period's discussion, since it refers to Martyr and Zanchi in defense of predestination. The crucial passage occurs in a discussion of <u>Romans</u> (9:10-19). On the promise to Sarah and the fate of Esau and Jacob, Martyr comments: "Paul here by sheweth that the hidden purpose of God moderateth and contracteth that which was promised generally. Not as though the election of God is repugnant unto the promise, yea rather it performeth & accomplisheth it, but yet in these in whom it is decreed to be performed." <u>Romans</u>, (1568), p. 247.

9. <u>Common</u> <u>Places</u> (1583), Part five, p. 93. 9 May 1554.

10. <u>Z</u>. <u>S</u>. <u>A</u>. EII (342), f. 324.

11. <u>Opuscula</u> (1582), cols. 35-48.J. Donnelly's unpublished, "Three Disputed Vermigli Tracts," proves Martyr's authorship.
12. Zurich Zentralbibliothek, MSC. <u>Car</u>. III 206g. See Brassel, <u>op</u>. <u>cit</u>., 476.

13. Joachim Staedke, "Drei umstrittene Traktate Peter Martyr Vermiglis," <u>Z</u>. XI (1962), 553.

14. <u>Opuscula</u> (1582), col. 9.

15. <u>Ibid</u>., col. 14.

16. <u>Ibid</u>., cols. 11-12. Lecture at Zurich 25 January 1560.

17. <u>Ibid</u>., col 42: regeneratos-renati.

18. <u>Ibid</u>., cols. 45-48 from <u>Samuelis</u> (1564), II. 1622. Martyr owned a copy of Theodoret's <u>De</u> <u>providentia</u>. See Ganoczy, 31 and 219 (Theodoret, <u>epitome</u> <u>Divinorum</u> <u>decretorum</u>). Samuel tract similar to disputed one.
19. Charles Schmidt, <u>Peter</u> <u>Martyr</u>, p. 276 f. 13 April 1561. <u>Opuscula</u> (1582), cols. 225-228.

20. <u>Opuscula</u> (1582), col. 225.

21. <u>Ibid.</u>, col. 226.

22. Schmidt, <u>op</u>. <u>cit</u>., pp. 278-81. Latin text in Hottinger VIII, 843-57.

23. Hottinger VIII, 855. See Donnelly, <u>op</u>. <u>cit</u>., pp. 302-303.

24. John Bray, <u>Theodore Beza's Doctrine of Predestination</u> (unpublished thesis) argues cogently that Beza may exceed Calvin in using predestination as a polemic because of Catholic opposition. See pp. 257-258. Donnelly has shown that Martyr is not Beza's agent for this scholasticism.

25. <u>C</u>. <u>R</u>. XLIV, 2591, cols. 403-404, February 1557.

26. <u>C</u>. <u>R</u>. XLIV, 2694. 1 September 1557.

27. <u>Common Places</u> (1583), Part five, p. 102. In March Martyr wrote to a friend: "We are all in good health; and I teach here as I was wont before time to do with you. God grant that I may not labor without fruit." <u>Ibid.</u>, p. 116. 15 March 1557.

28. <u>Ibid.</u>, p. 102. 29 August 1557. Beza wrote to Bullinger and Martyr on 24 August 1557 (<u>C</u>. <u>R</u>. XLIV, 2689), in which he also discussed the confession. See also Gorham, <u>op</u>. <u>cit</u>., p. 198 for letter of 11 November 1550 where Martyr mentions a confession to be drawn up by Laski. <u>C</u>. <u>R</u>. XLIV, 2668, cols. 545-546 assigns to Calvin the letter of Martyr to: <u>Amico quidam</u> inserted in the <u>Loci Communes</u> (1587). Here Martyr says of Beza's confession: "Neque in summa video in ista confessione usquam significari nostram coniunctionem veram cum Christo eiusmodi esse quae patiatur inter nos et corpus Domini locorum distantiam, ita ut realis aut substantialis eius praesentia hic iter non minime requiratur ad id ut vere cum ipso coniuncti simus." <u>Ibid.</u>, col. 546. This lack Martyr discussed at length in a letter to Beza found in <u>Common Places</u> (1583), Part five, pp. 105-106. Both of these letters I would assign to July of 1557 on the basis of <u>C</u>. <u>R</u>. XLIV, 2665, col. 543. Vermilius Bezae 20 July 1557. Text of Confession is in <u>C</u>. <u>R</u>. XLIV, cols. 470-472, where there is no reference to Laski. The Lambeth Palace Library document may be Laski's copy of the Göppingen confession.

29. <u>C</u>. <u>T</u>. <u>B</u>. II (<u>1556-1558</u>), p. 251.

30. On this social experiment see the account in W. K. Jordan, <u>Edward VI The Threshold of Power</u>, pp. 318-320.

31. <u>C</u>. <u>R</u>. XLIV, 2689, col. 577. 24 August 1557.

32. Geisendorf, op. cit., pp. 84-88. See the versions of Diller and Andreae in C. T. B. II, 243-248 and Robert Kolb, "Six Christian Sermons on the Way to Lutheran Unity," C. T. M. LXIV (1973), 261-274.

33. Raitt, op. cit., p. 3.

34. This copy in the Lambeth Palace Library is not used by the editors of Beza's letters though it is known to M. Dufour.

35. Geisendorf, op. cit., pp. 351-359. See also Raitt, op. cit., pp. 61-68. Rose Marie Muller - Streisand calls attention to a Declaratio of 1559 in which this confession is called substantia by Beza. See "Theologie und Kirchenpolitik bei Jacob Andreä bis zum Jahr 1568," Bl. f. w. KG. 60 und 61 (1960/61), 294 n. 223. Muller - Streisand says of the Göppingen Confession: Tatsächlick konnte diese unter Berücksichtigung aller württembergischen Anliegen in sechs Artikeln verfasste Confessio als eine brauchbare Grundlage für Einigungsbestrebungen betrachtet werden." Beza in his apology to Claude de Sainctes described Jacob Andreae as "modest, peaceful and obviously Christian." See Müller - Streisand, page 294 for above citation and page 294 note 222 for comment on Andreae.

36. Joachim Staedke, "Der Zurcher Praedestinationsstreit von 1560," Z. 9 (1944-1953), p.541 n. 23 quotes from Hottinger, "Non ignorare poterant Tigurini, Martyrem eo etiam nomine, quod profundius et solidus de Praedestinatione ageret, suspectum jam esse Argentinensibus." Martyr summarized the Zurich view on 29 December 1561 which supported Zanchi at Strasbourg. On Zanchi's thesis that "the elect unto life cannot be lost, so those not predestinated to life are necessarily damned," Martyr concurs. "God's decision is always just, but not always revealed." "The 'necessity' here is blameless, if we exclude necessity of force and accept only necessity of results. The result is the blessedness of the elect, therefore he who enjoys this, has certainty of salvation." McLelland, "The Reformed Doctrine of Predestination," p. 268 from Schmidt, op. cit., pp. 278-281. On Zanchi see Otto Gründler, Die Gotteslehre Girolami Zanchis und ihre Bedeutung für seine Lehre von der Pradestination.

37. Remains of Edmund Grindal, 236.

38. "Lever, or Leaver, Thomas," D. N. B. XI, p. 1021. See also O. L. I, p. 161. 4 January 1556 to Bullinger for a brief mention of Peter Martyr.

39. Paul Boesch, "Die englischen Fluchtlinge in Zurich unter Konigen Elizabeth I," Z. 9 (1949-53), 531-535. The standard account is still Theodor Vetter, Relations between England and Zurich during the Reformation.

40. See Martyr's letter to a certain English nobleman in Common Places (1583), Part five. On 5 November 1560 Martyr explained to Cooke how difficult it would be for him to reside again in England, yet "Anglia uero, quae mihi est altera patria." British Museum Add. MS. 29549, fol. 18^r.

41. O. L. I, p. 140. 20 January 1558.

42. O. L. I, p. 182. 8 April 1558. See on this complex question C. G. Bayne, Anglo-Roman Relations.

43. Loc. cit. C. R. XLV, 2855, col. 144. "Inauguratio novi Imperatoris, forma et ratione insolita et hactenus inaudita omnibus admirationem in credibilem peperit."

44. C. R. XLV, 2855, cols. 144-145. This is the sense of Martyr's text. Martyr also agreed with Calvin on predestination when comparing Calvin's views with his own Romans.

45. C. R. XLV, 2874, cols. 175-176. 22 May 1558. Calvin is pleased that he and Martyr concur on "The eternal providence of God."

46. Italian text in C. R. XLIII, no. 2018, col. 246 ff.

47. C. T. B. II, p. 15.

48. Ibid., p. 46.

49. C. R. XLIII, no. 2018, col. 247.

50. Loc. cit.

51. Philip E. Hughes, The Register of the Company of Pastors of Geneva in the Time of Calvin, p. 311.

52. Common Places (1583), Part five, p. 103. To Calvin, 11 June 1558. Dated to 11 July by Schmidt, op. cit., p. 208.

53. Benrath, Bernardino Ochino von Siena, pp. 306-307.

54. Gerdes, Scrinium Antiquarium III. II, 677. See letter printed in Bainton, Bernardino Ochino, p. 189.

55. O. L. I, p. 183. 10 July 1558.

56. O. L. I, p. 771. 20 August 1558 (26 August in Schmidt, p. 215).

57. Common Places (1583), Part five, p. 104. 16 September

(1559?). Martyr's congratulatory note on the refounding of the Genevan College dates this letter to 1559. On 4 October 1559 he praised Beza to Calvin for his work as rector of the Genevan Academy. "Omnia enim pro tua prudentia ac dexteritate, qua te Deus ornavit . . ." C. R. XLV, 3123, col. 654.

58. Z. L. II, p. 13. Sir Antony Cooke to Peter Martyr. 12 February 1559. Martyr wrote to Calvin on Elizabeth: "Tempus fortasse iam est ut in eo regno muri Ierosalem reaedificentur, ut ne tot martyrum sanguis videatur incassum tam largiter effusas." C. R. XLV, 2988, col. 391.

59. Common Places (1583), Part five, p. 58. Zanchi refers to Mary as "Jezebel" in a letter to Laski of January 1559: Gorham, op. cit., p. 402.

60. Ibid., p. 59.

61. Loc. cit.

62. Ibid., p. 60.

63. Unpublished letter in Lambeth Palace MS. 2010 translated by Huelin, op. cit., p. 117.

64. Gorham, op. cit., pp. 405-407. 7 January 1559. Martyr also wanted Utenhove to have booksellers purchase quantities at the Frankfurt Book Fair to distribute throughout Poland.

65. See Huelin, op. cit., pp. 131-138 for a brief survey of unpublished material relating to the Elizabethan Bishops and also the cautionary paragraphs in Claire Cross, The Royal Supremacy in the Elizabethan Church, pp. 71-72. Cross interjects contra Haugaard that the need to conciliate foreign powers governed Elizabeth's parliamentary religious actions during her first decade. See also the letter of Elizabeth to Cecil and her remark to the Spanish Ambassador cited in Conyers Read, Mr. Secretary Cecil and Queen Elizabeth, pp. 132-34.

66. Patrick Collinson, The Elizabethan Puritan Movement, pp. 61-62.

67. Patrick Collinson, "The Reformer and the Archbishop: Martin Bucer and an English Bucerian," J. R. H. 6 (1971), 305-330.

68. Z. L. I, p. 1. 17 December (1558?).

69. C. S. P. Elizabeth, 1558-1559 no. 297, p. 111.

70. Wallace T. MacCaffrey, "Elizabethan politics: the first

decade, 1558–1568," P. P. 24 (1963), p. 32.

71. Letter of 27 December 1973, p. 2.

72. Z. L. I, p. 7. 26 January (1559).

73. Strype, Annals, I, i, 29.

74. Z. L. I, p. 10. 20 March 1559.

75. Ibid., p. 11.

76. Z. L. I, p. 14. 6 April 1559.

77. Ibid., p. 11. 20 March 1559. Record of the debate may be found in F. A. Gasquet and Edmund Bishop, Edward VI and the Book of Common Prayer, pp. 397–443.

78. Ibid., p. 16. 6 April 1559.

79. Z. L. I, p. 17. 14 April 1559.

80. Ibid., p. 18. On 28 April Jewel mentions three letters from Martyr. They are not extant. Z. L. I, p. 19.

81. Translated in Huelin, op. cit., p. 117.

82. See the sensible article by L. H. Zuck, "The Influence of the Reformed Tradition on the Elizabethan Settlement," C. T. M. XXXI (1960), pp. 215–226.

83. Z. L. I, p. 23. No date.

84. Z. L. II, p. 25. 15 July 1559. This is no. 38 in Common Places (1583), Part five. Nos. 39, 40 and 41 are also to Sampson. See William P. Haugaard, "The Episcopal Pretensions of Thomas Sampson." H. M. P. E. C. XXXVI (1967), pp. 383–6.

85. Ibid., p. 26.

86. Ibid., p. 27.

87. Z. L. I, p. 40. 1 August 1559.

88. Z. L. I, p. 33. 22 May 1559.

89. Patrick McGrath, Papists and Puritans under Elizabeth I, p.79.

90. Z. L. I, p. 46. 2 November 1559.

91. C. S. P. Span. I, 105. The occasion was the marriage of one of the Queen's lady servants. The ambassador adds that the entire kingdom will soon see the same restoration of the crucifix.

92. Z. L. I, p. 55. 16 November 1559.

93. Loc. cit. Jewel's phrase. See letter of 5 November, Ibid., pp. 53-54, for Queen's inquiry about Martyr.

94. Z. L. II, p. 39. To Sampson. 1 February 1560. See Ibid., p. 47 to Sampson on 20 March 1560.

95. Z. L. I, p. 63. 6 January 1560. On Bullinger's warning to Beza about Sampson see Z. L. II, p. 152. 15 March 1567.

96. Z. L. II, p. 38. 1 February 1560.

97. Z. L. I, p. 67. 4 February 1560.

98. Ibid., p. 68.

99. Z. L. I, p. 71. 5 March 1560. See letter of 25 August 1560 from Randolf to Cecil. The Scot's Book of Common Reformation is now in transaction and will be sent to "Calvin, Viret and Beza in Geneva; and to Martyr, Bullinger and others in Zurich." C. S. P. Eliz. 1560-1561 no. 454, p. 259.

100. Z. L. I, p. 74. 1 April 1560.

101. John E. Booty, op. cit., p. 50.

102. Z. L. I, p. 92. 6 November 1560. On Jewel's Apology of the Church of England, see Booty, op. cit., pp. 51-5.

103. Common Places (1583), Part five, p. 134. 15 February 1561.

104. Peter G. Bietenholz, Basle And France In The Sixteenth Century, p. 210, n. 38.

105. Ibid., p. 149. 23 August 1561.

106. Ibid., p. 165. 1561.

107. W. M. Southgate, John Jewel, p. 76 n. 28. But see Strype, Annals I, 1, p. 381 who thinks that Thomas Duke of Norfolk invited Martyr.

108. Lambeth Palace Library, MS. 2010, f. 154. Translation in Huelin, op. cit., p. 137 and Latin text on p. 214. Nicolas Des Gallars,

pastor of the French Strangers Church in London, reported to the Bishop of London /Grindal/ on 29 October 1561: "That he and Peter Martyr often converse about the state of affairs and their friends in England!' C. S. P. Eliz. 1561-1562, no. 636, p. 382.

109. Alain Dufour, "Le Colloque de Poissy," 127-137 does not mention Martyr but gives a fine survey of the hopes expressed by the participants. See p. 137: Et de meme qu 'au XVIe siecle un tel espair etait soutenu par l'humanisme et son gout de revenir aux sources, de retrouver la primitive Eglise, de meme, de nos jours, le mouvement de rapprochement qui s' esquisse entre les confessions chretiennes est soutenu par un grand renouveau de l'exegese des textes bibliques." See Hotman to Bullinger of 12 April 1561 on Poissy in C. R. XLVI, 3372.

110. T. B. MS. 680: Reg. XXI: fol. 225.

111. Z. S. S. M. S. C. S. 239.21a. See translation by R. Dareste, "Francois Hotman. Sa Vie et sa Correspondance," R. H. II (1876), 28-30. Letter of 20 November 1560 reprinted in Donald Kelley, Francois Hotman, p. 343.

112. C. T. B. III, pp. 71-74.

113. The following account will attempt to bring up to date the study by Benjamin F. Paist, Jr., "Peter Martyr and the Colloquy of Poissy," P. T. R. 20 (1922), pp. 212-231; 418-447; 616-646. See also Joseph Roserot De Melin, "Rome et Poissy 1560-61," M. A. H. XXXIX (1921-22), 47-151. Martyr's letter to Calvin on the French Church is in C. R. XLVI, 3460, col. 579. 31 July 1560.

114. See Donald G. Nugent, "The Cardinal of Lorraine and the Colloquy of Poissy," H. J. XII (1969), pp. 596-605.

115. M. Chrital, "Odet de Coligny, Cardinal de Chatillon," B. S. H. P. F. LVII (1961), 1-12. Martyr inscribed a fine copy of the New Testament for Chatillon.

116. Paist, op. cit., pp. 422-23.

117. Ibid., p. 423.

118. Common Places (1583), Part five, p. 149. 13 July 1561.

119. A copy of the safe conduct is in C. C. C. C. MS. 119.6, dated 25 July 1561.

120. Ibid., p. 149. 13 August 1561. Dated 15 August by Paist. See letter of 12 August 1561 to Calvin in C. R. XLVI, 3516, col. 707. "Proposuit ad haec ipsa et Navarrenus confessionem Augustanam

tolerabiliorem videri. Ad haec ego respondi, nobis posse divinas literas sufficere."

121. C. R. XLVI, 3481, col. 610. 15 August 1561.

122. See letter from the Genevan Senate to the Zurich Senate of 21 July 1561. C. R. XLVI, 3450, col. 567. "Cest pour vous prier de permettre a spectable docteur Pierre Martyr de faire ung voiage en france pour se trouver en une assemblee quil vous dira."

123. Paist, op. cit., p. 423 gives fifteen days. I count thirteen days from August 29 to September 10.

124. Johann Wilhelm Baum, Theodor Beza nach handschriftlichen Quellen dargestellt, appendix, pp. 57-58. 29 August 1561.

125. Ibid., p. 57. Stuckius wrote to Conrad Hubert on 18 September 1561 from St. Germain. Here he states that Martyr left Zurich on 26 August, taking fifteen days for the journey to Paris.

126. Common Places (1583), Part five, p. 150. To Bullinger 12 September 1561. Martyr's Relatio colloquii Possiaceni is reprinted in C. R. XLVI, 3541, cols. 760-774. Martyr was impressed with the Cardinal's religion.

127. Loc. cit. See Phillipe de Felice, "Le Colloque de Poissy," B. S. H. P. F. CVII (1961), pp. 133-145 for a recent discussion of Beza's role. Beza's speeches of 1561 were published in Italian that year in three parts. One was the speech of 9 September 1561 at the opening session. The other was the letter of the same day to Catherine and the third is Cardinal Lorraine's response of 16 September 1561. See John A. Tedeschi and E. David Willis, "Two Italian Translations of Beza and Calvin," A. R. G. 55 (1964), 71-72.

128. Baum, op. cit., p. 62. 12 September 1561. Their conversation would have been in Italian.

129. Ibid., p. 63. "Dixi sacras Literas nobis debere sufficere et praeterea Confessionem Augustanam Papistis improbari et proscriptam esse."

130. Ibid., p. 66. 18 September 1561. Translation by Paist, op. cit., p. 427, n. 55. See also letter to Bullinger of 12 September 1561 in Common Places (1583), Part five, p. 151.

131. Common Places (1583), Part five, p. 150. See Andre Bouvier, Henri Bullinger reformateur et conseiller oecumenique le successeur de Zwingli, pp. 279-289: "Bullinger, Pierre Martyr et le Colloque De Poissy."

132. Loc. cit.

133. Baum, op. cit., p. 63. Martyr to Zurich Senate on 12 September 1561. See Beza to Calvin in C. R. XLVI, p. 687. On Beza's role at Poissy see Paul F. Geisendorf, Theodore De Beze, pp. 125-166 which makes use of Beza's Diary. See especially volume one of G. Baum et Ed. Cunitz, Histoire ecclesiastique des Eglise reformees au Royaume de France. Donald G. Nugent's published dissertation on Poissy, State University of Iowa, is an excellent corrective to some of Geisendorf's vigorous Protestant historiography on the motives of Lorraine.

134. Geisendorf, op. cit., p. 146. The Venetian Ambassador praised the speech, while charges of 'Blasphemy' rang out when Lorraine responded to Beza with the words, "non magis in coena quam in caeno," apparently misunderstanding what Beza had said.

135. Paist, op. cit., pp. 431-432. See Donald Ziegler, Great Debates Of The Reformation, pp. 211-242 for partial text of Colloquy in English.

136. Common Places (1583), Part five, pp. 151-152.

137. Baum, op. cit., pp. 282-293.

138. Common Places (1583), Part five, pp. 152 ff. Paist closely follows this account.

139. Loc.cit.

140. Loc.cit. "Teodoro Di Beza E Pier Martire Vermigli Alla Disputa Di Poissy," Rivista Cristiana 3(1875), 362.
141. Ibid., p. 154. Martyr to Bullinger of 2 October 1561. See the full account in Nugent, Ecumenism, pp. 204-219.

142. See Paist, op. cit., pp. 442-443 for report on the intervening days of Beza's attempted reconciliation with the Bishop of Valence under Catherine's direction. Geisendorf says of this affair in which Baum, op. cit., p. 342 blames Martyr for the failure to resolve the differences on the Eucharist: "L' Histoire ecclesiastique affirme que, lors do son examen par tous les pasteurs, il ne s'eleva jamais dispute ni differend quelconque sur le doctrine (I, 603-605), d'ou Baum a conclu, assez subtilement, qu'il y en eut peutetre . . . ailleurs que sur la doctrine." Ibid., pp. 158-59.

143. C. T. B. III (1559-1561), p. 164.

144. Paist, op. cit., p. 444 from letter of 2 October 1561 to Bullinger.

145. Loc. cit.

146. Loc. cit. Speech is in Monumenta historica Societatis Jesu VII, 759-768 according to Nugent.

147. De Melin, op. cit., p. 136. This Diary is based on two sixteenth-century copies and one seventeenth-century copy.

148. Loc. cit.

148a. Relatio colloquii Possiaceni, col. 771.

149. Ibid., p. 137.

150. Ibid., p. 138.

151. Ibid., p. 141.

152. Loc.cit. See Relatio, col. 772: "Quod ergo prius Christus docuerat quod rem, ut habetur 6 cap., in extrema coena voluit symbolis externis panis ac vini in perpetuam rei memoriam obsignare." The reference to John (6) is important when one remembers Marburg in 1529. Martyr cites from Augustine but not from Zwingli.

153. Baum, op. cit., p. 94, note 5.

154. Common Places (1583), Part five, p. 156. See Schmidt, op. cit., p. 265 to the effect that Martyr represented his colleagues and would not be misled.

155. Ibid., p. 141.

156. Latin text in Baum, op. cit., p. 395, n. 13.

157. Paist, op. cit., p. 622. "Obstinate" rather than "severe" would be a better translation of durus.

158. Ibid., pp. 628-29.

159. Geisendorf, op. cit., p. 163.

160. Oratio.

161. Paist, op. cit., pp. 634-35 gives the text of Catherine's letter to the Zurich Senate, thanking them for Martyr's presence at Poissy and certifying his good conduct. She was disappointed that no fruit came from the discussions. Such must await the infinite goodness of God "who alone rules such things." Is this a volte face on her part as a result of Martyr's final interview?

162. _Ibid._, p. 646. See Paulus, "Die stellung der protestantischen professoren Zanchi und Vermigli zur gewissensfreiheit," Strassburger Theologischen Studien II (1895), 83-102.

163. Common Places (1583), Part five, p. 157. 17 October 1561.

164. Ibid., p. 158 (misprinted as p. 152).

165. Loc. cit., 19 October 1561.

165a. C. T. B. V (1564), p. 31.

165b. Jill Raitt, The Eucharistic Theology of Theodore Beza,
pp. 61-68.

166. Common Places (1583), Part five, pp. 159-160. 6 November
1561 to Beza. Not long after, however, Caraccioli had to leave Troyes.
One wonders at Martyr's judgment of popular religious sentiment here
and in England.

167. Ibid., p. 160. 25 November 1561 to Beza.

168. Ibid., p. 161. 25 November 1561. The report of the
Venetian Ambassador in France on Poissy is interesting when he reports, "There is also expected Peter Martyr, who has a safe conduct
apart, because he is not of the kingdom, but an Italian, and dissents
from Calvin . . ." C. S. P. Ven. VII. 1558-1580, no. 278, p. 335.
23 August 1561.

169. See above note 108. See Bouvier, op. cit.,p. 417 who
shows that Martyr's commentary on Kings was cited at Geneva in the
1574 aftermath of St. Bartholomew's Eve 1572 during a dispute between
Geneva and Berne.

170. Published separately in 1573 under title, Trattato della
vera Chiesa cattolica e della necessita di vivere in essa according
to Benrath op. cit., p. 552. I have not seen a copy of the 1573
edition which is in the Gucciardini collection at Florence.

171. B. S. H. P. F. XXX (1881), p. 283 describes a work as
follows: Les noms de ceux qui ont donne advis sur ce fait, son mis
incontinent apres l'Epistre aux Lecteurs De l'imprimerie de Jean
Crespin. MDLVIII which has on pp. 37-39   le conseil de Pierre
Martyr: /see De Vitandis/ This is the second edition of the 1556
Pierre Alexandre work in Clare College Library, Cambridge. The
Musee historique de la Reformation, Geneva has the following item:
Epistre . . . a quelques fideles touchant leur abjuration et renoun-
cement de la verite . . . Plus un sermon de S. Cyprian . . . traitant
des persecutions et revoltes de son temps. - S. 1., sans impr: 8 .

Listed by Paul Chaix, Alain Dufour et Gustave Moeckli, Les Liveres
Imprimes a Geneve De 1550 A 1600, p. 81, under 1574. This is a French
translation of the letter to the Church at Lucca. The Bibliotheque
Nationale has an item called Lettres consolatoires envoyees a Madame
la Princesse de Conde durant sa maladie (Paris, 6 juillet 1564, et
Lyon, 19 Juin 1564), 8 LN²⁷. 4665. I doubt if these are by Martyr.
An inspection shows no reason to affirm his authorship on grounds of
internal evidence.

172. B. S. H. P. F. XLVI (1897), p. 237, n. 3. See Bouvier,
op. cit., pp. 344-45.

173. C. T. B. III (1559-1561), p. 240. See the illustration of
Poissy opposite the title page. On this discussion over images etc.,
see Geisendorf, op. cit., pp. 167-190. Same picture is reproduced
opposite p. 145.

174. Erdmann K. Sturm, Der junge Zacharias Ursin, pp. 168-219.
On the commentaries see p. 170 n. 10.

175. C. R. XLVII, 3691, col. 244. See Walter Hollweg, Heinrich
Bullingers Hausbuch, pp. 289-290. For Bullinger's brief to Martyr of
27 December 1561 and Zanchi's fourteen theses sent to Martyr on the
same date discussing predestination, see respectively Johan Hottinger,
Historiae ecclesiasticae Novi Testamenti (9 vols. 1651-1667); VIII,
pp. 833-35 and Zanchi Opera VII, 67f. See also G. B. Gallizioli,
Memorie istoriche e letterarie della vita e della opere di Girolamo
Zanchi.

176. Ibid., col. 245.

177. C. R. XLVII, 3840, col. 505. The following is identical in
wording to 3691, col. 245. "De iustificatione per fidam solam dicitur
non recte sentire. Praedicatur etiam docere, eam perfectionem in hac
vita obtineri ut operibus legi Dei satisfaciamus."

178. Marcus Kutter, Celio Secondo Curione, pp. 279-80. 16 June
1557. Basel Stadtsarchiv.

179. Durling, op. cit., p. 150.

180. Theodor Wotschke, Der Briefwechsel der Schweizer mit den
Polen, pp. 151-153.

181. C. R. XLVII, 3857, cols. 542-43. 24 September 1562. Z. S.
A. EII 367 (176/78).

182. Ibid., col. 544.

183. Letter of January 1562 may be found in Loci Communes (1626), pp. 802-803.

184. Common Places (1583), Part five, pp. 161-164. See A. Schweizer, op. cit., I, pp. 418-439 for controversy between Zanchi and Marbach.

185. Joseph Müller, Geschichte der böhmischen Brüder III, 102ff. Cited in J. K. Zeman, The Anabaptists And The Czech Brethren In Moravia 1526-1628, p. 260.

186. Z. S. A., EII (368), fol. 545^r. See also EII (367), fol. 367f where Paul Tileton wrote Bullinger from Frankenthal about his attendance in Martyr's classes. This letter printed in Bainton, Bernardino Ochino, pp. 197-201 is important as a reflection on Martyr's consistency in teaching a 'true presence.'

187. W. Köhler, Bibliographia Brentiana, p. 176.

188. J. C. McLellland, The Visible Words of God, p. 66.

189. Oratio (1582), sig. Rr. See Calvin's letter to Farel of 11 May 1541 that Brenz opposed the "wafer-god" at Ratisbon. L. C. I, 239. Martyr owned a copy of Brenz on Exodus (1544) and John (1546) which may explain his reluctance. See Ganoczy op. cit., p. 215.

190. Köhler, op. cit., pp. 185 ff. shows several Latin and German editions of 1562 as well as Latin editions of 1563 and 1565.

191. John Donnelly, S. J. is preparing a critical edition of the Dialogus. See McLelland, op. cit., pp. 206-220 on its content.

192. O. L. II, 544. 15 May 1550.

193. Oratio (1582), sig. Rrii.

194. Köhler, op. cit., p. 376. 22 November 1562. Z. S. A., E II (346).

195. Opuscula (1582), col. 232.

196. Oration. See also Hans Fischer, "Conrad Gesner (1515-1565) as Bibliographer and Encyclopedist," L. T. B. S., Fifth Series, XXI (1966), pp. 269-281. In a letter of 17 February 1564 Parkhurst sent Simler a catalogue of Patristic authors for Gesner, who was still editing texts. Z. L. I, p. 137. Simler describes Gesner's religious views in his 1566 life. "Primum itaque existimabat omnem de religione doctrinam ex sacris literis esse petendam, ideo eas libenter et saepe legebat, praecipue tamen Psalmorum lectione afficiebatur, quos saepe

Hebraice legebat: plurimum etiam Apollinarii Graeca par aphrasi
delectabatur . . . Tanto autem studio sacras literas legit, ut de
gravissimis controversiis religionis nostrae optime iudicare posset."
Josia Simler, Vita Clarissimi Philosophi et Medici Excellentissimi
Conradi Gesneri Tigurini (Tigurinus: Christoph. Froschoverus,
1566), p. 16ʳ. One of the works listed in Simler's appendix is an
edition of the patristic theologians printed in 1552 which includes
twelve letters of Ignatius. Ibid., p. 25ᵛ.

197. C. R. XLVIII, 3879, col. 585. 22 November 1562. Compare
Beza's comments about Bucer and Martyr in an important letter to
Cassiodore De Reina of 23 June 1565. Beza contrasted Bucer's prolixity on the Eucharist with advice to De Reina to use "the clearer
and more certain writings of our Martyr." C. T. B., VI, p. 115. On
27 June 1566 Beza wrote to Grindal about the excellent servant of
Christ, Peter Martyr. His commentaries were entirely endorsed by the
"Anglicana Ecclesia." Theodori Bezae Vezelii . . . Epistolarum
Theologicarum (1597), p. 67. The Plume Library at Maldon, Essex
contains six of Martyr's works. This private collection is representative of literature read in Elizabethan England. See S. G. Deed,
Catalogue of the Plume Library at Malden, Essex, 178-79. The volumes
were:
1. In duos libros Samuelis (fol. Tiguri, 1575).
2. Romanos (Heidelberg, 1613).
3. Genesis (Tiguri, 1569).
4. Corinthios (Tiguri, 1567).
5. Loci Communes (Heidelberg, 1622).
6. Melachim (Tiguri, 1581).

PART TWO: THE LEARNED STRANGER
(1542/53)

There is yet among us two great learned men, Petrus Martyr and Barnard Ochin, which have a hundred marks apiece: I would the king would bestow a thousand pound on that sort.

Hugh Latimer

CHAPTER VI

STRASBOURG LECTURES (1542/47)

When the nineteenth century historian R. W. Dixon called Peter

Martyr "a learned stranger" he was reflecting what Martyr's own con-

temporaries had said.[1] Edmund Grindal, Bishop of London wrote to Sir

William Cecil about Martyr's role at the Colloquy of Poissy:

> I am of your judgment, that no man alive is more fit than Peter
> Martyr for such a conference; and my lord of Canterbury, I trust,
> will communicate his opinion herewith . . . . the papists can win
> no honesty in any indifferent hearing; for he is better seen in
> old doctors, councils, and ecclesiastical histories than any
> Romish doctor of cristendom: he is also himself well seen in
> the civil and canon laws.[2]

A glance at Martyr's library preserved in Geneva as well as an exam-

ination of his *Romans* delivered as lectures while at Oxford will sup-

port Grindal's statement and Dixon's apt phrase. There can be no ques-

tion but that Martyr collected a useful library. That Martyr made good

use of his bibliographic tools can be seen especially in the commentary

on *Romans*.[3] There in the tract *Of Iustification* Martyr marshalled his

reading from Basil, Gregory of Nazianzus, Augustine, Chrysostom, Ambrose,

Cyprian, Origen, Jerome and the Church Councils including Trent.[4] In

fact the reference from *Corinthios* (1551) and Zanchi convinces one that

Martyr brought the text of his 1541 *Romans* lectures at Lucca with him

and revised them at Oxford in the light of his protestant experiences

in Northern Europe.

His chief opponent was the contemporary theologian Albert Pigge,

a perennial opponent of the new exegesis whether practiced by catholic

or protestant. Pigge could have been selected by Martyr for his attack on Martin Bucer of 1541 (republished in Mainz and Paris during 1543).[5]

More likely Martyr responded to Richard Smith's use of Pigge in the

1550 *Diatriba De Hominis Iustificatione*. There Smith attacked Bucer

on justification, mentioning Martyr by name only at page 156[r] though

the title page reads *Adversus Petrum Martyre . . . nunc apostatā in*

Anglia . . .

> And we will beginne first with Pigghius, because our adversaries
> count him for their Achilles or chief champion, and think that
> he only by his subtil sharp wit hath persed even into the inward
> misteries of the truth.[6]

In 1542 Pigge published a tract, *De Libero Arbitrio et divina gratia*,

which Calvin answered in the same year. Martyr would certainly have

known this while in Strasbourg. It is the *Defensio doctrinae de*

servitute arbitrii contra Pighium (Geneva: Gerardus, 1542). Still,

it is probably the exchange between Pigge, Bucer and Richard Smith

which animates Martyr's printed commentary. Calvin's response to Pigge

is in C. R. XXXV, cols. 233ff.

SOLA FIDE (1542/51)

The issue of *sola fide* did not always differentiate protestant

from catholic in the fourth decade of the sixteenth century.[7] Even

after the famous September debates on justification in 1546 at the

Council of Trent some catholic theologians still hoped for a moderate

atmosphere.[8] It would be helpful to describe here something of the

ambivalence during that decade in catholic theological discussion of

sola fide before examining Martyr's 1544 *Una Semplice Dichiaratione*.

One must also keep in mind the tract *De Schismate* in Martyr's Latin commentary on *Kings* delivered in Zurich after 1556. The question of

papal authority overrode any personal interpretation of faith for

sixteenth century catholics. In the biblical study of three catholic

scholars in Italy one can observe these tensions at work. These have

been selected because they represent the milieu from which Martyr came.

Marino Cardinal Grimani (1486-1546) served on the special committee

of cardinals which met twice a week during January 1546. As Jedin

comments, ". . . not only all questions about the programme of the

discussions . . . but even the drafts of decrees and the finances were

discussed by the Cardinals of the commission."[9] Since Grimani's life

parallels the pre-Tridentine search for reform and especially because

he is Venetian, his discussion of *sola fide* is important. Because

there is no history of this issue between 1520-1548, one could learn

much about the uncertainty in Italy over this central question from

documents such as Grimani's 1542 commentaries on *Romans* and *Galatians*.

Sola fide was not only a protestant distinctive in sixteenth century

Italy.[10]

In commenting on *Romans* (3:27) Grimani called the law of Christ

the law of faith.

> When all things which were required in the old law (such as the
> mandates which were subject to the senses themselves) were called
> the law of deeds, they were so by merit. Truly the law of Christ
> is called the law of faith when all things which are subject to
> it are held in hope.[11]

When St. Paul asked in this verse whether one abrogates the law by

faith, his own response was that faith confirms the law. Grimani's

printed marginal note reads, "They merit justice through the faith of

Jesus Christ alone."[12] At *Romans* (4:17) Grimani urged the necessity

of 'only faith'. Though "sola illius fides" is not the same as the

earlier Lutheran emphasis, it seems equally a denial of merit the-

ology.[13]

In the *Galatians* commentary Grimani at chapter three defined

justification by faith. At verse eleven Grimani utilized the *sola*

fide argument in a lengthy comment on the faith of Abraham. Abraham's

faith was "per solam fidem Christi."[14] Grimani urged that justifica-

tion before God was a far different matter than obedience to ceremonial

precepts in *Leviticus*.

> Justification before God, we conclude, is by faith alone, which
> Habakkuk authoritatively stated, saying 'Iustus ex fide vivit.'
> When therefore the Law is not of Faith, it is clear that justi-
> fication cannot be by the law . . ."[15]

That one needs to be careful in use of the term *sola fide* can be

seen from reading the commentaries of Clemens Aranis Ragnina (1482-

1559). His 1547 commentary on *Romans* published in Venice opposed

heretical ideas circulating in Italy at that time.[16] That this Domini-

can scholar was an eloquent foe of Lutheranism is clear from his fol-

lowing comment in the margin of folio 35 *recto*:

> It is not answering with bad deeds for the good – not a question
> of neglecting justification. Be aware, O Lutheran, that good
> works are necessary to salvation and not faith only. One an-
> swers that it is not at all according to faith alone – that you
> might understand what we say – but from faith according to works
> that 'the good man will be justified in (his) justification.'[17]

In addition to these opposing catholic views, – the dates 1542

and 1547 are revealing – one might cite from three additional catholic

commentators to catch the flavour of several variations on what current scholarship would have us believe is normative for Luther's lifetime to 1546. The formulae, 'quod in se est' and 'fides formata charitate' do distinguish theological discussions from 1512-1547, but do not in several instances separate protestant exegesis from catholic. They do distinguish a particular school of catholic exegesis from all other exegesis, particularly that influenced by Valla and Erasmus. This point is crucial for those who would examine Martyr's response to Pigge in the light of catholic variations on *sola fide* during the 1540's, even though Pigge died in 1542. Martyr's contention that the Church fathers taught *sola fide* (even Pope Gregory I) was another attempt to recover an evangelical understanding of faith for the Christian church in an age of acrimonious and tendentious theological discussion.

A reading of Girolamo Seripando (1492-1563), Ambrosius Catharinus (1484-1553) and the Benedictine scholar Isidore Clarius confirms the significance of Martyr's appeal to the patristic argument.[18] The point for this study of Martyr's exilic career is that his careful study of patristic and conciliar writings *contra* Pigge at Oxford reflects Martyr's orthodoxy rather than his apostasy. Subsequent analysis of Martyr's *De Schismate* will reveal that Martyr did not view himself as an apostate; it was the Roman Pope with some members of the Curia who had departed from evangelical truth.

Martyr did not abandon orthodoxy when he fled persecution; he joined Bucer in Strasbourg, Cranmer in England and Bullinger in Zurich to defend the gospel.[19] This positive trek through Martyr's biblical

writings is our main thesis, a pathway which Martyr trod despite his
opponent's calumnies over the Eucharist and deviations over the
Trinity. Martyr was not alone in his attempt to reconcile the obdurate
theologians of the post-Tridentine period. One must feel that even
until 24 August 1572 and the massacre of St. Bartholomew's Eve in Paris
such learned attempts were not all that heavyhanded nor devoid of
promise. Robert McNally points to the harm which the Tridentine theologians did to the spirituality of Loyola.[20] In spite of the theological arteriosclerosis at Trent there were converts to be won and believers to be confirmed. The significance of Martyr's *Romans* (1558)
with its political conservatism can be appreciated by seeing it as part
of a conciliatory genre originating with Contarini, Cortese, Pole,
Sadoleto, Seripando and other Paulinians of Sixteenth Century Italy.[21]

One should not forget that according to Simler members of this
group such as Hercules Gonzaga, Gaspar Contarini, Reginold Pole, Pietro
Bembo and Frederigo Fregoso intervened on Martyr's behalf. Martyr's
commentary of 1558 stands in a catholic genre of the sixteenth century
every bit as much as it rests on a catholic exegetical tradition of
the fifth and sixth centuries. What Erasmus praised in Lorenzo Valla's
philological notes on the New Testament text was to reverberate throughout in the sixteenth century among catholic and protestant scholars
alike. In this section these hermeneutical accents in Martyr's biblical
writings will be traced.

The nadir of catholic exegesis may be found in Ambrosius Catharinus' writings.[22] When Thomas de Vio Cardinal Cajetan attempted with

the aid of other scholars to produce a sensible commentary on *Romans*,
Catharinus levelled a vicious attack on Cajetan.[23]   In 1520 Catharinus
published an *Apologia*[24] against Martin Luther which he followed up
with another reply in 1521.[25]   Catharinus attacked Ochino as early as
1532 and in 1541 prepared for the expected general council by writing
against Contarini.   Since Catharinus occupied a prominent if controversial role in Cardinal Del Monte's committee at Trent,[26] his early
writings against Ochino[27] and Contarini[28] help one to see how negative
catholic exegesis could be.   When practiced by a Catharinus in the
1530's the issues were clearly drawn.

Ambrosius Catharinus' 1551 commentary on the Pauline Corpus[29]
assists one to understand the milieu in which Pigge attacked Bucer
and others in the protestant camp; consequently one can see what Martyr
sought to accomplish in his *Romans* lectures at Oxford when he selected
Pigge as the champion of catholic opposition to the protestant understanding of faith.   On the other hand, Catharinus and Pigge do not
represent the only option in catholic exegesis during the 1540's. This
does not mean that when one sketches in other possibilities for catholic
exegesis of *Romans* in this period one is thereby distorting Martyr's
purpose in responding to his opponents' use of Pigge.   On the contrary
one is thereby showing how Martyr's patristic argument fits into a
catholic tradition, albeit interrupted by the Council of Trent.[30]   At
Romans (1:17-18) Catharinus concluded that the impious first believe
and then have their faith accepted by God.[31]

Professor Kristeller has urged that more careful attention be given to monastic scholars in the sixteenth century. His valuable

article with a biographical checklist deserves careful attention.[32]

One of those monastic scholars was Isidore Clarius[33] who in 1536/37

prepared an oration on religious harmony which he sent to Gasparo

Contarini for a judgment. In 1538 Cochlaeus received the *Adhortatio*

ad concordiam from Clarius in Bautzen for publication,[34] objecting to

any printing of the treatise because the Protestants would use such

material to their advantage.[35] Morone, Bishop of Modena apparently

did not agree with these strictures since Gregorio Cortese endorsed

the treatise to Contarini as one means of resolving the religious

quarrel of the day.[36] Isidore Clarius who entered the Benedictine

Cassinese order on 24 June 1517 was one of the most learned biblical

scholars in Italy. Both Cortese and Contarini admired his exegetical

work which was incorporated in the seventeenth century *Critici Sacri*.

The treatise *Adhortatio ad concordiam* appeared in Milan, 1540,

Paris with no date and again in 1705.[37] Clarius nowhere mentioned

Luther or Melanchthon by name, but by implication abhorred Luther

while praising Melanchthon. He did not say that the Lutherans were

wrong, but did raise the question of utility or timing in Luther's

stress on predestination.[38] A fresh reading of the treatise reflects

Clarius' concern for bishops who would be learned in the scriptures.

Clarius dedicated the treatise to Contarini, naming Cortese as his

"praeceptor."

Clarius published some sophisticated biblical exegesis. A

representative selection of his work may be found in the 1542 *Vulgata*

Editio Novi, ac Veteris Testamentum . . . adiectis ex eruditis scriptoribus scholiis . . .(Venice: Petrus Scheffer, 1542).[39] In the scholia on *Romans* (3:28) Clarius observed that there was a great controversy in his time over the proper definition of works versus faith. The Apostle Paul together with the other Apostolic writers meant that Christ had abrogated the Jewish law. No one since could then be justified without the faith of Christ. Clarius went on to say that Paul meant to exclude circumcision as a requirement for faith. When Paul contended that a pure heart and faithful affection before God was required, Clarius maintained that no one could hold to a contrary opinion. He then summarized the biblical writings as follows:

> Jesus Christ is the true lamb and host who came to reconcile us to the Father, cancelling our sins' penalty in the cross for salvation and freeing us from servitude to the devil. As the adopted Son of God He gives true peace through faith, which the Father grants to us as sons. Faith is the gift of God by which we believe Christ has come into this world to save us from our sins . . . Faith and the Holy Ghost are given which all believe signifies our inheritance and spiritual testimony that we are sons of God, that is, by means of the love of God diffused in our hearts of which Paul writes to the Corinthians. For this reason we are justified by faith working through love, i. e., the Father Himself who is our agent receives us as sons justified by His grace, not imputing our shortcomings to us.[40]

This circle of biblical study in the Cassinese congregations reached many clerics during Cortese's years at San Giorgio Maggiore, Venice. It might well have touched Peter Martyr Vermigli. McNair argues convincingly that Martyr was in Rome during the meetings of the Reform Commission of 1536,[41] although his evidence is circumstantial. To McNair's evidence about Martyr's relationship to the signatories of the *Consilium de Emendanda Ecclesia* and to Simler's evidence in the

Oratio that Martyr while in Naples had these powerful friends in Rome, one can add the positive accents of their biblical study. By the time Martyr published his *Romans* commentary in 1558 at Basle, the confessional postures had hardened after Trent's decision on justification. Certainly in 1544 in his *Una Semplice Dichiaratione* there was the possibility of a *rapprochement* between catholic and protestant on the central theme of faith in St. Paul's letter to the Romans. In 1550/51 when Martyr delivered these lectures at Oxford he was attacking a particular group of adamant theologians whose chief proponent had been Albert Pigge. Not only did Martyr's biblical writings underscore in Jedin's phrase "the reality of the differences," they also continued "the dream of an understanding" by their rich recourse to patristic exegesis. One finds in Martyr's published lectures this sense of identity with the catholic exegetes of the fourth and fifth centuries which consoled him during bitter religious strife,[42] whether with the Lutherans Marbach, Osiander and Brenz, with Stephen Gardiner in England or Stancaro in Poland.

THESES AD DISPUTANDUM PUBLICE (1543/45)

In the letter to Lucca of 1542/43 Martyr's title is of great interest, e. e., *Grace and Peace from our Father-God through the Lord Jesus Christ-To The Faithful Lucchese Saints of the Universal Church.* In what respect did Martyr feel his pastoral responsiblity to the *Universis Ecclesiae Lucensis?* Martyr arrived in Basle during 1542 where there was no academic position for him. Neither Geneva nor Zurich offered him aid though Bucer did at Strasbourg. Near the end

of this Lucca letter Martyr gave the reason for his flight: to study
Sacred Scripture and expound Christian truth. "This is my benefit of
God, where I am able to interpret Holy Scripture, to console you by
letters and to encourage the preservation of the Gospel in its purity."[43]
Use of the phrase *Dei beneficio* would connote the *Benefits of Christ*
which Martyr likely read while still in Italy. The triple program outlined in the above passage sets the tone for a discussion of Martyr's
career in exile. He needed a position which would free him to be a
Biblical scholar, exercise pastoral care by correspondence to his
countrymen and defend the purity of the Gospel.

There are two published writings from 1543/45 in which Martyr
comments on the "Sacred Scriptures." They will be viewed in the following order: 1) *Theses D. Petri Martyris Pro/positae Ad Disputandum
Pvblice in Schol/la Argentinensi, Anno Domini M.D. XLIII.*[44] 2) *Vna
Sem/Plice Dichia/Ratione Sopra Gli/XII Articoli della Fede/Christiana*[45]
It does not seem likely that the oration on the study of scripture - a
sermon preached on *Malachi* (2) - was given in 1543 even though the
Dictionary of National Biography assigns it to that year. In the oration Martyr refers to the unclean fountains in the "Colleges in this
city," a clear reference to Oxford. Simler assigns two of the biblical
commentaries to this first period in Strasbourg. They are *Genesis* and
Lamentations which will be analyzed after the *Theses* and *Articoli*.

Luigi Santini uses the *Theses* of 1543 to show from 1543-1562
Martyr's consistent views on heresy and schism.[46] They also reflect
Martyr's exegetical method which was tied firmly to the Law/Gospel

motif.   This motif of 1543 perhaps explains in part why Martyr could

sign the Augsburg Confession in good conscience in 1553 during his

second period in Strasbourg.   The theses are propositions for public

discussion which perhaps later Martyr privately explained to his stu-

dents or even in sermons.   From *Genesis* (1) Martyr proposed, "Seeing

the holie Scripture is a declaration of the wisedome of God, we have

from thence the fountaine of our felicitie."[47]   This first proposition

is juxtaposed with III on the purpose of holy scripture.   Martyr in

his commentaries reiterated that the theologian must obey what he read

in scripture.   One example from the *De Schismate* will suffice here.

Martyr in that treatise accused his adversaries of perfidy, simony and

bellicose dreams of luxury and grandeur.   They were criminals who would

not enter the kingdom of heaven because they "neither devote themselves

to the word of God, nor preach it, nor feed the sheep."[48]   Thesis III

on *Genesis* (1) set forth this theme of obedience.   "The excellencie of

the holie scriptures is herein perceived, that it sendeth us to the

high cause of the will of God, which is revealed in them."[49]

From the fountain of scripture in which the will of God is reveal-

ed, Martyr drew out the twin themes of Law and Gospel.   From that funda-

mental premise Martyr went on to define the nature of faith.   Thesis

IV of *Genesis* (1) reads:

> The summe of those things which are conteined in the holie
> scriptures, is the lawe and the Gospell, which parts are
> indifferentlie contained as well in the new as in the old
> testament.[50]

The nature of faith depends for Martyr on the promises of God who through Christ illumined sacred and profane history. Sacred history

tells of things done by the Word of God, while profane history sets

forth the great works of God. Martyr summarized God's word, work and

promise by a reference to the person of Christ. This lent a continuity

to his exegesis which found all these themes in every part of scripture.

Martyr's proposition VI on *Genesis* (15) declared that, "Faith is a

firme assent of the mind unto the promises concerning Christ, through

the persuasion of the holie Ghost unto saluation."[51] The same point

is made during 1545 in thesis V on *Exodus* (2). There Martyr defined

the Church as the people of God selected by God's word and promise.

Martyr returned again and again to this theme. "We are not to deter-

mine of the People of God, according to the abundance of outward good

things, but onlie according to the promise and word of God."[52]

Certain themes in Martyr's exegesis are worth noting, i. e.,

assent to the promises of God in Christ, that law and gospel are con-

tained in Old and New Testament books alike and that profane history

sets forth the great works of God. Martyr could have read Melanchthon's

Loci Communes of 1521 in an early Italian version. That would be one

likely source for his dependance on these triple themes. There are

two known copies of this Italian translation which the *Corpus Refor-

matorum* prints as *I Principii/De La Theologia/di Ippofilo/da Terra/

negra*. It has no date, printer, year or preface given. The first

reference to this work as a Venetian imprint comes from Joseph Scaliger

in 1669 who heard it from Cardinal Seraphino. The first to cite the

title from first hand inspection was Christian Salig in 1735. Fontani

in 1753 ascribed the translation to Ludovico Castelvetro which
Tiraboschi rejected in 1781. Two other early Italian versions of
Melanchthon are known. Georg Strobel in 1776 mentions the annotations
on *Matthew* known from the Index as *Hippophili Melangaei Annotationes
in Evangelium Matthaei*. The Index of 1546 prohibited an interesting
work which excerpts from the Italian *Loci* under the title *Il sommario
della Scrittura*.[53] Italian translations speak of a familiarity with
Melanchthon in Italy which went beyond the Latin influence of the 1521
Loci Communes. On the other hand *Galatians* (3:13-29) contains such
views apart from any reading of Melanchthon.

On his deathbed in 1562 Martyr hesitated to oppose the Lutheran
Brenz "because hee knewe that Brentius did in other writings not altogether deserve ill of the Church . . . ." One reason for Martyr's
reluctance to speak out on Brenz may have been Martyr's use of Brenz
in preparing these Old Testament theses in 1543/45. In 1542 Brenz
published at Frankfurt a commentary on *Leviticus* and in 1544 one on
Exodus at Halle. Martyr owned copies of the 1544 *Exodus* and the 1552
Leviticus. The *Exodus* has marginalia in Martyr's hand. One can conclude therefore that theologically Martyr followed Paul in *Galatians*
(3:29) and exegetically appreciated Brenz.[54] Martyr also owned Bomberg's *Hebrew Bible* of 1517-1518 published in Venice with Rabbinic
comments as well as the second Venetian edition of 1524-27.[55] All of
this shows the care which Martyr took in preparing his Old Testament
lectures. Bomberg's second edition used Jacob ben Chayim on the

Massoretic text which in the sixteenth century established its printed
form for future scholarship. The Q^{e}re and K^{e}thibh were marked with a
marginal collation of these consonental and vowel preferences.

The full commentary on *Exodus* never appeared from Martyr's pen.
When one turns to Brenz on *Exodus*, the comments there parallel Martyr's
Propositions. At *Exodus* (1:1) for example, Brenz urged that "the truth
of God be commended where it warns us to hold fast to faith in the
promises of God and to endure in faith in all afflictions."[56] Again
in the first chapter Brenz urged his readers to consider the divine
promises and persevere in faith. In chapter two Brenz pointed to how
"Jacob fled from his own brother Esau and the land of promise." David
also fled from Saul and Christ told his Apostles to flee persecution
by flight into another city, for as Moses fled into the wilderness so
did God expect his servants to walk by faith rather than sight.[57] This
parallels Martyr's immediate flight from Italy in 1542. Taken with
the fact that Martyr annotated this 1544 *Exodus* commentary, Brenz's
Old Testament exegesis becomes one source for Martyr's own lectures
at Strasbourg. For this reason perhaps Martyr was reluctant to attack
Brenz by name in 1561.

Paul Fagius was a companion during Martyr's first stay in Strasbourg. Fagius' arrival at Cambridge in 1549 with Bucer and sudden
death in November of 1550 was a great loss to Bucer and Martyr. In
1541 Fagius published at Isny a study of 712 Hebrew, Aramaic, Arabic,
Greek and Latin terms from Levita's *Grammar*.[58] The title page gives
under the printer's device a Hebrew phrase which reads, "My hope is in

the Messiah who was sent, who will come in the future to judge the living and the dead." In 1542 Fagius saw in print his exegetical work called *Perousch, id est exegesis sive expositio dictionum Hebraicum literalis et simplex in quatuor capita Geneseos pro studiosis linguae hebraicae per Paulum Fagium*. In 1543 an expanded edition appeared in Constance with a German version and Latin translation for use in study. In 1544 Martyr would have seen Fagius' edition of Rabbi David Kimḥi's *Perush* and in 1546 at Strasbourg the *Targum* (Aramaic commentary) *Of Onkelos* on the Pentateuch. Many of these works were used by Martyr in preparing his Old Testament lectures[59] in addition to the Targum of Jonathan on *Judges*.

Martyr selected these historical books of the Old Testament for his lectures because he held to the importance of historical revelation. A clear example of this concern is the letter which Martyr sent to Elizabeth on her succession as Queen. In Marten's translation it reads as follows:

> If Bishops and Minsters of Churches shall not doe their duetie, if in handling of doctrine and administring of the Sacraments they forsake the iust rules of the holy Scriptures: who but a godlie Prince shall reuoke them into the right way? Let not your Maiestie expect, (as things nowe be) that those men are stirred up to these things of themselves; unlesse they be mooued thereunto by princely authoritie, they will not repaire the ruine of the Temple of God. *Ioas* a king of the Jewes, when he perceived that the Preestes perfourmed not this, took unto him the charge to amend the decaied buildings of Ϋ Temple. Go forward therefore O holie *Debora* of our times. Joine unto you ϲome godlie *Barac*. The Israelites which are diuers waies oppressed, deliuer you to the sincere and pure libertie of the Gospell. Bee not afraide, for God is not woont to leave these enterprises destitute of his fauour. Him you shall have with you: that you, like valiaunt Iahel may strike the head of Iabin with the hammer of your power, and fasten it to the ground from whence it came,

whereby he may cease to be troublesome unto your good nation.
We have verie great hope, that you shall bee the same Hester
which shall driue *Haman* unto hanging, which thirsteth for the
slaughter and blood of the people of God. Let these holie
women be an incouragement unto your Maiestie: and suffer not
your selfe to faint for this cause that you are not born a man
but a woman.[60]

Martyr reflected his classical training when in 1545 he endorsed pro-

fane history for its usefulness in demonstrating God's great works.

In the necessary proposition XIII on *Exodus* (8, 9, 10 and 11) Martyr

defended the study of scripture and ancient histories.

The holie and prophane histories, although they have manie
cases that be alike; yet herein they differ, that in the holie
histories, things are doone by the word of GOD, wherof in the
prophane histories there is no expresse mention made, and
yet neuerthelesse we acknowledge those things, which be there
set foorth to be the great works of God.[61]

These theses proposed at the start of Martyr's protestant career

in Strasbourg are important for the consistency with which they are

repeated and expounded in his subsequent writings. Together with the

prayers on the *Psalms* given as part of his public lectures during the

second Strasbourg sojourn, these propositions demonstrate a variety of

themes in Martyr's concern for a biblical theology which is historical

and philological in interpretation, yet dependent upon the firm

promises of God in Christ. Since Christ alone is the end of the law,

both Gospel and Law find their fulfilment in Him. Martyr's hermeneuti-

cal approach therefore is humanistic and Christological. For the

latter one must turn to the Twelve Articles on the Apostles Creed of

1544: for the former there is a concise point which Marten made in

his preface to the *Common Places* of 1583 when he urged that interpreters become multilingual as Martyr himself was.

> And they which give themselves to this studie, it shall be
> requisite that they have the knowledge of the toongs, especiallie
> of the Hebrue and Greeke; wherein the holie books of the scrip-
> tures were first written by the Prophets and Apostles: for he
> that dependeth altogither of interpreters, seeth with other mens
> eies, and speaketh in another mans mouth.[62]

Scripture therefore was Martyr's key to unlock the mysteries both

of the wisdom and knowledge of God. As a scholar of Christ[63] Martyr

was not satisfied to extract propositions from scripture for a *summa*

theologiae, nor did he seek to defend the truth of those writings by

public debate alone. Martyr intended that the scholar of Christ be

taught by what he read in scripture as well as teach it to   others,

a practice often done in private meetings in his home. Salvation was

not the only purpose for which the scholar was to immerse himself in

scripture, for he needed to express what he read in excellence of

life and holy works. Before one studies Martyr's Penteteuchal com-

mentary on *Genesis* it would be helpful to keep this emphasis on a

godly life in mind. Proposition XII from *Exodus* summarizes Martyr's

views that the law of God requires one to lead such a life.

> God's law requires of our perfect actions three things: first,
> that we be honest in outward affairs; next, that we avoid
> violence of our own accord; and finally, that we refer every
> good and spiritual impulse totally to God.[64]

Martyr gave the finest expression of his concern for an exemplary

and godly discipline in his *Encomium Verbi Dei* where he held up to

view Moses in *Deuteronomy* (32:2) as an example of a godly life. Then

he concluded with this prayer:

> So I good Lord most earnestly desire of thee that those thinges

which I shall teach thy children, may not be any stormes of errours, but desired and fruitful raines of the trueth: and that my interpretations may be no waters that should wast the Church and overthrow cosciences, but a deawie consolation, and a profitable edification of soules. And I beseech thee also that thou wilt hearken and graunt unto my prayer, that all those which be heere present, may heare the holie seede of thy word, not as the high way, nor as the thornes, nor as the stonie ground, but as the good lande and fielde prepared by thy spirite, they may out of the scriptures, which shall bee committed to the furrowes of their hearts, bring foorth fruite thirtie, sixtie and an hundreth fold.[65]

UNA SEMPLICE DICHIARATIONE (1544)

A reading of this early work acquaints one with Martyr's hermeneutical and theological approach to biblical study. In any event Martyr appreciated Bucer's hospitality and the freedom to explore the Hebrew text of the Old Testament with Paul Fagius. The 1544 explanation of the Apostle's Creed introduces one to the fundamentals of his thought.[66] Simon Goulart endorsed this work to Simler in 1574. Goulart translated Martyr's letter to the Luccan Church into French (ad fratres Italos Lapsos), and sought to edit Martyr's theological letters. This widely read exposition of the Apostle's Creed was praised for its simplicity.[67] Ambrogio Lusco in Caprodistria accused Vergerio on 25 January 1545 of owning a book by Martyr. This 1544 work was the only one of Martyr's books then in print.[68] The Sorbonne prohibited this 1544 work by Martyr in its 1551 list called *Collectio Judicorum De Novis Erroribus*.[68a]

On the first article Martyr urged that the purpose of creation was to give eternal life to the regenerate.

The similitude undoubtedlie, which the regenerate have with God their father, consisteth in wisdome, iustice, simplicitie of

mind, magnanimitie, charitie, and in other like heauenlie and
diuine affections of the mind: whereby they iudge themselves
to be made according to the image of GOD, as they were created
at the beginning. And the inheiritance, which they expect of
so excellent a father, is eternall and most blessed life.[69]

Martyr's reading of 'fortezza' is preferred to the Latin translation

'magnanimitate'. To link 'fortezze' with 'charita' seems to alter

Martyr's meaning of 'strength.'[70]

Felicity or eternal life depends on the Christ who rose again on

the third day to bring new life to those who have been grafted in Him.

Martyr's Christology is central to his interpretation of all canonical

biblical texts.

. . . let us reioise among ourselves; that it is brought to
passe by the goodnesse of God, that we be reckoned in so happie
a societie, under the banner of so noble a prince and valiant
brother; unto whom shall never want, either will or power to
help us.[71]

'Forze' here is translated 'power', a term for which Martyr was

fond and which could be used to translate *Romans* (1:4).[72] This resur-

rection theme then occurs in a lovely analogy which Martyr used to

express the certainty of future glory for the believer.

If in the winter time we see a bare tree without leaves, flowers
and fruit, so that by the outward rind it may be taken as
withered, and yet so long as the root sticketh fast in the
ground, it is aliue, and is not counted dead. But if a man cannot persuade himselfe thereof, let him expect until the spring
of the yeere, and then the truth of the matter will appeare by
the leaves and flowers which spring foorth. For by euident
effects it will be well knowne, that the life of that tree laie
hidden before. Euen so we, which here seeme to be as it were
the bootie of death, and in whom no tokens of sound life doo
apeare: if we be ingraffed in Christ, which is our root, who
liueth, and for our sakes is raised up againe, wherefore do we
now doubt of our resurrection to come? And this is that Paule
writeth in the epistle to the Colos. Ye are dead (saith he)
and your life is hidden in Christ with God: when Christ, which

is your life, shall be made manifest, then also shall ye be
made manifest with him in glorie.[73]

Martyr mentioned the benefits of Christ in the final part of this
section where he commented on the phrase, "Rose on the third day." The
term 'benefits of Christ' is reminiscent of the tract with that title
which circulated in Italy even prior to its first printed edition of
1543. Though this single phrase can not be conclusive for Martyr's
knowledge of the *Beneficio de Cristo* in 1544, it is known that Cardinals Cortese and Morone endorsed this treatise by Don Benedetto da
Mantua early in 1543.[74] Marc Antonio Flaminio had something to do
with the final draft as is clear from Carnesecchi's examination before
the Inquisition. Since Martyr was conversant with this circle before
his flight late in 1542, it is possible that he had seen a printed
copy or even a manuscript copy by 1544.[75]

In any event Martyr's summary with its theology of hope was a
sure consolation for all his confreres in exile. Martyr pointed to
the benefits of Christ which would enduce the Christian to benefit
his neighbor. The Holy Spirit renews the gifts of Christ in the elect
so that they might honor Him by a godly life, protected from all evil.

> Herein standeth the whole summe of Christianitie, that inwardlie
> we should be euer renewed, and that outwardlie as far as lieth
> in us, we should pleasure and benefit our neighbors: seeing
> Christ, being raised from the dead, hath so greatlie endued us
> with his benefits, by giuing from that time unto his children
> that pretious gift of the holie Ghost; and first went unto his
> father, where he continuallie beholdeth us, and offereth most
> acceptable prairers unto GOD for us. Life being renewed in him
> by his resurrection, he bountifullie and in heaped measure
> increaseth his gifts in his elect. He being exalted unto that
> most excellent power dooth now protect us from all eiuill, and
> filleth us with all goodnesses. Wherefore, our part is to

> bend all our care and diligence unto that end, that we may
> honor him after a godlie sort: not with earthlie ceremonies,
> or with sundrie inuentions of men; but with spirituall worshipp-
> ing, and with that which may be agreeable unto that heauenlie
> and spirituall state, whereunto Christ is now receiued. Before
> that he was come unto us and so long as he was conursant in the
> world after an humane sort, the shadowes and figures of the lawe,
> corporall worshippings, and wordlie ceremonies were in force:
> but now, we being raised up with Christ, it is meet, that even
> as we behold him both in the place and degree, wherein he is set;
> so also, that we should with lifted up eies of our mind, fasten
> our hope upon him.[76]

The above passage touches on the issue which Martyr raised in his letter

to Calvin of 8 March 1555.[77] The scriptural passage which Martyr used

there was *Hebrews* (2:14-15) which was repeated in correspondence with

Theodore Beza. The reference from *Hebrews* (2) in these later letters

may lie behind the above 1544 passage.

> Since all the Children share the same blood and flesh, he too
> shared equally in it, so that by his death he could take away
> all the power of the devil, who had power over death, and set
> free all those who had been held in slavery all their lives by
> the fear of death.

This passage was also cited in the 1543 *Beneficio di Cristo*.[78]

Two other sections of the 1544 tract will illustrate Martyr's

concern for inward renewal of the christian and the church. These

are the sections on the Holy Ghost and the Holy Catholic Church. After

this illustration from Martyr's early thought on the church, it will

be helpful to compare the treatise *De Schismate* from the 1566 Commen-

tary on I *Kings*. First of all one must examine Martyr's writings

given during 1542-1547. By proceeding chronologically one might pre-

serve the unity of Martyr's thought without too lengthy a disgression

from the historical setting. Since Martyr revised the lectures on

Kings and *Judges* while at Strasbourg and Zurich from 1553-1562, one can not separate strands of these commentaries by assigning them to various periods unless internal evidence permits one so to do. The reader should attend to the likely setting of some passages which seem to reflect on Martyr's experiences in Strasbourg and Zurich as he comes upon them.

On 29 December 1544 Martyr signed a letter issued by the Strasbourg Pastors to the church at Neuchatel in Switzerland. The letter describes the censure of ministers, whether there should be a public or private rebuke of ministers who were immoral. Such men were to be admonished in private and if they remained obstinant, were to be corrected singly and then before a group of ministers. One reminder is Paul's example, who challenged Peter in public.[79]

In his creedal exposition of the Holy Ghost Martyr urged the elect not to doubt the assurance of their salvation. The passage quoted below also seems appropriate as a comment on Martyr's flight from persecution in Lucca. Martyr did not suffer physical distress for he had a remarkable instinct for selfpreservation. There were elements of psychic anguish which Martyr continued to express long after he could no longer freely exercise his vocation in Lucca.

> To these things adde, if you will, that the comfort which
> springeth by the assurance of our saluation, is so great;
> as euen in the middest of troubles, miseries, calamities,
> and sorrowes of this world, we may lead a cheereful and merrie
> life. And that not without cause; seeing we feele in us that
> singular and noble gift, which Paule to the Ephesians calleth
> The pledge of our saluation. I see not now how anie man,
> upon iust cause, can doubt of his comming one daie into that
> state of Christ, when he perceiueth alreadie that his soule
> liueth by the same spirit of Christ.[80]

Such heavenly gifts would enable the christian to live a cheerful
and quiet life in the midst of persecutions. The hope of eternal life,
Martyr's 'leitmotif,' came by the grace of the Lord Jesus Christ.
Martyr gave thanks to such a benign and merciful God who by grafting
believers into Christ by the Spirit enabled them to be free, i.e.,
"destitute neither of strength, neither of force, neither of light,
neither of anie facultie to let us, whereby we should the lesse either
will or work aright."[81] Interestingly the translator here uses
'robore' for 'forza'. These passages in Martyr remind one of a similar
theme in the *Beneficio di Cristo*. There the strong Son of God became
the source of mortal strength and eternal felicity.

> Has He not spilt His blood to wash away all my iniquities? Then,
> my soul, why are you sad? Trust in the Lord, who loves you so
> much that He willed that His only son should die to free you from
> eternal death, who took upon Himself our poverty, to give us His
> riches, who took upon Himself our infirmity, to make us strong
> with His strength, who became mortal, to make us immortal, who
> descended to the earth, that we might mount into heauen, who be-
> came a son of man with us, to make us sons of God with Him.[82]

Martyr continued this theme of strength and holiness in his
comments on the article, "I believe in the Holy Catholic Church," for
he believed that strength in the Church came from the spiritual weapons of Word and Spirit rather than from the carnal weapons of war used
in military conquest. The universal body of the church comprised all
those who "embrace every good thing offered them in Christ." The
offices in the church must be defined and put into practice. With a
slight shift of Martyr's order one can see his emphasis that obedience
to Christ enriches the flock of Christ, who in turn retain holiness

and happiness in the Catholic Church. This triad of passages from

Marten's translation will summarize Martyr's teaching on the church

in 1544.

> Indeed this bodie is not destitute of his weapons, but these be
> spirituall, and not carnall weapons; namlie, the word and the
> spirit, with the which it overcommeth the wisdome of man, casteth
> it to the ground, leadeth captive the mind and cogitation to the
> obedience of Christ.[83]

The second passage urges the leaders of the church to fulfill

their godly vocation:

> If they be apostles, it perteineth unto their office to preach;
> if they be pastors, to feed; if they be schoole masters of the
> Church, to teach; if they be dispensors of the treasures of
> Christ, they ought to inrich their sheepe therewith: I meane
> not with their pardons, bulles, and blessings; but with the word
> of God, with continuell admonitions and corrections, by which
> meanes the infidels are converted into God, the faithful are
> stirred up from their sloth and idlenesse, and receiue comfort
> in the fernace of afflictions.[84]

When that vocation as a steward of the Word of God has been followed,

then the truth which has been revealed in the scriptures by the Spirit

will lead on to orthodoxy, i. e., right worship. In this passage one

can see Martyr's concern for faith, holiness, truth and worship. His

theology possesses a unity which can best be seen from studying the

exegetical writings in their entirety. The Catholic Church in Martyr's

view must devote herself to the truth of the scriptures and that lawful

worship which alone can be deduced from them. The Catholic Church is:

> . . . an uniuersall bodie, compact together of men of euerie
> state and condition; the which, in what parts soeuer of the
> earth they dwell, they reteine the same faith and grace, right-
> eousnesse, holinesse, and happinesse; and finallie, they embrace
> euery good thing offered them in Christ: and so, as they will
> never suffer themselues one iot to be led from that truth,
> which the spirit of God had reuealed to us in the holie

scriptures; but they will assure themselues of that onelie
worshipping to be lawfull and acceptable unto GOD, which hee
hath prescribed in those holie scriptures.[85]

In this brief treatise Martyr not only set down a confession of
faith, but also wrote an epistle of consolation for himself and his
fellow exiles. Martyr's concern for the truth of the gospel was based
on these themes of Law and Gospel, Word and Spirit. In the Pentateuchal
commentary on *Genesis* as well as in the Pauline commentary on *Romans*
Martyr constantly reiterated a program of reform for the Church.

Josiah Simler wrote that the lectures on the *Twelve Minor Prophets*
which Martyr gave in Strasbourg were never published, nor were those on
Exodus and *Leviticus*.[86] One would like to have the notes on *Amos* for
what they would contain by way of social comment on the hierarchy.

> Nowe while hee took eon him the office of teaching during those
> fiue yeares which he taught at *Strasborough* before hee departed
> into Englande, hee interpreted manie pookes of the Scripture.
> For first hee interpreted the lamentation of Ieremie. Next hee
> expounded the booke of the XII. Prophetes which are named the
> smaller Prophetes. After that hee beginning at the first booke
> of the Bible, he expounded *Genesis, Exodus* and a good part of
> *Leuiticus*.[87]

This study will restrict itself to a partial analysis of these writings
by focusing on the *Genesis* Commentary.[88] The general format will be to
select one complete commentary from each period of Martyr's protestant
career, illustrating that work by briefer references to other of his
writings from the same place and time. Klaus Sturm limits his analysis
to the first Strasbourg period. One fails to understand how the *Romans*
commentary can be assigned to that time in Martyr's career.[89] Its context is England rather than Strasbourg.

Martyr's work was appreciated not only for its patristic learning and philological acumen, but also for its spiritual tone. What one reads in the *Una Semplice* of 1544 about obedience to Christ and holy living shows itself in Martyr's larger published works and in his life as a lecturer. His comment to Melanchthon in a letter of 26 June 1556 bears this out.

> Wherefore, I will seeke and maintaine peace, as you admonish me, yet so nevertheless, that when occasion is offered, (not a snatched or sought occasion, but that which is iust and necessarie) I will teach and speake that which I iudge true cōcerning that matter wherein I know they disagree from me, and that with such moderation and temperance, as I will not greeue or bitterlie taunt anie man that is of an other iudgement. But as for commauding me to silence ɔr recantation, neitherhave I hitherto suffered it, neither will I now suffer it.[90]

GENESIS AND LAMENTATIONS (1545/47)

The *Genesis* commentary was known to John Milton, who seems to have used it with other Renaissance commentaries in the preparation of *Paradise Lost*.[91] Milton especially approved Martyr's political views in the commentary on *Judges*.[92] As Williams points out, it is difficult to assign sections of *Paradise Lost* to particular Renaissance commentaries.[93] Nonetheless, even here Martyr is important.

> If we seek, in order to understand the great epic, to know whose hands framed the great tradition of which *Paradise Lost* is the culmination, and whose hands passed it down to Milton, we can do no better than to go to those 'common Expositers' whom Milton condemned and praised, knew and used.[94]

Williams points to the commonplace in Martyr's *Genesis* where Joseph had Pharaoh's authority to monopolize the grain market and charge land owners twenty per cent rent. Martyr endorsed Joseph and condemned private citizens of his own time who charged exorbitant prices. Such greed is ignoble for a wise or noble man.[94a]

It would be useful to examine the *Genesis* commentary in those sections which expand on the theses of 1543. Though not published until 1569, Martyr quoted from his *Genesis* commentary in 1551.[95] It is possible that Bishop Hooper of Gloucester meant these expanded notes rather than the theses of 1543 in his letter to Bullinger of 27 October 1551. "Peter Martyr . . . is aliue and well, and boldly stands forth as a brave and godly soldier in the army of the Lord . . . . He has not yet determined to publish his annotations on Genesis; he is meditating something upon the epistle to the Romans."[96] One passage in particular is striking for its concise statement of Martyr's purpose.

> These faculties are distributed alike in the Old and New Covenant. The Old is Law, the new is Gospel. However, we must examine the definition of each member. The Law contains the traditional doctrines which God gave to lead men to Christ. The Gospel is the power of God to salvation: an expounder of the remission of sins through Christ. But there are no certain places in the Holy Scriptures & these books which are distinct or appear now in the New Testament to such a degree that they have not been discovered in the Old, for they pertain to both testaments. This must then be the distinction, that those evangelical doctrines which are in the Old Testament Books describe the future and are a counter promise. Those in the New echo the Law and lead to this introduction: there it preaches penitence which the Law before pressed on those who would believe. The Old Covenant comprises the prophets and other writings which interpret the Law . . . .[97]

Martyr then went on to say that all of the Old Testament contains deeds about the law and promise of the gospel.[98] The purpose of *Genesis* is to replace the source and head of sin (which is joined with mortal and venal sins) by the grace of many promises.[99] In commenting on *Genesis* (1:5) Martyr said, "This is the strength of our faith, that all rests on the word of God.[100]

In *Genesis* (15) Martyr elaborated the thesis of firm assent to the divine promises.[101] Faith is the firm assent of the soul to the divine promises since one is drawn by the Holy Spirit to salvation.[102] Martyr first proposed that "the law does not justify,"[103] secondly that no one would be justified by works of the law or morality[104] and concluded that justification is by faith.[105] Martyr defined in what way one is justified, that faith remits sins and imputes the justice of God.[106] What follows in the commentary relates imputation to the work of Christ, a theme which has already been observed as central to Martyr's thought in which the justice of Christ is communicated to the believer.[107]

The entire tract at *Genesis* (15) is similar to statements in I *Corinthians* (1551). Since Martyr lectured on I *Corinthians* before he left Italy it is a moot question as to which published commentary expresses the primary insight. Since the theses of 1543 had already set down the same position on faith and justification, it is conceivable that here in the *Genesis* commentary of 1569 is a passage which comes not from the 1551 commentary on I *Corinthians*, but from an even earlier lecture on *Romans* or I *Corinthians* given while Martyr was still in Italy. We have already seen that such thoughts were known prior to 1541 in the works of Valdes. What strikes the reader of the *Genesis* comment is the absence of *sola fide* which does occur in the I *Corinthian* commentary. By the time one reaches the full expansion of this doctrine in the *Romans* commentary, specific opponents such as Richard Smith and Albert Pigge are mentioned. Perhaps Martyr sharpened the argument as he faced bitter opposition in Oxford. In any event the *Genesis* passage is briefer than the other two and different in tone. Are these comments then an expansion of the 1543 theses? They were not altered after 1547, for if the *Genesis* passage had been altered then the two sections on justification in the New Testament commentaries would be reflected in the *Genesis* commentary.

Faith for Martyr rested on the promises of God communicated by the justice of Christ. Faith was not conditional.[108] This brief treatise written after *Genesis* (15:6) touches on themes to be found in other works of Peter Martyr. It would be tempting to conclude that here is a passage which is free from the controversial atmosphere in Oxford, i.e. the *sola fide* formula. Since Martyr quoted from his *Genesis* commentary in I *Corinthians* given from 1548 at Oxford, this passage probably comes from Martyr's first stay at Strasbourg or even earlier sermons in Italy. In it are contained Martyr's mature reflections on the central theological issue of his day. Unfortunately the fresh insight of Martin Luther and others into the patristic doctrine of *sola fide* was to become a shibboleth for the papacy which at Trent dessicated the very selfsame catholic tradition within which Martyr wished to work in Italy prior to his exile. His flight from persecution then was as well a flight from pestilence, the pestilence of the papacy which infected the truth of the Gospel with the sick and feverish activities of a self-justifying hierarchy. This illness Martyr would describe in his Latin Commentary on *Kings*.

The biographical section of this study touched on Martyr's epistle,

De Fuga in Persecutione. That theme of flight in the letter translated by Taddeo Duno was also discussed in the *Genesis* commentary where one can read Martyr's text in the context of his comments on justification. The passage is located in the commentary after *Genesis* (31).[109] Martyr cited the text from *Matthew* (10:23), "If they shall persecute you in one citie, flie ye into another."[110] Tertullian had thought that the precept was temporary until the Gospel had been preached to the whole of Jewry while Martyr obtruded the references which Christ made to His disciples which Christ did not abrogate, such as *Matthew* (10:9, 16 and 28), *Luke* (10:16) and *Matthew* (10:41). In such obligations as to be "wise like serpents, and simple as doues"[111] Martyr saw the continuing command of God. When persecution came therefore, the *Matthew* (10:23) passage also was to be obeyed. Then followed a poignant section in which Martyr gave the reasons why flight was so painful to the fugitive.

> In flieng awaie, we have good experience of manie discommodities; namely, of banishment, of the lacke of necessaries. In flieng awaie, we have the losse of our deere friends and countrie soile. Which things a man doth sometime take so greeuouslie, as he judgeth them more happie, which were slaine in the persecution it selfe, they hauing obteined the triumph of martyrdom.[112]

In another way Martyr was anxious to overcome Tertullian's objections to forced flight. The purpose of such flight was to serve the glory of God. Not only did such flight serve God's honour, but Martyr quoted with approval the Greek verse, " ὅ φυγῶν καὶ πάλίν μαχησεται."[113] Martyr did not flee away to flee yet again, though this did happen when Edward VI died. He fled to serve God

"more commodiouslie."[114] One of the *Psalms* which Martyr quoted in the
above treatise he also used for a prayer during the second period in
Strasbourg when times were not so calm. It summarizes his view on
constancy in faith during times of duress.

> There is no righteousnesse or puritie in our workes which we maye
> vaunt and boast off in thy presence: we francklye acknowledge
> and confesse that we have greatly strayed from thy holy precepts.
> Neuerthelesse yet pardon (according to thy accustomed woont and
> mercie the grieuous sinnes committed by vs, and vouchsafe of thy
> gracious fauour, to graūt and that we may hereafter liue as be-
> commeth thy chosen, blessed, and innocent people, so y̆ (on the
> other side) we may finde thee elect, holy and hurtlesse vnto us,
> throughe Jesus Christ our Lorde. Amen.[115]

During Martyr's first sojourn in Strasbourg he also lectured on
Lamentations. These notes were the last of the biblical lectures to
be published. In the prefatory letter to the 1629 edition Johann
Rudolf Stuckius told John Prideaux of Oxford that he found the autograph lectures in the library of Johann Guilielmi Stuckius.[116]

Martyr was disturbed among other things by defections from Christ
in his time.[117] These defections originated among those very men
whose lives were to be examples of saintliness.[118] In Martyr's view
since false teachers had created chaos within the Church, men were
needed to restore fruitful doctrine in the church who first had faith
and then both mortified the flesh and benefited their brothers in
love.[119] One can see from a glance at these brief notes that Martyr
viewed Jeremiah's /?/ calamities in terms of his own recent experiences
in Italy. This is perhaps why Martyr would be so inflexible in theology while at Oxford and yet be willing to live peaceably with all
men. Thomas Cranmer in a dispute with Richard Smith endorsed Martyr's

pilgrimage from Italy to Northern Europe.

> But as for Dr. Peter Martyr, hath he sought to please men for
> advantage? who, having a great yearly revenue in his own country,
> forsook all for Christ's sake, and for the truth and Glory of
> God came into strange countries, where he had neither land nor
> friends, but as God of his goodness, who never forsaketh them
> that put their trust in him, provided for him?[120]

NOTES TO CHAPTER VI

1. R. W. Dixon, History of the Church of England From the Abolition of the Roman Jurisdiction, II, p. 521. "But even from the beginning of Edward's reign, the prospect of England had drawn an invasion of learned strangers."

2. The Remains of Edmund Grindal, D. D., pp. 244-245. 11 August 1561. On Cranmer's library see Edward Burbidge, Remains of the Library of Thomas Cranmer, Archbishop of Canterbury, 1489-1556 (separation with marginal notes by the author, 1892).

3. Most lear/ned and fruitful Com/mentaries of D. Peter Martir/ Vermilius Florentine . . . upon the Epistle of S. Paul to/the Romanes . . . .

4. Ibid., pp. 384[V]-386[V]. This tract is the promised expansion of the treatise at the end of chapter I in the I Corinthian Commentary with the title, De Ivstificatione (pp. 15[V]-20[V]). There at p. 20[V] Martyr said, "Sed nunc redeundum est ad Pauli uerba, unde digressi sumus, atq̄; hac de re fusius & apertius dicemus in epistolam ad Romanos." See Philip McNair, Peter Martyr in Italy, p. 228 for citation from Zanchi's letter of 15 October 1565 to Philip of Hesse. Martyr lectured on Romans at Lucca in 1541.

5. Apologia A. Pighii . . . adversus M. Buceri calumnias, quas & solidas argumentis, et clarissimis rationibus confutat (Maguntiae, 1543: Parisiis, 1543). Since Martyr's response is in the context of a treatise on sola fide, the more likely source which he does not identify other than a chief source for 'our adversaries' might well be the Controversiarum quibus nunc exagitatur Christi fides et religio diligens et luculenta explicatio (Venetiis, 1541). Martyr's estimate of Pigge is confirmed by several other references to him in Romans (1558).

6. Romanes (1568), p. 392[V].

7. Ibid., p. 406[r]. Much of Martyr's library abandoned in Italy in 1542 did not reach Switzerland. See McNair, op. cit., pp. 270-71 who conjectures that they formed part of the rich monastic library of

S. Frediano. See McLelland, op. cit., pp. 267-271.

8. Reginald Pole abandoned all equivocation in his September draft on Justification and favoured "a view of justification which was in all essentials Lutheran." D. B. Fenlon, Reginald Pole and the Evangelical Religion: some problems of Italian Christian Humanism in the early Counter Reformation, p. 271. Unpublished 1970 Ph. D. dissertation in Cambridge University Library. Fenlon compares the De Iustificatio annotatio of 1546 with Pole's response to the Cardinal of Augsburg in 1554 where Pole interprets justification in the Tridentine sense. This accords with my own study of the 1546 Annotatio. See Marvin W. Anderson, "Trent and Justification (1546): A Protestant Reflection," S. J. T. 21 (1968), 385-406. N. B. pp. 401-402.

9. Hubert Jedin, A History of the Council of Trent II, 43.

10. Marino Grimani, Commentarii in Epistolas Pauli, ad Romanos et ad Galatas (Venetiis: Aldus, MD. XLII). See my documented study in C. H. 38 (1969), 26-33.

11. Ibid., fol. 33^r.

12. Ibid., fol. 34^v.

13. Ibid., fol. 36^v. "Dixerat, quod credenti in eum, qui iustificat impium, sola illius fides esset reputata illi ad iustificationem sine operibus carnis."

14. Ibid., fol. 148^v.

15. Ibid., fol. 149^v.

16. Expositio Fratris Clementis Aranei Ragusini Ordinis Praedicatorum cum resolutionibus occurrentium dubiorum, etiam Lutheranorum errores confutantium secundum subietam materiam, super epistolam Pauli ad Romanos (Venice: apud Nicolaus de Bascarinis, 1547).

17. Ibid., fol. 35^r. Used by permission of the editors of Church History. The marginal note on the left hand of folio 33^r reads, "sed salvamur sola fide. Sola fide sufficit. sola fide, quem per charitate operatus."

18. See Peter Fraenkel, Testimonium patrum: The Function of the Patristic Argument in the Theology of Philip Melanchthon. This important work deserves careful reading as a pattern for study of other sixteenth-century reformers. Unfortunately it lacks an index. See now Anselm Forster, Girolamo Seripando: De Iustitia Et Libertate Christiana (Corpus Catholicorum 30) (Münster Westfalen: Aschendorff, 1969). Forster edits these items written from 1553 to 1555. See

especially the section <u>Controversia de iustificatione prima</u> on p. 15:
"Cum omnis quaestio obscura et difficilis controversias parere
consueverit, nihil omnino mirum est, si multae et variae in Christi
ecclesia fuerunt (1) de iustificatione controversiae ac dissensiones
futuraeque etiam sint, donec in ea cum tritico paleae erunt admistae,
cum bonis scilicent mali et cum parvulis mundi sapientes atque
prudentas."

19. This aspect will be documented from Martyr's <u>De Schismate</u>.

20. Robert E. McNally, S. J., "The Council of Trent and the
Spiritual Doctrine of the Counter Reformation," <u>C</u>. <u>H</u>. 34 (1965), 36-
49. See especially p. 43: "He did not fit neatly into the categories
which his. opponents had assigned him."

21. Marvin Anderson, "Biblical Humanism and Roman Catholic Reform
(1501-1542): Contarini, Pole and Giberti," <u>C</u>. <u>T</u>. <u>M</u>. XXXIX (1968),
686-707. Now see James Bruce Ross, "The Emergence of Gasparo Contarini: A Bibliographical Essay," <u>C</u>. <u>H</u>. 41 (1972), 22-45.

22. That this is appropriate here can be seen from Ochino's
response to Catharinus, attributing to him the invective of "domini-
chia modestia." Cited in Roland Bainton, <u>Bernardino Ochino</u>. <u>Esule</u>
<u>E Riformatore Senese Del Cinquecento 1487-1573</u>, p. 57 from <u>Riposta di</u>
<u>messer Bernardino Ochino alle false calunnie e empie bestemmie di</u>
<u>frate Ambrosio Caterino</u> (Venice?: 1546).

23. T. A. Collins, "The Cajetan Controversy," <u>A</u>. <u>E</u>. <u>R</u>. 128
(1953), p. 90ff. See the literature cited in my article, "Thomas
Cajetan's Scientia Christi," <u>T</u>. <u>Z</u>. 26 (1970), 99-108.

24. Now edited by Jos. Schwiezer & Aug. Franzen, in <u>Corpus</u>
<u>Catholicorum</u> 27 (Munster: Aschendorff, 1956), <u>Apologia pro veritate</u>
<u>catholicae et apostolicae fidei ac doctrinae Adversus impia ac valde</u>
<u>pestifera Martini Lutheri dogmata</u>. First printed in Florence, 1520
& on 27 April, 1521.

25. <u>Excusatio disputationis contra Martinu ad vniversas</u>
<u>Ecclesias</u> (Florentae: Philippi Iuntae, April, 1521).

26. Neither Jedin nor George Tavard, <u>Holy Writ or Holy Church:</u>
<u>The crisis of the Protestant Reformation</u> utilize the biblical writings
of Catharinus.

27. See F. Lauchert, "Die Polemik des Ambrosius Catharinus gegen
Bernardino Ochino," <u>Z</u>. <u>K</u>. <u>G</u>. XXXI (1907), 23-50. The tract was
<u>Speculum Haereticorum contra Bernardinum Ochinum</u> published in Rome,
1532 and republished by Antonius Vincentius in Lyon, 1541.

28. De perfecto iustificatione a fide et operibus: ad cardinalem Gasparum Contarenum Venetum, listed in Jacques Quetif and Jacques Echard, Scriptores Ordines Praedicatorum recensiti . . . et ad hanc nostram aetatem . . . II, 144 col. i to 151 col. i.

29. Commentaria R. P. F. Ambrosii Catharine Politi Senesis, Episcopi Minoriensis, in Omnes Divi Pauli et Alias Septem Canonicae Epistolas (Venice: in officina Erasmiana Vincentii Valgrisii, 1541).

30. See Louis B. Pascoe, S. J., "The Council of Trent and Biblical Study: Humanism and Scripture," C. H. R. LII (1966), 18-38.

31. Commentaria . . . in Omnes Divi Pauli . . ., 15, col. ii: "Haec enim fides est donum Dei, et sic procedit ex fide in fidem, idest, ex fide sua, idest, actu priori donum est formatum charitate."

32. Paul Kristeller, "The Contribution of Religious Orders to Renaissance Thought and Learning," A. B. R. XXI (1970), Appendix B, pp. 31-55. See also T. Leccisotti, "Per la storia della Congregazione cassinese. Marginalia," B. XVI (1969), 136-143.

33. There is no modern biography of Clarius. See Magnoald Ziegelbauer, Historia rei literariae Ordinis S. Benedicti III, 344-347. See below note 39.

34. Freidrich Lauchert, "Der italienische Benedictiner Isidorus Clarius und seine Schrift fur den religiosen Freiden," S. M. G. B. O. XXVIII (1908), pp. 613-614.

35. Contarini responded on 8 November 1538 that "one must always act mildly and friendly toward the Protestants, but never offer any points that can be used to attack us." Lauchert, op. cit., p. 614.

36. Lettere Volgari, p. 129 (24 April 1540 from Polirone). These letters are located in G. A. Gradenigo, Greg. Cortesii, monarchi cassinatis et S. R. E. Cardinalis, omnia, quae hucusque colligi potuerunt, opera scripta sive ad illum spectantia I. See pp. 132-133 for additional letters.

37. I used the Paris edition, Isidori Clarii Brixioni, monachi Casinensis, ad eas qui a communi ecclesiae sententia discessere, adhortatio ad concordiam (Paris: Nicolai Divitem, n.d.).

38. Lauchert, op. cit., p. 617.

39. Gregorian university, Rome. Shelfmark PlI 135 B. I have since located a copy in the Corpus Christi College, Cambridge. The only recent biographical account known to me is the MS. in Foligno, F. 159 (F. 55.5-159), 'materials from Cardinal Alessandro Barnabo.'

c. 205; appunti biografici su Isidore Clario, Vescovo di Foligno. Cartaceo, rilegato in cartone di Carte non numerate 206, del sec. XIX. Mis. cm. 28 X 20. (Biblioteca Comunale di Foligno).

40. *Ibid.*, "Haec Docent Sacra Bibliarum Scripta," n.p. Clarius expanded this theme in the *Orationes quatuor habitae in Concilio Tridentino, nempe. Prima de Justificatione hominis Secunda de Imputatione Justitiae et Certitudine Gratiae et due de Gloria* (Venice, 1548).

41. McNair, *op. cit.*, pp. 133-318.

42. See the remark at the close of Martyr's *An Evangelici sint Schismatici, quod se alienauerint a Papistis*, p. 113[r] at the end of Chapter XII of the Commentary on Kings.

43. "Hic sum Dei beneficio, ubi possum S. literas interpretari, vos per literas consolari, atque ad retinendam Euangelii puritatem corhortari." *Opuscula* (1582), col. 198. I read the third clause without supplying another "vos."

44. Printed in the Basle edition of Martyr's collected works: *D. Petri Martiris Vermilii Florentini Proposita Dispvtata Pvblice In Schola Argentinensi ab anno M.D. XLIII. vsq: ad Annum XLIX.* (Basle: Petrus Perna, M.D. LXXXII). Pagination continuous from Tome III of this Basle *Opera*. The text here corresponds to that in several other printed editions of the *Loci Communes*.

45. Printed in Basle, 1544. The Latin translation in all editions of the *Loci Communes* varies from the printed Italian text of 1544. Consequently, when one cites Marten's 1583 English translation or the earlier 1578 English translation (S.T.C. 24663) which follow the Latin translation, one must check the Italian text of 1544. Dr. McNair communicated in privateconversation that perhaps Taddeo Duno translated this work as he did the letter to the Church at Lucca of 25 December 1542 and the *De fuga in persecutione*. On Duno see Albert Chenu, "Taddeo Duno (1523-1613)," *B. S. S. V.* 119 (1966), 55-61.

46. Luigi Santini, "'Scisma' e 'eresia' nel pensiero di P. M. Vermigli," *B.S.S.V.* XC (Giugno 1969), 27-43.

47. *Proposita*, p. 431. "Ex I Cap. Genesios. Necessaria. I. Cvm diuina scriptura sit expressio diuinae sapientiae, inde nos principium habemus nostrae foelicitatis." The translation quoted in our text is in each case that of Antonie Marten from the 1583 *Common Places*. Here it is from p. 143.

48. ". . . verbo Dei non vacant, non predicant, non pascunt

gregem, imo scandalis omnia replent." <u>Melachim</u> (1566), fol. 103^v.
Tract is at end of Chapter XII with the title, <u>An</u> <u>Evangelici</u> <u>Sint</u>
<u>Schismatici</u>/, <u>quod</u> <u>se</u> <u>alienaverint</u> <u>A</u> <u>Papistis.</u>

49. <u>Common</u> <u>Places</u> (1583), Part four, p. 143. "Praestantia
sacrarum literaru & in hoc attenditer, quod resoluit ad summam
causam diuinae voluntatis, quae in eis reuelatur," <u>Proposita</u>, p.431.

50. <u>Common</u> <u>Places</u> (1583), Part four,p. 143.

51. <u>Common</u> <u>Places</u> (1583), Part four, p. 149. "Fides est firmus
animi assensus diuinis promissionibus de Christo ex persuasione
Spiritus sancti ad salutem," <u>Proposita</u>, p. 442.

52. <u>Common</u> <u>Places</u> (1583), Part four, p. 158. "Non est de populo
Dei statuendum ex affluentia externorum bonorum, sed tantum ex
promisionibus & verbo Dei," <u>Proposita</u>, p. 458.

53. William Hammer, letter of 28 February 1974 to the author,
pp. 1-3. A Venetian printing would not be surprising.

54. Alexandre Ganoczy, <u>op</u>. <u>cit</u>., p. 215, no. 162. W. Köhler,
<u>Bibliographia</u> <u>Brentiana</u>, pp. 49 and 56, numbers 116 and 132.

55. Ganoczy, <u>op</u>. <u>cit</u>., p. 159, numbers 1 and 2.

56. John Brenz, <u>IN</u> <u>EXODVM</u>/<u>MOSI</u> <u>COMMEN</u>-/<u>TARII.</u>/<u>AVTORE</u> <u>IOANNE</u>/
<u>Brentio</u> (Halle: Petrus Brubachius, M.D.LXIII), sig. Av^r.

57. <u>Ibid</u>., sig. Avi^rand C^r.

58. Richard Raubenheimer, <u>Paul</u> <u>Fagius</u> <u>aus</u> <u>Rheinzabern</u>, p. 26.

59. See the list of Isny publications in Raubenheimer, <u>op</u>. <u>cit</u>.,
p. 38.

60. <u>Common</u> <u>Places</u> (1583), Part five, p. 61.

61. <u>Common</u> <u>Places</u> (1583), Part four, p. 160. "Historiae sacrae
& prophanae quamuis habeant multos consimiles casus, attamen hoc
differunt, quod in sacris verbo Dei res geruntur, cuius in prophanis
non habetur expressa mentio, & nihilominus quae ibi narrantur,
agnoscimus esse ingentia opera Dei," <u>Proposita</u>, p. 463.

62. <u>Common</u> <u>Places</u> (1583), "A briefe waie how Ministers should
order their studious exercises for to benefit themselues and their
flocks, and also what good vse they may haue by trauelling in the
Commonplaces of the Scripture, and in such bookes as are alreadie
gathered to this purpose," preface to Part one.

63. For Martyr's use of this term see Gorham, op. cit., p.133.

64. Proposita, p. 471.

65. Common Places (1583), "A prayse of the word of God taught in the scriptures, and an exhortation to the study of them," p. 43.

66. Marten's translation will be cited in the text with the 1544 Italian text compared in the notes with Duno's (?) Latin translation from Massonis 1576 Loci Communes. Where the Latin departs from the Italian, a few varients will be given. I have been unable to identify Martyr's biblical text with any of the extant Italian versions of the Quattrocento or Cinquecento.

67. Leonard Chester Jones, Simon Goulart 1543-1628. Etude Biographique et Bibliographique, p. 330. "Scripsit olim doctiss (imus) ille theologus italo sermone breuem expositionem in symbolum apostolorum quae si latine extaret a multis auide legeratur, etsi stilo simpliciore sit conscripta." 12 December 1574 from Geneva. Francesco Stella (1549) in Italy had a copy.

68. Schutte, Vergerio, p. 196.

68a. K. Sturm, Die Theologie Peter Martyr Vermiglis, p. 37 n.121.

69. Common Places (1583), Part two, p. 587. The Italian text has been separately studied and compared to the Latin versions in the Loci.

70. 'fortitude' might have better conveyed Martyr's phrase to the reader. "Perlequali simostra no essere" is hardly "alijsque eiusmodi coelestibus ac diunis animi affectionibus."

71. Common Places (1583), Part two, p. 616.

72. "Potenza" occurs a century later in Diodati's 1640 Genevan edition of the Italian Bible in the metrical version of Psalm I.

73. Common Places (1583), Part two, p. 624.

74. A typical phrase is the following comment on Christ's command to His followers that they should take up the cross daily and by self-denial follow Him. "Ma, perche la vita di Christo, della cui imitazione si tribolazioni, ignominie e persecuzioni, se vogliamo conformarci con la vita sua, ci bisogna portare di continuo la croce . . . " Cited from the helpful article by Mario Rosa, "Vita religiosa e pieta eucharistica nella Napoli del Cinquecento," R. S. L. R. (1968), 37-51. Quotation taken from p. 42. See the

translation of the _Beneficio di Cristo_ and a discussion of its
authorship by Ruth Prelowski, _Italian Reformation Studies in Honor
of Laelius Socinus,_ pp. 23-102. See also the fundamental analysis
by S. Caponetto, "Benedetto da Mantoua," _Dizionario Biografico Degli
Italiani_ 8, 437-441.

75. Martyr by 1548 may have known about the copy translated in
English by Edward Courtenay now in the Cambridge University Library
with additions in King Edward VI's hand. Could he have brought a
copy with him to England?

76. _Common Places_ (1583), Part two, p. 625.

77. "unto the elect, faith hath access at the appointed time
when they believe in Christ, and so they are not only forgiuen their
sins and are reconciled to God, which is the true and sound justification, but also there is added a renewing power of the spirit . . .
whereby our bodies also . . . become daily more and more . . . fasion-
ed unto Christ."

78. Prelowski, _op. cit._, pp. 59-60. The entire fourth chapter
of the _Beneficio_ deserves a careful reading as one background to
Martyr's concept of union with Christ. It is titled "On the Effects
of Living Faith And The Union of the Soul with Christ," _Ibid._, pp.
57-72. See also Nieto, _op. cit._, pp. 273-278, though Nieto shows
on p. 275 where Valdes abandoned the term 'union' for 'incorporation.'
The crucial text is I _Corinthians_ (2:14).

79. "Nostis exemplum Pauli reprehendentis Petrum, et praeceptum
iubentis incestum Corinthium increpari ab omnibus." _C. R._ XXXIX,
col. 817.

80. _Common Places_ (1583), Part two, p. 629.

81. _Loc.cit._

82. Maddison, _op. cit._, p. 144.

83. _Common Places_ (1583), Part two, p. 632.

84. _Common Places_ (1583), Part two, p. 633.

85. _Common Places_ (1583), Part two, p. 631.

86. McLelland, _op. cit._, p. 263 explains his modern attempt to
trace these lecture notes. They are not extant.

87. _Oratio._

88. In 1574 Simler added the following reference to these unpublished lectures. "Praeterea Comentarij Martyris in Exodum, in Prophetas aliquot Minores, Epistolae item & Orationes, alique nonnulla manuscripta seruantur a Iulio Terentiano.": in Conrad Gesner, Biblioteca Institvta Et Collecto Primvm A Conrado Gesnero. (1574), p. 560[b]. Johann Rudolf Stuckius in his dedicatory epistle to John Prideaux of Oxford on 20 February 1629 mentioned that he found the autograph of the In Lamentationes Sanctissimi Ieremiae Prophetae (1629) in the library of Johann Guilielmi Stuckius. The latter was Martyr's secretary at the Colloquy of Poissy.

89. Klaus Sturm, Die Theologie Peter Martyr Vermiglis während seines ersten Aufenthalts in Strassburg 1542-1547.

90. Common Places (1583),Part five, p. 95. There is a letter from Hedio, Martyr and Bucer of 6 December 1546 to the ministers of Zurich. In this letter Martyr set forth a view of the sacrament which would help the participant. From the text one can see that a grave issue was at stake, namely the religious well-being of young people in Strasbourg. Martyr's role is worth noting here, coming as it does from his pastoral concern. "D. Marbachius perturbatus, et iure, de ista adolescentis ingratitudine et inhumanitate, coepit eum officii sui leniter et ut pium praeceptorem decet admonere, ac deinde in pace dimisit." C. R. XL, col. 441. 6 December 1546. Marbach became a canon of St. Thomas in 1546. On the disagreement between Zurich and Strasbourg in 1547 see Rudolf Gualther, Οἰκέτης (1548).

91. Arnold Williams, "Milton and the Renaissance Commentaries on Genesis," M. P. XXXVII (1939-40), 263-278.

92. J. W. Ashton, "Peter Martyr on the function and character of literature," P. Q. XVIII (1939), 311-314.

93. Williams, op. cit., p. 275 and note 39 where Pareus quotes Martyr from the Commentary on I Corinthians (8) that meat was not eaten before the Deluge.

94. Ibid., p. 278.

94a. Arnold Williams, The Common Expositor: An Account of the Commentaries On Genesis 1527-1633, pp. 226-227.

95. Corinthios (1551), p. 153[v]. "De ea in meis Commentariis in Genesin fusius dixi. Descendit spiritus sanctus ad haec tradeda, quae sensus humanus iudicat subobscoena, cum tamen honestissima sint . . ."

96. O. L. I, 97.

97. Genesis (1569), fol. 1^{r-v}.

98. Ibid., fol. iv. "Si in vniuerso veteri instrumento agitur de lege & promissione Euāgelij . . ."

99. Loc. cit.

100. Ibid., fol. 3^{v}. "Hoc est rober nostrae fidae, omnia Dei verbo consistere."

101. See above, note 51. Ibid., fols. 59^{r}-61^{v}.

102. Ibid., fol. 59^{v}. "Fides est assensus firmus animi diuinis promissionibus, afflatu Spiritus Sancti ad salutem." For similar views see the exegetical writings of Seripando which were written in Naples before 1537. Martyr may well have perused them.

103. Loc. cit.

104. Ibid., fol. 60^{r}, "Ex operibus legis siue moralibus non habetur iustificatio."

105. Loc.cit.

106. Ibid., fol. 60^{v}.

107. Loc. cit.

108. Ibid., fol. 61^{v}.

109. Genesis (1569), fols. 128^{v}-130^{v}.

110. Common Places (1583), Part three, p. 287. "Si vos persequuti fuerint in vna ciuitate, fugite in aliam." Genesis (1569), fol. 128^{v}.

111. Common Places (1583), Part three, p. 287. Genesis (1569), fol. 128^{v}. Martyr is responding to Tertullian's De Fuga In Persecutione whose editio princeps was published by John Froben at Basle in 1521. On Matthew (19:23) Tertullian commented: "Hoc in personas proprie apostolorum et in tempora et in causas eorum pertinere defendimus, sicut subsequentes probabunt, qui non nisi in apostolos competunt: In viam nationum ne ieritis et in civitatem Samaritanorum ne introieritis, sed ite potius ad oves perditas domus Israëlis ." Consequently the Apostles were not to flee the nation of Israel. See the entire section in the Corpus Scriptorum Latinorum Paravianum, pp. 69-72. Section VI.

112. Common Places (1583), Part three, p. 289. Genesis (1569),

fol. 129^v. "Multa fugiendo experitur incommoda, exilium, rerum penuriam, cognatis, amicis & patriae solo destituitur fugiens, quae adeo interdum grauiter fert, vt foeliciores illos iudicet qui in ipsa persequutione occubuerint assequuti triumphum martyrij."

113. Ibid., p. 291. Genesis (1569), fol. 130^v.

114. Ibid., pp. 291 and 290. Genesis (1569), fol. 130^{r-v}.

115. Prayers (1569), sig. E2^{r-v}. (Final prayer on Psalm XVIII.)

116. Lament.

117. Ibid., p. 16. "A Domino defecerunt, qui eos consueverat pascere, vel in deserto. Et ideo nunc in urbibus ab eo sejuncti non possunt ali."

118. Ibid., pp. 119-120.

119. Ibid., p. 66.

120. Writings and Disputations of Thomas Cranmer, Archbishop of Canterbury, Martyr, 1556, Relative to the Sacrament of the Lord's Supper, pp. 374-375.

CHAPTER VII

OXFORD LECTURES (1547/53)

SERMONS

Peter Martyr's lectures on I *Corinthians* and *Romans* have been
somewhat neglected by scholars of the English Reformation, while the
1549 Oxford debate on the Eucharist has been analyzed.[1] What follows
will first examine Martyr's extant sermons from 1547 to 1553, secondly I *Corinthians* (1551)[2] and then give attention to the *Romans* commentary. This later work was near completion before Martyr left England though it was not published until 1558 at Basle. The date of
the *editio princeps* or its 1568 translation has led some historians
to assign this work to Elizabethan rather than Edwardian Tudor England.

The sermon on *Malachi* (2:4) sets forth Martyr's method while in
England. Though wrongly assigned to 1543 in the *Dictionary of National
Biography* it clearly belongs to the Oxford period.[3] These sermons
were well received. One other sermon which has been published by
Strype is on fasting in Lent. A third sermon is the unpublished *Sermon
on Thanksgiving*.

John Abell submitted the record of expenses for the journey of
Martyr and Ochino to England. The money was laid out for expenses
incurred from 4 November at Basle until 20 December at London.[4] One
item reads "p^d for the works of S. Augustine, Cyprian and Epithanius
for Petrus Marter at Basell."[5] Nicolas concludes that since Abell
looked for his payment to the Privy Council, "we may conclude that not
only was the visit of these eminent divines approved by the Government

but that the charges of their journey were defrayed by the Crown."[6]

Augustine and Cyprian are quoted in Martyr's New Testament commentaries. The works of 'Epithanius' were available in Basle during 1547. Abell meant of course Epiphanius, Bishop of Constantia in Cyprus whose works were published in Basle as early as 1529 and republished in 1543 and 1545 with a translation by Janus Cornarius.[7]

Cornarius was born in Zwickau in 1500 and had studied at Wittenberg in the 1520's. This physician (sometimes known as Hagenbut) like Conrad Gesner edited important patristic writings during the sixteenth century. Cornarius was a brilliant physician and Dean of the medical faculty at Jena where he died on 16 March 1558.[8] Among other works he edited in four parts the 1540 Basle folio of Basil's works.[9]

Abell's bill of expenses refers to the very popular *Contra Octoaginta haereses opus*, translated by Cornarius and published in Latin at Basle in 1543 and in Greek in 1544.[10] Martyr also had Cranmer's library at his disposal while living at the Lambeth episcopal residence. One can see why the busy Cranmer depended on Martyr for the two sermons of 1549 which Cranmer preached against the Devonshire and Cornwall rebels.

When one turns to three of Martyr's sermons given while in England some familiar themes reappear. The unpublished *Sermon on Thanksgiving*, for example, touches on the subject of how Christ and the christian are joined in the sacrament. The seventh saying makes this dependent on faith.

In the use of the Sacrament, there is great difference, between
the faithful and the wicked, for they that do believe when they
do commune, they uerely receiue the body and blood of Christ,
but they that be without faith and very ungodly, they receive
nothing else than but the tokens of bread and wine. This is the
reason of this saying because that this joining between Christ
and us is . . . by faith . . . ."[11]

The conclusions in Martyr's tract cover the ground taken up in debate

by Cranmer at Parliament House. Gasquet and Bishop go one step fur-

ther in assessing its significance.

It would appear more than probable that this manuscript was
actually designed for Somerset's help and guidance in the manage-
ment of the business.[12]

The Ash Wednesday Sermon gives a glimpse of Martyr's pastoral

concern for ecclesiastical discipline and popular reception. Strype's

account is also interesting from a bibliographical standpoint. Though

Martyr gave private sermons in Italian, Strype quotes from Humphrey's

Life of Jewel in a Latin version.[13]

Yet, notwithstanding these oppositions and discouragements of
Peter Martyr, the King's learned professor here at Oxford, he
steadily went on in the business committed to his trust; and
besides his public lectures, he sometimes preached at St. Mary's,
and had his private lectures, and his private sermons, in
Italian, at his house; whereunto resorted many auditors, and
Harding one of the chief; however he revolted in Queen Mary's
days. One Ash Wednesday he preached a public and seasonable
sermon concerning *fasting*; wherein he first defined a fast,
then divided it into parts, and distinguished all the kinds of
fasting, shewed the necessity of it, unfolded the causes, taught
the effects and benefits of it, and then excited the auditors
most earnestly 'to the keeping a true Christian fast; and accused
and blamed, in many respects, the *pharisaical* and *papistical*
fasting, whereby God was but superstitiously worshipped, a
snare cast upon the consciences of the weak, and death, damnation, and the torments of hell, denounced, if any did not observe
their frigid and pitiful constitutions, and if without their
leave and licence any ate flesh and milkmeats, God's clean
creatures, however moderately they did it, and soberly, with
thanksgiving, and sanctification of God's word, according to

the apostle's rule. Then he prayed and beseeched them to stand
fast in the liberty to which Christ had called them, and that
none should judge others in meats and drinks; that, being redeemed from the weak and beggerly elements of the world, they
became not the servants of men. And then, in a sad voice, he
cried out, Parcite sanguini Christi, parcite animabus vestris;
i. e. O. 'spare the blood of Christ, spare your own souls.'
And so came off with great applause and admiration of many,
and among the rest, of Dr. Henry Cole, of New College, that was
almost in an ecstasy at the hearing; yet one of the starters
aside afterwards.[14]

Cole preached the sermon on 21 March 1555/56 in St. Mary's Oxford

which first intimated that Cranmer would be executed.

The sermon on *Malachai* (2:4) describes Martyr's concern for

biblical preaching.[15] Martyr deplored the absence of public preaching

in Oxford in a passage which matches the sermon just quoted from

Strype.

Heere euen to this day after the feast of Easter are used no
sermons publikely. Heere are all things so clearly ridde of
the iuyce of the pure and syncere doctrine, that euen the fountains themselves growe drie and uncleane. Howe in a manner all
things are here infected with superstitious and peruerse opinions,
howsoeuer wee dissemble it, the thing itself cannot be hidden.
How manie Colleges (I beseech you) are in this Citie (let those
which bee distributers of the Almes declare) which either cannot
or will not yeelde so much as one professor or preacher of the
Gospell.[16]

The Exhortation for Young Men to studie the holie scriptures may

also have been given while Martyr was in Oxford. The sermon on *Haggai*

(1) and perhaps the sermon on *John* (20) might have been transcribed by

John Jewel.[17] It is interesting to compare at this point Jewel's sermon

on *Haggai* (1) with that of Martyr. Jewel selected verses 2--4 for his

sermon while Martyr chose verse 4. Both sermons build on the theme in

verse 4 where Haggai lamented that the people of God languished in sealed houses while the House of God lay waste. The sermons are not identical, though the development of the text is similar. Martyr's four points are: 1) The neglect of the temple on return from Babylon is blameworthy; 2) God laid punishments on the people for such a heinous sin; 3) the Holy Ghost showed by His Prophet what needed to be done; 4) How profitable was the sermon of 'our' prophet.[18] Jewel's three points are: 1) "our Church hath beene overgrowen with errours and abuses;" 2) "I will shew what things they be, that doe stay men from reedifying of this Temple;" 3) "After what sort this Church ought to be builded."[19] It may be that Jewel recalled Martyr's sermon while preparing his own.

Humphrey recorded that Martyr preached a sermon in St. Mary's, Oxford before the Bishop of Lincoln, Cox and other royal visitors (inquisitores) which Jewel transcribed. The text was *John* (16) where one reads, "In truth I tell you whatever you may ask in my Father's name I will give you it."[20] The first petition took up the twofold nature of true reform in England to have good laws implemented by the magistracy and to reform schools and Academies. The latter are the roots of the church. Such discipline is essential as *Haggai* noted long ago.[21] From the direct quotations one can assume that Humphrey had access to Jewel's transcripts of Martyr's sermons.[22] Jewel transcribed sermons while Martyr was at Oxford and seems also to have assisted Martyr with the *Romans* commentary. Martyr's role in the Edwardian Reformation is appreciated by Cox, Somerset and Cranmer.

The date of Martyr's *Exhortation for Young Men* is not given in

Marten. In any event apart from its date this homily guides one

seeking to understand the purpose behind Martyr's hermeneutical

practice. Scripture is a good treasure which opens for its readers

all things necessary for their salvation.[23] Such study is for Martyr

a lifetime occupation, for "the Holy Ghost hath there reserved many

things as yet secrete to himselfe, that he may have us to be scholers

euen till the ende of the worlde."[24] The Fathers are to be judged by

the touchstone of the scriptures[25] whose continual reading shall make

plain all those things necessary to salvation.

> Let us accustome our selves to the word of God, let us continuallie
> be occupied in the holie scriptures, let us be earnest in the
> reading of them: and by the benefite of Christes spirit, those
> things which be necessarie to saluatiō shal be plaine, direct and
> most manifest unto us.[26]

The Latin text uses *sermo* rather than *verbum*, a choice of terms with

significance when taken as part of Martyr's attempts at ecclesiastical

reform through the study of scripture.[27] One thinks of the Erasmian

translation of *sermo* at *John* (1:1).[28] Martyr used the Erasmian biblical

text for I *Corinthians* (1551) and *Romans* (1558). How Martyr put this

exhortation into practice appears in his commentaries on I *Corinthians*

and *Romans*.

I *CORINTHIANS* (1548/49)

In an unpublished letter to Richard Cox Martyr described his

lectures on I *Corinthians*.

> And when I had arrived at Chapter 7, where the Apostle writes a
> good deal concerning virginity and marriage, according as my
> opinions were regarding vows, I disputed at length.[29]

Immediately upon reaching the opening verse of I *Corinthians* (7)

that "it is good for a man not to join to a wife," Martyr accused the
Pope of tyranny for the Roman Bishop who made perpetual virginity the
teaching of I *Corinthians* (7:1) departed from St. Paul's text. Martyr
took these words in the sense of the Gospel injunction that eternal
life would be achieved by one who abandoned father, mother, wife, sons,
etc. to follow Christ thereby claiming that perpetual virginity could
not be supported by the Fathers since Jerome *Contra Iouianum*, Book I
said that Paul did not endorse premarital fornication nor prohibit
marriage.[30] In fact, St. Paul's proposition was indefinite, for elsewhere he praised matrimony.[31] Martyr argued that St. Paul meant three
things by *bonum*, i.e., "Vtile, honestum & iucundum."[32] By *Vtile* was
was meant the removal of "impediments" to the life of service to God.
Though Martyr could readily concede this, nevertheless he asserted
that St. Paul endorsed ministerial marriage. It was sophistry to
argue that the labor of marriage impeded prayer and was therefore a
burden.[33]

V. Norskov Olsen claims that Martyr follows a Lutheran pattern on
the divorce texts rather than Bucer's *De Regno Christi*. Olsen includes
the section on divorce from I *Corinthians* (7:10-11), but not on marriage and omits any reference to the *Defense of Sacerdotal Marriage
and Monastic Vows* which Martyr wrote against Richard Smith and published in 1559 at Basle. Olsen restricts himself to the divorce
question, though one could also consult with profit this *Defensio*
against Smith to see Martyr's existential response to a challenge of
his own marriage while at Oxford. Martyr also wrote a lengthy note

on the history of punishment for adultery.[34] The common place on
"Marraige, and Sole life; especiallie of Ministers" comes from the
1551 Commentary.[34a] Therefore one must turn to the commentary itself
and next proceed to the debate with Richard Smith *On Monastic Vows* to
see the reaction which Martyr's 1548 lectures created. Lack of space
precludes a study of that reaction here.

Chapter seven of the 1551 commentary was included in the 1568
The Fortresse of Fathers, which also translated Martyr on *Judges* (8),
I *Kings* (18), II *Kings* (12 and 2) and *Romans* (13). A brief selection
from this translation will introduce the commentary and its controversial character.

> There ar other bondages of Men whiche ought also to be eschewed;
> that for the getting and purchassing of Ritches, we shold not
> be Parasites, flalterers, or men pleasers, or we should not be
> to muche affraied, and for these causes should be turned to Idol
> seruice, and euell Kindes of worshipping. 'They ar greued vvith
> this kind of bondage, vvhich obey the naughty vvill of there
> vngody /sic/ Masters, or Lordes and set more by them then by God.'
> It appereth by these thinges, that the Corinthians cam to this
> opinion, that, such as cam to Christ shold chaung and ouertourn
> all thinges. And with this kind of folishnes ar the Religious men
> nowe a dayes sicke, which will have there garmentes, there manners,
> and the owtward codition of there liffe newe, in so much, as they
> must chaunge there old names also, where with they were named
> before. But Paul denieth that we shold do so, & he doth determine
> that those ar to be holden that ar not contrary vnto the word of
> God.[35]

Richard Smith also took exception to Martyr's view of thé Eucharist
in chapter eleven of the lectures. These published lectures of 1551
were given prior to the 1549 Oxford dispute on the Eucharist from which
came the 1549 *Tractatio* translated by Nicolas Udall.[36] The *Tractatio*
explains I *Corinthians* (11), but for our purposes the commentary of

1551 will be used to observe the range of exegesis which Martyr employed on this Epistle. Martyr did allude to a pure faith in his conclusions to the 1549 *Tractatio*. Udall's translation reads as follows:

> . . . We have dishonoured this sacraments two manier of wayes: partely in that of this so excellent and so singuler a gifte of Christe, we have erected and sette up an execrable Idoll: and partly for that we have usurped these holye mysteries with an unclene feith, with a conscience polluted with moste greuous synnes, without any due profe or exaimaction of our selues. Wherfore I beseche almighty god, that he wil take pitie upon this great calamitie, & that he vouce safe once to restore unto his Churche the Sacraments of *Eucharistia* truely receiued and restored.[37]

The 1551 commentary gained wide acceptance,[38] especially with Theodore Beza who praised the volume in a letter to Bullinger.[39] Beza referred both to the *Tractatio* and the commentary when he affirmed his accord with Martyr and Calvin on the meaning of substance in the Eucharist.[40] On 11 November 1550 Martyr told Bucer that Bergman of Cologne wanted to publish the commentary and that R. Wolf, King's printer of Greek, Latin, and Hebrew, could not then print it. It seems from other data that many eagerly awaited the printed version of these Oxford lectures.

The opening pages of Martyr's commentary defend scriptural authority. Martyr cited the call to Augustine, 'Tolle lege, tolle lege'.[41] The words of God were extraordinary. "In addition it is not possible to confirm the dogmas of the Christian faith apart from the reasoned authority of scripture."[42] Chrysostom was Martyr's introduction to that process.[43] In most instances Martyr cited Chrysostom as a commentator.[44] Martyr followed Chrysostom so that he might restore the authority of the word of God in a church whose authority had been eroded by

Papal audacity to claim such authority for itself.[45] No clearer statement of the doctrinal issue underlying the quest for reform can be
found among magisterial reformers than Martyr's defence of scriptural
authority following the example of Chrysostom and other patristic
writers.[46]

Martyr found patristic witness to *sola fide* in Ambrose and supported his interpretation of *Romans* (1:4) by just such evidence.[47]
Martyr read Paul's Greek text, accepted Chrysostom as a guide and
appealed to patristic evidence for *sola fide*. This makes his commentary invaluable as a source book for ascertaining the kind of biblical
study done in the 1550's. The decrees of Trent sought to halt this
form of renewal. One feels that because Martyr fled to the protestant
camp while some of his friends in Italy (chief catholic reformers) did
not is of utmost significance. It means that the problem of authority
divided the church every bit as much as *sola fide*. The experience of
Cardinal Seripando at Trent and Cardinal Pole's repudiation of *sola
fide* are clear examples of this phenomenon.[48]

Certain verses repeatedly occur in Martyr's commentaries. One
verse used for the understanding of I *Corinthians* (1:9) was *Hebrews*
(11:1). Martyr changed the "substantia" of the Vulgate to "funda-
mentum sperandarum rerum."[49] Martyr also used the annotations of
Erasmus, which appear to have been widely read by catholic and protestant biblical scholars from Colet to Martyr. Such use as both Seripando and Martyr made of these notes suggest that great importance must
be assigned to Erasmus as a biblical theologian in the decades after

his death. His comment on I *Corinthians* (1:25) is a prime example

of the fact that Martyr read Erasmus with discrimination.[50]

> Because the 'foolishness of God is wiser than men; and the
> weakness of God is stronger than men'. The meaning of this verse
> is: When to our reason, while listening to the story of Christ's
> cross, God seems to be foolish or unwise, in fact he is sur-
> passing all human wisdom. And again when men judge him to be
> either weak or feeble, in reality he is most powerful. Erasmus
> sees another meaning here; namely that 'the foolishness and weak-
> ness of God' should be understood not with a view to our judge-
> ment, but as referring to those heights of the divine perfection
> by comparison with which what we see, and what is shown to us in
> Christ, can be taken for folly and weakness. But the former
> meaning which we have suggested is clearer and easier. In this
> verse the Apostle sharply censures his friends at Corinth, by
> showing that God had thought human wisdom and power of so little
> value that in his dealings with us he had displayed just their
> opposite, while they were pursuing these with such a perverse
> devotion that for their sake they were dividing the Church.[51]

An important analysis of 'iustitia' may be found at I *Corinthians*

(1:31), filling pages 28-38. It is important for its careful linguis-

tic analysis of the primary authority of the biblical text, its de-

pendence on Chrysostom as a guide and the link it finds between *sola*

fide and the remission of sins. The occasion for the discussion was

Paul's admonition, "He that glories, let him glory in the Lord." Many

teach works of merit from this verse, claimed Martyr, who defined

justification to show that none could glory in God unless it be given

them by God. God alone enabled man to talk God-talk. All else was

philosophy based on reason, not theology based on faith.[52] To be

justified was הצדיק derived from צדק which was 'iustitia'.[53]

Martyr then called attention to the Old Testament usage in which the

verb pertained to civil justice opposed to the Hebrew הרשיע, which

was 'criminal and to declare depraved'. These verbs were in the conjugation which the Hebrews called hiphil.[54] There is a 'duplex

iustitia'. 'Iustitia Dei', however, is different.[55]

This phrase contains three meanings which possess an inner coher-
ence for Martyr. Its primary significance is the remission of sins
in which one might be just by the obedience of Christ who imputed his
living justice through that trust. Secondly, such a phrase meant that
grace and the spirit of Christ were accessible as gifts. Christian
action presupposed an imputation of the spirit of Christ. Finally
Martyr rejected 'Iustitia Dei' as an acquired justice since the ety-
mology of faith meant 'constant' and 'firm' in both Hebrew and Greek.[56]
The Hebrew phrase meant'firmum esse' while the Greek term for faith
meant to give constant assent to the word of God, "breathed by the
Holy Spirit for the purpose of saving belief."[57] Martyr found that
such imputation rested on the work of Christ.[58]

Martyr referred to Chrysostom ten times alone in the second chapter. Martyr followed Chrysostom in the 'crux criticorum' of I *Corinthians* (13) where he defined the nature of faith by further reference
to the patristic origins of *sola fide*. Martyr suggested that the universal understanding of this chapter was based on the 'charismata'
of the Holy Spirit whose superior action accomplished regeneration by
such charismatic gifts. One could not be justified apart from charity.
Martyr tested traditional exegesis by a reading of Chrysostom on this
point.[59] Chrysostom thought that all mysteries coufer love.[60] The
faith that moves mountains had two meanings for Martyr. Faith which
does not accompany charity does not justify. Martyr explained faith

as the gift of the Holy Spirit by which miracles were performed. It
is that which men had as a most firm confidence in the invocation of
God and the name of Jesus Christ. However, the 'genus fidei' did not
justify unless it embraced the whole Christ.[61] The word of God must
be understood in its totality, for what Chrysostom wrote on the twelfth
verse was not dogma but a sign. Martyr rejected Pigge on double justification because he understood this phrase in St. Paul to separate
faith from charity.[62] Chrysostom meant as did Paul that all faith was
required before charity could be possible. Now abide faith, hope and
charity. Paul's statement about a faith that works miracles is real.[63]
Martyr ended by citing Basil and Erasmus with Chrysostom.[64]

Martyr followed Erasmus in defining the relation of faith to
charity.[65] His questions were classic whatever his answers. First
of all, one must distinguish between opinion and belief, between
$\delta o \xi \acute{a} \zeta \epsilon \iota \nu$ and $\pi \iota \sigma \tau \epsilon \acute{u} \epsilon \iota \nu$. To believe was to offer firm assent
to the Divine Word inspired by the Holy Spirit through the authority
of God Himself.[66] Martyr then appealed to Hebrews (11:1) for the
clearest definition of faith. $\dot{v} \pi \acute{o} \sigma \tau \alpha \sigma \iota s$ was the basis or
existence of the things hoped, meaning that the content of evangelical
faith for Martyr was the remission of sins as the central hope of the
Christian man.[67] $\acute{\epsilon} \lambda \epsilon \gamma \chi o s$ meant 'firmus assensus', the only work by
which one was said to believe.[68]

Martyr also rejected the scholastic doctrine of 'fides formata
charitate' and 'fides informis'. Justification through faith was for
him a living faith[69] since Paul's advice to Timothy was not the

deadening logic of the scholastic technologian. A pure heart and a

good conscience required a faith 'non facta'. Martyr consulted

Augustine, Chrysostom, Jerome, Ambrose and Gregory's *Homily* CXII where

he said, "Quantum credimus, tantum diligimus."[70] Martyr summarized

scholastic arguments and rejected them in favour of Chrysostom, who

provided Martyr's exegetical motif that faith rules Christian living

which then acts in love.[71] Martyr concluded that charity was always

imperfect,for "love is never born any other way than of faith."[72]

The eschatological nature of I *Corinthians* (13:13) formed Martyr's

definition of hope "which was not different from fiducia."[73] Patristic

evidence, grammatical exegesis, a rejection of scholastic terminology

and the centrality of faith are the marks of this commentary which

formulated Martyr's exegesis. In this he was not alone.

The 1572 third edition claims on its title page to be an emended

edition. Some random selections using this edition demonstrate

Martyr's unchanged concern for the primacy of faith.[74] At chapter

eleven on the words, "not discerning the Lord's body," Martyr observ-

ed that faith would be necessary for a prudent judgment of the sacra-

ment.[75] Martyr's comments on the sacrament as communion with Christ

lie behind his letter to Calvin of 8 March 1555.

> Now the flesh and blood of Christ are immortal, possess eternal
> life and have nothing there which is corrupt or defective through
> sin. We do not in a proper sense communicate with Him unless
> faith is interposed, which is made effective in us through word
> and sacrament by the Holy Spirit.[76]

It is clear that Martyr at least since 1549 had urged that without

faith participants made the sacrament null and void. In I *Corinthians*

(12) there is a verse where one might expect Martyr to expand on his view of union with Christ.[77] On this unity which has been created by baptism through one Spirit Martyr confessed that there were two modes of union among members of the body. One mode was to retain what was essential among each other; the other was to hold to that which each had in Christ.[78] Martyr then concluded that union with Christ was first between His flesh and ours and then with His Spirit through Grace. Martyr quoted Cyril's *De Fide Orthodoxa* with approval that human flesh was 'consubstantial' with the flesh of Christ.[79]

Such union was nonexistant for Martyr apart from faith. A crucial sacramental passage follows the citation from Cyril. Martyr's Latin text reads as follows:

In Eucharistia etiam spiritū esse, quo uegetamur, Christus attestatus est, cum ait: Caro non prodest quicquam, spiritus est qui uiuificat. Id circo debent esse attenti, qui ad haec sacramenta se conferunt, ut concordiā & unitatem cū fratribus in primis colant. Docemur etiā hinc, in Eucharistia spiritualē esse manducationiē: ita ut qui sine fide ac spiritu accesserint, symbola tantū percipiant. Nam si spiritu careāt, quomodo Christo iungi possunt? Praedicatur hic adunatio ista in corpus Christi p̄ spiritum. Superest igitur, ab impiis & infidelibus tantū modo symbola percipi. Quemadmodum sacrae literae, licet aeternam uitam in se dicantur habere, non tamen omnes qui illas legunt & audiunt, aeternam uitam consequuntur. Et tamen sicut de Eucharistia dicitur, Hoc est corpus meū: ita Paulus de Euangelio dicit, quod esset uis Dei ad salutem. Et cum sit a Paulo mentio spiritus, ostenditur sacramenta opus hominū non esse, sed uere spiritus Christi.[80]

Julins Palmer was quite impressed by this commentary. When he sent one of his scholars to inquire about Bishop Hooper's death in 1555, the report shocked him. Later when Palmer saw Latimer, Ridley and Cranmer burned at the stake in Oxford, he burst out with this protest, "O raging cruelty! O tyranny tragical, and more than bar-

barous." John Foxe has written about Palmer's response to these

events.

> From that day forward he studiously sought to understand the
> truth, and therefore with all speed he borrowed Peter Martyr's
> commentaries upon the first to the Corinthians, of one of Magdalen,
> yet alive, and other good books of other men. And so, through
> hearty prayer and diligent search and conference of the Scriptures,
> at length he believed and embraced the truth with great joy . .
> . .[81]

ROMANS (1550/51)

During 1550 Peter Martyr lectured on *Romans* at Oxford from 9 to

10 A. M. each day.[82] Martyr himself in 1552 revised these lectures

for publication. What further delayed their appearance in print might

have been his work on the *Ecclesiastical Laws*, for his letter to

Bullinger mentions the commentaries on *Genesis* and *Exodus* in the con-

text of Martyr's appointment to the royal commission of thirty-two

members.

> But as to my other commentaries on Genesis and Exodus, I promise
> you, that as soon as I shall have had leisure to revise them, I
> will forward them to you to be printed; but I am now pressed by
> so much business as to be almost overwhelmed. I am also anxious
> to complete my commentaries on the epistle to the Romans, that
> they may be printed by you.[83]

A previous study of Martyr's commentary on *Romans* confines itself

to the important question of predestination.[84] The commentary as a

whole gives one a clear statement of Martyr's theology while in Eng-

land. The care taken in preparing these lectures can be seen by the

choice of πάντοτε in commenting on *Romans* (1): "In the gos-

pell of his sonne." It indicates that Martyr had examined several manuscripts.

> But Paule sayth now, that he alwayes maketh mencion of these men
> in his prayers: and in some bookes is added this aduerbe
> ΠάνΤοΤε , which signifyth euery where: althoughe some
> exemplars have put it out.[85]

Martyr's prefatory letter to Sir Anthony Cooke is dated August

1558. Martyr lamented that so great a hope of the gospel and of pure

doctrine in England "hath now in a maner utterly pearished."[86] A

reference to the Marian martyrs is followed by a prayer that the

church in England might yet be renewed by its holy confessors as has

the church in all ages. Martyr found aid and remedy for the church

in thoughts such as those and in the holy scriptures, "which we ought

alwais to have in our hands as a present remedy."[87] Peter Martyr

then described the purpose of his lectures. From what has already

been said, Martyr viewed his lectures as a means of reforming the

English church.

> Here have we a storehouse of GOD full stuffed with the plenty
> of all good things, and set abrod wyde open for us, thereout
> may euery man prouide for his owne want. Here is layde for us
> a table most plentifullye furnished, where the wisedome of God
> hath mingled for us most pleasant wyne, wherewith euery man
> may most plentifullye refreshe him. Here is set forth for
> euery man a garden and paradise more pleasant than the garden of
> Alcinoes & Salomon.[88]

Martyr also wrote against catholic adversaries. Martyr could

attack in print the works of opponents even if he never could in per-

sonal debate impugn any man's character. Much of the commentary is

irenic, though the following passage written to Cooke demonstrates

Martyr's feelings about the Roman theology of Albert Pigge. After a

reference to Hosiah, Martyr castigated those who were contemptuous of "Gods Bokes."

> Doubtles those children are to much degenerated, which count
> that voyce where-with theyr most louing parent calleth upon them
> to liue godly and vertuously, for a strange voyce: and contrari-
> wise do folow as theyr owne and proper voyce that which is in
> very dede a strange voyce: and so it commeth to passe, that after
> the maner of betels they refuse swete fauors, and go to stinking
> donghils. Wherefore it is not to be meruailed at, if they were
> rottē in the filthy puddle of worldly pleasures, if they be
> burnt up wyth unwoorthy and filthy cares, If they dispayre in
> adversities, and if at the laste they perishe in sinnes, and in
> a lyfe altogether corrupted.[89]

Such sentiments are not unique to the sixteenth century. In England

one is reminded of John Colet's famous 1512 sermon on *Romans* (12:1-2)

in which the gloomy Dean of St. Paul's lashed out at the English

clergy in similar terms.

Martyr alluded to other Renaissance commentators on *Romans* such

as Melanchthon, Bucer, Bullinger and Calvin. Martyr explained to

Cooke that the ancient church did not lack commentators on *Romans*.

Afraid that Cooke or some one else would ask "what neded you at this

time to take such great paynes in the interpreting of this epistle,"

Martyr answered in two ways. First of all Martyr did not "take in

hand this charge to write an exposition upon this epistle, for I knew

right well that the fathers both Grekes and lattines have with great

labour and fruite exercised themselues herein." Then Martyr gave his

opinion of Melanchthon, Bucer, Bullinger and Calvin.

> Neither was I ignorāt that there are of the latter writers,
> which have done the same. First Phillip Melancthon, a notable
> man, who elegantly and with an exquisite methode hath more then
> once explained this epistle. Afterward Martin Bucer, a man not
> onely endued with singular pietie and incomparable learning, but
> also so long as he liued coupled with me in most deare frendship,
> set forth upon the self some epistle a large and learned

commentary. And I had red also two other most shining lightes
of the church, Bullinger, I say, and Caliune, both most faithfull
pastors, the one of the church of Tigure, the other of the church
of Geneua, ether of which men hath with great trauaile to the
great profite of the flocke of Christ set forth most excellent
and most learned commentaries upon all the epistles of the
apostle . . . .[90]

One will observe that Melanchthon's format attracted Martyr and that

he knew of his several writings on *Romans*. Martyr then went on to say

that scripture was too rich to be confined to a solitary commentator.

One feels especially in the comments on *Romans* (4) that Martyr read

Melanchthon as did Bucer. Martyr did not intend that his lectures be

published since they were intended for private friends. When they

urged him to turn the lectures into commentaries, Martyr profited from

his protestant friends mentioned above.[91]

T. H. L. Parker has recently discussed Melanchthon, Bullinger and

Bucer in his study of Calvin's New Testament commentaries. Martyr

would have noted what Calvin said in his prefatory letter to the 1540

Romans. There to Simon Grynee of Basle Calvin outlined a method of

lucid brevity. Martyr's models would include Calvin.[92] Both Calvin

and Martyr resided with Bucer in Strasbourg.

Melanchthon's method of doctrinal explanation in the 1543 *Romans*

seems to have influenced Martyr in terms of content though unlike

Melanchthon Martyr restricted the number of separate places where he

elaborated doctrine. Martyr did weave *loci* into the text such as on

Predestination and Election after chapter nine and *sola fide* after

chapter eleven. In both cases Martyr placed these elaborations where

St. Paul in the text of *Romans* commented on the subject.

After the debate with Eck at Leipzig in 1519, Melanchthon vindi-
cated Luther's use of *Matthew* (16:18) that "the sense of scripture is
simple."[93] In the preface to his 1540 *Latin Grammar* Melanchthon wrote,
"It is a small thing, the figures of letters, and syllables . . . but
this small thing gains access to the knowledge of God . . . ."[94] His
Argumentum to Romans (1532) defends a view of catholicity which rests
as he felt on a proper exegesis of the *Epistle to the Romans*. Melanchthon used the text of *John* (1:17) that "the law was given by Moses,
but grace and truth were made by Jesus Christ." This he expanded in
a way that Martyr seems to have noticed from the significant number of
references to law and gospel in his own *Romans* commentary. Melanchthon
wrote: "Christ gives grace to us, that is, remission of sins by grace
and works in us true recognition of God, true love, true trust /fidu-
ciam/ and true prayer."[95]

Melanchthon shed all thought of human merit by his appeal to I
John (5). "Wherefore faith does not so signify historical knowledge
but rather indicates trust in the merciful promises because of Christ-
an assent to the divine promises."[96] One passage that Martyr read in
this 1532 commentary was Melanchthon's use of Chrysostom at *Romans*
(4). There Melanchthon said, "Chrysostom in his commentary on the
Epistle to the *Romans*, Chapter 4. 'By Faith', he says, 'not only do
we loue God, but also we belieue that he himself has loued . . .
and forgiven our sins . . . .'"[97] From the references to *promissio*
in Martyr's exegesis of *Romans* (4) one concludes that this Melanch-
thonian language somewhat foreign to Luther impressed Martyr. It may

even explain his fondness for the Augsburg Confession earlier at
Strasbourg.

At *Romans* (4:1) Martyr introduced the term promise which St. Paul
used in verse thirteen and in *Galatians* (3:29).

> And neither is it seen to be wrong to perceive what they affirm,
> that always the object of faith is the mercy and goodness of
> God, which in themselves are declared to be extraordinary, temporal
> and spiritual gifts.[98]

At *Romans* (4:13) Martyr cited Chrysostom on the meaning of promise as
he did at *Romans* (4:17) and again at the close of the chapter. It
seems that Martyr was as familiar with the patristic fathers as
Melanchthon and found his commentary very useful indeed.

Since Martyr did not cite his contemporaries in the *Romans* commentary, it would be difficult to go any further than this in tracing
the influence of Melanchthon, Bullinger, Bucer and Calvin. In spirit
Melanchthon more closely approximates Martyr's comments, though like
Calvin Martyr followed the Pauline text in exposition rather than
Melanchthon's doctrinal catagories. One might ask whether Bullinger
shaped the form of the lectures between 1556 and their printed form
of 1558, especially since Martyr knew Bullinger and moved to Zurich
in 1556. Martyr did not lecture on *Romans* in Zurich and seems to
have polished the lectures for the printer in 1552. On the other
hand, Bullinger's commentary on *Romans* was completed before Martyr
left Strasbourg for England in 1547 and lectured on *Romans* at Oxford
in 1550. Bullinger's *locus* on images after *Romans* (1:23) is matched
by a similar discussion in Martyr at *Romans* (1:23).[98a] This alone

illustrates that Martyr at times followed Bullinger's method in the 1558 *Romans*.

In the Preface Martyr quoted with approval from Chrysostom's commentary on *Romans* to the effect that continuous reading of scripture would make his own commentaries superfluous in the final analysis.[99] One way to examine this important commentary is by consecutive chapters so that something will be sensed of Martyr's own approach to the text of *Romans*. Citations will be to the 1568 translation. One example of the philological decisions which lie behind Martyr's exegetical solutions is his analysis of Λατρεία and δουλεία in *Romans* (1). These terms for worship are used in *Romans* (12:1-2) as acts of presentation for holy living. Martyr proceeded with care to distinguish Λατρεία from δουλεία. He adopted Augustine's distinction that Λατρεία was worship given to God, while δουλεία was worship given unto magistrates and princes.[100] Martyr then turned to Chrysostom's *Homily 33 on John* to understand that the creature worships while the creator is to be worshiped.[101] The Greek terms are crucial for Martyr who found them used interchangeably in Xenophon's *Cyropaedea*. Λατρεία was formed from Λα, meaning 'vehemency' and ΤΡειμ, 'which is to tremble.' Such worship was for God alone, not for images or idols.[102]

The bulk of Martyr's commentary mirrors the use of patristic argument during the midst of the sixteenth century. Especially in the treatise *On Justification* one notices Martyr's list of testimonia to the antiquity of *sola fide*.[103] Martyr pointed to Augustine and

Chrysostom more frequently than to any other extrabiblical sources.
Martyr early on began with a reference to the Pope.

> The Pope thundreth and lightneth with bulles, belles, gunnes,
> and weapons of warre: but Paule hath by the word of God, by
> admonitions, rebukings, wholesome doctrine, & by miracles thundred
> and lightned in the Church.[104]

That Martyr discussed the nature of faith with Bucer is clear from
a letter of 31 August 1550. Martyr commented on Bucer's dispute over
justification held on 18 August 1550 at Cambridge with Young.[105] Martyr agreed at every point with Bucer, i.e., that Cornelius in *Acts*
10(1-48) did not possess good works prior to his justification.
Augustine's opinion in his tract on Predestination is set forth by
Martyr as well as several other Augustinian references. In this case
Martyr saw how Augustine was wrong in his comments on the Centurion
Cornelius. "If, however, they shall say that Augustin opposes himself;
let him be left for reconciliation to those who prop themselves up by
the Fathers, leaving the Scriptures."[106] The influence of Bucer's
1536 *Commentary on Romans* seems a remote question since Bucer discussed the theological issues in person in greater detail than either
printed commentary. One could argue against the direct influence of
Bucer's antecedent published comments of 1536 on Martyr's commentary
without thereby separating their views. Since 1542 Martyr often had
direct contact with Bucer on this issue.

FAITH AND JUSTIFICATION

In defining 'saints' Martyr followed Ambrose. There can be little
doubt that the faith/works controversy permeates this commentary, even

when Martyr cited a patristic writer such as Ambrose who otherwise

did not view grace as did Augustine.

> Ambrose semeth to searche out, who are they which are called
> 'the beloued of God and called Sainctes'. And he aunswereth,
> that these are they, which thinke well of Christ. If thouwilt
> agayne demaund, what those are, he aunswereth: That those thynke
> well of Christ, which thinke that we ought to put our confidence
> in hym only, and that in hym is perfect saluation. And of it
> may be concluded as of contraries, that they thynke not well of
> Christ, which trust in theyr owne strengthes or workes:[107]

Such use of analogy as Martyr made in the above passage helps one to

understand what Martyr wrote in the midst of controversy. As elusive

as theological positions were in that period, Martyr can hardly be

guilty of what Quenstedt calls him when he said of Martyr in 1654,

"Theologus, ingenio & eruditione inter suos praestans, sed crassus

Calvinista . . ."[108] The chief point of the controversy was justifi-

cation, an issue on which many a Lutheran and Calvinist could agree

in Martyr's lifetime.[109] In an important passage for Martyr's thought

references may be found to law and gospel, mercy and promise.

> The righteousnes of the lawe is, to do and to worke. He that
> shall do these things, shall liue in them, sayd Moyses, as it
> is alleaged to the Galathyans: and shall in this Epistle be
> afterward intreated of in hys place. But contrarywyse the
> ryghteousnes and saluation of the Gospell is by fayth unto all
> the that beleue. For it is fayth which taketh hold of the mercye
> and promes of God.[110]

Peter Martyr described a three-fold righteousness when he commented

on the passage in *Romans* (3), "But now without the law is the righteous-

nes of God made manifest."[111] The first kind of righteousness was the

reception by Christ who forgave sin and imputed His own righteousness,

while the second was that which reformed the mind by the help of the

Holy Spirit. He inwardly renews the believer by grace. "Thirdly,

follow holy and godly workes, for they which are once come thus far

are most zelous and desirous of working well."[112] Martyr followed

on with a definition of law and gospel.

> These things make against the Anabaptistes, whiche make the
> Gospel to be nothing by good workes, and a most absolute conuer-
> sation. These men know not the chief and principall benefite of
> Christ, neyther make they any difference betwene the law and the
> Gospell. The law in deed commaundeth: but the Gospell ministreth
> strengths to accomplishe those thinges whiche are commaunded. The
> law accused the: The Gospel absolueth: The Gospell is grauen in
> the bowells: The law worketh anger: The Gospell maketh afeard,
> deiecteth the mind: The Gospell by comforting, erecteth it: The
> law is the ministry of death: The Gospell, of life: The law, is
> a schoolemaster: The gospel, is a perfect instruction: The
> whole lawe consisteth in this, that we should woork: The Gospel
> herein chiefly consisteth, that we should belieue: The law
> bringeth bondage: The Gospell, spirituall liberty: The lawe,
> is the letter: The Gospell, is the spirite: The lawe hath
> promises, but with this condition, if ye shall doo all those
> thinges: The promises of the Gospell, are free, and therefore
> firme.[113]

In the remainder of *Romans* (3) Martyr defined faith by an appeal

to Ambrose and Basil for support of the *sola fide* rubric. Where Paul

had said "And are justified freely by his grace," Martyr cited

Ambrose to the effect that, "We do nothying, we recompece not, by fayth

only are we iustified, which is the gift of God."[114] Martyr defined

faith as assent to the words of God obtained by the power of the Holy

Spirit and the authority of the speaker.[115] As an example of Martyr's

patristic argument, one ought to read his quotation from Basil's *De*

Confessione Fidei.

> 'We (sayeth he) have nothing whereof we may make our boast
> concerning righteousnes, forasmuch as we are iustified only by
> fayth in Christ'. Which wordes are not so to be understanded,
> as though the fayth wherby we are iustified, were alone, that

is not adorned with good and holy works: but because our workes
though they be neuer so holy, are not causes of the true right-
eousnes.[116]

SACRAMENTAL HOPE

Romans (4) provided Martyr with several texts to define the sacra-

ments and Christian hope. Sacraments are signs and seals of the gifts

and promises of God.[117] If faith is present, Martyr reasoned, then

both the outward sign and the thing signified were communicated to the

believer as happiness and blessedness from God.[118] Two teachings re-

pugnant to Martyr vis-a-vis the sacraments were that the sacraments

save or remit sins and that the sacraments were nothing more than

bare and naked signs. Martyr abhorred the thought that the sacraments

either remitted sins or were *nuda signa*.[119] The sacraments served to

separate true believers from other sects and to admonish them to lead

a holy life.

> But we will after a better sorte set forth these effectes
> of the sacraments. First, we say that they instruct us, which
> thing is alreadye said: Secondly, that they kindle in us fayth,
> & a desire of y̆ promises of God: Thirdly, that they knit us to-
> gether in a streighter bond of charity, for that we are all
> initiated with one and the selfe same mysteries. And to these
> may two other effects also be added. For by the sacraments, we
> are both separated from other sects, & also are admonised to
> lead an holy life.[120]

Martyr included in chapter four a discussion of Christian hope at

the verse where St. Paul said, "Which aboue hope beleued vnder hope."[121]

The subject of hope is continued in chapter five where the section from

folios 92^v-144^r describes hope as the incentive to a new life. This

dimension of union with Christ which leads to holy living is nowhere

more clearly set forth in Martyr's writings than here. Martyr followed

Chrysostom who said of the passage quoted above, "Aboue the hope (saith he) of man, and vnder the hope of God."[122]

Christian hope for Martyr authenticated the authority of the church. When his opponents objected with the words of Augustine, that they would not believe the gospel unless the authority of the church had moved them, Martyr countered that Augustine had in mind a ministry of the church committed to preaching and an inculcation of the gospel among all the faithful in the church. In Martyr's time the laity rightly complained that their pastors no longer preached. St. Bernard's well known saying was appropriately applied to them by men like Bishop Jewel at Salisbury: "They are not pastors, but impostors; not doctors, but seducers; not prelates but Pilates." Martyr gave a direct remedy:

> The laytie and simpler sort complayne of their pastors: for seing they lye snorting aslepe, it is not to be meruayled at, if others slepe. There can be no better remedy agaynst this so great negligence of the pastors, then that the lay men continually occupye themselues in the scriptures, and when they are in doubt of any thing to bring it to their pastors, and to aske of them in their iudgement, and to urge them. By that means it shall come to passe, that will they or nill they, they shalbe compelled to be diligent in study.[123]

St. Paul wrote that hope did not confound believers. Martyr accepted Basil's comment on *Psalm* (32) who there had excluded justification by works, and he rejected Peter Lombard who in the third book of the *Sentences* defined hope as a coming of God's grace and the merits which precede it.[124] Hope is to be distinguished from faith. By faith Martyr admitted the promises offered by God; by hope he would patiently wait for those promises to be performed.[125]

In *Romans* (5) Martyr challenged Pigge on original sin.[126] The

relationship of faith to hope and love as well as the work of the law
and of the Holy Spirit are crucial aspects of Martyr's theology. The
gift of the Spirit comes in regeneration: "for there, whilest by
fayth thou takest holde that Christ died for thee, thou are borne
agayne and made partaker of the nature of God."[127] The law was given,
said Martyr, so that "man might at the last be saved through grace".[128]
At this juncture Martyr parted company with the Pelagians whom he
asserted would make the acceptance of grace to depend on man's freedom
to give assent to or refuse to accept God's promises. Grace is free
of merit in both senses, as Martyr taught when he wrote,

> But yet we haue affirmed one thing, which is not yet confirmed
> by the scriptures: namely ϼ God doth not onely offer the promises
> which we have now spoken of, of his mere grace and beneuolence,
> but also with his spirit boweth the harte to receive them.[129]

The theme of a new life for the person grafted into Christ by the
promises of God occurs in *Romans* (6) in the context of Paul's baptismal passage. As Christ was raised up from the dead by God's glory,
so must the true believer also walk in newness of life. The theme is
continued in Martyr's comments on *Romans* (7). Two selections will
describe this kind of life.

> The glory of the father in this place signifieth the power of
> God, which was then chiefely declared, when Christ rose agayne
> from the deade: and in us it is manifestly shewed when we casting
> away sinnes do liue uncorruptly. And Paul by this word newness,
> doth oftentimes signifie the blameless life of Christians. For
> he saith, that we ought to put on the new man. And he saith that
> before God, circumcision, or uncircumcision is nothing, but only
> a new creature. And he admonisheth, that as touching the inward
> man we should be dayly more and more renewed. But by this word
> walking, he teacheth, that the purenes of life, that is to say,
> this newness hath certayne degrees: and we must have a care
> continually to profite more and more.[130]

In the second passage Martyr used the term 'grafted into Christ' to refute his opponents' teaching on merit. They cited from *Ecclesiasticus* (16) a passage which Martyr dismissed for two reasons; it was not in the Canon of scripture, and the Latin text was poorly translated from the Greek. If put into English their text from *Ecclesiasticus* (16) would read, "all mercy shall make place unto euery one accordyng to the merit of his workes." Martyr pointed to the Greek text which would read in English, "All mercy shall make place: eueryone shal finde according to his dedes." Such a reading has no mention of merit in it.[131] The grafting of the believer into Christ rather than meritorious works leads to a daily renewal of the Christian life. Martyr wrote a quite lovely description of this work of Christ.

> So we being in regeneracion grafted into Christ, ought to liue by his spirite, and with him both to die, and also to rise againe; that euen as Christ could not be holden of the sorrowes of death, so also can not the tiranny of sinne any longer hold us in bandes. Righteousness and pureness of lyfe shall daily be renewed in us: which thing is brought to passe, when we depart from sinne: for as long as we liue in sinne, we lead not a new life, but the olde life. There is no entraunce open unto the lyfe of the resurrection, but by death.[132]

Martyr's sacramental teaching is an intensely personal emphasis with its insistence in such passages that only death to sin and resurrection with Christ can validate the visible words of God in the Dominical Sacraments. The Holy Spirit whose work it is to renew believers in body and in soul is the agent of such reconciliation. Such activity of the Spirit will display "new and unaccustomed workes" since one work of the Holy Spirit is to renew believers in body and in soul.[133] These remarks also reflect Martyr's attempt to reform persons

by preaching and the English nation through the *Ecclesiastical Laws*
and the revised *Prayerbook*.

Martyr returned to the patristic arguments of Ambrose and Chrysostom when he sought to understand *Romans* (8). His comments here are
valuable for their discussion of righteousness. Both here and in the
treatise on justification inserted at the end of *Romans* (11) Martyr
not only answered his opponents but also described righteousness in
terms agreeable to Calvin and other reformed theologians. What
follows will be an attempt to link Martyr's thought in the *Romans*
commentary with the tract on justification reprinted in the *Loci*
Communes of 1576 from the end of *Romans* (11).

HOLY SPIRIT AND GOSPEL POWER

Christ delivered Paul from the dominion of sin and death. When
Martyr came to Paul's passage on Christian freedom from sin and death,
he turned to the work of the Holy Spirit to explain Paul's meaning.
It is important to notice that Martyr used another Pauline passage in
I *Corinthians* to explain Paul's statement in *Romans*. One feels that
Martyr had selected these two Pauline letters because they touched on
the nature of faith and its priority to sacramental obedience. When
one cites treatises from the *Common Places* (1583) or editions of the
Loci Communes (1576-1656), one must not forget that Martyr lectured
on these subjects before 1542 while still in Italy. The published
commentaries of 1551 and 1558 represent positions which Martyr held
on arrival in England and perhaps before 1542. Martyr long held to
the position first published in 1558 where he commented,

. . . the Gospell, so long as it doth but outwardly only make
a sound, neither is the holy ghost inwardly in the hartes of the
hearers, to moue and bowe them to beleue, so long (I say) the
Gospell hath the nature of the killying letter, neyther differeth
it any thyng from the Lawe, as touchying efficacye unto saluation.
For althoughe it conteyne other tynges then the Lawe dothe, yet
it canne neyther geue Grace, nor remission of synnes unto the
hearers. But after that the holy ghost hath once moued y̆ harts
of the hearers to beleue, then at length the Gospell obtayneth his
power to make safe.[134]

Chrysostom interpreted Paul to mean that the presence of the Holy

Spirit delivered the Christian from sin and death. Martyr elaborated

on that theme by ascribing to the Holy Spirit such help "with the

strength of the spirite, and instrumente of heavenly giftes that we

suffer not this lawe of naturall corruption to raigne in vs."[135]

Martyr defined $\delta\iota\kappa\alpha\iota o\sigma\acute{u}v\eta$ as an antithesis to sin and as the life

of God. He was careful to check the Greek text, however, for the

Latin text read, "propter iustificatione͞," as though the Greek text

were $\delta\iota\grave{\alpha}\ \delta\iota\kappa\alpha\iota\acute{\omega}\sigma\iota v$. Even though Chrysostom took the reading

as $\delta\iota\grave{\alpha}\ \delta\iota\kappa\alpha\iota\acute{\omega}\sigma\iota v$ rather than $\delta\iota\grave{\alpha}\ \delta\iota\kappa\alpha\iota o\sigma\acute{u}v\eta v$, Martyr

approved his interpretation.

'That the body is the at the last dead, when we are no more
affected with the motions thereof, th͞e we are moued by our Karkases
being now buried and hid under grounde'. And thys he saith, is
the communion with the death of Christ, because Christ dyed, to
dissolue the body of sinne.[136]

Hope still waits, said Martyr, for the perfect restitution and full

delivery from all evil. He could agree with St. Paul's conclusion in

Romans (8) that "We are saued by hope."[137]

Martyr concluded with St. Paul that Christian hope was bound up

with the incomparable love of Christ.

And he useth an interreogation, thereby to signify a constant
certaynty. And the wordes which he useth, are not placed by
chance, or at all a ventures, but with exceding greate conning
of the holy ghost. The first word, is $\theta\lambda\iota\pi\iota\varsigma$, that is, afflic-
tio, deriued of this verbe $\theta\lambda\iota\beta\epsilon\iota\nu$, which signifieth to
breake, or vehemently to presse. For first, thinges being well
ordred are accustomed to be brused or broken: and afterward he
encreaseth the euill and addeth $\varsigma\epsilon\upsilon\alpha\chi\omega\rho\iota\alpha$, that is,
anguishe, where thinges are brought to so narrow a streight,
that a man can not tell what counsell to take, or which way to
turne himselfe.[138]

By this reasoning of Paul we may easely gather, ỹ the Church shal
neuer utterly fall away frō God, neither shall there euer come any
euils of so great might, that they can utterly ouerthrow it. Which
thing Christ inother words promised unto Peter saying: 'The gates
of hell shall not preuayle agaynst it.' For it is as it were a
certayne moste strong rocke, whiche although it be striken with
waues and floudes, yet can not be moued out of this place. For
the church pertayneth to predestination, and hath to hys protection
the loue of God. Wherefore no creature is able to preuayle
against it.[139]

PREDESTINATION

At the end of *Romans* (9) Martyr wrote a definition of predestination

and election. In the Latin edition of 1558 it occupies folios 404-441.

In the context of *Romans* (9) Martyr at verse ten on Esau and Jacob found

the source of election in God's will. McLelland has shown that at

Romans (9:13) Martyr noted the problem of hatred as well as love in

God's will.

I affirm with the holy Scriptures that God truly and indeed loues
and hates . . . . since we cannot understand the force and power
of the loue and hatred of God in themselues, we consider them by
the effects: namely either by His gifts or by His punishments.
But the ground of the question is, whether the loue comes of merits,
or freely.[140]

Martyr noted that in verse sixteen St. Paul said that it came from the

mercy of God. Then Martyr gave his own definition of the controversy,

"whether God wills felicity to the elect by works foreseen, or not:

and how he wills it not to the reprobate."[141] McLelland noted

Martyr's solution, that man is moved according to his nature. Since

the elect have different natures than others, God only confirms each

will but never compells it.

The *locus* which occupies so many folio pages at the end of *Romans*

(9) refers to this controversy current in France. Predestination was

of great consolation to Martyr because it advanced God's glory and

confirmed man's justification. Calvin spoke in the *Institutes* (1539)

of predestination to damnation (XIV:1) while Martyr said something

quite the opposite, namely that "I separate the reprobate from the

predestinate, because the Scriptures nowhere that I know of, call men

that shall be damned predestinate."[142] Martyr taught that the repro-

bate and the predestinate partook of different benefits of God.[143]

Martyr finally argued the necessity of predestination. Outward

necessity was the pagan doctrine of Fate which compelled one by

violence, while inward necessity was that advanced by scripture where

God made certain His compulsion. The predestinate could not commit

anything which would overthrow their salvation nor could the reprobate

be compelled against their will to salvation. Martyr concluded:

> Let no man be offended with the doctrine of predestination, when
> rather by it are we led to acknowledge the benefits of God, and
> to give thanks unto Him alone. Let us also learn not to attribute
> more unto our own strength than we ought: and let us have a sure
> persuasion of the good will of God towards us, by which He would
> elect His before the foundations of the world were laid: let us
> moreover be confirmed in adversities, knowing assuredly that
> whatever calamity happens, it is done by the counsel and will of
> God, and shall at last by the government of predestination turn
> us to good, and to eternal salvation.[144]

It is these matters which Calvin praised in his letter of 22 May 1558 to Martyr. They agreed on predestination as defined in the long delayed version of this *Romans* commentary. Calvin would wrench the commentaries on *Genesis* and the *Prophets* from Martyr's hand if he were only in Geneva.

At *Romans* (9) Martyr defined two principles of the church, namely, God's election and God's Word. These rather than the authority of the multitude or the "gorgeousness of this world" should define the word of faith which St. Paul preached in *Romans* (10).[145] Not only was the chief part of the Apostolic ministry concerned about the righteousness of faith but it was also communicated by preaching. At *Romans* (10: 17) Martyr quoted from Basil's *De Confessione fidei* on the necessity of public proclamation of the Word and the inner direction of the Spirit.[146] Martyr lauded St. Paul's quotation from *Isaiah*, "But how shall they heare without a preacher?"[147] In a poignant passage Martyr lamented the lack of preaching by the hierarchy.

> Behold with how excellent a title the ministers of the Church are adorned: they are called *κηρυκες* that is, the ambassadors of God. This is theyr chiefest worke to published abrode the wordes of God. But they have utterly lost this dignity, which are of this minde that the highest and singulariest honor is to consecrate (as they vse to speake) the sacrament, or to transubstantiate bread and wyne. They are not so described in the holye scriptures, but that they shoulde preache, and doo the office of ambassadors.[148]

SOLA FIDE: GATE TO NEW LIFE (*ROMANS* 11-12)

The *Loci Communes* of 1576 as expanded in further continental editions until 1656 assembled *loci* such as Martyr's discourse on justification at *Romans* (11). It is helpful to examine the immediate context

of each *locus* in its own commentary, for in what preceeds and follows
this *locus* one can see that justification meant the gateway to new
life in Christ. To use the section from the *Common Places* in isola-
tion from its origin might mislead a reader to think that Martyr has
set forth another arid dispute for which the sixteenth century is
often blamed. The 'Scholar of Christ' as Martyr called himself was
to act out his faith as the Holy Spirit directed him. In *Romans*(10)
Martyr concluded that such men made up the kingdom of Christ.

> But herein consisteth hys kingdome, that we be directed by the
> word and spirite of God. After these two maners Christ raygneth
> in us. The woord sheweth what is to be beleued, and what is to
> be done. The spirit impelleth and moueth us to doo these
> thinges.[149]

Three features of this tractate merit comment. First of all, this
is the third such discussion in Martyr's commentaries after the other
two in the *Genesis* and I *Corinthian* commentaries. Secondly, Martyr
utilized a catena of patristic citations on *sola fide*. Finally, his
tractate was a response to Albert Pigge, "because our adversaries count
him for their Achilles."[150] A brief glance at the two similar passages
in *Genesis* and I *Corinthians* shows that the patristic citations and
response to Pigge are unique to this tract *On Iustification*.

Archbishop **Thomas Cranmer** assembled such a list of *Testimonia* in
preparing his *Homily of Salvation, Homily of Faith* and *Homily of Good
Works*. The dating of the *Notes on Justification* has depended on their
similarity to the three homilies. The original manuscript, however, is
not dated.[151] It is of interest to compare Martyr's list of patristic
authorities with those used by Cranmer when one recalls that Martyr

prepared the list of quotations for Cranmer's sermons against rebellion of 1549. Some variations occur in the listing. Martyr cited
from Cyril, *Against Julian* and from Popes Leo and Gregory. Cranmer
cited Prosper, Bruno and Hugo of St. Victor. Both Martyr and Cranmer
used Bede's comments on *James*. Our conclusion is that Martyr prepared
his own list which varies considerably from that of Cranmer. The method
of citation however demonstrated their unanimity on this vital issue.
Martyr would not have used Cranmer's *Homilies* since he did not read
English. Certainly they would have talked over the passages in both
lists at Lambeth during 1547-1553. Peter Alexander's two folio volumes
of quotations were available by March of 1550.

Martyr taught that justification was freely accomplished apart from
merit but that good works follow on as a consequence of that act. Mar-
tyr would prove that teaching by citing an impressive list ranging from
Basil, *De Baptismo* to the Council of Trent.[152] After answering Pigge[153]
Martyr turned again to patristic citation.[154] At the end of this list
Martyr gave additional sources of some interest for his readers.

> Whome these things suffice not let him reade *Genuadius* upon the
> 5. chap. to the Romanes: *Cirillus* in his 9. booke 3. chapiter
> upon *Iohn*: *Theodoretus* upon the 5. chapiter to the Romanes.
> *Didimus* upon the 2. chapiter of *Iames Eusebius* in his Ecclesi-
> asticall history the 3 booke and 27, chap. *Ciprian* (or whatso-
> euer he were, in his exposition of the simbole: *Liranus* upon
> the third to the Galathians: The ordinary glosse upon the epistle
> unto *Iames*: *Haimo* upon the Gospell of Circumcision: *Sedulius*
> upon the 1. and 2. chapiters unto the Romanes. *Thomas* upon
> the 3. to the Galathians. Bruno upon the 4. unto the Romanes.
> *Arnobius* upon the 106 Psalme.[155]

Gennadius, Bruno, the ordinary gloss on *James*, Cyril on *John*,

Thomas on *Galatians*, Lyra on *Galatians* 3 and Theodoret on *Romans* (5)

are all in Cranmer's list.[156] The lists are close enough to suggest

that Martyr and Cranmer drew from a common source, and that Martyr

added from them to his own list. The common source would be Peter

Alexander's 1549 manuscript volume, Lambeth MS. 1108 though Martyr's

tract may have been composed prior to his arrival at Lambeth late in

1547. Strype preserves an account of Peter Alexander which may help

on this point. On the advice of Cranmer, Alexander read over the

ancient fathers in order to collect extracts from them pertaining to

current religious issues.

> One folio volume of these Collections, taken out of Dionysius,
> Ignatius, Irenaeus, Tertullian and Cyprian, he presented this
> year 1549 to the Archbishop: which he took in very good part at
> his hands, approving and commending his diligence therein, as
> tending to the profit of the church, and the benefit of the
> studious; which encouraged the said Peter to go on in the same
> method with the ecclesiastical writers, next in order of time to
> them; so that by April 1550, he presented the archbishop with
> another great folio of Notes extracted out of the works of Origen,
> Athanasius, and Epiphanius; before which he set an Epistle
> Dedicatory to the same. . .[157]

Strype adds that this volume was among the rare collection of manu-

scripts belonging to Dr. More, late Bishop of Ely /sic. John Moore

(1646-1714)_/. When Dr. Moore's library was sold to King George I, he

presented it to the University of Cambridge. This volume in 1971 was

Ee.2.8. in the Cambridge University Library Anderson Room. It is

possible that Alexander's list was the sort of reading which Martyr

himself had already noted.

The references in Alexander's *Collectanae* to Epiphanius came from

the *Contra Haereses*. Martyr could have used this volume in preparing

his *Romans* commentary. The other volume mentioned by Strype is Lambeth

Palace Library MS. 1108. In his dedicatory letter to Cranmer Alexander said that the first volume contained extracts from Dionysius, Ignatius, Irenaeus, Tertullian and Cyprian. Now he has extracted from Origen, Athanasius and Epiphanius "for the use of the Church and convienience of scholars in the tabernacle of the Lord . . . ." The letter gives the reason for the collection, "because the works of these Fathers are prolix." Dated 28 April 1550. Lambeth.[158]

Two additional lists of patristic citations available to Martyr were those of Robert Barnes, _Sententiae Ex Doctoribus Collectae_ (1530) and the anonymous Herman Bodius, _Unio dissidentium_(1531). Barnes cited from Origen and Ambrose on _Romans_ (3), Augustine, Athanasius, Gregory, Bernard, Erasmus and Orbellus. The _Unio_ lists the following names: Augustine, Ambrose, Jerome, Gregory, Cyprian, Origen, Chrysostom, Hilary, Bernard, Fulgentius, Athanasius, Cyril, Theophylact, Tertullian, Bede, Clement and Lactantius. A comparison of Cranmer and Martyr shows references unique to Martyr not in the _Unio, Sententiae,_ Cranmer or Alexander. One can conclude from these comparisons that Martyr drew on a vast fund of reading and reflection which Cranmer used to great advantage. The _Unio_ is now thought to originate among the Strasbourg reformers on the basis of Hedio's 1537 German translation.[159]

Jean Crespin published a volume in 1556 containing a letter of Alexander to the English Church in Diaspora. The letter is little known since only one copy exists of the second 1558 edition and two copies exist of the first edition. The two first edition copies are in Vienna and Clare College, Cambridge. The volume is a French translation of the 1549 *De Vitandis Superstitionibus* with additional selections. The contributors are Oecolampadius, Zwingli, Melanchthon, Bucer, Martyr, Calvin, Musculus, Sultzer, Laski, Ochino, Bullinger, Gualter, Werdmullerus, Pelican, Bibliander, Curione, Viret, Borrahus, Myconius and Dillerus.[160] A close association between Alexander, Cranmer and Martyr is shown by the existence of these printed and manuscript volumes.

One would expect to find Augustine's *De Spiritu et litera* used by Martyr, who focused his attention on chapter 24 concerning the inward persuasion of the Holy Spirit.[161] One reference from Bede is of interest because it seldom appears in catholic commentaries sympathetic to *sola fide*. Martyr quoted the passage from *James* where Bede cited the experience of Cornelius.

> We came not, (sayeth he) to fayth by workes: but by fayth we attayne unto vertues. For Cornelius the Centurion came not vnto fayth by workes: but by fayth came vnto workes.[162]

Albert Pigge wrote *De Fide Operibus et Iustificatione Hominis* which was published in 1541. Together with the *De Peccato Originis* and *De Ecclesia*, these treatises as defended by Richard Smith in 1551 are the likely source for Martyr's response to Pigge in the commonplace on *Justification*.[163] A selection of Martyr's comments on Pigge would help to understand Martyr's theological methodology. Pigge realized the importance of *sola fide* controversy when he summarized protestant doctrine as teaching that God saves and redeems through Christ the Saviour by faith alone. Justification and salvation were simply free and to be accepted as a certainty by the believer.[164] Martyr deplored

the subtile craft of this Achilles who sought to separate faith from

justification.[165]

> But Pighius afterward demaundeth, why we take away from workes
> the power of iustifieng. Unto this we could make answere with
> one word, that we do it because the holy ghost in the holy scrip-
> tures so teacheth us: namely that men are iustified by fayth
> without workes.[166]

Martyr rejected Pigge's proof that love justified rather than faith

because love was superior to faith as a theological virtue. This St.

Paul seemed to teach in I *Corinthians* (13:13).[167] Martyr marveled at

the implications of this interpretation that a man must be perfect be-

fore he could be justified. This misunderstanding on the part of

sixteenth century theologians had wide ramifications. When the Council

of Trent seemed to endorse a position on justification which made the

sola fide argument its chief target, men like Martyr felt the need to

return to the sourcebook of the church's understanding. Martyr used

the patristic argument and an exegesis of St. Paul's *sola fide* to lead

a christian to holy living. His summary of Pigge's doctrine must be

seen in this light of a concern to insist that purity of life could

only derive from purity of doctrine and worship.

> To be briefe, he reckeneth up all those things which we before
> declared under the name of ẙ Synode of Trent, but in the last
> place he sayth, succedeth a sincere & pure loue of God, which
> altogether beareth dominion in our heartes: and unto this he
> saith is ascribed iustification. I can not inough meruaile at
> the deuise of this man. For he affirmeth that a man is in a
> manner perfecte before he can be iustified. For which he be-
> leueth, feareth, hopeth, repenteth, and sincerely loueth God,
> what wanteth he to perfection? But this man holdeth, that a man
> without Christ, a straunger from God, and not yet iustified, is
> able to accōplish those things: which undoubtedly in no wise
> agreeth with ẙ holy scriptures.[168]

Martyr held that all deeds of man prior to justification were in the
words of *Colossians*, "occupied in euil works, & wandreth in the hatred
of God."169

At the same time that Martyr took care to demonstrate the validity
of the *sola fide* argument in the writings of the Fathers, he also set
forth in his commentary the Pauline emphasis upon conformity to Christ.
In a lovely passage at *Romans* (12:1-2) Martyr compared the life of a
christian to Christ's sacrifice.

> If Christ would for our sakes be made an oblatiō, it ought not
> to seme greuous to any of us, if we on the other side be made
> oblations, & be sacrificed unto God. For hereto are we predes-
> tinated, to be made like unto the image of the Sonne of God. And
> euen as he is not a good citezin which cannot be content with the
> common condition of other citezins, so or rather much les is he
> to be counted for a good Christian which refuseth to take upon
> him the condition of his head or first borne brother.170

On occasion Martyr chose alternate readings of the Greek text to
explain his choice of categories such as the distinction between law
and gospel or faith and works. On St. Paul's concern at *Romans* (12)
that the Romans ought to give themselves to hospitality Martyr observed that some manuscripts read μνείκς rather than χρείας Origen's
interpreter preferred the former reading as did Ambrose.171 Martyr by
selecting χρείκς, read the passage as 'necessities of the Saints',
rather than 'memories'.

> The kingdome of God is geuen for election and the promises sake,
> which the saints receive by faith. But bicause those things are
> hidden from mannes eyes, therefore are brought forth good workes:
> which are the proper and manifest effectes bothe of our faith,
> and of the election of God.172

THE SCOPE OF THEOLOGY

The *Romans* commentary is notable for its irenic tone where it discusses the views of Martyr's opponents. Elsewhere Martyr sometimes digressed in his *loci*, though in this commentary the only extended common places are on justification and predestination. Even in these lengthy theological comments Martyr maintained a lively pace, argued with skill and marshalled his evidence. In his lectures on that perennial textbook of Medieval theology, the *Nichomachian Ethics* of Aristotle, Martyr defined the relation of theology to philosophy.

Martyr was freed from lectures on Aristotle at Zurich because Conrad Gesner gave the Aristotelian lectures at the Carolinum. This gave Martyr leisure to revise for publication what he had written for private use in Strasbourg.[173] The introduction to the *Ethics* indicates something of his theological method.[174] "All our knowledge is either revealed or acquired. In the first case it is Theology, in the other it is Philosophy."[175] This method of commenting on Aristotle's *Ethics* explains how Martyr interpreted the Biblical texts in his *Romans* Commentary. Martyr first set forth the text followed by an explanation of its scope through the use of *loci*, then he turned to grammatical and textual matters and gave finally an exposition. Martyr compared the teaching of Aristotle with the Divine Writings.[176] Though Martyr used this method in his commentaries, in practice he left out of the published lectures most grammatical or textual analysis. Martyr went on to approve of St. Paul who in his letters not only set forth speculative dogmatic teaching but also proceeded to moral instruction and "ad uitam componendam."[177]

This moral dimension and emphasis upon a Christian life in which the benefits of Christ are shared among true followers of the Cross are the characteristic themes of Peter Martyr's biblical lectures. The "learned stranger" in King Edward's England could with good cause call himself the "Scholar of Christ." This term was used by John Ponet in his 1553 Catechism, where the Master said to the Scholar, "Doest thou then confess thyself to be a follower of Christian godliness and religion, and a scholar of our Lord Christ?"[178] Or again as Edmund Grindal wrote to Sir William Cecil, no man alive was more fit than any Papist to restore honesty to theological discussion.

NOTES TO CHAPTER VII

1. J. C. McLelland, The Visible Words of God, pp. 273-76.

2. Marvin W. Anderson, "Word and Spirit in Exile (1542-61): The Biblical Writings of Peter Martyr Vermigli," J. E. H. XXI (1970), 193-201.

3. Martyr mentions colleges in the plural.

4. Nicolas Harris Nicholas, "The Bill of the Expences attending the Journey of Peter Martyr and Bernardinus Ochin, from Basil to England, in 1547," A. XXI (1827), pp. 469-473 from Ashmole's MSS. 826 in the Bodleian Library, Oxford.

5. Ibid., p. 471.

6. Loc. cit.

7. Ibid., p. 470.

8. On Cornarius see the notice in Biographie Universelle Ancienne Et Moderne, Nouvelle Edition, IX, pp. 216-217. Also Otto Clemen, "Janus Cornarius," N.A.S.G.A. 33 (1912), 36-76. There are three letters to Pflug in Christian G. Mueller, Epistolae Petri Mosellani (1802). An interesting work by Cornarius is his Theologiae vitis viniferae libri tres (Heidleberg, 1614). On Gesner see the 1543

prefatory letter to his edition of Stobeius: "non enim dubito, quin
uos ipsi pro uestra prudentia sat intelligatis, ueterum licet ethni-
corum, in rebus humanis sapientiam Christianae professioni non tantum
non aduersari, sed eam potius iuuare." Ioannis Stobei Sententiae ex
thesauris Graecorum delectae. Martyr lectured on Aristotle's Ethics
from 1553-1555 while in Strasbourg.

9. The Omnia Opera were translated by Cornarius, and published
by Hieronymus Frobenius and Nicholaus Episcopius in 1540.

10. Epiphanii . . . de prophetarum vita et interitu commentarius
Graecus, una cum interpretatione e regione Latina, A. Torino inter-
pretate. This was published with Erasmus' edition of Sophronius &
Jerome, libellus de vita evangelistarum, Parabolae et miracula quae
a singulis evangelistis narrantur. The work on Heresies was first
published as the Contra octaginta haereses opus (Basle: Robertus
Vuinterus, Sept. 1543) and in Greek at Basle in 1544. Cornarius'
translation was reprinted in Basle in September, 1545 by Winter and
in 1560 by Ioannes Oporinus & Heruagius. There were several Paris
editions.

11. Of The Sacrament of Thanksgiving. A Short Treatise of
Peter Martyr's Making. (British Museum Royal MSS. 17. C.V.), fol.
45^V-46^r. This sacramental treatise was prepared for the Lord Protector Somerset to guide the 1549 debate in Parliament on the Prayer
Book. The 1580 Lutheran Formula of Concord excoriates Beza and Peter
Martyr for calling unworthy eating of the sacrament, "two hairs of a
horse's tail and an invention of which even Satan himself would be
ashamed; just as they describe the majesty of Christ as "Satan's dung,
by which the devil amuses himself and deceives men.' These phrases
are so terrible that a pious Christian should be ashamed to translate
them." The Book of Concord, p. 582. Tappert does not identify these
"terrible phrases" nor have I found them in any of Martyr's extant
writings.

12. F. A. Gasquet and E. Bishop, Edward VI and the Book of Common
Prayer, pp. 159-160. Gasquet and Bishop think that the translator was
Turner, Somerset's chaplain.

13. John Strype, Ecclesiastical Memorials (1816), II, XXV, pp.
336-337. Text in Laurence Humphrey, Ioannis Ivelli Angli . . . vita
et mors . . ., pp. 131-32.

14. Humphrey refers to Harding on pp. 138-39 where he says,
":qui Pet. Martyrem Oxoniae tantum non adorauit: qui non solum publice
eu legentem, sed etiam in aedibus Italice concionante audiuit: qui ex
Italia reversus, Francesco Guauarrae viro optimo dixit, Margaritas ceu
Mercator vndiq; coquisiui, & ecce praestantissiamam domi inueni, Pet.
Martyrem, quo nihil habet Europa doctius . . ." This parallels

Harding's own account to Jewel.

15. An Oration or Sermon out of the 2 Chapter of Malachie, of
the profit and worthiness of the holy Ministerie, in Common Places
(1583), Part five, pp. 27-32. The 1587 Zurich edition published by
Froschouer is used since neither the 1580 nor 1583 Latin editions
were accessible at the time.

16. Common Places, (1583), Part five, pp. 29-30.

17. See the brief life prefixed to the translation of Jewel's
Works (1609): "among others, Peter Martyr, as a spirituall Bezeliel,
was by his Maiestie appointed Professour of Diunitie in Oxford, 'vt
verbi diuini gemmas exculperet fideliter coaptaret, adornaret
sapienter, adijceret gratiam splendorem uenustatem,' to point, fit
and polish such pearles. Whose excellent skill herein, and rich shop
full of all choise and pretious knowledge, as all admired, so
especiallie Iewel, who repaired unto this cunning Ieweller, and
(seeking to be perfited by him) observed his arte, copied out his
Sermons and Lectures . . ." There seems to be some question about the
provenance of the seven sermons included in this edition, since they
were found unsigned among the papers of Jewel. They might be transcripts of Martyr's private sermons.

18. Common Places (1583), Part five, p. 12.

19. See John Jewel, Works, p. 172.

20. Humphrey, op. cit., p. 41.

21. Ibid., pp. 43-44.

22. The Zurich Zentralbibliothek lists a Conciones et Epistolae
Variae with no date or place of publication. Pembroke College, Oxford
owns a volume whose spine is labled, "Peter Martyr, Paralipomenon."
It is a commentary by Ludvig Lavater. I could not locate in Zurich
this Conciones which seems to be an inaccurate entry in the 18th
century catalogue.

23. Common Places (1583), Part five, p. 32.

24. Ibid., p. 33. ". . . multa sibi referuauit Spiritus sanctus
adhuc ibi clausa, vt nos vsque ad orbis consummationem discipulos
habeat." Loci Communes (1587).

25. Ibid., p. 34.

26. Loc. cit.

27. *Loci* *Communes* (1587), p. 1050.

28. C. A. L. Jarrot, "Erasmus' *In* *Principio* *Erat* *Sermo*: a Controversial Translation," *Studies* *in* *Philology* XLI (1964), p.35.

29. 22 August 1559 in Huelin, *op.* *cit.*, p. 49.

30. *Corinthios* (1551), p. 147$^\text{v}$.

31. *Ibid.*, p. 148$^\text{r-v}$.

32. *Ibid.*, p. 149$^\text{v}$.

33. *Ibid.*, p. 154$^\text{v}$.

34. V. Norskov Olsen, *The* *New* *Testament* *Logia* *on* *Divorce*, pp. 88-94. On punishment for adultery see *Common* *Places* (1583), pp. 482-495.

34a. *Common* *Places* (1583), Part three, pp. 192-203.

35. *The* *Fortresse* *of* *Fathers* (1566), sig. B2$^\text{v}$-B3$^\text{r}$.

36. See also G. A. Starr, "Antedatings from Nicholas Udall's translation of Peter Martyr's 'Discourse,'" *N.Q.*, new series XII (1966), 9-12.

37. *Discourse* (1550), fol. CX$^\text{r}$.

38. Few copies of either the 1551 *Corinthians* or the 1558 *Romans* have survived in European or English libraries. Martyr himself lamented the lack of copies in England of the Corinthian Commentary.

39. *C.* *T.* *B.* III (1559-1561), p. 38 note 17.

40. *Ibid.*, p. 36. "Et quum dicit Dominus: Hoc est corpus meum, et Paulus, panem esse communcationem corporis, an de corpore aliquo intelligunt quod sit substantiae èxpers? Denique non aliter substantiae vocabulo velim uti quam explicavit D. Martyr sua praefatione ad Cantuariensem, et in Commentariis ad Corinthios fol. 302, initio prioris paginae, a quo ne tantillum quidem dissentio, ac proinde neque a te ut existimo, neque a vestrum quoquam."

41. *Corinthios* (1551), 2$^\text{v}$.

42. *Ibid.*, 2$^\text{v}$-2$^\text{r}$. Margin reads "Solae scripturae dogmata confirmant."

43. *Ibid.*, 3$^\text{v}$-4$^\text{r}$: "Hoc vero non ignoratio facit, sed quod

nolint beati huius viri scripta in manibus assidue habere." Cf.
Migne, Patrologia Graeca LX, 329 which seems to correspond to
Vermigli's argument.

44. Ibid., 6^v.

45. Ibid., 9^r.

46. See Common Places (1583), Part one, pp. 39-44.

47. Ibid., 11^v. "Et Ambrosius, dum hanc particulam interpretatur,
id non dissimulat. Inquit enim: Quia hoc constitutum est a deo, ut
qui credit in Christum, saluus sit sine opere, sola fide, gratis
accipiens remissionem peccatorum." I have been unable as yet to
identify this quotation among Ambrose's writings.

48. On Seripando and Pole see this author's articles in C. T. M.
XXXIX (1968) and C. H. 38 (1969).

49. Ibid., 13^v. "Neque, spes concepta de promissionibus dei,
unquam pudefacit, imo bonum quod abest . . . ."

50. Ibid., 23^v where Martyr cited from Erasmus, Adnotationes.
See Roland Bainton, "The Paraphrases of Erasmus," A. R. G. 67 (1966),
67-75.

51. Ibid., 23^v.

52. Ibid., 29^v.

53. Loc. cit.   I have not modernised Martyr's orthography.

54. Loc.cit.

55. Loc.cit. See Martyr to Bullinger, August 1562, where he
objects to comments on Romans (9) by reference to I Corinthians (10):
C. R. XLVII. 3840, col. 505.

56. Ibid., 29^r: " . . . tum iustitia sic acquisita improbatur."

57. Corinthios (1551), 29^r.

58. Ibid., 35^v. Margin reads, "In iustificatione peccata nobis
non imputantur, et iustitia Christi nobis imputatur."

59. Ibid., 349^r.

60. Loc. cit.

61. Ibid., 350^{r-v}.

62. Ibid., 350^r.

63. Ibid., 351^v.

64. Loc. cit.

65. Ibid., 351^r.

66. Loc. cit.

67. Ibid., 352^v.

68. Loc. cit.

69. Ibid., 353^v.

70. Ibid., 353^r.

71. Ibid., 355^v.   Chrysostom, Third Homily on Titus.

72. Ibid., 357^v; cf. 359^v.

73. Ibid., 371^v.

74. Corinthios (1572).

75. Ibid., p. 166^v.

76. Ibid., p. 136^v.

77. Ibid., p. 178^r. "Cap. XII (Etenim per unum Spiritum nos omnes in unum corpus baptizati sumus, siue Iudaei, siue Graeci, siue serui, siue liberi, & omnes unum Spiritum hausimus)."

78. Loc. cit. "Duplex autem coniunctio in membris huius corporis observuatur. Vna est, quam retinere debet inter sese: altera, quam cu Christo habeat oportet." 1551 Edition, p. 337^v, identical text.

79. Ibid., p. 178^v. "Et certe cum Christo ita coniungimur, ut dicamur caro ex carnibus eius, & os ex osibus /sic./ eius. Quia per illius incarnationem eiusdem generis atq̄; speciei effecti sumus cum illo: postea uero accedente spiritu eius & gratia, spiritualium eius conditionum atq̄; proprietatum particpes reddimur, ut superius explicatum fuit. Vnde Cyrillus scribens ad Regnias de fide orthodoxa, dixit, carnem nostram consubstantialem carni Christ, & eos qui aliter sentiant, habet pro anathemate." 1551 edition, p. 337^v, identical text.

80. Ibid., p. 179[r],

81. The Acts and Monuments of John Foxe (1877), VIII, pp. 205-206. Galeazzc Caraccioli heard Martyr preach in Naples during 1540 on I Corinthians. Martyr also lectured on this epistle at Lucca according to Zanchi. For the conversion of Caraccioli see McNair, Peter Martyr in Italy, pp. 154-156 and 176-177.

82. O. L. II, p. 419. John ab Ulmis to Rodolph Gualter, Oxford, 5 November 1550. "from nine to ten Peter Martyr lectures upon the epistle to the Romans."

83. O. L. II, p. 504. Peter Martyr to Bullinger. 8 March 1552. From the House of the Archbishop of Canterbury. The Latin text appeared in 1558 at Basle, printed by Peter Perna. On this native of Lucca now see Leandro Perini, "Ancora sul libraio-tipografa Pietro Perna e su alcune figure di eretici italiani in rapporto con lui negli anni 1549-1555." N. R. S. 51 (1967), 363-404.

84. McLelland's useful article in the Scottish Journal of Theology examines only the views on predestination in Romans (9). See also Amedeo Molnar, "Romani 13 nella interpretazioni della primi Riforma," P XXIV (1969), 65-76.

85. Romanes (1568), p. 1[v]. Where it is crucial to the argument the Latin text of the 1558 Basle edition will appear in the notes.

86. To The Right Honorable/and Vvorthy Sir Anthony Cooke/Knight, Peter Martir Vermilius of Florence, Professor of Divinitie In The Schole of/Tigure, Vvisheth Health.

87. Ibid., sig. A3[r].

88. Loc. cit. This Homeric reference together with the Biblical Solomon is interesting. Alcinoüs was the ruler of the Phaeaces to whom Odysseus came in his wandering. ODYSSEY VI-VIII. Alcinoüs had the fairest of orchards on the island of Scheria.

89. Ibid., sig. A4[r].

90. Loc. cit.

91. Prefatory letter to Cooke, sig. A5[r-v].

92. T. H. L. Parker, Calvin's New Testament Commentaries, pp. 26-48. See Rolf Schafer, "Melanchthons Hermeneutik im Romerbrief-Kommentar von 1532," Z. T. K. 60 (1963), 216-217.

93. C. R. I:114.

94. C. R. XX: 228–229.

95. C. R. XV: 498.

96. C. R. XV: 503. Bucer quotes this in his 1536 Romans with approval. See section nine translated by David Wright, Common Places of Martin Bucer, p. 172 and following. Bucer's appeal to Melanchthon also appears in the structure of this section such as the comment on the authority of the Church. Martyr's use of Chrysostom in particular goes beyond Bucer's commentary.

97. C. R. XV: 519.

98. Romanos (1558), f. 99.

98a. Reference to Bullinger provided by T. H. L. Parker, Calvin's New Testament Commentaries, p. 42. For Martyr's comments see Romanos (1558), fols. 33–35.

99. Prefatory letter to Cooke, sig. B3^v.

100. Romanes (1568), p. 8^r.

101. Loc. cit.

102. Ibid., p. 8^v.

103. Ibid., pp. 384^v–386^v. We shall discuss Martyr's sources for this information in chapter eight.

104. Ibid., p. 3^r.

105. Gorham, op. cit., pp. 168–175. Bucer's account is in Scripta Anglicana, pp. 797–803.

106. Ibid., p. 172.

107. Romanes (1568), p. 5^v.

108. Iohannes Andreas Quenstedt, Dialogus De Patris Illustrium Doctrina et Scriptis Virorum, p. 311.

109. Romanes (1568), p. 15^r.

110. Loc. cit.

111. Ibid., p. 59^v.

112. Ibid., p. 60^r.

113. <u>Ibid</u>., p. 61^r.

114. <u>Ibid</u>., p. 63^v. "Nihil, inquiens, facimus, non rependimus vices, sola fide iustificamur dono Dei." fol. 85. Same text in third edition (1560), p. 191.

115. <u>Ibid</u>., p. 62^v.

116. <u>Ibid</u>., p. 63^v.

117. <u>Romanos</u> (1558), fol. 105.

118. <u>Romanes</u> (1568), pp. 79^r-80^r.

119. <u>Ibid</u>., p. 80^r.

120. <u>Loc</u>. <u>cit</u>.

121. <u>Ibid</u>., p. 92^v.

122. <u>Loc</u>. <u>cit</u>.

123. <u>Ibid</u>., p. 95^v.

124. <u>Ibid</u>., p. 101^r.

125. <u>Ibid</u>., p. 103^r.

126. <u>Ibid</u>., pp. 120^r-128^v.

127. <u>Ibid</u>., p. 104^v.

128. <u>Ibid</u>., p. 136^r.

129. <u>Ibid</u>., p. 140^r.

130. <u>Ibid</u>., p. 144^r.

131. <u>Ibid</u>., p. 159^v.

132. <u>Ibid</u>., p. 144^r.

133. <u>Ibid</u>., pp. 162^v-163^r.

134. <u>Ibid</u>., p. 192^r.

135. <u>Loc</u>. <u>cit</u>.

136. <u>Ibid</u>., p. 200^v.

137. Ibid., p. 220^r.

138. Ibid., p. 232^r.

139. Ibid., p. 235^r.

140. J. C. McLelland, "The Reformed Doctrine of Predestination according to Peter Martyr," S. J. T., VIII (1955), 259. Romanos (1558), f. 355. The phrase begins, "Hic ego non pugno: quamvis cum id concedo, vere asseram cum sacra scriptura . . ."

141. Loc. cit.

142. Ibid., p. 262.

143. Romanos (1558), f. 431.

144. McLelland, op. cit., p. 265. Romanos (1558), fol. 441. Martyr uses moderatione which here I would translate "restraint."

145. Romanes (1568), p. 236^{r-v}.

146. Ibid., p. 324^v.

147. Ibid., p. 322^v.

148. Loc. cit.

149. Ibid., p. 324^{r-v}. Iain Murray, The Puritan Hope, pp. 41–45, points to the influence of Martyr's argument in chapter 11 on seventeenth century speculation about conversion of the Jews.

150. Ibid., p. 392^v.

151. Henry Jenkyns, The Remains of Thomas Cranmer, D. D. Archbishop of Canterbury (1833), II, p. 121. Jenkyns observes that Stephen Gardiner in his letters to Somerset assigns the Homily of Salvation to Cranmer. The homilies were first printed on July 31, 1547. Inivncci/ons geue by the moste ex/cellent prince, Edward the/sixte, by the grace of God,/kyng of England, Frauce/and Ireland: defender of/the faythe, and in earthe/under Christ, of the chur=/che of Englande and of/Ireland the supreme/hedde: To all and/singuler his lo=/uyng subiec=/tes, aswell/of the/Clergie, as of the/Laietie. (London: Rychard Grafton, M.D. XLVII). The colophon dates the printing at the end of July, before Martyr and Ochino arrived in England.

152. Romanes (1568), pp. 384^v-386^v and 387^v-388^r.

153. Ibid., pp. 392^v-403^r.

154. Ibid., pp. 403^v-410^r.

155. Ibid., p. 410^r. This list is identical to that on p. 1324 of the third edition (1560).

156. Jenkyns, op. cit., pp. 121-137.

157. John Strype, Ecclesiastical Memorials (1816), II, p. 334.

158. See J. R. Gilmont, "Una pseudonyme de Pierre Alexandre, Simon Alexius," S. H.P. B. ser. 5, livre 6 (1970), 179-188. I am grateful to M. Alain Dufour for calling this article to my attention.

159. Robert Peters, "Who compiled the Sixteenth-Century Patristic Handbook Unio Dissidentium?," S. C. H. II, p. 250, and Robert Peters, "The Use of the Fathers in the Reformation Handbook Unio Dissidentium," S. P. 9 (1966), 570-577.

160. Les/Conseils et Ad/vis De Plvsievrs Ex/cellens & suans personnages, sur le faict/des Temporiseurs. Et comment le fidele/se doit maintenir entre les Papistes. Item/vne Epistre Consola/taire aux freres & membres de l'eglise de Ie/sus Christ, qui fut en Angleterre durant le/regne du bon Roy Edourd: escrite par M./Pierre Alex. (Geneva/: Chez Iean Crespin M. D. LVI). See Osw. Michotte, Un reformateur. Pierre Alexandre, These Neufchatel, 1913 (129 p.). The letter is not mentioned by Rod. Reuss, Notes pour servir a l'histoire de l'eglise de Strasbourg (Paris: 1880), 37-50.

161. Romanes (1568), p. 407^v.

162. Ibid., p. 406^r. Bede's New Testament commentaries were first printed at Paris in 1521. Cornelius was the subject of discussion with Bucer in 1550. See above, note 106 in situ.

163. Martyr does not identify these sources in his printed response.

164. "Docent per solam fidem, a Deo, in Christo saluatore, redemptorecq nostro, omnem iustitiam, & salutem mere gratis, expectare nos oportere, & derto accipere." Pigge, De Fide Operibus. (op.cit.), p. XLVIII^r.

165. Romanes (1568), p. 393^r.

166. Ibid., p. 396^r.

167. Ibid., pp. 396^r-399^v.

168. Ibid., p. 397^r.

169. Loc. cit.

170. Ibid., p. 412^r.

171. Ibid., p. 421^v.

172. Ibid., p. 422^r.

173. "Cum uero in ea schola philosophicam doceat Conradus Gesnerus uir (ut omnes norunt) in omnia philosophia & arte Medica exercitatissimus." Preface to Ethics (1563).

174. On the wider background see the fundamental study by Neal W. Gilbert, "The influence of Humanism on Methodology in the Various Subjects of the University Curriculum," Renaissance Concepts of Method.

175. "Omnis nostra noticia vel est reuelata vel acquisita: in primo membro Theologia, in altero Philosophia." Ethics (1563), p.1.

176. Ibid., p. 7. "Primum partiar propositum Aristotelis textum: secundo scopum & propositionem loci assumpti exponam cum eius probatione: tertio sensum & verba excutiam, quae visa fuerint expositione indigere: quarto quae dubia fuerint ostendam: & ad extremum pro locis communibus admonebo quid cum diuinis literis, quae allata fuerint, vel consentiant vel dissentiant." The term 'scopus' is a technical one used by Aristotelian commentators such as Elias. See Richard Walzer, "Zur Traditionsgeschichte der Aristotelischen Poetik," Greek Into Arabic, p. 134.

177. Ibid., p. 8. "Ita Paulus in epistolis demonstrat: prius enim tractat dogmata, postea descedit ad morum instructionem & ad uitam componendam." Compare above, note 13 where Martyr used a similar method in his sermon.

178. John Ponet, A Short Catechism (1865), p. 8.

PART THREE: THE CHRISTIAN SCHOLAR
(1553/62)

I am of your judgement, that no man alive is more fit than Peter
Martyr for such a conference /Colloquy of Poissy, 1561/; and my
lord of Canterbury, I trust, will communicate his opinion herewith
. . . . for he is better seen in old doctors, councils, and
ecclesiastical histories than any Romish doctor of cristendom: he
is also himself well seen in the civil and canon laws.

Edmund Grindal to Sir William Cecil

CHAPTER VIII

MARTYR'S LIBRARY AND LECTURES (1553/62)

A SCHOLAR'S TOOLS

A glance at Peter Martyr's commentaries on I *Corinthians* and
Romans has shown the care with which Martyr examined patristic literature. Three examples will reflect how Martyr used his sources and
obtained his data. Prior to his flight from Italy Martyr visited
libraries to copy down unpublished manuscripts. The letter to Conrad
Hubert about the Theodosian letters is one illustration of this scholarly interest; a second is Cranmer's use of Chrysostom's Ad *Caesarium*
Monachum to attack transubstantiation. Martyr brought a copy of it
with him to England.[1] A third example would be Martyr's use of secular and sacred authorities in the commentary on *Judges* (1561). Martyr
owned copies of Bomberg's *Hebrew Bible* and knew the Medieval Rabbi
David Kimhi as a commentator.

At *Judges* (1:16) Martyr gave his readers information on the city
of Palms and the Kenites. Some commentators thought the city was
Engaddi /Engedi/ on the western shores of the Dead Sea where the
scented henna blossoms grew. Martyr thought most commentators meant
Jericho, citing Josephus and the *Paraphrastes Chaldaicus* as well as
Deuteronomy (34:3) for his authorities. Strabo testified that Jericho
possessed a grove of Palms one hundred furlongs in length; Kimhi
thought Jericho had been conquered after Hebron and Debir while Jerome
confirmed that the Kenite in *Judges* (1:16) was the father-in-law of
Moses.[2] Martyr then described what such peregrinations had meant for

the ancients and his contemporaries.

The reference to *Paraphrastes Chaldaicus* would be to the Aramaic paraphrase of *Judges* known as the *Targum of Jonathan*. Kimhi commented in Hebrew which Martyr also read. Whether Martyr read Aramaic is of great interest for if so it would set Martyr among a select group of Renaissance Christian Hebraists. Martyr owned Sebastian Münster's *Chaldaean Dictionary* of 1527.[3] Münster issued in 1527 the first Aramaic grammar written by a Christian. Martyr's friend Paul Fagius at Strasbourg knew Aramaic because he translated the *Targum of Onkelos* on the Pentateuch. Münster's *Chaldaica Grammatica* was based on the earliest surviving Aramaic dictionary, the *Arukh* by Nathan Ben Jehiel, head of the yeshiva of Rome. The *Arukh* is a comparative dictionary of mishnaic Hebrew, Galilean Aramaic, Babylonian Aramaic and the Aramaic of Onkelos. Modern dictionaries find it a pattern for citation of some excellent readings from Babylonian geonic sources.[4] Such a blending of Rabbinic, classical and patristic sources together with the context from other portions of the Old Testament left his auditors and readers convinced that Martyr was a diligent commentator.

Martyr refused to accept the famous 'Johannine Comma' about the three heavenly witnesses in I *John* (5:7), for in I *Corinthians* (1551) Martyr observed that Jerome omitted the text in his Latin translation even though he maintained it in the Greek. Cyril, Augustine and Bede omitted it though Erasmus found it in a British codex and a Spanish manuscript. Martyr could not then from these observations use this text to construct a proper argument.[5]

Martyr's interest in the history of the early church led him to choose a wide range of texts to support his views in the commentaries. For example the Greek text of Theodoret's *Ecclesiastical History* (1:7) is given on the use of scripture at Nicaea.

> And the Emperor Constantine in the Nicene Synod which Theodoret has in his history, book one, chapter seven, required that the Bishops when they turned to controversy must define (issues) out of the Old and New Testaments.[6]

Another often quoted work was Socrates' *Tripartite History*. Martyr cited the example of Spyridon, Bishop of Tremithus in Cyprus (d.c. 348) from this objective if dull text.[7] In the *Romans* commentary Martyr chose Socrates as his source for a list of historical data on images, a passage which illustrates Martyr's range in reading.[8] In two other places Martyr cited from historical sources: Paphnutius on the Nicene Synod,[9] and "Zacharias Papa ut in quarto sententiarum scribitur" on the question of adultery.[10] This Pope from 741-752 held a synod at Rome in 743. I have not been able to identify these references.

When Martyr traveled to England he purchased a set of Epiphanius. A check of the I *Corinthian* commentary shows twelve separate references to this important writer. Pierre Fraenkel describes the significance of Epiphanius' *Panarion* for Philip Melanchthon.[11] Jerome translated some of the letters of this monk (d.403) who had sought to counter the influence of Origen. His work against heresies was important for Martyr since it was the most extensive ancient account. Fraenkel claims that Epiphanius attributed ancient errors to excessive zeal and cataloged them because the Nicene formula opposed them.[12]

The range of citations to Epiphanius in I *Corinthians* (1551) is impressive though Martyr may well have seen Peter Alexander's folio index on Epiphanius. The citations are to the *Raziae historia, Aduersus Aerium, Aduersus Arrian, Contra Semiarrios, In Doctrina Compendiaria, De ponderibus & mensuris, On Heresies, Contra Valesios haereticos, Against Heresies, Against the Anchorites* (twice) and *On the Nicene Synod.*[13] One gains from all of the above why *Calvin* should say that Martyr left nothing to be desired when it came to patristic study, for the context in which Martyr used these quotations demonstrates his critical reading of the requisite text.

Peter Martyr gave his endorsement to three outstanding classical authors in the *Romans* commentary. Where St. Paul spoke of the natural order in chapter one Martyr selected three examples among those who best recognized nature's wonders. These were Aristotle, Plato and Galen.[14] The letter from John Warner on Bucer's illness and Simler's reference that Martyr discussed his fatal fever with the Zurich physicians document this reference to Galen as well as a reference to Galen's *De Usu et Partium* in I *Corinthians* (1551). A look at parts of his library extant in Geneva will explain to some extent how Martyr marked the volumes in his personal library. Polman observed that this kind of study was crucial to an understanding of the Protestant Reformation. Veluanus in his 1557 *Vom Nachtmal Christi Bericht Adami Christiani* employed the patristic citations used by Martyr and Bullinger[15] and the 1556 Genevan work of Jean Crespin under the title

L'estat de l'Eglise avec le discours des temps depuis les Apostres jusques au present cites from Martyr on pp. 141, 145 and 150 as historical argument.[16] There can be little doubt that Martyr's contemporaries were aware of his patristic learning. They could scarcely ignore this Christian scholar whose works penetrated to the core of the religious controversies in the mid-sixteenth century.

A SCHOLAR'S TOOLS

When Peter Martyr traveled from Strasbourg to Lambeth in 1547 John Abel submitted a bill of expenses for the purchase among other items of a set of Augustine, Cyprian and Epiphanius in Basle for Peter Martyr.[17] By 1572 the Genevan Academy purchased the bulk of Martyr's library.[18] Alexandre Ganoczy's study of the 1572 Academy catalogue assigns additional volumes to Peter Martyr than did Gardy.[19] An examination of the patristic volumes in the Genevan University Library assigned to Martyr by Gardy and Ganoczy shows that in some cases the identification cannot be positive. Ganoczy assigns an index in Vadian to Martyr even though Martyr never used its orthography for the sibilant found in that index. The temptation is strong to say that Martyr indexed this *In Christo naturas diversas* which seems a likely source for Martyr's response to the Polish nobility against Stancaro in 1556.[20] Indeed observation based on an analysis of Martyr's hand may be erroneous since the index could have been made by a friend. In that case it is Martyr's source for the 1556 letter and perhaps the *Dialogus De Utraque In Christo Natura* of 1561.

Ganoczy observes that Martyr's library can be divided into three categories based on the number of volumes from each which Martyr possessed. Primacy must go to the patristic works which are beautifully bound in contemporary Italian blind-stamped pigskin. Second in importance are the ancient Greek and Latin works, including a Greek Plato, Aristotle, Plutarch, Aristophanes, a Latin Plato, Demosthenes, Polybius, Sophocles, Pindar and Hesiod.[21] The third category is the number of works on biblical studies with a preponderance of Old Testament volumes[22] such as Musculus' and Calvin's 1554 commentaries on *Genesis*.[23] The latter must be the volume mentioned in Martyr's letter to Calvin of 6 September 1554.[24]

It seemed helpful to analyze the annotated sections in Martyr's patristic holdings because in many places the marginalia are either corrections of the printed text or a summary of the argument which then give one a glimpse into Martyr's mode of study. Such corrections can be observed in folio 137 of Martyr's copy of Justin Martyr.[25] For this reason it seems well to comment on the passages marked rather than only the notations. For example, one can see what interested Martyr most in the Greek edition of Basil when all the marginalia are in the letters of Basil to Libanius.[16] Of particular importance to Martyr was the letter on reading from folio 668. Such annotations may reflect Martyr's interest in effective communication of Holy Scriptures in works such as the *Exhortation For Young Men to Study the Holy Scriptures*, or *A Prayse of the Word of God*, or again an *Oration Concerning the Study of Divinity*.[27] Libanius' gift of eloquence impressed Martyr.

One very important source for Martyr appears to be the 1550

Greek and Latin edition of Gregory Nazianzus.[28] The annotations are

to the Latin translation. Martyr underlined and asterisked a passage

in the life of Gregory which reads in Musculus' translation.

> nihil enim tam est hominibus /sic/ iucundum, atque aliena
> loqui: & maxime, si uel beneuolentia quodam uel odio rapiantur.
> unde sit, ut ab illis ueritas frequenter occulatur.[29]

This marked passage provides a backdrop to Martyr's discussion of

these virtues in letters to Melanchthon and Calvin. Gregory's orations

have been numbered in Martyr's copy where oration seven seems espe-

cially significant for its relation to Martyr's views on godly living

and learning. Folio 35 is marked with notes at lines 4, 16, 37 and

45. Lines 45-46 read as follows: "in qua celebrantur uulnera, &

uincula, & tormenta, & ignis minae, & gladiorum acies, & bestiarum

ferocitas, & tenebrae . . ."[30] Martyr was impressed by this descrip-

tion of Gregory's brother Caesarius in argument with Julian the Apos-

tate:

> That noble man, fortified with the sign of Christ, and defending
> himself with His Mighty Word, entered the lists against an
> adversary experienced in arms and strong in his skill in argu-
> ment . . . . The judge on one side was Christ, arming the athlete
> with His own sufferings: . . . Didst thou not fear for Caesarius,
> lest aught unworthy of his zeal should befall him? Nay, be ye
> of good courage. For the victory is with Christ, who overcame
> the world.[31]

Gregory's *Oration on Athanasius* contains a note by Martyr which

reads, "Cardinalis Caraffa." This reference to the future Pope Paul

IV dates the note prior to Caraffa's 1555 elevation to the Papacy.

That the life of Athanasius is heavily annotated is not surprising

when on recalls the chequered career of this often exiled bishop and
theologian. The reference to Caraffa comes at the lines which read:
"et priusquam purgentur purgant. hieri sacrilegi, hodie sacerdotes
hieri sacroru expertes, hodie in sacres duces: ueteres in malitia,
at tenues in pietate."[32] Martyr read very carefully the epistles of
Gregory and especially one to Nectarius of Constantinople on the
Apollinarian controversy.[33]

Martyr used Cornarius' translation of Epiphanius' *Contra Octaginta
haeresos opus*. The *epistola scripta et epistola rescripta ad Acacium*
are heavily marked as though Martyr had proofread them. There are no
other marginalia in this volume. Martyr also seems to have read the
Compendia uera doctrina de fide catholicae & Apostolicae Ecclesiae
from the reference to this section in I *Corinthians* (1551).[34] An
important marginal note reads "Contra Nicodemitas."[35]

Martyr apparently made good use of Tertullian[36] in the Christological controversy with Stancaro and Brenz since he carefully marked
the passage on *John* (17) in *De Trinitate*,[37] the section on the predestination of Christ[38] and the final three pages of the tract.[39] In
addition Martyr carefully read the *Aduersus Praxean Liber*.[40] Such
background reading indicates something of those passages which Martyr
consulted when preparing his lectures and treatises.

One must not here use an *argumentum ex silentio* in noting that
Martyr marked Jerome's commentary on *Jeremiah* to Chapter (21)[41] and
Ezekiel[42] as well as *Zechariah*.[43] Perhaps this indicates his pre-
paratory reading for Old Testament lectures on the Prophets or even

sermons which are no longer extant. Martyr had cited Jerome's New
Testament commentaries in his own tractate *On Justification*[44] so that
for this reason the presence or absence of *marginalia* in Martyr's
personal library can not of itself be definitive for assessing his
theological development. On the other hand when Martyr annotated
Jerome's *De Laude Vitae Solitariae*[45] to Heliodorus and underlined the
De Vita Clericorum including the scholia, one sees with what care
Martyr examined certain ecclesiastical practices from which he dissented in the *De Votis Monasticis* against Richard Smith. Martyr also
carefully marked the *Adversus Pelagianos*.[46]

On occasion Martyr approved of specific passages in his reading
where the clearest example seems to be Cyprian's *Sermo De Coena Domini
et Prima Institutione consummantis omnia sacramenta*.[47] From the
volume of notations underlining and summary one can see that this
sermon very early (1540 edition) influenced Martyr. One passage in
particular is approved by underlining. It reads as follows: "Haec
quoties agimus, non dentes ad mordendum acuimus, sed fide syncera
ponem sanctū frangimus & . . ."[48] Another complete work which Martyr
carefully marked is Basil's *Quod Deus non est Autor Malorum*.[49] Martyr
summarized Book IV of Basil's *Contra Apologeticum Eunomii* in the
margins as well as the letters on folios 655-755.[50]

Two summaries of Christian doctrine seem to have been important
sources for Martyr's thought: Damascene's *De Fide Orthodoxa*, where
at folio 32 Martyr underlined a Greek passage and commented on
substantia[51] and the contemporary confession by Stanislaus Hosius.

Martyr appended a note to a lengthy passage that Hosius "contra nostra
dogmata sit statunt . . ."[52] This passage serves as a conclusion to
a brief survey of Martyr's patristic library and reading[53] since it
is likely a volume sent to Martyr from Poland by Utenhove or Lismanini.
Small wonder Thomas Martin placed Martyr with Oecolampadius in attacking the protestant scholar's hierarchy. Would Jerome if he lived in
Martin's time: "have spoken lesse of Oecolampadius, Capito, Bucer,
Munster, Peter Martyr, the founders of our newe fonde religion, who
agreing with their master Luther both in life and doctrine, became
all of friers or monkes maried men . . . ."[54]

    SECOND EXILE: STRASBOURG (1553/56)

    Peter Martyr needed the calm of Zurich to continue what he felt
to be his life's work. In an unpublished letter to Albert Hardenberg
one can read his rage over the inflexible Saxon theologians. Martyr
rested his case on his own 1549 Oxford Disputation and Calvin's 1555
consensuses.His comment bears repeating.

> But the Saxons are so inflexible, I will not say anything more
> severe, that they endure hearing no one except one who speaks
> most stupidly, and they want men to swear, not so much by their
> own opinions, as by phrases and words. Now, as you rightly say,
> all these things incline towards papistry . . . Let them cleave
> the Church in sunder and tear it to pieces as they will, there
> will remain, whether they like it or not, those who are of God.[55]

    On 7 July 1556 Martyr told John Calvin that the Magistrates of
Strasbourg were not willing to permit open disputation about the
Eucharist in the schools.[56] This action disturbed Martyr since it
prohibited him from discussion while his opponents were able to raise
the issue in the schools. Martyr's letter to Wolfgang Musculus

gives this as a reason for Martyr's dissaffection at Strasbourg.[57]

The chronicler John Sleidan described Martyr's transition to Zurich

where he could exercise to the fullest his calling as a Scholar of

Christ.

> Peter Martyr, a florentine of whome we have spoken before, what
> tyme the dissention about the Lordes supper was kindled againe,
> & he in certen bokes was touched by name, wēt from Strasburg to
> Zurich, that he might handle that matter frely both in teaching
> and writing. That time Conrade Pellicane died at Zurich: And
> therfore the Senate being requested by the ministers of the
> churche, wryting their letters to the Senate of Strasburg,
> praye earnestly that he might be sent them. So he departeth at
> the third Ides of July not without the sighing and grief of
> many, whiche loved him for his incomparable learning, his moste
> exacte iudgement, his great gentlenes and modestie and his
> other vertues.[58]

This section which follows will describe Martyr's activity as a

Christian scholar. An examination of his relationship to Bullinger

and Calvin is involved in such a description, for Martyr not only

continued his scholarly activities while in Zurich (1556-1562), but

also participated in the growing consensus of Reformed Theology.

One's task is not to describe that influence beyond Martyr's lifetime

though it is of interest to note the attack on Calvinism by Cornelius

Schulting in 1602. In five books Schulting examined Calvin's *Insti-

tutes of the Christian Religion* and Peter Martyr's *Loci Communes*.[59]

One further example of Martyr's identity with pejorative Cal-

vinism is the sermon preached ·by William Barrett of Caius College

Cambridge. In his sermon of 1595 Barrett attacked predestination

for which he was forced to recant at Great St. Mary's. As a result

of Barrett's attack the Articles of Lambeth were framed on 20 November

1595 which repudiated Barrett for asserting among other heresies,
viz.,

> IX. Calvin, Beza, Luther, P. Martyr, and Junius, were false
> guides. And he mervailed that we taught not so; and bewailed
> the iniquity of our time, that we should be so misled by such
> young teachers.[60]

Through a careful study of Martyr's correspondence with Bullinger
and Calvin one can see the stature which Peter Martyr had among these
leaders of Reformed Theology.[61] It would be wrong to label him
Zwinglian, and premature to mark Martyr as a Calvinist.

Heinrich Bullinger in his letters and *Diary* gave some detailed
information about Peter Martyr's arrival in Zurich during July of
1556. From this information one can see that Martyr quickly returned
to his studies after he settled in Zurich. Bullinger's *Diary* for
1556 adds to Simler's account.

> In the year of the Lord 1556 April 30. Peter Martyr is received
> by the Senate; a letter of dismissal is sent from Strasbourg.
> He came on July 17, lodging with me. On July 20 he was pre-
> sented to the Senate and on the 28th he took the oath. He first
> profited us on August 24 when he began to lecture on I Samuel.[62]

Bullinger went on to say that Martyr left his house on 6 August and
began lectures on 24 August.[63] Martyr took up residence across the
square from the Grossmünster, a stone's throw from Bullinger's
dwelling. Wolfgang Musculus wrote Bullinger on 25 August 1556 to
console him on the death of Pellican and to endorse Martyr and Ochino
as "equally most learned and faithful athletes of Christ."[63a]

Martyr's lectures are models of clarity which even his opponents
recognized. Cornelius Schulting gave this reason for singling out

Martyr's *Loci Communes* to compare with *The Institutes* of John Calvin.
Martyr's greater clarity contrasts with the many obscure and intri-
cate passages in the *Institutes*.[64] Then, too, Schulting inquired
whether Calvin changed his *Institutes* as he became acquainted with
Martyr, "an Caluinus sit sua mutuatus magna ex parte a Petre Martyre
. . . ."[65] In reading Schulting one notices that Calvin's text is
usually under discussion. Schulting apparently assumes without documentation that Martyr influenced Calvin. A careful rereading of
their correspondence will show the equanimity shared by these two
theologians after 1555.[66] A comparison of Calvin's *Institutes* and
Martyr's *Una Semplice Dichiaratione* convinces one that Schulting has
made a telling point in his comparison of Martyr and Calvin. Martyr
was held in great esteem by his own contemporaries as a clear exponent
of Reformed Theology. It is quite possible that Calvin borrowed from
Martyr for the 1559 edition of the *Institutes*.

One event which demonstrates Martyr's wider influence in Europe
was the synod in Pinczow which on 7 August 1559 judged the doctrine
of Francesco Stancaro. In a second meeting of 19 August 1559 the
synod used the writings of Martyr, the Lausanners and Zurichers.[67]
Heinrich Bullinger on 23 August 1556 (the day before Martyr resumed
lectures in Zurich) described his two companions Bibliander and Martyr
as incomparable in their understanding of history and clear in their
narration of the Prophets. Martyr was noted for his rare knowledge
of languages and eloquence in teaching[68] which after one discounts
the hyperbole of a friend is an endorsement that endures under

scrutiny. Bullinger's judgment gains further credence as one turns
to study some special themes in Martyr's Old Testament commentaries.

ROMANS (13) AND SECULAR MAGISTRATES

In analysing Martyr's commentaries on *Kings* and *Judges* it seems
useful to restrict attention to a few themes which will illustrate
Martyr's involvement in his contemporary world. Already it is clear
that Martyr abhored turmoil in theological dispute or political
activity. His notes for Cranmer's sermons against the Devonshire
Rebels of 1549 mingle themes of stability and calm reason. In his
Cogitationes on the 1549 Rebellion Martyr concluded with a threefold
analysis of its origin. First came religious change and then oppression of the poor. Finally robust men grew weary of true leisure.[69]
Martyr returned to the questions of heresy and rebellion in his
comments on *Romans* (13) where he argued from efficient causes and the
end or purpose of God's command in *Romans* (13:1-2) that every person
must be subject to the magistrate for sake of conscience. It was not
lawful for private men to kill a tyrant.

> Wherefore seeing that euen in wicked Princes (Nero) shineth
> forth much good, it is very manifest, ẙ theyr power also is of
> God: neither is it lawfull for any priuate man to kill a tiranne:
> Dauid when he mought, yet notwithstanding would not kil Saule,
> although he used himself like a tyranne: yea rather he com-
> maunded that Amalechite to be slaine, which bosted that he had
> killed Saule: and he put them to death, also, which had slaine
>   baseth Saules sonne. And doubtles if it should be lawful
> for every man at his pleasure to destroy a tyranne, there would
> not want wicked men, which under the pretence of the condemning
> of tyranny, would doe violence unto godly Princes: and so should
> nothing be left holy and unviolated.[70]

On the other hand Martyr permitted inferior magistrates to put down superior powers.[71]

JUDGES AND SACRED HISTORY

Keeping to the sequence in which Martyr lectured on the substance of the text later published in his commentaries, one ought now to turn to the lectures on *Judges*. The prefatory letter is to the governors of the College of St. Thomas at Strasbourg and is dated 22 December 1560.[72] Martyr refers to Marbach by implication for his friend Zanchi was involved in a dispute on predestination as well as on the Eucharist.

> The cause of my departure I wyll not nowe speake of bicause it is to all men knowen well inough. Thus much onely wil I say, that I do both vehemently desyre, and also hope, that this stop or let may be taken away out of the field of the Lord.[73]

The translation "stop or let" does not do full justice to Martyr's term. 'Maceria' could mean either a wall (enclosure) or affliction. Affairs in Strasbourg in 1556 had been a hindrance to Martyr's work and in 1560 were still an affliction. The commentary is dedicated to the College because Martyr lectured there on *Judges*: "As I have taught it in your Schoole, I have determined to dedicate it to your name. . . ."[74] Proof that Martyr gave these lectures during 1554/56 can be seen from examining a 1555 English translation of Martyr's comments on *Judges* (1:36f.). McLelland pointed out that A *Treatise of the Cohabitacyon of the faithful with the vn-faithfull* (1555) was a translation of *An Christianis Liceat Cum Infidelibus Habitare* which appeared in the *Judges* (1561) commentary. Since these lectures were given while several Marian exiles were in Strasbourg, its translator is difficult to identify.

It is also of interest to see that sermon five in the Elizabethan
Book of Homilies (1563) is in part from Martyr's commentary on *Judges*.
These sermons were probably prepared by 1562. Sermon five is usually
assigned to James Pilkington (by Tomlinson) or to Edmund Grindal
(*Oxford Dictionary of the Christian Church*). Blench points out that
sermon five of the second *Book of Homilies* is a translation from the
Martyr's *Judges* (1561). See the "Homily against Gluttony and Drunk-
eness" in *Certain Sermons Appointed By The Queen's Majesty*.[75] St.
Johns and Trinity Colleges, Cambridge have copies of this second *Book
of Homilies* dated 1563. Sermon five based on Peter Martyr was one of
those read at every parish service in England if the priest had not
prepared his own homily. John Jewel seems to have prepared most of
these. Martyr's sermon was given official status as a homily because
it inculcates discipline as the third mark of a reformed church.

The scriptural references are noted in the margin as *Genesis* (19:
1-23), II *Samuel* (13:28,29), *Judith* (13:2,8) and I *Maccabees* (16:16)
from the *Apocrypha*, *Exodus* (32:6), I *Corinthians* (10:7), *Matthew* (14:
6-10), *Luke* (16:19-25), and *Ezekiel* (16:49).

> If God spared not his servant Lot, being otherwise a godly man,
> nephew unto Abraham, one that entertained the angels of God;
> what will he do to these beastly belly-slaves, which, void of
> all godliness or virtuous behaviour, not once, but continually
> day and night, give themselves wholly to bibbling and banqueting?
> But let us yet further behold the terrible examples of God's
> indignation against such as greedily follow their unsatiable
> lusts. Amnon the son of David, feasting himself with his brother
> Absalom, is cruelly murdered of his own brother. Holofernes, a
> valiant and mighty captain, being overwhelmed with wine, had his
> head stricken from his shoulders by that silly woman Judith.
> Simon the high priest, and his two sons, Mattathias and Judas,
> being entertained of Ptolemy the son of Abobus, who had before

married Simon's daughter, after much eating and drinking were traitorously murdered of their own kinsman. If the Israelites had not given themselves to belly-cheer, they had never so often fallen to idolatry. Neither would we at this day be so addict to superstition, were it not that we so much esteemed the filling of our bellies. The Israelites, when they served idols, *sate down to eat and drink, and rose again to play,* as the scripture reporteth; therefore seeking to serve their bellies, they forsook the service of the Lord their God. So are we drawn to consent unto wickedness, when our hearts are overwhelmed by drunkenness and feasting. So Herod setting his mind on banqueting, was content to grant, that the holy man of God, John Baptist, should be beheaded at the request of his whore's daughter. Had not the rich glutton been so greedily given to the pampering of his belly, he would never have been so unmerciful to the poor Lazarus, neither had he felt the torments of the unquenchable fire. What was the cause that God so horribly punished Sodom and Gomorrha? was it not their proud banqueting and continual idleness, which caused them to be so lewd of life, and so unmerciful towards the poor?[76]

In this sermon one should compare Martyr's comments on Alexander the

Great. *Of VVine and Droonkennesse* describes the famous leader as

follows:

Alexander of Macedonia, the conqueror of the world, was most shamefullie overcome with wine, and being droonke, slue Clytus his most valiant and faithfull friend, whose dilligence, industrie, labour, prudence, & strength, he had long time used in the wars, to his great commoditie. . . . . Wherefore Seneca, in his 84 epistle alreadie alledged, writeth, that Alexander, which had escaped so manie dangers, and ouercome the hardest enterprises, perished through intemperance of drinking, and by the fatall cup of Hercules.[77]

One can surmize that since Martyr's comments *On Wine and Inebriation*

were translated for the *Book of Homilies,* Martyr influenced another

official document of the English Church. One might observe that in

such a homily Martyr had the welfare of his students in mind as can

be seen from Sturm's admonitions in Strasbourg. Other factors than

theological lectures appealed to student interests, for they often

missed classes, fought, drank and carried out "nocturnal ambula-
tions."[78]

Martyr interpreted *Judges* as secular and sacred history in an
approach which VViganus Orthius endorsed in a letter to Zanchi of 13
July 1561.[79] Christ could not be excluded from this Old Testament
sacred history because it clearly preached Christ to its readers.[80]
Therefore special attention will be given to *De Seditione* after
Judges (12:6). Another reason for this selection is that this passage
seems not to be in any edition of the *Loci Communes* and also ante-
dates the text from I *Kings* (17) which is included in the *Loci Communes*. From *De Seditione* the narrative will turn to *De Dolo* and *De
Magistratu* before viewing Martyr's attitude toward scripture in this
commentary.

Martyr defined sedition in commenting on *Judges* (12:6) which
reads that when the fugitives of Ephraim could not pronounce "shibboleth" but only "sibboleth", the men of Gilead slew forty-two
thousand of them as rebels.

> In summe, the chiefly is sedicion, when by a tumult, they which
> are of one & the selfe same company and body, doo mete out of
> sundry partes, to fight together. This vice is in especial
> contrary to peace and civil concord. For in sedicion there are
> manye partes of one people, and the unitye of Citizens is
> troubled and endaungered.[81]

The benefits of God were twofold for Martyr. God gave to His own
people the revelation of the gospel, faith, justification and eternal
life. Temporal or common gifts were given to evil and good men
alike.[82] Consequently even an evil prince has been ordained of God

to put down sedition though such activity may end in civil war.

> Wherfore Iiphtah made ciuill war, but yet not vniust warre.
> For he had the sword, wherewith his duty was to punish not
> onely the enemies, but also the citizens, when they offend
> either against the lawes of man, or the lawes of God. God
> had geuen him the victory.[83]

Martyr would not permit every citizen to initiate civil war even

though lesser magistrates might do so. Private subjects ought not to

displace their Princes of either dignity or degree.[84] If a tyrant

invade a kingdom, he ought to be resisted; if on the other hand a

tyrant has gained control, it is not right for private men to put him

down.[85] Even though the ancient philosophers seem to approve of

tyrannicide, Martyr dissented from them because he desired to pre-

serve civic concord. No ruler would be safe if private citizens

tasted of royal blood! In *Judges* (3) after verse thirty Martyr

cautioned rebellious spirits that neither godliness nor the holy

scriptures could condone their actions.

> And although I know right well $\overset{e}{y}$ the Ethniks in the Old time
> appointed rewardes for such as killed Tirannes, yet I have
> answered that godlines and the holy scriptures do not allow
> the same. Undoubtedly if it be lawful for the people to put
> down kings that raigne uniustly, no kinges or Princes should at
> any time be in safety. For although they raygne iustly and
> holily, yet they cannot satisfy the people.[86]

Martyr gave a full explanation of this political conservatism in

defense of magistracy in the commentary on *Romans* (13). A magistrate

is

> . . . .A person elected by the institution of God, to kepe the
> lawes as touching outward discipline, in punishing trasgressors
> with punishment of the body, and to noorish and defend the
> good.[87]

Because in Martyr's view the office cannot be separated from the person, such views are important observations on the relationship of civic to religious duties. From a definition that princes are called pastors while magistrates are called fathers,[88] Martyr moved on to attack the papal plenitude of power developed by papal extremists like Pope Boniface VIII and the canon lawyers. The bull *Unam Sanctam* in particular came under Martyr's scrutiny for there could not be two swords in the church. Martyr argued that there could be no exemption from St. Paul's words in *Romans* (13) that every soul must be subject to the higher powers.

Martyr spoke not only of the *fact* of rebellion by using such examples as Solomon in I *Kings* (2) who deposed Abiathar and substituted Sadok as high priest; he also claimed the right of the magistrate so to act. By not excluding any private person from St. Paul's admonition, Martyr sought to reverse the role of the Pope and place him under the civic magistrate.

> But the Papistes, and they which will be called Ecclesiastical men, wyll not heare these things. For they cry that they are exempted from publike and ordinary powers, when as yet the Apostle vsed no exception when hee sayde: Let euerye soule be subject vnto the higher powers. And: He whiche resisteth the power resisteth the ordinance of God. Yea and Chrisostome also vpon that place saith that the Apostles, Prophetes, Euangelistes, and Moonkes, are compreheded vnder that lawe. And Chrisostome wrote these thinges of Ecclesiastical persons, when as yet he was Bishop of Constantinople, and there were then also Christian Emperours.[89]

Martyr had sixteenth century England in mind when he lectured in Strasbourg as well as fourth century Antioch and Constantinople. An unpublished letter of 10 December 1554 to Bullinger commented on the

above opinion[90] by noting Cardinal Pole's return as papal legate to
England. The papal desire to subject England to catholicism smacked
of political and religious conspiracy: "Cardinalis Polus est in
Anglia, et ibi legatum Antichristi agit."[91]

Martyr in *Judges* also added that ministers must be subject to
the magistrate concerning their religious function. Purity of teaching would be ensured by a magistracy which would regulate ecclesiastical function.[92] Small wonder Martyr lamented bitterly the death
of Edward VI and rejoiced at the coronation of Elizabeth. His work
on the *Ecclesiastical Laws* helps one to understand Martyr's similar
concerns in these lectures at Strasbourg on *Judges*. That this is in
fact what Martyr thought can be seen from the comments and prayer at
the end of *Judges* (21). Martyr's own time was beset by problems
similar to those in ancient days when Israel had no kings. Martyr
concluded:

> Wherefore let us praye vnto God our most louying father throughe
> his sonne Jesus Christ, that euen as from the begynning he hath
> holpen and noorished hys Churche in most great daungers, so also
> he would now keepe and defende it, when it is almoste ouerwhelmed
> with euils and calamityes. Let us desyre him also, that euen
> as he from tyme to tyme stirred up Judges and deliuerers vnto
> the Hebrues by whom he restored both liberty and health: and as
> in our tyme he hath geuen Heroicall and most excellent men,
> namely Luther, Zuinglius, Oecolampadius, Phillip Melanchton and
> suche like setters forth of the doctrine of the Gospel, so he
> would vouchsafe to go forewarde, and in conuenient tymes stirre
> vp certayn lyghtes, by whiche he may illustrate the mindes of
> hys elect, and kindle their heartes to keepe & amphlifie the
> Church of Christ, that at the lĕgth he may have it raygning
> with him in heauen, without spot or wrinkle. Amen.[93]

Peter Martyr's conception of biblical precedence for political
authority certainly affected John Jewel as he transcribed them for

Peter Martyr. Jewel's *Apology* with Martyr's letter of endorsement

pertains to many of these issues. Martyr claimed that the most dan-

gerous error of Antichrist was to assert that the church brings auth-

ority to the holy scriptures, when the contrary is true.

> For what soeuer authoritie or estimation cometh vnto the
> Churche, that all whole commeth of the worde of God. It
> is horrible to be heard, that the holy oracles and wordes of
> god should get their credite by men which are otherwise lyers.[94]

Because Martyr held that secular history could not be studied

apart from its sacred dimension, the political affairs of ancient

Israel during the period of the *Judges* seems to be an extended comment

on his beloved England without a protestant king. Did Martyr in his

letter to Bullinger forget that the catholic Mary who had gained

control was to be supported by private citizens? One must interject

an important qualification to Martyr's biblical interpretation of

political affairs thus far by pointing out that for Martyr rulers must

possess pure faith.

> Because Iudah and Simeon obtayned the victory according to
> the promyses of the oracle, it shalbe our part diligently to
> consider and marke, that they which worke with faith by the
> woorde of God do without doubt obtaine his promises.[95]

Though given as lectures in Strasbourg and delivered with the recent

religious and political turmoil of England in mind, Martyr needed the

comparative calm of Zurich to prepare his manuscript for publication.

As his prayer put it at the end of *Judges* (21): Martyr had been

given convenient times to illustrate the minds of the elect. In *A*

Treatise of the Cohabitacyon of the faithfull with the unfaithfull

of 1555, Martyr asserted the right of lesser magistrates to chall-

enge unfaithful rulers. Thomas Becon may have been the translator.

The new *Short Title Catalogue* entry 24673.5 gives W. Rihel, Strasbourg as the publisher.

> Now will I speake of those princes and Rulers/which ar under these chief Rulers. Whome I do deuide into two sortes. Eyther they are such as have Jurisdiction/oure/an auctoritie/which commeth to them by discent frō theyr Auncetours/ or els committed unto them of Emperours/Kinges/ and common welthes: Eyther els they have no Jurisdiction nor Rule ouer others . . . . . For it is not lawfull for them/no not at the commaundement of theyr hygher Princes and Lords/to compell those subiectes ouer whom they have rule/to receyve wicked Religion and supersticion/neyther to permitt the unfaithfull in the places where they do beare Rule/to have theyr ungodly Idolatries and supersticions.[96]

INFERIOR MAGISTRATES

The *Judges* locus is quite explicit about resistance against wicked rulers. Martyr made a distinction between sedition and the defense of true religion in which *Romans* (13) should encourage the lesser magistrates.

> All these sentences do confirme the courages of the inferiour powers, that they should be nothing afearde of the superiour power, when they in defending of religion obey it not.

> But thou wilt say: by what lawe doo inferiour Princes resist either the Emperour or Kynges, or elles publique wealthes, when as they defend the syncere religion and true faith? I aunswer by the law of the Emperour, or by the lawe of the king, or by the law of the publique wealth. For they are chosen of Emperours, Kings and publique wealthes, as helpers to rule, whereby Justice may more and more flourishe. And therefore were they ordeyned according to the office committed unto them, rightly, iustly, and godly to gouerne the publyke wealthe. Wherefore they doo according to their duty, when in cause of religion they resist the higher power. Neither can that superiour power iustly complain, if in that case the inferiour power fal from it.[97]

Professor Hans Baron has traced this right of the lesser magistrates to resist ungodly rulers to the biblical lectures of Martin

Bucer on *Matthew* (1530) and *Judges* (1554).[98] Baron is correct that

Bucer ventured his opposition to monarchy for religious reasons rather

than political ones. When the posthumous *Lectures on the Book of*

Judges appeared in Geneva in 1554, Calvin did seem to incorporate them

in his own *Sermons On Deuteronomy* of 1555/56. One should add that

many who heard Martyr lecture on *Judges* during 1553/56 would have

conveyed this information to their friends in Geneva. One might

query whether Calvin followed Martyr as much as Bucer in these matters.

It has recently been shown that Lutheran writers also supported

the right of lesser magistrates to resist higher authorities. Richard

Benert's 1967 dissertation traces the doctrine of lesser magistrates

to legal theories of the time. More recently Benert (1970) has shown

how Lutheran resistance theory followed three levels of argumentation

in which first out of love for God one could "stand armed on rare

occasions in history against the legions of Satan."[99] From the level

of natural law in the second place all men were obligated to defend

their families in times of danger. The lowest level was that of

positive law in which estates could resist when the Emperor violated

his contract with them. Feudal law then supported Lutherans who

appealed to the expected Church Council against Charles V as a judge.

Oliver Olsen concludes that Magdeburg was the center which trans-

mitted this resistance theory to the monarchomachs after 1572. Beza

and Hotman then follow a Lutheran theory of 1536 used at Magdeburg

over Calvin's practice.[100] The operative idea of Huguenot resistance

in this view comes from Lutheran sources rather than Bucer, Calvin or

Martyr. In 1550/51 these theories became reality as Magdeburg

fought for its life with its troops singing on the streets:

> Do as the Maccabees did
> And strive for God's word.
> Attack the land's betrayer;
> Avenge the gross murder
> Done in the German land.[101]

The *Magdeburg Confession* is the document which Beza expounded in

1574 as *De Jure Magistratuum in Subitos*.[102]

It seems clear that Martyr resisted sedition by private persons,

also rejected tyrannicide and warned students like Ponet and Sampson

against political rebellion. On the other hand Martyr made use of

the lesser magistrate doctrine which Bucer discussed in the *Matthew*

commentary. Martyr expanded this in his own commentary on *Judges*

at Strasbourg. Simler remarks that Martyr read Bucer on the Four

Gospels while in Naples, and Carnesecchi confessed to the Inquisition

that at Naples he also read Bucer on *Matthew*.[103] Naples would be the

terminus a quo.

In all of this one must keep in mind that Martyr placed reli-

gious ideals above political reality. When one reads this commentary

and rereads the letter to Queen Elizabeth three conclusions emerge

from all of the above. Private citizens have no recourse to rebell-

ion since St. Paul in *Romans* (13) forbade such action. Superior

powers are to be obeyed even if they are wicked men like Nero. Lesser

magistrates were to interfere with political authority if their right

of religious self-determination was attacked. This they did by

virtue of their office given them by the higher authority (Emperours and Kings) and the consent of the "publique wealthes." Martyr did

not teach religious toleration; he simply condemned tyrannicide and

public rebellion as contrary to God's explicit command in scrip-

ture.[104]

It is intriguing to notice this appearance in English trans-

lation of portions of Martyr's lectures five years before they were

published in Latin. It indicates that Martyr greatly influenced

men like Becon, Ponet and Sampson during the Marian exile.

A TREATISE OF THE COHABITACYON . . .

In 1555 politicians and theologians cast their nets for some

very strange schools of fish. That year saw the famous religious

peace of Augsburg in which the Lutherans achieved legal recognition.

As Professor Spitz observes somewhere, Suleiman was cast in the bibli-

cal role of King Cyrus of Persia whom God used to free Israel. The

Duke of Alva beseiged Rome in 1556, fighting Pope Paul IV while pay-

ing him reverence. Leopold Von Ranke mused over such strange bed-

fellows when he wrote:

> And who were those by whom the pope was defended against such
> good Catholics? The most effective among them were Germans,
> and Protestant to a man! They amused themselves with the
> saintly images on the highways, they laughed at the mass in the
> churches, were utterly regardless of the fast days, and did
> things innumerable, for which, at any other time, the pope
> would have punished them with a death. I even find that Carlo
> Caraffa established a very close intimacy with that great
> Protestant leader, the Margrave Albert of Brandenburg.
> (*History of the Popes*, trans. E. Foster: London, 1847,I,p.222)

Various sources were linked to political documents in this era

of the hot gospelers. The radical statements in John Ponet's

A *Shorte Treatise of Politike Power* (1556) and dedication of the
Geneva Bible of 1560 to Queen Elizabeth of England reflect different
answers to the critical question of the gospel's relation to political
action. Among the more curious matches was the publishing in 1555 of
Reginald Pole's *Defense of the Unity of the Church* under protestant
auspices in Strasbourg. Pier Paolo Vergerio edited Pole to replace
Stephen Gardiner's *De Vera Obedientia* against the supreme authority
of the Roman pontiff. Pole's defense of the papacy against Henry VIII
had first appeared in 1537/38 without Pole's permission. Since Pole
was in 1555 busy restoring catholicism in England it is surprising to
see this defense of the papacy printed together with comments of
Martin Luther, Flaccus Illyricus, Franciscus Vilierius, Philip
Melanchthon, John Calvin, Martin Bucer and Wolfgang Musculus - - all
directed against papal supremacy.[105]

Strasbourg in 1555 was the home of several exiles from England.
Many of these congregated with Peter Martyr, himself twice an exile,
from Lucca in Italy (1542) and from London in 1553. Martyr was in
Strasbourg for a second time after a previous five years there with
Martin Bucer (1542-1547) and six years with Thomas Cranmer in England
(1547-1553). Martyr's lectures on *Judges* were well attended by
Marian Exiles such as John Ponet, Thomas Sampson and John Jewel his
secretary and amanuensis. James Pilkington described Martyr's importance in a letter to Heinrich Bullinger of 27 June 1556. Pilkington
approved Martyr's move to Zurich as Conrad Pellican's successor.
Many in Strasbourg applauded Bullinger's invitation to Martyr since

they "are promising themselves great things concerning him, when
they perceive how great an accession he will be to the cause of
truth . . . ."[106]

Sir Richard Morison was also in Strasbourg during this time.
In 1551 he had preached an evangelical sermon before Charles V at
Brussels. Morison established contact with John Ponet late in 1554
and in the fall of 1555 when Sir John Cheke arrived the three directed their energies against Queen Mary Tudor. That Morison and Cheke
influenced Ponet can be seen in the similarity of Starkey's *A Dialogue between Cardinal Pole and Thomas Lupset* and John Ponet's
Politike Power.[107] Ponet coauthored with Thomas Sampson a lesser
known *Confession of the Banished Ministers* in 1554. Miss Garrett has
shown that Peter Martyr wrote to Thomas Sampson expressing his chagrin
at this work. Martyr could scare believe that such matters, i.e. of
political unrest, "were circulated in our name."[108]

Martyr's rejection of this *Confession* was based not only on his
prior experiences in England under the 1549 rebellion but also came
from his exegesis of *Romans* (13) given in Oxford during 1550 and
Judges at Strasbourg during 1555. Latin editions of *Judges* were
printed in 1561, 1565, 1571, and 1582 at Zurich and in 1609 at Heidelberg. In 1564 John Day published an English translation of *Judges*
in London. It is with great interest that a portion of Martyr's
lectures were translated and published at Strasbourg in 1555, six
years prior to the Latin *editio princeps* of 1561 in Zurich and nine
years before the whole appeared in English. One surmises that Martyr's

friends recognized the importance of his exegesis for their political

views. In any event it was published with a sermon of Heinrich Bull-

inger on the confessing of Christ. This work was titled, A *Treatise*

of the/Cohabitacyon of the/faithful with the vn=/faithfull (Stras-

bourg: J. Rihel (?), 1555).

Martyr supported princes who defended the gospel and urged lesser

magistrates to exercise their gospel duty to check chief princes who

had forfeited their genuine office. First of all, it was lawful for

the unfaithful to live with the faithful if the magistrates did not

force or compel the faithful to join with the unfaithful in worship.[109]

To enforce this would be the work of Antichrist. Secondly, the un-

faithful must not use their "supersticions and wicked idolatries which

are c̄otrarie vnto Godds worde."[110] Thirdly, "the princes and rulers

which do suffer these vnfaithfull m̄e to dwell Ī their dominions sholde

prouide that they mighte be taughte the truthe."[111] Finally Martyr

allowed that the magistrate should not infect the people committed to

their care.

> I say that when they have prouided that these vnfaithfull
> ha=ue bene taughte a good whyle and truly instructed/they must
> then enforce and compell them vnto tho=se holye and pure rytes
> and worshippinges of Godd, which are commaunded in the scrip-
> tures: for princes and rulers must not always/nor yet to longe
> suffer theyr cytyzens and subiectes/to lyue without exercise of
> godlynes and vertue. The ende of politicall gouernemente is/
> that the subiecte both shold lyue in felycytie/ād also in the
> practyse of god=lynes/because that godlines and the true wor-
> shipp of God is the chefest of all vertues.[112]

Toleration of the godly by the ungodly, elimination of idolatry,

teaching of the truth and enforcing of scriptural worship occur in

Martyr's lectures on *Judges* to the College of St. Thomas and the
Marian Exiles. Such exegesis served the existential needs of exiles
seeking to restore Jerusalem in England's green and pleasant land.
While in Zurich Martyr prepared a lengthy defense of the Eucharist
against Stephen Gardiner, Bishop of Winchester. Here Martyr told
why his exegesis was central to his Eucharistic views. Martyr was
serious that the stem and stern of salvation did not consist in
preoccupation with the external sacraments of the church.

> We acknowledge that the use of Sacraments hath some weight in
> promoting our salvation; - not "the chief." The Death of Christ,
> the Holy Spirit, our Calling, Faith, Justifiation, have much
> greater weight in promoting salvation than Sacraments have.
> But our INCONSTANT is such a subtle theologian, that he will
> have both the prow and the stern of our Salvation to be con-
> stituted in external things.[113]

When Peter Martyr refers to lesser magistrates it is clear that
he never sanctions indiscriminate use of force. When Sir William
Maitland quoted Luther, Melanchthon, Bucer, Musculus, and Calvin
against John Knox, he might also have included Peter Martyr. The
theology of dissent in Martyr's biblical writings does not allow for
use of the Magdeburg Monarchomachy. Peter Martyr taught that the
inferior magistrate was superior to every private person. On the
other hand, even though a tyrant should be resisted when he invades
a territory, once even a Nero is in power he was to be obeyed as the
instrument of God for conscience's sake. Martyr argued that the magistrate could and should resist ecclesiastical power though in no
case should private citizens or public magistrates invoke tyrannicide.
To flee from persecution was legitimate; to fight against flesh and

blood was seditious, as when the prophets in Ancient Israel worshipped Baal. False worship fosters sedition; the Gospel promotes unity.114

Professor Kingdon prints from the *Loci Communes* (1576), p. 1087 a passage which endorses the right of inferior magistrates to constrain the Prince by war if necessary that he may perform his covenant with the commonwealth. This appears to contradict what Martyr says elsewhere. Kingdon does not resolve the contradiction between this passage and Martyr's toleration of tyrants given on p. 1014. Martyr may be describing the situation permitted by the Imperial Constitution without condoning such action. Does the "Iis" refer only to "Electoribus Imperii" or also to "aliis Regnis"? It would seem to endorse the right of lesser magistrates to resist their Prince. One should check the context of that passage in the setting of Martyr's defense. In the 1549 *Sermon on Rebellion* which Cranmer preached from Martyr's Latin draft, sedition is defined as private persons rebelling against magistrates. That Martyr did not condone the views of Ponet andSampson may mean that he continued to advocate that God alone would punish the slack magistrate as the 1549 Sermon states. In religious matters inferior magistrates need not obey their Prince if he forces the mass on them. Martyr summed it all up in his definition of a valiant man who says "This I will not do," rather than, "This I will not suffer." The latter is mediocrity; the former, honesty and God's will. The ungodly magistrate is to be endured while the godly magistrate is to enforce true religion. Martyr may recognize the reverse axiom but seems reluctant to encourage revolt by the godly magistrate against the Prince. A tentative

solution may be that Martyr is rejecting pacifism of the Anabaptists

a la article 36 of the Forty-Two Articles rather than rationalizing

a wide use of the lesser magistrate political argument for rebellion.

Even Theodore Beza as late as 1560 in his *Confession of Faith* for-

bade inferior magistrates to resist by force of arms.

A distinction must be made based on the fact that this common-

place cited by Kingdon comes from the lectures on I *Corinthians*

(1551) at chapter five, given earlier at Oxford in 1548/49. It is

on excommunication. The passage on excommunication from folios 67^v-

68^r is identical in the 1551 commentary with the text accurately

given by Kingdon from the 1576 *Loci Communes*. One should turn else-

where to see Martyr's developed views on lesser magistrates.

Martyr did discuss the right of clergy to bear arms in his com-

ments on II *Kings* (II) of 1566, folio 280^{r-v}, sig. A_a4^{r-v}. "Whether

it be lawful for Ecclesiastical men to deale in material affaires."

> But why in times past both the principalitie and Priesthood
> were ioyned together, this may be declared the cause, namely
> that in those persons Christ was shadowed: to whom was due both
> the true Priesthood and soueraine kingdome. But after his
> comming upon the earth, we have no other Priest but himselfe,
> our onely mediatour and redeemer. Undoubtedly those ministers
> of the Church which are instituted by him, are appointed to
> preache the Gospell of the sonne of God, and to administer the
> sacraments. Wherefore it is meete that they shoulde abstaine
> (sic.) themselves from outward principalitie and administration
> of ciuill affaires, since they have bin so instructed by Christ.
> For he said vnto his Apostles, the Princes of the nations have
> dominion over them, but it shall not be so among you.[115]

Martyr then proceeded to discuss *Matthew* (20:25), *Luke* (12:13) and

II *Timothy* (2:4). The Gospel texts urged the disciples not to lord

it over one another as did the Gentiles, nor to be covetous in divid-
ing an inheritance. St. Paul warned Timothy that no soldier of
Christ should entangle himself with secula affairs. Martyr then
analyzed the right of ministers to bear arms. These conditions
raised by Martyr are crucial to an understanding of his political
views in the *Kings* lectures revised in 1562 and published in 1566.
Small wonder Queen Elizabeth was pleased by the above statement.

Martyr taught that Arms should not be "utterly taken away from
the Ministers of the Church: because so it may otherwise befall, as
it shall be lawful for them to exercise the same."
These conditions were as follows:

(1) If in a desert place murderers set on a minister and no
magistrate is present, violence for violence is a "blameless defense."

(2) If thieves come armed in the night season to a house and
are killed by the owner, God will not "decree an unjust thing."

(3) If there is a scarcity of men in a town in time of danger,
then ministers may defend the gates or walls.

(4) Ministers may serve as chaplains to preach where there is
greatest need of God's word. That word is to reprove the evil acts
dependent on war and to encourage the minds of the fighters.[116]

Thomas Erastus' 1589 *Explicatio Gravissimae Quaestiones Utrum
Excommunicatio* was published in London by Giacopc Castelvetro. On
page 182 of this Latin work Erastus quoted Peter Martyr from his
commentary on I *Samuel,* chapter eight. Erastus preferred against
Beza Martyr's view that ministers are subordinate to the civil

magistrate. One sees here how Martyr's political views influenced a
man whose name is synonymous for state supremacy over the church.[117]
That Martyr's views were otherwise understood in England a century
later can be seen in John Milton's use of the *Judges* commentary.

> Peter Martyr /in *Judges* (3)/ declares that those who choose a
> superior magistrate and on definite terms make him ruler of the
> State, as do today the Electors of the Empire, may, if the
> prince does not abide by his covenants and promises, treat him
> as an ordinary citizen and compel him by force to fulfill the
> conditions and covenants which he had promised, and that they
> may have recourse to arms if other means fail. To support this
> he cites a statement of Polydorus that our people sometimes
> compelled their kings to give an account of the misuse of public
> funds.[117a]

This Milton wrote in his *Common Place Book* found in 1874 which
is now British Museum MS. Add. 36354. The next entry is from Machiavelli's *Discorso* which urges tyrannicide.

Martyr himself supported the young Josiah-Edward VI, fled from
Jezebel-Mary Tudor and prayed for Deborah-Elizabeth I. The reason
for Martyr's support of the godly magistrate was his experience of a
godless hierarchy whose use of the Inquisition forced Martyr to
flight. When he fled in order to fight again, it was to join in a
logomachy rather than a monarchomachy – to rely on the Word of God
instead of the weapons of men. Martyr eagerly accepted magisterial
support of that Word. If on the other hand the magistrate rejected
the Word, Martyr would distinguish between toleration and persecution.
In no case would he tolerate idolatry.

Martyr felt that he could not accept in the papacy the false
presence of the Kingdom when its King was absent. The problem did not

seem to lie with either hierarchy or sacrament. Both needed to be
defined as vehicles which communicate Christ the Word. Like Martin
Luther before him Martyr would seek for Christ nowhere else than in
the poor tokens of the canonical scriptures and the hearing of the
Word alone. To remain free for that task Italy's greatest protestant
theologian left his native soil in 1542, Strasbourg in 1547, England
in 1553 and Strasbourg in 1556. Only in Zurich did Martyr find refuge from flight. There he was pursued by the writings of John
Brenz on Christ's two natures and Stancaro's attack on the Christology of his *Romans* commentary. Martyr never shrank from a defense
of the truth which would always be challenged in his lifetime. That
certainly was his own view of a Christian scholar's vocation.[118]

ZURICH SCHOLAR (1556/62): FORTITUDE AND FAITH

Questions of conscience in matters of faith exercised the Puritans
of New England in the seventeenth century. One work of 1648 in its
preface mentions Martyr's answer to the question of flight.

> It is a case of Conscience frequently put, and oft resolved by
> holy Bradford, Peter Martyr, Philpot and others, in Queen Maries
> bloody dayes, viz. Whether it was lawfull to flee out of the
> Land: To which their answer was, that if God gave a spirit of
> courage & willingness to glorify him by sufferings, they should
> stay; but if they found not such a spirit, they might lawfully
> fly . . .[119]

From the number of times that Martyr mentions exile, flight,
persecution and fortitude, one can assume that these matters exercised him greatly as he labored in one protestant centre after
another during his twenty years of exile from Italy. In the lectures
on I & II *Samuel* given from 24 August 1556 in Zurich, Martyr touched

again these questions of fortitude and constancy in faith, recalling

the letters to his friends in Lucca in which Martyr urged them to

endure what had come to pass. Behind these discussions was always

the cause celebree of Francesco Spira which had been popularized in

Curione's (?) 1550 volume[120] and mentioned by Sleidan in his *Chron-*

icle.[121] To continue a thematic approach, one should analyze Martyr's

treatise *On Fortitude* found in II *Samuel* (10:12). A comparison of

this with the well known *De Cruce*[122] will enable one to see Martyr's

response to this question of conscience. This theme of constancy in

the lectures on *Samuel* marks a transition from the question of rebell-

ion in the commentary on *Judges* to the nature of schism in the com-

mentary on *Kings*. "Fortitude therefore is an habit of our mind,

whereby (according to right reason for iustiæ and honestie sake) we

hold a meane betweene feare and boldnes."[123]

Such a mean between fear and boldness explains Peter Martyr's

preoccupation with these questions; for quite rightly he felt that

fear could vitiate faith, but that boldness ought to be tempered by

reason.

> Now then we must thus order the matter, that a ualiant man is
> bold, but yet with reason; namelie, when it behooueth him, and
> when reason beareth rule ouer the feare that is in him. But he
> is a rash fellowe, which is bold to doo anie thing rashlie: for
> he putteth forward himselfe to perils, but without reason: in
> deed he hath not set aside all feare, but the greatest part he
> hath.[124]

The overcoming of fear is the crux of fortitude, though this conquest

of fear must be a matter of choice. If one is shipwrecked, Martyr

reasoned, such disaster could be suffered patiently even though that

kind of endurance was not fortitude, "for these things are not taken
upon us by choise."[125] Fortitude was rather more difficult than
endurance because it suffered danger voluntarily. One can not help
but feel that here Peter Martyr added another dimension to his earlier
exegesis of *Matthew* (10:13) in the letter *De Fuga in Persecutione*, a
dimension of choice which enabled him to determine when to exercise
fortitude and when to avoid rash action. John Calvin had written a
similar letter on flight in 1537.[126] Martyr might have seen this
famous letter while in Strasbourg with Bucer late in 1542, though
Calvin discussed idolatry and persecution rather than flight. Martyr
turned to Plutarch and Menander the poet to define his own view of
fortitude. The following selection is integral to one's understanding
of Peter Martyr's peregrinations from 1542-1562.

> It is not (saith he) the part of a ualiant man, to saie, This
> I will not suffer; but, This I will not do. For the other thing
> .s not put in our power. Wherfore the subiect of fortitude, is
> that part of the mind, wherein is conuersant, feare, and boldnes.
> The obiect which it hath respect unto, is perill. And these two
> belong unto the matter. The forme is mediocritie. The end is
> honestie and goodnesse, and the will of God.[127]

Martyr's treatise *De Cruce* continues his theme of voluntary
exile as a token of a godly life and obedience to the will of God.[128]
Patience and moderation prepare the mind for better things, not as
rules in a monastery, but with the intent to help one's neighbor.
This common place from I *Corinthians* (1551) fits well between the one
on fortitude from II *Samuel* and on flight from *Genesis*. Martyr's
definition of patience depended on St. Paul's words to the Corinthian
Church that one carries in his body the death of Christ to make known

His life /II Corinthians (4:10)/.

> And to speake in few words, the crosse is no other thing but
> aduersities, heauie haps, temptations, and sorrowes, as well
> of the mind, as of the body; the which are laid upon us by
> God, for the glorie of his owne name, and for our saluation.[129]

Martyr followed Chrysostom's comments on II Timothy (2:11): "If we
die togither with him, we shall reigne togither with him." Chrysostom added that since God freely gives many things, surely after many
sorrows and calamities God will yet provide excellent gifts for
those that believe in Him.[130]

Martyr knew Conrad Gesner in Zurich whose bibliographical and
patristic expertise matched his fame as a naturalist. It is worth
noting and commenting here on Gesner's advice to a friend on this
subject of consistency in faith. This document is remarkable for
its candor about the nature of faith and for its selfcritique of
protestant exegesis. That Gesner had a concern for religious questions and a competence to analyze them has already been noted. Less
well known are his own religious writings. Gesner wrote after
Martyr's death urging Zanchi to fill Martyr's position in Zurich.[131]
Gesner's letter to James Dalechamp[132] is dated 8 January 1562. He
gave an analysis of the religious controversy and a solution which
would enable Dalechamp to avoid despair and apostasy. The themes
are similar to those developed in Martyr's commentaries where the
point of departure is Christ's advice to seek the Reign of God and
all else will be added to those who do that first.[133]

The chief proponent of earthly power and honour for Gesner was

the Roman Pontif, whose activities earn him the title of Antichrist![134]
Dalechamp may dispute this designation, though Gesner reminded him
that the chief sign of Antichrist was "to usurp what is of God and
Christ - to condone human sins . . ."[135] Prayer to the Lord God
would enable one to understand that He has given all honor and glory
to Christ who is the way to truth and life.[136] The imperfect decrees
of the Fathers, Councils and Popes are no consolation for they are
not sufficiently true. The article of faith called the Symbol of the
Apostles is defective as a guide to salvation.[137] Gesner concluded
that mortals need to depend on other aids than post-apostolic and
papal accretions to divine literature. Gesner on the basis of that
evidence urged Dalechamp to depend on scripture and prayer.[138]
Gesner in this letter went on to discuss the psychological and physio-
logical concomitants of abandonment to Christ in prayer. Dalechamp
ought not to forget the power of tears!

A remarkable passage follows Gesner's advice on prayer. He
reminded Dalechamp not to rely on Calvin, Luther, Viret and others
who had recently written on the sacred scriptures.[139] Gesner made
a simple admission: "I see that those are human and able to err."[140]
One ought to depend first on the ancient Old Testament as an unwavering witness to the truth[141] and in addition to those hoary writings
Gesner would send his friend to the New Testament whose purpose was
to teach about the Patriarchs, Prophets, Apostles and Christ himself.[142] The Spirit of Christ could illumine Dalechamp's mind if he
would pore over the prayers, precepts and difficult passages in

scripture. The scriptures contained for Gesner and his friends who
shared such views all things necessary for salvation. In this way
they were to be taught by God who desired men to love Him.[143]

A theme close to Martyr's concept of fortitude may be found in
this letter: Christ alone gives eternal life. Gesner urged Dalechamp to know Christ in whom alone there was salvation. The Holy
Spirit would fan that piety which remained into a flame of grace
despite Dalechamp's despair.[144] "Sequere, sequere, Christus te vocat
ad tuam felicitatem et suam gloriam."[145] Conrad Gesner as the greatest bibliographer of the sixteenth century was well versed in patristic and other theological literature. It is conceivable that Peter
Martyr and scholars who visited Zurich and signed his *Liber Amicorum*
discussed similar themes with Gesner as well as joining him in weekly
ascent of Swiss mountain peaks.

This letter enables one to penetrate behind the scenes of public
controversy and academic life to see what were the chief concerns of
Peter Martyr's close friend in Zurich. Martyr would concur with
Gesner's advice to Dalechamp that the holy scriptures have the authority to confer faith in Christ.[146] As a matter of fact, Martyr's
orations on the study of scriptures are quite similar in tone to
Gesner's letter with its advice that only scripture was authoritative
for salvation.[147] Gesner closed his letter with a reference to
Galen.[148]

I *KINGS*: SCHISM AND PAPACY

In the aftermath of the massacre of the Huguenot party on St.

Bartholomew's Eve (24 August 1572) political pressures forced many

to seek arguments from scripture in self-defense. From November of

1572 La Rochelle forced a full eight month seige as the center of

French protestant resistance. Francois Hotman asked Bullinger at

Zurich whether such a persecuted city had the right to resist royal

authority and assert its ancient rights. Hotman raised the issue of

the ancient Hebrew city of Libna which in II *Kings* (8:22) took up

arms against Joram, son of Ahab. Hotman claimed that Martyr himself

had noted this example.[149]

Peter Martyr's letter to Reginald Pole written when he fled from

persecution in Lucca in 1542 has not survived. It is possible that

Martyr's letter contained comments very similar to what one reads in

the Latin commentary on *Kings*. Macaluso describes Pole's *De Summo

Pontifice* which draws the opposite conclusion about the papacy than

did Martyr,[150] though Pole like St. Bernard can counsel humility for

the Vicar of Christ.

> This submission of Christ teaches us all how we should be, and
> is the first example of what the Vicar of Christ should show
> forth in himself: that although he is the greatest of all in
> dignity on earth, yet as often as he sees or hears, by his
> counsel or by his work, that the least and most abject of
> sinners can be saved, he should humble himself, and become a
> little one that he can counsel his salvation, which Paul
> testified that he had done in these words: "We have become
> little ones in your midst, for this reason; that the least
> might become the greatest, that they become sons of God who
> before had been his slaves and enemies."[150a]

From the unpublished letter already cited in which Martyr refers to

Cardinal Pole's legation in England as that of Antichrist, one can

see that Martyr was in no mood to compromise the truth of *sola scriptura, sola fide* and the sacramental views which were for him a logical consequence of such insights. The issue at stake for Peter Martyr was the wrong use of authority by the Roman Pope. A positive affirmation of the truth of the gospel required that Martyr separate from such evil men and their vicious doctrines. Such actions were not heretical. In the Latin Commentary on *Kings* published posthumously in 1566 Martyr set forth his mature judgment on the papacy. It is clear that among other works Martyr had read Cardinal Pole's *Pro Defensione de unitate Ecclesia* (1536) written to Henry VIII.[151] A careful look at Martyr's tract will enable one to understand the context in which he could say after making his will and confession of faith on his death bed: "This is my faith, and those that teach otherwise, to the withdrawing of men from God, God will destroy them."[152] Martyr's presence at Poissy and concern for French protestantism may have hardened his mind against the Guise.

In the prefatory letter to *Kings* John Wolph mentioned that part of Martyr's commentary had been published from manuscript sources and part from dictation. In his letter to Frederick, Count Palatine and Duke of Bavaria[153] Wolph wrote, "ut eos ipsos etiam absoluerem, ne si non perficerentur, ecclesiam thesauro tanto fraudaremus."[154] The theme of the church is taken up by Martyr as the central argument on schism.[155] Martyr divided his defence into three parts, viz., 1) Just causes for separation from the Papacy, 2) the necessity of such separation and 3) that he has not departed from the Church but returned to it.[156]

Martyr first d fined the several species of schism. Schism is
the separation of parts from the whole. When the whole is infected
it is not schismatic to separate from that which is evil in order to
avoid corruption and contamination. It was a good separation when
the proselytes left idolatry to join the ancient people of God. So
was it a good thing, reasoned Martyr, when Christ and the Apostles
separated themselves from the Jews.[157] An evil schism would arise
when a man separated from the whole which was good to join defiled
parts separated in schism. Since such actions demolish the church
Martyr warned against that kind of deadly activity.[158] "Now it must
be seen whether our separation is evil or good. I affirm that it is
good".[159]

Martyr's conclusion that his separation from the papacy is good
follows the thesis that the whole or centre of the church has become
evil. The first reason adduced is that his adversaries have cast
away the faith. Their departure appears in their adherence to traditions which neglect the Word of God.[160] As Martyr proceeded with his
reasons for separating from a defective hierarchy one can see why he
devoted himself to scholarly activity. It was exactly that freedom
to learn from Christ through a study of sacred scripture which would
have been denied him had he remained in Italy. Inquisition or inquiry; as a 'scholar of Christ' Martyr felt that a choice was necessary
to defect from the Roman Antichrist and his sub-Christian minions.
The following paragraphs will describe how Martyr sought to justify
that fateful decision to flee Italy.

Martyr's fourth reason for separation from the Papacy was to
ensure purity of worship.

> Fourthly, Papists suffer us not to worship God purelie and
> sincerelie, if we be conuersant with them. Because they neither
> suffer that the Gospell shoulde be preached by us; neither graunt
> they the pure administration of the Sacraments, as they be
> instituted of Christ.[161]

Martyr's tenth reason gave a concise definition of the church. In

the church some things were necessary, some were free and others were

wicked. Discipline in the administration of the sacrament was neces-

sary so that men might live godly and holy lives. But in the church

the freedom to live this necessary life was denied by teachers who

corrupted doctrine by asserting that men were not justified by faith

only.[162]

When Martyr came to the twelfth reason for separation from the

Roman hierarchy he outlined all those deeds which were antipathetic

to his own view of the Christian life.

> Further our adversaries are most manifestly founde to be
> plunged in those crimes of which the Apostle hath pronounced,
> 'that they which doe such things, have no part in the kingdome
> of God'. What place therefore shall we giue them in the Church?
> Undoubtedlie they be Simonites, Sorcerers, Bloud suckers,
> raisers of warres, men giuen to lust, they abound in more than
> Persian or Sybariticall riotousness: They haue no leasure for
> the word of God, they preach not, they feed not the flocke,
> naie rather they fill all things full of offences. And in the
> meane they did nothing but iangle of Peters and Pauls, from
> whom they are more distant than heaven is frō earth.[163]

Such a catalogue of crimes describes Martyr's chief co.cern that the

hierarchy had failed to fulfil its apostolic commission of preaching

and teaching the Word of God as stated in Christ's prayer for

unity in *John* (17:20). This is far deeper than a proto-pietistic protest against administrative distraction. Martyr accused his ad-

versaries of deliberately distorting the priorities of the faith.

This is precisely the point which Martyr made in his 1559 *Defensio*

against Stephan Gardiner.

> We acknowledge that the use of Sacraments hath some weight in
> promoting our salvation; – not the chief. The Death of Christ,
> the Holy Spirit, our Calling, Faith, Justification, have much
> greater weight in promoting salvation than the sacraments have.
> But our INCONSTANT is such a subtle Theologian, that he will
> have both the prow and the stern of our Salvation to be con-
> stituted in external things.[164]

Martyr's controversy centered on the doctrinal deviation of

clerics who could not bring themselves to admit that the Church or

their interpretations in the Church could err.

> To conclude, this controversie is betweene us and our aduerseries:
> namelie, whether ỹ Church can erre: We ioyne thereunto the worde
> of God: by which if it deale and define, we will gràunt that the
> same doeth not erre. But the Papists iudge that it is so great-
> lie ruled by the holie Ghost, that although it decree anie thing
> besides or against the worde of God, it doeth not erre: and there-
> fore they will, that the same should rather be beleeued than the
> Scriptures of God. But while they stand to that opinion, they
> dissent the whole world ouer from the fathers, who alwayes in
> their Councels confirmed their decrees by diuine Oracles.[165]

When one recalls the patristic argument in Martyr's biblical commen-

taries one is reminded of the careful study which lies behind such

a judgment.

Martyr went on to argue that the church indeed ruled certain

early literature such as the *Gospel of Nicodemus* and the *Acts of Peter*

as non-canonical. That decision however did not mean for Martyr that

the authority of the church could exceed that of the Four Gospels

which it endorsed. The church is like a notary which testifies to

the authority of scripture.[166] After giving particular examples where
the "Romanists" had misunderstood scripture such as the phrase in
Matthew (26:27) - Drink ye all of this -, Martyr went to the heart of
the matter. Could the Papacy in its teaching office err *in materia
fidei*? Martyr answered in the affirmative.

Martyr began his analysis of defective papal teaching by citing
the example of Pope John XXI who affirmed that men's souls perish with
their bodies.[167] Martyr also denied that Peter was translated from
the Bishopric of Antioch to that of Rome.[168] Martyr's explanation
depended on his interpretation of "Tu es Petrus" - *Matthew* (16:16)
and "Pasce oues meas" - *John* (21:15).

Martyr used Zwingli to refute the Romanist claim that in the
Petrine command of *John* (21:15) Christ granted to Peter's successors
an authoritative teaching over the church. Martyr appealed to
Zwingli's *De Vera et Falsa Religione* to demonstrate apostolic response
when in *John* (6:67) Christ asked the twelve disciples whether they
also would leave after the seventy had departed. Peter answered in
the plural for himself and his fellow disciples.[169] Martyr then
adduced the example of the Corinthian Church which Paul wished to be
saved from corruption by hearing the gospel.

> So lykwise in the Church of *Corinth*, the word of God was openly
> published and the Sacraments were soundlie administered. And
> thus although manie were infected with sinnes and grieuous
> corruptions, yet did they not all straie from faith & holiness:
> wherefore the Church ceased not to be at *Corinth*.[170]

Martyr tempered his judgment of ecclesiastical foibles with this
example of a pure church in Corinth which functioned in the midst of

a corrupt though quite religious society.

Martyr reserved a final argument to answer the accusation that he had destroyed the unity of the church by his flight and subsequent teaching. Martyr cited St. Paul from *Ephesians* (4:3) on One Lord, one faith, one baptism and the priestly prayer by Christ for unity in *John* (17) to assert:

> The unitie of the Church therefore by the places alleaged consisteth in the spirit, in the worde of God, in the Sacraments, and in a most neere bond with Christ, who is the head of all the members of the Church. Such a unitie haue we not broken, but we with euerie manner of waie that it maie be maintained safe and sound.[171]

In such a unity with the church Peter Martyr found both a consolation for his years in exile and a confirmation of his vocation to heal a depraved and decaying Roman Church.

At I *Kings* (22:5) Martyr described Jehosophat the righteous ruler who kept the divine law in the Word of God. God blessed his reign.[172] Martyr then turned to ancient Rome which solemnly consulted haruspices and omens for public and solemn occasions. Nevertheless it abandoned the source of true piety and ancient religion. Cyrus, Alexander of Macedonia and David on the contrary were good princes. "Quorum diligentiam & studium, nunc Iephosaphatus imitatur."[173]

Sedition and calamities arrived in Ancient Israel when the prophets worshipped Baal. Martyr in his comments on I *Kings* (18: 15-18) blamed Ahab[174] who condoned false worship which in turn fostered the crime of sedition. The nation fought against itself. The same accusation had been falsely laid to Christ, Paul and the

evangelical preachers.[175] John the Baptist opposed Herod for many
of the same reasons that lead Elias to forecast the decay of Ahab.
Martyr mused that these rulers in abandoning their ancient faith
scorned precepts and laws by actions which deliberately fomented
revolt. Martyr applied these historical precedents to the papacy of
his time. The popes were authors of the same sedition which Ahab and
Herod spread when they neglected true worship of the ancient faith.[176]

The Biblioteca Nazionale, Florence, Guicciardini 20-2-79 contains a 1572 Italian work under the title, *Trattato della Vera Chiesa
e della Necessita di Vivere in Essa, dell' eccellente Theologo M.
Pietro Martire Vermiglio Fiorentino.* It is not clear whether this
work reprinted by E. Comba in his 1884 *Biblioteca della Riforma
italiana* IV, 73-162 is a free simple translation of the commentary on
Kings or an expansion by Martyr himself and published posthumously.
I have not seen the Guicciardini copy. Delio Cantimori quotes from
the prefatory letter, A' *fratelli nel Signore essuli per il suo santo
evangelio*, "Prego . . . . et resister a le lusinghe et all rabbia di
Satana . . ."[177] This letter is by the translator and would appear
to use Martyr's non-violent treatise from *Kings* in the context of the
St. Bartholomew's Eve panic of 1572. A French translation of 1646
in Geneva speaks about Martyr's impact in this treatise.

The only study known to me of this tract in Florence occurs in
a 1949 unpublished thesis.[178] Di Gangi's sampling indicates the
similarity of the text to the 1566 commentary. Vermigli thanked
God for all those men like Luther and Zwingli who loved the true

church and had quickened her from ashes and ruins. No longer did
the Roman church remain apostolic or catholic since it had abandoned
all contact with primitive Christianity by its innovations which went
beyond the text of scripture. The evangelical reformers have restored
the truth to the church so that those who left Rome have come to the
true church.[179]

Martyr turned from these examples of schism and sedition to
unity. Paul urged the Corinthian Church in his first epistle not to
be schismatic (1:10).[180] Martyr quoted the words of the Latin poet
Virgil[181] to define the duty of a magistrate who was to execute the
laws of God from the Word of God. The godly magistrate would pass
honest civic decrees, judge matters of indifference and look to the
grave and difficult issues.[182] It is clear that Martyr would have the
godly magistrate reform the church when its religious rulers were
defective in morality and *in materia fidei*. This same historical
argument may be found in Martyr's letter to Queen Elizabeth. Small
wonder that Bishop Jewel in his *Apology* and Lambert Danaeus both were
impressed by these lectures on *Judges* and *Kings*.

Ancient Israel became in these lectures Martyr's example for
a Christian commonwealth. In these lectures Martyr found justification for abandoning the papacy and consolation for the difficulty
which his theological opponents had caused him in Oxford and Strasbourg. One feels that the controversy intensified in proportion to
Martyr's importance for both his friends and opponents. Because
Martyr by 1556 was held in such esteem one ought not to be surprised

at the sharpened controversy. Eucharistic controversy is but a part of Martyr's greater concern with the essentials of salvation. Nothing was more important to Martyr than the person of Christ.

NOTES TO CHAPTER VIII

1. McLelland, op. cit., p. 269. The tract was rediscovered in 1680. Martyr mentioned this manuscript from Florence in his Tractatio (1549), p. 31.

2. Judges (1564), fols. 27^r-28^r. The Massoretic text can be read as either father-in-law (Jethro) or brother-in-law (Hobab). The adjectival form Kenite needed an article which was missing from the Hebrew text.

3. Ganoczy, op. cit., p. 154.

4. "Nathan Ben Jehiel of Rome", Encyclopedia Judaica 12, cols. 859-860.

5. Corinthios (1551), p. 333^v.

6. Ibid., p. 94^v.

7. Ibid., p. 209^r. See also 210^r and Romanos (1558), pp. 13 & 23.

8. Romanos (1558), p. 41.

9. Corinthios (1551), p. 155^v. I cannot identify this reference.

10. Ibid., p. 164^v.

11. Fraenkel, Testimonium Patrum, p. 23. Toward the end of 1529 Melanchthon received a manuscript from Lang at Erfurt, the source of the editio princeps (Basle: Oporinus: 1544).

12. Pierre Fraenkel, "Histoire Sainte Et Heresie Chez Saint Epiphane De Salamine D'Apres Le Tome I Du Panarion," R. T. P. 12 (1961), 175-191. See p. 176.

13. Corinthios (1551), 82^r, 83^v, 84^v, 110^v, 112^r, 183^r, 119^v, 155^v, 192^v, 252^v, and 335^v, 336^r. De Ponderibus et mensuris was a dictionary of the Bible which discussed Canon and Translations of the Old Testament, biblical measures and weights, and the geography of Palestine. The Ancoratus (374) contains two creeds, one the baptismal creed of Salamis and the other by Epiphanius himself.

14. Romanos (1558), p. 41.

15. Pontien Polman, L'Element Historique Dans La Controverse religieuse du XVIe Siecle, p. 143, n.2. See Biblioteca Reformatoria Neerlandica IV, p. 397.

16. Jean de Hainault /Jean Crespin/. Copy in Bibliotheque Nationale, Paris. This work was reprinted several times.

17. A. XXI (1827), pp. 469-473.

18. F. Gardy, "Les livres de Pierre Martyr Vermigli conserves a la Bibliotheque de Geneve," A. S. G., n.s. 17 (1919), 1-6.

19. Alexandre Ganoczy, "La Bibliotheque De Pierre Martyr," La Bibliotheque de l'Academie de Calvin, pp. 19-27.

20. Ganoczy, op. cit.,p. 218: "Dans I egalement: annotations marginales de la main de P. Martyr. Il est complete par un index ms. calligraphie par une note de la main de P. Martyr." 170 on p. 218. Martyr to my knowledge does not use ∫ in his manuscript letters or other notations. The index may be in the hand of a secretary. In any event the notes are sparse.

21. Ibid., p. 22, note 4.

22. Ibid., p. 23.

23. In Mosis Genesim plenissimi commentarii (Basle: Ioannes Heruagios, Aug. (Sept.) 1554), A volume of 861 folio pages. In Primum Mosis librum qui Genesis vulgo dicitur (Paris: R. Estienne, 1554).

24. C. R. XLIII, 2003, col. 220.

25. The following numeration refers to the 1572 bibliographic list in Ganoczy; op. cit., pp. 159-313. See 27.

26, Ganoczy 28. En Amice lector, thesaurum damus inaestim-abiliem D. Basilium vere magnum . . . Erasmi Roterodami praefationem . . . (Basel: Froben, 1532). See Nicene and Post Nicene Fathers VIII, pp. 320-326.

27. Common Places (1583), and in all editions of the Loci Communes from 1576.

28. Ganoczy 38. Divi Gregorii . . . Opera . . . (Basle, Ioannes Heruagius, 1550).

29. Ibid., fol. 1. Folio 22 on Jonah reads in the margin, "causa cur fugavit Jonah."

30. Ibid., fol. 35. Lines 4-5, 16 and 37-38 are as follows: 4-5 "& de meis diiudicant laboribus, sermonem tanquam aes alienum, sine ulla recusatione exigentes": 16. "qui in multis laborant sermonibus emendari, & haec de sermonibus ipsis afferunt." 37-38. "nunquā ab oculis lippitundinem detergemus? Nunquam cogitabimus quae nam uerae sint diuitiae?"

31. Henry Wace and Philip Schaff, A Select Library of Nicene and Post Nicene Fathers of the Christian Church. Second Series, VII, p. 233.

32. Gregorii Opera, fols. 229-230.

33. Ibid., fols. 229-230. See Wace and Schaff, op. cit., pp. 438-439.

34. Ganoczy, 48. D. Epiphanii episcopi Constantiae Cypri, Contra Octoginta haereses opus, Panarium siue Arcula aut Capsula Medica appellatum. . . Iano Cornario medico physico interprete . . . (Basel: R. Winterus, 1545), fol. 515.

35. Ibid., fol. 19.

36. Ganoczy, 52. Qui Septimi Florentis Tertulliani Carthaginensis presbyteri . . . Scripta . . . B. Rhenani annotationibus . . . (Basel: Froben, 1550).

37. Ibid., fol. 622.

38. Loc. cit.

39. Ibid., fols. 632 (entire page marked), 633 & 634. This is by Novatian.

40. Ibid., fols. 405-420.

41. Ganoczy, 61. Omnes quae extant D. Hieronymi Stridonensis lucubrationes . . . per Des. Erasmum digestae . . . in novem tomos (Basel: Froben, 1533), tome 5, fols. 262-317.

42. Ibid., fols. 409-457.

43. Ibid., tome VI, chapter IX.

44. Jerome on Philemon & Galatians. See Romanes (1568), pp. 384^v-386^v and 403^r.

45. Jerome, Tome I, fols. 1-2.

46. Ibid., Tome I, fols. 250-265.

47. Ganoczy, 62: Divi Caecilii Cypriani episcopi Carthaginensis et martyris Opera . . . repurgata per Des. Erasmum . . . (Basel: Hervagius, 1540), fol. 443-451. Martyr knew from his copy of Melanchthon's works that the Cyprianic authorship of the De Coena was suspect, as in Sententiae Veterum.

48. Ibid., fol. 450. I am not suggesting here that Martyr purchased the volume in 1540.

49. Ganoczy, 65: Omnia D. Basilii Magni Archiepiscopi Caesareae Cappadociae Quae ad nos extant opera . . . ad Iano Cornario interpretata . . . (Basel: Froben, 1552), fols. 177-183. (4 tomes in 1 volume.)

50. Ibid., fols. 306-351 entirely marked.

51. Ganoczy, 36: Beati Ioannis Damasceni Orthodoxae fidei accurata explicatio . . . Iacobo Fabro Stapulensi interprete . . . (Basel: Henric-Petri, 1548).

52. Ganoczy, 176: Confessio catholicae fidei christiana . . . in Synodo . . . quae habita est Petrikoviae . . . (1541) . . . (Poznan: Ioannes Petruus (imprime a Mayence par Franciscus Beham), 1557).

53. Ganoczy, 176, fol. XXIV.

54. Thomas Martin, A Traictise declaryng and plainly prouyng, that the pretended marriage of Priestes, and professed persones, is no marraige, but altogether unlawful, and in all ages, and al countreies of Christendome, bothe forbidden,and also punyshed. (London: Robert Coly, May 1554), sig. Aiii[v].

55. Biblioteca Nazionale Centrale Vittorio Emanuele II, Roma. Fondo Autografi, Busta 153, n. 23. Copy in Thesaurus Baumianus, Bibliotheque Nationale et Universitaire de Strasbourg. Albert Hardenberg of Bremen (1510-1572) was educated by the Brethren of the Common Life at Groningen. When taking his doctorate at Mainz in 1537 or 1539 he met John Laski. From 1547 until his expulsion for denial of the Lutheran doctrine of the Eucharist Hardenberg was cathedral preacher at Bremen. The standard account is still Bernard Spiegel, D. Albert Rizaus Hardenberg. Ein Theologenleben aus der Reformationzeit (Bremen: Ed. Muller, 1869). In addition to some tracts and letters printed in Gerdes, Scrinium Antiquarium there are some letters in E. S. Cyprianus, Catalogus codicum manuscriptorum

Bibliothecae (Leipzig: 1714). A letter in C. C. C. C. MS. 119:98
of Hardenberg to Bucer is dated 7 September 1550 from Lambeth, indicating Albert's visit to England at that time. See also Wilhelm
Neuser, "Hardenberg And Melanchthon. Der Hardenbergische Streit
(1554-1560)," J. G. N. K. G. 65 (1967), 142-186.

56. C. R. LXIV, 2494, cols. 221-222. Martyr to Calvin.
Zurich. 7 July 1556: "Non vult magistratus ut quaestio haec in
schola disputetur . . .".

57. Staatsbibliothek Zofingen, Epistolae Autographae Variorum
eruditione celebrium virorum saec. XVI. ad Musculos aliosque
scriptae, MS. I, fol. 23^{r-v}. 11 September 1556.

58. Ioannes Sleidani, A Famouse Cronicle of oure time (1560),
fol. CCCCLXIX^v.

59. Cornelius Schulting, Bibliothecae Catholicae Et Orthodoxae
(1602), five vols. in two.

60. John Strype, The Life and Acts of John Whitgift, D. D.
(1822), III, p. 320. D. N. B., article "Barrett, William." See also
Strype, Annals of the Reformation, IV. 320. The Lambeth articles
have been reprinted in Philip Schaff, The Creeds of the Evangelical
Protestant Churches, pp. 523-24.

61. Marvin Anderson, "Peter Martyr, Reformed Theologian
(1542-1562): His letters to Bullinger and Calvin" S. C. J. IV
(1973), 41-64.

62. Emil Egli, Heinrich Bullingers Diarium (Annales vitae)
der Jahre 1504-1574, p. 48: "Anno Domini 1556 Aprilis 30, re-
cipitur a senatu d. Petrus Martyr; mittitur tabellio Argentinam.
Venit Iulii 17. deuertit apud me. Praesentatur senatui 20. Iullii;
iurat 28. eiusdem. Primo profitetur Augusti die 24; orditur I
lib. Samuelis."

63. Ibid., p. 49. Simler added in 1575 additional comments
about Martyr's arrival in Zurich. See Iosias Simler, Narratio De
Ortu, Vita, et Obitu Reverendi Viri, D. Henrici Bullingeri (1575),
p 29^r: "In eius locum (i.e. Pelican) successit Petrus Martyr
Vermilius, quo nescio an aluim Bullingerus chariorem habuerit.
Coniunxit eos non tantum summa in omnibus doctrinae partibus con-
sensio, sed quaedam etiam morum & vitae similitudo. Cum enim ambo
essent summi viri, tanta tamen erat utriusque modestia & humanitas
vt alterum sibi praeferret: erat in Martyre magnum acumen in
enucleandis grauissimis quaestionibus, singularem habebat gratiam
siue in schola disputandum siue docendum esset:"

63a. <u>Z</u>. <u>S</u>. <u>A</u>. EII (360) fol. 209 reprinted in Bainton, <u>Bernardino Ochino</u>, p. 179.

64. Schulting, <u>op</u>. <u>cit</u>., I, sig. A^1: "praeterea in locis Communibus Martyris maior est dictionis perspicuitas. Caluinus est magis in Institutionibus, quam in Commentariis in scripturas, idque de industria, & studiose vt imponat & fallat lectorem tortuosus serpens in tot maeandros & formas se vertit vt cauda apprehendi & teneri vix possit: si hic constringas, ibi elabitur."

65. <u>Loc</u>. <u>cit</u>.

66. Calvin's attention had been drawn to Martyr as early as November of 1542. Bucer wrote to Calvin about Martyr on 28 October 1542. <u>C</u>. <u>R</u>. XXXIX, 430, cols. 456-457: "Aduenit ex Italia vir quidam graece hebraice et latine admodum doctus, et in scripturis feliciter versatus, annos natus quadraginta quatuor, gravis moribus et iudicio acri, Petro Martyri nomen est."

67. Francesco Ruffini, <u>Francesco Stancaro</u>, p. 212.

68. <u>Bullingers Korrespondenz mit den Graubündnern</u>. I Teil. <u>Januar 1533-April 1557</u>, p. 452. 319. Heinrich Bullinger an Johannes Travers. Zurich, 23 August 1556: "Profitentur igitur nunc alternatim viri sane incomparabiles D. Theodorus Bibliander et D. Petrus Martyr, et hic quidem historias enarrat, ille prophetas explicat; utrique rara est linguarum cognitio, scriptuarum peritia; uterque eloquens est in omnibus artibus et disciplinis exercitatissimus, unde et summa cum laude profitentur."

69. <u>C</u>. <u>C</u>. <u>C</u>. <u>C</u>., MS. 102:31, fol. 512.

70. <u>Romanes</u> (1568), p. 430^{r-v}.

71. <u>Ibid</u>., p. 430^v.

72. Martyr had prepared his confutation of Stephan Gardiner before the publication of this volume in 1561.

73. <u>Judges</u> (1564), sig. B. IV. I am grateful to the Perne librarian of Peterhouse, Cambridge, Mr. E. F. Kenney, F. B. A., for permission to consult the first editions of Martyr's commentaries on <u>Judges, Samuel</u> and <u>Kings</u>. See <u>Iudicum</u> (1561), fol. 2^v: "Causam discessus nõ commemborabo: quod omnibus perspecta sit. Id tantum dicam, me tum uehementer optare, tum etiam sperare, hanc maceriam ex agro domini sublatum iri."

74. <u>Judges</u> (1564), sig. B. i^v. <u>Iudicum</u> (1561), fol. 2^v: ". . . ut illum in uestra schola docui, eum etiã uestro nomini dedicare statui . . . ."

75. J. W. Blench, <u>Preaching In England</u>, p. 101.

76. <u>Certain Sermons Or Homilies</u>, p. 268. The examples in this
selection are the ones given in the <u>locus</u> "Of VVine and Droonkennesse"
in <u>Common Places</u> (1583), Part two, pp. 497-503. In <u>Judges</u> (1564)
Alexander was "most filthely ouercome with wine." fol. 163^v. Marten
in the <u>Common Places</u> (1583) translated it as "most shamefullie ouercome with wine."

77. <u>Judges</u> (1564), fol. 163^v.

78. From the ordinance of magistrates, 18 December 1559, cited
in Donald Kelly, <u>Francois Hotman</u>, p. 86.

79. <u>Operum Theologicorum</u> . . . <u>Zanchi, Tomus Septimus</u>, p. 338.
This phrase is quoted in the preface of Lambertus Danaeus, <u>Politicorum
aphorismorum silva, ex</u> . . . <u>graecis</u>, . . . latiuis scriptoribus . . .
collecta . . . .

80. <u>Iudicum</u> (1561), col. 3^r. "Cum enim sit finis legis, & summa
diuinae scripturae,   hic liber ad lege pertinet, & pars est diuinae
scripturae, tam Christum ipsum lectoribus ostendit, ac euidentissime
praedicat."

81. <u>Judges</u> (1564), fol. 197^v. <u>Iudicum</u> (1561), f. 142^r: "In
summa tum maxime seditio est, quando per tumultum concurrunt ex
diuersis partibus, qui sunt eiusdem coetus & corporis, ut inter
sese pugnent. Aduersatur hoc uitium cumprimis pace & ciuili con-
cordiae. Sunt enim in seditione plures partes unius populi, ten-
taturque ac periclitatur ipsa unitas ciuim."

82. <u>Iudicum</u> (1561), fol. 143^r.

83. <u>Judges</u> (1564), fol. 299 (sic. 199) $^{r-v}$. <u>Iudicum</u> (1561),
fol. 143^v: "Proinde Iiphtah bellum ciuile gessit, non tamen iniustum.
Gladium quippe habuit, quo non solum hastes, uerumetiam ciues
coercere debuit, cum in leges humanas uel diuinas peccarent. Deus
ei iuctoriaɯ concesserat:"

84. <u>Iudicum</u> (1561), fol. 59^v.

85. <u>Ibid.</u>, fol. 60^v.

86. <u>Judges</u> (1564), fol. 91^r. <u>Iudicum</u> (1561), fol. 61^{r-v}.

87. <u>Judges</u> (1564), fol. 255^r. <u>Iudicum</u> (1561), fol. 183^r:
"Persona diuino instituto delecta, ut quo ad externam disciplinam
leges custodiat, poena corporis transgressares plectendo, & bonos
foueat atque amplectator."

88. *Iudicum* (1561), fol. 183^V.

89. *Judges* (1564), fol. 257^r. *Iudicum* (1561), fol. 184^V.

90. Letter to Bullinger. *Z. S. A.* EII (340), fol. 215.

91. *Ibid.*, lines 9-10. See D. M. Loades, "The Enforcement of Reaction, 1553-1558," *J. E. H.* XVI (1965), 54-66.

92. *Judges* (1564), fol. 258^V.

93. *Ibid.*, fol. 288^V. *Iudicum* (1561), fol. 208^r.

94. *Judges* (1564), fol. 5^r. *Iudicum* (1561), fol. 3b(v).

95. *Judges* (1564), fol. 13^V. *Iudicum* (1561), fol. 9b(v).

96. *Cohabitacyon*, pp. 47^{r-v}. Information on printer and place of publication communicated in a letter of 16 September 1971 from Miss Katharine Pantzer, The Houghton Library, Harvard University. *Judges* (1564), fol. 44^V-59^V.

97. *Judges* (1564), fol. 56^r.

98. Hans Baron, "Calvinist Republicanism And Its Historical Roots," *C. H.* VIII (1939), 35-37.

99. Richard Benert, "Lutheran Contributions To Sixteenth Century Resistance Theory," unpublished lecture, p. 2.

100. Oliver Olsen, "Theology of Revolution: Magdeburg, 1550-1551," *S. C. J.* III (1972), 56-57.

101. *Ibid.*, p. 70.

102. See partial text in Julian H. Franklin, *Constitutionalism and Resistance in the Sixteenth Century*, 98-135. Professor Kingdon in 1955 pointed to use of the Magdeburg *Bekenntnis* in Beza's 1554 response to Castellio. See Robert M. Kingdon, "The First Expression of Theodore Beza's Political Ideas," *A. R. G.* 46(1955), 93.

103. Philip McNair, *Peter Martyr In Italy*, p. 149.

104. Richard Benert devotes chapter four of *Inferior Magistrates In Sixteenth-Century Political and Religious Thought* to Calvinist literature before 1572. Martyr's Judges in the 1571 edition is cited on pages 135-138. Martyr did not specify the legal origin of his views, though his "non-noble" view of lesser magistrates sets him apart from what Benert calls a Lutheran view (p. 137).

105. Joseph G. Dryer, Pole's Defense of the Unity of the Church, p. 342. On the religious justification for rebellion developed by Lutheran thinkers see Oliver K. Olsen, op. cit., pp. 56-79. Vergerio's hostility to Pole, who enjoyed a reputation for conciliation with the Lutherans, was an attempt to discredit Pole with Duke Christoph who thought Pole was really on their side. In 1555 the Epistolae duae in its second letter bitterly attacked Pole. This rare De Studio, et Zelo pietatis Cardinalis Poli contrasted Pole's former moderation with his current persecution of English Protestants. Vergerio then published the De Unitate to discredit the papal delegates to Augsburg and to avoid just that compromise achieved by Duke Christoph in 1555 at Augsburg. See Dermot Fenlon, Heresy and Obedience in Tridentine Italy - Cardinal Pole and the Counter Reformation, pp. 266-69.

106. Original Letters Relative To The English Reformation, Written During the Reigns of King Henry VIII, King Edward VI, and Queen Mary: Chiefly From The Archives of Zurich, p. 137.

107. W. Gordon Zeeveld, Foundations of Tudor Policy, pp. 248-49. Zeeveld also cites several other works by Starkey.

108. Christina M. Garrett, "John Ponet and the confession of the banished ministers," C. Q. R. 137 (Oct.-Dec. 1943), 47-74; 137 (Jan.-Mar. 1944), 181-204.

109. Cohabitacyon, sig. f. iii^r.

110. Loc. cit.

111. Ibid., sig. f. iv^v.

112. Ibid., sig. fv^r. See Barrett L. Beer, "London and the Rebellion of 1548-1549," J. B. S. XII (1972), 15-38.

113. Defensio Doctrinae Veteris & Apostolicae De Sacrosancto Evchariistiae Sacramento . . . (1559), p. 229.

114. Melachim (1566), fol. 113^r, and fol. 145^r. Robert Kingdon, "The Political Resistance of the Calvinists in France and the Low Countries," C. H. XXVII (1958), pp. 226-227 argues that Paul's injunction in Romans (13:1-3) applies only to private individuals. Martyr does not seem to make that distinction ubiquitous. In the 1566 Fortress of Fathers Peter Martyr's comments on Romans (13:1) are included together with I Corinthians (7:23), Judges (8) and II Kings (10). When Robert Crowley cited Martyr from Romans (13:1) in his A Briefe discourse/against the outwarde apparell/and Ministring garmen-/tes of the popishe church, Matthew Parker cited Martyr against Crowley. This would argue for the conservative understanding of Martyr's political views in 1566 in England if not in

1572 in France! Archibishop Parker's response to Crowley's attack on his own Advertisements partly for due order . . . and the apparrell of all persons ec-/clesiasticall . . . . (London: R. Wolfe, 1564) would be the An Examination . . . of a certain Declaration (London: 1566). Trinterud's observation of this background to the Fortress of Fathers endorses how Martyr's English readers construed his political views.

115. Common Places (1583), IV, 327ff.

116. Ibid., pp. 327-328.

117. Donnelly, op. cit., p. 327, n. 79.

117a. John Milton, Commonplace Book, p. 183.

118. For location of Professor Kingdon's passage see Robert Kingdon, Geneva and the Consolidation of the French Protestant Movement 1564-1572 (Madison: University of Wisconsin Press, 1967), p. 219.

119. Thomas Allan & Thomas Shepard, A/Defence/of the/answer made unto the Nine Questions/or Positions sent from New-England, Against the/Reply Thereto/by/That Reverend servant of Christ,/Mr. John Ball . . ., (London: Andrew Crooke, 1648), The Preface.

120. Francesci Spierae, Quiquod Susceptam semel Euagelica ueritatis professione abnegasset, damnassetque, in harrendam incidit desperationem, HISTORIA, A quatuor summis uiris, summa fide conscripta: cum clariss uirorum Praefationibus, Caelii. S. C. & Io. Caluini, & Petri Pauli Vergerii Apologia: in quibus multa hoc tempore scitu digna grauissime tractantur. (Basel: M. D. L. n.p.)

121. Sleidan, op. cit., fols. CCCXXVII^v-CCCXXVIII^r.

122. Reprinted between John Calvin's De Crucis tolerantia and Bullinger's De Calamitatibus in TheophilusGeruasius, Panoplia (1588).

123. Common Places (1583), Part three, p. 270. fol. 231^v: "Est ergo fortitudo habitus animi nostri, quo secundum rectam rationem, propter iustum & honestum, mediocritatem tenemus inter metum, & audaciam."

124. Common Places (1583), Part three, pp. 270-271.

125. Ibid., p. 271.

126. Ioannis Calvini, Verbi Dei, In Ecclesia Geneuensi, fidelissimi ministri, Epistolae duae . . . Prior,De Fugiendis impioru illicitis sacris, & puritate Christianae religionis obseruanda (Geneva: M.D.L., n.p.), Prefatory letter dated pridie

Idus Ianuarii. Anno 1537. First edition published in Basle: Lasius & Platter, 1537. 4 . Translated by Robert Horne in 1553 and printed again in 1576 and 1584 with Horne's apology.

127. Common Places (1583), Part three, p. 271. Samuelis (1564), fol. 231^V.

128. Marten continues the treatise On Fortitude from Il Samuel (10:12) with a translation of De Crucis found in the Loci Communes (1576) and taken from I Corinthians (9:27). The De Fuga from Genesis (32) has already been discussed in section II. On Fortitude is not in the Loci Communes (1576), but is published separately from De Crucis on pp. 656-657 of the Loci Communes (1583). De Crucis begins in Marten's translation with "3. But mortification" on p. 272 of part three. In Corinthios (1551) it commences at fol. 233^V, line 26: ". . . & septimo ad Romanos." A Collation of the third edition of 1572 shows no departure from the text of the first edition (fols. 123^r-124^r). Masson has rearranged the text from its order in the commentary i.e. the text goes from "wantoness of the flesh" directly to "But of the first principall point." Marten's translation does not follow the textual order in either of the first three Latin editions of I Corinthians (1551, 1567, 1572).

129. Common Places (1583), Part three, p. 273. Corinthios (1551), fol. 233^V; "Et ut paucis, dicamus, crux nil est aliud quam aduersitates, tristes casus, tentationes, dolores tam animi quam corporis, qui a deo irrogantur ad gloriam sui nominis & nostra salutem."

130. Loci Communes (1576), p. 731. Marten proceeds from I Corinthians (9: 27) to Romans (8:17) and (8:31). Masson in the 1576 Loci Communes arranged the text in that order on pp. 729-740. The passage from I Corinthians in its new order may be found on pages 729-730. At 4. on page 730 Masson refers to the Romans Commentary (8:17), i.e., "Sed vt ad priorem illam mortificationis speciem redeamus." At 12. on page 736 Masson points to Romans (8:31), i.e., "Capite autem octauo ad Romanos: Postquam Paulus infinitis rationibus." At 17. on page 740 he apparently used the Judges commentary. This example of how the Loci Communes shifted the order of Martyr's writings demonstrates why one must consult the Commentaries as well as the Loci Communes in representing Martyr's views on a given topic.

131. Operum . . . Theologicorum . . . Zanchi, Tomus Septimus, p. 286.

132. Jacobus Dalechampius Cadomensus was born in Caen, 1513. From 1552 until his death in 1588 he was a noted scholar and Botonist at Lyons. In 1552 he published at Lyons a Latin version of Athanasius with the Greek text and Commentary as well as Viviers, De Peste libri tres. In 1566 he prepared a French edition of Galen

and in 1588 edited the text of Pliny. He was most famous for editing
a general history of plants called Historia Lugdunensis. Charles B.
Schmitt hopes soon to publish the letters between Gesner and Dalechamp
preserved in MS. Paris, BN. Lat. 13,063. See Charles B. Schmitt,
"Some Notes. Jacobus Dalechampius and his Translation of Theophrastus
(Manuscript: BN. Lat. 11, 857)," G. 26 (1969), 36-53. See p. 44, n.32.

133. Letter is printed in Museum Helveticum I (1746), pp. 133-
150. For similar correspondence see Conradin Bonorand, "Humanismus
und Reformation in Sudbunden im Lichte der Korrespondenz der Churer
Prediger mit Joachim Vadian und Konrad Gessner," Festschrift 600
Jahre Gotteshausbund, pp. 439-88. Some additional Gesner letters
were printed in Caspar Bauhinus, De plantis a diuis sanctis've nomen
habentibus (Basel: C. Waldkirch, 1591). See also letter of Ursinus
to Gesner of 22 March 1562 informing Gesner of religious studies in
Heidelberg: Z. S. A. EII (363), fol. 81. See R. J. Durling, "Conrad
Gesner's Liber Amicorum 1555-1565," G. 22 (1965), pp. 134-159 for
names of guests and Gesner's comment. Also see J. Staedtke, "Conrad
Gesner als Theologe," G. 23 (1966), pp. 238-65, and reference in letter
of Robert Horn and Richard Chambers to Bullinger of 3 feb. 1556: "We
think master Gessner, whose kind offices to us were unnumberable, must
be no means be passed over." O. L. I, p. 130.) Zanchi described,
Gesner as πολλακις η δοξα βιαζεται την αληθειαν, αλλ' εν
Γεσνηρω, η αληθεια βιασεται την δοξαν.
(Often one's glory forces the truth but in Gesner the truth seizes
the glory). Gesner's list of Froschouer's publications is of great
bibliographic importance. J. C. Bay, "Conrad Gessner (1516-1565) the
father of bibliography," P. B. S. A. X (1916), 53-86. Froschouer
published Gesner's study of the Church Fathers, particularly Maximus
the Confessor, Theophilus of Antioch and Tatian in 1546. Martyr may
have obtained some of his patristic material from Gesner. He could
scarcely be unaware of Gesner's lectures on Aristotle at the Carolinum
and his own students in Zurich who visited Gesner and signed the Liber
Amicorum. See also Bernhard Milt, "Conrad Gessners theologische
Enzyklopadie," Z. VIII (1948), pp. 571-87. Gesner signed a letter
of 27 December 1534 to Bullinger, "in aedibus Buceri." C. R. XXXVIII,
23, cols. 42-44.

134. De Constantia in fide, p. 136.

135. Loc. cit.

136. Ibid., p. 137. The hendyidas of via, vertias & vita I take
from the Greek text.

137. Ibid., p. 138.

138. Ibid., p. 139.

139. _Ibid._, p. 140. Viret is perhaps included with Luther and Calvin because Gesner spent three years in Lausanne. See E. Olivier, "Les Annees Lausannoises (1537-1540) de Conrad Gesner," S̲. Z̲. G̲. (1951), 369-428,

140. _Loc. cit._

141. _Loc. cit._ "ad solum vetus Testamentum te remitto, quo ut nihil antiquius in ullis literarum monumentis, ita nihil verius a condito mundo, una eademque veritate . . ."

142. _Loc. cit._

143. _Ibid._, p. 141.

144. _Ibid._, p. 142.

145. _Loc. cit._

146. _Ibid._, p. 143: "autoritatem Scripturae stabiliat tibi ipsi evidentia rerum et eventuum certitudo, tum illorum, qui olim euenerunt, et suis in Veteri Testamento Prophetiis responderunt per omnia in Novo . . . ."

147. _Ibid._, p. 145: "Soli Sacrae Scripturae plenam authoritatem tribuendam, inque ea, quod ad salutem sit necessarium, desiderari nihil:"

148. _Ibid._, p. 150. In a letter Ad̲ Laelii Socini fratres of 6 January 1561 Gesner also touched on the theme of constancy in faith. See especially pp. 353-355 in Johannes Hanhart, _Conrad Gessner._

149. Donald R. Kelley, _Francois Hotman_, p. 228. Bullinger responded to Hotman on 10 January 1573 that "Nec dum videre possum quomodo defectionem suam defendere possint, qui a magistratu suo licet tyrannico, sine expresso Dei mandato, aut argumentis alioqui irrefrogabilibus deficiunt." See Bouvier, _op. cit._, p. 537.

150. Peter F. Macaluso, _Kingship And Papacy In The Thought of Reginald Pole, 1500-1558,_ (unpublished thesis) pp. 153-175.

150a. _Ibid._, p. 158.

151. "An Evangelici Sint Schismatici, quod se alienauerint a Papistis," fols. 102[r]-113[v] in _Melachim_ (1566). Reference to Pole is found on fol. 106[v].

152. _Oratio_ (1563).

153. <u>Melachim</u> (1566), <u>Praefatio</u>, fol. 2^r. "Cumcque essent inuenti in schedis Martyris eius praelectionum commentarij, partim ab eo dictari, partim eius manu scripti."

154. <u>Loc</u>. <u>cit</u>.

155. See the background sketched by L. Santini, "'Scisma' e 'eresia' nel pensiero di P. M. Vermigli," <u>B</u>. <u>S</u>. <u>S</u>. <u>V</u>. XC (Guigno 1969), 27-43.

156. <u>Melachim</u> (1566), fol. 102^r: "Defensionem in tria capita distribuam, Primum ostendam nostrae separationis iustissimas causas intercessisse. Deinde necessariam fuisse nobis hanc separationem confirmabo. Tertio planum faciam, nos ab Ecclesia non discessisse, verum potius ad eam accessisse."

157. <u>Loc</u>. <u>cit</u>.

158. <u>Melachim</u> (1566), fol. 102^v: "In malo itaque Schismate qui se separant, & seipsos perimunt, & (quantum in eis est) Ecclesiam demoliuntur, nisi Christus adesset, qui eam & restituit & conservat. Cauendum est itaque vitium hoc, vt exitiosum."

159. <u>Loc</u>. <u>cit</u>.

160. <u>Loc</u>. <u>cit</u>. "Quare non potest inter eos & nos intercedere coniunctio."

161. <u>Common Places</u> (1583), Part four, p. 69. <u>Melachim</u> (1566), fol. 102^v.

162. <u>Melachim</u> (1566), fol. 103^r. "Doctrinam vtique corruperunt: non enim fide sola (vt scripturae statuunt) non iustificari docent, sed etiam operibus."

163. <u>Common Places</u> (1583), Part four, page 71. <u>Melachim</u> (1566), fol. 103^v.

164. <u>Defensio</u> (1559), p. 229.

165. <u>Common Places</u> (1583), Part four, p. 73. <u>Melachim</u> (1566), fol. 104^r,

166. <u>Melachim</u> (1566), fol. 104^v.

167. <u>Ibid</u>., fol. 106^v.

168. <u>Loc</u>. <u>cit</u>. This question arose very early among the Protestant reformers. Its significance can be seen in the treatise of 1522

written by the Benedictine Abbot Gregorio Cortese for Pope Adrian
VI. Conrad Gesner included Cortese's treatise in his bibliography of
theological works.

169. <u>Melachim</u> (1566), fol. 109^r: "In eo sane argumento Zuinglius
bonam operam nouauit. Is de uera religione, capite vbi de Clauibus
Ecclesiae agit, loca plura collegit, quae ad rem praesentem commodo
faciunt. In Ioanne cap. 6 cum 70. discipuli abijssent, Christus con-
uersus ad 12. illis ait, Nunquid & vos abire vultis? Ibi Petrus
omnium vice respondit, Domine ad quem ibimus? Verba vitae aeternae
habes. Ipsi nouimus & credimus, quod tu es Christus filius Dei."

170. <u>Common Places</u> (1583), Part four, p. 95. <u>Melachim</u> (1566),
fol. 113^r.

171. <u>Ibid.</u>, p. 96. <u>Melachim</u> (1566), fol. 113^r.

172. <u>Melachim</u> (1566), fol. 175^r. "Collaudandum est porro
studium Iehosaphati erga uerbum Dei Erat diuina lex magnopere cordi
huic regi: qua uolebat Deus in rebus grauissimis consuli, quo pro
vero & summo eius gentis rege haberetur, vt qui eam peculiariter
gubernare constituerit."

173. <u>Loc. cit.</u>

174. <u>Ibid.</u>, fol. 145^r. Particular passage is: (Qui respondit,
Non conturbaui Israelem, sed tu & domus patris tui, quum dereliquer-
itis mandata Iehouae, 7 ambulaueritis post Baalim.)

175. <u>Loc. cit.</u> "Primo congressu nequaquam salutauit, nec
Prophetae quicquam fausti precatus est, imo grauissimum crimen seditionis impegit, quasi perturbasset Israelem, ac in seditionem prorsus
uertisset."

176. <u>Ibid.</u>, fol. 145^v. "Causam adijcit Elias, cur Ahabus &
maiores eius turbauerint Israelem, nempe, quod verum & patrium Deum
reliquerint, eiusq; praecepta & leges contempserint, dijsq; alienis
inseruiuerint. Hoc inquit fuisse principium, fontem, & radicem
turbationis. Et quia res haec magna est, & cognitio eius plurimum
commodat hisce temporibus, quibus Papistae aiunt nos esse perturbatores Ecclesiae, ac seditionis autores, nosq; vicissem regerimus, ab
illis haec mala orta esse, operae pretium erit, vt causa posit
dijudicari, de Turbatione vel seditione aliquid in medium afferre."

177. Cantimori, <u>Ginevra e l'Italia</u>, p. 189, n. 13.

178. Mariano Di Gangi, <u>Pietro Martire Vermigli 1500-1562</u>
(unpublished thesis), pp. 93-109. Copy furnished by Di Gangi.

179. <u>Ibid</u>., p. 109. See Comba, <u>op</u>. <u>cit</u>., p. 152: "Ma essendo gia a Dio piaciuto di suscitare uomini illustri quali furono Lutero e Zuinglio, i quali piantarano chiese unnumerevoli, avendo lasciato i sepolcri, le ceneri e alcune poche vestigie della Chiesa, fu convenevole che molte pie persone vi andassero quivi, dove secondo la Parola di Dio e operare e vivere potessero, e in questo modo continuassero in se stessi per successione la fide e vita apostolica, congiungendo se stessi ai loro passati, i quali diretta-mente e sinceramente erano vissuti nella primitiva Chiesa."

180. <u>Ibid</u>., fol. 146[r].

181. <u>Ibid</u>., fol. 146[v].

182. <u>Ibid</u>., fol. 147[r]: "Sed quoniam Magistratus est lex animata, & vices Dei gerit, qui aduersus eos insurgunt, ij merito dicuntur seditiosi. Nam & legum executionem & imaginem Dei, quantum in ipsis est, auferunt. Suspiciendus itaque Magistratus est, nec aduersandum illi tantisper dum imperat ex verbo Dei, aut ex honestis decretis ciuilibus, vel etiam dum ἀδιάφορα mandat, etiam si grauia & dura interdum videantur."

CHAPTER IX

THE PERSON OF CHRIST

Klaus Sturm summarizes the soteriological aspect of Martyr's Christology[1] by selecting terms from Martyr's writings such as *potentia patris, exemplum, signum, Dominus, reconciliatio* and *exaltatio*.[2] This selection reminds one that Martyr went beyond the sacraments to find the birth of the Christian Church and its believers in the resurrection of Christ. The sacraments are seals therefore of the promise and election of God. When Sturm turns to Heidegger one feels that the context within which Martyr worked has been discarded. Neither Martyr nor St. Paul read *Sein und Zeit*[3] or the Neo-Kantian philosophy of modern German university life. Heidegger's example of a turn signal which uncovers an existential intent for a driver is used by Sturm to update Martyr for his readers. Tylenda warns against this process when he urges that one drop all use of "real presence" in favour of true presence. "Though they declare that Calvin taught a real presence their real has a twentieth-century meaning and not that of the sixteenth century; and furthermore, it is being used in an age most concious of unity and not in the age of polemics."[4] This section on *exemplum* in Sturm needs to be read with Corda's thesis title in mind, *Veritas Sacramenti*. Sturm's summary however is a good reminder that Martyr "described factually all that concerns the life of Christ for Christians, i.e., what a Christian man thanks God for as he participates in salvation offered through Christ via the work of the Holy Spirit."[5] The effects gave Martyr a fresh concept of

the Word of God, the sermon, sacraments and the teaching of justification and sanctification. From Martyr's understanding of the Holy
Spirit follows his dogmatic framework in which immediacy to God is
the most promient feature. Such immediacy forms a pious self-aware-
ness in which faith possesses the knowledge of God, a true understanding of the Bible and is governed by the Holy Spirit.[6] The consistency
between the *De Fuga* and Martyr's final exegetical work depends on his
view of Christ as risen and regnant in the Church of which He is the
Head. Martyr surely knew the triple designation in the *Apocalypse*
where Christ was praised as "the faithful martyr, the firstborn from
the dead and the ruler over the kings of the earth."

The motto on the frontispiece of Martyr's commentary on I *Corinthians* (1551) selects St. Paul's great affirmation that one ought only
to glorify in the cross of Christ. This confession from *Galatians*
(6:14) sums up Martyr's own Christological affirmation in his 1544
exposition of the Creed, the Oxford sermons and the debates with Stancaro. It seems appropriate therefore to sketch in conclusion some-
thingof Martyr's views on the person of Christ. In the midst of constant challenge over his Eucharistic views Martyr felt a close relation
to the risen Christ which enabled him consistently to defend the
Chalcedonian formulae. That is to say, Martyr did not always view the
person and work of Christ as a formula to be defended in academic
disputations alone for a glance at his sermon on *Philippians* (2) clearly reflects the positive thrust of Martyr's personal faith. Martyr
knew that though every day he faced death as a mortal, one day he

would see the Resurrected Christ face-to-face.

> So as God hath tempered for us a medicine out of the death and resurrection of Christ, whereby we be delivered, and death perisheth: in like maner as a wise Physician drinketh unto the patient of the medicine, wherewith he is releeued, and the ague or disease extinguished. And, of this wholesome medicine we drinke healthfullie, while as either by reading, or by preaching, there is mention made of the death and resurrection of the Lord, and we with a liuelie faith embrace the same: and also, when we make pretestation of our faith by the sealing of baptisme and receiuing of the Lords supper. For in these holie actions, both the death and resurrection of Christ are celebrated. In the treatise of this place, Paul added; that Death is swallowed vp by victorie; namelie, of Christ.[7]

OXFORD SERMONS

In his sermon on *Philippians* (2) Martyr reminded his audience

that those who think about the powers of the mind ought to recall that

it extols the memory when committed to writings. Such an incomparable

treasury of the mind is given by God who exhorts his followers to keep

in mind the mighty acts of salvation done for them. Martyr in com-

memorating the death of Christ was expounding to his listeners the

infinite love of Christ who suffered death for their sake.[8]

> This Christological hymn meant for Martyr three things, i.e.:

> First therefore he sheweth, who this is that we ought to follow, to wit God & man. Secondly wherein he was obedient, namely unto death, euen the death of the crosse. Thirdlie what he obtained for these things, euen a name which is aboue euerie name.[9]

The trinitarian confession was part of Martyr's interpretation of this

passage. Martyr used especially Chrysostom's Homily, *De Consubstan-*

tialitate Trinitatis to attack the Arian interpretation of the term

$\lambda o \gamma o s$.[10] As Christ served both God and man, so Martyr reasoned,

"we which haue the spirit of faith doe receiue Christ in this ignominie: yea and we see that he by his afflictions sanctified all

aduersities."[11]

This theme of Christ as the humble man and the Hidden God per-

meated Martyr's thinking. The strong Son of God who was obedient unto

death humbled Himself in the form of a servant. His death on the

cross was for Martyr the means of identification with mankind.

> The death of the Crosse is a new kinde of sacrifice, and there-
> fore a new altar. He fastened to his crosse the handwriting of
> ordinances that was against us, and he triumphed ouer his enemies.
> This is the triumphant chariot of Christ.[12]

Not only did Martyr urge the suffering Christ as an example, he

also preached the risen Lord as a means of triumph over tribulation.

The *Oration concerning the Resurrection of Christ* seems to be a com-

panion sermon to that on *Philippians* (2) since it refers to a sermon

on the death of Christ.[13] First Martyr mentioned that Christ is risen,

secondly that Christians are risen with Him, and in the third place

"what we must now doe being raised up."[14] This final theme of new

life in Christ relates directly to the issue of union with Christ

which Martyr raised in his letter of 8 March 1555 to John Calvin.

Martyr taught a view that Christ's resurrection enabled a be-

liever to perform good works which signify an entrance to eternal

life. "They are degrees whereby God draweth us unto a perfect life."[15]

Christ has not only risen in history, claimed Martyr, but he has also

risen in those who believe and are thereby obedient.

> All things are subdued unto Christ: so ought we to ouercome
> all thinges and to faint in nothing. Let us stande out in
> temptations and triumph ouer our tribulations.[16]

POLISH CHURCH AND STANCARO

One of Martyr's opponents between 1556 and 1562 was the Italian Hebraist Francesco Stancaro born in Mantua in 1501. Stancaro achieved fame for his 1530 *De modo legendi Hebarice instituto brevissima* published in Venice.[17] After he became a language teacher at Padua in 1540, Stancaro left the Roman Church only to suffer eight month's imprisonment. Stancaro escaped and fled to Italy in 1542 and in 1544 was given the chair of Hebrew at Vienna though he was dismissed at King Ferdinand's command in March 1546. In 1547 Curione failed to gain Stancaro a position at Basle even though Stancaro took the Basle doctorate in theology. After much controversy in the Rhetian league Stancaro appeared in Poland as the founder of the first Reformed parish in that land.

In 1550 Stancaro succeeded in having Lord Nicholas Olesnicki drive out the monks from Pinczow in support of a Reformed synod.[18] In March 1555 Felix Cruciger became the first Polish superintendent of Reformed Churches. The Synod of Kozminek met from 24 August to 1 September 1555 to unite the Polish Church of the Little Poles and the *Unitas Fratrum*. On 15 September 1555 at Pinczow Francis Lismanini was unanimously elected as co-superintendent with Cruciger. Lismanini had been former Franciscan provincial general in Poland and was in Geneva when elected.[19]

In 1549 Stancaro as professor of Hebrew at the University of Cracow caused an uproar by his lectures on the *Psalms*. Stancaro escaped after eight months imprisonment in the episcopal palace via

a rope ladder to take refuge in Pinczow. Williams remarks that
Stancaro was a born controversialist whose next action in Poland was
to be banned. In Ducal Prussia Stancaro became professor of Hebrew
at Konigsberg University[20] where he was asked to settle the debate
over Osiander's teaching that one is justified by the inherent justice
of Christ. The disputants carried firearms to the lecture hall where
Stancaro solved the issue by asserting that Christ was mediator only
according to his divine nature. In 1559 Stancaro attacked Melanchthon
in a bitter ten-page document and assumed in a letter to Calvin of 4
December 1560 that the Polish Calvinists taught tritheism.[21]

The 1559 tract would be an answer to Melanchthon's 1553 *Responsio
de controuersiis Stancari*. In Stancaro's 1559 *Collatio doctrinae Arrii
et Philippi Melanchthonis* he accused Melanchthon of Arianism. In 1552
Stancaro as Professor of Hebrew in Frankfurt on the Oder attacked
Osiander. In the same city Andreas Musculus in May of 1552 published
his own propositions that Christ was mediator both as God and man, so
affecting the atonement that He died as God. Stancaro in his *Apology
Against Musculus* (1552) concluded that only if one excluded the divine
nature of Christ in His propitiatory death could the impassibility of
God be defended. His opponents then were forced into such a defense
of divine mediatorship in Christ that they seemed to dissolve the
Nicene formula.[22] The Elector of Brandenburg urged Melanchthon to
solve the controversy. Melanchthon endorsed Musculus' appeal to the
Communicatio idiomatum and condemned Stancaro's restriction of
mediatorship to Christ's divine nature.[23]

The issue became clear when Melanchthon responded again to
Stancaro.   In 1560 Melanchthon composed a *Corpus doctrinae* of his
most important writings.   The 1553 *Response of Philip Melanchthon
about The Stancaro Controversy* joined the altered *Augsburg Confession*,
the *Apology*, the *Saxon Confession*, the *Loci*, *Examination of Ordinands*
and the *Reply to the Bavarian Inquisition*. That this document is
among Melanchthon's most cherished writings reflects the seriousness
with which Stancaro was taken.[24]   Stancaro called Melanchthon "The
Arius of the North." Melanchthon had said in the 1553 *Response*:

> We say therefore that Christ is concretely man, the logos is man,
> Christ is wounded, Christ is dead, God is dead_. . . . Clearly
> then it has been _said that the communication /exchange of the
> natures in Christ_/ is in the concrete and not in the abstract.
> It is necessary therefore to acknowledge two natures in the
> Christ born of a virgin in order that one may of_necessity retain
> the unity of persons or the hypostatical union.[25]

The Polish Calvinists charged Stancaro in turn with Sabellian modalism.
This was a misnomer since Sabellius taught as a corollary that the
Father suffered as the Son, i.e., patripassianism.[26]

In his 1560 preface to the *Corpus doctrinae christianae*
Melanchthon reiterated his judgment now to be seen in the context of
Stancaro's bitter 1559 pamphlet.

> Staphylus and Stancaro stitch together purely false accusations
> and their allies. In order that it might be said they really
> are acting responsibly /actum agentes/, they create creaking
> sounds and raise dust like the pantomimes of old women.[27]

Stancaro's letter to Calvin of 4 December 1560 was also addressed
to Peter Martyr. In 1562 Stancaro dismissed the ministers of Zurich
and Geneva outright.

Peter Lombard alone is worth more than a hundred Luthers, two hundred Melancthons, three hundred Bullingers, four hundred Peter Martyrs, and five hundred Calvins, and all of them ground in a mortar with a pestle would not amount to an ounce of true theology.[28]

Lismanini learned of the spreading Servetian doctrines in Poland and in turn Lismanini informed Calvin about five questions in a letter of 15 September 1555. These are 1) a debate between Hislebius and Andreas Musculus over the *communicatio idiomatum*; 2) the dogma of Osiander on essential justice stemming from Christ's humanity; 3) Philip Melanchthon's defense of the mediatorship of Christ according to both natures; 4) whether Christ can be denied as the Son of God according to his humanity; 5) the errors and doctrines of Servetus which are held by some.[29]

The reference to Servetus is important for it reflects the internal divisions among these Italian countrymen who like Martyr fled the Italian inquisitors. Martyr was concerned while at Zurich with two of his countrymen. Giorgio Blandrata was called to the Polish court in 1540 as personal physician to the Queen Bona Sforza of Milan. This scion of a noble family in the Piedmont took his medical degree at Montpellier in 1533 where he specialized in female diseases. After a dozen years Blandrata returned to Italy only to fall under suspicion of the Inquisition. In 1556 Blandrata fled to Geneva, became one of the four elders of the Italian congregation and ran afoul of the Consistory after he raised several questions about the deity of Christ with Calvin. Calvin wrote out an answer in full in 1557 which appeared verbatim in part in the 1559 *Institutes* as a general condemnation of Anti-trinitarian views a la Servetus.[30] Antonio

Rotondo has argued that Calvin in confusion lumped together in his

1559 *Institutes* (I, xiii,23) "certain rascals" with Servetus. Calvin

was wrong for there never was a linear developement in radical views

of the Trinity from Servetus to the Socini.[31] Both Willis and

Friedman think differently. Willis points to the need for greater

attention to Lelio Socini's *Brevis Explicatio* of 1561 with its novel

explication of the prologue to the Fourth Gospel. The rich diversity

of this movement which compelled Calvin to alter his 1559 *Institutes*

is underlined in Rotondo by Willis who at the same time would distin-

guish between the Arianism of Servetus, the Sabellianism of Blandrata

and the modalism of Stancaro.[32] Stancaro would accuse Blandrata of

tri-theism. Friedman on the other side absolves Calvin of confusion

or linear thinking on this question since the secret prologue to *John*

was not well known in Geneva (1560?) and Rotondo underestimates

Servetus.[33] Friedman concludes that such eclectic views which circu-

lated among the Italian radicals can not be associated with any one

family.

Blandrata held several conferences with Martyr in 1558. Martyr

confided to Calvin on 11 June 1558 that these men confessed a multitude

of Gods by their distinction of diversity in the divine essence.[34]

The context was a public meeting of the Italian church which asked

Calvin for help. On 18 May 1558 a confession of faith which all were

expected to sign was introduced. In a heated three hour meeting with

Calvin Blandrata and Aciati made a bad impression and left Geneva without signing the confession.[35] Blandrata visited Berne where

Zurkiden wrote about him to Calvin. Calvin responded on 4 July 1558.

> That madman, when he had annoyed me a whole year, did not offend
> me so deeply by his impious ravings from which I endeavored to
> recall him, as by his perfidy, which though I have always ab-
> horred I did not for all that abstain from admitting him to
> private conferences . . . . Because he furtively distilled his
> venom among his countrymen, he became at length intolerable to
> the pastor and company of elders . . . . I even pardoned his
> wicked slander of which he was openly convicted in presense of
> the whole Italian congregation.[36]

Martyr also interviewed Blandrata in Zurich but could not con-

vince him of any theological error. The nature of the issue can be

read in Calvin's *Response To The Questions of George Blandrata*. One

such question Calvin answered was whether the view was ambiguous that

the eternal Word of God was another substance from but still essential

to the Father. Calvin thought the question was not ambiguous for

though he conceeded that the Word (*Sermo*) was another hypostasis, it

was truly God and the same essence.[37] Calvin on 19 December 1558

urged Lismanini in Poland to "warn the good brethren, before they

learn by experience what a monster Giorgio Blandrata is, or rather,

how many monsters he fosters, to beware of him."[38] All of this gives

one a glimpse into Martyr's private interview with Blandrata in June

of 1558.

The debate with Stancaro was not private, for Martyr in letters

to Poland and in alterations to the *Romans* commentary sought to

answer an important question raised by Stancaro. For the first time

in centuries this theological issue surfaced in Poland in 1556 at the

Synod of Secemin. Martyr then participated in this debate with real

interest since it involved his own countrymen. There could be no
compromise on Martyr's part with Catherine de Medici at Poissy who
in 1561 would use theologians to further her political and dynastic
concerns. Likewise Martyr would not desert his congregation in Lucca
by using theology to further his all too human desire to seek identity
with God through the humanity of Christ alone. The irony lay in the
Italian birth of these three who in foreign lands worked out their
own peculiar salvations with fear and trembling.

On 21-29 January 1556 the Synod of Secemin had the doctrine of
the trinity proposed for discussion by the Lithuanian pastor Piotr
Goniadz.[39] Among other objections, Goniadz queried the trinitarian
formulae of the early ecumenical councils. "Surely faith in One
Father God was not in doubt for four centuries. But woe, the /concept
of the/ Deity of the Son, however, long after the death of the
Apostles sharply separated the Christian World by means of its superstition."[40]

On 14 February 1556 Peter Martyr sent a letter to the Polish
nobility and ministers in which he warned them against Arianism. Martyr
responded to five questions raised by Lismanini for the Polish Church.[41]
First Martyr denied that Christ suffered at all in His divine nature.
Secondly, he confessed that Christ was mediator with respect to both
his human and divine natures. In the third place Martyr asserted
that Christ by nature was both the Son of God and the son of man. In
the fourth place Martyr rejected the essential justice of Osiander
who taught that imputed righteousness was not sufficient.[42] If one

takes Martyr's closing statement on Servetus as point five then his
letter to the Polish nobility is an answer to the five points raised
by Lismanini in Calvin's letter and demonstrates Calvin's dependance
on Martyr in this Polish question. It appears that Martyr answered
Lismanini's letter to Calvin.

Martyr closed his letter with a condemnation of Servetus.

> About Servetus the Spaniard I have nothing else to say than that
> he was a genuine son of the Devil whose fatal and detestible
> doctrine has been exposed for what it was - a prostitution of the
> truth. There is no reason to fault the magistrate who sent that
> one to his death, since when he was accused there were no signs
> of amendment in him. His blasphemy was totally intolerable.

In spite of Martyr's attack on Servetus' doctrine and life, Celsi
cited Martyr in his 1577 *In haereticis coercendis*. Celsi used Martyr
perhaps because Celsi reserved the sword only for rebels against
public authority and was attacking Beza's 1554 *De haereticis a civili
magistratu puniendis libellus*. That Martyr charged Servetus with
blasphemy rather than heresy is significant. One could on those
grounds proceed to instant execution based on *Leviticus* (24) rather
than force a heretic to relapse based on *Titus* (3:10). In this Martyr
seems to follow Musculus rather than Beza. Musculus thought the only
mistake Geneva made was to burn Servetus on a charge of heresy rather
than blasphemy.[43]

In 1560 Calvin responded to Stancaro that Christ's divinity played
a crucial role in his office as mediator. The joint statement of the
Genevan ministers read as follows:

Indeed, the manner in which Stancaro strives to weigh down this

teaching saying that Christ would be less than the Father, if
he interceded with him according to his divinity, is foolish
and of no account. As long as Christ sustains the role of
mediator, he does not hesitate to submit himself to the Father.
He does this not because his divinity had lost its rank when
he was clothed in the flesh but because he could not in any
other way interpose himself as intermediary between us and the
Father without the Father's glory, in the present dispensation,
becoming clearly visible in the person of the mediator. Nor
should Christ's saying that he is less than the Father (*John*
14:28), a statement concerning his humanity, be referred to the
whole person; neither does he unite his humanity with the Father's
divinity, but links the present state with the future, in which
the glory of his divinity will be perfectly revealed. Now, the
entire divinity is denoted under the name of the Father, whose
plenitude is in Christ (*Col.* 1:19, 2:9), and that not only is
the distinction between the persons of the Father and the Son
to be maintained, but also that admirable counsel of God by which
it came about that God's only begotten Son should descend to
us. /341/ So Stancaro discusses worthless quibbles by which he
wants to spread mists, scattering it about that it is not fitting
that the Son of God be mediator according to his divinity because
he would be interceding with himself. Even though the divinity
in the Holy Spirit is the same as in the Father, nevertheless,
we do not say that Christ intercedes with the Spirit, but only
with the Father. In this matter we must consider the economy
of divine wisdom and not give free rein to our speculations.
Christ, for this reason, is said to send the spirit from his
Father (*John* 16:7) to raise us, by degrees, up to the Father.
Finally, on the last day the Son will hand over his kingdom to
God the Father (I *Cor.* 15:28), because then, as I say, the splendor of the glory of God the Father will be instantly visible to
us, the glory which now appears in Christ, his living image.

Would that Stancaro be moved by these words. Then, at length,
it may be hoped that natural endowment, which was raised too much
on high by boasting, may incline him to gentleness and moderation.
We believe, honorable brethren, the matter is sufficiently
proven. May God always govern you by his spirit, and bless
your holy labors.[44]

A second response was twice the length and concentrated on the Logos

as the son of God and eternal.

These two facts, that the $\lambda\acute{o}\gamma o\varsigma$ and eternal son of God is equal
to the Father and that the mediator is less than the Father are
no more incompatible than these two, that the $\lambda\acute{o}\gamma o\varsigma$ by itself and separately is a divine person and, nevertheless, that

the one person of Christ the mediator is constituted by two
natures. Stancaro argues ineptly: if Christ, mediator in two
natures, is less than the Father, then he is less according to
both natures. We have taught above that what truly and suitably
belongs to the totality ought not to be divided and assigned
to the natures, just as the intermediary position which Christ
the Redeemer occupies does not in the least derogate from his
divine essence. The reasons which Stancaro brings forward from
the office of mediator carry no weight since they are drawn
from a part and applied to the whole.[45]

In 1561 the Zurich Pastors addressed two letters to Poland in
which they responded to the synodical endorsement of Stancaro at
Pinczow on 7 August and 19 August 1559. The later meeting used Martyr's writings in arriving at their decision.[46] The letters have on
their title page the verse from I *Timothy* (2:5): "Vnus est Deus, unus
etiam mediator. Dei & hominum, homo Christus Iesus, qui dedit sem-
etipsum pretium redemptionis pro omnibus."[47] Prior to these two letters, Stancaro had written from Poland defending himself against
Arianism. This letter was endorsed by Stanislaus Ostrorog on 10
December 1560.[48] Stancaro mentioned Martyr's letter of 14 February
1556 and sought to exonorate himself from the charge of heresy.[49]

Jan Utenhove had already alerted Martyr to the controversy in
Poland in a letter of 18 September 1558. Utenhove reported his own
participation in the controversy between the Polish nobility and their
ministers about Christ's mediatory activity. A second question arose
over impiety. Utenhove then requested a copy of Martyr's book on
matrimony.[50] Utenhove identified one of the nobles who was addicted
first to Luther and then to Laski. The person was "D. Stanislao ab
Ostrorog Castellano Medzerecensi ex antiquissima ducum familiae."[51]

On 29 November 1559 Martyr answered Utenhove that the number of alien

sects was incredible. A just God brought this on Christendom "be-

cause of our sins." Martyr consoled himself that the *Romans* com-

mentary had been published. He was especially proud of his *Defensio*

against Gardiner. "It is a very large book, and I hope that every-

where it will clearly be esteemed on this universal question

/Eucharist/."[52]

Enough of the issue can be read in these letters and printed

tracts to enable one to see how important a matter this was for Martyr.

Stancaro objected that the Arian heresy was scarcely to be seen in

Poland, a heresy which taught that there were three separate Gods

and three separate human beings.[53] Stancaro himself defended the

catholic doctrine and faith concerning the Trinity and Mediator accord-

ing to Acts 4, 8, 10, 16, and 18 in the sixth synod of Constantinople.[54]

In his confession, Stancaro used the terms *Unus Deus, unius essentiae,*

unius voluntatis et unius operationis of the Christ. Ostrorog in his

defense of Stancaro thought it incredible that anyone could question

his orthodoxy. He went on to answer, viz:

> In your doctrines concerning the trinity and mediation (of
> Christ) it is not at all clear from your books how to determine
> what is determined as orthodox by the Church from the Word of
> God.[55]

The charges of inconsistency rankled Martyr and his supporters

for Stancaro questioned two passages in particular in Martyr's writ-

ings. From Simler one learns that a passage in Martyr's *Corinthian*

Commentary (1551) had been questioned by Stancaro. He had interpreted

Martyr at I *Corinthians* (12) as praying to the Holy Spirit and thereby subordinating God.[56] The letters of the Zurich pastors accused
Stancaro of altering quotations from "our commentaries," a possible
reference to Martyr and Bullinger as well as Simler.[57] Stancaro perhaps objected to this phrase in his letter of 4 December 1560.

The second letter from Zurich dated March 1561 describes Stancaro's
teaching as a version of the Nestorian heresy, i.e., that the humanity
of Christ was only a vehicle for divinity (cuius humanitatas hospitium
uel templum fuerit, ut Nestorius imaginabatur).[58] Stancaro in a
printed response of 1562 accused Martyr of a change in view between
1556 and 1561. The passage in question occurs in Martyr's commentary
on *Romans* (8), page 323. Stancaro dismissed the letter of 27 May 1560
by accusing Martyr of inconsistency.[59] The title, colophon and motto
on the title page of this response are all provocative. Stancaro and
his Polish supporters felt that Bullinger, Calvin and Martyr led a
unified opposition to the true understanding of Christ and His work.

Stancaro again sought to clear himself of the charge of Arianism
when his prefatory letter to the Polish nobility pointed out that
Calvin's preface to the commentary on *Acts* accused Blandrata of
Arianism.[60] Calvin's prefatory letter of 1 August 1560 was addressed
to Duke Nicholas Radziwill. This Commentary was first published in
1552. Stancaro meant the combined second edition of 1554 and 1560.
Calvin nowhere uses the term Arian in this letter, but accused Stancaro and Blandrata of Servetus' ungodliness. Stancaro was tumultuous,
ambitious and delerious.[60a] Bullinger, Martyr and the other Zurich

pastors asked whether Stancaro held that the Father, Son and Holy Spirit were one God, one will and one operation. That is to say, they questioned Stancaro whether or not he believed that the Father, Son and Holy Spirit were three consubstantial persons, coequal and co-eternal who possess the same essence, will and operation. This manner of speaking bothered Stancaro since the Nicene, Constanti-nopolitanean, Ephesian and Chalcedonian synods which defined Christ thus taught definitions or formulae which were not found in the Holy Scriptures.[61]

Stancaro seems to have approached his anti-Trinitarian position from his study of the Old Testament Hebrew names for God. A rare work of 1551 gives fifty-four assertions on the Trinity in which Stancaro depended on Rabbinic exegesis. He first concluded that God was "one divine essence, that is, one God, eternal and incorporeal, maker of heaven and earth . . . ."[62] Conclusions twelve and thirteen make much of the Hebrew term for God used in Exodus (3), Psalm (50) and cited in the Apocalypse. The tense is quoted in the New Testament as extending from alpha to omega, i.e., "Who is, who was and who is to be." This argument based on "Ehyeh" seems to conclude that the essence of God is described in a future or "piel" conjugation. Stancaro then asserted the immutable nature of God's essence to deny any Trinitarian understanding.[63] This transferral of Rabbinic exegesis to Hellenistic concepts of essence would appear to be something not done by the Rabbis themselves. Even Philo kept to a personal God when using Hebraic terms for the divine name. Stancaro introduces the term essence

into exegesis for negative purposes as his opponents had done so for
positive ones. That Stancaro noted the divine name "Ehyeh" in *Psalm*
50 indicates his powers of observation since few published works on
the *Psalms* make a similar observation on *Psalm* 50.

Stancaro preferred to speak of two natures, wills and operations
in the one Lord Jesus Christ which neither conflicted nor contradicted
each other. He accused the church of departing from the true Apostolic
way when it devised the Nicene and successive formulae.[64] Stancaro
upset several theologians in Hungary as well. In 1554 the Lutheran
synod of Szek condemned Stancaro and ordered him to leave the country.
Toth points to two in particular who noted the pseudo-historical ten-
dencies of his teaching. Francis David wrote in 1555:

> Stancarus considers it irrational that God should be a mediator
> toward God or that an equal should approach an equal with
> supplications and from this concludes that the Son of God could
> not be a mediator in His divine nature. This conclusion
> resembles an unloosed broom for Holy Scripture shows the
> mediator as one who is a true God and man.[65]

Stancaro's language grew more abusive as he singled out Martyr
for attack as a heretic and agent of Satan.[66] Had Martyr changed his
views between the time of the 1556 letter and the *Romans* commentary
of 1558? Earlier Martyr condemned prayer to Christ according to His
divine nature as Arianism while now Martyr according to Stancaro
accepts this in the *Romans* commentary at chapter eight, page 323.[67]
Stancaro's reference is to the 1558 Basle edition where Martyr wrote
of Christ's prayer to the Father in *John* (17:21). "Abba pater:"
"Arriani eo detorserunt hunc locum, vt ostenderent, filium patre

minorem esse: quod apud eum intercedat. precari enim, & esse

supplices, inferiorum esse, non aequalium." Martyr then observed

from Ambrose that in this passage 1) The persons are distinct, and

2) The Father is the font and prime principle of all things. "Nam

si filius orat Patrem, necesse est, aliam eius personam esse, aliam

patris." The 1560 third edition varies this text by reading: "Nec

bene affirmabant Ariani, Paulum dicere, spiritum sanctum intercedere

apud filiu. Ex eo enim illi impie inferre volebant, vt sicut

statuebant, filiu esse minore patre, ita spiritum sanctu minore esse

filio," p. 711. On p. 340 of the fourth edition (Basle: Petrus

Perna, 1568) the revised reading of the third edition is maintained.

Martyr's argument was quite sophisticated in its analysis of patristic

teaching. Simler in fact published an examination of the early synods

in 1571 as a contribution to this very significant conflict.[68]

Stanislaus Paclesius who was minister and superintendent of the

Church at Lublinensius wrote to Martyr about Stancaro on 18 August

1562, disturbed that the dogmas of Stancaro troubled the Polish con-

gregations. His deliria meant that several antichrists infiltrated

the churches (eruperunt in penetralia ecclesiae).[69] As late as 1567

Stancaro sought to answer Simler whose 1563 refutation summed up

the entire affair for the Swiss. Stancaro died at Stobinica, Poland

on 12 November 1574.

In all of this lengthy debate which lasted from 1556 until after

Martyr's death in 1562 one finds that Bullinger, Calvin and Martyr

were agreed that the ancient Trinitarian creeds of the church expressed a reality whose denial was dangerous to faith in the living

God. It was such tortuous denials that Martyr sought to expose

during his entire protestant career in exile. In this controversy

Martyr drew closer to Bullinger and Calvin as an orthodox theologian

of ecumenical stature. Stancaro's letter of 4 December 1560 to Calvin,

Musculus, Martyr and Bullinger provoked a response from Beza to

Gualter at Zurich on 27 February 1561.[70] The Genevans also made public

Calvin's letter of 9 June 1560. Calvin wrote *Dilucida explicatio*

against Hesshusius. Beza's letter of 5 August 1567 argued that

Stancaro was Arian for restricting the mediatorship of Christ to His

human nature.[71] There can be little question therefore that Stancaro

posed a threat to orthodox Christology in the minds of Martyr, Calvin,

Beza and Bullinger.

A prayer on *Psalm* (2) given while under constant attack in Stras-

bourg from 1553-1556 summarizes Martyr's view of the person of Christ.

> Althoughe (moste good and myghtie God) the Deuill fret, the
> powers of the worlde stande up daylie, and the fleshe wyth all
> hir seruitors conspire against the kingdome of thy onely sonne
> Jesus Christ our Lord: let us yet understande, yea let us be
> perswaded through a constant fayth that thou doest deryde and
> contemne all such: who (so soone as it pleaseth thee) are hable
> to destroye them in thy wrath and whote displeasure. But alack,
> seing in this confidence we are oftentimes unstable and moueable,
> in so much as we (being led away by dyuers terrours) doe obey thy
> commaudements lesse then it becommeth us, we beseeche thee of thy
> fauorable and bountifull goodnesse to bee mercifull unto us, so
> that we may ground our selves stedfastly upō this rock of faith,
> that thy sonne our king and redeemer hath in thee of all thinges
> the highest power and gouernement, for when thou didst beget him,
> thou gauest all Nations to hym, to rule and gouerne them by
> right of inheritance. Graunt therefore, that we maybe once at
> length be so godlye, wyse, and so ryghtly instructed, as (seru-
> ing thee wyth all reuerence and humble feare) wee bee not at
> the last daye lyke a potters vessell, consumed and brought to

naught wyth the rod of thy indignation: through Jesus Christ
oure Lorde. Amen.[72]

Martyr scarcely qualified as an apostate. He felt that God alone
would reveal those whom He had chosen through Christ and sealed in the
visible signs of Baptism and Eucharist by the promise of the Holy
Spirit.

CONCLUSION

On 10 March 1561 the Heidelberg theologian Zacharias Ursinus
described Martyr to his friend Abel Birkenhahn. Ursinus' contemporary
assessment will summarize this study of Peter Martyr's biblical
writings.[73] Ursinus said that Martyr was clearer than Zwingli or
Oecolampadius and gave as an example a passage from Martyr's commentary on *Romans*. This praise of Martyr's judgment by his opponents
and supporters alike requires sober reflection. To them Peter Martyr's
writings were essential documents of the mid-sixteenth century. Future
studies might well explore how vital these writings were for the Protestant Reformation from 1562-1600. One thinks of letters like that
of Roger Ascham thanking Queen Elizabeth for a copy of the *Kings* commentary in 1566, or again Walter Haddon to Archbishop Matthew Parker
on 13 June 1566 from Bruges about the 1550 letters in the 1566 *Brief
Examination*: Bucer and Martyr are "perfectissimi theologi."[74]

One who followed Martyr out of Italy was Jerome Zanchi who had
known Martyr since 1536. This theologian best known for predestinarian
views at Heidelberg, near the end of his life penned a family confession. One can see here the continuity of Martyr's faith as held

by Zanchi. Shepherd shows how Gründler has edited Zanchi to make

him more bibliocentric/scholastic than Zanchi himself. Zanchi under-

stood that faith was assent not only to the whole word of God re-

vealed in scripture but also to the Gospel. "bearing the joyful news

of redemption accomplished through Christ, we truly recognize,

assuredly know, and lovingly embrace God in it, and the will of God,

Christ the Mediator and his benefits . . . ."[75]

Zanchi remained at Strasbourg to marry Curione's daughter and

taught there when Martyr died. In 1563 he became pastor of the

Italian Church at Chiavenna and in 1568 Zanchi went to Heidelberg for

a decade until John Casimir appointed him head of the new academy at

Neustadt. Zanchi died on a visit to Heidelberg in 1590. In Colonial

New England both Martyr and Zanchi were read by the Puritan ministers.

So did Melanchthon's theme, "To know Jesus Christ is to know his

benefits," travel from Wittenberg, England and Northern Europe to New

England through men like Martyr and Zanchi.[76] The doctrine of the

knowledge of God in Calvin, Martyr and Zanchi rests not only on a

literal interpretation of scripture in their biblical commentaries

but also on a knowledge of God in the person of Jesus Christ crucified.

William Perkins for example included a *Brief discourse, taken

out of the writings of Her. Zanchius* in his 1595 discussion on *How A

Man May Know Whether He Be A Child Of God Or No.*

> neither David for his adultery and murder, nor Peter for his
> threefold denial, did despair of their election: which
> appeareth, in that being plunged in the very gulfs of their
> temptations, they held fast their faith as an anchor, and
> called upon God . . . ."[77]

Brian Armstrong follows Gründler in an attempt to interpret Martyr and Zanchi as those who altered Calvinism in a scholastic direction. "Men like Martyr, Zanchi, Beza, Antoine de Chandieu, and Lambert Danaeus represent this divergence from a theology which had been carefully constructed by Calvin to represent faithfully the scriptural teaching."[78] Armstrong argues that these men would focus on one element in Calvin's thought, destroy his tension and create a scholasticism which reigned at the dawn of the seventeenth century "in all the leading Reformed academies outside France."[79] A reviewer challenges Brian Armstrong's attitude toward Martyr and Reformed Orthodoxy.[80] Calvin's positive evaluation of Martyr seems more to the point than any critique of his friends four centuries later.

From Martyr's initial arrival in Strasbourg which Bucer reported to Calvin until his death Peter Martyr affected the lives of several important protestant reformers in leading centres of dissent. Previous studies have concentrated on Martyr's patristic expertise or his ability to debate the nature of the Eucharist. This study has chosen to demonstrate why Martyr pursued these twin tasks with a rare facility. Behind the learned debates at Oxford and the vigorous treatises against Smith, Gardiner, Brenz and Stancaro one ought to search for Martyr's view of the christian life. One will find in such a quest Martyr's rationale for theological controversy in which the *furor theologicus* was all about the meaning of the death of Christ. Justification for Martyr's flight from persecution is fully expressed in his biblical lectures. Like St. Paul before him who withstood St. Peter to his face, Peter Martyr sought glory only in the cross. Though Martyr may have been no more successful in imitating Christ than many a humble peasant of Oxfordshire or printer of Lyon, the leaders of reformed theology such as Bucer, Bullinger, Beza, Calvin and Cranmer praised Martyr for showing them how to experience in this life the death and resurrection of Christ. That Martyr's biblical writings were invaluable guides for their own lives and work would be reason enough for a study of this Reformer in Exile from 1542-1562.

Martyr's impact on the Elizabethan Bishops calls for a final reflection. Patrick Collinson reminds us that in the summer of 1603 there was substance to the hopes that a Scots' king would honor the Millenary petition of the Puritan party at Hampton Court. This conference aroused echoes of similar formal meetings which in the past solidified religious change. In July 1603 the King even wrote to the vice-chancellors of Oxford and Cambridge to announce acceptance of the puritan remedy for an unlearned ministry.[81] It is tragic that Peter Martyr's influence in England, the puritan aspirations for a godly ministry and the extension of the continental reformation were vitiated by James I in 1604. This study of Peter Martyr documents a vital segment of Anglican history whose recollection may serve to honor the memory of the young king, Edward, the learned Archbishop Cranmer and the gifted reformer, Peter Martyr.

Edward VI's annotated *Benefits of Christ* now in the Cambridge University Library, Archbishop Cranmer's *Homily of Salvation* and Peter

Martyr's biblical writings - - *Romans* and I *Corinthians* in particular

- - prove that once the *Ecclesia Anglicana* almost committed herself

to the Continental Reformation. The young Josiah, Archbishop Cranmer

and Peter Martyr for a few brief months attempted to build the Kingdom

of Christ in England, a task which in Martyr's own words to Utenhove

was the most difficult one in the world. Time and again the English

Parliament proved the accuracy of Martyr's observation.

Martyr's biblical writings enunciate that only reformed men can

reform a church. No one in sixteenth century Europe more clearly

articulated that concern which Martyr and Cardinal Contarini must have

shared in Lucca during the fall of 1541. Like the bishops at Chalcedon

Peter Martyr did not hesitate to add disciplinary canons to doctrinal

definitions even though Martyr, like Contarini, never realized the

goal of sixteenth century reform attempts:

Purga Romam, purgatur mundam.

In the only extant letter from Martyr's Italian period, he de-

scribed his reasons for flight into exile to the Canons of S. Frediano

in Lucca. This letter of 24 August 1542 concludes with the phrase, "I

am free from Hypocrisy through the grace of Christ."[82] The consistency

of Martyr's protestant career in exile rested on this heartfelt freedom

to serve and defend evangelical truth.[83]

John Wesley prepared his *Christian Library* in 1753 for itinerent

Methodist preachers. In volumes **twenty-six** and **twenty-seven** Wesley

included abridged versions of Samuel Clarke's 1683 *The/Lives/Of sundry/*

Eminent Persons/In This/Later Age . . . . Among these lives is that of Peter Martyr which Clarke prepared from Simler and/or Melchior

Adam. Wesley comments:

> Perhaps it may be useful . . . to observe how the same Spirit
> works the same Work of Grace in Men upright of Heart, of what-
> ever Denomination . . . . How far distant soever they are from
> each other, with Regard to the Circumstances of Worship, they
> all meet in the Substance of all true Worship, *the Faith that
> worketh by Love.*[84]

John Wesley placed Martyr between Melanchthon and Calvin, a fitting

position for Pietro Martire Vermigli, Theologian of the Italian Refor-

mation.

Josiah Simler prefaced his *Oration* with a letter to John Jewel,

Bishop of Salisbury in Marytr's *altera patria*. Simler reminded

Jewel how much like a father Martyr had been to this his spiritual

son and closed the *Oration* itself with a prayer which sums up the

impact Martyr made on his many friends in protestant lands.

> Regard (we beseeche thee) thy little flocke, and gouerne it
> according as thou hast promised, and defend it against Wolues.
> Giue it no hyrelings, but faithfull Pastors which may leade thy
> sheepe vnto wholesome pastures and to the fountaines of liuely
> water . . . .[85]

NOTES TO CHAPTER IX

1. Klaus Sturm, <u>Die Theologie Peter Martyr Vermiglis</u>, pp. 127-175.

2. <u>Ibid.</u>, p. 128n.88; p. 132 n. 111; p. 139; p. 148 n. 209; p. 115 n. 267; p. 161 n. 314.

3. <u>Ibid.</u>, pp. 139-142.

4. Joseph Tylenda, "Calvin And Christ's Presence In The Supper-True Or Real," <u>S. J. T.</u> 27(1974), 74.

5. Sturm, <u>op. cit.</u>, p. 267.

6. <u>Ibid.</u>, pp. 266-268.

7. Common Places (1583), Part three, p. 355.

8. Common Places (1583), Part six, p. 1.

9. Ibid., p. 2.

10. Loc. cit.

11. Ibid., p. 3.

12. Ibid., pp. 5-6.

13. Ibid., p. 9.

14. Loc. cit.

15. Loc. cit.

16. Ibid., p. 12.

17. In 1547 Stancaro published two other grammatical works: Ebreae grammaticae instituto and Suae Ebreae grammaticae compendium. The same month saw publication in Basle of his Opera nuoua della Riformatione. The following account depends on Ruffini, op. cit., and George H. Williams, The Radical Reformation, pp. 570 passim.

18. Williams, op. cit., p. 640.

19. Ibid., p. 641. Lismanini apparently published the 68 page Exemplvm Literarvm Ecclesiae Tigurinae ad Ecclesias Polonicas which is number 1380 in the catalogue: Theodoro Wierzbowski, Polonica XV ac XVIss. Sive Catalogus Librorum Res Polonicas Tractantium Vel A Polonis Conscriptorum Qui In Bibliotheca Universitatis Caesarea Varsouiensis Asservantur (Varsouiae: C. Kowalewski, 1891), p. 109. Item 5 in the Exemplvm is a rare 1559 copy of Martyr's 1556 letter to the Polish church: Petri Martyri Florentini, professoris theologiae in Argentinensi schola, ad ecclesiam Polonicam, Argentiae, 14 Februarii 1556 (Pinczoviae: Apud Danielem Lancicium, MDLIX). Used by permission of Librarian.

20. Ibid., p. 653.

21. C. R. LXVI, 3288, col. 260.

22. George Williams, Radical Reformation, p. 655. E Morse Wilbur, Socinianism and Its Antecedents, p. 298. Wilbur cites from the Collatio though no copy is now extant. See C. T. B. II, 220.

23. Ruffini, op. cit., pp. 215-217.

24. Robert Stupperich, <u>Melanchthon</u>, p. 125.

25. Melanchthon, <u>Responsio</u> (1563), sig. A4^r. See <u>Melanchthons Werke in Auswahl</u> VI, 262-263.

26. Williams, <u>op</u>. <u>cit</u>., p. 656.

27. <u>Melanchthons Werke in Auswahl</u> VI, 10.

28. Williams, <u>op</u>. <u>cit</u>., p. 660.

29. <u>C</u>. <u>R</u>. XLIII, 2350, Col. 869. To Calvin. 15 September 1555. See on Calvin, O. Bartel, "Calvin und Polen," <u>R</u>. <u>H</u>. <u>P</u>. <u>R</u>. 45 (1965), 93-108.

30. E. Morse Wilbur, <u>A History of Unitarianism</u> I, 223-226.

31. Antonio Rotondo, <u>Calvin and the Italian Anti-Trinitarians</u>, p. 28.

32. E. David Willis, "Miszelle," <u>A</u>. <u>R</u>. <u>G</u>. 62 (1971), 279-282.

33. Jerome Friedman, "Servetus . . . A' Propos Antonio Rotondo," <u>B</u>. <u>H</u>. <u>R</u>. XXXV (1973), 544.

34. <u>Common Places</u> (1583), Part five, p. 103.

35. Wilbur, <u>op</u>. <u>cit</u>., pp. 224-225.

36. <u>L</u>. <u>C</u>. III, 430.

37. <u>Calvini Opera</u> (1667), VIII, f. 586.

38. Wilbur, <u>op</u>. <u>cit</u>., p. 225.

39. A. Rotondo, <u>Calvin and the Italian Antitrinitarians</u>, p. 15. See <u>Acta Synodow roznowierczych w Polsce</u> I, 46-52: "Actus Gonedzii Petri, novi Ariani et Servetiani Hoc Tempore prodiit in medio congregationis Petrus Gonedzius, qui ex Lithuania venerat cum litteris illustrissimi d. palatini Nicholai Radziwitt, ducis de Olyka, qui offerbat confessionem per se scriptam, plenam blasphemiarum in Filium Dei et gloriam eius. Eius confessionis haec summa est: Primo, confitetur Trinitatem non esse, immo hoc vocabulum noum et excogitatum esse. Secundo, <u>Symbolum</u> Athanasii a multis temporibus receptum consonumque verbo Dei impugnabat et humanum commentum esse dicebat et penitus abiciebat. Tertio, Deum Patrem esse solum Deum et praeter eum nullum esse alium Deum. Hanc suam sententiam probabat uerbo Christi illo loco: Haec est, inquit, vita aeterna, ut cognoscant te, Pater, solum Deum et quem misisti Iesum Christum. Quarto, Christum

asserebat esse minorem Patre, immo servum Patris, dictum illud Christi repetens: Quia tu me misisti, Pater, etc. Quinto, asserebat esse Verbum invisibile immortale et tempore suo conversum in carnem in utero Virginis. Illud vero invisibile Verbum dicebat esse semen Felii /sic/ incarnati. Sexto, consubstantialitatem denegabat Iesu Christi, quam habet cum Deo Patre in divinitate." Ibid., p.47.

40. Stanislaus Lubieniecio, Historia Reformationis Polonicae, p. 114.

41. Common Places (1583), Part six. p. 90.

42. An interpretation of Osiander seen in Martyr's response, Ibid., p. 91.

43. Opuscula (1582), Sig. G3^v. 14 February 1556. Strasbourg. On Celsi see Cantimori, Eretici Italiani, pp. 295-306 and Peter G. Bietenholz, "Mino Celsi and the Toleration Controversy of the Sixteenth Century," B. H. R. XXXIV (1972), 42 and 46.

44. Joseph Tylenda, "Christ The Mediator: Calvin Versus Stancaro," C. T. J. 8 (1973), 15-16.

45. Joseph Tylenda, "The Controversy On Christ The Mediator: Calvin's Second Reply to Stancaro," C. T. J. 8 (1973), 153.

46. Francesco Ruffini, Francesco Stancaro, p. 212. A copy of the Synod's resolution may be found in Stancaro's De Trinitate & Mediatore of 1562.

47. Epistolae Dvae, Ad Ecclesias Polonicas, Iesv Christi Euangelium amplexas, scriptae a Tigurinae ecclesiae ministris, de negotio Stancariano & mediatore dei & hominum Iesu Christo, an hic secundum humanam naturam duntaxat, an secundum utranque mediatore sit (Tiguri: Christophorus Froschouerus, mense Martio 1561).

48. Both letters are in C. R. XLVI, 3288 & 3290 respectively. The autographs are in the Z. S. A. EII (371), fol. 815 and EII (371), fols. 816-817. It is not clear from the C. R. that Stadnicius is Stanislaus Ostrorog. Stancaro addressed letter 3288 to Musculus, Martyr, Calvin and Bullinger while Ostrorog sent his endorsement to Calvin, Musculus, Bullinger, Martyr and the Lausanners.

49. Z. S. A. EII (371), fol. 815^r.

50. "liberos suos matrimonio iungant cum infidelibus." Z. S. A. Eii (371), fol. 719^r. Raptim prope Cracouiam. This would be the Defense of Clerical Marriage Against Richard Smith, published at Basle in 1558.

51. <u>Loc. cit</u>. See Theodor Wotschke, "Stanislaus Ostrorog, Ein Schutzherr der grosspol nischen euangelischen Kirche" <u>Z. H.G. P. P.</u> XXII (1907), 1-76.

52. Daniel Gerdes, <u>Scrinium Antiquarium</u> III, II, 677-78.

53. <u>C. R.</u> XLVI, 3288, col. 260. <u>Z. S. A.</u> EII (371), fol.815[r].

54. <u>Ibid.</u>, cols. 261-262. <u>Z. S. A.</u> EII (371), fol. 815[r-v].

55. <u>C. R.</u> XLVI, 3290, col. 266. <u>Z. S.A.</u> EII (371), fol. 816[v]. See also the report of Gregorius Paulus to Martyr and Bullinger from Cracow on 24 September 1562. <u>Z. S. A.</u> EII (367), fols. 176-178. Here the interpretation of I <u>John</u> and the Sabellian controversy was an issue.

56. <u>Responsio ad Maledicum Francesci Stancari Mantuani Librum aduersus Tigurinae ecclesiae ministros, de Trinitate & Mediatore Domino nostro Iesu Christo, auctore Iosia Simlero Tigurino</u> (Tiguri: Christ. Froschouerus, M. D. LXIII), Part II, p. 23[v]-24[r]. I have not seen Simler's <u>De Aeterno Dei Filio</u> . . . <u>et de Spiritu sancto</u> (1568). Simler's letter of 1563 to the Polish Church is reproduced in <u>Valentini Gentilis teterrimi Haeretici impietatum ac triplicis perfidiae & periurii, breuis explicatio</u> (1567), pp. 65-74.

57. <u>Epistolae Duae</u>, "Epistola Prior," p. 9. Dated 27 May 1560. "Caeterum si Stancarus ex nostris libris aliquid decerpit, quo nos ostendat a se stare, in eo tam se quam alios fallit. Sed quae loca ex nostris Commentariis arripat, si nobis a fratribus demonstretur, ea facile poterimus explicare: ita ut ueritati, non autem mendaciis aut perturbationibus ecclesiarum seruire intelligant."

58. <u>Ibid.</u>, "Epistola Posterior," p. 25. March 1561.

59. <u>Franciscvs Stancarvs Mantvanvs De Trinitate & Mediatore Domino Nostro Iesu Christo, Aduersus Henricum Bullingerum, Petrum Martyre & Ioannem Caluninu, & Reliquos Tigurinae ac Genuesis Ecclesiae Ministros, Ecclesiae Dei Perturbatores</u>. The colophon reads: "Cracouiae in Officina haeredum Marci Scharfenbergi. Anno Virginei partus M. D. LXII. I Corint. 3. Si quis templum Dei prophanat, quae est ecclesia, hunc perdet Deus."

60. <u>Ibid.</u>, n.p.

60a. John Calvin, <u>Commentariorum in Acta Apostolorum, Libri Duo</u> (1560), sigs. iii[v]-iiii[r]. Calvin's text reads as follows: "Sic dum Stancarus homo tumultuasi ingenii, pro suo ambitione, qua totus flagrat, deliria sua apud vos spargit, hinc erupit contentio quae dissipationem aliquam minatur: & expositi fuistis multorum probis, quia creditum fuit sectam eius latius grassari. Ecce ex altera parte medicus quidam Georgius Brandata, Stancaro deterior, quo magis detestabili errore imbutus est, & plus occultae virulentiae in animo alit." See Delio Cantimori, "Profilo di Giorgio Biandrata Saluzzese," B. S. B. S. 38 (1936), 352-402 and Antonio Rotondo,"Giorgio Biandrata e Johan Sommer," C. S. VIII (1969), 363-400,

61. Stancaro, De Trinitate & Mediatore (1562), sig. Aii^v-Aiii^v.

62. Frances/ci Stancari Man=/Tvani Sacrae Theologiae,/ & Ebraicae linquae in Aca=/demia Regiomontana/Prussiae, publici pro=/ fessoris,/ DISPVTATIO DE/TRINITATE, HABITA/20 IUNIJ 1551,/ . . . CVM EPISTOLA/EIVSDEM STANCARI AD=/monitoria aduersus Epistolam Ga=/latini praeliminarem, sig. A2^r.

63. Ibid., sig. A3^r.

64. Stancaro, De Trinitate & Mediatore (1562), sig. B^r. "Cum duas autem naturas, duasque naturales uolentates, & duas naturales operationes confitemur in uno Domino nostro Iesu Christo non contrarias eas, nec aduersas ad alterutru dicimus (sicut a uia ueritatis errantes Apostolicam traditionem accusant, absit haec impietas a fidelium cordibus . . ."

65. William Toth, "Trinitarianism versus Antitrinitarianism in the Hungarian Reformation," C. H. 13 (1944), pp. 256-257.

66. De Trinitate & Mediatore (1562), sig. D. ii^r.

67. Ibid., sig. D. vi^r. "Hanc enim interpretationem reiicit Petrus Martyr ut Arrianam & haereticam, quam hic nunc adducit, & laudat in commentariis suis Epistolae ad Rom. 8. pag. 323 in illud Apostoli de Christo, qui & intercedit pro nobis."

68. Scripta Vetervm Latina, De Vna Persona et Dvabvs Natvris Domini et Seruatoris nostri Iesu Christi, aduersus Nestorum, Eutychen & Acephalos olim aedita (Tigvri: Christophorvs Froschovervs, M.D. LXXXI). The catholic defense of the Trinity by the Bishop of Gnesen also made good use of patristic evidence. See Jacobus Vchanski, Brevis Avgvstissimi Ac Svmme Venerandi Sacrosanctae Missae Sacrificii ex sanctis patrib. contra impium Francesci Stancari Mantuani scriptum, assertio (Coloniae Agrippinae: Arnoldus Brickmannus, M.D. LXXVII). An interesting feature of this work is its use of Rabbinical literature. See the list of Rabbis cited in the "Catalogus Authorum."

69. Theodor Wotschke, Der Briefwechsel der Schweizer mit den Polen, pp. 151-153.

70. C. T. B. III, 86-88.

71. Beza, _Epistolarum Theologicarum_ (1597), p. 275.

72. _Psalms_ (1569), sig. Biii^{r-v}.

73. "Abschrift, Briefsammlung des Jakob Monau." Paris, Biblio-theque Ste Genevieve, MS. 1458, Epistolae haereticorum V, 463^v-470^r. First published by Erdmann Sturm, "Brief des Heidelberger Theologen Zacharias Ursinus Aus Wittenberg und Zurich (1560/61)," _H. J._ XIV (1970), 85–119. Reference is from pp. 90–91. On Ursinus see Wulf Metz, _Theologie Des Zacharias Ursinus_ (Zurich: Zwingli Verlag, 1970).

74. Rev. Dr. Giles, _The Whole Works of Roger Ascham_, II, 133. On Ascham's letter see _Works_ III, 69 (edited by James Spedding, London, 1883–92).

75. Norman Shepherd,"Zanchius On Saving Faith," _W. T. J._ XXXVI (1973), p. 36. On details of Zanchi's life see Philip McNair, _Peter Martyr In Italy_, pp. 227–228. Donnelly, _op. cit._, p. 328 n. 87 is the first to see from Martyr's letter to Peter Sturm of 13 April 1561 the "vigentiquinque annis" phrase.

76. Spini, _op. cit._, 451–489. Martyr's memorial to Zanchi is in Hottinger VIII, 843–57.

77. John Coolidge, _The Pauline Renaissance in England_, p. 123.

78. Brian Armstrong, _Calvinism And The Amyraut Heresy_, pp. 37–38.

79. _Ibid._, p. 38.

80. _B. H. R._ XXXIII (1971), 428. For a detailed critique see review by Geoffrey Nuttall, _J. E. H._ XXII (1971), 153–154. See also David Sabean in _A. R. G._ 62 (1971), 327 who points to Armstrong's central thesis that Amyraut preserved Calvin's humanistic emphasis. That is Donnelly's point about Martyr.

81. Patrick Collinson, _The Elizabethan Puritan Movement_, pp. 449–450.

82. Philip McNair, _Peter Martyr In Italy_, p. 288.

83. _Loc cit._

84. John Wesley, _A Christian Library_ (1753), XXVI, pp. vi-vii.

85. _Oratio_ (1563).

APPENDIX I

REGISTER EPISTOLARUM VERMIGLII

This checklist is preliminary to an index complete with
incipits in preparation for the Kingdon-Donnelly Bibliografia
Vermigliana. The reader will note that no attempt has been made
to list every occasion on which a letter appears in the multiple
editions of the Loci Communes. Translations of Latin autographs
and copies may be located from this checklist as well as the range
of sources in which Martyr correspondence is extant. I am grateful
to Dr. Philip McNair who loaned his similar list in 1971 to check
against mine.

SIGLA:

Ascham - Epistolae Rogeri Aschami (1703)

A.S.T. - Archives Du Chapitre De St. Thomas De Strasbourg

B. - Bodleian, Oxford

Baum - J. W. Baum, Theodor Beza (1843-1851)

B. Ste. Gen. - Bibliotheque Ste Genevieve, Paris

Bindseil - Philippi Melanchthonis Epistolae (1874)

B.N.C.V.E. - Biblioteca Nazionale Centrale Vittorio Emanuele II, Rome

B. U.P. - Bibliotheque Universitaire Publique, Geneva

C.C.C.C. - Corpus Christi College Cambridge

C.P. (1583) - Common Places (Marten translation)

C.R. - Corpus Reformatorum

C.T.B. - Correspondance De Theodore De Beze

C.U.L. - Cambridge University Library

G. - G. C. Gorham, Gleanings (1857)

Goode.- William Godde, An Unpublished Letter (1850)

H. - C. Hopf, Martin Bucer (1946)

Her. - Herminjard, Correspondance des Reformateurs

Hott. - Hottinger, Historiae Ecclesiasticae Novi Testamenti

Huelin - Peter Martyr And The English Reformation (1955)

L.C. - Loci Communes (1576-1656)

L.L. - Lambeth Palace Library, Selden Papers

M.H.R. - Musee Historique de la Reformation, Geneva

Muller - J.A. Muller, Letters of Stephen Gardiner (1933)

Norton - An Epistle Unto Somerset (1550)

O. - Gerdes, Scrinium Antiquarium (1753)

O.L. - Original Letters (Parker Society Edition, 1846-1847)

Parma - Archivio di Stato, Parma

S.A. - Scripta Anglicana (1577)

Strype - Memorials of Cranmer (1694), Ecclesiastical Memorials (1812)

S.S. - Simmlerische Sammlung, Zurich Zentralbibliothek.

T.B. - Thesaurus Baumianus, Strasbourg

Tig. - Epistolae Tigurinae (Parker Society Edition)

Wotschke. - Der Briefwechsel der Schweizer mit den Polen (1908)

Z.L. - Zurich Letters (Parker Society Edition, 1842-1845)

Ficker - Ficker und Winckelmann, Handschriftenproben . . . nach
     Strassburger Originalen (1905).

Kelley, Francois Hotman (1973).

White, John, Diacosio-Martyrion (1553)

	Date	Place	Correspondent	Location
	1542			
1.	14 January,	Basle	Bullinger	Z.S.A., E II 340 (111)
2.	24 August,	Fiesole	San Frediano	Parma
3.	5 October,	Basle	Bullinger	S.S. MS. C.S 52 /14/ ZSA, E II 340 (112)
4.	17 October,	Basle	Bullinger	SS, 52 (86)
5.	19 December,	Strasbourg	Bullinger	S.S. MS. C.S. 52(86)
	1543			
6.	8 January,	Strasbourg	San Frediano	L.C. (1582)/C.P.(1583)
7.	14 July,	Strasbourg	Melanchthon	C.R. 5, 143
	1544			
8.	13 April,	(Strasbourg)	Bucer	T.B. MS674: Reg. XV. 32-33 A.S.T. 40.21.28.
9.	29 December,	Strasbourg	Neuchateloise	C.R. 39,597 Her. IX: 436-441
	1545			
10.	7 July,	Strasbourg	Bullinger	Z.S.A., E II 340(157^{r-v})
11.	23 December,	Strasbourg	Bucer	T.B. Reg. XVI, 158th
	1546			
12.	6 December,	Ratisbon	Bucer/Zurich Pastors	T.B. Reg. XVII, 130-133 U. 159-161 C.R. 40
	1547			
13.	22 August,	(Lambeth)	Dryander	T.B. Reg. XVIII, 87 A.S.T. 92 y. 40, fol.837
14.	5 October,	(Lambeth)	Dryander	T.B. Reg. XVIII, 102 A.S.T. 40, fol. 839

1548

15.	21 September, Oxford	Utenhove	O III.II, 662-664/G.
16.	26 December, (Oxford)	Bucer	T.B. Reg XIX, fol. 125-127 A.S.T. 159: 83,84,85 Tig., O.L. II

1549

17.	3 January	Dryander	T.B. Reg XX, 2-3 A.S.T. 40, 881^{r}
18.	15 January	Utenhove	O. III. II. 664-666
19.	22 January	Bucer	T.B. Reg. XX, 14-15 Tig./O.L. II/A.S.T.
20.	1 February	Dryander	T.B. Reg. XX, 18 A.S.T.
21.	9 May	Utenhove	O. III. II. 666-667
22.	15 June	Bucer	T.B. Reg. XX, 87 A.S.T. 177: 87-96 (German text and letter of 20 June) G./Strype/S.A./L.C. (1627), f. 760.
23.	20 June	Bucer/Martyr	A.S.T. 177: 87-96 T.B. MS. 679 Reg. XX, 92-96. S.A. 546-550 G.
24.	13 August	Cecil	T.B. MS. 679 Reg. XX,132
25.	August	Bucer	G.
26.	10 September	Strasbourg Pastors	C.C.C.C. MS. 119:89
27.	18 December	Bucer	C.C.C.C. MS. 102,107-110 G.
28.	?	Tower of London	Gardiner/Martyr B.M. Arundel MS.100 Muller, Letters of Gardiner, 445-6

<u>1550</u>

29.	10 January	Bucer	T.B. MS. 679, Reg. XX, 161-162 Ascham, 437f.
30.	27 January	Bullinger	Z.S.A. EII 369 (84) Tig./O.L.II.
31.	March	Somerset	Norton/G.: 128-140
32.	31 March	Bucer	G/C.C.C. MS. 119,119-20.
33.	1 June	Bullinger	Z.S.A. E II 369(83) Tig./O.L.II
34.	1 June	Gualter	Tig./O.L.II
35.	10 June 11 June	Bucer	G/C.C.C. MS. 119, 107-08 C.C.C.C. MS. 119,117-118
36.	1 July	A Friend	(Cheke? Strype, <u>Cranmer</u>) L.C. (1582)/C.P. (1583)/ L.C. (1587)/L.C. (1603)/G.
37.	31 August	Bucer	G./C.C.C. MS. 102, 91-94
38.	6 September	Bucer	G./C.C.C. MS. 119, 106y-106
39.	10 September	Bucer	G./TB/B.M.Add.MS.19,400, no.3.
40.	20 September /T.B. 20 October/	Bucer	C.C.C. MS.119,106E B.M. Add. MS. 19400, fol. 20/T.B. MS.679: Reg. XX, fol. 212.
41.	17 October	Hooper/Bucer & Vermigli	2 Hooper XIV Strype (1812) II/ii.455
42.	25 October	Bucer	H/Bod. MS. New College 343, f. 14-15
43.	4 November	Hooper	L.C. (1582)/C.P.(1583) L.C. (1587)/L.C.(1603) G./B.M.

44.	11 November	Bucer	C.C.C.C. MS.119, 106 -106 G.
45.	1 December	Cooche	C.P. (1583)

1551

46.	10 January	Bucer	T.B. Reg. XX, 237-38. C.C.C.C.119, 106 G./Ascham/Mem.Cranmer II
47.	Preface I <u>Corinthians</u> (1551)	Edward VI	C.U.L.
48.	28 January	Bullinger	Tig./O.L.II
49.	/2/ February	Bucer	B.M. Add. MS.28571, fol. 47-48 G. (Not in any L.C.)
50.	8 March	Rosenblatt	T.B. MS. 679, Reg. XX, 252/L.C. (1580), 572 L.C. (1613), 1088-89
51.	8 March	Hubert	A.S.T. 165: 207, 208 (2 copies) T.B. Reg. XX, 249-50 L.C. (1624) Tig./O.L. II
52.	8 March College St.Thomas		G./L.C. (1576)/L.C. (1582)/C.P. (1583)
53.	10 March	Cheke/Martyr	G./Strype, <u>Cheke</u> (?)
54.	March	Bucer's Widow	L.C. (1576)/L.C.(1582) C.P. (1583)
55.	/March?/	John Warner/ Martyr	C.C.C.C. MS. 119:109
56.	25 April	Bullinger	O.L. II/Tig.
57.	25 April Oxford	Gualter	L.C. (1582) 25 October C.P. (1583)/L.C.(1587) L.C. (1603)/G.
58.	6 August	Bullinger	O.L. II/Tig.
59.	7 September	Hubert	A.S.T. 41, 97-98 T.B. Reg. XX,262-63

60.	26 October		Bullinger	O.L. II/Tig.
61.	23 November		Heinrich, Count Palatine	SS 76:93/Huelin

1552

62.	23 February		Hubert	A.S.T.41: 103-05-07 T.B., Reg. XXI, 10-11.
63.	6 March,	Lambeth	Gualter	O.L.II/L.C.(1576)/Tig. L.C.(1582)/C.P.(1583) L.C.(1587)/L.C.(1603)
64.	7 March,	Oxford	Cecil	Strype, Mem. Cran. (1694), II, 228-9
65.	8 March,	Lambeth	Bullinger	O.L.II
66.	14 June,	Oxford	Bullinger	2 Brad.403 (Parker Soc.) Goode/G.
67.	10 September		Hubert	A.S.T. 41: 115,117,119 T.B., Reg. XXI, 25-26
68.	4 October,	Oxford	Bullinger	G./Z.S.A.

1553

69.	/8 Jan?/		Hubert	A.S.T. 41: 123,125
70.	1553?			T.B. Reg. XXI, 42
71.	7 March,	Oxford	Cecil	BM./Strype, Cranmer, 228-9
72.	18 April,	Oxford	Haddon	B.M./Strype, Cranmer,227
73.	23 April		Hubert/Martyr	Hubert, Historia vera, 195
74.	9 May,	Oxford	Utenhove	G./O.
75.	20 July		Hubert	A.S.T. 41: 127-129 T.B., Reg. XXI,54-55
76.	29 October		Bullinger	Schmidt
77.	3 November,	Strasbourg	Calvin	L.C.(1582)/C.P.(1583) L.C.(1587)/L.C.(1603) L.C.(1613)/C.R. 1842

78.	3 November		Bullinger	Z.S.A./O.L.II/Tig.332
79.	15 December		Bullinger	Z.S.A./O.II/Tig.
80.	30 December		Bullinger	Z.S.A., E II 340(225/26)
81.	27 December /L.C.(1582)7Aux scolarques			A.S.T. 346, 62-63
82.	30 December		Lavater	L.C.(1576)/L.C.(1582) C.P.(1583)/L.C.(1587) L.C.(1603)

1554

83.	22 January,	Strasbourg	Students St. Thomas	A.S.T.346, fol. 119
84.	22 January		Bullinger	Z.S.A./O.L.II/Tig.
85.	21 February		J. Sturm	A.S.T.173: 110
86.	24 February		Bullinger	O III.II.668-69 Z.S.A./O.L.II./Tig.
87.	13 March		Bullinger	S.S. MS.C.S. 81/1077 Z.S.A. E II, 340 (214)
88.	3 April		Bullinger	Z.S.A./O.L.II/Tig.
89.	9 May,	Strasbourg	Calvin	L.C.(1582), Cols. 231-232 C.P.(1583)/L.C.(1613) -
	/1 January 1554 in G. 310-117			8 May/C.R. 1953/G.
90.	29 May		Melanchthon	Bindseil, #382 Z.S.A. E II 356(197-98)
91.	26 June		Friend /Melanchthon7	L.C.(1576)/C.P.(1583) L.C.(1587)/L.C.(1603)/G.
92.	27 August		Calvin/Vermigli	Constable, 59
93.	6 September,	Geneva	Calvin/Vermigli	C.R. 2003
94.	24 September,	Strasbourg	Calvin	C.R. 2014
95.	30 September,	Strasbourg	Omnibus Anglis	L.C.(1582)/C.P.(1583)
	/McNair dates 1555 - dated 1554 in			L.C.(1587)/L.C.(1623)
	L.C.(1627) fol. 270-717			L.C.(1627)/C.R.2014
96.	12 October		Foxe/Martyr	Strype, Ecc.Mem. VII (1816), 153-54.

97. /1554/	Foxe/Martyr	Strype, Ecc. Mem.VII, 151-152
98. 20 October	Bucer	T.B.Reg. XX, 212.
99. 29 October	W. Musculus	A.S.T. 159: 93,94 T.B., Reg. XXI, 93+ Zofingen MS.I, fol.24^r-v. (auto)
100. 18 November	Beza	C.T.B. I, 147 L.C. (1580)/L.C.(1582) C.R.2049/C.P.(1583)
101. ?	A Friend	L.C.(1582)/C.P.(1583)/G.
102. 27 November, Geneva	Calvin/Vermigli	Z.S.A., EII 358 C.R.2053/Constable 98
103. 10 December	Bullinger	Z.S.A., E II 340(215)
1555		
104. 18 January, Geneva	Calvin/Vermigli	C.R.2089/Constable 121
105. 29 January	Bullinger	S.S., MS. C.S.84 /49/ Z.S.A., E II 340(216/17)
106. 17 February	Bullinger	Z.S.A.,E II 340 (220/22)
107. 8 March	Calvin	C.R.2142/L.C.(1576) L.C.(1582)/C.P.(1583) L.C.(1587)/L.C.(1603) L.C.(1623)/G.
108. 8 March (Internal date)	Beza	C.T.B. I, 153-155 L.C.(1576)/L.C.(1580) L.C.(1582)/C.P.(1583), 105-106.
109. 16 April	Bullinger	Z.S.A., E II 359(2950)
110. 18 June	Alexandre	L.C.(1576)/L.C.(1582) C.P.(1583)/L.C.(1587) L.C.(1603)
111. 3 July	Bullinger	C.R. 2237
112. 8 August, Geneva	Calvin/Martyr	C.R.2266/G/Constable 217

113. 23 September,Strasbourg Calvin   C.R. 2301/C.P.(1583)
     L.C.(1582) dates 23 Sept.
     L.C.(1587) dates 25 Sept.
     L.C.(1603)
     L.C.(1613) dates 23 Sept.

114. 25 September   Hardenberg   Rome, B.N.C.V.E.II,Busta
     153, n. 23

115. 8 December   Calvin   C.R.2357

116. 31 December   Bullinger   Tig.338-39/O.L.II/Z.S.A.

117. ? (1555)   Cranmer   2 Cran 457(Parker)/O.L.I

1556

118. 13 January   Calvin   C.R.2377/B.U.P.
     MS. Lat. 112 f. 1-2

119. 14 February   Polish NobilityL.C.(1582)/C.P.(1583).

120. 16 February   Calvin   C.R.2390/L.C. (1576)
     L.C.(1580)/L.C.(1582)
     C.P. (1583)/L.C.(1583)
     L.C. (1587)/L.C.(1603)
     L.C.(1623)/G.

121. 1556 Fragment   Calvin   C.R.2390/L.C.(1583)

122. 17 February   Bullinger   S.S. MS. C.S.86/150/

123. 18 February   Wolf   Tig./O.L.II

124. 15 March   Grindal   Strype, Cheke, 130=
     C.P. (1583)

125. 4 April   Lavater   L.C.(1582)/C.P.(1583)
     L.C.(1587)/L.C.(1603)
     L.C.(1623)/L.C.1624),784

126. 5 April,   Strasbourg Bullinger   S.S. MS. C.S.87/70/
     Z.S.A. E II 359 (2951)

127. 16 April /1556-C.R./1559L.C.(1576)/   L.C.(1582)/C.R.3092
     Calvin   C.P.(1583)

128. 21 April,   Zurich   Calvin   L.C.(1576)/L.C.(1582)
     C.P. (1583)

129. 1 May	Bullinger/ Vermigli	Z.S.A. E II 347, S.323
130. 7 May	Bullinger	G./L.C.(1582)/C.P.(1583 L.C.(1587)/L.C.(1603) L.C.(1623)
131. 7 May	Burg.Rat/Zurich	Z.S.A. E I 1(3)
132. 22 May	Bullinger	G./C.P.(1583)/L.C.(1587) L.C.(1603)/L.C.(1623)
133. 7 June	Utenhove	O III.II., 670-71
134. 14 June	Calvin	C.R.2479
135. 29 June	Bullinger	G./L.C.(1582)/C.P.(1583) L.C.(1587)/L.C.(1603) L.C.(1623)
136. 30 June 3 June /C.P.(1583)/	Lavater	L.C.(1580)/L.C.(1582) C.P.(1583)/L.C.(1587) L.C.(1603)/L.C.(1613), 1117/L.C.(1623)/G.
137. 7 July	Calvin	B.U.P. Ms. Lat. 112 f.3-4/C.R.2494
138. 3 August	Friend(see 120)	C.P. (1583)
139. 14 August	Sleidan	176:551 A.S.T.24:338,339
140. 11 September	W. Musculus	Zofingen: MSI, fol.23^{r-v}.
141. 1556	San Frediano	L.C.(1576)/L.C.(1582) C.P.(1583)/M.H.R.: H. Mar 3

1557

142. February, Geneva 31 January (Constable)	Calvin/Martyr	S.S. MS. C.S.89/32/ S.S. MS. C.S.89(37) C.R.2591/Con.III 313
143. 15 March, Zurich	Friend	G./L.C.(1582)/C.P.(1583) L.C.(1587)/L.C.(1603) L.C.(1623)
144. 19 March	Stump	S.S. MS. C.S. 313(107)

145. 8 April	Calvin	C.R.2614/L.C.(1582) C.P.(1583)/L.C.(1587) L.C.(1603)/L.C.(1623)
146. 21 April/McNair//1553?/	Calvin	C.P.(1583)
147. 29 May	J. Crato	Z.S.A E II 361(289)
148. 5 June	Poullain	C.T.B.II, 251-252
149. 8 June	Magistrat.Stras.A.S.T.43:313,314	
150. 10 June	Utenhove	O.
151. 16 June	Curione	Kutter, 279-30
152. 23 June	Utenhove/Martyr & Bullinger	O.L. II, 596-604
153. 1 July	Calvin	Hottinger VIII, 829 Gotha, Bib. Ducale MS.405, f.328
153a.15 July	Maria Ponet	O.L. I, 118.
154. 20 July	Beza	C.T.B. II, 79/C.R.2665
155. 20 July	Calvin	C.R.2667
156. /July 1557?/	Calvin	C.R.2668
157. 24 August	Beza-Bullinger/ Vermigli	Z.S.A. E II 348(461) C.T.B.II, 86-93/C.R.2689
158. 29 August	Calvin	C.R.2690/L.C.(1582) C.P.(1583)/L.C.(1583) L.C.(1603)/L.C.(1623)
159. 1 September	Calvin/Zurich Pastors	Constable 353
160. 13 October	Calvin	C.R.2742
161. 20 October	Melanchthon	C.P.(1583)/L.C.(1587) 1120/L.C.(1603)/L.C.(1613) L.C.(1623)

1558

162. 20 January	Cooke	O.L.I

163. 8 April	Sampson	O.L.I
164. (?) 8 April (same as 1557?)	Calvin	L.C.(1583)
165. 28 April	Calvin	C.R.2855
166. 6 May	Laelius Socinus	Z.S.A. EII374(297)
167. 22 May	Calvin	C.R.2874
168. $\underline{/22 \text{ May}/}$	Calvin/Martyr	Constable, 421
169. 10 June	Utenhove	O.III.II.,671-74
170. 30 June $\underline{/10 \text{ June}?/}$	Utenhove	Schmidt
171. 10 July	Sampson	Tig.121/O.L.I.
172. 11 July	Calvin	L.C.(1576) 11 June L.C.(1582) 11 June C.P.(1583)/L.C.(1587) L.C.(1603)/L.C.(1613) 11 July/L.C.(1623)
173. 20 August 26 August in Schmidt, 215	Goodman	Z.S.A. E II 368(258/59) O.L.II. 768
174. 26 August	Bullinger	Z.S.A. EII346a(389/90)
175. 18 September	Utenhove	Z.S.A. EII371(718-19)
176. 16 September	Calvin	C.P.(1583)
177. 19 September	Bullinger	Z.S.A. EII 374(323,40 & 350-60)
178. 15 October	Cooke (?)	B.M. Add. Ms. 29549, f16-16 Autograph
179. 14 November	Negri/Martyr	T.B. MS.680 Reg. XXI, f.202/S.S. MS. C.S.93$\underline{/118/}$
180. 29 November	Utenhove	O.III.II, 676-78/G.
181. 1 December $\underline{/1558/}$	Calvin	C.R.2988 G./L.C.(1582)/C.P.(1583), 94/L.C.(1587)/L.C.(1603) L.C.(1623)

182.	1̲7̲ December /S̲imler, 18 Decembe̲r̲/	Sampson	Z.L.1,1.
183.	22 December	Elizabeth I	B.M./G./L.C.(1582) C.P.(1583)

1559

184.	7 January	Utenhove	O.III.II.674-76 G., 405-407
185.	18 January	Viret	Z.S.A. E II 371(737) C.R. 3001
186.	26 January	Jewel	4 Jewel(Parker)/Z.L.I,6
187.	27 January	Polish Reformers	S.S.
188.	12 February	Cooke	Z.L.II, 13/Z.S.A./Tig.8
189.	6 Nonnes March	Calvin/Vermigli	C.R.3048/Z.S.A.
190.	20 March	Jewel	4 Jewel (Parker)/Z.L.I,9 Tig.5
191.	6 April	Jewel	4 Jewel (Parker)/Z.L.I,13 Tig.7
192.	14 April	Jewel	4 Jewel (Parker)/Z.L.I,17 Tig.9
193.	16 April	Calvin	C.R.3042/L.C.(1583) L.C.(1587)/L.C.(1603) L.C.(1623)
194.	28 April	Jewel	4 Jewel (Parker)/Z.L.I,19
195.	1559 /d̲ate?̲/	Jewel	4 Jewel (Parker)/Z.L.I,23 Tig.11
196.	4 May	Viret/Vermigli	C.R.3048/Z.S.A.
197.	6 May	Olevian/Vermigli	C.R.3049
198.	29 May	Melanchthon	Z.S.A.EII356(197/198)
199.	13 June	Utenhove	S.S.
200.	13 June /1̲560?̲/	Blauer	Z.S.A.EII357(458ff.)
201.	18 June	Sandys	L.L. MS. 2010
202.	15 July	Sampson	L.C.(1582)/C.P.(1583) Z.L.II,25/L.C.(1587) L.C.(1603)/L.C.(1623)/Tig.15

203.	1 August	Jewel	4 Jewel(Parker)/Z.L.I,38 Tig.22
204.	16 August	Blauer	Z.S.A. EII 437(471-74)
205.	22 August	Cox	L.L. MS. 2010,**Defensio**(1559)
206.	26 August	Calvin	L.C.(1583)
207.	31 August	Cox	L.L.MS. 2010
208.	26 September	Calvin	L.C.(1582)/C.R.3119 L.C.(1583)
209.	4 October, Zurich	Calvin	T.B. Reg.X,36/C.R.3122
210.	4 October, Zurich	Beza	C.T.B.II,25/C.R.3123 L.C.(1580),580/C.P.(1583)
211.	10 October, Geneva	Calvin/Vermigli	C.R.3122
212.	2 November	Jewel	4 Jewel (Parker)/Z.L.I,44 Tig.25
213.	4 November	Friend /Sampson/	L.C.(1582)/C.P.(1583) Z.L.II,32 (Mentions letter of 27 August not extant)
213a.	5 November	Jewel	Z.L.I.52/Tig 30
214.	16 November	Jewel	4 Jewel (Parker)/Z.L.I,54 Tig.33
215.	29 November	Utenhove	O.III.II.676-78
216.	1 December	Jewel	4 Jewel (Parker)/Z.L.I,59

1560

217.	6 January	Sampson	Z.L.I,62
218.	22 January /1561/	Hotman	Dareste, 28-30
219.	28 January	Grindal	L.L. MS.2010/B.M. MS.32091 f.179
220.	1 February	Sampson	L.C.(1582)/C.P.(1583) Z.L.II,38 (Mentions letter of October 1559 not extant)
221.	4 February	Jewel	4 Jewel (Parker)/Z.L.I,67
222.	5 March	Jewel	4 Jewel (Parker)/Z.L.I.,70 Tig.40

223. 20 March	Friend /Sampson/	L.C.(1582)/Z.L.II,47 C.P.(1583)
	(Mentions letter of 6 January extant)	
224. 1 April	Sandys	Z.L.I,72/Tig.42
225. 5 May	Calvin	C.R.3196
226. 9 May	Folkertzheimer /Wolf/	C.R.3195/S.S.MS.C.S.97 /32/ T.B. MS. 680:Reg.XXI,225
227. 13 May	Sampson	Z.L.I,75/Tig.44
228. 22 May	Jewel	4 Jewel (Parker)/Z.L.I,77 Tig.45
229. 1 June	Jewel	4 Jewel (Parker)/Z.L.I,80
229a.13 June	Blauer/Martyr	Z.S.A.,E II,437(a)(475-90)
230. 18 June	Martyr/Cox	L.L.MS.2010
231. 18 June	Sandys	L.L.MS.2010
232. 17 July	Jewel	4 Jewel (Parker)/Z.L.I.
233. 31 July	Calvin	C.R.3460
234. 5 November	Cooke	B.M.Add.MS.29459,f.18^r
235. 6 November	Jewel	4 Jewel (Parker)/Z.L.I,91 Tig.54
236. 4 December	Stancaro/ Martyr, et. al.	C.R.3288/Z.S.A.E II 371(815)
237. 10 December	Stanislaus Ostrorog	Z.S.A. E II 371 (816/17)
238. /Dec. 1560?/	Certain Friend	C.P.(1583) Not dated in L.C.editions
238a./June (?)/ 1561	Cox/Martyr	Z.L.I.,65-67/Tig.38
239. (1561?)	Hubert	A.S.T.
240. January 22 (1560)	Hotman/Martyr- Beza-Bullinger	S.S. MS. C.S.239/21a/ Z.S.A. E II 356a(860) Revue Historique II (1876),29 Kelley, 343.
/November 20/ 241. 15 February	Stranger's Church	L.C.(1582)/C.P.(1583)

242.	13 April	Peter Sturm	L.C.(1582)/C.P.(1583) L.C.(1587)/L.C.(1603) L.C.(1623)
243.	23 April	Peter Sturm	T.B. MS.681 Reg.XXII,5
244.	29 May	Crato/Vermigli	Z.S.A., E II 361(289)
245.	July	Earl of Bedford	G./C.P. (1583)
246.	12 July	Hotman/Martyr	Z.S.A. E II 345(489)
247.	12 July	John Sturm	S.S. MS.C.S. 239(215a)
248.	12 July	Hubert	A.S.T.4.206 or 233.
249.	13 July 31 July	Calvin	C.P. (1583) L.C. (1582)/L.C.(1656)
250.	21 July	Peter Sturm	A.S.T.159:95,96,97
251.	22 July	Prince in England	L.C.(1582)/C.P.(1583) Z.L.II,57
252.	July	Farel/̄Dubious̄/	C.R.3462 S.S. MS.C.S.239/̄223b̄/
253.	12 August	Calvin	C.R.3516
254.	13 August	Calvin	L.C.(1583)
255.	15 August	Calvin	L.C.(1582/C.R.3481 C.P.(1583) Same as 13 August (?)
256.	15 August	Jewel	L.L.MS.2010
257.	17 August	Calvin	C.T.B.II/C.R.3483 Baum
258.	20 August	Zurich Senate	Baum, 57-58
259.	23 August	Parkhurst	L.C.(1582)/C.P.(1583)
260.	29 August	Zurich Senate	Z.S.A. E I, 13
261.	12 September	Zurich Senate	Baum 62/63
262.	12 September	Bullinger	L.C.(1582)/C.R.3517 C.P. (1583)

263.	12 September	Calvin	C.R.3516
264.	19 September	Zurich Senate	Baum
265.	19 September	Bullinger	L.C.(1582)/C.P.(1583) Z.S.A.E II 374(332-40&350-60)
266.	24 September	Bullinger	C.R.3544
267.	30 September	Exhibita	Baum/L.C.(1582)
268.	2 October	Bullinger	L.C.(1582)/Baum,395(13) C.P.(1583)
269.	4 October	Zurich Senate	Z.S.A. E I 1(L3)
270.	4 October	Calvin	C.R.3547/L.C.(1582) C.P.(1583)/L.C.(1587) L.C.(1603)/L.C.(1623)
271.	6 October	Randolf/Martyr	S.S.MS. C.S.239/$\overline{324a}$/
272.	17 October	Zurich Senate	L.C.(1582)
273.	17 October	Bullinger	C.R. 3579/L.C.(1582) C.P.(1583)/L.C.(1587) L.C.(1603)/L.C. (1623
274.	19 October	Lavater	L.C.(1582)/C.R.3576 C.P.(1583)/L.C.(1587) L.C.(1603)/L.C.(1623)
275.	20 October	Bullinger	L.C.(1582)/L.C.(1583) L.C.(1587)/L.C.(1603) L.C.(1623)/C.R.3578
276.	24 October	Bullinger	Z.S.A. E II 358(352-53)'
277.	6 November, Troyes 6 October in C.T.B.III,209 Martyr in Troyes on 5 November	Beza	C.R.3602/L.C.(1580),582 L.C.(1582)/C.T.B.III,209 C.P.(1583)/L.C.(1587) L.C.(1603)
278.	25 November	Beza	C.T.B.III,230/L.C.(1580) 582/L.C.(1582)/C.P.(1583) L.C.(1587)/L.C.(1603)
279.	25 November	Calvin	C.R.3625/L.C.(1582) C.P.(1583)/L.C.(1587) L.C.(1603)/L.C.(1623)

280. 25 November	Gallasius	C.T.B.II,/Z.S.A./ E II 368(545/Baum
281. 14 December	Beza/Vermigli	C.T.B.III, 239-40
282. 31 December	J. Sturm	Zanchi Epist. I, 486

1562

283. January	Peter Sturm John Sturm	A.S.T.165: 312-313 L.C.(1623), 802-803
284. January	Bullinger	C.R. 3691
285. 7 February	Jewel	4 Jewel (Parker)/Z.L.I,99
286. 16 March	Calvin	C.R.3743
287. 19 March	Hubert	T.B. MS.681.Reg.XXII,f.48
288. 22 May 24 May	(Same Letter?) Dist.Gentleman Peter Sturm	Z.S.A. /89a/ L.C.(1582)/L.C.(1656), 904-905. Baum/O.T.Z./C.P.(1583)

Copy in Zurich Zentralbibliothek MS. Car. XV.20(79-88)/ M.H.R:
H.MAR. 2 (French)

289. 26 June	Cooke	Opera Zanchi, 108 Z.L.II, 76
290. 1562?	Hubert	T.B., Reg.XXIII,288-289
291. 15 July	Hubert	A.S.T.41:225
292. 5 August	Bullinger	C.R. 3840
293. 5 August	Cox/Martyr	S.S. MS. C.S.239(213a)
294. 14 August	Jewel	4 Jewel (Parker)/Z.L.I,117
295. 18 August	Stanislaus Paclesius	Z.S.A.E. II 367 (185-188) Wotsche
296. 24 August	Jewel	L.C.(1582)/C.P.(1583) Z.L.I, Appendix L.C.(1587)/L.C.(1603)
297. August	Bullinger	C.R.3840

298. 19 September   Bullinger   Bib.Ste.Gen.MS.347, 47 f. 158

299. 24 September, Cracow   Paulus/Vermigli—C.R.3857 Bullinger   Z.S.A. E II 367(176-78)

300. 1 October   Cox   B.M.

301. 4 October   Cox   L.L. MS.2010

302. 17 November /̄ ?̱/   Bullinger   Z.S.A. E II 367(179-181)

Martyr died on 12 November.

303. 4 May 1556,Zurich   Senate/Martyr   Archives de la Ville de Strasbourg AA. 1816.61

304. 26 May 1562, Geneva   Calvin/Martyr   A.S.T. II. 92(92)11

305. 1553?   White/Martyr   Diacosio-**Martyrion**

LETTER TO WOLFGANG MUSCULUS

9 September 1556

Clarissimo Viro Domino Volphango Musculo, diuinarum litterarum
professori atque fratri in Christo mihi plurimum obseruando. Gratia
Pax A Deo Patre, per Jesum Christum Seruatorem nostrum.[1]

Quas litteras ad me,[2] uir clarissime, mihique pietatis ac
doctrinae merito longe charissime, per Johannem Hallerum, ecclesiae
uestrae ministrum colendissimum, dedisti, lubenti sane atque grat-
ulabundo animo accepi. Non enim[3] parum sum laetatus, quod a uiro
ista eruditione ac sanctitate praedito sic amanter salutarer, nam
etsi de facie te non uideo in litteris tamen quandam tuae dulcissimae
conversationis umbram experior. Quamobrem ista de causa et gratias
ago et humanitati tuae plurimum debere me sentio meaeque tarditatis
nonnihil piget et pudet, quod in hoc scribendi officio me anteuerteris,
cum tamen de tua praestantia non raro, sed frequenter in mentem
uenerit. Argentinensis Ecclesia, de qua interrogas, et erga quam
hactenus fui et hodie sum mirifice affectus, meretur, et quidem
permultis de causis, me judice, ut non uulgariter ametur: magistratum
quippe habet insignem, florentem scholam, et ministros aliquot
pietate ac eruditione praeclaros; quibus omnibus rebus efficitur ut
licet inde recesserim, de ea nihilominus dilectione, qua eam pro-
sequebar dum illic eram, nihil sit imminutum. Quid igitur, inquies,
inde te commouisti? Quoniam illi, qui primas in ea Ecclesia hodie
habent, in sacramentaria doctrina Saxonicae, ut ita dixerim, factioni
tam uehementer sunt addicti, ut piam ueramque sententiam huius

doctrinae uexandi atque dilacerandi pro concionibus nullum finem

faciant eoque Senatum alioqui pium et bonum impulerunt, ut pati

nolit ab homine docenti sacras litteras quid ea de re sentiendum

uideatur in schola perspicue atque aperte tradi et disputari. Quare

cum leges parum honestae quoad hoc essent impositae, atque compedes

non modo linguae sed etiam calamo iniectae, quando pia iustaque

occasio se obtulit, in libertatem non quidem carnis, uerum Christiani

spiritus, decreui me asserere: siquidem ita manendo ueritatem

silentio meo uidebar prodere, iamque a nonnullis inconstantiae, ne

dixerim perfidiae accusabar, quasi palinodiam tacendo canerem nec ex

mea uocatione qua deberem παρρησία uterer. Quamobrem discessu

meo perspicum facere statui me nullius quietis, honoris, emolumenti

causa mutasse animum, sed idem omnino sentire quod alias et scriptis

et docendo sum professus. Non tamen id tacebo, summo praceptorum

dolore, permultis discipulorum lachrymis, et Senatu diu reluctante

missionem impetratam fuisse, quam tamen ego non sic importune

flagitabam, quasi uellem omnino abire, imo ad manendum ea conditione

me offerebam, ut docendi, scribendi, ac disputandi salua et integra

libertas relinqueretur. Quod cum reclamantibus aduersariis et

rationibus ciuilis administrationis impedientibus obtineri non

posset, post diuturnam cunctationem potestas abeundi tandem facta

est. Ideoque ad hos sanctissimos fratres, a quibus huc aduocabar,

me contuli, cum quibus tranquilla et pacatissima conscientia iam

uiuo. Summam negotii habes, de qua forsitan alii plura scripsissem,

uerum tibi, qui es huiusmodi casibus aliquando exercitatus, haec

nimis multa iudicaui quae animum tuum, uti spero, non parum incit-
abunt ad coelestem patrem una cum caeteris piis orandum, ne bonam,
iustam et ueram causam ita proscindi, conculcari, iacere sinat
digneturque istam maceriam qua sic misere diuidimur a fratribus
tandem auferre, ut aliqundo in ueritate idem sentiamus et dicamus.
Quod tamen aetate nostra difficulter posse fieri animaduerto,
quando tantus ignis ambitionis atque contentionis accensus est et
a nonnullis non pro eruenda ueritate, sed premendis partibus
acerbissime dimicatur. Sed quo minus de humana ratione speratur, eo
ad caeleste auxilium petendum studiosius debemus confugere. De
Zancho uero amantissimo atque doctissimo fratre quid sit futurum
nescio. Erit nihilominus in statione sua quamdiu poterit, et
aliquandiu, ceu arbitror, durabit. Neque enim[4] in iuuenes quemadmodum
in senes animaduerititur; tamen quoad fieri potest, precibus iuuandus
est. Ego uero portum hunc senectutis mihi etiam atque etiam gratulor
et oro Deum immortalem, ut quae faustissima salutatione mihi precaris,
ab illo tua quoque intercessione consequar. Uotis denique omnibus te,
Uir sanctissime atque doctissime, Christi Ecclesiae ac Sancto
Euangelio amplificando incolumem seruari diutissime opto, meque
synceritate christiano offero ad ea omnia sedulo praestanda, quibus
tibi quoquomodo possim gratificari. Uale atque me ut facis ama:
nam ego quoque te in oculis fero, atque in comino plurimum diligo.
Nonis Septembris. 1556. Tiguri. Dominus Bernardis tibi officio-
sissime salutem dicit.

Tui studiosissimus

Petrus Martyr[5]

1. Autograph letter in Ms. I, fol. 23[r-v], Epistolae Autographae variorum eruditione celebrium uirorum saec. XVI. ad Musculos
aliosque scriptae, Staatsbibliothek Zofingen, Switzerland. Published
by permission of the Director.

2. This letter is not extant. I am grateful to Mr. Richard
Kerr of the Cambridge University Library who checked the transcription of this and the following letter. The spelling has been
modernized. Martyr's punctuation is at best tenuous. Tagged 'e'
(ȩ)has not been retained.

3. Text reads '.n.' "nimirum" is a possible reading.

4. "nimirum" possible reading.

5. Seal on letter indicates Martyr was in Zurich. Musculus
was then in Bern.

APPENDIX III

LAMBETH PALACE LETTERS

During the course of research for my thesis <u>Peter Martyr</u> <u>and</u> <u>The</u>
<u>English Reformation</u>[1] which was awarded the degree of Doctor of Philos-
ophy of the University of London in 1955, I had the good fortune to
come across a number of what were up to that time unknown letters of
Peter Martyr, addressed by him to certain bishops of the Anglican
Church during the early years of the reign of Elizabeth I. At the
time when I was studying them they were temporarily housed in the
Library of St. Paul's Cathedral London, but after various vicissitudes
which have been described by the present Librarian of Lambeth, Mr. G.
Bill,[2] they have found their way to the Lambeth Palace Library where
they form part of one of its most important manuscript accessions in
recent years.[3]

The letters, seven in all, are as follows:

No. 82 to Richard Cox, 22 August 1559

No. 83 to Richard Cox, 31 August 1559

No. 73 to Edmund Grindal, 28 January 1560

No. 84 to Edwin Sandys, 18 June 1560

No. 85 to Richard Cox, 18 June 1560

No. 86 to John Jewel, 15 August 1561

No. 87 to Richard Cox, 4 October 1562

It will be seen that the earliest and the latest of the letters were
written to Richard Cox, Bishop of Ely, a man with whom Martyr had
been closely associated during the years when he had been Regius
Professor of Divinity at Oxford. The last letter was in fact,

written less than six weeks before Martyr's death. Another copy of
the letter to Edmund Grindal may be seen in the manuscript department
of the British Museum in London.[4]

Prior to the discovery of this collection, only two letters
appeared to have survived from what must have been a very considerable
correspondence. Hence, in attempting to assess the relationship
between Martyr and the Elizabethan bishops one had to depend almost
entirely on the letters which they addressed to him. The Lambeth
letters not merely throw additional light upon the Reformer's estimation of these bishops, but also illustrate how he endeavoured to
meet the agonising questions of men who, having endured years of
exile and hardship abroad on account of their religious opinions, now
found themselves occupying important positions under a sovereign with
whose Via Media outlook they were not always in sympathy.

Martyr's enthusiasm for the new queen shows itself frequently in
these letters. It was, he wrote to Cox, her piety and wisdom that had
restored the religion of England to a happier and better state,[5] and
to Sandys, a month later, he spoke of her as a child of God in spirit.[6]
Nevertheless, he himself did not display much eagerness to return to
England; and although in his letter to Grindal, he affirmed his desire
to be of as much service as he could both to the English church and
kingdom, he made it clear that his position in Zurich was such that he
was likely to remain there.[7]

Martyr also gave his opinion on the various matters which caused
the bishops some concern. One such matter was the fact that Elizabeth

had demanded of them the surrender of church lands. Well, Martyr
wrote to Grindal, at least it would be plain to people that in
accepting office the bishop had not been moved by reason of personal
gain.[8] Another cause of grievance was the retention by the queen of
the cross and candles on the altar of her private chapel. Martyr
sympathised with Cox in lamenting this and said he was sure that the
bishop was doing everything in his power to put the matter right.[9] In
his letter to Sandys, the bishop of Worcester, Martyr rejoiced that
the removal of superstitious images had been secured, and went on to
express the hope that the same would eventually happen in the case of
the vestments, adding that he was sure that with the help of the
zealous bishop this would be so.[10]

The sentiments expressed in Martyr's letters to the English
bishops shows his regard for them and his confidence that they would
be faithful in promoting the Reformation ideals in their country which
was just recovering from the Catholic reaction under Mary Tudor. In
his letter to Cox of August 22, 1559 he spoke of his delight that
Elizabeth had given to the not merely faint but almost dead church of
her kingdom bishops who were both learned and distinguished for their
piety.[11] In encouraging Sandys in what he realised was a far-from-
easy position, Martyr referred to a bishop as being like a rock in
the sea beaten by nearly every wave; and he prayed that the bishop of
Worcester and his colleagues would be given a rock-like firmness as
regards the Word of God. He moreover urged that they should guard
with unwearying zeal the treasury of wholesome doctrine which had

been committed to them by Christ.[12] To Grindal, Martyr expressed his

joy that men such as he who were specially instructed in religion and

were pillars of the church had not refused office at a time when

their church was most in need of them.[13]

No reference has so far been made to the longest of these letters:

that addressed to John Jewel, the newly-appointed bishop of Salisbury.[14]

Much of this letter concerns the Ubiquitarian controversy in which

Martyr became involved with the German Protestant theologian Johann

Brentz. To Martyr, whose mind was then fully occupied with this latest

adversary, it was a source of satisfaction that England had been pre-

served from the Ubiquitarian teaching concerning the body of Christ in

the Eucharist. At the same time Martyr makes some complimentary re-

marks on the Elizabethan bishops in general, and on Jewel in particular

who, he says, shines like the brightest star among the rest. Recalling

both the days which he and Jewel had spent together at Oxford, and the

years of exile in Strasbourg when Jewel had lived under his roof and

the two men had studied and conversed together, Martyr expressed the

opinion that no one could speak with more knowledge than himself of

Jewel's virtues, the contest which he had entered in the cause of

true religion, the purity of his life, his genius, eloquence and

studiousness, and above all his modesty and moderation. Any future

biographer of John Jewel will surely find in this hitherto untranslated

letter some immensely valuable material for a character study.

Of all his friends in England it was perhaps Richard Cox for whom

Martyr had the tenderest regard. Not only did he dedicate to the

bishop his book concerning vows[15] and commend to his care his own
faithful servant Julius Terentianus,[16] but he clearly never forgot
the kindnesses and favours which Cox had shown on his behalf during
the Oxford days, as well as his efforts to further the reformation
under Edward VI.[17] It was to Cox that Martyr addressed what is, as
far as is known, the last letter he ever sent to England: and in it
he spoke once more of how much he owed to him.[18]

This, then, is a brief survey of the letters which follow. In
addition to providing important information on the closing years of
the man who forms the subject of Dr. Marvin Anderson's book, they
also give a picture of some of the leading bishops of the England of
Elizabeth I, beset by various difficulties and turning for advice to
an old colleague then far away in Zurich, but still one on whose
guidance and friendship they were certain they could rely--Peter Martyr.

NOTES

1. This unpublished thesis is in the University of London Library,
Senate House, London.

2. I am indebted to Mr. Bill for allowing me to include the
letters here in an English translation. He has himself told something
of the remarkable story of how they finally reached Lambeth in an
article Lambeth Palace Library, contained in The Library (Transactions
of the Bibliographical Society) 5th Ser. Vol. XXI, 1966, pp.201-202).

3. Lambeth Palace Library

4. Brit. Mus. Add. Ms. 32091 f. 179.

5. No. 82

6. No. 84

7. No. 73

8. _Ibid._

9. No. 85

10. No. 84

11. No. 82

12. No. 84

13. No. 73

14. No. 86

15. No. 85

16. _Ibid._

17. No. 82

18. No. 87

NOTE BENE

Dr. Huelin has permitted me to publish these letters without the full study which illness prevented him from doing. Letters 82 to Richard Cox and 86 to John Jewel have been published as prefaces to the 1559 _Defensio_ against Richard Smith and the 1561 _Dialogus_ against John Brenz. Since copies of these letters are all but inaccessible, it seemed wise to include them as a unit with the other five letters which taken as a whole, reflect facets of Martyr's mood while a respected protestant divine in far off Zurich. The triple reference to the underworld judges Aeacus, Minos and Rhadamanthys (letter 86) marks our now revered theologian as incurably classical in his outlook, a point seen in an inspection of Martyr's library in Geneva and underlined in the same letter to Jewel by the extended reference to Marcus Cato's judgement on the Roman knights who neglected their horses.

One is reminded of the *Romans* commentary where in St. Paul's first
chapter Martyr cited Aristotle, Plato and Galen as examples of those
who best recognized nature's wonders. In viewing scripture as a
veritable paradise, Martyr mentioned the splendors of Solomon and the
garden of Alcinoüs in the same sentence.

More than the learned references of a classical scholar, these
letters bespeak Martyr's hopes for royal and episcopal reform under
the aegis of a holy Deborah. Martyr had dedicated his commentary on
Romans to Queen Elizabeth in whom he placed great hope for evangelical
purity in stark contrast to his opinion of Catharine De Medici, pol-
itique and Queen regent of France. Queen Elizabeth would protect the
realm from another Haman and like Esther would see the persecutor
hanged on his own gallows. To Grindal in letter 73 Martyr spoke about
the wolves of Anti-Christ.

The patience of this refugee who could yet hope for the conversion
of Brenz to evangelical truth must be matched with the acid remarks
against Richard Smith. A good bit of Martyr's sojurn in England is
hinted at in these bitter comments to Cox who also was a married
cleric at Oxford. These feelings are human after all and remind one
that "not all that has happened has been recorded by historians."
These seven letters describe in their candor what Martyr meant when
he wrote to Sir Anthony Cooke that England was his other fatherland
(*altera patria*).

Monsignor John Sankovitz did yeoman service in translating letter
82 after note 2 and all of letter 86 at the last moment. The Greek

expressions in letter 86 were not clear to us at all points. Minimal

identification of persons and events has been added to assist the

reader.

Martyr's classical study was cited by John Sanderson when

Cambridge University sought to expel him in September 1562. The chief

points raised by this fellow of Trinity are in manuscript. C.C.C.C.

MS 106(223), 537 reads:

> Was I reprehended for bringing in Plato? sayth he. I think
> not, because the Scripture and St. Augustine, Peter Martyr,
> and Stephen Gardiner use profane writers.[1]

---

1. J. E. Booty, "The Expulsion of John Sanderson: Trouble in
an Elizabethan University," Historical Magazine of the Protestant
Episcopal Church XXXVI (1967), 238.

LETTER No. 82

To the reverend father in Christ Dr. Lord Richard Cox, by the
grace of God an English bishop, M. Peter Martyr professor of sacred
letters in the school of Zurich, grace and health from God the father
through Jesus Christ our Saviour.[1]

I once expounded at Oxford, reverend bishop, in the reign of
Edward VI of England, in whose name I still live, the First Epistle of
Paul to the Corinthians, at which time you governed most happily as
rector of that college (or, as they call it Chancellor). And when I
had now arrived at chapter 7 where the Apostle writes a good deal
concerning virginity and Marriage, I disputed at length according as
my opinions were regarding vows. There was often present in the
schools, indeed constantly, Smith, in whose place at the sacred letters
I had been substituted by order of the king. He not only listened
attentively to what was said by me, but also as far as he could noted
it down in writing. The same was done by him when in explaining
chapter 7 of the same Epistle I taught concerning the mystery of the
Eucharist those things which I believed to be the more true and
sincere: for as he had done before, he took exception to all these
things as well. Indeed, because to him (as it is with a disordered
mind and corrupt opinion) the things which I had said were approved
of very little, on a day when I was not suspecting it, a certain man
in the lecture-room itself urged with a very great disturbance of his
making, that at the hour when I was daily accustomed to engage in my

teaching function, I should go down unexpectedly and suddenly with an arranged escourt to a sacred disputation. I, indeed, sufficiently perceived that the whole affair was full of danger: for nothing was then easier than that everything should eventuate into discord, and indeed the most turbulent discord. For the works of that man through the whole school, because he had been intimately connected with it, presented themselves ready at any time to make disturbance, and to throw into confusion; and by as much as they could not extinguish the truth, they oppressed it in every way by circulating, feigning and inculcating that the victory was theirs.

Wherefore, I was unwilling to accept that condition which, as I content myself with saying, was offered to me. Nor did it appear that the great discord he intended would satisfy the raving man. No one would have been so blind that he could not easily see that nothing fruitful would come either to the school or to the church from such a disputation: indeed, neither to the hearers nor to myself was it sufficiently evident concerning which questions there was a difference: for truly at that moment he had concealed those things; nor, as the custom is, did he propose disputing the question in the clear light of day. We all generally understood that he wished to argue against me concerning the sacrament of the Eucharist, but not enough time seemed to be allowed for the examining of so great a matter. Indeed it was now after nine o'clock, and it was not possible in the one hour which remained that a disputation could be resolved which afterwards was held for four days, and even then could only with difficulty be brought to an end. Moreover, it happened inconveniently that neither judges nor any other moderators had been summoned by whose judgement the whole matter might be directed: likeise, no clerks had been appointed who is good faith we insist upon, that they might take down with diligence those things which are said in disputation between one party and another. Wherefore indeed, that all things might be done rightly and orderly that deliberation was postponed to an appropriate day. But our Smith secretly withdrew himself from England and was to that extent absent at the agreed time of the disputation as he had wished to be present. Moreover, he went to Louvain and wrote against me two no less impertinent than venomous letters concerning the celibacy of priesthood and monastic vows.[2] I recognized, when I received them, that I had already published a commentary on the 1st Epistle to the Corinthians. But in order that an edition which not only my friends but many honorable men were requesting might not be put off any longer (sed improbe efflagitabatur), I thought I would set aside my treatise on vows and my reply to Smith to another time.[3] But I had been well received by my students in the past when I had lectured on chapter seven. Then, I found some leisure time and decided to answer that trickster. Moreover, because I thought that the zeal of our followers had already been enkindled at the prospect of such a debate, I had already decided to burn the midnight oil over what I had written in order to crush that unjust non-entity. And some of my friends as well as other outstanding men urged me to go ahead. Indeed, I was not allowed to follow my original plan, for they either had

read my commentary or placed me in their debt by now reading it and
have formed a coalition of sorts. They urged me to forget my original
resolve and to break my former promise. I am unable to resist any
longer their insistent requests, reluctant though I am, and have
decided to do now what I promised to do later on. And I have nominated
you, Reverend Father, Bishop and most learned man, as the patron of my
labors--a title I could rightfully attribute to you for many reasons.
First of all, because of all the memories I have of you from days
gone by, especially from our days together at Oxford where you held
a position of authority and so often led as well as took part in
activities there. Then I am bound to you closely and forever because
of your outstanding personal qualities, your awesome learning and the
many honors and high offices conferred on me (through you?). This
nefarious critic whose attack I am answering bitterly dishonors your
reputation as well as me and other honest men. By his writings this
mad man flails and wounds and destroys you, a man whose learning and
dignity he should readily recognize. Criticism from virtuous and
learned men does not disturb me, but I can't stand it from ignorant
men of low moral standards. Last of all, when I wanted to congratulate
you not only on your return to your country but also on receiving your
bishopric, it seemed to have this result: no matter how modest the
tribute might be, the splendor and dignity of your name - to whom it
was addressed - would add to its intrinsic worth much more than it
possessed of itself. At least that is what I dared promise myself.

Now as to the order and plan followed in writing and replying, I shall say nothing; it seems to me that the reader will find these satisfactorily set out in my preface. Likewise I shall not apologize for the style nor blush over phrases which might offend your sensitive ears; neither shall I boast about my hard work, for I depend upon you to be the just and friendly patron you have always been and I shall experience the same affection I have always known in the past.

Now in this letter I come to those things which I often think about concerning you - and not without great pleasure: namely, the delight I took in your return to England. I can't adequately put it into words nor do I think anyone would believe me if I tried to do so. What more can I say? I am as pleased as I can be. I now plainly see ahead to a life of equal prosperity and adversity. It will have a certain or reciprocal quality as best expressed in the vivid image of the death and resurrection of Christ. Servants of God are at times held in honor and esteem, and at times destined like sheep for slaughter in the name of Christ. God is to be praised and glorified forever who willed to dispel the darkness and in His goodness allowed the light to shine again in the kingdom of England. He preserved our most powerful Queen Elizabeth safe to the present day, through whose piety and wisdom we are blessed with the happy and favorable time. For she recalls religion to the purity of the gospel, abolishes superstition more and more each day, and commands the word of God, the foundation of all good things to be preached and taught everywhere throughout the realm. May God continue to bless her so that she may complete what she has begun in holiness and truth until at last all

is perfected. May (Amorrheorum) remain in the people of God so that
superstition may be completely eradicated from the hearts of men.
She is endowed with both wisdom and grace and has councillors who
excel in zeal and true doctrine. Among them I firmly believe that
you will continue to fulfill faithfully your duty to God and your
loyalty to the Queen.

As for me I continue to command Queen, Church, and the realm of
England to the Son of God in every prayer I offer and rejoice daily
in the good news of your most happy restoration. But among the many
things her majesty the Queen has accomplished in reviving religion,
this seems to me to be of particular importance and affords me particular satisfaction - - that she has given to the churches of her kingdom bishops outstanding in both learning and piety at a time when
these churches were languishing and almost dead. You are named among
them rightfully and because of your merits to govern the church of
N.[4] I do not congratulate you on this advancement as though you have
achieved some greater dignity or honor than ever before. For I am
positive that you have never sought out such honors because you have
always known and possessed them in abundance. However, if I do rejoice
it is because I know how much you can do for the church in the arena
(palestra).[5] I know how you burn with desire to restore true devotion.
I know finally with what prudence and skill you went about your work
when Edward, King of England of happy memory was still alive and your
student. You enkindled in his heart a pure love of God and your deeds
and dedication filled his ears with truly Christian music. Under your

instruction and example that truly divine prince although still a
young boy, grew in grace and in pure Christian teaching and that of
the Gospel. I pass over your many public accomplishments while you
were teaching at Oxford, and what you accomplished in private at
Christ College before you lost it. I pass over also your works of
faith and charity toward the poor in distributing alms. I pass over
them, I say, and refuse to proclaim them to one and all. But I recall
them now to you, for they have moved me and all others who like myself confidently expect great things from you for the good of the
church. We foresee and predict that your ministry will be a most
fruitful one for the flock of Christ, for you appear to be appointed
to bring forth fruit in abundance from the plain flooded with the
riches of your teaching: that the love of Christ might be spread far
and wide you will plant and water with great diligence. God the
fount of all that is good will most abundently bless with his protection
your hard work and dedication; our hope is that your fresh efforts
will bring forth not the 30 or 60 fold harvest but the 100fold unto
the kingdom of heaven.[6]

The foundation is laid: Christ Jesus the Son of God. The Roman
antichrist is overthrown. Therefore you will build more eagerly and
soundly than ever before upon Christ - - not hay or straw or wood but
gold, silver and precious stones.[7] And although without you your
flock has been orphaned for a long time, like the good father of a
family you will offer them the abundant treasure of Holy Writ and the
commandments of faith. This treasure you have assimilated with great

effort, the treasury of salvation in the teachings of the New and
Old Testaments. You will share this with the flock in your care,
using those talents God has given you in such abundance and which you
have cultivated so zealously. You will double them in your mission
and as the servant of Christ and most faithful steward your name will
resound with such just praise that we can think of nothing more
pleasing or more deserved.

This, Reverend Bishop, is some measure of the deep respect I have
for you. and of how I desire to offer my congratulations. I beg God,
the Father of our Lord Jesus Christ, that just as He once supported
you while you bore your cross of exile with great fortitude, preferring
to obey His Word rather than impiety - - so now He would guide you
with his Spirit as you occupy my See, (ea sede) to which He brought
you through the choice of her majesty the Queen.

Farewell, honored master (antistes) and most devout father in
Christ Jesus. I have dedicated my little book in your name hoping
that you would not only accept it but make it your own in mind and
heart. I have dared send it to you from Zurich on August 22, 1559.

NOTES

1. This letter was published as the preface to Martyr's Defensio
ad Riccardi Smythaei . . . de Caelibatu sacerdotum & Votis monasticis
. . . . (Basilea apud Petrum Pernam M.D.LIX). See letter 83 of 31
August 1559. It is not printed in Opusula (1581) Cols. 1653-1654.

2. Martyr refers to Smith's Defensio coelebatus sacerdotum,
contra P. Mart. (Louvain, 1550) which contained a Confutatio quorundam
articulorum de votis monasticis Pet. Martyris Itali. Both were
reprinted by Reginald & Claude Calderius in Paris, (1550) under the
title Defensio Sacri Episoporū/& Sacerdotum Coelibatus, contra impias
&/indoctis Petri Martyris Vermili nugas, & /calumnias . . . . Smith

fled to St. Andrews where he addressed letters to Cranmer, dated 11
and 14 February /1550/. See Martyr's letter to Bucer of 10 June 1550
for further comment on Smith.

3. Reference seems to be to the Romans commentary where Martyr
would also respond to Smith's Diatriba/De Hominis Ivstife=/catione
printed in Louvain in October of 1550.

4. See letter 83 where Martyr was uncertain about the place
where Cox was bishop. It was Ely.

5. "Wrestling Ring", i.e., either Convocation or Parliament.
Martyr knew all about the delay over implementing reform under Edward
VI.

6. Matthew (13:8); Mark (4:8) & (4:20).

7. I Corinthians (3:12-15).

LETTER No. 83

Greetings. Since, reverend father, and most esteemed lord, I have dealt with many things in that letter to you which, with a little book on vows I prefixed with a dedication in your name, it is not that I write now more copiously, and certainly I should have omitted to write had not a twofold cause driven me to do so. First, I did not wish to give occasion that a book without my letters should be presented to you.[1] Then a certain mistake concerning you on my part is to be deprecated, which however, is not my fault but of those who at different times carried letters from England; they all affirmed indeed that you had been made a bishop, but they did not agree however as to the place or church over which you preside. Wherefore it might have been written following the last letters, and before it was made known in writing that letter by hurt ($T\eta\varsigma\, T\rho\omega\mu\alpha\, T\iota\eta\varsigma$?) I easily fell and it may be that I did not ascribe the true name of your church. Truly whatever that is of error, whatever human ardour among friends, I trust will again be condoned by you on my behalf that I may obtain what I ask and value.

Farewell; do not allow yourself to forget your Martyr, who, if you do not know, now has a wife, and in fact one with child.[2] I ask that you support him with your prayers.

My Julius greets you indeed most courteously. I truly wish to salute your most excellent wife in my name. Zurich. August 31st 1559.

Your most respectful

Peter Martyr

To my most esteemed Dr. Rich. Cox, Doct. of Theol and most faithful

minster of the word of God and my most dear friend.

NOTES

1. This letter seems a companion to one by Cox in Z.L.I, 65-67/
Tig. 38 which would be dated after 21 December 1559.

2. On May 9th 1559, Martyr married his second wife, Catherine
Merenda, by whom he had three children. As he tells Sandys in the
following letter (No. 84) the child whom his wife was expecting here -
a boy - died only eight days after birth.

LETTER No. 73

Greetings; because reverend and most excellent lord (for so to me you seem worthy to be called, since undoubtedly you are now a bishop) you wrote to me so kindly and courteously, I thank you warmly, and I solemnly assure you of this, that nothing more pleasant has befallen me at this time than your letters. Because I am replying slowly to them I beg you not to regard it as my fault. You in fact dated them October 29 but I received them on January 24.[1] As to your decision not to forsake the church nor to refuse the positions offered, I strongly approve it. For if you who by the grace of God are especially instructed in religion and are pillars of that church, in such a dearth of ministers withdraw your hands and arms from the task, by whom then will the work proceed? Only you will not be driven to admitting or approving of any superstition. What I hope is that the piety of the Queen's Majesty is no less; and that it will be particularly clear as far as you are concerned that you have not been led as though moved by what was advantageous on account of the estates offered: for that would have brought shame on your profession and order. If you had been asked to cast away good things of that kind from the churches the matter would then have required greater and more serious consideration, but you do not obtain this and you are without blame.

What you say afterwards concerning external matters that they did not seem to you sufficiently contentious for you to refuse a calling, you seem to me to speak piously and correctly. As to the episcopal

dress and apparel which may have so much a civic reason particularly
in that kingdom, it is not in my judgement of such importance that
it should allow us to reject sacred office. The things which pertain
to ecclesiastical rites, those I would desire to be as simple as
possible. If you do not yet have these, you will possibly at some
time recover them when you are truly in your appointed vocation. But
if you give way to the wolves of anti-Christ, what you have will not
become so much better, but you will with difficulty retain to that
extent what has so far been won.

I will discuss these things with you my Grindal more intently,
and pour into the bosom of my very great friend.[2] He I know indeed
will not discuss my councils. But I write nevertheless, as I would
write to one who thinks well, and as I would give shoes to one who is
running correctly. In this same spirit I have written to our Sampson,[3]
how much indeed I may influence him I do not know.

I came to the last topic of your letters in which you ask me that
if I am called I shall not refuse the journey or the task. I want you
to know, my Grindal most dear brother and lord in Christ, that I am so
disposed towards that church and kingdom that I desire to serve it as
much as my strength allows. And would that I could give you such
fruit as I would desire you to enjoy from me. Just as the will is not
only ready but also prompt to all your advantages. Nevertheless you
ought to reflect on this that I am a citizen here and a canon of this
church. And I cannot go away without the goodwill of both. Hence,
I am bound to the country as well as to the church. And I cannot

go away without the goodwill of both. Hence, if I am called to the
position which is offered, I answer to the wish and pleasure of the
church and Senate. Nor can I (as you yourself realise) do otherwise
in that matter. I have no doubt that you and others like you are
convinced of my mind. For since I am begetting many sons in Christ
here, and I have through many who esteem me greatly, I cannot be
bestowed on you as well I might be. Wherefore it is well for me and
I rejoice exceedingly since concerning your affairs they signify to
me what I desire to hear. Therefore I beg whatever your affairs are,
you will not allow me to be ignorant.

Farewell, most dear brother and lord in Christ. Master Bullinger
and my Julius greet you. You indeed will not delay to greet my
brothers in my name: nor yet Cecil when you see him. Again farewell;
pray for me and love me as you do. Zurich 28 January 1560.

Your reverend piety's most devoted

Peter Martyr.

To one outstanding in piety and learning, namely most faithful
minister of the Word of God and my most dear friend in England.

NOTES

1. Letter of October or November 1559 is not extant.

2. **Christ**

3. Letter of 4 November 1559.

LETTER No. 84

Greetings because to me reverend bishop and brother in Christ

most dear: you have not recently written and it was not that you are

without any excuse. For I am not ignorant with what and how many

waves of cares you have been tossed. A bishop is like a rock in the

sea which almost all the waves beat upon. I pray that there may be

given to you and your colleagues a rock-like and as-firm-as-possible

constancy in the word of God, in which I rejoice that you are constant

to this day. May God think it worthy to perfect the work which he

has begun, and erect at length in England his church which is cleared

away again from all errors and abuses.

What concerns me is that the exceedingly scarce or tardy writing

is satisfactory. Although (as I indeed own) I cannot earnestly desire

concerning you and your affairs to know anything in what way it has.

This is the natural mark of a true friend, concerning him whom in

Christ closely and truly he loves to know perpetually or frequently.

However, because I know both by great and careful troubles so much I

did not put out of sight, therefore because they bear your reasons to

accept with a fair mind, I however rejoice and fully approve that

you have entered into the episcopal office: for the field of Christ

has not been abandoned in such poverty of labours and fruits. May

God bless the labours of you and your colleagues, although I have

begun a wonderful delight in a sound, pure and unchanged doctrine

of the Eucharist which you hold fast. That to me is so agreeable that

it is not unknown to me that this truth is beseiged by very many

wiles and races. Stand therefore as a light of the Church of England
and a treasury of the sound doctrine entrusted by Christ to you with
unwearied endeavour and strength maintained.

Because from the scandal and superstition of images you have now
been satisfactorily relieved by the grace of Christ, I give great
thanks to God. It was that stain of your church now burned away which
affected pious men with the greatest sorrow. But as you write it
does not remain. It delights all good men that you have got ride of
it: would that concerning the vestments the same may at length
happen. It will indeed happen if you give aid zealously.

I do not doubt that your queen is a daughter of God in spirit.
I know she will not refuse it and because it is not yet perfect, she
may complete it (absolvet) in the ministry of your preaching. Nevertheless that caring for me in mind which you promise me, that I shall
not be coming to you soon will not I know be anything but troublesome
to you. But for me you know that all things are ruled and governed
by the providence of God who, with a most careful eye, does see better
than us in what places the functions of ministers are seemly.

What matters to me whether I am in Zurich or England is that I
live and serve Christ. Nor if I do not agree am I less a friend to
your kingdom and church than before. On the contrary, you may conclude
that I burn more and more with vehement love towards England.

As you congratulate me on my new wife, so I pray for you my most
dear (friend) a happy and auspicious marriage. God gave me a little
son, but after eight days he called him again to himself. Herman[1]

has departed for France, although he stayed a little while at Geneva.
Bullinger particularly greets you, together with my other fellow-
ministers. My wife, Julius with her, as well as Paul and Martyrillus
remember you well and that teaching which you had and inculcated with
great labour.

We all together bid you greet your most dear wife. Farewell
reverend bishop and most dear lord. May God long preserve you safe
to your church.

18 June 1560

Your most dedicated

Pet. Martyr

To the reverend father in Christ and Doctor of Divinity Edwin Sandys,
Bishop of Worcester, and to his most dear lord: in England.

NOTES

1. Herman Folkertzheimer /Wolf/. See letter of 9 May 1560 in
C.R. 3195.

LETTER No. 85

Greetings especially in Christ. Your letters, most reverend
bishop, have so far refreshed me, that by your return to England I
could not receive more agreeable. Since, for a long time, I heard
nothing of you, that to me was more bitter inasmuch as I have always
loved and esteemed you among the first. But now your most truly
human letter has compensated aboundantly for the long silence; on
account of which I give you great thanks.[1] It happened moreover that
you received a book concerning vows which I dedicated in your name
with a cheerful mind; for which success I congratulate myself, and
value your kindness greatly. For the favour which we show to friends
now and then delights us, when we consider to have been pleasant with
them. I see therefore my night work has not been wasted when I under-
stand its offering $\lceil \pi \rho o\ \theta\omega\mu\eta\sigma\tau\nu$ to be pleasant to you. I indeed
rejoice exceedingly that I may use you as a kind and willing patron.
And this I promised myself to be as well. For you indeed are not of
those who bear thanks with such contempt that they despise inscriptions
in books however discourteous. By you indeed it is wisely and Chris-
tianly done, who even if you are tossed by varying storms, and are
experienced in the many chances of this world, have nevertheless,
retained your old humanity, which to me afterwards you declare most
fully since you say that you yourself hope to do me another service;
as if by such a favour, grace and zeal you can thereby accompany me in
no other way. You have not only so greatly furnished me with kindnesses, but have so loaded me that I cannot ever hope to be able to

repay. Because indeed you have laboured by all means on behalf of
my Julius in order that you could well perceive a benefit. For he
and I love and respect you very much for it. And as I was devoted to
you very much before, now by your liberality I am bound all the more.
Concerning my support, you indeed speak of it lovingly, beautifully
and correctly. Indeed concerning that, whether renewed or left, I
desire you to use first your counsel, then your help. This however,
I want you to know for certain: that I do not wish to ask for that
again for myself; but whether there may be a hope that it may be
transferred to Julius but I bring it up again in order that it might
be transferred to Julius. For indeed, when I consider in my mind
his state, I would altogether desire for him something to look forward to: for truly he has served me both long and faithfully. Therefore it is fitting that unless I should wish to be most ungrateful
to him who is poor and has a wife and child, I should have regard
for him in some way. But what concerns me, I never did anything, I
have no means to give help. I have lived perpetually with another
family where opportunities by which I could have provided for him
were lacking. There is no need for me to tell you of his honesty and
ability. I know that he has not degenerated in himself, but rather
since his departure from England, his piety, prudence and judgement
have not a little increased. As long as I live I shall take care
that there is nothing lacking for him and his, so far as is not
wanting. But he is now of a mature age, and while he served me he
gained nothing for himself. Therefore it is fitting for me to

consider his welfare. You have the reason for my consideration.
Accordingly what ever counsel you offer for what can be done in this
matter, or what is best to do, I respect that you may have difficulty
relating it to me /‾ ne significare graueris/. I do not however wish
to cause you trouble, because if I appear to myself to have written
too much, your kindness invites me to this. This I go about places
me in the greatest joy, because religion with you so as you write has
been restored.

Concerning the crucifix and the image of Christ, what we hear from
you and others we cannot but bewail. But we also hope from that cross
in some manner other deliberations. In which matter you, reverend
patron, I observe and assert that you do not spare in your industry
and labour.

I know that you have taken the bit between your teeth as much
as you can, and are helpingaccording to your powers.

May God bless what you do with the most abundant fruit, and not
allow your labours to be frustrated. As you congratulate me on a new
wife, so I wish that by your prayers you may obtain off spring. She
indeed bore me a little son who died after eight days. What henceforth
God shall give, I await with a quiet mind. My wife, Julius with her,
most dutifully give you greeting, and together we greet your most dear
wife from the heart. Dr. Bullinger also wishes that I send you greeting in his name.   18 June 1560.

To you from my heart /ex animo/ you most zealous and beloved

                                               Peter Martyr

To the Reverend Father and Lord in Christ, Dr. Richard Cox, Bishop

of Ely and most devoted Servant of his Lord.

NOTES

1. This would be the undated letter of Cox in Z.L. I, 65-67 and would date it between 21 December 1559 and 18 June 1560.

2. Julius Terentianus is mentioned in four of these letters. Of all Martyr's references to his devoted servant the most important is that contained in the present letter. in the spring of 1561 Julius visited England once more and called on many of his old acquaintances. It seems that this visit was concerned with the matter which Martyr raises here. On his return to Zurich, Julius acted as messenger, conveying to his master letters from English friends. A letter from Grindal to Bullinger of 31 July 1570, where he refers to having paid the pension of Julius to Froschauer the Zurich printer, in whose service Julius was then employed, makes it clear that Martyr's request in respect of his faithful servant was granted.

LETTER No. 86

To the reverend father in Christ, John Jewel, by the grace of
God Bishop of Salisbury and most devoted servant of his Lord, Peter
Martyr Vermigli professor of Sacred Scripture in the school of
Zurich, sends greetings, that is, desire for complete happiness in
Christ.

Those who have disputed among themselves for such a long time
now finally are looking for critics and (guides?) who can put an end
to their quarrel by rendering judgment upon the long drawn-out quarrel.
Two men especially, Pantachus and Orothetes,[1] have been disputing over
a serious question for a long while; they have now asked me to find
them a judge, one who is both completely honest and one who has some
knowledge of the matter in dispute. Therefore thou, my reverend
patron, came to mind as one whose judgment is swayed neither by favor-
itism nor dislike. And because you are thoroughly schooled in both
divine and human disciplines, ignorance is not likely to obscure your
judgment. Thus it occured to me to expose these two gentlemen to
your scrutiny, especially since you are thoroughly acquainted with
the topic under discussion.[2]

The Ethnics had Aeacus, Minos, and Rhadamanthys[3] as their supreme
judges; in you we have all three in one, since we benefit from your
intelligence, dignity, and sense of justice. I felt no desire to look
for any one but you as judge in this case, particularly because you
use as your standard of judgment only the word of God. Consequently,
I call upon your great generosity not to refuse to serve in this

whole case. Neither of the litigants (if they are wise) will object
to the judgment of a man like you. To acquaint you with the case I
have sent you the arguments of both sides so far as I was able to
(in good faith). No bishop as estimable as you are will be able to
refrain from this obligation. (incomplete?) I write these words fully
aware of your great (many?) and sacred duties and aware also that to
interrupt you in their performance is to do serious harm to the church
of Christ. Thus I have assembled a clear and detailed summary so that
you might learn their arguments and reasoning and almost with one
glance easily make your own the essence of the dispute. Aristotle
once excused himself to Alexander by saying he had built his writings
(ἀκροαματικα: I have produced and I have not produced -- to this
extent, that those who would grasp what he wrote would have heard him
as he taught them. [4] Moreover he wrote further that he should console
the king because he had been unwilling to see such matters made known
to the public.

I worked as hard as possible to see that this Dialogue of mine
be crystal clear. For it seemed more desireable to engage the reader
for a longer period of time than to torture him with the obscurities
of condensation. I cannot agree with the opinion Neoptolemus
Enninanus[5] espoused: Wisdom comes packaged in few words. Brevity
rarely pleases one because highly condensed ideas are either obscure
or demand lengthy explanation. Rarely can we achieve speech which is
both brief and clear. I have always thought that we should strive
for brevity only if there is no lessening of clarity: we should aim

at concise phrasing only if we avoid shrouding difficult ideas in
darkness.

Augustine tells us that Alypius[10] was extremely angry at a certain
difficult and important court case where one party asked that the
(verdict?) on the whole case be rendered in as few words as possible;
he declared that it was possible to explain obscure issues only in
the clearest prose, and he found it difficult to equate clear prose
with brevity. In this kind of writing brevity cannot prevail: for
we must build our own case while destroying that of our opponents.
The pagans were emphatically in error when they not only worshiped
Jupiter but Anti-Jove along with him: they went to Jupiter for help
in their own needs and to Anti-Jove to counter their opponents. This
practice of theirs was discredited completely since there is only one
deity who bestows on mortal men innumerable blessings and likewise
punishes them for their lapses from justice. Therefore godly men
rightly condemn this pagan practice. Nonetheless, we can learn something from it in our daily activity: let us devote all our efforts
to retaining and conserving the   useful while at the same time
suppressing all that is evil, false and useless. This should be our
practice in general but above all in all disagreements and debate over
religion.

In religion sound teaching must be emphasized and strengthened
while at the same time deceit, snares, and sophistry must be rooted
out and destroyed. This applies to my Dialogue if it is to be of any
help to simple souls. Therefore I could not employ the brevity which

I wanted to use and which the reader would have wanted to find there.

Next I want you to know that when you read my work, your gentle soul? will not be offended: I have eliminated all insults, stinging remarks, and angry words. I have not even mentioned my opponent's name since I would prefer to see him corrected and repentant than condemned and derided. I see myself as the enemy of error, not the erring. Debate over truth should not in my opinion harm one's opponent. Far be it from me, either, to advance the name and reputation of anyone when I write this way. More than any other goal, I tried to keep this in mind throughout, to show that the humanity of Christ is not found everywhere (which reasonable and orthodox belief is not even doubted by Catholics). I also tried to refute with all my strength the arguments of my opponent which would make me out to be a deceiver of the ignorant and unwary. How well I have succeeded in using this sort of argumentation I leave to the judgment of others and especially to you, knowing full well how your judgment will reflect our mutual esteem.

I am certainly not compelled to write this treatise either because of avarice or lust for combat; you know better anyone else that I am free of any such compulsion. First of all my brothers and colleagues in the ministry of the church in Zurich asked me to do it repeatedly. I was unable to refuse them since their ties of good will are almost as great as ours. Otherwise it would have . en possible for me to turn it over to a committee and escape the obligation. Besides, your recent letter to me[8] mentions that there some among your people who are now starting to think about ubiquity. But you added a remark

which restored my spirits, namely that we need not fear that any
such teaching will ever take root in either church or realm. Those
words made me very happy.

These then are the reasons why I took on this onerous duty and
why I wanted your distinguished name in mind as patron: not that I
thought I could teach you something new nor even that I could
strengthen our friendship with greater affection. For you have a fine
grasp of the other teachings of our religion and especially of this
doctrine; and for many years you have been my constant support in an
overwhelming outpouring of affection. Indeed, in this project I took
particular delight in writing against the ones who deserve to be
chastened (flogged) of whom there seem to be more than a few. I knew
I had brave, wise, and most friendly patron who would defend me tire-
lessly against the bitter attacks of malevolent men. It was not your
affection for me alone which prompted you to support me in this
project, but your sanctity and learning, that two-fold grace of God
you possess in such abundance. Nor am I afraid, while speaking of
you in this way, that the phrase "blind is the love of that which is
loved" of Theophrastus[6] will work against me. Indeed because of
your excellent training you would be able to refute without effort
even the grossest error or most bitter fruit of the wild summer fig.

Another point: your own sense of reverence which yearns most
ardently for the practice of pure divine worship will not permit such
less than accurate teachings (to be charitable about them) to grow
unchecked withing your churches. The danger is that they will take

root. And I am fully persuaded that your colleagues and brother
bishops in England, that land so blessed by God, also hold this same
position now. They are chosen by the grace of God. They adorn the
church splendidly with their piety and learning. (But you, my
reverend patron, shine among them like the biggest star.) May you
all devote every effort to preserving the teaching on the Lord's
Supper pure and undefiled. You know how many times terrible distor-
tions and foul errors have misled and devastated the church of the
son of God because that very doctrine was obscured, twisted or
corrupted. This new teaching of ubiquity, as you well know, seeks
nothing other than to mislead the unwary by falsified reasoning and
logic that the body and blood of the Lord is present in the bread
and wine of the sacred meal (as they say) truly, really, corporally,
substantially, secretly, and in a heavenly fashion. For if the
human nature of Christ is established as present everywhere, will
there be any position left in this falsified reasoning except to confess exactly what is at stake in our whole debate - - that he is
present in the bread and wine. It is absolutely necessary that all
of us worship Christ in pure and sound faith (?with hands and feet?)
in order that the vineyard of the Lord be purged of every kind of
thorn and bramble. When that has finally been accomplished, it will
be able to bring forth good and tasty fruit for its owner. But this
seems a legitimate and proper work for bishops, our pastors and
teachers. Therefore, you and all the others who by divine choice
guard and guide the ship of the church must watch carefully lest our

inheritance from Christ be corrupted from within by some new sort of
error. The devil detests nothing more than to hear the holy Gospel
of the son of God preached in church without change or diminution.

Therefore he tries desperately within the reformed churches,
directly and through deceit, to mix truth and falsehood, to disguise
lies with deceptive honey-coating, to cajole the faithful people of
Christ into believing and professing new and most outrageous teaching
so that he might expose them to the ridicule and condemnation of their
sworn enemies, the papists and to prudent men as well. I have done
all I can in this cause out of a sense of duty. However, I recognize
my limitations and willingly turn the project over to you in its
incomplete state, knowing that it will return to me completed in every
detail. Please add or change anything you think I may have missed.
Don't think that I (suggest) this because of Scripture's warning to
fear and worship the Lord. Rather, as you know, I am influenced by
the example of a wise man among the pagan writers, Marcus Cato. Cato
was an ancient author who testified (as Aulus Gellius notes in Book
12, Chapter 12 of Attic Nights) as follows: if any one has let one
of his lambs grow filthy through neglect and shows no sign of greater
diligence despite repeated warnings; or he has neglected his trees or
his vineyard, he shall see the punishment of being deprived of his
vote by the censors. Furthermore, these same censors would seize
publicly owned horses from Roman knights who had allowed them te grow
sick, thin, and filthy, and demoted those same knights in rank because
they had been convicted (ut ille scribit) of carelessness and

negligence. I write these things to show you, O Praetor, that I have
not fulfilled my office in writing this Dialogue until the church is
purged of disfiguring flaws and rendered more attractive. And you
will be fulfilling your duty as Bishop if you see to it with all your
energies that strange and false opinions of this sort be ejected from
the sheep-fold of Christ. Two reasons will prompt you to accept this
task: to protect my little book (if I may call it that) from the
envious and to substitute more suitable phrases where they are needed.

I have already set forth in a few words what I would like you to
do, my reverend and most learned friend. All that is left now (as
is the custom in literary dedications) is to praise your sterling
qualities to the entire Christian world. If I were to summon up
enough courage to do this, I would find myself running out of words
before I exhausted the subject. And no one can be found better able
to speak of your character and admirable life than I, for I speak not
from second hand evidence but what I actually heard and saw and experienced. I speak of the quality of your genius, your eloquence and
devotion, your capacity for hard work and the struggle for true
religion, and above all, your modesty and moderation. When you and I
were together at Oxford, I realized you had these qualities to an
eminent degree. But since we were togethr there for only a short time,
many began to think me a liar or dupe. For sly men usually give the
impression of possessing many fine qualities when in reality they were
filled with corruption. But later on, after you had moved to Germany
from England, and lived for many years in the same house with me, there

(at the same table with snakes!) we studied and conversed together

every day. I believe that of all men I alone can accurately testify

to your sincere faith, high moral standards, single-minded devotion

and unwavering courage, not to mention the native ability, self-disci-

pline, and sound judgment which I found to be *αὐτωπτη*. If I

were to enter upon a lengthy description of these attractive qualities

and say what I really think of you, I would not only exceed the limits

of proper correspondence but grieviously offend one whose ears have

never been attuned to compliments and praise of himself. Moreover,

I would be saying less than the facts call for, since your good

example, upright life, and thorough commitment to your duties contri-

bute more to your exalted reputation than anything a man could write.

Hence it is opinion that you are already at that point (or not far from

it) which Jerome speaks of regarding Pammachus in the prologue to his

two books on Hosea: he refers to the reputation of Marcus Cato as

such that no one could add to it with praise or harm it with criticism

even though men of great talent tried both. His reference is to the

writings of Marcus Cicero and Gaius (Julius?) Caesar: the former

wrote in praise, the latter in criticism of Cato. Therefore I decided

not to attempt the impossible, a useless task and one displeasing to

you.

Finally, I shall appeal to you, my dear friend, a pillar of

Christ's church and its most splendid ornament, to consider my little

gift to you as a compliment and accept it with a grateful heart. And

if indeed I did omit many things which might have been pertinent to the matter before us, remember this, that I was forced to cover over warp, woof, and whole cloth of my friend Pantachus' work. Perhaps someone will come after me to repeat and confirm what I said and even it bolder and stronger in order to stamp out this new danger more easily. Also, I am happy to say that Henry Bullinger, an excellent man and outstanding minister of the Zurich church, my most reverend brother in Christ, has recently been occupied with this same subject. Thus it was well that I get on with my own work and omit or at least treat only superficially things which he would deal with more at length. Indeed I might possibly even have skipped the task completely, once he published his work on mansions revisited;[7] but then a publication came out which made it almost mandatory that I respond to it—as I have said so often. I would ask one last favor of you based on our longlasting friendship: please continue your prayers for me to our heavenly Father for a fruitful and salutary outcome to this venture. I would not want to run in vain. Rather, I hope to aid the growth of Christ's church which the Lord will credit as gain to me.

Farewell, reverend Bishop; may God safeguard you as a bulwark to both kingdom and church for as long as possible.

Written at Zurich. August 15, 1561.[9]

NOTES

1. Letter of Martyr to Parkhurst, 23 August 1561. "Pantachus . . . sustains the person of Brentius, and Orothetes, myself."

2. Letter of Jewel to Martyr, 7 February 1562, answers this letter. Palaemon, the moderator in the _Dialogus_, is Jewel.

3. Aeacus was the son of Zeus who as king of Aegina ruled the

Myrmidons whom Zeus created out of ants to people the isle. When
Greece suffered a drought Aeacus interceeded with Zeus for rain. The
grateful Greeks built him a temple in Aegina. Minos was the mythical
king of Crete thought by Hesiod to be the mightiest king of all
mortals as the framer of the older Cretan constitution. Homer placed
Minos in Hades to judge the shades with a golden sceptre. Rhadamanthys
was the son of Zeus and Europa, brother of Minos. He was praised for
his wisdom, piety and justice. Homer /Od. iv 564/ described
Rhadamanthys as resident in the Elysian fields. Martyr's point about
Jewel combining the qualities of these three classical judges bespeaks
his hopes for renewal of piety in England and compares the reign of
Mary Tudor to the shadowy world of Hades.

    4. Martyr's reference is to an exchange of letters between
Aristotle and Alexander recorded by Plutarch. When Alexander berated
Aristotle's publishing of oral doctrine, Aristotle retorted in
Plutarch's account "And Aristotle, soothing this passion for pre-
eminence, spoke, in his excuse for himself of these doctrines as in
fact both published and not published . . . ." Plutarch goes on to
say useless for those already conversant in that manner of learning,
hence they are unpublished in that sense.

    5. Neoptolemus, son of Achilles, was a hero of the Wooden Horse
at Troy where he alone remained undaunted and killed the aged Priam
at the taking of Troy. Martyr's reference is to Brenz against whom
this Dialogus is written.

    6. Theophrastus (C.371-C.286 B.C.), disciple and successor of
Aristotle who in logic introduced indirect moods for the first figure
of the syllogism. Martyr's reference may be to one of these patterns
of converting universal negative propositions of possibility. Martyr
would then be using Theophrastus' Metaphysics to attack the doctrine
of ubiquity. When Aristotle introduced the changeless changer as the
source of all movement, Theophrastus analyzes the difficulties of
assuming either a single or plural changer in Metaphysical Fragments
(4-7). Aristotle had used the ubiquitous terms of potentiality and
actuality in De Anima III. 5,430a22. Martyr in this reference means
however that Jewel is his disciple as Theophrastus was the pupil of
Aristotle. That is a remarkable reference since it confirms Martyr's
Aristotelian training at Padua. One might note that beyond that
personal reference the use of Theophrastus does pertain to the doctrine
of ubiquity. The term apeiron (boundless) was developed by Aristotle
from Anaximander who first used arche in a philosophical sense.
Theophrastus reports that Anaximander introduced the concept of the
boundless and denied peras or the boundary. This should be kept in
mind when one reads the Diaogue itself.

    7. Builinger refuted Brenz in a work of that title to answer

Brenz who in turn used that phrase in his 1562 response to Martyr
and Bullinger. See W. Köhler, Bibliographia Brentiana, pp. 185ff.
Martyr's copy of Bullinger's 1561 work is in Geneva: Tractatio
verborum Domini In Domo Petris mei mansiones multae sunt etc . . . .
(Zurich: Froschauer, 1561).

8. Letter of 6 November 1560. Z. L. I 91/Tig.54. "That volatile
Ubiquitarian doctrine cannot by any means gain footing among us,
though there have not been wanting from the first outset those who
had the subject much at heart."

9. I am grateful to John Donnelly for sending a copy of the
printed letter appended to the Dialogus. Greek phrases have been
translated where their reading seemed plausible.

10. Event contained in letter of Augustine to Alypius, Bishop
of Tagaste (A.D. 411). At the end of A.D. 410 the wealthy widow
Albina left Rome for Tagaste with her daughter and son-in-law Pinian.
He visited Hippo where the people impressed by his piety or wealth
exacted an oath under duress not to leave Hippo or ever be ordained
elsewhere. When Pinian returned to Tagaste and a trial for perjury
ensued, Augustine wrote: "For it is difficult to express a brief
sentence in words which convey the exact obligation of one who takes
the oath." Patrologia Latina XXXIII, col. 476, lines 4-6.
These kinds of references have a wider significance. Alypius was
converted with Augustine (Confessions VI) and Theophrastus was the
disciple of Aristotle. Jewel is Martyr's Aristotelian and Augustinian successor for readers of the Dialogus.

LETTER No. 87

Greetings. After I had already sealed up your former letters,
most reverend patron, yours arrived for me, which, as they were a
sign of your singular kindness towards me were thus for me completely
crammed and, for a long time, very pleasant. Moreover, the same
opinion which I notice that you have urged somewhat, was frequently
in my mind also, namely, that the great distance between us has not
commended any letters; because one may understand it not to have
been done from another place, except that we are separated from you
by a great distance and there is an incredible lack of couriers; for
neither at Zurich nor at Strasbourg have we merchants of your nation
who delight us with letters sent in England, as they used to do.
However, it was both very troublesome, and altogether I decided that
for whatever reason it could be done with so great inconvenience, I
would persuade you it was done eagerly by me. Meanwhile, I ask you,
reverend Bishop, do you think it is on that account that I have seldom
written to you? What shall ever destroy for me the most sweet memory
of you? I remember constantly, I remember I say, how much I owe to
you, and it assuredly increases this memory that you continue stead-
fastly your purpose in loving me. Whence it happens that you desire
letters to be sent between us mutually in order that you may delight
in my written words, which moreover, having been lovingly selected
by which you embrace me, cannot satisfy your sharp and keen judgment,
that you may continue to follow me with your noted liberality. I
have since indeed, received with one of your letters twenty sun-struck

Gallic crowns. From which I understand that your kindness to me
does not only remain in the mind, or only show itself in words and
letters, but also, as is demonstrated by a liberal gift. To these
kindnesses assuredly I have not the wherewith to respond, except
that I may only be able to promise two things. First, I pray God,
of whose riches there is no measure nor end, that he will restore
to you most fully, because you have given liberally to me. Then, as
I proceed with the task of the interpretation of the scriptures,
that I may give it as much diligence as I can. For I am devoting
myself entirely to my commentaries on both Samuel and Kings, now to
the reviewing, now again to the copying, in order that they may be
produced as quickly as possible. I am moreover, projecting that the
Dialogue which I published against the Ubiquity of Brentz shall not
be shown to you as I had previously instructed, but possibly expanded.
(redditur). Farewell, most esteemed father. May God preserve you
safely to the Church and State for a long time. 4th October 1562,
Zurich. Bullinger asks me to greet you exceedingly.

Your most devoted

Peter Martyr.

To the reverend in Christ father and lord Dr. Richard Cox, Bishop
of Ely: to his most dear lord: in England.

BIBLIOGRAPHICAL ESSAY

In the year after Martyr's first published work at Basle (1544), the civic authorities at Lucca prohibited the *libri dicti* of Martyr and Ochino. In 1574 the Elector of Saxony required that students of the University of Wittenberg subscribe to written oath not to purchase or read Vermigli's sacramental works. Whether on an Italian index or Lutheran, Martyr's writings were controversial; that they were also helpful to his contemporaries has been the theme of this study, whether for Cranmer who used them in compiling the 1552 Prayer Book and the *Forty Two Articles* or for Calvin who would wrench from Martyr his biblical writings if he would only come to Geneva.

When Professor Robert Kingdon of Wisconsin completes the *Bibliographia Vermigliana* with the aid of John Donnelly, S. J. one will be able to see for the first time how extensively Martyr's writings circulated in Europe from 1544-1656. Donnelly provided me with a preliminary list of titles after my own European research for this study turned up more than fifty separate Martyr imprints. The Kingdon/Donnelly list shows over one hundred and ten printed editions of Martyr's works extant. The task of collating these must await their location and identification as would be true of the three hundred and one letters listed in appendix I.

One should approach Martyr's protestant career bibliographically for a number of reasons. One would be to correct data cited by recent scholars such as V. Norskov Olsen, who for example, in *The New Testament Logia on Divorce* writes on page 89 "Peter Martyr's first lectures at Oxford were on the First Epistle to the Corinthians,

but his commentary on this epistle was printed posthumously in 1567,
as most of his other commentaries were." His evidence for this is
the British Museum Catalogue even though other libraries list this
commentary in two printings in 1551 at Zurich. J. C. McLelland
gives the first edition as 1562 which is a misprint for the third
edition of 1572. Another example of the need for collation of editions
is the procedure of Robert Masson, French pastor in London, who
collected Martyr's *loci* into the pattern of Calvin's *Institutes*.
Masson or the proof-readers depart from the sequence of Martyr's text
as printed in the several editions of the *Corinthian* commentary.

The *Romans* commentary first appeared at Basle in 1558. A study
of the Basle edition of 1560 shows a significant variant in the
controversy with Stancaro over prayer to the Holy Spirit in the
interpretation of *Romans* (8). That problems still remain can be seen
from McLelland's note that the Basle edition exists in two tomes and
the Zurich edition of 1559 is folio. My own copy of the 1558 Basle
edition is in folio. Kingdon/Donnelly have photographed title pages
of the following Latin copies: Basle 1558, Zurich 1559, Basle 1560,
1568, 1570, Heidelberg 1612, 1613 and of course London in English,
1568. That in itself speaks for the wide circulation of the *Romans*
commentary certainly used at Heidelberg with the *Loci* of 1603, 1613,
and 1622 as texts. The commentary on *Kings* was also printed at
Heidelberg in 1599 as were *Genesis* in 1606 and *Judges* in 1609. Eight
Heidelberg editions of these commentaries and the *Loci* speak
volumes about Martyr's influence there via Zanchi. The Library of

Congress reports no copies of the Latin *Romans* in the United States

listed in the forthcoming entry on Vermigli in its *National Union*

Catalogue, Pre-1956 Imprints.

Unfortunately Klaus Sturm's Bonn dissertation arrived too late

for me to incorporate it at length. Sturm's study raises the question

of chronology. The *Romans* was given as lectures in Oxford during

1550/51 and revised with Cranmer at Lambeth 1552, the Marian Exiles

at Strasbourg from 1553/56 and finally edited in Zurich 1558. The

context therefore is Oxford, Strasbourg II and Zurich, not Strasbourg

I (1542/47) as in Sturm. Sturm also used I *Corinthians* to develop

Martyr's theology under Bucer's influence in that early period while

on the contrary their personal contact at Cambridge seems more

pertinent than an extrapolation from the years at Strasbourg. There

are documents from their English encounter not used by Sturm.

My study proceeds bibliographically and chronologically to

creat a *Sitz im Leben* parallel to Schmidt (1858) and preliminary to

that of a future monograph which must be built on Donnelly, Corda,

Sturm and the Kingdon bibliography. The greatest *desideratum* apart

from work on Martyr texts is progress on the mature Bullinger and

the Zurich pastors like Lavater, a process which under the careful

hand of Professor Fritz Büsser and his Zurich team will take three

generations to edit the vast Bullinger correspondence in more than

100 volumes.[1]

Anyone citing from the 1583 *Common Places* should check the

English text against the thirteen Latin editions from 1576 at London

to 1656 at Amsterdam/Frankfurt. On should then collate the various
editions of the commentary from which it comes and assess the context
in each commentary to arrive at Martyr's message. Logistical problems
make that procedure difficult since no one library has copies of all
Martyr editions. Therefore, the reader can see why I prefer the term
interim study since it was not possible to document my several
attempts to do that with the commentaries cited in this study. The
documentation would have buried my narrative beyond recognition. A
future study can be written after a scientific edition of Martyr's
corpus has been prepared in which every *locus* in the editions of the
Loci Communes can be read *in situ* from the commentaries themselves.
One might better see then that Martyr deserves to be called the
theologian of the Italian Reformation. At the end of such a process
scholars may be less inclined to view Martyr as a scholastic and more
as a rhetorical humanist like Calvin and Melanchthon. One major
difference between Martyr and these friends would be his use of
Rabbinic sources.

Donald Nugent's *Ecumenism In The Age of the Reformation* reached
my desk as these final lines were typed. Nugent concludes that a
theology of hope can transcend in our day the barriers erected in
the sixteenth century by theologians like Peter Martyr. Eschatology
would seem to favour Nugent's view of ecumenism. But one could
reflect with Robert McNally,S.J. on the past mystery of disintegration
as well as appeal to the future miracle of reintegration with Donald
Nugent. Both scholars muse over the meaning of dialogue between

catholic and protestant traditions now of four centuries' duration.

Martyr moved from dialogue in Italy to dissent in Northern Europe

so that he might pursue the truth as he experienced it. The integ-

rity of that protest has been impressive to observe in the life of

the Florentine reformer, Pietro Martire Vermigli. To set forth

Martyr's explanation of his exile and protest has been a central

concern of this study, which to ignore would be to conclude with

observations foreign to Peter Martyr and to follow a procedure not

very scientific in its conception.

The range of scholars who aided me in this study has transcended

those ideological barriers which have their origin in Martyr's epoch.

The Methodist Gordon Rupp and Anglicans Peter Brooks and Patrick

Collinson have joined the Jesuit Father John Donnelly and Monsignor

John Sankovitz in assisting this study. Martyr has his charm for all

of these scholars who like myself have been drawn into the orbit of

Martyr's world. John Sankovitz in particular has labored over his

translation of Martyr's letters and invited me twice to speak on

Martyr at St. Paul Seminary. His gracious spirit is a sign of pro-

gress from the turmoil of the sixteenth century and bespeaks a

desire to see the truth as understood by Martyr set forth in all its

clarity. I trust that for all my collaborators the words of St.

Augustine may ring true which John Calvin added at the foot of his

preface to the fifth edition (1550) of the *Institutes of The

Christian Religion*: Ego ex eorum numero me esse profiteor qui

scribunt proficiendo et scribendo proficiunt. I profess that I am of the number who write as they progress and progress by writing.

Schmidt's 1858 study concludes that Martyr had neither the fiery constitution of Farel nor did he become the focus of a church movement (kirkenbildend) like Luther, Calvin or Bullinger. Nonetheless, his lectures and exegesis found several followers through their "freedom from gross vulgarity, their choice and sought after elegance, simplicity, clarity, precision and classical charm."[2]

It might be that Martyr was most appreciated by the beleaguered citizenry of La Rochelle, for Brunet lists a 1581 French edition of Martyr's *Psalms* printed in La Rochelle. These Huguenots knew their *Psalms* as Battle-hymns of the Lord.[3] So did a papal exile become a son of consolation for the Israel of God in Sixteenth Century France.

1. Fritz Büsser, "Reformation History Research in German speaking Switzerland," Renaissance and Reformation IX (1972), 26-27. Studies of Gualther, Stucki and Wolf would also help one to understand Vermigli.

2. Charles Schmidt, Peter Martyr Vermigli. Leben und ausgewählte Schriften, p. 293. "Seine Rede war eben so frei von roher Gemeinheit als von gesuchter Eleganz, sie war einfach, klar, bestimmt, und doch voll klassischer Anmuth."

3. William S. Reid, "Battle hymns of the Lord; Calvinist Psalmody of the Sixteenth century," Sixteenth Century Essays and Studies II (1971), 36-54.

BIBLIOGRAPHY OF SOURCES AND REFERENCE TOOLS

I. MANUSCRIPTS

A. Cambridge

1. Corpus Christi College

Corpus Christi College, Cambridge. MS. 102:29, "A Sermon concernynge
the time of rebellion." The original is MS. 340:4, Sermo Petri
Martyri manu propria scriptus in seditionem Devonensium.

Corpus Christi College, Cambridge. MS. 102:31, fol. 512.
Peter Martyr on Rebellion.

Corpus Christi College, Cambridge. MS. 119: fols. 109-114.
John Warner to Peter Martyr, March (?) 1551, from Oxford,
autograph.

Corpus Christi College, Cambridge. MS. 119:98.
Albert von Hardenberg to Martin Bucer, 7 September 1550 from
Lambeth, autograph.

Corpus Christi College, Cambridge. MS. 119:6.
Safe conduct from King Charles IX for attendance at the Colloquy
of Poissy, 25 July 1561.

2. University Library

Anderson Room. Ee. 2.8. Collectanae, MS. folio volume compiled by
Pierre Alexandre for Thomas Cranmer, Archbishop of Canterbury.

3. Gonville and Caius College

MS 53/30. Letterbook of Bishop Cox of Ely.

B. London

1. British Museum

Add. MS. 21, 524. /19400, f.20/
Bucer, 20 September 1550 & 10 September 1550.

Add. MS. 29549 (13), fol. 18^r.
Sir Anthony Cooke, 5 November 1560.

Add. MS. 32091, fol. 179. Edmund Grindal, 28 January 1560.

Arundel MS. 100. GARDINER, STEPHEN, In Petrū Martyrem florentinum
malae tractacionis querela Sanctissimae Eucharistiae nōīe
edita, authore Stephano Winton.

Harleian MS. 426, Plut, LXV.C; fol. 211^r.
Foxe, John, Collection of Letters and Papers on Theological and Political Matters.

Harleian MS. 426. C.
Reformatio Legum Ecclesiasticarum

Landsdowne MS. 3(22), p. 44.
Haddon to Cecil.

Royal MS. 17.C.V., fol. 45^v-46^r.
Of The Sacrament of Thanksgiving. A Short Treatise of Peter Martyr's Making.

Royal MS. 18 B. xi fol. 1.
Udall's answer to the Commoners of Devonshire and Cornwall.

2. Lambeth Palace Library

SELDEN MS. 2010.
/John a Lasco, De Sacrament. 14 May 1557 signed by Farel and Beza./ Epistolae Virorum Doctorum de Rebus ecclesiastices tempore Elizabethae reginae.

SELDEN MS. 2010, No. 82.
Peter Martyr to Richard Cox, 22 August 1559 from Zurich.

SELDEN MS. 2010, No. 83.
Peter Martyr to Richard Cox, 31 August 1559 from Zurich.

SELDEN MS. 2010, No. 73.
Peter Martyr to Edmund Grindal, 28 January 1560 from Zurich.

SELDEN MS. 2010, No. 84.
Peter Martyr to Edwin Sandys, 18 June 1560 from Zurich.

SELDEN MS. 2010, No. 85.
Peter Martyr to Richard Cox, 18 June 1560 from Zurich.

SELDEN MS. 2010, No. 86.
Peter Martyr to John Jewel, 15 August 1561 from Zurich.

SELDEN MS. 2010, No. 87.
Peter Martyr to Richard Cox, 4 October 1562 from Zurich.

C. Modena

Archivio di Stato, Modena
Giurisdizione ecclesiastica Vescovi Vicario Modena, Busta 265.

Archivio privato Cortesi Busta 209 et 210.
By special permission of Professor Antonio Rotondo and the
Archivist.

       D. Paris

          1. Bibliotheque Nationale

MS. Paris, BN. Lat. 13,063.
    MS. letters between Conrad Gesner and James Dalechamp.

          2. Bibliotheque Ste Genevieve

MS. 347, No. 47 (f. 158).
    Peter Martyr to Heinrich Bullinger, 19 September, 1562. Copy.

       E. Parma

Archivio di Stato Parma, Raccoldi MSS., busta n. 135, Cardinali
    pergamene e lettere autographe, "Pole (Card.) Rêginaldo --
    1537 -- S.A.," n. 3.

       F. Perugia

Archivio di Stato, Perugia: Documenti Scientifici Storici e
    Letterarii. Archivio privato: Ansidei Miscellanea, no. 25.
    By special permission of Director, Roberto Abbondonza.

Lettere di Giovanni Domenico Sigbaldo Vicario di Mons. Giovanni
    Morone Vescovio di Modena scritte da Modena negli anni 1540-
    1541 ad esso Morone che era Nuncio Apostolico Appresso il Re
    de Romani.

       G. Oxford

Bodleian Library MS. 29279

       H. Rome

             1. Biblioteca Nazionale Centrale Vittorio
                Emanuele II. Fondo Autografi, Busta 153,
                n.23 Peter Martyr to Albert von Hardenberg,
                25 September 1555 from Strasbourg, autograph.

             2. Biblioteca Apostolica Vaticana.
                Codices Vaticani Latini 10755, 21.
                Acta Diaectae Ratisbonensis.

I. Strasbourg

1. Archives Municipales Du Ville De Strasbourg

<u>Archives Du Chapitre De St-Thomas De Strasbourg</u>, 40, fol. 837^{r}.
Peter Martyr to Francesco Dryander, 22 August 1547 from Oxford,
autograph.

<u>Archives Du Chapitre De St-Thomas De Strasbourg</u>, 40, fol. 839^{r}.
Peter Martyr to Francesco Dryander, 5 October 1547 from Oxford,
autograph.

<u>Archives Du Chapitre De St-Thomas De Strasbourg</u>, 40, fol. 881^{r}.
Peter Martyr to Francesco Dryander, 3 January 1549 from Oxford,
autograph.

<u>Archives Du Chapitre De St-Thomas De Strasbourg</u>, 40, fol. 883^{r}.
Peter Martyr to Francesco Dryander, 1 February 1549 from Oxford,
autograph.

<u>Archives Du Chapitre De St-Thomas De Strasbourg</u>, 41, fol. 97.
Conrad Hubert to Peter Martyr, 7 September 1551 from Strasbourg,
autograph.

<u>Archives Du Chapitre De St-Thomas De Strasbourg</u>, 346, fol. 114.
Peter Martyr to Governors of the College of St. Thomas, 22
January 1554 from Strasbourg, autograph.

<u>Archives Du Chapitre De St-Thomas De Strasbourg</u>, 43, fols. 313-314.
Peter Martyr to Zurich Burgorat, 8 June 1556 from Strasbourg,
autograph. Copy dated 7 May 1556 in Zurich Staatsarchiv.

2. Bibliotheque Nationale et Universitaire de
Strasbourg

<u>Thesaurus Baumianus</u>, MS. 674: Reg. XV: fol. 32-33. Peter Martyr
to Martin Bucer, 13 April 1544 from Strasbourg, copy.

<u>Thesaurus Baumianus</u>, MS. 675, Reg. XVI: fol. 158. Martin Bucer to
Fellio, Martyr and Fagius, 23 December 1545 from Ratisbon,copy.

<u>Thesaurus Baumianus</u>, MS. 680, Reg. XXI: fol. 225. Hermann
Folkertzheimer to Peter Martyr, 9 May 1560, copy.

J. Zofingen Staatsbibliothek

<u>Epistolae Autographae variorum eruditione celebrium virorum saec.</u>
<u>XVI. ad Musculos aliosque scriptae.</u>

MS. I, fol. 24^{r-v}. Peter Martyr to Wolfgang Musculus, 29 October 1554 from Strasbourg, autograph.

MS. I, fol. 23^{r-v}. Peter Martyr to Wolfgang Musculus, 11 September 1556 from Zurich, autograph.

K. Zurich

1. Staatsarchiv

EII (340), fol. 111. Peter Martyr to Heinrich Bullinger, xiiii Kl. Januarias M.D. XLII, from Strasbourg, autograph.

EII (340), fol. 112. Peter Martyr to Heinrich Bullinger, III Nones October 1542 from Basle, autograph.

EII (340), fol. 157^{r-v}. Peter Martyr to Heinrich Bullinger, 7 July 1545 from Strasbourg, autograph.

EII (156), fol. 34. Francesco Dryander to Heinrich Bullinger, 8 May 1547 from Strasbourg, autograph.

EII (340), fol. 215. Peter Martyr to Heinrich Bullinger, 10 December 1554 from Strasbourg, autograph.

EII (342), fol. 323. Peter Martyr to Heinrich Bullinger, 1 May 1556 from Strasbourg, autograph.

EII (371), fol. 815^{r}. Francesco Stancaro to Musculus, Martyr, Calvin and Bullinger, 10 December 1560 from Cracow, autograph.

EII (368), fol. 545^{r}. Nicholas Gallasius to Peter Martyr, 25 November 1561 from Edinburgh, autograph.

EII (363), fol. 81. Zacharias Ursinus to Conrad Gesner, 22 March 1562 from Heidelberg, autograph.

EII (367), fols. 176-178. Gregorius Paulus to Martyr and Bullinger, 24 September 1562 from Cracow, autograph.

2. Zentralbibliothek

a. Simmlerische Sammlung

Simmlerische Sammlung MSC. S. 52. Peter Martyr to Heinrich Bullinger, III Nones October 1542 from Basle. Copy.

Simmlerische Sammlung MSC. S. 52(86). Peter Martyr to Heinrich Bullinger, 19 December 1542 from Strasbourg, copy.

<u>Simmlerische Sammlung</u> MSC. 76:93. Peter Martyr to Otto Heinrich, Count Palatine, 23 November 1551 from Lambeth, copy.

<u>Simmlerische Sammlung</u> MSC. 79:188. Wolfgang Musculus to Heinrich Bullinger, November 1553 from Basle, copy.

<u>Simmlerische Sammlung</u>, MSC. 239, 21a. Francois Hotman to Peter Martyr, 22 January 1561, copy.

b. Car. XV.20S.89-97.

<u>Ad peregrinae ecclesiae apud Francfordienses fratres, de baptismo a Lutheranis administratio.</u> Peter Martyr to Refugee Church at Frankfort, 30 September 1554, copy with title in Bullinger's hand.

II. MARTYR IMPRINTS
(BY DATE OF PUBLICATION)

<u>UNA SEM-/PLICE DICHIARA-/TIONE SOPRA GLI/XII ARTICOLI DELLA FEDE/ CHRISTIANA. Di Mar/tyre Vermigli Firentino./Non moriar, sed vivam, et narra-/bo opera Domini./Psal. 117.</u> (nella inclyta Basilea, 1544).

<u>TRACTATIO/DE SACRAMENTO EV-/charistiae, habita in celeberrima vni-/ uersitate OXONIENSI in Anglia, per/D. PETRVM MARTYREM/VERMILIVM FLOREN-tinum, Regium ibidem/Theologiae professorem, cum/iam absoluisset interpre=/tationem. 11 capi=/tis prioris/epistolae D. Pauli Apostoli/ ad Corinthios./Ad Hec./DISPVTATIO DE EODEM/EVCHARISTIAE SA-/CRAMENTO, in eadem Vniuersitate/habita per eundem D.P. MAR./Anno Domini/M.D.XLIX</u> (Londini: ad aeneum serpentem). Collated with 1552 and 1562 Zurich editions.

<u>DE VITANDIS SUPER-/STITIONIBUS, quae/cum sincera fidei/confessione/ pu-/gnant./Libellus Ioannis Calvini./Eiusdem excusatio ad pseu-/ donicodemos./Philippi Melancthonis,/Martini Buceri,/Petri Martyris responsa/de eadem re./Calvini ultimum responsum,/cum appendicibus</u> (Genevae, per Ioannem Girardum, 1549).

<u>A discourse or traic=/tise of Petur Martyr Ver/mill a Floretine, the publy=/que reader of diuinitee in/the Uniuersitee of Oxford/wherein he openly declared/his whole and determinate/iudgemente concernynge/ the Sacrament of the Lordes supper in/the sayde Uni=/uersitee.</u> (Imprinted at London by Robert Stough=/ton dwellinge within Ludgate at the signe/of the Bysshoppes Miter for Nycolas/Udall) 1550?/1551.

<u>An Epistle Vnto the right honorable and christian Prince, the Duke of Somerset, written unto him in Latin anone after hys deliueraunce out of trouble by the famous clearke Doctour Peter Martyr, and</u>

translated into Englyshe by Thomas Norton. Anno a verbo incarnato.
M.D.L. Regni Edwardi sexti iii. (London: Gwalter Lynne, M.D.L.).

IN SELECTISSIMAM S. PAVLI PRIOREM AD CORINTH/IOS/ EPISTOLAM D. Petri
Martyris, Florentini, ad Sereniss. regem Angliae, &c. Eduardum VI.
Commentarij doctissimi . . . .(Tiguri ex officina Christ. Froschoueri,
Anno M.D.LI). /First edition/ Two printings appeared in Zurich,
1551 with varient title pages. Text checked against Zurich editions
of 1567, 1569, 1572 and 1579.

Dispvtatio de Evcharistiae sacramento habita in celeberr. Vniuersitate
Oxonien. in Anglia, antea quidem illic excusa, iam uero denuo cum
triplici indice in lucem edita. (Tigvri, Apvd And. Gesnervm, F. & R.
Vuysenbachium. Anno M.D. LII.).

A treatise of the cohabitacyon of the faithful with the vnfaithfull.
Wherunto is added. A sermon made of the confessing of Christe and
his gospell (Strasbourg: W. Rihel, 1555). Reprinted in 1642.

IN EPISTOLAM S. PAVLI APOSTOLI AD ROMANOS D. Petri Martyris Vermilii
Florentini, Professoris diuinarum literarum in schola Tigurina,
commentarii doctissimi . . . . (Basilea apud Petrum Pernam M.D.LVIII).
Text check against Zurich edition of 1559 (Cambridge University
Library), and the Basle editions of 1560 (Pet. D.5.35.) and
1568 (Pet. N.5.6.). A textual varient occurs on p. 711 in
Romans 8 of the 1560 edition. Text collated with Heidelberg
editions of 1612 and 1613.

Petri Martyri Florentini, professoris theologiae in Argentinensi
schola, ad ecclesiam Polonicam, Argentiae, 14 Februarii 1556
(Pinczoviae: Apud Danielem Lancicium, MDLIX).
    Checked against text of 1561 Zurich edition in Cambridge
    University Library.

DEFENSIO D. PETRI MARTYRIS VERMILII FLORENTINI diuinarum literarum
in schola Tigurina professoris, ad Riccardi Smythaei Angli, olim
Theologiae professoris Oxoniensis duos libellos de Caelibatu
sacerdotum, & Votis monasticis . . . . (Basilea apud Petrum Pernam
M.D. LIX). Text collated with Basle edition of 1581.

DEFENSIO DOCTRINAE VETERIS & APOSTOLICAE DE SACROSANCTO EVCHARISTIAE
SACRAMENTO, D. Petri Martyris Vermilij, Florentini, diuinarum
literarum in schola Tigurina professoris, in quatuor distincta
prates, aduersus Stephani Gardineri, quondam Vuintoniensis Episcopi,
librum, quem ille primum quidem sub huius modi titulo edidit,
Confutatio cauillationum, quibus sacrosanctum Eucharistiae Sacra-
memtum ab impijs Capernaitus impeti solet, authore M. Anton.
Constantio, & C. deinde uero comme titia hoc nemine ixpuncto,
proprique suo ipsius nomine apposito ac expresso, euulgauit.

(ZURICH: Froschauer, 1559).
Text checked against Zurich edition of 1562 and Basle edition
of 1581.

Epistolae Dvae, Ad Ecclesias Polonicas, Iesv Christi Euangelium
amplexas, scriptae a Tigurinae ecclesiae ministris, de negotio
Stancariano & mediatore dei & hominum Iesu Christo, an hic secundum
humanam naturam duntaxat, an secundum utranque mediatore sit
(Tiguri: Christophorus Froschouerus, mense Martio 1561).

In Librvm IVDICVM/D. PETRI MARTYRIS VERMILIJ FLO=/RENTINI, PROFESSORIS
DIVINARUM LITE=/RARVM IN SCHOLA TIGURINA, COM/MENT ARIJ DOCTISSIMI,
CUM TRACTATIONE PERUTILIRE=/RUM & LOCORUM (TIGURI/EXCUDEBAT CHRISTOPH.
FROSCHVERVS./M.D.LXI).
Text checked in rare 1609 Heidelberg edition. Peterborough
Cathedral Library collection, Pet. N.5.1^2.

In Primvm,/Secvndvm, Et Ini/tivm Tertii Libri Ethi/corvm Aristotelis
ad Nicoma/chvm, Clariss & doctiss viri D. Petri Marty/ris Vermilij,
Florentini, Sacrarum literarum in/Schola Tigurina Professoris, Com/
mentarius doctissimus (Tigvri: Christophorus Froschouerus Iunior,
Mense Augusto, Anno M.D. LXIII).

Most fruit/full & learned Comenta=/ries of Doctor Peter Martir Ver=/
mil Florentine, Professor of Deui=/nitie, in the Universitye of
Tygure,/ with a very profitable tract of the/matter and places./
(Imprinted at London by John/Day, dwellyng ouer Aldersgate. 1564).

Scripta quaedam D. Petri Martyris de/Euchariftia, nunquam antehac
edita/ in ORATIO/DE VITA ET OBI=/TV CLARISSIMI VIRI ET PRAESTAN-/
tifsimi Theologi D. PETRI MARTYRIS VER/MIL II diuinarum literarum
profefforis in fcho-/la Tigurina, habita ibidem a I O S l A/S I M
L E R O Tigurino./ITEM (TIGVRI APVD CHRISTOPHORVM/Frofchouerum
Iuniorem, Anno M.D.LXIII.).

PRECES/SACRAE EX/PSALMIS/DAVIDIS/DESVMPTAE per D. Pe-/trum Martyrem
Vermi-/lium Florentinum, sacrarum lite-/rarum in schola Tigurina/
professorem./ (Tiguri: excludebat Christophorus Froschouerus,
Anno M.D. LXIIII).
Text checked against 1566 Zurich edition, Pet. E.6.63.,
1578 Zurich edition and 1582 Basle edition.

A briefe examination for the tyme, of a certaine declaration, lately
put in print in the name and defence of certaine Ministers in London,
refusying to weare the apparell prescribed by the lawes and orders
of the Realme. In the ende is reported, the iudgement of two notable
learned fathers, M. doctour Bucer, and M. doctour Martir, sometyme in
eyther vniuersities here of England the kynges readers and professours
of diuinitie, translated out of the originals, written by theyr owne

handes, purposely debatyng this controuersie. (London: Richard Iugge, 1566).

IN DVOS LIBROS SAMUELIS PROPHETAE quie uulgo Priores Libri Regum appellantur D. Petri Martyris Vermilii Florentini, professoris diuinarum literarum in schola Tigurina, Commentarii doctissimi . . . . (Tiguri excludebat Christophorus Froschouerus,Anno M.D.LXIIII).

    Text checked against Zurich editions of 1564, 1567, 1575 (Pet. N.5.5.) and 1595.

Melachim/Id Est REGVM LIBRIDVO/posteriores cum Com/mentarijs/Petri Martyris Vermilii/Florentini Sacrar. Literar. in Schol/la Tigurina Professoris in primum totum & se/cundi priori XI capita (Tigvri/Excludebat Christophorus Froschouerus, Mense Martio/Anno M.D.LXVI:)
    Text checked against Zurich editions of 1569 (Pet. N.5.1'), 1571, 1581 (Dr. Williams Library) and Heidelberg edition of 1599 (University of Pennsylvania).

VVHETHER it be mortall/sinne to transgresse ciuil lawes,/which be the commaun-/dementes of ciuill/Magistrates./The iudgement of Philip Me-/lancton in his Epitome/of morall Philo-/sophie./The resolution of. D. Hen. Bullin-/ger, and. D. Rod. Gualter, of. D. Mar-/tin Bucer, and. D. Peter Martyr,/concernyng thapparrel of/ Ministers, and other/indifferent/thinges./ (London: Richard Iugge, 1566).

Most lear/ned and fruitfull Com/mentaries of D. Peter Martir/Vermilius Florentine, Professor of Diuinitie in the Schole of Ti/gure, upon the Epistle of S. Paul to the Romanes: wherein are diligent/ly & most profitably entreated all/such matters and chiefe common/places of religion touched in/the same Epistle (trans. H.B., London: Iohn Daye, 1568).

In Primvm Librvm/Mosis, Qui VVLGO GE-/nesis Dicitvr Commentarii/ doctissimi D. Petri Martyris Vermilii Florent-/tini, professoris diuinarum literarum in/schola Tigurina, nunc primum/in lucem edita (Tigvri: excludebat Christophorvs/Froschoverus, M.D. LXIX).
    Text checked against Zurich edition of 1579, Pet. N.5.1' and 1606 Heidelberg edition, Ely Cathedral Library.

Glemhan, Charles, Most Godly prayers compiled out of Dauids Psalmes by D. Peter Martyr (London: William Seres, 1569).

In Selectissiman/D. Pavli Priorem Ad Co/rinthios Epistolam. D. Petri/ Martyris Vermilii Florentini, ad Sereniss./Regem Angliae, & C. Edvar/DUM VI, Commentarii/doctissimi (Tiguri: Christophorus Froschouerus, M.D.LXXII.) /Third edition/.

Epistre . . . a quelques fideles touchant leur abjuration et
renouncement de la verite . . . . (sans impr., 8), Musee historique
de la Reformation, Geneva. 1574.

PETRI MARTYRIS VERMILII, Florentini praestantissimi nostra aetate
theologi, Loci commvnes. Ex varijs ipsius aucthoris & libris in
vnum volumen collecti, & quatuor classes distributi (ed. Robert
Masson, Londini, ex typographia Ioannis Kyngstoni, 1576) /First
edition/.

Loci commvnes d. Petri Martyris Vermilii . . . ex variis ipsius
authoris scriptis, in vnum librum collecti, & in quatuor classes
distributi. Accesservnt huic aeditioni ab ipso authore P. Martyre
scripti, nec antea publicati, Loci de libero arbitrio . . . adhaec
orationes siue conciones, nec non quaestiones aliquot & responsa:
epistolae . . . (Tigvri: C. Froschovervs,MD.LXXX).

PETRI MARTYRIS/VERMILLII/Locorum Communium/Theologicorum, ex ipsius
diurfis/Opufculis collectorum/TOMVS SECVNDUS/(Basileae: Ad Perneam
Lecythvm, MDXXCI).

D. Petri Martyris Vermilii Florentini Analysis Libri De Evcharistia
contra Gardinerum, in Petri Martyris Vermilii Locorum Communium
Theologicorum, ex ipsius diuersis Opusculis collectorum, Tomvs
Secvndvs (Basle: Pernea Lecythus, MD XXCI). First printed in Simler,
Oratio (1563).
        Separate title page bound with second volume.

D. Petri Martiris Vermilii Florentini Proposita Dispvtata Pvblice In
Schola Argentinensi ab anno M.D. XLIII. vsq: ad Annum XLIX
(Basle: Petrus Perna, M.D. LXXXII).
        Bound in volume III of Basle edition.

PETRI MARTYRIS/VERMILII/Opuscula Theologica/omnia partim noua, partim/
prius quoque edita./ TOMVS TERTIVS./In quo reliqua omnia eius Opuscula,
tam/edita quam antea non edita/continentur (Basileae: Ad Perneam
Lecythvm, M.D.XXCII).

THE/COMMON PLACES/of the most famous and/renowned /sic/ Diuine
Doctor/Peter Martyr, diuided/into foure principall parts; with/a
large addition of manie theo-/logicall and necessarie dis-/courses,
some never/extant before./Translated and partlie gathered by/
Anthonie Marten, one of the/Sewers of hir Maiesties/most Honourable/
Chamber./ Meliora spero./ . . . (London: Imprinted at the costs and
charges of Henrie Denham, Thomas Chard, Vvilliam Broome, and Andrew
Maunsell, 1583).

Loci commvnes/D. Petri/Martyris Ver-/milii, Florentini, sacrarvm/
literarum in Schola Tigvrina/Professoris: ex varijs ipsu-/is
authoris scriptis, in vnum/librum collecti, & in quatuor classes
distributi./ Qvam multa ad priorem editionem accesserint, ex
admoniti-/one quam prima pagina exhibebit, faci-/le lector deprehendet.
/ . . . (Londini, excudebat Thomas Vautrollerius typographus, 1583).

Loci communes D. Petri Martyris Vermilii Florentini . . . (Tiguri: In
Officina Froschoviana, M.D. LXXXVII).

Geruasius, Theophilus, Panoplia/Christiana/Seu/Adversvs Varias Ten/
tationes et Afflictio/nes, quibus pij in mundo/exercenter,/MVNIMENTA
ET REMEDIA (Geneva: Eustachius Vignon, M.D. LXXXVIII).
    De cruce et afflictionibus perferendis (pp. 356-387) from
Martyr, I Corinthians (9:27) on 233-234 /1551 edition/.

Loci Commvnes/D. Petri Mar-/tyris Vermilii Flo-/rentini Sacrarvm
Lite/rarum In Schola Tigurina/Professoris . . ./quam multa ad priorem
editionem accesserint . . . (Heidelbergae: apud Iohannem Lancellotum,
impensis Andreae Cambieri, 1613).

Münster, Joannis a, Collectanea Variorum Authorum De Sortibus et Ludo
Aleae in Pascasii Justi, Alea, siue De Curanda in Pecuniam Ludendi
Cupiditate, libri duo, una cum collectaneis, tam uterum, quam recentium
authorum de sortibus, aleae, taxillorum, et chartarum ludo (Neapoli
Nemetum: Henricus Starkius, MDC.XVII).
    De Ludis (pp. 115-121) from Martyr, Judges XIV /1561 edition/,
and De Sortibus (pp. 121-124) from Martyr, I Samuel (19:19)
/1566 edition/.

Loci commvnes Petri Martyris Vermilii: ex variis ipsivs avctoris
scriptis in vnum volumen collecti & in quatuor classes iuxta veram
methodum distributi. Quibus appendicis loco adiiciuntur loci quidam
peculiariter ab auctore traditi: item theses, orationes, epistolae
de variis rebus theologicis scriptae; nec non tres confessiones de
S. Coena, quarum duae olim amplissimo senatui Argentinensi exhibitae
fuerunt . . . (Heidelbergae: Sumptibus D. & D. Aubriorum, M.DC.
XXII).

Loci commones Petri Martyris Vermilii: ex varies ipsivs anthoris
scriptis in vnum librum collecti, in quatuor classes distributi Hvnc
postremae ed., . . . ingens eiusden m.p. aliguot commonibus, qui
hactenus desiderabartur, additis. Adiectis praeterea thesibos
nonnullis gvaestionibus/etc./. Qvid hac editione accesserit
triplici cruce adnotatum reperies (Genevae: sumptibus & typis P.
Avberti, M.DC.XXVI).

Loci Commvnes/Petri Martyris/Vermilii Florentini/Theologi Celebrerrimi: /Ex Variis Ipsius Avthoris Scriptis,/in Vnum librum collecti, & in quatuor classes distributi (Geneva: Petrus Avbertus; M.DC.XXVII). Genevan editions checked against Geneva text (1624).

In Lamentationes/Sanctissimi/Ieremiae Prophetae,/D. Petri Martvris/ Vermilii, Florentini,/Sacarum Literarum/quondam in Schola Tigurina/ Professoris,/Commentarjvm./Hoc Demvm Lamentabili et/lugubri tempore, ex autographo collectum, cor-/rectum, et in lucem editum,/Cum Notis et Indice./Matth.24. Videte turbemini: oportet enim omnia fieri (Tigvri: excludebat, Ioh. Iacobus Bodmerus, M.D.C.XXIX).

TVrrettin, Benedict, Brief/Traicte,/Auquel est monstre/, Que Celuy Qui a La Cognois-/sance de l' Euangile, est necessairement oblige/de sortir de l' Eglise Papistique/Romaine./Plus quelques Fragments tires d'un traicte'/du docteur P. Martyr Florentine./(n.p.)/M.DCXLVI:37-49: On Demande, Si nous qui faisons profession de la Religion Reformee Auons bien fait de nous separer de l'Eglise Romaine. Musee Historique de la Reformation, Geneva.

Loci Communes/D. Petri Martyris/Vermilii Florentini Sa-/crarum Literarum In Scho-/la Tigurina Professoris/quondam celeberrimi (Prostant Amstelaedami & Francofurti Apud Joannema Ravensteyn Bibliopolam. M.DC.LVI).

Goode, William, AN UNPUBLISHED LETTER/OF/PETER MARTYR, REG. DIV. PROF. OXFORD,/TO HENRY BULLINGER;/Written from Oxford Just After the Comple- tion of/THE SECOND PRAYER BOOK OF EDWARD VI.;/ . . . . (London: J. Hatchard and Son, 1850).

An Homily Against Gluttony and Drunkenness (1563) in Certain Sermons or Homilies Appointed To Be Read In Churches In The Time Of Queen Elizabeth . . . (Philadelphia: Edward Biddle, 1844).

III.   EARLY PRINTED SOURCES

Acta Synodow roznowierczych w Polsce (edited by M. Sipaylto: Warsaw, 1966), I.

Adam, Melchior, Decades DVae Continuentes Vitas Theologorum Exteriorum Principum, Qui Ecclesiam Christi Superior Seculo Propagarunt et propugnarunt (Francofurti: Typis Nicolai Hoffmanni, M.D.C. XVIII). Latin text of Simler's Oratio.

Alexandre, Pierre, Les/Conseils et Ad/vis De Plvsievrs Ex/cellans & suans personnages, sur le faict/des Temporisaurs. Et comment le fidele/se doit maintenir entre les Papistes. Item/vne Epistre Consola/taire aux freres & membres de l'eglise de Ie/sus Christ,

qui fut en Angleterre durant le/regne du bon Roy Edouard:
escrite par M./Pierre Alex. (Geneva/: Chez Iean Crespin
M.D.LVI).

Allan, Thomas & Thomas Shepard, A/Defence/of the/answer made unto
the Nine Questions/or Positions sent from New-England, Against
the/Reply Thereto/by/That Reverend servant of Christ,/Mr. John
Ball . . ., (London: Andrew Crooke, 1648).

Ascham, Roger, Epistolarum, Libri Quatuor (Oxford: Henry Clements,
MDCCIII).

The Whole Works of Roger Ascham, Now First Collected and Revised,
With A Life of the Author, edited by Rev. Dr. Giles (London:
John Russel Smith, 1864), II.

/Barnes, Robert/, Anglus, Antonius, (Pseud.), Sen-/tenciae Ex Doc-/
toribus Col-/lectae Qvas papistae ualde im-/pudenter ho-/die
dam-/nant (Wittenberg: J. Clug, 1530).

Bauhinus, Caspar, De plantis a diuis sanctis've nomen habentibus
(Basel: C. Waldkirch, 1591).

Baum, G. et Ed. Cunitz, Histoire ecclesiasticque des Eglise
reformees au Royaume de France (Edition nouvelle, Paris, 1883-
89).

Baum, Johann Wilhelm, Theodor Beza nach handschriftlichen Quellen
dargestellt (Leipzig: Wedimann'sche Buchhandlung, 1843).

De Beze, Theodore, Correspondance De Theodore De Beze (edited by F.
Aubert, H. Meylan and A. Dufour) Tome II (1556-1558)
(Geneve: Librairie E. Droz, 1962). Also Tome III (1559-
1561), Tome IV (1562-1563), Tome V (1564), Tome VI (1565) and
Tome VII (1566) (Geneve: E. Droz, 1963-1973).

_____, THEODORE//BEZAE VEZELII, VI-//GILANTISSIMI PASTORIS
//ET FIDELISSIMI DOCTORIS EC-//clesiae Geneuensis,//EPISTOLARVM
THE-//OLOGICARVM,//LIBER VNVS.//Editio tertia, ab ipso auctore
re-//cognita.// (HANOVIAE//Apud Giulielmum Antonium,//MDXCVII).

Bodius, H. /Pseudonym/, Vnio Dissidentium Libellus Omnibus unitatis
ac pacis amatoribus utilissimus ex praecipuis Ecclesiae
Christianae doctoribus, per Uenerabilem patrem Hermannum Bodiū
verbi diuini concionatorem eximum selectus ac per eundem
Secundo recognitus (Köln: T. Symnicus, Sept. 1531).

Brenz, John, IN/EXODVM/MOSI COMMEN-/TARII./AVTORE IOANNE/Brentio
(Halle: Petrus Brubachius, M.D.XLIIII).

Bucer, Martin, Praelectiones Doctiss. In Epistolam D.P. ad Ephesios, eximij doctoris D. Martini Buceri, habitae Cantabrigae in Anglia, Anno MD. L. & LI (Basle: Petrus Perna, M.D. LXII).

_____, Martini Bvceri Scripta Anglicana Fere Omnialis etiam, quae hactenus vel nondum, vel sparsim, vel peregrino saltem idiomate edita fuere (Basileae: Ex Petri Pernae Officina, MD. LXXVII).

Bullinger, Heinrich, Heinrich Bullingers Briefwechsel mit seinen Sohne Heinrich, zu Strassburg und Wittenberg, pp. 75-158 in Friedrich Franz, Merkwürdize zuge aus dem Leben des Zürcherischen Antistes Henrich Bullinger, nebst dessen Reiseinstruktion und Briefen an seinen Ältesten Sohn Heinrich, auf den Lehranstalten zu Strassburg und Wittenberg (Bern: J. J. Burgdorfer, 1828).

_____, Heinrich Bullingers Diarium (Annales vitae) der Jahre 1504-1574 (edited by Emil Egli, Bassel: Adolf Geering, 1904).

_____, Bullingers Korrespondenz mit den Graubündnern. I Teil, Januar 1533-April 1557 (Traugott Schiess; Basel: Adolf Geering, 1904) (Quellen Zur Schweizer Geschichte 23).

_____, A treatise or Sermon of Henry Bullinger, much fruitfull and necessarye for this tyme, concernynge magistrates and obedience of subiects. Also concernyng the affayres of warre, and what scryptures make mension thereof (London: Gwalter Lynne, 1549).

Calendar of State Papers, Foreign Series, of the Reign of Elizabeth 1558-1559 (edited by Joseph Stevenson, London: Her Majesty's Stationery Office, 1863).

Calendar of State Papers, Foreign Series, of the Reign of Elizabeth 1560-1561 (edited by Joseph Stevenson, London: Her Majesty's Stationery Office, 1865).

Calendar of State Papers and Manuscripts, Relating to English Affairs, existing in the Archives and Collections of Venice, And in other Libraries of Northern Italy (edited by Rawdon Brown and G.C. Bentinck, London: Her Majesty's Stationery Office, 1890), Vol. Vii. 1558-1580.

Calvin, John, Commentariorum in Acta Apostolorum, Libri Duo (Geneva: Johannes Crispin, M.D.LX).

_____, Commentary on the Epistles of Paul the Apostle to the Corinthians II (translated by John Pringle, Grand Rapids: W.B. Eerdmans, 1948).

_____, An epistle/both of Godly Consolation and/also of advertissemente, written by John/Caluine the pastour and preacher/of Geneua, to the righte noble prince/Edwarde Duke of So=/merset, before the time/of knowledge had/of his trouble, but de=/lyuered to the sayde/Duke, in the/time of hys/trouble,/ and so translated out of frenche by the same/Duke hymselfe, in/ the tyme of his/imprieson=/mente (London: E. Whitechurche, 1550).

_____, Institutio Christianae religionis (Geneva: Oliva Roberti Stephani, M.D.LIX).

_____, Letters of John Calvin Compiled From the original manuscripts and edited with Historical Notes by Dr. Jules Bonnet I-IV (1858 edition). Reprinted by Burt Franklin, New York, 1972.

_____, Ioannis Calvini Opera quae supersunt omnia (edited by G. Baum, Ed. Cunitz and Ed. Reuss, Brunsvigae: Schwetschke et filii, 1863-1900). Volumes XXIX-LXXXVI of Corpus Reformatorum.

_____, Secunda Defensio Piae et Orthodoxae De Sacramentis Fidei, Contra IoachimWestphali calumnias (Geneva?: Ioannis Crispini, M.D. LVI).

_____, Ioannis Calvini, Verbi Dei, In Ecclesia Geneuensi, fidelissimi ministri, Epistolae duae . . . Prior, De Fugiendis impioru illicitis sacris, & puritate Christianae religionis obseruanda (Geneva: M.D.L., n.p.).

Cartwright, Thomas, A Replye to an Answere made of M. Dr. Whitgifte Agaynste the Admonition to the Parliament (No imprint 1573? /McAlpine/, 1574? /S. T. C./).

Catharinus, Ambrosius, Apologia pro veritate catholicae et apostolicae fidei ac doctrinae Adversus impia ac valde pestifera Martini Lutheri dogmata. First printed in Florence, 1520 & on 27 April, 1521. Edited by Jos. Schweizer & Aug. Franzen, in Corpus Catholicorum 27 (Munster: Aschendorff, 1956).

_____, Commentaria R. P. F. Ambrosii Catharine Politi Senesis, Episcopi Minoriensis, in Omnes Divi Pauli Et Alias Septem Canonicae Epistolas (Venice: in officina Erasmiana Vincentii Valgrisii, 1541).

Clarius, Isidore, Isidori Clarii Brixioni, monachi Casinensis, ad eas qui a communi ecclesiae sententia discessere, adhortatio ad concordiam (Paris: Nicolai Divitem, n.d.).

_____, Vulgata Editio Novi, ac Veteris Testamentum . . . adiectis ex eruditis scriptoribus scholiis . . . (Venice: Petrus Scheffer, 1542).

Contarini, Gasparo. Scholia In Epistolas Divi Pauli (Paris: Sebastian Nivellius, 1571).

Cranmer, Archbishop Thomas, Miscellaneous Writings and Letters of Thomas Cranmer, Archbishop of Canterbury and Martyr 1556 (edited John Cox, Cambridge: Parker Society, 1846).

_____, The Remains of Thomas Cranmer, D. D. Archbishop of Canterbury (edited by Henry Jenkyns, Oxford: At the University Press, M. D. CCCXXXIII), II.

_____, Writings and Disputations of Thomas Cranmer, Archbishop of Canterbury, Martyr, 1556, Relative To The Sacrament Of The Lord's Supper (edited for the Parker Society by Rev. John Edmund Cox, Cambridge: The University Press, M.D. CCC.XLIV).

Danaeus, Lambertus, Politicorum aphorismorum silva, ex . . .graecis, . . . latinis scriptoribus . . . collecta . . . (Antwerp: Chr. Plantius, 1583).

Dorcastor, Nicolas, THE HVMBLE and vnfained confessio of the belefe of certain poore banished men, grounded upon the holy Scriptures of God, and upon the Articles of that undefiled and onlye undoubted true Christian faith, which the holy Catholicke (that is to say universal) Churche of Christ professeth (Wittonburge Strasbourg: XIII May, M.D. LIIII).

Edward VI, King, The Chronicle and Political Papers of King Edward VI (edited by W. K. Jordan, London: George Allen and Unwin Ltd., 1966).

Florio, Michelagnolo Fiorentino, CATHE=/CHISMO, CIOE FOR=/ma breue per Amaestrae i fanciul=/li: La quale di tutta la Christiana disciplina cot/tiene la somma: E perl' autorita del Serenissimo/ Re d'Inghilterra etc. messa in luce: e con or=/dine che tutta i maestri di scuola a disce=/poli loro l'insegnino: e in quella/con diligenzia amaestrino/Tradotta di Latino in lingua/ Thoscana per M. Michelagnolo/Florio Fiorentino, (London: Stephen Mierdman, 1553?).

The Fortresse of Fathers, ernestlie defending the puritie of Religion, and Ceremonies, by the trew expositio of certaine places of Scripture: againste such as wold bring in an Abuse of Idol stouff, and of thinges indifferent, and do appoinct th' aucthority of Princes and Prelates larger then the trueth is.

Translated out of Latine into English for there sakes that
vnderstand no Latine by I. B. (Geneva?: no printer, M. D.
LXVI).

Foxe, John, Actes and Monuments of matters most speciall and memorable, happenyng in the Church, with an Vniuersall history of
the same, wherein is set forth at large the whole race and
course of the Church, from the primitive age to these latter
tymes of ours, with the bloudy times, horrible troubles, and
great persecutions agaynst the true Martyrs of Christ, sought
and wrought as well by Heathen Emperours, as nowe lately
practised by Romish Prelates, especially in this Realme of
England and Scotland (Revised ed., London, October 1583).
/Fourth English Edition/.

_____, The Acts and Monuments of John Foxe (Fourth Edition
by Josiah Pratt, London: The Religious Tract Society, 1877),
Vols. VI and VIII. Also 1838 edition edited by S. R. Cottley
(London: R. B. Seeley and W. Burnside).

Gentile, Valentine, Valentini Gentilis teterrimi Haeretici impletatum
ac triplicis perfidiae & periurii, breuis explicatio (Geneva:
Franciscus Perrinus, M.D. LXVII).

Gerdes, Daniel, SCRINIUM ANTEQUARIUM/SIVE/MISCELLANEA GRONINGANA/
NOVA AD HISTORIAM REFORMATIONIS/ECCLESIASTICAM PRAECIPUE/
SPECTANTIA/INSERUN TUR/TRACTATUS VARII GENERIS./EPISTOLAE.
ORATIONES./BIOGRAPHIAE.ETSIM./SIVE/NUMQUAM ANTEA EDITAE,/
SIVE/ITA factae Rariores ut Pro/Inedites Haberi/Possint./
(Groningen and Bremen: Corn. Barlingkhof & G. W. Rump, 1753),
Tomi III. Pars II.

Gesner, Conrad, Biblioteca Institvta Et Collecto Primvm A Conrado
Gesnero, Deinde in Epitomen redacta & nouarum Libroru accesione
locupletata, iam vero postremo recognita, & in duplum post
priores editiones aucta, per Iosiam Simlerum Tigurinum (Tiguri:
apud Christophorvm Froschovervm, Mense Martio, M. D. LXXIIII).

_____, "Conradi Gesneri Epistola: De Constantia in Fide,"
Museum Helveticum I (Zurich, 1746).

Gradenigo, G. A., Greg. Cortesii, monarchi cassinatis et S. R. E.
Cardinalis, omnia, quae hucusque colligi potuerun·, opera
scripta sive ad illum spectantia (Padua: A. Comino, 1774), I.

Grimani, Marino, Commentarii in Epistolas Pauli, ad Romanos et ad
Galatas (Venetiis: Aldus, MD.XLII).

Grindal, Edmund, The Remains of Edmund Grindal, D. D. (edited by
Rev. William Nicholson, Cambridge: At the University Press,
M.DCCC. XLIII).

Gualther, Rudolf, *OὶΚΕΤΗ5* siue servus ecclesiasticus, i. e. de
officio ministrorum ecclesiae oratio: dicta in conventu
ministrorum urbis et agri Tigurini (Tiguri: Christophorus
Froschouerus, 1548).

Henry VIII, King, The Letters of King Henry VIII (edited by M. St.
Clare Byrne, London: Cassell, 1968).

Hollweg, Walter, Heinrich Bullingers Hausbuch (Verlag der Buchhandlung des Erzielungsvereins Neukirchen Kreis (Moers, 1956).

Homilies, Book of, Inivncci/ons geue by the moste ex/cellent prince,
Edward the/sixte, by the grace of God,/kyng of England, Frauce/
and Ireland: defender of/the faythe, and in earthe/under
Christ, of the chur=/che of Englande and of/Ireland the supreme/
hedde: To all and singuler his lo=/uyng subiec=/tes, aswell/
of the/Clergie, as of the/Laietie (London: Rychard Grafton,
M.D. XLVII).

Hooper, Bishop John, Later Writings of Bishop Hooper, together with
His Letters and Other Pieces (edited for the Parker Society
by Rev. Charles Nevinson, Cambridge: The University Press,
M. DCCC.LII).

Hubert, Conrad and Sir John Cheke, Historia uera; de vita M. Buceri
& P. Fagii. Item historia Catharinae Vermiliae (Argentinae:
Paulus Machaeropoeum, 1562) & J. Catfhill, London: 1561.

Hughes, Philip Edgecumbe, The Register of the Company of Pastors of
Geneva in the Time of Calvin (Grand Rapids: William B.
Eerdmans, 1966).

Humphrey, Laurence, Ioannis Iuelli Angli, Episcopi Sarisburiensis
vita et mors . . . (Londoni: Apud Iohannem Dayum, 1573).

Jewel, John, The Works of the Very Learned and Reverend Father in
God, Iohn Ievvell, not long since Bishop of Sarisburie (London:
John Norton, 1609).

Kennedy, W. P. M., Elizabethan Episcopal Administration III.
Visitation Articles and Injunctions, 1583-1603 (London: A. R.
Mowbray & Co., Ltd., 1924).

Kimhi, Rabbi David, The Commentary of Rabbi David Kimhi on Psalms
CXX-CL (edited and translated by Joshua Baker and Ernest W.
Nicholson. Cambridge: At the University Press, 1973).

Knox, John, The Works of John Knox IV (edited by David Laing. Edinburgh: Wodrow Society, 1855).

Latimer, Hugh, Sermons by Hugh Latimer, Sometime Bishop of Worcester, Martyr, 1555 (edited for the Parker Society by George Corrie, Cambridge University Press, 1844).

Laws, Lucca, "1545. Legge riguardante le nuove opinioni religiose, e divieto di libri ereticali," Archivio Storico Italiano X (1847), Documenti, pp. 165-168.

Lismanini Francesco, Exemplvm Literarvm Ecclesiae Tigurinae ad Ecclesias Polonicas (1561).

Lubieniecio, Stanislaus, Historia Reformationis Polonicae (Friestad: Johannes Anconius, 1685).

Martin, Thomas, A Traictise declaryng and plainly prouyng, that the pretended marriage of Priestes, and professed persons, is no marriage, but altogether unlawful, and in all ages, and al countreies of Christendome, bothe forbidden, and also punyshed (London: Robert Coly, May 1554).

Melanchthon, Philipp, Philippi Melanchthonis Epistolae, Iudicia, Consilia, Testimonia Aliorumque Ad Eum Epistolae Quae In Corpore Reformatorum Desiderantur (edited by Henricus E. Bindseil, Halle: Gustavus Schwetschke, MDCCCLXXIV).

_____, RESPONSIO/DE CONTROVER=/SIIS STANCARI,/SCRIPTA A/PHILIPPO MELAN./ANNO M.D.LIII. (Leipzig: Valentine Papa, 1563).

Original Letters Relative to the English Reformation (edited by Rev. Hastings Robinson for the Parker Society, Cambridge:The University Press, M.DCCC.XLVI) I (1537-1558).

Original Letters Relative to the English Reformation (edited by Rev. Hastings Robinson for the Parker Society, Cambridge: The University Press, M.DCCC.XLVII) II (1537-1558).

Philpot, John, The trew re-/port of the dysputacyon/had & begone in the con-/uocacyo hows at london/among the clargye there/assembled the xviij. da-/ye of October in the/yeare of our lord/M.D. LJJJJ /Sic. 1553/ . . . . (Basil: Alexander Edmunds, 1554?).

Pigge, Albert, Apologia A. Pighii . . . adversus M. Buceri calumnias, quas & solidas argumentis, et clarissimis rationibus confutat (Maguntiae, 1543: Parisiis, 1543).

Pocock, Nicolas, Troubles Connected with the Prayer Book of 1549.
See Udall, Nicholas.

Pole, Reginald, Epistolarum Reginaldi Poli S. R. E. Cardinalis et
Aliarum ad Ipsum III (edited by Angelo Maria Quirini. Brescia:
Joannes-Maria Rizzardi, 1746).

Ponet, John, A Notable Sermon concerninge the ryght use of the
lordes supper and other thynges very profitable for all men
to knowe preached before the Kynges most excellent Mayestye and
hys courte at Westmynster the 14. daye of Marche . . . 1550
(London: Gwalter Lynne, 1550).

Public Record Office, Calendar of the Patent Rolls, Edward VI, Vol.
I, A. D. 1547-1548 (London: His Majesty's Stationery Office,
1924).

Quenstedt, Iohanne Andrea, Dialogus De Patriis Illustrium Doctrina
et Scriptis Virorum (Wittenberg: Michael Wendt, 1654).

Ragnina, Clemens, Expositio Fratris Clementis Aranei Ragusini Ordinis
Praedicatorum cum resolutionibus occurrentium dubiorum, etiam
Lutheranorum errores confutantium secundum subietam materiam,
super epistolam Pauli ad Romanos (Venice: apud Nicolaus de
Barcarinis, 1547).

Reformatio Legum Ecclesiasticarum, ex Authoritate primum Regis
Henrici. 8. inchoata: Deinde per Regem Edouardem 6. provecta,
adauctaque: in hunc modum, atque; nunc ad pleniorem ipsarum
reformationem in lucem aedita (Londini: ex officina Johannis
Daij, 1571).

Schaff, Philip, The Creeds of the Evangelical Protestant Churches
(London: Hodder and Stoughton, MDCCCLXXVII).

Schulting, Cornelius, Bibliothecae Catholicae Et Orthodoxae, Contra
Summam Totius Theologiae Calvinianae in Institutionibus Ioannis
Calvini, Et Locis Communibus Petri Martyris, breuiter comprehensae (Coloniae Agrippinae: Stephanus Hemmerdem, M.DC.II),
five vols. in two.

Scrimger, Henri, Francesci Spierae, Quiquod Susceptam semel Euagelice
ueritatis professione abnegasset, damnassetque, in harrendam
incidit desperationem, HISTORIA, A quatuor summis uiris, summa
fide conscripta: cum clariss uirorum Praefationibus, Caelii.
S. C. & Io. Caluini, & Petri Pauli Vergerji Apologia: in quibus
multa hoc tempore scitu digna grauissime tractantur (Basel:
M.D.L. n.p.). Also Geneva: Ioannem Geradus, 1550).

Seripando, Girolamo, De Iustitia Et Libertate Christiana (Corpus Catholicarum 30) (Münster Westfalen: Aschendorff, 1969).

Simler, Josias, Narratio De Ortu, Vita, et Obitu Reverendi Viri, D. Henrici Bullingeri, Tigurinae Ecclesiae pastoris . . . (Tiguri: excudebat Froschouerus, 1575).

ORATIO/DE VITA ET OBI=/TV CLARISSIMI VIRI ET PRAESTAN-/tifsimi Theologi D. PETRI MARTYRIS VER/MILII diuinarum literarum profefforis in fcho-/la Tigurina, habita ibidem a I O S I A/ S I M L E R O Tigurino./ITEM Scripta quaedam D. Petri Martyris de/Euchariftia, nunquam antehac edita/ (TIGVRI APVD CHRISTO-PHORVM/Frofchouerum Iuniorem, Anno M.D.LXIII.).

_____, Responsio ad Maledicum Francesci Stancari Mantuani Librum aduersus Tigurinae ecclesiae ministros, de Trinitate & Mediatore Domino nostro Iesu Christo, auctore Iosia Simlero Tigurino (Tiguri: Christ. Froschouerus, M.D.LXIII).

_____, Scripta Vetervm Latina, De Vna Petsona et Dvabvs Natvris Domini et Seruatoris nostri Iesu Christi, aduersus Nestorum, Eutychen & Acephalos olim aedita (Tigvri: Christophorvs Froschovervs, M.D.LXXI).

_____, Vita Clarissimi Philosophi et Medici Excellentissimi Conradi Gesneri Tigurini (Tigurinus: Christoph. Froschoverus, 1566).

Sleiden, Johannes, A Famouse Cronicle of oure time, called Sleidane's Commentaries, concerning the state of Religion and common wealth, during the raigne of the Emperour Charles the fifth (trans. Ihon Daus, for Nicholas Englande: London. M.D. LX).

Smith, Richard, Diatriba/De Hominis Ivstife=/catione Aedita Oxoniae/ in Anglia, anno a nativitate Domini no/stri Iesu Christi. 1550. Mense Februario/aduersus Petrum Martyre Vermilinū, o-/lim Cartusianū Lucensem in Italia, nunc/apostatā in Anglia Oxoniae, accerrimum/improborum dogmatum asserto-/rem, sed imperitum, & impud-/dentem cum primis./ (Lovanii: Apud Antonium Mariam Bergaigne Typogra. Iurat., Anno Domini, 1550. Mense Octobri.).

Stancaro, Francesco, Francisvs Stancarvs Mantvanvs De Trinitate & Mediatore Domino Nostro Iesu Christo, Aduersus Henricum Bullingerum, Petrum Martyre & Ioannem Caluninu, & Reliquos Tigurinae ac Genuesis Ecclesiae Ministros, Ecclesiae Dei Perturbatores (Cracouiae: in Officina haeredum Marci Scharfenbergi, Anno Virginei partus M.D. LXII).

_____, Frances/ci Stancari Man=/TVani Sacrae Theologiae,/
& Ebraicae linguae in Aca=/demia Regiomontana/Prussiae, publici
pro=/fessoris,/DISPVTATIO DE/TRINITATE, HABITA/20 IUNIJ 1551,/
. . . CVM EPISTOLA=/EIVSDEM STANCARI AD=/monitoria aduersus
Epistolam Ga=/latini praeliminarem. Admonitio ad lectorem data
15 Junii 1551.

_____, Rabinorum recentiorum, et anabaptistarum falsa
opinio de duobus messiis, priscorum Thalmudistarum autoritatibus
confutata (Neuburg: Donau, 1547).

Stobeius, John, Ioannis Stobei Sententiae ex thesauris Graecorum
delectae (Tiguri: Christophorus Froschauerus, M.D. XLIII.).

STRYPE, JOHN, MEMORIALS/of/The Most Reverend Father in God/THOMAS
CRANMER,/sometime/Lord Archbishop of CANTERBURY./ . . . (London:
Printed for Richard Chriswell, at the Rose and Crown/in St.
Paul's Church-Yard. MDCXCIV).

Sturm, John, D. Ioannis/Stvrmii Rectoris/Argentinensis/Antipappi
Tres,/Contra D. Ioannis Pappi/Charitatim Et/Condemnationem/
Christianam (M.D.LXXIX).

Tertullian, Quintus Septimius Florens, "De Fuga In Persecutione,"
Corpus Scriptorum Latinorum Paravinnum (edited Iosephus Marra,
1957).

Vchanski, Jacobus, Brevis Avgvstissimi Ac Svmme Venerandi Sacrosanctae
Missae Sacrificii ex sanctis patrib. contra impium Francesci
Stancari Mantuani scriptum, assertio (Coloniae Agrippinae:
Arnoldus Brickmannus, M.D. LXXVII).

Udall, Nicholas, Udall's Answer to the Commoners of Devonshire and
Cornwall (Royal MS. 18B. xi fol. 1. British Museum) printed
in Nicholas Pocock, Troubles Connected with the Prayer Book of
1549 (London: Camden Society, 1884, New Series, Vol. XXXVII).

Valdes, Juan De, Commentary On The Gospel of St. Matthew, translated
by John Betts (London: Trübner & Co., 1882).

Vergerio, Pier Paolo, LA FORMA DELLE/PVBLICHE ORATIONI, ET/della
cõfefsione, & Affolutione, la qual/fi usa nella chiesa de
forestieri, che e nuouamente ftata inftituita in Lon/dra
(per gratia di Dio) con l'/autorita & cofentimen/to del Re.
Microfilm of Dr. 12020, Westdeutsche Bibliothek Marburg,
deposited in Foundation For Retormation Research, St. Louis,
Missouri.

Wace, Henry and Philip Schaff, A Select Library of Nicene and Post
    Nicene Fathers of the Christian Chruch. Second Series (Oxford:
    James Parker and Company, 1894), VII.

Williams, C. H., ed. English Historical Documents, Volume V, 1485-
    1558. (New York: Oxford University Press, 1967).

Wood, Thomas, A Brieff discours off the troubles begonne at Franck-
    ford in Germany Anno Domini 1554. Abowte the Booke off common
    prayer and Ceremonies/and continued by the Englishe men theyre/
    to thende off Q. Maries Raigne/in the which discours/the gentle
    reader shall see the uery originall and beginninge off all the
    contention that hathe byn/and what was the cause off the same
    (Zurich: Christopher Froschouer?, M.D. LXXV).

Zanchi, Jerome, Opervm/Theologicorvm/D. Hieronymi/Zanchii/Tomus
    Septimus,/Miscellaneorvm Partes/DVas Complectens: QVarvm/
    Posterior NVNC Primvm Prodit in LVcem (Geneva: Excludebat
    Petrvs AVBertvs, M.DC.XIII).

The Zurich Letters A.D. 1558-1579 (edited by Rev. Hastings Robinson
    for The Parker Society, Cambridge: The University Press,
    M.DCCC. XLII).

The Zurich Letters (Second Series) A.D. 1558-1602 (edited by Rev.
    Hastings Robinson for the Parker Society, Cambridge: The
    University Press, M.DCCC.XLV).

IV.   SECONDARY WORKS

Adam, Jean, Inventaire Des Archives Du Chapitre De St-Thomas De
    Strasbourg (Strasbourg: Imprimerie Alsacienne, 1937).

Adams, H. M., Catalogue of Books Printed on the Continent of Europe,
    1501-1600 in Cambridge Libraries, I & II (Cambridge: Cambridge
    University Press, 1967).

Armstrong, Brian G., Calvinism And The Amyraut Heresy (Madison:
    University of Wisconsin, 1969).

Bainton, Roland, Bernardino Ochio. Esule E Riformatore Senese
    Del Cinquecento 1487-1573 (Firenze: G. D. Sansoni, 1939).

Bayne, C. G., Anglo-Roman Relations (Oxford: At the Clarendon Press,
    1968 reprint).

Benrath, Karl, Bernardino Ochino von Siena, 2 verbesserte Auflage (Braunschweig: C.A. Schwetschke und Sohn, 1892).

Berengo, Marino, Nobili e mercanti nella Lucca del Cinquecento (Torino: Giulio Einaudi, 1965).

Bietenholz, Peter G., Basle and France In The Sixteenth Century (Toronto/Geneva: University of Toronto/Librairie Droz, 1971).

Biographie Universelle Ancienne Et Moderne Nouvelle Edition, edited by A. Thoisnier Desplaces; (Paris: M. Michaud, 1852).

Bishop, William Warner, A Checklist of American copies of "Short-title catalogue" books, 2d edition (Ann Arbor: University of Michigan Press, 1950).

Blench, J. W., Preaching In England in the late Fifteenth and Sixteenth Centuries. A Study of English Sermons 1450-C.1600 (New York: Barnes & Noble Inc., 1964).

The Book of Concord (translated by Theodore G. Tappert; Philadelphia: Muhlenberg Press, 1959).

Booty, John E., John Jewel as Apologist of the Church of England (London: S.P.C.K., 1963).

Bouvier, Andre, Henri Bullinger reformateur et conseiller oecumenique le successeur de Zwingli (Neuchatel: Delachaux & Niestle S. A., 1940).

Bradshaw, Paul F., The Anglican Ordinal (London: S.P.C.K., 1971).

Brooks, Peter, Thomas Cranmer's Doctrine of the Eucharist (London: MacMillan, 1965).

Brunet, Jacques Charles, Manuel du libraire et de l'Amateur de livres. 5.ed. originale entirement refondue et augm. d'un tiers (Paris: F. Didot, 1860-80), 9 vols.

Burbidge, Edward, Remains of the Library of Thomas Cranmer, Archbishop of Canterbury, 1489-1556 (separation with marginal notes by the author, 1892).

Burnet, Gilbert, The History of the Reformation of the Church of England (London: Richard Chiswell, MDCLXXXI), Part II, and 1843 edition(New York: D. Appleton and Company).

Cantimori, Delio, Eretici Italiani Del Cinquecento (Firenze: G. C. Sansoni, 1939).

Cantu, Cesare, Gli Eretici D'Italia (Torino: Unione Tipografico-
Editrice, 1866), Volume Secondo.

Camporeale, Salvatore I. Lorenzo Valla Umanesimo E Teologia (Firenze:
Nella Sede Dell' Istituto Palazzo Strozzi, 1972).

Cioranesco, Alexandre, Bibliographie de la Litterature francaise du
XVIe siecle (Paris: Klincksieck, 1959).

Chaix, Paul, Alain Dufour et Gustave Moeckli, Les Liveres Imprimes
a Geneve De 1550 A 1600 (Geneve: Librairie Droz, 1966).

Cochrane, Arthur C.,Reformed Confessions of the 16th Century
(Philadelphia: The Westminster Press, 1966).

Collinson, Patrick, The Elizabethan Puritan Movement (London:
Jonathan Cape, 1967).

Coolidge, John S., The Pauline Renaissance In England (Oxford: The
Clarendon Press, 1970).

Croce, Benedetto, Un Calvinista Italiano. Il Marchese Di Vico
Galeazzo Caracciolo (Bari: Gius. Laterza & Figli, 1933).

Cross, Claire, The Royal Supremacy in the Elizabethan Church (London:
George Allen and Unwin Ltd., 1969).

Cutts, Edward L., Turning Points of English Church History (London:
S.P.C.K., 1887).

Cyprianus, E. S., Catalogus codicum manuscriptorum Bibliothecae
Gothanae (Leipzig: 1714).

Davies, Horton, Worship and Theology in England From Cranmer to Hooker
1534-1603 (London: Oxford University Press, 1970).

Deed, S. G., Catalogue of the Plume Library at Malden, Essex (Malden:
Plume Library Trustees, 1959).

Dixon, R. W., History of the Church of England From the Abolition of
the Roman Jurisdiction II. (London: George Routledge and Sons,
1881 and III 1885).

Ferguson, Arthur B., The Articulate Citizen And The English
Renaissance (Durham: Duke University Press, 1965).

Ficker, Johannes, und Otto Winckelmann, Handschriftenproben des
Sechzehnten Jahrhunderts nach Strassburger Originalem (Strassburg: Karl J. Trübner, 1905), Zweiter Band (Tafel 47-102).

Fraenkel, Peter, Testimonium patrum: The Function of the Patristic Argument in the Theology of Philip Melanchthon (Geneve: E. Droz, 1961).

Franklin, Julian H., Constitutionalism and Resistance in the Sixteenth Century (New York: Pegasus, 1969).

Gagliardi, Ernst, and Ludwig Forrer, Katalog Der Handschriften Der Zentralbibliothek Zurich II. Neuere Handschriften seit 1500 (Zurich: Buchdruckerei Berichthaus, 1931-1967).

Gallizioli, Memorie istoriche e letterarie della vita e della opere di Girolamo Zanchi (Bergamo: Franchesco Locatelli, 1785).

Garrett, C. H., The Marian Exiles 1553-1559 (Cambridge: At the University Press, 1938).

Gasquet, F. A., and E. Bishop, Edward VI and the Book of Common Prayer (London: John Hodges, 1890).

Geisendorf, Paul F., Theodore De Beze (Geneve: Labor Et Fides, 1949).

Gilbert, Neal W., Renaissance Concepts of Method (New York: Columbia University Press, 1960).

Gilmore, Myron P., "Boniface Amerbach," Humanists And Jurists: Six Studies In The Renaissance (Cambridge: Belknap Press of the Harvard University Press, 1963), pp. 146-177.

Gorham, George Cornelius, Gleanings of a Few Scattered Ears, During the Period of the Reformation in England and of the times immediately succeeding, A.D. 1533 to A. D. 1588 (London: Bell and Daldy, 1857).

Graesse, J. G. T., Orbis latinus oder Verzeichnis der wichtigsten lateinischen Orts-und Ländernamen, 3rd edition (Berlin: Schmidt, 1922).

Gründler, Otto, Die Gotteslehre Girolami Zanchis und ihre Bedeutung für seine Lehre von der Pradestination (Neukirchen-Vluyn: Neukirchener Verlag des Erziehungsvereins BmbH, 1965).

Haag, Eugenie & Emmanuele, La France Protestante ou Vies des Protestants Francais (Paris: Joel Cherbuliez, 1846-59), 10 volumes.

Hanhart, Johannes, Conrad Gessner. Ein Bentrag zur Geschichte des wissenschaftlichen Sirehens und der Glaubensuerbesserung im 16ten Jahrhundert (Winterthur: in der Steinerischen Buchhandlung, 1824).

Hardwick, Charles, A History of the Articles of Religion (London:
George Bell & Sons, 1904).

Hauben, Paul J., Three Spanish Heretics and the Reformation: Antonio
Del Corro, Cassiodoro De Reina, Cypriano De Valera (Geneve:
Droz, 1967).

Historical Manuscripts Commission, Guide To The Reports of the Royal
Commission on Historical Manuscripts 1911-1957. Part II:
Index of Persons, Volume III (edited by A. C. S. Hall, London:
Her Majesties Stationary Office, 1966).

Hopf, Constantin, Martin Lucer and the English Reformation (Oxford:
B. Blackwell, 1946).

Horst, Irvin B., The Radical Brethren. Anabaptism and The English
Reformation to 1558 (Nieuwkoop: B. De Graaf, 1972).

Hottinger, Johan, Historiae ecclesiasticae Novi Testamenti (Zurich:
M. Schufelberger, 1651-1667): VIII.

Jedin, Hubert, A History of the Council of Trent (Edinburgh: J.
Nelson, 1951).

Jones, Leonard Chester, Simon Goulart 1543-1628. Etude Biographique
et Bibliographique (Geneve/Paris: George & Cie et Edouard
Champion, 1917).

Jordan, W. K., Edward VI. The Threshold of Power (Cambridge: Harvard
University Press, 1970).

_____, Edward VI: The Young King. The Protectorship of the
Duke of Somerset (London: George Allen & Unwin Ltd., 1968).

Kelley, Donald R., Francois Hotman A Revolutionary's Ordeal
(Princeton: Princeton University Press, 1973).

Köhler, W., Bibliographia Brentiana /1904/ (Nieuwkoop: B. De Graaf,
1963).

Kristeller, Paul O., Iter Italicum I (London: Warburg Institute,
1963), and II (London: Warburg Institute, 1967).

Lewins, M., The Life of Bernard Gilpin, Generally Known as the Apostle
of the North; Also, of Peter Martyr, An Eminent Reformer (London:
Simpkin and Marshall, MDCCCXXXVI).

Lindboom, J., Austin Friars History of the Dutch Reformed Church in
London 1550-1950 (translated by D. De Iongh, The Hague:
Martinus Nijhoff, 1950).

Lorimer, Peter, John Knox and the Church of England (London: Henry S. King, 1875).

McConica, James K., English Humanists And Reformation Politics Under Henry VIII and Edward VI (Oxford: At The Clarendon Press,1965).

McDonnell, Kilian, John Calvin, the Church, and the Eucharist (Princeton: Princeton University Press, 1967).

McGrath, Patrick, Papists and Puritans under Elizabeth I (London: Blandford Press, 1967).

McLelland, Joseph C., The Visible Words of God: An Exposition of the Sacramental Theology of Peter Martyr Vermigli A. D. 1500-1562 (Grand Rapids: William B. Eerdmans Publishing Company, 1957).

McNair, Philip, Peter Martyr in Italy: The Anatomy of an Apostasy (Oxford: At the Clarendon Press, 1967).

Maddison, Carol, Marcantonio Flaminio, Poet, Humanist & Reformer (London: Routledge and Kegan Paul, 1965).

Mazzini, Giovanni, Libri Stampati Palatini Vaticani Latini 2670-2830 (Citta Del Vaticano: Tipografia Poliglotta Vaticano, 1953).

Metz, Wulf, Theologie Des Zacharias Ursinus (Zurich: Zwingli Verlag, 1970).

Milner, Benjamin Charles, Jr., Calvin's Doctrine of the Church (Leiden: E. J. Brill, 1970).

Milton, John, Commonplace Book: The Works of John Milton, volume XVIII (New York: Columbia University Press, 1938), pp. 128-227.

Muller, James Arthur, The Letters of Stephen Gardiner (Cambridge: At the University Press, 1933).

_____, Stephen Gardiner and The Tudor Reaction (New York: The MacMillan Company, 1926).

Murray, Iain, The Puritan Hope (London: Banner of Truth, 1971).

Neale, J. E. Elizabeth I and Her Parliaments 1559-1581 (London: Jonathan Cape, 1953).

Nieto, Jose C., Juan De Valdes and the Origins of the Spanish and Italian Reformation (Geneve: Librairie Droz, 1970).

Nineham, D. E.,The Church's Use of the Bible, Past and Present (London: S.P.C.K., 1963).

Norwood, Frederick A., The Reformation Refugees as an Economic Force (Chicago: The American Society of Church History, 1942).

_____, Strangers and Exiles, A History of Religious Refugees, I (Nashville & New York: Abingdon Press, 1969).

Olin, John C., The Catholic Reformation: Savonarola to Ignatius Loyola; Reform in the Church 1495-1650 (New York: Harper and Row, 1969).

Olsen, V. Norskov, The New Testament Logia on Divorce, A Study of the Interpretation from Erasmus to Milton (Tubingen: J.C.B. Mohr-Paul Siebeck, 1971).

Parker, T. H. L., Calvin's New Testament Commentaries (Grand Rapids: William B. Eerdmans, 1973).

Pettit, Norman, The Heart Prepared: Grace and Conversion in Puritan Spiritual Life (New Haven and London: Yale University Press, 1966).

Polman, Pontien, L'Element Historique Dans La Controverse religieuse du XVIe Siecle (Gembloux: J. Duculot, 1932).

Prescott, H. F. M., Mary Tudor (New York: The Macmillan Company, 1954).

Primus, John H., The Vestments Controversy (Kampen, 1960).

Raitt, Jill, The Eucharistic Theology of Theodore Beza (Chambersburg: American Academy of Religion, 1972).

Ramage, David, A finding-list of English books to 1640 in libraries in the British Isles . . . . (Durham: Council of the Durham Colleges, 1958).

Raubenheimer, Richard, Paul Fagius aus Rheinzabern (Grünstadt (Pfalz): Emil Sommer, 1957).

Read, Conyers, Mr. Secretary Cecil and Queen Elizabeth (London: Jonathan Cape, 1965).

Reuss, Rod., Notes pour servir a l'histoire de l'eglise de Strasbourg (Paris: 1880).

Richardson, Cyril, Zwingli and Cranmer on the Eucharist (Cranmer dixit et contradixit) (Evanston: Seabury-Western Theological Seminary, 1949).

Ridley, Jasper, Thomas Cranmer (Oxford: The Clarendon Press, 1962).

_____, John Knox (Oxford: The Clarendon Press, 1968).

Rose-Troup, Frances, The Western Rebellion of 1549 (London: Smith, Elder & Co., 1913).

Rotondo, Antonio, Calvin and the Italian Anti-Trinitarians (translated by John A. and Ann Tedeschi, St. Louis: Foundation For Reformation Research, 1969).

Ruffini, Francesco, Francesco Stancaro in Studi sui Riformatori Italiani di Francesco Ruffini (edited by A. Bertoli, L. Firpo, & E. Ruffing. Turin: Ramella, 1955).

Rupp, Gordon, Six Makers of English Religion 1500-1700 (London: Hodder and Stoughton, 1964).

de Schickler, Fernand, Les Eglises du Refuge en Angleterre (Paris: Fischbacher, 1892), 3 vols.

Schmidt, Charles, Peter Martyr Vermigli, Leben Und ausgewahlte Schriften (Elberfield: R. L. Friderichs, 1858).

_____, La Vie Et Les Travaux De Jean Sturm (Nieuwkoop: B. de Graaf, 1970).

Schweizer, Alexander, Die Protestantischen Centraldogmen in Ihrer Entwicklung Innerhalf Der Reformirten Kirche I (Zurich: Bei Orell, Fuessli und Comp., 1854).

Societe Generale Suisse d'Histoire, Dictionnaire historique et biographique de la Suisse (Neuchatel: Admin. du Dictionnaire, 1921-34), volumes 1-7 and supplement.

Smyth, Charles H., Cranmer and the Reformation under Edward VI (Cambridge: The University Press, 1926).

Southgate, W. M., John Jewel and the Problem of Doctrinal Authority (Cambridge: Harvard University Press, 1962).

Spiegel, Bernard, D. Albert Rizäus Hardenberg, Ein Theologenleben aus der Reformationzeit (Bremen: Ed. Muller, 1869).

Strohl, Henri, Le Protestantisme en Alsace (Strasbourg: Editions Oberlin, 1950).

Strype, John, Annals of the Reformation and Establishment of Religion and Other Various Occurances in the Church of England During Queen Elizabeth's Happy Reign (Oxford: The Clarendon Press, 1824).

Strype, John, Ecclesiastical Memorials Relating Chiefly to Religion, And Its Reformation, under the Reigns of King Henry VIII. King Edward VI. and Queen Mary The First (London: Samuel Bagster, MDCCCXVI), II.

_____, Memorials of the Most Reverend Father In God Thomas Cranmer (Oxford: The Clarendon Press, 1812), vol. I.

_____, The Life and Acts of John Whitgift, D. D. (Oxford: At the Clarendon Press, MDCCCXXII), Vol. III.

Stupperich, Robert, Melanchthon (Berlin: Walter De Gruyter, 1960).

Sturm, Erdmann K., Der junge Zacharias Ursin. Sein Weg vom Philippismus zum Calvinismus (1534-1562) (Neukirken-Vluyn: Neukirchener Verlag, 1972).

Sturm, Klaus, Die Theologie Peter Martyr Vermiglis wahrend seines ersten Aufenthalts in Strassburg 1542-1547 (Neukirken-Vluyn: Neukirchener Verlag, 1971).

Tedeschi, John A., The Literature of the Italian Reformation (Chicago: The Newberry Library, 1971).

Vetter, Theodor, Relations between England and Zurich during the Reformation (London: Elliot Stock, 1904).

Walzer, Michael, The Revolution of The Saints (London: Weidenfeld and Nicolson, 1966).

Walzer, Richard, Greek Into Arabic (Oxford=Bruno Cassirer, 1962).

Wendel, Francois, Calvin. The Origins and Development of His Religious Thought (translated by Philip Mairet, London: Collins, 1963).

Wierzbowski, Theodoro, Polonica XV ac XVIss. Sive Catalogus Librorum Res Polonicas Tractantium Vel A Polonis Conscriptorum Qui In Bibliotheca Universitatis Caesarea Varsouiensis Asservantur (Varsouiae: C. Kowalewski, 1891).

Wilbur, E. Morse, A History of Unitarianism I, Socinianism And Its Antecedents (Cambridge: Harvard University Press, 1947).

Williams, Arnold, The Common Expositor: An Account of the Commentaries on Genesis 1527-1633 (Chapel Hill: University of North Carolina Press, 1948).

Williams, George H., The Radical Reformation (London: Weidenfeld and Nicholson, 1962).

Wotschke, Theodor, Der Briefwechsel der Schweizer mit den Polen (Leipzig: M. Heinsius, 1908).

Young, M., The Life and Times of Aonio Paleario (London: Bell and Daldy, 1860).

Zeman, Jerold Knox, The Anabaptists And The Czech Brethren In Moravia 1526-1628 (The Hague. Paris: Mouton, 1969).

Ziegelbauer, Magnoald, Historia rei literariae Ordinis S. Benedicti (completed by Oliverius Legipontius, O. S. B., Augsburg: M. Veith, 1754), III.

V.   PERIODICAL LITERATURE

Anderson, Marvin, "Biblical Humanism and Roman Catholic Reform (1501-1542): Contarini, Pole and Giberti," Concordia Theological Monthly XXXIX (1968), 686-707.

_____, "Gregorio Cortese and Roman Catholic Reform," Sixteenth Century Essays and Studies I (1970), 75-106.

_____, "Laurentius Valla: Renaissance Critic and Biblical Theologian," Concordia Theological Monthly XXXIX (1968), 10-27.

_____, "Peter Martyr on Romans," Scottish Journal of Theology 26 (1973), 401-420.

_____, "Peter Martyr, Reformed Theologian (1542-1562): His letters to Bullinger and Calvin," Sixteenth Century Journal IV (1973), 41-64.

_____, "Pietro Martire Vermigli on the Scope and Clarity of Scripture," Theologische Zeitschrift 30 (1974), 86-94.

_____, "Thomas Cajetan's Scientia Christi," Theologische Zeitschrift 26 (1970), 99-108.

_____, "Trent and Justification (1546): A Protestant Reflection," Scottish Journal of Theology 21 (1968), 385-406.

_____, "Word and Spirit in Exile (1542-61): The Biblical Writings of Peter Martyr Vermigli," Journal of Ecclesiastical History XXI (1970), 193-201.

Ashton, J. W., "Peter Martyr on the function and character of literature," Philological Quarterly XVIII (1939), 311-314.

Bainton, Roland, "The Bible In The Reformation," pp. 1-37 in The
    Cambridge History of The Bible. The West From The Reformation
    To The Present Day, edited by S. L. Greenslade (Cambridge: At
    The University Press, 1963).

Bakhuizen van den Brink, J. N., "Ratramn's eucharistic doctrine and
    its influence in sixteenth-century England," Studies In
    Church History II, 54-77.

Baron, Hans, "Calvinist Republicanism And Its Historical Roots,"
    Church History 8 (1939), 30-42.

Bartel, O., "Calvin and Polen," Revue D'Histoire E De Philosophie
    Religieuses 45 (1965), 93-108.

Beesley, Alan, "An unpublished source of the Book of Common Prayer:
    Peter Martyr Vermigli's Adhortatio ad Coenam Domini Mysticam,"
    Journal of Ecclesiastical History XIX (1968), 33-38.

Bein, Alexander, "Nathan Ben Jehiel of Rome," Encyclopedia Judaica
    (New York: MacMillan, 1972) 12, cols. 859-860.

Belladona, Rita, "Sperone Speroni and Alessandro Piccolomini on
    Justification," Renaissance Quarterly XXV (1972), 161-172.

Benrath, Karl, "Vermigli, Pietro Martire," Realencyclopedie für
    protestantische Theologie und Kirche (ed. Albert Hauck, Dritte
    Auflage, Leipzig, J. C. Hinrichsische Buchhandlung, 1908),
    550-552.

Berchtold, Jacob, "Die Grundquelle von Stumpfs und Bullingers
    Reformationschronik," Schweizerische Zeitschrift für Geschichte
    VII (1927),314-330.

Bietenholz, Peter G., "Mino Celsi and the Toleration Controversy of
    the Sixteenth Century," Bibliotheque D'Humanisme Et Renaissance
    XXXIV (1972), 31-48.

Bill, E. G. W., "Records of the Church of England recently recovered
    by Lambeth Palace Library," Journal of the Society of
    Archivists III (1965-69), 24-26.

Boehmer, Eduard, "Francesci Dryandri, Hispani, epistolæ quinquaginta",
    Zeitschrift für die Historische Theologie XL (1870), 387-442.

Boesch, Paul, "Die englischen Fluchtlinge in Zurich unter Konigen
    Elizabeth I," Zwingliana 9 (1949-53), 531-535.

Bonorand, Conradin, "Humanismus und Reformation in Sudbunden im Lichte der Korrespondenz der Churer Prediger mit Joachim Vadian und Konrad Gessner," Festschrift 600 Jahre Gotteshausbund (Chur: Otto P. Clavendetscher, Calven Verlag, 1967), 439-488.

Booty, John E., "Preparation for the Lord's Supper in Elizabethan England," Anglican Theological Review XLIX (1967), 131-148.

Bornkamm, Heinrich, "Martin Butzers letzter Brief. Sein Urteil uber die englische Reformation und seine Stellung zum Interim in Deutschland," Archiv für Reformationsgeschichte 38 (1941), 239-249.

Boy, J. C., "Conrad Gessner (1516-1565), the father of bibliography," Papers on the Bibliographical Society of America X (1916), 53-86.

Brassel, Thomas, "Drei umstrittene Traktate Peter Martyr Vermiglis," Zwingliana I (1959-63), 476.

Büsser, Fritz, "Reformation History Research in German-speaking Switzerland," Renaissance and Reformation IX (1972), 23-27.

Cantimori, Delio, "Nicodemism and the Expectations of a Conciliar Solution to the Religious Question," The Late Italian Renaissance 1525-1630 (edited by Eric Cochrane, London: MacMillan and Co. Ltd., 1970), 246-247.

_____, "Profilo di Giorgio Biandrata Saluzzese," Bolletino Storico-bibliografico subalpino 38 (1936), 352-402.

Caponetto, S., "Benedetto da Mantoua," Dizionario Biografico Degli Italiani (Roma: Istituto Della Enciclopedia Italiana, 1966), 8, 437-441.

Carbonnier, Jean, "Le Colloque de Poissy," Foi et Vie 60 (1961), 43-52.

Chenu, Albert, "Taddeo Duno (1523-1613)," Bolletino Della Societa Di Studi Valdesi 119 (1966), 55-61.

Chrital, M., "Odet de Coligny, Cardinal de Chatillon," Bulletin Societe De L'Histoire du Protestantisme Francais LVII (1961) 1-12.

Clemen, Otto, "Janus Cornarius," Neues Archiv für Sachsische Geschichte und altertumskunde 33 (1912), 36-76.

Collins, T. A., "The Cajetan Controversy," American Ecclesiastical Review 128 (1953), 90-100.

Collinson, Patrick, "The Authorship of a Brieff Discours off the Troubles Begonne at Frankford," Journal of Ecclesiastical History 9 (1958), 201-208.

_____, "The Reformer and the Archbishop: Martin Bucer and an English Bucerian," Journal of Religious History 6 (1971), 305-330.

Cowell, Henry J., "English Protestant Refugees in Strasbourg, 1553-1558," Hugeonot Society of London, Proceedings XV (1933-37), 69-120.

_____, "The Sixteenth Century English speaking refugee churches at Geneva and Frankfort," Hugeonot Society of London, Proceedings XVI (1939), 209-30.

_____, "The Sixteenth Century English speaking refugee churches at Strasbourg, Basle, Zurich, Aarau, Wesel and Emden," Hugeonot Society of London, Proceedings XV (1937), 612-65.

Dantine, Johannes, "Les Tabelles sur las Doctrine de la Predestination par Theodore De Beze," Revue De Theologie et De Philosophie, troisieme serie, Tome XVI (1966), 365-377.

Dareste, R., "Francois Hotman. Sa Vie et sa Correspondance," Revue Historique II (1876), 28-30.

Dufour, Alain, "Le Colloque de Poissy," Melanges D'Histoire Du XVIe Siecle Afferts a Henri Meylan (Geneve: Librairie Droz, 1970), 127-137.

Durling, R. J., "Conrad Gesner's Liber Amicorum 1555-1565," Gesnerus 22 (1965), 134-159.

Evenett, H. O., "Claude D'Espence et son Discours Du Colloque De Poissy" Revue Historique 164 (1930), 40-78.

_____, "Three Benedictine Abbots at the Council of Trent," Studia Monastica I (1959), 343-377.

de Felice, Philipe, "Le Colloque de Poissy," Bulletin de la societe de l' histoire du protestantisme Francais CVII (1961), 133-145.

Firpo, Luigi, "La Chiesa Italiana Di Londra nel Cinquecento e i suoi rapporti con Ginevra," Ginevra e l' Italia (edited by Delio Cantimori et al.: Firenze: G. C. Sansoni, 1959), 309-412.

Fischer, Hans, "Conrad Gesner (1515-1565) as Bibliographer and Encyclopedist," The Library, Transactions of the Bibliographical Society, Fifth Series, XXI (1966), 269-281.

Fraenkel, Pierre, "Histoire Sainte Et Heresie Chez Saint Epiphane De Salamine D'Apres Le Tome I Du Panarion," Revue De Theologie Et Philosophie 12 (1961), 175-191.

_____, "Ten Questions Concerning Melanchthon, The Fathers And The Eucharist," 146-164 in Vilmos Vajta, Luther and Melanchthon In the history and theology of the Reformation (Philadelphia: Muhlenberg Press, 1961).

Fragnito, Gigliola, "Gli spirituali" e la fuga di Bernardino Ochino," Rivista Storica Italiana 84(1972), 777-813.

Friedman, Jerome, "Servetus and Antitrinitarianism: A' Propos Antonio Rotondo," Bibliotheque De Humanisme et Renaissance XXXV (1973), 543-545.

Ganoczy, Alexandre, "La Bibliotheque De Pierre Martyr," La Bibliotheque de l' Academie de Calvin (Geneve: Librairie Droz, 1969), 19-27.

Gardy, F., "Les livres de Pierre Martyr Vermigli conserves a la Bibliotheque de Geneve," Anzeiger für Schweizerische Geschichte, n.s. Tome 17 (1919), 1-6.

Garrett, Christina M., "John Ponet and the confession of the banished ministers," Church Quarterly Review 137 (Oct.-Dec. 1943), 47-74; 137 (Jan.-Mar. 1944), 181-204.

Gilmont, J. F., "Una pseudonyme de Pierre Alexandre, Simon Alexius," Societe de'histoire du protestantisme belge, ser. 5, livre 5 (1970), 179-188.

Gordon, Alexander, "Vermigli, Pietro Martire," Dictionary of National Biography (edited by Sir Leslie Stephen and Sir Sidney Lee, Oxford: University Press, 1960 reprint of 1917 edition), 253-256.

Green, Lowell, "The Bible in Sixteenth-Century Humanist Education," Studies In The Renaissance XIX (1972), 112-134.

Hall, Basil, "Biblical Scholarship: Editions And Commentaries," pp. 38-93 in The Cambridge History of The Bible. The West From The Reformation To The Present Day, edited by S. L. Greenslade (Cambridge: At The University Press, 1963).

Huelin, Gordon, "Vermigli, Pietro Martire," p. 1151 in Twentieth Century Encyclopedia of Religious Knowledge, edited Lefferts A. Loetscher (Grand Rapids: Baker Book House, 1955).

Hugelshafer, W., "Zum Porträt des Petrus Martyr Vermilius," Zwingliana 5 (1929-33), 127-129.

Jarrot, C. A. L., "Erasmus' In Principio Erat Sermo: a Controversial Translation," Studies In Philology LXI (1964), 35-40.

Joachimson, Paul, "Loci Communes/Eine Untersuchung zur Geistes-geschichte des Humanismus und der Reformation" Luther=Jahrbuch VIII (1926), 27-97.

Jorgensen, K. E. Jordt, "Fejden mellem Lipomano og Radziwill i Wilno 1556," Festskrift til Jens Nørregaard, edited N. K. Anderson, et al. (Kobenhavn: G. E. C. Gad, 1967), 96-111.

Jones, William M., "Reformers from Wittenberg, Strasbourg, Zurich, and Geneva in England: 1547-1549," Iliff Review XXVII (1970), 69-73.

Kingdon, Robert, "The Political Resistance of the Calvinists in France and the Low Countries," Church History XXVII (1958), 220-233.

_____, "The First Expression of Theodore Beza's Political Ideas," Archiv für Reformationsgeschichte 46 (1955), 88-99.

Kolb, Robert, "Six Christian Sermons on the Way to Lutheran Unity," Concordia Theological Monthly XLIV (1973), 261-274.

Kristeller, Paul, "The Contribution of Religious Orders to Renaissance Thought and Learning," American Benedictine Review XXI (1970), 1-55.

Lauchert, Freidrich, "Der Italienische Benedictiner Isidorus Clarius und seine Schrift fur den religiosen Freiden," Studien und Mitteilungen Zur Geschichte Des Benediktiner-Ordens XXVIII (1908), 613-614.

_____, "Die Polemik des Ambrosius Catharinus gegen Bernardino Ochino," Zeitschrift für Katholische Geschichte XXXI (1907), 23-50.

Leccisotti, T., "Per la storia della Congregazione cassinese. Marginalia," Benedictina XVI (1969), 136-143.

"Lever, or Leaver, Thomas," Dictionary of National Biography XI, 1021.

Levine, Mortimer, "The last will and testament of Henry VIII: a reappraisal appraised," Historian 26 (1964), 471-485.

Loades, D. M., "The Enforcement of Reaction, 1553-1558," Journal of Ecclesiastical History XVI (1965), 54-66.

Logan, F. Donald, "The Henrician Canons," Bulletin of the Institute of Historical Research XLVII (1974), 99-103.

Logan, O. M. T., "Grace and Justification: Some Italian Views of the Sixteenth and Early Seventeenth Centuries, Journal of Ecclesiastical History XX (1969), 67-78.

MacCaffrey, Wallace T., "Elizabethan politics: the first decade, 1558-1568," Past and Present 24 (1963), 25-42.

McGee, J., "The Nominalism of Thomas Cranmer," Harvard Theological Review 57 (1964), 189-206.

McLelland, J. C., "The Reformed Doctrine of Predestination according to Peter Martyr," Scottish Journal of Theology VIII (1955), 257-265.

McNair, Philip and John A. Tedeschi, "New Light on Ochino," Bibliotheque D'Humanisme Et Renaissance XXXV (1973), 289-301.

_____, "Ochino on Sedition. An Italian Dialogue of the Sixteenth Century," Italian Studies XV (1960), 36-49. Text reproduced on pp. 46-49.

McNally, Robert E., S. J., "The Council of Trent and the Spiritual Doctrine of the Counter Reformation," Church History 34 (1965), 36-49.

Mason, A. R., "Rebellion in Norfolk, 1549," Contemporary Review (March, 1959), 164-167.

De Melin, Joseph Roserot, "Rome et Poissy 1560-61," Melanges D' Archeologie et D'Histoire XXXIX (1921-22), 47-151.

Mesnard, Pierre, "The Pedagogy of Johann Sturm (1507-1589) and its Evangelical Inspiration," Studies In The Renaissance XIII (1966), 200-219.

Milt, Bernhard, "Conrad Gessners theologische Enzyklopadie," Zwingliana VIII (1948), 571-587.

Molnar, Amedeao, "Romani 13 nella interpretazioni della prima Riforma," Protestantesimo XXIV (1969), 65-76.

Monter, William E., "The Italians In Geneva, 1550-1600: A New Look," Geneve et l'Italie, edited Luc Monnier (Geneva: Droz,1969).

Morreale, Margherita, "Juan De Valdes as Translator and Interpreter of St. Paul: The Concept of GNOSIS," Bulletin of Hispanic Studies XXXIV (1957), 89-94.

Mueller-Streisand, Rosemarie, "Theologie und Kirchenpolitik bei Jacob Andreä bis zun Jahr 1568, Blätter Für Württembergische Kirchengeschichte 60/61 (1969/61), 224-395.

Neuser, Wilhelm, "Hardenberg und Melanchthon. Der Hardenbergische Streit (1554-1560)," Jahrbuch der Gesellshaft für niedersäch-sische Kirchengeschichte 65 (1967), 142-186.

Nicolas, Nicholas Harris, "The Bill of the Expences attending the Journey of Peter Martyr and Bernardinus Ochin, from Basil to England, in 1547," Archaeologia (Society of Antiquaries of London), XXI (1827), 469-473.

Niesel, W., "Calvin wider Osianders Rechtfertigungslehre," Zeitschrift für Kirchengeschichte 46 (1928), 410-430.

Norwood, Frederick A., "The Marian Exiles = Denizens or Sojourners?" Church History XIII (1944), 100-110.

_____, "The Strangers' 'Model Churches' in Sixteenth-Century England," Reformation Studies In Honor of Roland H. Bainton (edited by Franklin H. Littell, Richmond: John Knox Press, 1962), 180-196.

Nugent, Donald G., "The Cardinal of Lorraine and the Colloquy of Poissy," The Historical Journal XII (1969), 596-605.

Olivier, E., "Les Annees Lausannoises (1537-1540) de Conrad Gesner," Schweizerische Zeitschrift für Geschichte (1951), 369-428.

Olsen, Oliver K., "Theology of Revolution: Magdeburg, 1550-1551," Sixteenth Century Journal III (1972), 56-79.

Opie, John, "The Anglicizing of John Hooper," Archiv für Reformations-geschichte 59 (1968), 150-177.

Paist, Benjamin F., Jr., "Peter Martyr and the Colloquy of Poissy," Princeton Theological Review 20 (1922), pp. 212-231; 418-447; 616-646.

Parris, J. R., "Hooker's doctrine of the Eucharist," Scottish Journal of Theology 16 (1963), 151-164.

Pascal, A., "Da Lucca a Ginevra," Rivista Storica Italiana (1933).

Pascoe, Louis B., S. J., "The Council of Trent and Biblical Study: Humanism and Scripture," Catholic Historical Review LII (1966), 18-38.

Paulus, "Die stellung der protestantischen professoren Zanchi und Vermigli zur gewissensfreiheit," Strassburger Theologischen Studien II (1895), 83-102.

Perini, Leandro, "Ancora sul libraio-tipografa Pietro Perna e su alcune figure di eretici italiani in rapporto con lui negli anni 1549-1555," Nuova Rivista Storica 51 (1967), 363-404.

Peters, Robert, "Who compiled the Sixteenth-Century Patristic Handbook Unio Dissidentium?", Studies In Church History II (edited G. J. Cuming. Edinburgh: Thomas Nelson and Sons, 1965), 237-250.

_____, "The Use of the Fathers in the Reformation Handbook Unio Dissidentium," Studia Patristica 9(1966), 570-577.

Pocock, Nicholas, "The condition of Moral and Religious Belief in the Reign of Edward VI," English Historical Review X (1895), 417-444.

_____, "Preparations for the Second Prayer Book of Edward VI," Church Quarterly Review 37 (1893), 137-166.

Prelowski, Ruth, "The Beneficio di Cristo," Italian Reformation Studies in Honor of Laelius Socinus (edited by John A. Tedeschi; Firenze: Felice le Monnier, 1965), 23-102.

Pope, Hugh, O. P., "The Oxford and Cambridge Disputations on the Holy Eucharist 1549," Irish Ecclesiastical Record 54 (1942), 403-424.

Price, F. Douglas, "Gloucester diocese under Bishop Hooper, 1551-3," Transactions of the Bristol and Gloucestershire Archaeological Society 60 (1938), 51-151.

Ratcliff, E. C., "The Liturgical Work of Archbishop Cranmer," Journal of Ecclesiastical History VII (1956), 189-203.

Reid, William S., "Battle Hymns of the Lord; Calvinist Psalmnody of the Sixteenth Century," Sixteenth Century Essays and Studies II (1971), 36-54.

Richardson, Cyril C., "Cranmer and the Analysis of Eucharistic Doctrine," Journal of Theological Studies 16 (1965), 421-437.

Ross, James Bruce, "The Emergence of Gasparo Contarini: A Bibliographical Essay," Church History 41 (1972), 22-45.

Rotondo, Antonio, "Atteggiamenti Della Vita Morale Italiana Del Cinquecento La Pratica Nicodemitica," Rivista Storica Italiana 79 (1967), 991-1030.

_____, "Giorgio Biandrata e Johan Sommer," Critica Storica VIII (1969), 363-400.

Rosa, Mario, "Vita religiosa e pieta eucharistica nella Napoli del Cinquecento," Rivista Di Storia E Letteratura Religiosa IV (1968), 37-54.

Rott, Jean and Robert Faerber, "Un Anglais a Strassbourg au milieu du XVIe siecle: John Hales, Roger Ascham et Jean Sturm," Etudes Anglaises 21 (1968), 381-394.

Rupp, E. Gordon, "The Bible in the Age of the Reformation," pp.73-87 in D. E. Nineham, The Church's Use of The Bible Past and Present (London: S.P.C.K., 1963).

_____, "Patterns of Salvation in the First Age of the Reformation," Archiv für Reformationsgeschichte 57 (1966), 52-66.

Santini, Luigi, "Appunti sulla ecclesiologia de P. M. Vermigli e la edificazione della Chiesa," Bollentino della Societa di Studi Valdesi, CIV (1958), 69-75.

_____, "'Scisma' e 'eresia' nel pensiero di P. M. Vermigli," Bolletino Della Societa Di Studi Valdesi XC (Guigno 1969), 27-43.

_____, "La Tesi della fuga nella persecuzione nella teologia di P. M. Vermigli," Bolletino della Societa di Studi valdesi 108 (1960), 37-49.

Saulnier, V.L., "Autour Du Colloque De Poissy Les Avatars D'Une Chanson De Saint-Gelais A Ronsard Et Theophile," Bibliotheque D'Humanisme Et Renaissance XX (1958), 44-78.

Schäfer, Rolf, "Melanchthons Hermeneutik im Romberbrief-Kommentar von 1532," Zeitschrift für Theologie und Kirche 60 (1963), 216-235.

Schmid, Walter, "Johannes Stumpfs Schweizer und Reformationschronik," Zwingliana 10 (1954-58), 502-506.

Schmitt, Charles B., "Some Notes. Jacobus Dalechampius and his Translation of Theophrastus (Manuscript: BN. Lat. 11, 857)," Gesnerus 26 (1969), 36-53.

Selwyn, D. G., "A Neglected Edition of Cranmer's Catechism" Journal of Theological Studies 15 (1964), 76-91.

Shepherd, Norman, "Zanchius on Saving Faith," Westminster Theological Journal XXXVI (1973), 31-47.

Smith, Lacey Baldwin, "Henry VIII and the Protestant Triumph," American Historical Review LXXXI (1966), 1237-1264.

_____, "The last will and testament of Henry VIII: a question of perspective," Journal of British Studies 2 (1962), 14-27.

Spaulding, James C., "The Reformatio Legum Ecclesiasticarum of 1552 and the Furthering of Discipline in England," Church History XXXIX (1970), 162-163.

Spini, Giorgio, "Riforma italiana e mediazioni ginevrine nella nuova Inghilterra puritana," Ginevra e I'ltalia (edited by Delio Cantimori and others, Florence: Sansoni, 1959), 451-489.

Staedtke, Joachim, "Conrad Gesner als Theologe," Gesnerus 23 (1966), 238-265.

_____, "Miszellen Drei umstrittene Traktate Peter Martyr Vermiglis," Zwingliana XI (1962), 553-554.

_____, "Der Zürcher Praedestinationsstreit von 1560," Zwingliana 9 (1944-1953), 536-546.

Starr, G. A., "Antedatings from Nicholas Udall's translation of Peter Martyr's 'Discourse'", Notes and Queries, new series CII (1966), 9-12.

Strasser, Otto Erich, "Der Consensus Tigurinus," Zwingliana 9 (1949), 1-16.

Sturm, Erdmann, "Brief des Heidelberger Theologen Zacharias Ursinus Aus Wittenberg und Zurich (1560/61)," Heidelberger Jahrbücher XIV (1970), 85-119.

"La Pietas litterata de Jean Sturm et le developpement a Strasbourg d' une pedagogie oecumenique (1538-1581)," Bulletin de la Societe d'Historie Du Protestantisme Francais CXI (1967), 281-302.

Tedeschi, John, "Florentine Documents for a History of the 'Index of Prohibited Books'," Anthony Molho and John Tedeschi, Renaissance Studies In Honor of Hans Baron (Dekalb: Northern Illinois University Press, 1971), 579-81.

_____, "Genevan Books of the Sixteenth Century," Bibliotheque d'Humanisme et Renaissance XXXI (1969), 173-180.

_____, "Italian Reformers and the Diffusion of Renaissance Culture," Sixteenth Century Journal V (1974), 79-94.

Tedeschi, John A. and E. David Willis, "Two Italian Translations of Beza and Calvin," Archiv für Reformationsgeschichte 55 (1964), 70-74.

Telfer, W., "The Codex Verona LX (53)," Harvard Theological Review XXXVI (1943), 169-246.

Thomas, Morley, "Tunstal-Trimmer or Martyr?," Journal of Ecclesiastical History XXIV (1973), 337-355.

Thurian, Max, "The Real Presence," 197-222 in Christianity Divided, edited by Daniel J. Callahan, et al. (London: Sheed and Ward, 1962).

Toth, William, "Trinitarianism versus Antitrinitarianism in the Hungarian Reformation," Church History 13 (1944), 255-268.

Tylenda, Joseph, "Calvin and Christ's Presence In The Supper-True Or Real," Scottish Journal of Theology 27 (1974), 65-75.

_____, "Christ The Mediator: Calvin Versus Stancaro," Calvin Theological Review 8 (1973), 5-16.

_____, "The Controversy On Christ The Mediator: Calvin's Second Reply To Stancaro," Calvin Theological Review 8 (1973), 131-157.

VanderMolen, Ronald J., "Anglican Against Puritan," Church History 42 (1973), 45-57.

Vinay, Valdo, "Riformatori e lotte contadine. Scritte e Polemiche relative alla ribellione dei contadini nella Cornouaglia e nel Devonshire sotto Edoardo VI," Rivista di Storia e Letteratura religiosa III (1967), 203-251.

Walser, Peter, "Glaube und Leben bei Heinrich Bullinger," Zwingliana
    XI (1959-63), 613-614.

Walzer, Michael, "Revolutionary ideology: The case of the Marian
    exiles," American Political Science Review 57 (1963), 643-654.

Williams, Arnold, "Milton and the Renaissance Commentaries on Genesis",
    Modern Philology XXXVII (1939-40), 263-278.

Williams, George Hunston, "Camillo Renato (c. 1500? 1575)," Italian
    Reformation Studies in Honor of Laelius Socinus (ed. John A.
    Tedeschi, Firenze: Felice Le Monnier, 1965), 103-83.

Willis, E. David, "Miszelle. Calvin and the Italian Anti-Trinitarians,"
    Archiv für Reformationsgeschichte 62 (1971), 279-282.

Witte, J. L., "Die Christologie Calvins," 487-529 in Das Konzil von
    Chalkedon III: Chalkedon Heute, edited by A. Grillmeier
    (Würzburg: Echter-verlag, 1954).

Wotschke, Theodor, "Stanislaus Ostrorog, Ein Schutzherr der gorsspol
    nischen euangelischen Kirche," Zeitschrift der Hist. Gesell.
    fur die Provinz & Posen XXII (1907), 1-76.

Yost, John K., "Hugh Latimer and the Reformation Crisis in the
    Education of Preachers," Lutheran Quarterly XXIV (1972), 179-189.

Zonti, G., "Francesco Negri l'eretico e la sua tragedia 'Il libero
    arbitrio,'" Giornale storico della letteratura Italiana
    LXVII-LXVIII (1916), 265-324; 108-160.

Zuck, L. H., "The Influence of the Reformed Tradition on the
    Elizabethan Settlement," Concordia Theological Monthly XXXI
    (1960), 215-226.

VI UNPUBLISHED DISSERTATIONS

Anderson, Marvin W., Biblical Humanism and Roman Catholic Reform
    1444-1563: A Study of Renaissance Philology and New Testament
    Criticism From Laurentius Valla to Pietro Martyre Vermigli.
    Unpublished 1964 Ph.D. dissertation in Kings College Library,
    University of Aberdeen, Scotland.

Benert, Richard R., Inferior Magistrates In Sixteenth-Century
    Political and Religious Thought. Unpublished 1967 Ph.D. thesis,
    University of Minnesota.

Carlson, A. J., The Bishops and the Queen: A Study of 'Puritan' Episcopal Activity in Early Elizabethan England, 1558-1566. Unpublished 1962 Ph.D. thesis, Princeton University.

Di Gangi, Mariano, Pietro Martire Vermigli 1500-1562. Unpublished 1949 B.D. thesis Presbyterian College, Montreal, Quebec.

Donnelly, John Patrick, S. J., Peter Martyr On Fallen Man: A Protestant Scholastic View. Unpublished 1971 University of Wisconsin Ph.D. Thesis.

Fenlon, D. B., Reginald Pole and the Evangelical Religion: some problems of Italian Christian Humanism in the early Counter Reformation. Unpublished 1970 Ph.D. dissertation in Cambridge University Library. Published by Cambridge, 1973 as Heresy and Obedience In Tridentine Italy.

Gleason, Elizabeth, Cardinal Gasparo Contarini (1483-1542) and the Beginning of Catholic Reform. Unpublished 1963 Ph.D. Thesis, Stanford University.

Haggard, Theodore Merrill, The Church and Sacraments in the Theological Writings of Juan De Valdes. Unpublished 1971 Ph.D. thesis, Emory University.

Heal, Felicity, The Bishops of Ely and their Diocese during the Reformation Period: Ca. 1515-1600. Unpublished 1972 Ph.D. thesis, Cambridge.

Hoak, D. E., The King's Council in the reign of Edward VI. Unpublished 1971 Cambridge Ph.D. Thesis.

Huelin, Gordon, Peter Martyr and the English Reformation. Unpublished London University Ph.D. Thesis, 1955, University of London Library.

Ives, Robert B., The Theology of Wolfgang Musculus (1497-1563). Unpublished 1965 Ph.D. Dissertation in Manchester University Library.

Keep, D. J., Henry Bullinger and The Elizabethan Church. Unpublished 1970 Sheffield Ph.D. Thesis.

Macaluso, Peter F., Kingship and Papacy in the Thought of Reginald Pole, 1500-1558. Unpublished 1973 New York University Ph.D. Thesis.

Salgat, Anne-Marie, Aspects of The Life and Theology Of Pierre
    Viret (1511-1571). Unpublished 1972 Union Theological Seminary
    Th.D. Thesis.

Schutte, Anne Cole Jacobson, Pier Paolo Vergerio: The Making of
    An Italian Reformer. Unpublished 1969 Ph.D. Thesis, Stanford
    University.

Storer, S. F., The Life and Times of Edwin Sandys, Archbishop of
    York. Unpublished M. Phil. Thesis in progress (1972), University
    of London.

Vander Molen, Ronald Jay, Richard Cox (1499-1581), Bishop of Ely.
    Unpublished 1969 Ph.D. Thesis, Michigan State University.

Vogt, Herbert, Martin Bucer und die Kirche von England (Diss.
    Münster, 1966), 1968. Printed copy deposited in Cambridge
    University Library.

VII.   PRIVATE CORRESPONDENCE

Patrick Collinson, 27 December 1973. Sidney, Australia.

James Spaulding, 28 November 1973. Iowa City, Iowa.

Katharine Pantzer, 16 September 1971. Cambridge, Massachusets.

VIII.   UNPUBLISHED LECTURES

Benert, Richard, "Lutheran Contributions to Sixteenth Century
    Resistance Theory," Annual Meeting of American Historical
    Association, 30 December 1970.

Donnelly, John Patrick, "Calvinist Thomism", read at Western Michigan
    Conference on Medieval Studies 1974.

_____, "Italian Influences On the Developement of
    Calvinist Scholasticism," revised copy of lecture read in October
    1973.

_____, "Three Disputed Vermigli Tracts" Myron Gilmore
    Festchrift (1976?).

INDEX I.

SCRIPTURE REFERENCES

A.   OLD TESTAMENT

Genesis

1	280
1:5	296
9:20-23	181
15	281,297
19:1-23	384
31	299

Exodus

1:1	283
1:5	241
2	281
3	451
8-11	285
32:6	384

Leviticus

24	446

Deuteronomy

32:2	286
34:3	369

Judges

1:16	369,418n2
1:36f	383
3	387,402
8	320
12:6	386
21	389,392

I Samuel

8	401

II Samuel

10:12	404
13:28,29	384

I Kings

2	388
17	386
18	320
18:15-18	415
22:5	415

II Kings

2	320
8:22	409
12	320

Psalms

1	307n72
2	454
18	300
34	339
50	451,452
56	168
106	348

Isaiah

6:9-10	219

Ezekiel

16:49	384

Haggai

1	316

Malachi

2	279
2:4	313,316

B.   APOCRYPHA

Judith		Ecclesiasticus	
13:2	341	16	341
13:8	384		
		1 Maccabees	
		16:16	384

C.   NEW TESTAMENT

Matthew		John	
3:7-10	73	1:1	318
8	136	1:7	332
10:1-16	116n19	3	348
10:9	66n19,299	5:39	59
10:13	405	6	64,242,262n152
10:16	66n19,299	6:67	414
10:23	50	10:30	222
10:28	66n19,299	14:28	447
10:41	299	15	191
14:6-10	384	16	317
15	63	16:7	447
16:16	414	17	376,415
16:18	332	17:21	452
19:23	310n111	20	316
20:25	400	21:15	414
26:26	241		
26:27	414	Acts	
		4	449
Mark		8	449
4:11-12	219	10	449
6:7-10	50,116n19	10:1-48	335
		16	449
Luke		18	449
		23	28f
9:1-5	50,116n19	28:26-27	219
10:16	66n19		
12:1-12	50,116n19	Romans	
12:13	400		
14:6-24	153	1	328,334,348
16:19-25	384	1:4	288,322

1:10	168
1:17-18	275
1:23	333
2	348
3	56,336,337,350
3:27	271
3:28	277
4	195,331,332,338,348
4:1	333
4:13	333
4:16	24
4:17	272,333
5	55,192,193,339,348
6	340
7	340
7:15	216
8	55,342,343,450
9	147,215,247,342,344,345,346 359n55
9-10-19	252 n8
9-11	219
9:13	344
10	346,347
11	56,342,346
12	346,353
12:1-2	330,331,334,353
13	56,110,152,320,382,387,388 391,393,396
13:1-2	382
14	184

I Corinthians

1:9	188,322
1:10	417
1:25	323
1:31	323
2:14	172,308n78
3:15	74
6:12	184
7	318,319
7:14	205n80
8	309n93
10	247,251n6,359n55
10:7	384
10:16-17	61,97,101
11	56,63,103,320
12	326f.,450
13	324

13:13	326,352
15	55,192,193
15:28	447

II Corinthians

4:10	405f.

Galatians

3	272,348
3:13-29	282
3:29	333
6:14	58,436

Ephesians

2:19	88
3:6	194
3:9-12	191
4:3	415

Philippians

2	436,437,438
2:6ff.	248

Colossians

1:19	447
2:9	447

I Timothy

2:5	448

II Timothy

2:4	400
2:11	406

Titus

3:10	446

Hebrews

2:14-15	290
2:15	187

11:1   322,325   I John

James   5   332
                                      5:7   370
       2   348,351

PERSONS & PLACES

Abell, John, 313,314,373.
Abraham, 193,272.
Aciati, 443.
Adam, 192,193,194.
Adam, Melchior, 460.
Adrian VI, Pope, 36.
Aeacus, 496,520,529n.3.
Agricola, Rudolph, 68n46.
Ahab, 409,416.
Alcaraz, Pedro Ruiz De, 73.
Alcinoüs, 497.
Alexander The Great, 385,415,521,
530n4.
Alexander, Peter (Alexandre,Pierre)
198,348,349,350,351,372.
Alva, Duke of, 394.
Alypius, 522.
Ambrose, Saint, Bishop of Milan,269
322,326,335,336,337,342,350,353,
453.
Amerbach, Bonifacius, 77,169.
Ananias, 28.
Andreae, Jacob, 217,218,245,254n35.
Anaximander, 530n6.
Anti-Jove, 522.
Antwerp, 27.
Apollus, 222.
Aristophanes, 374.
Aristotle, 53,54,175,177,178,185,
354,372,374.
Arius, 195.
Armstrong, Brian, 457.
Arrau, 163,164,220.
Ascham, Roger, 81,455.
Athanasius, St., 349,350,375.
Augsburg, 171.
Augustine, St., Bishop of Hippo, 44
132,216,242,269,313,314,321,326,
334,335,336,339,350,351,370,373,
522.
Aylmer, John, 178.
Ayre, John, 178.

Badia, Thomas, Cardinal, 37,40.
Bainton, Roland, 26.
Bale, John, Bishop, 180.
Barnabas, 214.

Barnes, Robert, 350.
Baron, Hans, 391,392.
Barrett, William, 379,380.
Barth, Karl, 60.
Basil, St., 269,314,325,337,339,
346,348,374,377.
Basle, 76,77,138,153,163,164,170
247,278,439.
Bataillon, Marcel, 73.
Bates, Gordon, 193.
Bautrad, 236.
Bavaria, Duke of, 410.
Beaumont, Robert, 220
Becon, Thomas, 178,390,394.
Bede, 348,350,351,370.
Bedford, Earl of, 233.
Beesley, Alan, 127,138.
Bembo, Pietro Cardinal, 37,38,74
274.
Benert, Richard, 392.
Bentham, Thomas, 220.
Bergman of Cologne, printer, 321
Bernard, St., 339,350,409.
Berne, 170,186,220.
Beza, Theodore, 51,54,55,56,97,
133,165,189,194,208n129,217,
218,221,234,235,237,238,239,
240,245,246,260n127,266n197,
290,321,356n11,380,392,400,401
446,454,457,458.
Bibliander, Theodore, 110,169,
213,214,351,381.
Biel, Gabriel, 66n17.
Bill, E.G.W., 495.
Birkenhahn, Abel, 455.
Bishop, E., 315.
Blandrata, Giorgio, 222,442,443,
444,450.
Blauer, Ambrosius, 80.
Bodius, Herman, 350.
Boesch, Paul, 220.
Bologna, 40,41,43,49.
Bolsec, 213.
Bomberg, Daniel, printer,282,369
Bona Sforza, Queen of Poland,442
Boniface VIII, Pope, 388.
Bonner, Edmund, Bishop, 91,100.

Booty, John, 153.
Borrahus, Martin, 351.
Boston (New England), 48.
Bozza, Tommaso, 46.
Bradford, William, 151.
Bradshaw, Paul, 114.
Brandenburg, Electoral, 96.
Brassel, Thomas, 215.
Bremen, 186.
Brenz, John, 26,27,74,174,217,233,
   239,248,249,278,282,283,376,403,
   457,496,497,530n7,533.
Brinkelow, Henry, 111.
Brooks, Peter, 128,137,538.
Brunfels, Otto, 78,117n30.
Bruno, St. (C.1032-1101), 348.
Bucer, Martin, 23,48,51,54,56, 62,
   72,74,76,77,78,79,80,81,82,84,85
   90,91,92,94,99,101,104,105, 106,
   107,108,110,111,114,127,129,130,
   132,133,136,138,139,140,143,161,
   169,170,175,185,187,189,190,192,
   216,225,249,250,270,273,275,278,
   283,287,319,321,330,331,333,335,
   351,372,378,392,393,395,398,455,
   458.
Büsser, Fritz, 536.
Bullinger, Heinrich, 33,51,52, 56,
   57,76,77,80,86,97,108,110, 112,
   113,114,129,130,134,138,139,140,
   143,145,148,165,166,170,171,174,
   177,178,179,180,181,182,183,185,
   198,212,213,214,215,216,217,218,
   221,229,234,235,236,237,239,241,
   242,243,244,246,247,248,249,273,
   296,321,328,330,331,333,334,351,
   372,379,380,381,382,388,390,395,
   409,442,450,453,454,458,512,515,
   518,529,530n7,533.
Butterfield, Herbert, 58.
Byrchman, 140.

Caesar, Manus, (julius), 528.
Caesarius, St., of Nazianzus, 375.
Gajetanus Thomas de Vio, Cardinal,
   274,273.
Calvin, Johan, 30,38,48,51,52,54,55
   56,57,59,60,63,72,77,78,79,80,97
   101,108,109,129,130,138,146,150,

   164,170,173,174,178,179,180,185
   186,187,188,189,190,191,192,193
   194,196,197,198,199,212,213,214
   216,217,218,219,220,221,222,224
   233,234,235,240,242,246,248,249
   250,270,290,321,326,330,331,333
   342,345,346,351,372,374,375,378
   379,380,381,392,395,398,405,407
   435,438,440,441,442,443,444,446
   450,453,454,456,457,458,460.
Cambridge, 83,127,129,132,139,151
   161,189,250,283.
Cano, Melchior, 229.
Canterbury, 161.
Cantimori, Delio, 51, 416.
Capito, Wolfgang, 175,378.
Carafa, Giovanni Pietro, Cardinal
   (Pope Paul IV), 76,375,376.
Carnesecchi, Pietro, 49,72,289,
   393.
Car accioli, Antonio, 187,236.
Cartwright, Thomas, 55,56,231.
Casimir, John (Palatinate), 456.
Castellio, Sebastian, 28,214,219,
   223,247.
Castelvetro, Ludovico, 41,42,282,
   401: Giacopo.
Catharinus, Ambrosius, 273,274,
   275.
Catherine of Aragon, 23.
Catherine de' Medici, 234,238,243
   445,497.
Cato, Marcus, 496,526,528.
Cecil, Sir William, 135,145,167,
   230,256n65,258n99,269,355,512.
Celsi, Mino, 446.
Cervini, Marcello, Cardinal (Pope
   Marcellus II), 43.
Chadsey, William, 105.
Chambers, Richard, 93,165,166,180
Chandieu, Antoine de, 457.
Charles V, Emperor, 57,161,229,
   392,396.
Charles IX, King of France, 234.
Chatillon, Odet de, Cardinal, 235
   236,238,243.
Chauny, 246.
Chayim, Jacob ben, 282.
Cheke, Sir John, 110,129,133,134,

135,143,145,178,396.
Christopher of Württemberg, Duke,
226.
Chrysostom, John, St., 90,169,269,
321,322,323,324,325,326,332,333,
334,335,339,342,343,350,369,406,
437.
Cicero, 528.
Clarius, Isidore, 46,273,276,277.
Clarke, Samuel, 459,460.
Clement of Alexandria, 350.
Cochlaeus, Johannes (Johann
Dobenek), 276.
Cole, Henry, 316.
Cole, Thomas, 178.
Cole, William, 220,227.
Colet, John, 322,330.
Coligny, Gasparo de, Admiral, 235,
244.
Collinson, Patrick, 114,225,226,
227,458,538.
Comba, E., 416.
Conde, Prince of, 236,237,244.
Constance, 171.
Constantine, The Great Emperor,371
Contarini, Gasparo, Cardinal, 23,
24,25,35,37,38,41,42,43,46,47,48
49,51,74,75,76,274,275,276,459.
Cooke, Sir Anthony, 135,152,178,
220,329,330.
Corda, Sergio,   60,435,536.
Cornarius, Janus, 314,376.
Cornelius, 335,351.
Cortese, Gregorio, Cardinal, 25,35
36,37,38,39,40,42,43,45,46,48,49
51,274,276,277,289.
Cotton, John, 48.
Coverdale, Miles, Bishop, 100,113,
162,164.
Cowell, Henry, 178.
Cox, Richard, Bishop, 103,105,106,
162,163,164,179,180,181,225,228,
233,317,318,491,492,293,494,496,
497,499-507,508-509,516-519,532-
533.
Cracow, 247,439.
Cranmer, Thomas, Archbishop, 48,51
52,56,57,85,86,88,89,90,91,92,95
96,97,98,99,100,101,104,105,106,

107,108,109,110,111,127,128,129
133,134,135,136,137,138,139,143
144,145,146,147,148,149,150,151
152,153,161,163,185,216,219,251
273,300,314,315,316,317,327,347
348,349,350,369,382,395,399,458
459,534.
Crato, 246.
Crespin, Jean, printer, 350,372.
Crowley, Robert, 426n114.
Cruciger, Felix, 439.
Curione, Celio Secondo, 247, 351,
404,439,456.
Cyprian, St., 269,313,314,349,350
373,377.
Cyril of Alexandria, St., 64,191,
327,348,350,370.
Cyrus, King of Persia, 394,415.

Dalechamp, James, 406,407,408.
Damascene, St. John, 24,377.
Dampmartin, Catherine, (Martyr's
first wife), 84,94,143,149.
Danaeus, Lambert, 417,457.
David, King of Israel, 224,283,
415.
David, Francis, 452.
Davies, Horton, 138.
Day, John, 396.
Deborah, 402.
De Ferriere, Jean, 245.
Del Monte, Giovanni Maria,
Cardinal-bishop, 275.
De Loene, Peter, 232.
Demosthenes, 374.
De Reina, Cassiodore, 266n197.
Di Gangi, Mariano, 416.
Dillerus, Michael, 351.
Diodoti, Giovanni, 88.
Dionysius, 349,350.
Dixon, R.W., 91,128,269.
Donnelly, John Patrick, S.J., 49,
57,60,467,534,535,536,538,585.
Dorcastor, Nicolas, 203n62.
Dryander, Francis, 85,89,98,99.
Dudley, John, Earl of Warwick &
Duke of Northumberland, 99,100.
Dufour, Alain 259n109,365n158.
Dugmore, C.W., 127,135,136.

Duno, Taddeo, 299,305n45.
Durham, 150.

Eck, John, 23,332.
Edward VI, Tudor King, 56,61,85,86
    87,88,89,91,95,98,99,100,101,106
    113,136,137,139,142,149,150,152,
    168,169,173,228,299,389,402,458,
    499,504.
Elector of Saxony, 534.
Elias (Elisha), 416.
Elizabeth I, Tudor Queen, 92,98,
    151,165,212,220,224,225,226,227,
    230,256n65, 284,389,393,395,401,
    402,417,455,497,503-04,510,514.
Elyot, Thomas, 99.
Emden, 163,164,165,180.
Epiphanius, 313,314,349,350,371,
    372,373,376.
Erasmus, Desiderius, 27,72,77,99,
    219,273,274,322,323,325,350,370.
Erastus, Thomas, 401.
Esau, 252n8,283,344.
Este, Ippolito, d'Cardinal,239,241
    244.
Esther, Queen, 497.
Etherege, George, 92.
Exeter, 113.

Fagius, Paul, 83,85,99,129,283,284
    287,370.
Farel, Guillaume, 108,130,133,217,
    218,245.
Farnese, Alessandro, Cardinal
    (Pope Paul III), 76.
Farreus, J., Venetian printer, 90.
Fenlon, Dermot, 37,48.
Ferdinand of Austria, Emperor, 221
    439.
Ferguson, Arthur B., 111.
Ferrara, 40,75.
Ferrara, Duke of , 40.
Firpo, Luigi, 87.
Flaminio, Marc Antonio, 289.
Florence, 49,76,90.
Florio, Michael Angelo, 87,120n73,
    222,223.
Foligno, 304n39.
Folkertzheimer, Herman, 234,514-515

Fontani, 281.
Formula of Concord (1580),356n11.
Fortress of Fathers (1566),
    426n114.
Foxe, John, 97,137,179,219,328.
Foxe, Richard, 93.
Fraenkel, Pierre, 192,371.
Fragnito, Gigliola, 76.
France, 27.
Francis I, King, 27,234.
Francois, Maitre, 222.
Frankfurt, 97,163,166,177,179,180
    181,182,183,184,185,219,223,224
    282.
Frectus (Frecht, Martin of Ulm,80
Frederick, Count Palatine & Duke
    of Bavaria, 410.
Fregoso, Frederigo, Cardinal, 36,
    75,274.
Frideswyde, St., 84.
Friedman, Jerome, 443.
Froschouer, Christopher, printer,
    178,519n2.
Fulgentius, St., 350.

Galen, 372,408,497.
Gallars, Nicolas des (Gallasius)
    248,258n108.
Ganoczy, Alexandre, 373.
Gardiner, Stephen, Bishop, 64,90,
    91,97,98,99,100,106,107,127,136
    137,162,166,168,177,194,197,225
    228,278,395,398,413,449,457.
Gardy, F., 373.
Garnerius, 198.
Garrett, Christina M., 176.
Gasquet, F.A., 315.
Geisendorf, Paul, 243.
Gellius, Aulus, Attic Nights 12:
    12, 526.
Geneva, 29,42,48,55,59,77,88,90,
    163,164,165,170,180,186,187,212,
    216,217,220,221,222,223,224,229,
    269,373-378.
Genoa, 38.
George I, of England, 349.
Gesner, Conrad, 53,110,247,250,
    265n196, 313,354,355n8,406,407,
    408,429n133.

Gibson, Thomas, 178.
Gilbert, Felix, 47.
Gilbert, Neal, 26.
Glastonbury, 161,217.
Gleason, Elisabeth, 46,47.
Gloucester, 100,109,113.
Göppingen Confession (1557),   133,
   217,218,245,253n28.
Coniadz, Piotr, 445,462n39.
Conzaga, Frederico, Duke, 38.
Conzaga, Hercules, Cardinal, 37,74
   274.
Goodman, Christopher, 223,224.
Coulart, Simon, 287.
Grafton, Richard, 146.
Creco, Franceso, 41.
Gregorio da Milano, 76.
Grogory of Nazianzus, St., 269,326
   350,375,376.
Gregory I, Pope, 273,348.
Gribaldi, Matteo, 221,222.
Grillenzoni, Giovanni, 41.
Grindal, Edmund, Bishop, 114,135,
   146,162,163,177,178,180,219,225,
   232,258n108,269,355,384,492,493,
   510-512,519.
Grison, 87.
Gründler, Otto, 456.
Grynee, Simon, 331.
Gualter, Rudolf, 56,114,140,143,
   215,351,454.
Guicciardini, Francesco, 416.
Guise, Duke of, 238.

Haddon, James, 178,180.
Haddon, Walter, 455.
Haemstede, Adriaan van, 232.
Hagebut, see Cornarius, Janus.
Haggard, Theodore, 73.
Hall, Basil, 26,47.
Haman, 497.
Hardenberg, Albert, 186,378,421n55
Harding, Thomas, 93,315.
Hardwick, Charles, 145.
Harpsfield, John, 92.
Harpsfield, Nicholas, 92.
Haugaard, William P., 120n74.

Hedio, Caspor, 84,85,171,350.
Heidelberg, 179,217,455.
Heidegger, Martin, 435.
Heinrich, Otto von (Count
   Palatine), 155n7.
Heliodorus, 377.
Henrician Canons (1535), 154n5.
Henry VIII, Tudor King, 23,56,85,
   86,89,128,395,410.
Herbert, Peter, 248.
Herod, 416.
Hesiod, 374.
Hesshusius, 454.
Hilary, St., 191,192,350.
Hills, Richard, 122n95.
Hislebius, 442.
Hoak, D.E., 101.
Homer, 44.
Hooper, John, Bishop, 100,107,109
   110,113,114,115,134,141,145,181
   296,327.
Horn, Robert, 165,166,178,220.
Horst, Irwin, 232.
Hosius, Stanislaus, Cardinal -
   bishop, 377,378.
Hotman, Francois, 234,392,409.
Hubert, Conrad, 81,143,169,199,
   236,370.
Huelin, Gordon, 73,141,496.
Hugo of St. Victor, 348.
Humphrey, Laurence, 114,175,183,
   185,220,315,317.

Ignatius, St., 349,350.
Illyricus, Flacius, 111,395.
Ipswich, 48.
Irenaeus, St., 191,349,350.
Isny, 283.
Italy, 30,35,37,38,46,47,48,51
   58,77,89,171,172,281,289.

Jacob, 241,252n8,283,344.
Januarius, 44.
Jedin, Hubert, 271,278.
Jehiel, Nathan Ben, 370.
Jehosophat, 415.
Jelsma, A. J., 232.
Jeremiah, 300.

Jerome, St., 269,319,326,350,369, 370,376,377,378,528.
Jerusalem, 78.
Jesse, Pierre-Jean, 222.
Jewel, John, Bishop, 52,92,93,94, 175,177,178,185,212,220,225,227, 228,229,230,231,233,316,317,339, 384,389,390,395,417,460,494,496, 520-29,529n2,530n6.
Jezebel, 402.
Joachimsen, Paul, 68n46.
Job, 139.
John XXI, Pope, 414.
John The Baptist, 416.
Jonathan, Targumist, 284.
Joram, 409.
Jordan, W.K., 86,91,101.
Joseph, 295.
Josephus, 369.
Josiah, King, 402.
Julian The Apostate, 375.
Julius II (Pope), 161.
Junius, Franciscus (?),380.
Jupiter, 522.
Justin, Martyr, St., 374.

Kerquefinen, Claude de, 233.
Kerr, Richard, 490.
Killigrew, Henry, 226.
Kimhi, David, 284,369,370.
Kingdon, Robert, 399,400,467, 534, 535,536.
Knox, John, 100,109,138,139, 146, 162,163,164,179,180,181,224,398.
Kristeller, Paul, 275.
Krusche, Werner, 192.

Lactantius, 350.
Lambeth, 52,89,132,134,138,139,144 146,161,216.
Lancaster, Thomas, 135.
Lancelloto of Modena, 40.
Lang, August, 418n11.
LaRochelle, 409,539.
Laski, Jan, 87,88,91,99,113,132, 133,136,145,161,162,167,351,448.
Latimer, Hugh, 89,91,163,327.
Latomus, Bartholomäus, 102.
Lausanne, 29,31n16,220.

Lavater, Ludwig, 171,178,198,245, 536.
Laynez, Diego, 239,240,241,242.
Leipzig, 111.
Lennox, Fourth or Twelfth Earl of (Stewart, Matthew)?, 180.
Leo X, Pope, 36,348.
Lever, Thomas, 111, 178,180,220.
Libanius, 374.
Lindau, 171, 172.
Lismanini, Francis, 195,439,442, 444,445,446.
Logan, O.M.T., 24.
Lombard, Peter, Bishop, 339,442.
London, 86,87,99,100,101,105,107, 108,109,112,113,131,138,139,145 150,151,161,175,227,231,313.
Lorimer, Peter, 139.
Lorraine, Cardinal of, 235,238-41
Louvain, 102,103.
Lovell, Thomas, 137.
Loyola, Ignatius, 239,274.
Lucca, 35,39,46,49,58,75,76,78,83 195,196,269.
Lusco, Ambrogio, 287.
Luther, Martin, 53,54,60,101,127, 170,172,175,187,216,239,248,273 275,276,298,332,378,380,395,398 403,407,416,442,448.
Lynne, Gwalter (Walter), 108.

Macaluso, Peter, 409.
MacCaffrey, Walter, 226.
McConica, James, 92.
McDonnell, Kilian, 189.
McGrath, Patrick, 229.
Machiavelli, Niccolo, 226,402.
McLelland, J.C., 60,90,106,134, 141,216,233,344,345,383,535.
McNair, Philip, 37,39,49,76,91, 277,467.
McNally, Robert, S.J., 274,537-38
Maisonneuve, Jean de la, 222.
Maitland, Sir William, 398.
Magdeburg, 392-393.
Manelfi, Pietro, 49.
Mantua, 35,37,38,42.
Mantua, Don Benedetto da, 46,289.
Marbach, John, 81,82,130,170,171,

173,174,182,184,198,200,217,278,
309n90,383.
Marburg, 64,87,88,174,248.
Marcion, 242.
Margurite of Navarre, 27.
Marten, Sir Anthoney, 57,284,285,
293,318.
Martin, Thomas, 378.
Martinego (Celsus Brixiensis),186
187,221.
Martyr, Catherine see Dampmarten,
Catherine, 1st wife, Merenda,
Catharine, 2nd wife.
Martyr, Peter, 24f,26,29,30,33,35,
37,38,46,47,48,49,50,51,52,53,54
55,56,57,58,59,60,61,62,63,64,72
73,74,75,76,77,78,79,80,81,82,83
84,85,86,87,88,89,90,91,92,93,94
95,96,97,98,99,101,103,104, 105,
106,107,108,109,110,111,112,113,
114,127,128,129,130,131,132,133,
134,135,136,137,138,139,140,141,
142,143,144,146,147,148,149,150,
151,152,153,154,161,162,164,166,
168,169,170,171,172,173,174,175,
176,177,178,179,180,181,182,183,
184,185,186,187,188,189,190,191,
192,193,194,195,196,197,198,199,
200,221,222,223,224,225,226,227,
228,229,230,231,232,233,234,235,
236,237,238,239,240,241,242,243,
244,245,246,247,248,249,250,251,
264n171,269,270,271,273,274,275,
277,278,279,280,281,282,283,284,
285,286,287,288,289,290,291,292,
293,294,295,296,297,298,299,300,
301,313,314,315,316,317,318,319,
320,321,322,323,324,325,326,327,
328,329,330,331,332,333,334,335,
336,337,338,339,340,341,342,343,
344,345,346,347,348,349,350,351,
352,353,354,355,369,370,371,372,
373,374,375,376,377,378,379,380,
381,382,383,384,385,386,387,388,
389,390,391,392,393,394,395,396,
397,398,399,400,401,402,403,404,
405,406,408,409,410,411,412,413,
414,415,416,417,418,435,436,437,

438,439,442,443,444,445,446,448
449,450,452,453,454,455,456,457
458,459,460.
Mary, Tudor Queen, 52,100,149,151
161,162,163,164,165,167,168,185
220,228,315,390,396,402,403.
Masson, Robert, 60,213,428n128,
535.
Matheson, Peter, 47.
Maximilian of Bohemia, 221.
Meaux, 27.
Melanchthon, Philip, 23,35,42, 68
n68,72,77,78,85,111,166,171,173
174,175,182,184,185,192,200,217
248,276,281,282,295,330,331,332
333,351,371,375,395,398,440,442
460.
Memmingen, 171.
Menander, 405.
Merenda, Catharine, (Martyr's 2nd
wife), 212,236,508-09,514,515,
518.
Mesnard, Pierre, 82.
Micronius, Martin, 86,124n120.
Milano, Alessandro, 41.
Milner, B.C., 192.
Milton, John, 295,402.
Minos, 496,520,530n3.
Modena, 30,35,37,38,39,40,41,43,
45,46,48,49,75.
Mommeja, Bernard, 246.
Montbeliard, 218,245.
Moore, John, Bishop, 349.
More, Thomas, St., 92,99.
Morgan (Philipps), 105.
Morison, Sir Richard, 135,396.
Morone, Giovanni, Cardinal, 39,40
42,43,276,289.
Morreale, Margherita, 115n7.
Morwen, John, 92.
Moses, 82,283,286,369.
Münster, Sebastian, 378.
Musculus, Andrea, 440,442,446,454
Musculus, Wolfgang, 59,60,61,160n
79, 179,180,200,351,374,375,378
380,395,398,487-90.
Myconius, 85,351.

Naples, 25,37,49,72,73,74,75,190, 194,278.
Navarre, King of, 234,235,236.
Nectarius of Constantinople, 376.
Neoptolemus, 521,530n5.
Nero, Emperor, 393.
Neuchatel, 82,84,236.
Niesel, Wilhelm, 191,192.
Nieto, Jose, 72,73.
Niger, Theobald, 85,130.
Nimes, 29.
Noah, 181.
Northumberland, Duke of, see also Dudley, John, 100, 109,110,112, 149.
Norton, John, 48.
Norwich, 59,231.
Norwood, Frederick, 163,165,166.
Nowell, Alexander, 178.
Nugent, Donald, 239,537,538.

Ochino, Bernardino, 47,50,51,56, 57,76,83,91,99,110,132,136,195, 220,223,275,313,351.
Oecolampadius, 68n46,127,128,215, 248,351,378,455.
Oglethorpe, Owen, 103.
Olesnicki, Nicholas, 439,440.
Olsen, Oliver, 392.
Olsen, V. Norskov, 319,534,535.
Onorato, Fascitelli, 40.
Orange, 29.
Orbellus, 350.
Origen, 63,269,349,350,353,371.

Osiander, Luke, 169,191,195,245, 278,442,445.
Ostrorog, Stanislaus, 448,449.
Oxford, 29,30,52,53,56,61,63,83, 84,87,89,90,91,92,93,95,97,98, 101,102,103,104,105,106,107,110 111,112,113,128,130,131,132,135 139,140,141,142,146,151,152,154 161,169,177,178,194,216,218,229 230,250,251,269,273,275,279,300 313-353.

Paclesius, Stanislaus, 247,453.
Padua, 24,35,37,51,178.

Paget, Sir William, 109.
Paist, William, 244.
Palatine, Count (Otto von Heinrich), 410.
Palmer, Julins, 327,328.
Paolo Lacizi da Verona, 76.
Paphnutius, 371.
Paris, 244,274.
Parker, Matthew, Archbishop, 426n 114,455.
Parker, T. M., 99.
Parkhurst, John, Bishop, 220,231, 233,249,529n1.
Parma, 30n1.
Pammaclus, 528.
Parr, William, 167.
Parto, Francesco, 40.
Pastor, Ludwig von, 36,39,40.
Paul, St., 24,25,28,43,54,63,64, 85,88,95,107,110,168,184,188, 190,191,192,193,194,195,214,215 219,222,271,277,278,291,319,320 323,325,331,333,337,338,339,340 342,343,344,346,352,353,354,372 388,393,401,405,414,415,417,435 436,457.
Paul III, Pope (Alessandro Farnese), 24,35,36,38,39,46,47, 48,49,88.
Paul IV, Pope (see Carafa, Giovanni Pietro), 375,394.
Paulus, Gregory, 247,464n55.
Pedder, John, 178.
Pellican, Conrad, 178,197,199,351 379,380,395.
Perkins, William, 456.
Peter St., 291,414,458.
Philip of Hesse, 301n4.
Philip of Saxony, 221.
Philo, 451.
Philpot, John, 403.
Pigge, Albert, 54,269,270,275,278 297,325,329,339,347,348,351,352
Pilkington, James, 212,220,384, 395.
Pinczow, 439,440,448.
Pindar, 374.
Pisa, 75.
Plato, 372,374,497.

Plume LIbrary, Maldon, England,266 n197.
Plutarch, 374,405,430n4.
Pocock, Nicholas, 131,136,147.
Poissy, Colloquy of (1561), 52,212 218,233,234-244,245,269.
Polanco, Jean, 240.
Poland, 195,223,225,247,439-453.
Pole, Reginald, 23,24,37,38,40,42, 43,46,48,49,51,74,76,84,99,274, 322,389,395,409,410.
Polman, Pontien, 372.
Polybius, 374.
Ponet, John, 35,100,165,166,177, 178,180,355,393,394,395,396,399.
Pope, Hugh, 124n122.
Poullain, Valerand, 85,99,161,162, 163,217.
Prescott, H.F.M., 163,167.
Prideaux, John, 300.
Priuli, Alvise, 24.
Prosper, St., 348.

Quenstedt, Iohannes Andreas, 336.

Radziwill, NIcholas, Duke, 450.
Ragnina, Clemens Aranis, 272.
Randolf, Thomas, 226,258n99.
Ranke, Leopold Von, 394.
Ratcliff, E.C., 96.
Ratisbon/Regensburg, 23,46,47,48, 51.
Ratramn, 137.
Reggio, 76.
Reinhard, Wolfgang, 37.
Renard, Simon, 161.
Renato, Camillo, 40,75.
Reniger, Michael, 178.
Rhadamanthys, 496,520,530n3.
Rhetica, 186.
Ridley, Nicholas, 97,100,110,137, 138,139,163,177,327.
Rihel, W., 391.
Rochester, 100,109.
Rome, 24,38,39,40,41,42,43,45,46, 50,74,75,168.
Rosenblatt, 143.
Ross, J.B., 47.
Rotondo, Antonio, 443.

Rüger, Jacob, 214.
Rupp, Ernest Gordon, 26,45,58,60, 204n79,538.

Sabellius, 441.
Sacramental Disputation (1550) /B.M.Add.MS.21,524/, 156n21.
Sadoleto, Jacob, Cardinal, 36,41, 42,43,274.
St. Andrews, 507.
Salig, Christian, 281.
Salisbury, 92,175,231,460.
Sampson, Thomas, 114,175,176,177, 220,223,225,226,227,228,229,230 393-96,399,511.
Sandys, Edwin, Bishop, 162,178, 220,230,493,513-515.
Sankovitz, John, 497,538.
Santini, Luigi, 229.
Saul, King of Israel, 213,217,283
Scaliger, Joseph, 281.
Scambler, Edmund, Bishop, 59.
Schmidt, Charles, 216,536,539.
Schulting, Cornelius, 55,379,380, 381.
Scory, John, Bishop, 162,164,165, 180.
Scotland, 101,225,226,248.
Scot's Book of Common Reformation 258n99.
Seripando, Girolamo, Cardinal, 48 115n5,273-74,302n18.
Seraphino, Cardinal, 281,322
Servetus, 195,244,249,442-43,446, 450.
Shepherd, Norman, 456.
Siena, 89.
Sigbaldo, Giovanni Domenico, 39, 40,42.
Simler, Josiah, 37,59,72,74,80,81 82,84,212,236,244,249,250,265n 196,274,277,279,287,294,372,380 393,449-50,453,460.
Sleidan, John, 379,404.
Smith, Richard, 92,101,102,103, 106,152,229,251,270,297,300,319 320,351,377,457,496-97,499-502, 506-07.
Smyth, Charles H., 128,136.

Socinus, Laelius, 79,120n70,443.
Socrates, 371.
Solomon, King of Israel, 388,497.
Somerset, Duke of, 95,96,97,99,100
   103,106,108,109,112,128,130,136,
   315,317.
Sophocles, 374.
Soto, Dominic, 229.
Spaulding, James, 148.
Speroni, Sperone, 24.
Spiera, Francesco, 78,404.
Spitz, Lewis, 394.
Spyridon, 371.
Staedke, Joachim, 214,215.
Stancaro, Francesco, 55,195,247,
   278,373,376,381,403,436,439-41,
   443-44,446-54,457,535.
Staphylus, 441.
Stapulensis, Faber, 27.
Starkey, Thomas, 396.
Stella, Francesco, 307n67.
Strabo, 369.
Strasbourg, 29,30,48,52,53,73,74,
   76,77,78,79,80,81,82,83,84,85,90
   93,104,140,141,142,143,150,153,
   163,166,168,169,170,171,172,173,
   174,175,176,177,178,180,182,183,
   184,185,194,196,197,198,199,200,
   211,212,216,218,219,220,223,227,
   247,273,279,280,283,285,294,378-
   391,456.
Strobel, Georg, 282.
Strype, John, 90,164,165,166,313,
   315,316,349.
Stuckius, Johann Guilielmi, 236,
   300.
Stumphius, John Rodolph, 141.
Sturm, Jacob, 171.
Sturm, Jean (John), 29,80-82,169-
   72,243,247,385.
Sturm, Klaus, 294,435,536.
Sturm, Peter, 199,216,249.
Suffolk, Duke of, 167.
Suleiman, 394.
Sultzer, 351.
Sunningwell, 93.
Sylvester, 223.

Tassoni, Giambattista, 42.

Tedeschi, John, 25,87.
Tertullian, 50,242,299,349,350,
   376.
Terrentianus, Julius, 106,141,149
   236,495,508,512,515,517-19.
Theodoret, 90,120n79,371.
Theodosius, Emperor, 89.
Theodosius, Monophysite Patriarch
   of Constantinople, 120n79.
Theophylact, 350.
Theophrastus, 524,530n6.
Throckmorton, Nicolas, 226.
Tileton, Paul, 265n186.
Timothy, 85,325,401.
Tiraboschi, 282.
Titus, 85.
Torrance, T.F., 60,192.
Tremelius, Emanuel, 190.
Trent, 24,36,37,48,169,269,275.
Tresham, William, 90, 105.
Troyes, 245.
Tunstal, Cuthbert, 96,149,150.
Turner, William, 178.
Tylenda, Joseph, 435.
Tyndale, William, 99, 136.

Udall, Nicholas, 64,105,110,123n
   108,320,321.
Ulmis, John ab, 141,149,151.
Urbino, 38.
Ursinus, Zacharias, 52,246,455.
Utenhove, Jan, 61,62,98,104,161,
   162,163,223,225,232,448,449,459

Vadian (Joachim von Watt), 77.
Valdes, Juan de, 25,50,51,72,73,
   74,194,297,308n78.
Valence, Bishop of, 261n142.
Valla, Laurentius, 273,274.
Vanden Brink, Bakhuizen, 137.
Van der Delft, Spanish Ambassador
   57.
Vchouski, Jacobus, 465n68.
Veluanus, 372.
Venice, 24,35,38,39,46,90,91,271,
   272,277,281,282.
Vergerio, Pier Paolo, 50,51,87,88
   226,287,395,426n105.
Verona, 76.

Vilierius, Franciscus, 395.
Vinay, Valdo, 108,111.
Viret, Pierre, 179,180,351,407.
Virgil, 417.
Viterbo, 40,72.

Walton,Brian, 26.
Warner, John, 140,250,372.
Werdmullerus, 351.
Wesel, 163,164.
Wesley, John, 459,460.
Westphal, Joachim, 197,198,248.
Whitgift, John, Archbishop, 55.
Whitingham, William, 151.
William of Occam, 57.
Williams, Arnold, 295.
Williams, George H., 440.
Willis, David, 443.
Winchester, Bishop of, (See
   Gardiner, Stephen), 59,102.
Wisdom, Robert, 178.
Wittenberg, 46,53,127,172,174.
Wolf, John, 198,410.
Wolf, R., 321.
Wood, Thomas, 179.

Worms, 38,49,51.
Worth, 178.
Wyatt, Thomas, 185.

Xenophon, 334.
Ximenes De Ciscernos, Francisco,
   Cardinal, 27.

Young, John, 335.

Zanchi, Jerome, 25,175,197,199,
   214,216,221,247,254n3-6,269,301
   n4,383,386,406,429n133,455-57,
   535.
Zurich, 29,30,48,52,53,55,76,77,
   84,93,97,114,130,140,141,143,
   163,166,170,177,178,180,186,187
   197,198,199,200,211,212,213,214
   215,216,217,218,219,220,221,222
   223,229,239,246,247,248,250,273
   403-418.
Zurkiden, 444.
Zwingli, Ulrich, 26,27,57,58,64,
   72,74,125n135,127,248,351,414,
   416,455.

SPECIAL SUBJECT INDEX

Beza, Theodore
  Armstrong on Calvin, 457.
  Bullinger converts B.
  Colloquy of Montbeliard and
    1593 *De Controversiis*, 245.
  Confession of Faith (1560),400.
  Elders in Cartwright's A *Replye
    to . . . Dr Witgifte* (1573).
  Erastus prefers Martyr, 401.
  Formula of Concord (1580) de-
    grades Beza & Martyr, 356n11.
  Göppingen Confession (1557),133
    217-218.
  Letters:
    De Reina and Grindal on
      Martyr, 22n197.
    1564 to Jean De Ferriere,245.
    Martyr on Christ (1555), 189,
      194.
    Martyr on St. Germain(14 Dec.
      1561), 246.
  Magdeburg resistence theory,392
  Martyr:
    clarity, 51,54.
    Two Adam Christology, 55.
    Commentary on I *Cor.*(1551)321
    Gribaldi's confession, 221.
    learning, 57.
  Poissy:
    Cardinal of Lorraine response
      238.
    Martyr's arrival, 235.
    Martyr's invitation, 234.
    Speech of 9 Sept. 1561, 237.
    Speeches in Italian versions,
      260n127.
    Protest of 26 Sept. 1561,240.
  Stancaro on Arian, 454.
  Summa totius Christianismi, 208
    n129.
  Toleration, 446.

Bucer, Martin
  Alexandre's French *De Vitandis*
    of 1556/58, 351.
  Arrival in England 1549, 91.
  Ascham offers Sturm a life of

  B., 81.
  Martyr's 1549 Oxford Tractate.,
    249.
  Brief Examination (1566), 455.
  Brunfels, Otto, 78.
  Calvin complains about popery
    (1549), 108.
  Cambridge dispute on justifica-
    tion (1550), 335.
  Cartwright quotes in 1573.
  Collinson on B. and Grindal,225
  Commentary on *Gospels* & *Psalms*
    at Naples, 71.
  Cotton, John, on (1652), 48.
  Cranmer appeals about Hooper
    (1550), 110.
  Davies on 'virtualism', 138.
  Defection to Martyr 'weakens'
    Cranmer, 136.
  De Regno Christi, 319.
  De Vitandis (1545), 78.
  Dryander's 1547 letter on civic
    unrest at Stras., 85.
  Dugmore on Bucer, 127.
  Eucharistic letter to Zurich 6
    Dec. 1546, 84.
  Lectures at Strasbourg on N. T.
    82.
  lesser magistrates in *Matthew*
    (1530) & *Judges* (1554),392-93
  Maitland, Sir William, quotes
    B. against Knox, 398.
  Mss. in England, 169.
  Martin's opinion, 378.
  Martyr:
    on B. character (155), 84.
    on B. as commentator of
      Romans, 330-31.
    on B.'s death, 140.
    on B.'s house, 79-80.
    reads B. in Naples.
    to Bullinger about B., 77.
    on Cambridge disputations
      (1550), 132.
    on *Censura* to revised Prayer
      Book, 133-34.
    confidant, 51.

Bucer, Martin (cont.)
   on Eucharist 26 December 1548,
      94.
   on Fagius' death, 129.
   on Laski's confession, 132.
   lectures excell B., 80.
   on Leipzig *Adiaphora*, 111.
   letter on Oxford colleagues
      (155), 92.
   on Oxford theology 1549, 104-5
   on Papists (1549), 62.
   on printing of I *Cor.* (1551) 321
   on Richard Smith (10 June 1550)
      101-103.
   stipend (1542), 79.
   Strasbourg call, 76.
   Strasbourg home, 83.
   to Warner on B. illness, 250.
Niger on Martyr's piety, 130.
Oxford Disputation (1549), 106.
Patristic study, 90.
prolixity, 54.
Quid sit Ecclesia: Ephesians (4)
   189-90.
Ratisbon Articles (May 1541), 23.
Response to Martyr's 1549 propositions on Eucharist, 104.
Sententiae Veterum and Hilary,
   192.
Vergerio edits anti-papal com-
   ments in 1555., 395.
Wittenberg Concord (1536), 170,
   174-75.
Worried about presence in
   Martyr's Eucharistic thought,
   107.

Bullinger, Heinrich
   Alexandre's French *De Vitandis*
      (1552/56), 351.
   Beza on *Göppingen Confession*,
      217-18.
   Beza on Gribaldi (1556), 221.
   Beza praises *Tractatio* (1549) and
      I *Corinthians* (1551), 321.
   Greets English Bishops, 512,515,
      518,533.
   Brenz attacks (1562), 249.

Brenz on ubiquity, 174.
Cartwright quotes in *Replye* . .
   Whitegifte (1573), 56.
Chambers, Richard, and Robert
   Horn on Marian England (1556)
   165.
Colloquy of Poissy (1561) 234-45
Consensus (1551), 213.
Davies on 'virtualism', 138.
Diary, 215.
Diary (1556) on Martyr's move
   to Zurich, 380.
Frankfurt exiles appeal (1555),
   179-81.
Herbert, Peter, meets on *Unitas
   Fratrum* (156), 248.
Hooper's letter 27 Feb. 1549 on
   Forty Two Articles, 145.
Hooper on Martyr's *Genesis*
   (1551), 296.
Hotman on Martyr's *Kings* (1561)
   and civic resistence, 409.
Jewel on Oxford ruination, 229.
Marian Exiles, 177-78.
Martyr:
   debates Bibliander, 214.
   in B.'s house, 212.
   on B.'s *Romans*, 333-34.
   confidant, 51.
   endorses *Consensus Tigurinus*,
      129-30.
   contacts 5 Oct. 1542, 76-77.
   praises *Decades*, 110.
   on *Ecclesiastical Laws*, 148.
   on English reform and Oxford,
      112-114.
   on Eucharist, 134.
   letter to Frankfurt (30 Sept.
      1554), 181-83.
   on *Genesis* and *Exodus* (1552),
      328.
   learning, 381-82.
   on Oxford and I *Cor.*, 139-40.
   on Pole as Antichrist (1554),
      388-89.
   Predestination (1553), 171.
   on religious conflict in
      Stras. (1545), 80.

Bullinger, Heinrich (cont.)
   on *Romans* (1553), 213.
   leaves Stras.(1556), 198.
   on temporary stay at Stras.
     (1553), 170.
   on Wyatt's rebellion, 185.
Micronius reports on London
   Stranger's Church (155), 86-87
Pilkington on Martyr (1556),395.
Ponet, John, on exile, 166.
Second Helvetic Confession(1561)
   247.
*Sermon . . . concernynge magis-
trates* (1549), 108.
Stancaro, 442, 450.
Tractatio (1561) against Brenz,
   529,530n7.
Veluanus uses patristic
   citations, 372.

Calvin, John
   Acts (1560) on Stancaro &
     Blandrata, 450.
   Alexander's French *De Vitandis*
     (1552/56), 351.
   Blandrata in *Institutes*, 442.
   Blandrata condemned to Zurkiden
     444.
   Bucer writes about Martyr, 28
     Oct. 1542, 77.
   Bullinger on Brenz, 249.
   Bullinger eulogizes Martyr, 250.
   Cartwright cites *Institutes* in
     Replye . . . Whitgifte (1573),
     56.
   Cortese reads *Institutes*, 38.
   Cotton, John, on Calvin (1652)48
   Damnation, 345.
   Davies on 'virtualism', 138.
   letter on flight (1537), 78.
   Forty-Two Articles (1553),
     Article XVII, 146.
   Frankfurt exiles appeal, 179-80.
   Gribaldi and Company of Pastors,
     222.
   Grynee, Simon, preface to *Romans*
     (1540), 331.
   Martin, Thomas, 378.

Martyr:
   at one with C., 246.
   confidant, 51.
   on Catherine de Medici, 224.
   endorses *Consensus* to Harden-
     berg (1555), 186.
   Eucharist tract (1555),54-55.
   Geneva visit (1553), 170.
   Geneva Invitation, 187.
   Second invitation to Geneva,
     216-17.
   on Imperial coronation, 221.
   plucked out of Lion's mouth,
     150-51.
   lectures on *Minor Prophets*,80
   on Poissy (27 Sept. 1561),240
   letter on Poissy (4 Oct.1561)
     242.
   on predestination and
     Castellio, 213-214.
   on *Romans* & Eucharist,196-200
   letter on Union with Christ,
     63.
   Unio Christi, 188-194.
Berates Melanchthon on Stras.
   silence (27 August 1554), 173
Nicodemites 1543,1544, 405.
Response to Pigge, 270.
Rupp on *Institutes*, 60.
Bishop Scambler orders Norwich
   diocese to read *Institutes* in
   1589, 59.
Schulting on Calvin & Martyr,
   381.
Socinus, Laelius, on **Martyr**
   (1549), 79.
Letter to Somerset (1550), 108-
   09.
Stancaro's letter on Polish
   tritheism (4 Dec. 1560), 440-
   41.
Response to Stancaro (1560),446
Letter to Strasbourg exiles
   (June 1555), 178.
Tylenda on 'real presence',435.
Wesley, John, places Martyr be-
   tween Melanchthon & C., 460.
Zanchi on Zurich, 196-200.

Cranmer, Thomas, Archbishop
  'Black Rubric', note to Privy
    Council, 139.
  Book of Homilies (1547), 99.
  Cecil (19 Sept. 1552) on *Forty-
    Two Articles*, 145.
  Cole's sermon announces execu-
    tion (21 March 1555/56), 316.
  Commonplace Books, 127.
  Commons bill of 1535 opposed,128
  Davies on 'virtualism', 138.
  Declaration Concerning the Mass,
    (1553), 150.
  Eucharistic explanation (1548),
    96-97.
  Eucharistic questions (1540),105
  Forty-Five and *Forty-Two*
    Articles, 146-147.
  Gardiner answered 1550-1559,107.
  Gardiner thinks C. translates
    Martyr on Eucharist, 97-98.
  Grindal to Foxe on C.'s view of
    Eucharist (28 Dec. 1557), 219-
    20.
  Liturgical reform 1544 Litany,
    88-89.
  Martyr:
    Censura (1550) sent to Cranmer
      133.
    C. endorses M. to Bucer (1548)
      94.
    Chrysostom's *ad Caesarium
      Monachim*, ms., 90, 369.
    Ecclesiastical Laws, 148-149.
    Parliamentary residence at
      Lambeth (1552), 144.
    prayer of invitation: 1552
      Prayer Book, 56-57.
    exhortation in Prayer Book
      (1552), Cranmer's version,
      153-54.
    sermon on rebellion (1549),
      notes, 382,399.
  Palmer, Julins, upset at martyr-
    dom, 327-28.
  property offered to secure

    Martyr, 151.
  Protestant leaders invited to
    England, 91.
  Sermons on Rebellion (1549) 108
  Response to Smith (1556), 152,
    251,300-301.
  Testimonia on *sola fide*,347-350

Jewel, John, Bishop
  amanuensis of Martyr, 52, 177,
    395.
  Apology, 390,417.
  Ayre, John, on Jewel, 178.
  Disputation of 5 Feb. 1560,230.
  exile at Strasbourg, 175.
  Harding, 94.
  Martyr's prefatory letter to
    Dialogus, 520-31.
  Oxford career, 93.
  Oxford pupil of John Morwen,92.
  patristic study with Martyr,185
  Peace in England (1560), 231.
  prepares Martyr's sermons, 384.
  Salisbury Diocesan visit (1559)
    229.
  Sermon on Haggai (1), 316-17.
  Simler's 1563 letter on Martyr,
    460.
  Westminster disputation (1559),
    227-28.

Martyr, Peter
  *Adhortatio ad Coenam Domini
    Mysticam*, 138,153-54.
  Amerbach's aid, 77.
  Aristotle's Ethics (1563), 354-
    55.
  Ash Wednesday Sermon, 315-16.
  Augsburg Confession, 170-71.
  Earl of Bedford, invites M
    Martyr's return to England,
    233.
  Bibliander, 214- 216.
  Bibliography of printed
    writings, 545-51.
  Biblical comments, 24-26, 29-30

Martyr, Peter (cont.)
  Biblical Commentaries:
    Genesis 25,66n19-20,67n25,79,
      221,241,279-81,286,294-99,
      310n112,328,346-47,384,405.
    Exodus 52,79,241,281-86,294,
      384,451.
    Leviticus 79,294,446(Brenz,282)
    Deuteronomy 286,369,392.
    Judges 25,153,175-78,291,295,
      320,369-70,382-92,395-98,402
      404,418n2.
    Samuel 25,212-13,233,384,401,
      403-04.
    Kings 25,56,83,212,234,246,271
      290-91,298,305n42,320,386,
      388,401,404,408-18,455.
    Job 107
    Psalms 26,51,88,168,212,285,
      300,307n72,339,348,451-52,
      454.
    Prophets (*Minor*) 79-81,169,212
      221,294,346.
    Lamentations 26,79,279,300,376
    Haggai, *Sermon on* 316-17.
    Malachi (2),*Sermon on* 279,313,
      316.
    John (16), *Sermon on* 316-17.
    Romans 25,53-54,67n27 & 30, 74
      110,144,146-7,152-3,158n67,
      168,176,184,192-93,195-6,213
      215,216,219,221,228,246,247,
      252n8,255n44,269,272,274,278
      294,297,301n5,313,320,322,
      328-55,358n38,359n55,382,444
      450,452,455,459.
    I Corinthians 25,37,49,55-6,58
      61,63,74,97-8,101,128,140,
      143,169,189,191,192-4,205n80
      215,309n95,318-28,347,368-72
      376,384,400,405f.
    Philippians (2),*Sermon on* 53,
      251,436-38,436-38.
  Blandrata, 443-44.
  Brenz, John, 248-50,520-29.
  A *Brieff Discours* . . . *at Frank-
    ford*, 179-185.

Bucer as bishop, 79-80.
Bucer's death, 140.
Bucer as example, 84.
Bucer on Eucharist (26 Dec.1548)
  94.
Bucer on *Censura*, 133-34.
Bullinger, Heinrich, 530n7.
Calvin & *Unio Christi*, 186-194.
Cartwright on Martyr, 56.
Cogitationes (1549), 111.
Contarini, conversations at
  Lucca 1541, 46.
I Corinthians (1548/51),318-28.
Cox, Richard, 502-03,508-09,516-
  19,533-33.
Cranmer & 'black rubric', 139.
Catherine Dampmartin (1st wife)
  84.
De Libero Arbitrio (1560), 215-
  16.
Declaration Concerning The Mass
  (1553), 150.
A *Dialogue Between Custom and
  veritie*, 137-38.
*Dialogus de utraque in Christo
  natura* (1561), 232-33.
Dryander letters (1547), 89.
Ecclesiastical Laws, 148-149.
Edward VI, Tudor King, 131,504-
  05.
Elector of Saxony prohibits
  writings, 534.
Elizabeth I, Tudor Queen, Let
  Letter of 1558, 224-225.
Elizabeth I, Tudor Queen, 503-
  04.
Epistola ad Caesarium Monachum
  90.
Exhortation For Young Men. . .
  317-18.
Flight from England, 150-51.
Flight from Italy, 49-51.
Forty-Two Articles (1553)
  Article XVII, 145-147.
Frankfurt Letter on Lutheran
  baptism (1554), 181-185.
Gardiner responds on Eucharist,

Martyr, Peter (cont.)
  Gardiner, 106-107.
  Garnarius, 198.
  Genesis, 295-300.
  Göppingen Confession (1557),217-
    18.
  Gregorio da Milano on flight (24
    August 1542), 76.
  Gribaldi, 221-222.
  Grindal on Martyr's lectures,177
  Grindal, Edmund, letter of 28
    January 1560, 510-12.
  Hooper, letter on vestments, (4
    November 1550), 114.
  Hubert, Conrad, letters on
    Strasbourg, 169.
  Inferior magistrates, 391-403.
  Jewel, John, 178,520-31.
  Jewel on Elizabethan Church,227-
    231.
  Judges, 383,403.
  I *Kings*: Schism, 408-18.
  Lambeth Palace Letters descrip-
    tion, 491-98.
  Lamentations, 300-01.
  Laski,132-33.
  Letters, Register of, 467-86.
  Library in Geneva, 373-78.
  London Italian Church, 87-88.
  London Stranger's Church &
    Virgin Birth, 231-232.
  Lucca - on flight, 75.
  Lucca letter, 195-96.
  Lutheran baptism, 56.
  Marbach, John, 171-175.
  Melanchthon's letter (14 July
    1543), 77.
  Minor Prophets, 80.
  Musculus, Wolfgang, letter of 9
    Sept. 1556, 487-90.
  Naples - I *Corinthians*, 74-75.
  Neuchatel letter on ministerial
    discipline,(29 December 1544),
    84-85.
  Nicodemism (*De Vitandis*), 78-79.
  Norton, John on Martyr (1652),48
  Ochino, 222-23.

Oxford:
  Bullinger on lectures, 113.
  colleagues, 92.
  Dryander letter - Eucharistic
    debate, 3 January 1549, 98.
  Eucharistic debate, 101-105.
  Harding on Martyr's house,93-
    94.
  Jewel, John, 93.
  Rebellion of 1549, 107-111.
  Smith, Richard, 101-103.

Palmer, Julins, on I *Cor.*(1551)
  328.
*Oration Concerning the Resurrec-
  tion of Christ*, 438.
*Oration Concerning the Study of
  Divinity*, 168.
Poissy (1561), 234-46.
Pole, missing letter of 1542.
  75-76.
Ponet, John, on exile, 166.
*Prayer against Eucharistic
  Idolatry*, 141-42.
Prayerbooks (1549-52), 127-139.
Protestant career, summary,52-
  64.
Psalms, 300.
Psalm (2), 454-55.
Psalm (56), 168.
Romans (1558) preface to Cooke,
  152-53.
Romans (1550-58), 328-54,535.
Romans (13), 382-83.
Sampson, Thomas, letter,176-77.
Sandys, Edwin, 513-515.
Schmidt, Charles, assessment of
  Martyr's writings, 539,539n2.
Sermon on Haggai (1), 316-17.
Sermon on John (16), 317.
Sermon on Malachai (2:4), 316.
Sermon on Philippians (2), 437-
  38.
Sermon of Thanksgiving (1548),
  95.
Servetus, 446.

Martyr, Peter (cont.)
  Simler, letter to Jewel in
    Oratio (1563), 460.
  Smith & Cranmer's defense, 152.
  Smith, Richard, 499-502,506n1-2,
    507n3,508.
  Somerset Letter (1550), 112-113.
  Stancaro, 439-53.
  Strasbourg:
    lectures, 81-82.
    Martyr's home, 83.
    Senate, 211-212.
  Terentianus,Julius, 517-18,519n2.
  Tetropolitan Confession, 172-73.
  Theodoret, *Eranistes* (1549), 90-
    91.
  Theses Ad Disputandum Publice
    (1543/45), 278-87.
  Una Semplice Dichiaratione (1544)
    287-295.
  Una Semplice (1544) proscribed at
    Lucca 1545, 83.
  Ursinus, Zacharius, 246.
  Valdes, 71-74.
  Wesley, John, 459-60.
  Zanchi, 455-57.
  Zurich Pastors, letter (6 Dec.
    1546), 84.

Melanchthon, Philip
  Alexander's French *De Vitandis*
    (1552,56), 351.
  Calvin writes M. on Strasbourg
    (27 August 1554), 173.

Castelvetro translates *Loci*,42.
Clarius, Isidore, 276.
De Vitandis (1549), 78.
Epiphanius' *Panarion*, 371-72.
Hippophili Melangaei Annota-
  tiones in Evangelium Matthaei
  282.
Maitland, Sir William quotes
  against Knox, 398.
Marburg, (1529), 248.
Martyr:
  Letter to Martyr (14 July
    1543), 77, 85.
  Letter on Marbach (24 May
    1554), 173-182.
  Letter of June 1554, 185.
  Letter to Melanchthon (26
    January 1555), 173.
  Letter of 26 June 1556, 295.
Ponet's, John, comforter, 166.
I Principi De La Theologia di
  Ippofilo da Terra negra, 281-
  82.
Responsio de controversiis
  Stancari (1553), 440-42.
Romans (1532), 330-33.
Sententiae Veterum & Hilary,192
Il sommario della Scrittura,282
Theological method, 68n68.
Vergerio edits (1555), 395.
Wesley, John places Martyr be-
  tween Melanchthon and Calvin,
  460.

DATE DUE

GAYLORD			PRINTED IN U.S.A.